THE HUMAN RIGHTS OF PERSONS WITH INTELLECTUAL DISABILITIES

Stanley Sholom Herr, 1945 - 2001

THE HUMAN RIGHTS OF PERSONS WITH INTELLECTUAL DISABILITIES

Different But Equal

Edited by
STANLEY S. HERR
LAWRENCE O. GOSTIN
HAROLD HONGJU KOH

OXFORD

UNIVERSITY PRESS

OXFORD

UNIVERSITY PRESS

Great Clarendon Street, Oxford OX2 6DP

Oxford University Press is a department of the University of Oxford.
It furthers the University's objective of excellence in research, scholarship,
and education by publishing worldwide in

Oxford New York

Auckland Bangkok Buenos Aires Cape Town Chennai
Dar es Salaam Delhi Hong Kong Istanbul Karachi Kolkata
Kuala Lumpur Madrid Melbourne Mexico City Mumbai Nairobi
São Paulo Shanghai Taipei Tokyo Toronto

Oxford is a registered trade mark of Oxford University Press
in the UK and in certain other countries

Published in the United States
by Oxford University Press Inc., New York

© Stanley S. Herr, Lawrence O. Gostin and Harold Hongju Koh 2003

The moral rights of the authors have been asserted
Database right Oxford University Press (maker)

First published 2003

British Library Cataloguing in Publication Data
Data available

Library of Congress Cataloging in Publication Data
Data available
ISBN 0-19-826779-7
ISBN 0-19-926451-1 (pbk.)

1 3 5 7 9 10 8 6 4 2

Typeset by Newgen Imaging Systems (P) Ltd., Chennai, India
Printed in Great Britain
on acid-free paper by
Biddles Ltd., Guildford and King's Lynn

Foreword

MARY ROBINSON

The notion of equality has evolved into something we all, in theory, respect. Our systems of law, both international and domestic, are built upon it. The human rights movement was born out of it.

Article 1 of the Universal Declaration of Human Rights affirms that we all are born free and equal in dignity and in rights. Traditionally, this affirmation has been advanced through efforts to eliminate all forms of discrimination. Even so, some forms of prejudice have received less of our attention than others. In the early years of the human rights movement, discrimination against the disabled was virtually neglected. It was in part due to the hard work of individuals like Stanley Herr, to whom this book is dedicated, that this oversight has slowly been reversed.

Stanley Herr devoted his life to ensuring that the approach surrounding the disabled became one of rights instead of an exclusively humanitarian, social, or welfare issue. Court cases he argued in the 1970s led to the passing of the Education for All Handicapped Children Act of 1975 (later called the Individuals with Disabilities Education Act), which effectively allowed the one million children previously excluded from the public school system due to mental handicaps (perceived or real) the ability—and right—to return to school and be educated. In his later years, Herr was a frontrunner in the campaign to abolish capital punishment for the mentally retarded, and advocated on behalf of the homeless, another largely voiceless group. For his tireless efforts to ensure the enjoyment of human rights for everyone, no matter how invisible or silent, Herr serves as an inspiring example to us all.

As I look back on developments over the past decade, I am struck both by the advances that have been made, and the continuing dire state of human rights of the mentally disabled. Individuals with intellectual disabilities still rank among the most vulnerable segments of all societies. While much disability reform has taken place at the international level in recent years—from the General Assembly's adoption of the Standard Rules on the Equalization of Opportunities for Persons with Disabilities in 1993, to the appointment of a Special Rapporteur on disability in 1994, to the recently published study commissioned by the Office of the High Commissioner for Human Rights to expressly evaluate the effectiveness of existing international mechanisms on the rights of the disabled, to the European Union declaring 2003 as the European Year for People with Disabilities—the vast majority of the world's disabled still live in deplorable conditions. This is clearly visible in the numbers. Over 600 million people, or 10% of the world's population, are disabled. Two-thirds of them live in developing countries, which is not surprising given the clear linkages between poverty, malnutrition, and retardation. Of the children in this group, a mere 2% are likely to receive any education or rehabilitation.

By coincidence, I wrote a preface recently for a book published by University College, Dublin, Ireland on 'Health and Women with Intellectual Disabilities'. A happy coincidence, because it means there is more attention being paid at last to the many issues that need to be addressed. That publication looked at particular difficulties faced by women, including older women in the context of greater life expectancy.

Our information society has allowed us to know that significant social and physical barriers still prevent the mentally disabled from integrating and participating fully in the larger society. Establishing that people with intellectual disabilities are entitled to the same basic human rights as the rest of the population is important. Ensuring that they actually enjoy those rights remains a major challenge. The information society has enabled us to see how much of the world lives in dire poverty and lack of opportunity. We have a duty towards all segments of the wider global community to improve the basic living conditions of affected populations. This duty cannot be shirked when it comes to the disabled.

It is intolerable that any man, woman, or child go through life segregated and deprived of their rights for any reason, much less because they were born into a body or mind that our global society may deem too different to accommodate. That their separation is due to a physical or mental disability, as opposed to one of the more 'traditional' or visible classifications like race or religion or gender, makes the violation of their rights no less severe. True equality for the disabled means more than access to buildings and methods of transportation. It mandates a change in attitude in the larger social fabric—of which we are all a part—to ensure that they are no longer viewed as problems, but as holders of rights that deserve to be met with the same urgency we afford to our own. Equality puts an end to our tendency to perceive 'flaws' in the individual, and moves our attention to the deficiencies in social and economic mechanisms that do not accommodate differences. Equality also propels us to confront the manner in which our own fears and ignorance turn the intellectually disabled into an 'other' completely separate from ourselves. By looking at how each one of us contributes to the trend of discrimination towards the disabled, we can in turn discern how to facilitate the group's active participation in all aspects of society.

At the most basic level, we must ensure the intellectually disabled have access to knowledge. It is arguably the most precious commodity a human can possess. Article 27 of the Universal Declaration not only guarantees all people the right to education, but it guarantees education that facilitates 'the full development of the human personality'. In the case of the intellectually disabled, this may mean tailoring educational programs to the particular needs of these students. International human rights instruments require governments to progressively realize human rights within the limits of their available resources. This being said, even in resource rich societies adequate funding may not be available to make the necessary changes. But enhancing educational opportunities for the intellectually disabled should be given the highest priority among the possible choices.

Education is crucial because it enables intellectually disabled people to help themselves by learning a trade or a skill that can secure their place in the workforce. It in turn allows them to be acknowledged as useful and productive citizens who are both accepted and respected in their societies. Research shows that adults with intellectual disabilities need just as much stimulation and/or work as a normal part of their lives as other adults do. Consistent activity prevents depression and other emotional problems in this population that ultimately can become the responsibility of the State. It is imperative that States continue to prioritize education as a way to meet the rights of the intellectually disabled, and thus allow them to participate in the larger society. With current technologies making information more and more accessible to people at an unprecedented rate, there is no excuse to deny anyone the right to education and knowledge.

Along with access to education comes participation. States must conceptualize involvement in the decision making that affects one's life as itself a right. There is growing understanding that this approach is crucial to creating an equal and fair society in which one may assert and embed one's rights. Each and every individual is entitled to challenge their own condition, and in doing so, command the respect and dignity that constitutes the heart of equality. This is particularly important in the case of individuals who are institutionalized or live in other residential care facilities. Without attention to the ways in which mental disabilities can reinforce power imbalances, we allow abuse in these settings to flourish in our complacency. Thus it is the responsibility of those who can assert control over their own lives to empower those who are not so easily heard.

We must work for the laws and policies that encourage the right to be heard and the right to participate in the direction of our own lives. We must encourage the codification of the concepts that enshrine the unfettered equality articulated in the Universal Declaration of Human Rights. We must encourage our lawmakers to continue to accept that intellectual disability is a rights issue first and a medical matter second. We must utilize the existing UN human rights treaties and their monitoring bodies to target existing instances of disability discrimination. Already, the United Nations Human Rights Committee has found under the Optional

Protocol to the International Covenant on Civil and Political Rights that States must accommodate the special needs of disabled prisoners. The normative precedent set by this ruling is an important victory in the struggle to translate rights-based rhetoric into real improvements that actually improve the lives of those living with disabilities.

But as we work to combat discrimination in general, we must not treat the intellectually disabled as a homogeneous group lest we violate the rights of its individual members. Mental disabilities afflict the old and the young, women and men. People with disabilities live in the richest and the poorest nations on earth. They come from all racial and ethic minorities and majorities. They are both refugees, and those who have never seen war. All of these sub-groups need support and protection unique to the issues they face. The Convention on the Rights of the Child includes a clause devoted specifically to the rights of children with disabilities. It is promising that the phenomenon of double discrimination in relation to disabled women was discussed at last year's World Conference against Racism, Racial Discrimination, Xenophobia, and Racial Intolerance. As life spans increase and our population ages, the special needs of the elderly with intellectual disabilities are being recognized increasingly and dealt with. And we can no longer ignore the degree to which persons affected by war and post-war situations are especially vulnerable to mental health problems.

A recent United Nations report concluded that the issue of the human rights of persons with disabilities could be mainstreamed better into the current human rights system through the creation of a new international convention. The new document would not undermine existing treaty law, but aim to bolster its effectiveness by concentrating directly on the rights of the disabled. Whether or not the treaty will come to pass remains to be seen, but I encourage any meaningful addition to the human rights dialogue aiming to ensure equal rights for those with mental and physical disabilities.

We know from experience that language can serve either to reinforce or to undermine human dignity and worth. This is precisely why I am happy to introduce this particular volume, as it will for the first time address comprehensively the rights of persons with intellectual disabilities in the language of standing comparative and international law. It is my hope that the discussion it fosters will fuel the growing international movement advocating treatment of the rights of the intellectually disabled as fundamental human rights. And it is my wish that this volume will help us to recognize that people with mental disabilities should not be denied equal treatment simply because they are different.

MARY ROBINSON

Dedication: In Memory of
Stanley Sholom Herr, 1945–2001

It was the mid-1970s in Harley Street in London when an imposing figure entered the conference room of MIND (the National Association of Mental Health). The young Stanley Herr demanded reform of the British Mental Health Act and the establishment of an advocacy group for persons with mental disabilities. Stan would work with MIND for several years to achieve both dreams.

Those years in England began a remarkable career dedicated, in Stan's own words, to transforming 'wrongs to rights'. Stan was awarded a D.Phil. from Balliol College at Oxford University, having already earned a JD from Yale. He would go on to hold the most influential positions in American advocacy, ranging from a Kennedy Public Policy Fellowship at the Clinton White House to the presidency of the American Association on Mental Retardation.

Speaking for all who knew, loved, and respected him, Stan Herr was truly a man for all seasons. We saw him as a teacher, leader, mentor, colleague, and friend. His brilliance shone through with every deed and endeavor. Stan's mind seemed always to be working creatively and with the pure impulse of looking to do good. He represented the advocate and law professor committed to social justice. For Stan this meant dedicating his thirty-year career to righting injustices to the most vulnerable of the vulnerable, namely persons with intellectual disabilities, homeless people, and defendants on death row.

Stan had an uncommon passion for family and community. Professionally, he dedicated himself to making this a more just world. He was the supreme champion of disability rights through scholarship, teaching, and activism. He argued several high-profile cases noted for winning civil rights for people with disabilities. The *Pennhurst* case went to the Supreme Court and led to the closure of a notorious Pennsylvania institution that mistreated persons with intellectual disabilities. The *Mills* case established a right to a free and appropriate public education for children with disabilities. Stan was influential in the passage of the Education for All Handicapped Children Act of 1975 (now called the Individuals with Disabilities Education Act). He also waged a legal battle in Maryland, which led to the state barring the execution of prisoners with intellectual disabilities. Most recently, he continued his vocal and legal opposition to the death penalty by contesting Texas' plans to execute a person with intellectual disabilities.

Stan knew he was blessed with an exceptional family. He often told us how fortunate he was to wake each day to Raquel and their three almost-teenage darlings, David, Deborah, and Ilana. Stan was a huge presence in their lives and he rejoiced in sharing his work with family especially when combining vacation and human rights work in Israel and Europe.

Stan's schedule was packed tight. He juggled more than most and had an impressive resume. Stan continued to balance numerous writing projects right through his year-long battle with cancer. He left us with homework assignments, including the completion of this book, which meant so much to him. When asked how a clinician could publish more than a hundred articles and five books, Stan was fond of saying that he owed much to his family for allowing him to pursue his special niche as a scholar.

Within the clinic at the University of Maryland, Stan moved quickly and often appeared as a blur. He could be seen racing down the hall to the old-fashioned xerox machine where he would retrieve his latest draft before speeding back to his office to answer a ringing phone and prepare for his next student appointment. Stan had great admiration and respect for students. He was an extremely well prepared teacher who enlivened his classes with films, news clips, clients, and outside experts. Not surprisingly, students often left his two-hour seminar feeling invigorated and refreshed. Stan had a special relationship with students and unabashedly invited many to join his work projects. Together they filed friend of the court briefs for virtually every United States Supreme Court disability case within the last decade, including an amicus brief that the *New York Times* considered 'a moving account for abolishing the death penalty for young persons with mental retardation'. Surely, one of Stan's great legacies is having influenced an army of former students to join the struggle for equality within the disability community where he was recognized nationally and internationally.

Stan's many accomplishments included being the Commissioner of the American Bar Association Commission on Mental and Physical Disability and co-founder of Baltimore's Homeless Persons Representation Project. He also received numerous prizes, including the 2001 American Bar Association's Hearn Award, the University of Maryland Regents 2000 Award for Excellence in Public Service, the Maryland State Bar Association's 1999 Rights of the Disadvantaged Award, and the Baltimore Association for Retarded Citizens Distinguished Professional Service Award. As a 1991 Fulbright Senior Scholar, Stan inspired the creation of Israel's Human Rights Center for People with Disabilities. Years later as a United States Department of Education Switzer Distinguished Research Fellow, Stan lobbied and testified in favor of Israel's Equal Rights for Persons with Disabilities Law.

Somehow within this whirlwind of activity, Stan found the time to be a supreme teacher, loving husband and father, and active sportsman.

He could often be seen jogging through beautiful wooded trails of the Baltimore suburbs. Stan's optimistic, soothing, and fully-engaged approach is enveloped in his four-part mantra: calmness, belief, love, and energy.

CALMNESS. While Stan's boundless energy and ability to juggle many balls in the air are legend, he always seemed to project a sense of calmness. He was not afraid to express strong and passionate views, but there also was a simple truth about Stan: when he spoke he delivered wise counsel and was a master at building consensus and finding common ground.

Stan could be counted on to take the best of what others had to offer and mold a workable solution. While respecting his colleagues' zeal and passion, Stan convinced them to discard what was not important. He spoke in a voice that resonated with respect and reasonableness. Stan was the consummate problem solver. While others became overwhelmed with details, Stan fixed things and made them better.

Stan's sense of calmness taught us to listen and to be diplomatic. Left to ourselves we would have had a front-end collision with an opposing party we knew was wrong and suffered bruised feelings or worse. Rather than beginning with guns-a-blazing and directly confronting injustice, Stan's calm advice oozed through as he gently suggested: 'Maybe you want to begin by showing understanding rather than clobbering the person.' Empathy was one of Stan's strong suits. He always delivered a strategy for avoiding that unnecessary confrontation.

BELIEF. Stan's overwhelmingly optimistic and forward-looking spirit extended to his belief in colleagues, students, friends, and family. He believed we, too, could achieve and become agents of change and progress. Repeatedly, Stan reminded his family and friends that they could do things they did not think were possible. He constantly challenged people and seemed to know their capabilities even as they were expressing doubt. He hung in there during the rough times. Ultimately he convinced us we could succeed at what we had started, pursue our dream job, repair a damaged relationship, and climb new mountains. He believed we were that good.

LOVE. Stan expressed his love in many ways. By taking an interest in our lives, we knew he cared about our future and could be counted on to help with an immediate crisis. Stan shared in our accomplishments. He took great pride when a student, colleague, or friend would achieve a new job, a promotion, a milestone event. Stan had a talent for bringing people together, people who didn't always choose to work together. He showed the possibilities for working collectively, and taught us about persistence, vigilance, and motivation to excel. Stan was an activist who welcomed us to join the extraordinary civil rights movement for persons with disabilities of which he was a vital part.

During Stan's illness, he maintained his love and generosity. He amazed us. When we visited, he focused on our problems. From his hospital bed, he made phone calls to check on clients going through hard times. He also never lost his sense of charm. During one hospital stay, the nursing staff, which found him irresistible and seemed to do all the extra things, had turned down his request for a sushi dinner. Stan's smile usually won them over but not this time. On these rare occasions, Stan was not above invoking other strategies. Lawyers know about judge shopping and the search for a person in black robes who understands justice the same way you do. Stan's nurse shopping meant finding someone in white garb who would honor his request. It was not long before he was eating his sushi dinner.

ENERGY. Of course, Stan's work energy will always be legend. He achieved more in his shortened life than three ordinary people living a full life. Stan was a Boston and New York City marathon runner before he learned to jog, a jogger before he learned speed walking. He always led the way, challenging us to keep up. Stan would set the pace but slowed enough for us to travel with him. He even entertained us at parties (and at every other occasion when we encouraged him to sing).

Stan's energetic and positive attitude allowed him to handle his illness in a courageous spirit. He never wanted crying visitors, but always sought lively conversation and personal exchanges. Stan mustered the energy to fight the cancer and did it with humor to lighten the trail for those who loved him. Indeed, one of his running gags was how he would recruit every visitor to help him complete one of his five ongoing articles.

Stan should still be with us. He should have had another quarter century of living the full and rich life he led. His children should have had him by their side as they grow to adulthood. And we should have had the joy and benefit of his love, friendship, wisdom, and dedication. Instead he has left us many gifts to sustain us. The gift of being an incredibly positive and creative thinker. The gifts of knowing how to get things done, and of moving forward and not getting stuck. It is now for us to take that good spirit and energy wherever we travel and keep Stan alive in our memories as we continue to do good work for others.

DOUGLAS L. COLBERT
University of Maryland

LAWRENCE O. GOSTIN
Georgetown University

HAROLD HONGJU KOH
Yale University

Acknowledgements

This book began its development at the International Symposium on the Rights of People with Mental Retardation: Should Difference Make a Difference?, held at the Yale Law School, 24 March 1995. Stanley S. Herr and Harold Hongju Koh chaired the symposium, which was held in connection with the Special Olympics World Games in New Haven, Connecticut. The Kennedy Foundation generously sponsored the event.

The conference attendees drafted and signed an important human rights document—the Yale Declaration (see Appendix). This Declaration enunciates general human rights principles, provides an account of the entitlements of persons with intellectual disabilities, and urges a more robust international recognition of these rights.

In the summer of 2001, Stanley S. Herr informed us of his fight with cancer and asked us to complete this book. He passed away that autumn, but saw this volume as the culmination of a life's work. He made a remarkable difference in the lives of persons with mental disabilities through his scholarship, litigation, and advocacy. We dedicate this volume to Stanley and his wife, Raquel Schuster Herr. The book has been a labor of love, but we had a great deal of help from our colleagues and students.

This book is the product of three great institutions dedicated to international human rights—Yale University, the University of Maryland, and Georgetown University. Yale Law School's Orville Schell, Jr. Center for International Human Rights (which Harold Hongju Koh directed in 1995) was the driving force behind this project. Dean Anthony Kronman, Associate Dean Stephen Yandle, Associate Dean Carroll Stevens, Ronald Slye, and Stephen Pincus all played vital roles in organizing and supporting the 1995 Yale symposium. Tim Shriver of the Special Olympics gave marvelous leadership in helping to put the conference together. Robin Tooneh also made an important contribution to the project. We also thank Yale law students Rebekka Bonner, Renee DeMatteo, Kris Kavanaugh, and Jessica Sebeok for their help with the manuscript.

Stan was very much a part of the Maryland Law School community and his legacy continues to live in that institution. Dean Karen Rothenberg and Associate Dean Dianne Hoffman have worked to make Stan's dream a reality. On 4 October 2002, Maryland hosted the 'Stanley S. Herr Conference on Disability Rights and Social Justice', and the *Maryland Law Review* is publishing the proceedings. Maryland law professors Douglas L. Colbert and Joan L. O'Sullivan graciously contributed to the book's development. Maryland law students Heesun Choi, Mark Machi, Andrew May, Luciene Parsley, Alan Sachs, and Joseph Ward provided research assistance.

Much of the work to make the book a reality took place at the Georgetown University Law Center with the gracious support of Dean Judith Areen. Janice Hoggs and Laura Kidd managed the process, intellectually and organizationally, for more than a year. The book never would have been completed without their exceptional leadership. Stephen Barbour, Kevin Haeberle, James G. Hodge, Jr., Anna Selden, Lesley Stone, and Lance Gable also made important contributions.

Most of all, we want to thank the many advocates and self-advocates throughout the world who have fought for the human rights of persons with intellectual disabilities. As we note in our Introduction, this book brings together the two great international movements of the twenty-first century—disability rights and human rights. Many of the world's most admired advocates and self-advocates offer their insights, experience, and passion in the pages of this book.

LAWRENCE O. GOSTIN

HAROLD HONGJU KOH

Contents

Notes on Contributors   xviii

Introduction: The Human Rights Imperative   1
Harold Hongju Koh and Lawrence O. Gostin

I. Conceptualizing Intellectual Disabilities: History and Terminology

1. Meeting the Needs of People with an Intellectual Disability: International Perspectives   25
   Peter Mittler

2. Terminology and Power   49
   Ruth Luckasson

3. Cross-Cultural Perceptions of Disability: Policy Implications of Divergent Views   59
   Alison Dundes Renteln

4. Social Policy Toward Intellectual Disabilities in the Nineteenth and Twentieth Centuries   83
   David L. Braddock and Susan L. Parish

II. The Human Rights Movement: International Norms and Standards

5. From Wrongs to Rights: International Human Rights and Legal Protection   115
   Stanley S. Herr

6. Disability as a Subject of International Human Rights Law and Comparative Discrimination Law   151
   Theresia Degener

7. Liberty, Due Process, and the Pursuit of Happiness   185
   Michael W. Smull and Luciene Parsley

III. The Disability Rights Movement: Anti-discrimination Legislation

8. The Potential of Disability Non-discrimination Laws   203
   Stanley S. Herr

9. When Legislation Should Take Intellectual
    Disabilities into Account   237
    Dan Shnit

10. Statutory Changes in Disability Policy:
    Types of Legislation, Policies, and Goals   263
    Robert Silverstein

        IV. Equality and Difference: Social Policy Perspectives

11. On Second Thought: Constructing Knowledge, Law,
    Disability, and Inequality   287
    Marcia H. Rioux

12. Respecting Persons with Disabilities and Preventing
    Disability: Is there a Conflict?   319
    Adrienne Asch, Lawrence O. Gostin, and Diann M. Johnson

13. Studying the Emerging Workforce   347
    Peter Blanck and Helen A. Schartz

14. The Economics of Equality: An Exploration of
    Country Differences   387
    John H. Noble, Jr.

15. Out-of-Home Placement of Children with Intellectual
    Disabilities: The Need for a Family Support Policy   415
    Arie Rimmerman

16. Self-Determination, Autonomy, and Alternatives
    for Guardianship   429
    Stanley S. Herr

                V. Future Goals and Aspirations

17. Voices of Self-Advocates   453
    Mitchell Levitz

18. Recognizing Existing Rights and Crafting New Ones:
    Tools for Drafting Human Rights Instruments for
    People with Mental Disabilities   467
    Eric Rosenthal and Clarence J. Sundram

19. Recommendations for the United Nations and
    International NGOs   503
    Ronald C. Slye

Appendix: Yale Declaration   517

Index   527

Notes on Contributors

EDITORS

Professor Lawrence O. Gostin, Professor of Law, Georgetown University, Professor of Law & Public Health, Johns Hopkins University, Director, Center for Law & the Public's Health, Georgetown University Law Center, 600 New Jersey Ave., NW, Washington, DC 20001, 202-662-9373 (P), 202-662-9408 (F), gostin@law.georgetown.edu

Professor Stanley S. Herr (Posthumous), Professor of Law, University of Maryland, School of Law, 515 W. Lombard Street, Baltimore, MD 21201

Professor Harold Hongju Koh, Professor of International Law, Yale Law School, 127 Wall St., P.O. Box 208215, New Haven, CT 06520–8215, 203-432-4932 (P), (203) 432-1040 (F), harold.koh@yale.edu

CONTRIBUTORS

Professor Adrienne Asch, Wellesley College, 106 Central Street, Wellesley, MA 02181–8295, 781-283-3248 (P), (H), 781-283-3671 (F), aasch@wellesley.edu

Professor Peter D. Blanck, Professor of Law, Professor of Psychology and of Public Health, University of Iowa, College of Law, Director, Law, Health Policy & Disability Center, Iowa City, IA 52242, 319-335-9043 (P), 319-335-9019 (F)

Professor David L. Braddock, Associate Vice President for Research, University of Colorado System, Executive Director, Coleman Institute for Cognitive Disabilities, 586 Sys, 4001 Discovery Dr., Boulder CO 80309, 303-492-0639 (P), braddock@cu.edu

Professor Douglas L. Colbert, Professor of Law, University of Maryland School of Law, 500 West Baltimore Street, Baltimore, MD 21201, 410-706-0683 (P), 410-706-5856 (F), dcolbert@law.umaryland.edu

Professor Dr. Theresia Degener, Professor of Law, Administration and Organizational Science, Evangelische Fachhochschule, Rheinland-Westfalen-Lippe, Bochum, GERMANY, +49 234 3 69 01-0 (P), +49 234 3 69 01-100 (F), degener@efh-bochum.de

Ms. Diann Marie Johnson, Senior Auditor, Department of Health and Human Services, Office of Inspector General, 19134 Highstream Drive, Germantown MD 20874, diannmarie29@yahoo.com

Mr. Mitchell Levitz, Westchester Institute for Human Development/ UCDD, Westchester Medical Center & New York Medical College, 3B Atrian Court, Courtland Manor, NY 10567, 1-800-871-2181 (W) jlevitz@bellatlantic.net

Professor Ruth Luckasson, Regents' Professor, Professor of Special Education, The University of New Mexico, College of Education, Albuquerque, NM 87131-0001, 505-277-7231 (P), 505-277-7601 (F), ruthl@unm.edu

Peter Mittler, Emeritus Professor, Centre for Educational Support and Inclusion, University of Manchester, 3 Knightsbridge Mews, Manchester, England M20 6GX, +44-161-434-5625(P/F), mittlerpeter@interfree.it, peter.mittler@man.ac.uk

John H. Noble Jr., Endowed Professor for Social Justice, The Catholic University of America, National Catholic School of Social Service, Washington, DC 20064, 202-319-5459 (P) jnoble4@cox.net

Dr. Susan L. Parish, Postdoctoral Research Fellow, Waisman Center, University of Wisconsin-Madison, 1500 Highland Avenue, Madison, WI 53705-2280, 608-262-9145 (P), parish@waisman.wisc.edu

Luciene Parsley, Maryland Disability Law Center, The Walbert Building, 1800 N. Charles Street, 4th Floor, Baltimore, MD 21201, 410-272-6352 (P), 410-727-6389 (F)

Professor Alison Dundes Renteln, Department of Political Science, University of Southern California Von Klein Smid Center, 327, Los Angeles, California 90089-0044, (213) 740-3248 (P), (213) 740-8893 (F), arenteln@usc.edu

Professor Arie Rimmerman, Chair of Social Policy & Planning, Social Welfare and Health Studies, University of Haifa, Faculty of Social Welfare and Health Studies, Mount Carmel, Haifa, ISRAEL 31905, 972-4-8249950 (P), 972-4-8249946 (F), rimmer@research.haifa.ac.il

Dr. Marcia H. Rioux, Chair & Professor, School of Health Policy & Managment, Atkinson Faculty of Liberal & Professional Studies, York University, 4700 Keele St., Toronto ON M3J, 1P3 CANADA, 416-736-2100 x22112 (P), 416-929-3539 (F), mrioux@yorku.com

Ms. Mary Robinson, United Nations High Commissioner for Human Rights, OHCHR-UNOG, 8-14 Avenue de la Paix, 1211 Geneva 10, Switzerland, +41-22-917-9000 (P)

Mr. Eric Rosenthal, Executive Director, Mental Disability Rights International, 1156 15th Street, N.W., Suite 1001, Washington, DC 20005, 202-296-0800 (P), 202-728-3053 (F), eric.rosenthal@erols.com

Professor Helen Ann Schartz, Director of Research, Associate Research Scientist, Law, Health Policy and Disability Center, University of Iowa College of Law, Iowa City, IA 52242-5000, 319-335-4695 (P), helen-schartz@uiowa.edu

Professor Dan Shnit, Tel Aviv University, Shapell School of Social Work, Ramat Aviv, 89970, ISRAEL, 972-3-6409130 (P), 972-3-6409182 (F)

Mr. Robert Silverstein, Director, Center for the Study and Advancement of Disability Policy, 1331 H Street, NW, Suite 301, Washington, DC 20006, 202-783-5111 (P), 202-783-8250 (F), bobby@csadp.org

Professor Ronald Slye, Seattle University Law School, 900 Broadway, Seattle, Washington, 98122, 206-398-4045 (P), slye@seattleu.edu

Mr. Michael W. Smull, Support Development Associates, Community Support Unit, 3245 Harness Creek Road, Annapolis, MD 21403, 410-626-2707 (P), 410-626-2908 (F), mwsmull@cs.com

Clarence J. Sundram, Special Master, United States District Court, 28 Tierney Drive, Delmar, NY 12054

Introduction: The Human Rights Imperative

HAROLD HONGJU KOH AND LAWRENCE O. GOSTIN

This is the first book comprehensively to address the rights of persons with intellectual disabilities from the perspectives of comparative and international human rights law.

We dedicate it to our late co-author, Professor Stanley Sholom Herr, who was both an American and a global pioneer in framing the concerns of persons with intellectual disabilities as a human rights imperative. This book grew out of a conference held in March 1995 in connection with the Special Olympics World Games in New Haven, Connecticut, which Stan Herr and Harold Hongju Koh co-sponsored at Yale Law School's Orville Schell, Jr. Center for International Human Rights, and at which Larry Gostin was a principal speaker. Although sadly, Stan did not live to see the final publication of this volume, his spirit moves throughout these pages.

This book brings together two great social movements of the past half-century: the international human rights movement and the disability rights movement. Since the Second World War, international human rights have been defined as embracing those universally recognized inalienable rights to whose enjoyment all persons are entitled solely by virtue of being born human. The list of universal rights is specified in the 1948 Universal Declaration of Human Rights, and elaborated in the International Covenants on Civil and Political Rights and on Economic, Social and Cultural Rights, both of which have been almost universally signed and ratified throughout the world (although the United States, prominently, has not ratified the Economic, Social and Cultural Rights Covenant). At the 1993 Vienna Conference on Human Rights, nearly all nations of the world joined in a declaration that called these rights universal, indivisible, and interdependent.

During the last half-century, the promotion of human rights has come to be recognized not simply as an American or Western value, but as a universal value with internationally recognized meaning. In fact, countries with entrenched traditions of socialism and social democracy have more broadly embraced notions of economic, social, and cultural rights than have such market capitalist countries as the United States. Those in the United States who are wary of economic, social, and cultural rights have generally argued that the guaranteed provision of housing,

We are grateful to Jessica Sebeok of Yale Law School for her help in preparing this introduction.

schooling, health care, and the like would have broad redistributive implications and would place impossible burdens on federal, state, and local governments to provide social services. While these skeptics rarely object to guaranteeing the 'freedom from' rights—eg, freedom from genocide, torture, discrimination, arbitrary punishment, and other forms of overt government invasion—they contend that similarly guaranteeing 'freedom to' rights—such as rights to housing, education, and health—would create unsustainable burdens on the public fisc. In so asserting, their hesitation has been reinforced in US domestic law by judicial decisions by the Burger and Rehnquist Courts, which have drawn the constitutional line between strong protection of civil and political rights and a refusal to recognize constitutional rights to health care and education. This mindset has created a growing schism—both between the United States and developing nations and within the United States—between wealthy and underprivileged groups who see securing economic, social, and cultural rights as a practical precondition to meaningful enjoyment of civil and political rights.

For more than half a century, the international human rights movement has focused almost entirely on the activities of the able-bodied and able-minded. But over the last two decades, existing human rights networks have finally turned from the rights of 'traditional and visible minorities'—including people of color, ethnic and religious minorities, women, children, and refugees—to the rights of what might be called 'invisible, underprotected minorities', particularly persons living with HIV/AIDS, gays and lesbians, and persons with physical or mental disabilities. Discrimination against each of these groups has become a serious and neglected problem that affects large numbers in every society. Because each of these groups has traditionally been hidden from mainstream society, each has long been subjected to widespread, unredressed discrimination, which traditionally has been neither well-chronicled nor subjected to sustained public scrutiny or criticism. From a human rights perspective, the intellectually disabled rank among the world's most vulnerable and at-risk populations both because they are different and because their disability renders them less able either to assert their rights or to protect themselves against blatant discrimination.

In dealing with persons with intellectual disabilities, many governments fail to distinguish between two groups with distinctly different problems and needs: those with mental retardation and those with mental illness. According to the American Association on Mental Retardation, '[*m*]*ental retardation* refers to substantial limitations in present functioning. It is characterized by [three characteristics: 1] significantly subaverage intellectual functioning, [with an IQ tested below 70] existing concurrently with [2] related limitations in two or more of the following applicable adaptive skill areas: communication, self-care, home living, social skills, community use, self-direction, health and safety, functional academics, leisure, and work. [and 3] Mental retardation manifests before age 18.'[1] Mentally ill persons, by contrast, may exhibit very high intelligence, shifting adaptive skills, and may become afflicted (or cured) at any time during their lives.[2]

Like the disabled at large, the vast majority of the world's intellectually disabled still live in horrifying conditions. As Mary Robinson, who recently stepped down as United Nations High Commissioner for Human Rights, has noted, 'We know that persons with disabilities frequently live in deplorable conditions, and face physical and social barriers, which prevent their integration and full participation in the community. As a result, millions of adults and children throughout the world are segregated, deprived of virtually all their rights, and sometimes lead wretched and marginalised lives....'[3] Because of their incapacity to protect or even to understand their own interests, the intellectually disabled are at the greatest risk. Mental institutions and psychiatric hospitals worldwide stand in dismal condition, and patients often contend with inhumane and unsanitary living conditions, where they are treated as subhuman prisoners, and receive little or no medical care. Incredibly, in the United States of America, until the Supreme Court's landmark decision in June 2002 in *Atkins v Virginia*,[4] those with mental retardation were still subject to capital punishment, a state of affairs that existed in no other country in the world.

The thesis of this book is that Article I of the Universal Declaration of Human Rights, which declares that all humans are born free and equal in dignity and rights, carries special meaning in the context of disability. Collectively, the essays in this volume argue that, however different persons with disabilities may be, they are nevertheless born free and equal in dignity and rights, and hence are entitled to equality of respect and treatment, even if that equality does not entail identical treatment under all circumstances.

Making concrete the principle of 'different but equal' raises challenges for both governmental and nongovernmental organizations at both a national and international level. National and international organizations share a joint responsibility to ensure that rights proclaimed in international norms and national legislation are translated into genuine and concrete improvements in the lives of persons with intellectual disabilities. Human rights workers need to learn how to help intellectually disabled persons speak up for their own rights and how to integrate the language, tools, strategies, and networks of the international human rights movement into their daily struggle for dignity, equality, and justice.

For human rights advocates, this is a familiar task. In building global human rights regimes, a pattern has emerged, whereby advocates focus on five priorities: first on reconceptualizing the disability question as a human rights issue; second, on developing knowledge; third, on developing transnational issue networks to address problems; fourth, on developing legal precedents under domestic law; and fifth, on using that reconceptualization, knowledge, and domestic precedent to help crystallize international normative standards.

Such a pattern has begun to unfold with respect to the intellectually disabled, as advocates have sought first, to reconceptualize disability as a human rights issue, and only secondarily as a medical issue.[5] Treating intellectual disability as a human rights issue directly addresses, and seeks to readjust, the power relationships that shape the unequal treatment of the disabled. As Mary Robinson put it:

The most important tool in tackling inequality is to enable those experiencing it to remedy the power relationship, to take some control. This is a concept of rights that requires that those who are furthest from the cabinet table own the rights that inhere to them by virtue solely of their humanity. Ownership of this kind enables them to describe their condition, then to challenge it, and then to ensure that any decisions taken in the organisation and the ordering of their lives are made 'by and with' them, not 'about and for' them.[6]

The second step has been the formation of what one of us has elsewhere called a 'transnational human rights network'[7] that has worked to expose worldwide discrimination against persons with intellectual disabilities. That global network of human rights nongovernmental organizations (NGOs) now includes such organizations as Inclusion International, Mental Disability Rights International, Rehabilitation, and Sister Witness International (as well as such 'general-purpose NGOs' such as Human Rights Watch), all dedicated to investigating, publicizing, and calling for action on international disability issues in such countries as Russia, Romania, Latin America, and Kosovo. In August 2002, for example, one of those NGOs, Mental Disability Rights International, grabbed headlines around the world by releasing a report about psychiatric hospitals in Kosovo. That report demonstrated that, even under UN supervision, women are raped by male patients while staff watch; that mentally ill patients sit in prolonged enforced idleness in conditions of appalling filth; and that patients are often drugged rather than counseled, threatened with retaliation for charges of abuse, and frequently left without meaningful treatment or instruction.[8]

A third step has been to litigate discrimination issues involving the intellectually disabled under domestic law. Domestic advocates in Ireland, for example, have made high-profile use of international law in *O'Donoghue v Minister for Health*, in which the High Court concluded that the government had deprived a child with a disability of a free appropriate education in violation of broad guarantees of a free required education under Ireland's Constitution.[9] In *Department of Health and Community*

Services v J.W.B. (In re Marion), the High Court of Australia severely restricted a guardian's right to authorize the involuntary sterilization of a person with an intellectual disability.[10] These issues have also been extensively litigated in the United States, particularly in the well-known *Pennhurst* and *Mills* litigations.[11] These court cases eventually spurred enactment of the Education for All Handicapped Children Act of 1975 (later called the Individuals with Disabilities Education Act), which effectively allowed the return of some one million children previously excluded from the American public school system due to their perceived mental handicaps.

Fourth, these domestic efforts have spurred nascent efforts to develop and harden an international standard regarding the rights of the mentally disabled, which should someday ripen into a ratifiable treaty barring such discrimination.[12] Throughout this process, the United Nations has played an increasingly proactive role in working for global recognition of human rights of people with intellectual disabilities: by launching the International Year of Disabled Persons, the World Program of Action and the Decade of Disabled Persons, and the World Summit on Social Development. In 1971 the UN General Assembly adopted a Declaration on the Rights of Mentally Retarded Persons. In 1975 the UN endorsed a Declaration on the Rights of Disabled Persons that covers some one-half billion persons who suffer from a mental or a physical disability. In 1993 the General Assembly adopted the Standard Rules on the Equalization of Opportunities for Persons with Disabilities. This led in 1994 to the appointment of a UN Special Rapporteur on Disability, as well as to a recently published study commissioned by the Office of the UN High Commissioner for Human Rights to expressly evaluate the effectiveness of existing international mechanisms on the rights of the disabled.

What should constitute the core elements of this international standard? That issue is discussed throughout this volume. But the core elements are now commonly recognized to include such rights as *access* to tools for exercising individual agency; *participation* and *inclusion* in critical decisions that affect the disabled person's life and future; and freedom for disabled individuals proactively to exercise their rights, both personally and through agents. Advocates have also made a powerful case that those with mental retardation should have their own legal authority to make their own decisions about *having and raising children*.[13] For those with mental illness, the *right to treatment* remains a paramount concern. Many societies continue to regard the mentally ill as outcasts, rather than as patients in need of health care, institutionalizing the curable and driving millions suffering from mental illness from seeking help for fear of long-term detention or social stigmatization. Also not to be forgotten are the distinctive needs of individuals whose intellectual disabilities only exacerbate their existing human rights vulnerabilities, for example, refugees and children who suffer from mental health problems.[14]

The Yale Declaration, announced in March 1995 at the end of the Yale Conference that gave rise to these essays (and reproduced in the end of this volume), represents perhaps the most progressive effort thus far to enumerate the elements of an authoritative international human rights instrument that could forthrightly address this issue. It is our sincere hope that this volume will help fuel the growing international movement to treat the rights of the intellectually disabled as fundamental human rights. In time, we hope that this volume will be remembered as only the first of many works to recognize Stan Herr's vision: that a genuine commitment to human rights requires that people with intellectual disabilities be treated as different, but equal.

THE PLAN OF THIS BOOK

This volume proceeds in five parts.

Part I addresses the problem of *conceptualizing* the needs of persons with intellectual disabilities as a human rights issue. The four chapters in this part address the question from four different perspectives: international, terminological, cross-cultural, and historical.

In the opening chapter, Peter Mittler, an international pioneer in this area, provides a *tour d'horizon* of the field of intellectual disability, highlighting advances in the recognition of the rights of intellectually disabled persons and identifying challenges for the future. Mittler sees a world trend toward an internationally agreed upon human rights perspective, which redefines intellectual disability as residing not in an individual's handicap, but rather, in the limitations imposed on the individual by societal institutions. The field has experienced a major paradigm shift, he argues, away from a 'defect model'—which emphasizes defects in the individual—toward one emphasizing that individual's interactions with the environment and the nature and intensity of the supports that individual needs to engage successfully with that environment. Mittler notes several worldwide shifts of emphasis: from segregated custodial services to community living and access to mainstream services, an increasingly powerful global self-advocacy movement, more effective partnership between professionals and parents of the disabled, and the rapid growth of organizations of and for people with intellectual disability, which have in turn, created partnerships with other local, national, and international human rights NGOs. Progress, Mittler concludes, depends largely upon developing these partnerships so that empowered and committed families and the disabled themselves can enjoy equal opportunities to assert their rights. The key issues for the future, he sees, are promoting self-advocacy and inclusion, a strategy that helps change stereotypes through increased interaction.

Throughout his discussion, Mittler highlights terminology. Terminology, he argues, signals the general public about the need to respect the dignity and self-respect of those with intellectual disabilities by avoiding degrading or stereotype-reinforcing language that denies their individuality. This theme is picked up in Chapter 2, on 'Terminology and Power', in which Ruth Luckasson analyzes the role of power in shaping the 'terminology' of intellectual disabilities. Historically, she notes, those with intellectual disabilities have been named by others; their current attempts to influence how they are named is merely a microcosm of their much broader struggle to take control of their own destinies through personal agency. The term 'mental retardation' has long held a pejorative and stereotypical connotation, which carries with it a false assumption of homogeneity among the disabled. By including those with intellectual disability in the process of naming themselves, advocates would promote the goal of maximizing the participation of the mentally disabled in any proposed decisions and actions that affect their welfare and societal perception.

Chapter 3, by Alison Dundes Renteln, examines the divergent cross-cultural perceptions of disability, and demonstrates that cultural differences in the understanding of disability have significant policy implications. Like Mittler, Renteln notes that a shift from a medical to a socio-political model of disability has challenged the notion that disability is a condition inhering in the individuals, as opposed to a failure of society to make the environmental adaptations necessary to ensure the full participation by persons with disabilities. The central question, she asks, is 'how do conceptualizations of disability influence the disposition of actual disputes in society?' Across societies, she finds common and disturbing trends: elites generally display profound ignorance about the meaning of disabilities for ethnic minorities and the public at large; there is widespread official intolerance for disabilities, as well as a general inability to appreciate culturally specific disabilities. Renteln concludes by suggesting that comparative studies reveal the 'contingent nature of "normalcy"'. Future cross-cultural research, she says, should focus on gaining insight into culturally diverse methods of addressing various kinds of disabilities, with the goal of identifying best practices and yielding more humane approaches to social issues like disability.

Concluding Part I, David Braddock's and Susan Parish's Chapter 4 provides a historical policy survey of the treatment of people with intellectual disabilities in America and in Europe. In the nineteenth and early twentieth century, they demonstrate, social policy toward the intellectually disabled flowed primarily from a segregative, 'asylum' model—the growth of physical institutions to house the intellectually disabled and a cruel and

invasive debate over eugenics and the control of reproduction by those
with such disabilities. But after the Second World War, that model gave
way to the idea of state-supported de-institutionalized family care based
on contemporary family, community, and rights-based models of support.
During the 1970s, particularly in the United States, the 'de-institutionalization' movement merged with a parallel notion of a right to treatment,
which ultimately led in 1990 to the enactment of the Americans with
Disabilities Act (ADA), a watershed event for disability rights globally.
The ADA has since served as an international model for improving international standards of treatment in the United Kingdom and helped engen-
der the United Nations General Assembly's Standard Rules and World
Program of Action. Thus, assertive political activism by disabled persons
and their families created cross-disability coalitions that helped spur passage of domestic legislation and promoted a new emphasis on civil rights
and social participation that now cuts across national lines.

Having clarified how the issue of intellectual disabilities entered the
human rights rubric, Part II turns from what Stanley Herr calls 'wrongs to
rights': how the violation of the human rights of the intellectually disabled can be redressed through international and comparative law.
Stanley Herr's Chapter 5, entitled 'From Wrongs to Rights: International
Human Rights and Legal Protection', reviews the history and principles
underlying international human rights law and suggests strategies for
extending these principles further into the disabilities area. As Herr notes,
there are currently over 180 disability-related UN human rights documents relevant to the disabled. The two most significant are the UN
Declaration on the Rights of Mentally Retarded Persons, which recognizes those with mental retardation as entitled to the same rights as other
humans, as well as enjoying rights *to* services and proper legal safeguards, and the UN Declaration on the Rights of Disabled Persons, which
grants broad egalitarian and dignitary rights—both civil and political and
economic and social—to disabled persons regardless of degree, origin,
and type of disability. Following Mittler, Herr highlights how these
instruments have recognized the critical importance of *advocacy and
empowerment* to the disabled and their families. Herr further canvasses the
full array of international treaties, UN human rights statements, and the
work of UN Specialized Agencies and world conferences, to show both
the progress made in placing disability rights concerns on the world stage
and the extent to which disability issues still lag behind other global
human rights advances. Herr reviews successful strategies applied by
NGOs, foreign aid packages, domestic litigation,[15] national legislation,
and national disability plans. He demonstrates that successful human
rights advocacy for the disabled must pursue what one of us has called a
strategy of 'legal internationalization', that is, seeking to incorporate

human rights principles into national and local laws as well as into the customs and interactions of people who apply human rights principles in other settings.[16]

Moving to a comparative perspective, in Chapter 6—'Disability as a Subject of International Human Rights Law and Comparative Discrimination Law'—Theresia Degener examines how strong global trends towards discrimination laws protecting people with disabilities have spurred a paradigm shift from a medical to a human rights model in comparative and international disability law. That legal shift flowed from a recognition that the exclusion and segregation of the disabled do not follow inexorably from their 'impairments'. Rather, exclusion results from political choices that view disability as a problem of the individual, not society's failure to accommodate human differences. Laws that seek to effect the desegregation and de-institutionalization of disabled people thus counteract this defect by promoting instead the human rights values of *equality, dignity, autonomy,* and *solidarity*. While these values can be protected by a variety of approaches embodied in disability discrimination laws around the world—including constitutional, criminal, civil, or social law—a civil rights perspective, which depends largely on the judiciary to give meaning to the concept of equalization of opportunities for the disabled, has emerged as the most effective way for the disabled proactively to play a major role in enforcing their rights and dismantling the structural discrimination against them.

In their chapter on 'Liberty, Due Process, and the Pursuit of Happiness', Michael W. Smull and Luciene Parsley similarly seek to unpack the human rights values underlying the disability rights movement. Their chapter calls for change in the current treatment of the intellectually disabled. The current structure and philosophy of treatment, they claim, too often understates what is important *to* people with disabilities and overstates what is important *for* them. They argue that the concept of due process, as it has been clarified by the US Supreme Court, creates an emerging legal duty for professionals to ensure that the liberty of a person with a disability is not unduly restricted. The authors argue that professionals are morally, ethically, and legally obligated to understand and implement the lifestyle preferences of the disabled through techniques such as 'person-centered planning'. Moreover, they argue in favor of shifting from rigid *program services*—designed to keep a person safe, provide basic care and support to the person, and to teach the person skills that increase independence—toward a better practice: more flexible, individualized *support services*, which support the individual with disabilities to live the life he or she wants to have. Rather than seeking to manage behavior, support services focus on listening to the needs and desires of the disabled themselves; and giving disabled persons the support they need to attain and maintain control over the desired lifestyle. When others determine how someone else will live, they argue, personal liberty is restricted and due process is required to remedy the situation. Person-centered planning, which is applied in programs running in the United States, Canada, and the United Kingdom, allows for more accurate and reliable determination of individual preferences, and seeks to balance the desired lifestyle of the person against the health and safety needs of the individual and others; and the resources that are available to support the individual. Thus, equality of treatment can be accorded to people with intellectual disabilities not just in theory, but also in practice, by adopting individualized programs that vary from individual to individual, but share the goal of maximizing personal liberty, autonomy, and the pursuit of happiness.

In Part III, the volume shifts focus toward how the disability rights movement has pursued national anti-discrimination legislation as its primary vehicle for promoting human rights progress. In his chapter 'The Potential of Disability Non-discrimination Laws', Stanley Herr analyzes how the United States, Israel, and the United Kingdom each implemented laws to remedy disability-based discrimination in turn reinforcing campaigns to develop international treaties on disability rights. Thus, rather than focusing on the kind of 'internalization analysis', which describes how norms trickle down from the international to the national level, this chapter addresses how techniques incorporated into national laws—for example, the use of alternative dispute resolution methods to minimize or eliminate disability discrimination—can bubble up to become part of an emerging international standard. Herr outlines the uses and limitations of disability non-discrimination for disabled persons and explores the origins of the US Americans with Disabilities Act, a vigorous legal and social enterprise that has sought to counter the medicalized stereotypes that had historically discriminated against people with disabilities. Herr further traces the development of the Israeli 'equal rights for the disabled' law and the UK Disability Discrimination Act, and presents a *tour d'horizon* of disability laws in dozens of countries, identifying commonalities and appraising limitations. Some laws, for example the Israeli statute, contain language permitting affirmative action to correct prior or present discrimination against the disabled or to promote their equality. Other statutes range, Herr notes, from 'non-discrimination statutes to constitutional non-discrimination provisions, from highly specific protections and prohibitions to more hybrid social welfare laws with some anti-discrimination language, from penal laws to those with civil characteristics, and from generic non-discrimination to disability-specific laws'.[17] Herr closes with recommendations for how enforcement of disability non-discrimination norms can be improved, particularly by combining prudent test-case litigation with less adversarial methods of dispute resolution, non-litigation strategies that can be used by grassroots activists, and quasi-governmental initiatives. He singles out the Israeli experience with Disabilities Rights Commissions as illustrating how strong, independent oversight and enforcement agencies can advance the cause of disability non-discrimination law, an approach that he recommends be implemented in the United States through creation of a centralized White House Office on ADA Implementation and Disability Rights. A universal human rights strategy for promoting intellectual disability rights, Herr reasons, must include strategies for developing pride and empowerment; for creating authentic expectations for rights and quality of life, and for developing new mechanisms for implementation of disability non-discrimination laws.

Dan Shnit's chapter, 'When Legislation Should Take Intellectual Disabilities into Account' builds on Herr's argument by examining potential spheres where countries should adopt specific or general anti-discriminatory legislation that can address the needs of persons with intellectual disabilities. If the goal is maximum integration of persons with intellectual disabilities into community life, Shnit reasons, societies should grant equal rights to disabled persons in a number of specific domains: access to services, tailored assistance and treatment, non-discriminatory legal status (with respect to contracts, criminal responsibility, and freedom and dignity), and various kinds of protective legislation. Shnit distinguishes between *specific legislation*, which is intended to regulate a specific set of issues pertaining to the rights or status of people with intellectual disabilities; *comprehensive legislation*, which is intended to regulate issues pertaining to the rights of people with a variety of disabilities; and *universal legislation*, which is applicable to all citizens of the country. Countries should seek a balance, he argues, between general legislation aimed at ensuring civil rights and personal freedoms of the intellectually disabled and specific legislation aimed at finding solutions addressing the special needs of those individuals. Wherever possible, however, he argues that it is preferable to enact general legislation with a broad application. Requiring specific legislation, he fears, unnecessarily reinforces paternalistic, segregative trends. In addition, governments should create the tools and conditions for the enforcement and implementation of the statutory provisions, including creating agencies with legal powers to enforce the law, to educate and inform, and to encourage public and private NGOs who can lobby for the rights of those with disabilities.

Robert Silverstein refines this analysis even further by distinguishing among five general categories of laws affecting people with disabilities: civil rights statutes (eg, ADA), entitlement programs (eg, 'open-ended' programs such as SSDI, SSI, Medicare and 'close-ended' programs such as the Children's Health Insurance Program under Title XXI of the Social Security Act), discretionary grant-in-aid programs (formula-grant programs and competitive grant programs), regulatory statutes (eg, National Voter Registration Act of 1993), and other provisions, including appropriations, tax legislation, and loans (eg, Disabled Access Tax Credit, Targeted Jobs Credit). Collectively, these statutes promote equality of opportunity, full participation, independent living, and economic self-sufficiency. Silverstein's chapter seeks to demonstrate that a convergence and harmonization of these statutes from many different spheres—non-discrimination, other civil rights, and social services laws—will better achieve basic equality by furthering the goal of taking difference into account.

The chapters in Part IV explore social policy perspectives on equality and difference. Marcia H. Rioux's chapter 'On Second Thought: Constructing Knowledge, Law, Disability, and Inequality' seeks to unpack prevailing notions of disability and equality by exploring how such differing conceptions necessarily incorporate inherent biases towards particular standards of policy, program, and legal status. Disabled people continue to be subject to violations of their human rights, she argues, both because of the way in which human rights norms and standards are constructed; and the way in which nations do or do not meet their commitments to the codified standards. Rioux contrasts formulations of disability based on individual pathology, a biomedical approach in which the disability is assumed to be caused by a preventable or ameliorable mental or physical condition, with formulations based on social pathology, which assume that disability is not inherent to the individual independent of social structure and environment. Whenever perceptions of disability change, understandings of equality also change from models based on notions of equality of treatment, to equality of opportunity, to equality of resources. Distinguishable typologies of disability have emerged, each with its own clear standard of social responsibility, inherent ethical foundation, and justification of rights. These range from a civil disability model, which emphasizes the social responsibility to protect the disabled, to a compensatory privilege model, which focuses on paternalism, to a 'well-being' model, which would allocate treatment, care, and resources based on a notion of equal outcomes for people with disabilities. Rioux argues that distinguishing among these models can provide important insights into the interplay and interpenetration of national and international declarations of human rights and rehabilitation systems.

In Chapter 12, 'Prevention of Disability: Is There a Conflict between Public Health Prevention and Respect for Persons with Disabilities', Adrienne Asch, Lawrence O. Gostin, and Diann M. Johnson bring immediacy to Rioux's analysis by focusing on a profound moral dilemma: should public health systems seek to prevent disabilities by intervention, and would such intervention promote the goal of improving the societal status of persons with disabilities? Public health programs, they assert, face a tension in addressing the issues of disabilities: on the one hand, they attempt to prevent disability; on the other hand, they should seek to elevate the status of persons with disabilities in society. Certain primary prevention activities, such as prenatal testing and selective abortion, tend to undercut the goals of equality and full inclusion for people with disabilities. While the authors support a mother's right to decide whether the fetus should be aborted, they are also troubled by such a choice made without rules of professional practice or moral guidance. In fact, they note, these decisions are too often made under severe economic and personal influences—such as pressure from pharmaceutical companies that market prenatal tests; cost-cutting pressures faced by physicians and managed care organizations; physicians' fears of 'wrongful life' malpractice suits—as well as professional, societal, and governmental influences such as public health practices and policies, funding decisions, and overt coercion about screening, sterilization, and abortion decisions. While the authors reject a Darwinian view and instead argue that society should respect diversity in all its incarnations, they also explore the meaning of the inherent importance in maintaining diversity of physical and mental capacities in society. With modern technological advances, they note, disability could become a function of wealth and resources worldwide, with developing countries, which have the fewest resources, producing the most disabled people. While admitting that it is necessary to take cost into account, the authors stress as fundamental the notion that the absence or presence of a particular disability or personal trait cannot be the basis for treating one person as superior to another. Accordingly, maternal or parental decisions with respect to prevention measures should be insulated from outside pressures with parents receiving unbiased and complete information so that they can make morally informed and well-reasoned decisions. Society, they argue, needs to study the issues of selective abortion to ensure government neutrality in a woman's choice, as well as to strive fully to integrate those with intellectual disabilities more fully into society.

The strong focus on moral reasoning in Asch, Gostin, and Johnson's chapter is followed by an empirical chapter, 'Studying the Emerging Workforce', by Peter David Blanck and Helen A. Schartz. That chapter stresses the importance of inter- and cross-disciplinary research as a means of informing policymakers and citizens about issues relating to the development of national disability employment policies. Noting the lack of systemic comparative research in the field of disability employment policy creation, implementation, and evaluation, the authors attempt to trace the shift in disability laws and policies over the past twenty-five years. They discern evolution from a model of charity and compensation, to medical oversight, and finally to a 'civil rights' approach to disability, which conceives of disabled persons as a minority group entitled to the same hard-won legal protections granted other racial, ethnic, and gender minorities. The authors argue that a comparative approach to assessing disability employment laws and policies would highlight different perspectives and assumptions in a way that would reconcile apparently conflicting outcomes. To prove this point, the authors present the findings of a lengthy investigation of employment of intellectually disabled individuals, begun in 1989, to demonstrate the implementation of and compliance with ADA prescriptions. Using outcome measures, they discover both positive change and 'chronic stagnation' in employment and the economic status of intellectually disabled persons during the period from 1990 to 1999, grouped under five headings: (1) employment integration; (2) economic opportunity; (3) individual growth; (4) the 'black hole' effect whereby even employed disabled persons remain in non-integrated settings; and (5) perceptions of rights and ADA implementation. Based on this empirical examination, the authors conclude that policymakers often have difficulty distinguishing between cases where change is actually occurring or where there is simply an illusion of change. Surveying the various strategies developed and implemented around the world, the authors examine Canada; the EU; Ireland; Germany; the UK; non-EU parts of Europe; Israel; Latin America; and such Asian countries as China, Japan, Australia, and India. The authors conclude by reiterating that comparative approaches to the definition of disability may not only help to avoid and resolve disputes, but also may aid policymakers in gauging the effectiveness of national disability legislation. Comparative study suggests that the implementation of disability employment policy is neither unduly costly nor burdensome so long as there is greater international understanding about what enhances the effectiveness of national disability legislation.

John H. Noble, Jr.'s chapter on 'The Economics of Equality: An Exploration of Country Differences' applies an economic perspective to estimate both the *direct* and *indirect* costs borne by society in addressing mental illness or mental retardation. Direct costs, Noble argues, are the resources society spends to achieve well-being—eg, custodial, remedial, habilitative, educational, and other services—over what would have been spent on a similarly situated, non-disabled person. Indirect costs refer to other, less quantifiable ways in which mental illness or retardation interferes with a person's normal functioning, thereby reducing his or her well-being. In applying cost-benefit analysis, Noble candidly recognizes that the lives of the intellectually disabled have not had the same value for everyone everywhere; different choices have been made in different countries about who is allowed to join the moral community of humanity for whom equality of opportunities is universally accepted. Noble also raises the familiar human rights question of cultural relativism—how will the economics of equality be operationalized in different countries, and to what extent will equality be made contingent on culture, resource availability, or national development? Culture and economics both help explain cross-cultural inequalities in the treatment of persons with physical and mental disabilities, Noble concludes, because 'economic means more than any alternative explanatory factor determines the extent to which a society can provide disability services in order to reduce the indirect cost burden of disability on individuals, families, and the community.'[18] Redressing differences in economic means, he suggests, calls for a strategy that combines economic development and debt forgiveness; foreign aid; and interdependent sharing of goods, services, and information.

The final chapters of Part IV turn to life choices for persons with disabilities. In 'Out-of-Home Placement of Children with Intellectual Disabilities: The Need for a Family Support Policy', Arie Rimmerman surveys the research done in the United States and Israel on the out-of-home placement of children with intellectual disabilities. In particular, he examines the implications of such placements for family support policy and human rights. Placement, the author suggests, is a process, not a single outcome, with placement determinations usually being made by parents in response to stressful life events and internal resources, such as locus of control, hardiness, and sense of coherence and external resources such as social support, family cohesion, and adaptation. Not surprisingly, parents who apply for placement tend to lack internal and/or external resources and desperately need such local social support services as (1) respite care services; (2) extended hours in schools to allow parents to work and pursue a normal life; (3) recreation programs for adolescents and adults; (4) individual and group support services for families in crisis; and (5) training and guidance programs for parents. Inevitably, human rights tensions arise. A child's right to live with his or her natural parents can conflict with the right of the parents to obtain placement as a means of conserving their own well-being. Parents with a 'low sense of coherence' are most likely to accede to external, governmental pressures in giving up their child.

In his third and final chapter in this volume, on 'Self-Determination, Autonomy, and Alternatives for Guardianship', Stanley Herr similarly applies a comparative law perspective to examine ways to minimize the use of legal guardianship. How, Herr asks, can society both maximize an individual's autonomy and offer community support services that help the individual to participate in society's decision-making processes? In the United States, he maintains, guardianship has become an overused legal institution in danger of collapse. Instead, he argues, humane twenty-first-century societies must empower individuals by recognizing that people's capacities are dynamic and listening to people with disabilities, rather than dictating to them based on ostensibly 'professional' expertise and superiority. The chapter contrasts the US position with the Swedish view, which has made steady progress in moving disabled people into the societal mainstream. Legal reforms and legal institutions, he argues, have played significant parts in these advances: ranging from access to the courts, ensuring administrative remedies, replacing a law focusing on mental retardation with one that addresses the full range of severe disabilities, and abolishing guardianship and replacing it with a continuum of supportive services, none of which disenfranchise adults. Herr notes that in Germany, a 1992 law replaced guardianship with flexible measures sensitive to principles of the least restrictive alternative and procedural justice. In a prescient note, he closes by arguing that the movement for enhanced self-determination is gaining momentum throughout the world. It now finds expression in international human rights documents, the rise of self-advocacy groups, and a plethora of legal reforms. As leading NGOs have long recognized, the US's social programs have reached their limits. Too many people, Herr concludes, are needlessly suffering under disenfranchising plenary guardianships when less intrusive and more consensual forms of support are available and would easily suffice.

The fifth and final part of the book features chapters that address the future goals and aspirations of the intellectual disabilities rights movement. The part begins with 'Voices of Self-Advocates' by Mitchell Levitz, the gripping personal story of a young man with Downs syndrome who became self-sufficient by age 31. Levitz's story reveals that independence and self-sufficiency are critically important for the personal development and dignity of the individual, but that environmental factors are equally crucial—eg, access to public transportation. Independent living is only possible if, on the one hand, the disabled person is not controlled by the government or even family or friends; on the other hand, independent living does not mean rejecting public services and family support. Instead, disabled individuals must be both recognized and must be able to see themselves as part of the larger community, what Levitz calls a Circle of Support or Circle of Friends, which is a planning process that emphasizes the interdependent nature of relationships. The sum total of these changes, he concludes, is that people with disabilities will gain a sense of control over their lives, identity, and future, while gaining as well a greater network of relationships that will lead them to greater inclusion and the feeling of full citizenship. Self-advocacy thus can be seen as the first step toward becoming a successful advocate for others, which entails being vocal, and calling for early intervention, quality education and inclusion, employment opportunities, and full integration into society.

The final two chapters of the book explicate the 1995 *Yale Declaration*, reproduced in the back of this volume, as an important source of policy guidance to legislative and treaty drafters in this area. In 'Recognizing Existing Rights and Crafting New Ones: Tools for Drafting Human Rights Instruments for People with Mental Disabilities', two skilled advocates, Eric Rosenthal and Clarence J. Sundram, chronicle the growing interest in drafting new domestic and international human rights laws to protect the rights of disabled people. They note how the Yale Declaration recognizes the dangers of new legal instruments that fail to reflect the binding nature of human rights law relating to disabled people. A specialized international convention on the rights of the disabled, they argue, is now necessary to make it clear that extant international human rights law creates binding obligations on governments, so that the recognition of disability rights is not left to the discretion of individual domestic governments. The chapter discusses the genesis of the Yale Declaration, its guiding principles, as well as the increasing attention it is being given by the international community. Their discussion tracks the most important features of the Declaration, particularly its recommendations concerning full enforcement of existing human rights law until a new United Nations Disability Rights Convention can be adopted and can come into force. The Yale Declaration, which cites the Standard Rules, further states that all human rights and fundamental freedoms are universal and therefore include people with disabilities, thereby explicitly bringing disability rights within the embrace of existing international human rights instruments. The Declaration goes on to state that all States must immediately begin to reform their laws and public policies to 'achieve or exceed' international standards. The Yale Declaration links the concept of human rights protection with a rehabilitative concept—that of community integration—and calls on both governments and international development programs to promote best practices of service in the most integrated settings possible. Because community integration is a right per se, the authors argue, development of the best and most integrated services systems should be seen as a human rights prerogative.

The authors compare the Yale Declaration with the Inter-American Convention on Disability, noting its flaws while recognizing that it is also a major step forward as a matter of law, as a statement of principle, and as a form of public education which can provide useful guidance to drafters of the UN Convention on Disability. They also analyze in detail the 2001 World Health Organization Study by Rosenthal and Sundram—'The Role of International Human Rights in Domestic Mental Health Legislation'— which was drafted to assist legislators on the domestic level to understand existing protections under international human rights law. The WHO Study describes the core minimum obligations on governments under extant human rights covenants to protect rights of the intellectually disabled. Those obligations include recognizing the right to community integration under international law as part of the protection against discrimination and the right to the highest attainable standard of physical and mental health. The authors further suggest that a series of rights are implicit in existing international human rights instruments: (1) a right to the highest attainable standard of physical and mental health,[19] (2) protections against discrimination on the basis of disability,[20] (3) protections against inhuman and degrading treatment,[21] (4) a right to liberty and security of the person,[22] and (5) safeguards required to protect rights under both the ICCPR and the ICESCR. There are two international principles, they argue, that are absolutely essential to ensure the human rights of disabled persons: first, a right to the highest attainable standard of health ('right to health'), which entails access to appropriate and professional services, right to individualized treatment, right to rehabilitation and treatment that enhances autonomy, right to independence and social integration, right to least restrictive services, and a right to community-based services; second, a 'right to protection against discrimination', which connotes both affirmative action and reasonable accommodation and a rule of proportionality coupled with due process protections. Applications of the right to protection against discrimination in mental health law, they argue, include a right to community integration and to prevent the improper imposition of guardianship.

The authors close by concluding that a new disability rights convention, based in good measure on the Yale Declaration, that spells out the rights of the disabled under existing international human rights conventions, would aid compliance by clearly notifying governments as to their international obligations. Any new instrument should represent, per the Yale Declaration, 'best practices' likely to garner the support of the people it is intended to protect. Such a convention could also be internalized into domestic law by assisting legislators or activists who seek to draft new domestic legislation to conform to the full requirements of international human rights law. Creation of a new UN treaty monitoring body would provide continuous oversight of governmental performance under the new instrument. To avoid some of the errors of the past, they suggest, the drafters of a new human rights convention should frame it in general language and should consult extensively with the disability rights community to achieve a final text.

In the closing chapter, 'Recommendations for the United Nations and International NGOs', Ronald C. Slye highlights the core recommendations issuing from the March 1995 Yale Law School Conference 'Should Difference Make a Difference?' that were eventually delivered to the UN and international NGOs. Slye divides the Conference recommendations into five core categories. The first is collection and dissemination of information, a recommendation which suggests that dissemination of the Standard Rules should be used as a guide to create an inclusive process for reforming state laws and policies. The second is for enhanced monitoring, of both the implementation of international norms, such as the Standard Rules, and violations of the rights of persons with intellectual disabilities. The recommendations suggests that issues relating to the rights of the intellectually disabled be included in the US Department of State's annual Country Reports on Human Rights Practices, a recommendation that one of us (Koh) was able later to implement while serving as Assistant Secretary of State for Democracy, Human Rights and Labor in the Clinton Administration. Third, the chapter makes recommendations regarding advocacy, including the notion that the UN and international NGOs support the development of locally-based advocacy organizations and foster leadership and public discourse on the rights of the intellectually disabled. Fourth, the chapter follows Rosenthal and Sundram by urging more efforts toward standard setting, particularly increasing the number of authoritative statements linking international human rights with disability rights to promote the long-term goal of creating a binding treaty on the rights of the intellectually disabled. Fifth and finally, the chapter recommends internalization: the incorporation of disability rights concerns into international development programs and other planning processes, with international development assistance being made more inclusive so that people with intellectual disabilities can take advantage of them; focusing democratization programs on persons with intellectual disabilities; fostering relevant civil society programs that incorporate the views of the disabled, their families, and their advocates, and the like.

Although some progress has been made in each of the five areas since the Yale Conference, Slye concludes that much work remains to be done. Since 1995, the United Nations and some international NGOs have created useful websites collecting information on the use of the Standard Rules and 'best practices'. But the mainstreaming in practice of rights of people with intellectual disabilities has remained minimal. Even though major international human rights organizations have finally begun to focus on the rights of the intellectually disabled, their focus has been neither comprehensive nor systematic. Similarly, some progress has been made towards creating binding international agreements to protect the rights of the intellectually disabled. Most critically, the idea of a binding treaty was finally endorsed by the General Assembly in December 2001. Nevertheless, persons with intellectual disabilities are still not seen as on par with able-bodied and able-minded individuals, as full-fledged subjects and objects of the international human rights movement.

CONCLUSION

This extended review leaves us with a question: whither the human rights and intellectual disabilities movement? What have we gained from promoting this interchange between international human rights and disability rights movements? Three conclusions emerge.

First and most obviously, the rights of persons with intellectual disabilities clearly stand at the cutting edge of the international human rights movement. That movement rests on two core notions: first, that persons acquire certain inalienable rights solely by virtue of being born human, and second, that governments have no right to treat human beings as less than fully human—or less deserving of equal treatment and dignity—solely because of the physical or mental characteristics with which they were born or acquire later in life.

Second, we plainly benefit from examining the needs and rights of people with mental retardation from both an interdisciplinary and cross-cultural perspective. We cannot create or influence better-informed twenty-first-century public policy, national legislation, or a new and more relevant generation of international human rights standards if we rely on the scientific, ethical, moral, or legal understandings of the twentieth century. To make genuine progress, we must learn from the United Nations, regional organizations and nongovernmental organizations, from the developing as well as the developed nations. We need interdisciplinary understanding as well: the insights of lawyers and scientists, scholars and advocates, experts and self-advocates, and economists and educators, to understand and respond to the complex and multifaceted problem of making disability rights a human rights imperative. While law has evolved slowly, the disability rights movement is plainly a social and scientific movement that has continued rapidly to progress. The scientific causes of mental retardation and mental illness have become better understood. Techniques of remediation and habilitation have been refined. Service delivery has progressed. Domestic non-discrimination legislation has proliferated. Compliance with existing standards has started to improve.

Third, tensions remain within the disability rights movement: between those who favor segregation or assimilation as ideals, between prevention strategies or claims for diversity, between remediation or habilitation, and on questions of capacity versus choice. Domestic legislation has walked a fine line in balancing these tensions, and so too, must the international standard setting that is still to come. But that having been acknowledged, the two movements have finally begun to mix their insights and now stand at the threshold of a new global law-making exercise. As treaty-makers finally start to consider how our laws should treat those who are different, we hope that the essays in this volume will persuade them to keep the norms of equality and respect for human dignity at the forefront of their thinking. For difference need not mean legal difference, when those with intellectual disabilities are treated as they should be—as human beings who are different, but fully equal.

NOTES

1. *Mental Retardation: Definition, Classification, and Systems of Supports* (9th edn, Washington, DC: AAMR, 1992) 5. The American Psychiatric Association's definition similarly states: 'The essential feature of Mental Retardation is significantly subaverage general intellectual functioning (Criterion A) that is accompanied by significant limitations in adaptive functioning in at least two of the following skill areas: communication, self-care, home living, social/interpersonal skills, use of community resources, self-direction, functional academic skills, work, leisure, health, and safety (Criterion B). The onset must occur before age 18 years (Criterion C). Mental Retardation has many different etiologies and may be seen as a final common pathway of various pathological processes that affect the functioning of the central nervous system.' American Psychiatric Association, *Diagnostic and Statistical Manual of Mental Disorders* (4th edn, Washington, DC: American Psychiatric Association, 2000) 41. 'Mild' mental retardation is typically used to describe people with an IQ level of 50–55 to approximately 70. ibid 42–43.
2. For the compelling, well-publicized story of one such individual, the brilliant mathematician John F. Nash, who overcame mental illness and won the Nobel Prize in Economics, see S Nassar, *A Beautiful Mind: A Biography of John Forbes Nash, Jr.* (New York: Simon & Schuster, 1994).
3. M Robinson, UN High Commissioner for Human Rights, Video Message to the International Seminar on Human Rights and Disability (Stockholm, 5 November 2000, excerpt of transcript available at http://www.un.org/esa/socdev/enable/stockholmnov2000a.htm).
4. 122 S Ct 2242 (decided 20 June 2002).
5. M Robinson, quoted in 'No More Exclusion', *World Disability Report* (Geneva: International Disability Foundation, 2002) available at http://www.dpi.org/old_site/report.html.
6. M Robinson, 'Equality and Rights', available at http://www.equality.ie/pdf/NEWSLETT.PDF.
7. See generally HH Koh, 'Bringing International Law Home' (1998) 35 *Houston Law Review* 623.
8. See 'Forgotten by the U.N.', *Washington Post*, 18 August 2002 at B06; EM Lederer, 'Report of Abuse in Kosovo Clinics', *Washington Post*, 8 August 2002; O Burkeman, 'UN "Ignored" Abuse at Kosovo Mental Homes', *The Guardian*, 8 August 2002.
9. [1996] OR 20.
10. 106 ALR (High Court of Australia, 6 May 1992).
11. *Mills v Board of Education* 348 F Supp 866 (DDC 1972); *Halderman v Pennhurst State School and Hospital* 446 F Supp 1295 (ED Pa 1977), aff'd 612 F 2d 84 (3d Cir 1979), reversed and remanded 451 US 1 (1981).
12. LO Gostin, 'Human Rights of Persons with Mental Disabilities: The European Convention of Human Rights' (2000) 23 *International Journal of Law & Psychiatry* 125.

13. See generally MA Field and VA Sanchez, *Equal Treatment for People with Mental Retardation: Having and Raising Children* (Cambridge, Mass: Harvard Univ Press, 1999).
14. In her address to the October 2000 International Consultation on Mental Health of Refugees and Displaced Populations in Conflict and Post-Conflict Situations, High Commissioner Mary Robinson explained: 'We also have a better understanding now of the degree to which persons affected by conflict and post-conflict situations are especially vulnerable to mental health problems. Professionals involved in complex emergencies must address the delicate issues arising with regard to mental health. Victims themselves must be able to recognize that the trauma of conflict can cause mental health problems. Both should be able to seek support, without fear of stigmatization.' The International Consultation on Mental Health of Refugees and Displaced Populations in Conflict and Post-Conflict Situations: From Crisis through Reconstruction, WHO headquarters, Geneva, Switzerland, 23 to 25 October 2000, available at http://www.whomsa.org/it/text8/04_statement.html.
15. In American case law, the high water mark was *Wyatt v Stickney* 244 F Supp 387 (MD Ala 1972), which cited the 1971 UN Declaration and included reference to international human rights standards in making its decisions. In general, US courts have seldom used international human rights law to redress human rights abuses, though now they are increasingly more willing to do so. See generally HH Koh, 'Transnational Public Law Litigation' (1991) 100 *Yale Law Journal* 2347. In other countries, as Herr's chapter chronicles, judges have made strong use of human rights declarations for persons with intellectual disabilities.
16. See generally HH Koh, 'How is International Human Rights Law Enforced?' (1999) 74 *Indiana Law Journal* 1397.
17. Herr ch 8 at p. 213.
18. Noble ch 14 at p. 405.
19. ICESCR, art 12.
20. ICCPR, art 26 and ICESCR, art 2(2).
21. ICCPR, art 7.
22. ICCPR, art 9.

Part I
Conceptualizing Intellectual Disabilities: History and Terminology

1

Meeting the Needs of People with an Intellectual Disability: International Perspectives

PETER MITTLER

All of us have experienced and will continue to experience difficulties in learning. These difficulties may be transient and affect only a few aspects of living and learning. But for some, the difficulties appear to be pervasive and permanent, leading to labels such as intellectual disability or mental retardation.

The moment such labels are imposed or are even being considered as appropriate, there is a major risk that the abilities of the individual will be underestimated and that decisions will be made which are likely to result in reduced access to society's institutions and services, including education in mainstream schools, paid employment, and opportunities to contribute to society and to the community. In many countries of the world, people with intellectual disabilities lose their civil rights and are forced to live at or beyond the margins of society, as inmates of institutions, vagrants, beggars, and prostitutes.

We have hardly begun to understand how human beings learn or fail to learn. It is one of the unresolved mysteries of life itself. The study of learning difficulties and how these can be overcome or alleviated must therefore be seen as one of the major challenges not merely for science, medicine, or education but for humanity itself.

I. GLOBAL TRENDS

The field of intellectual disability has changed out of all recognition since the end of the Second World War and will no doubt do so again in the next half century. Although the nature and pace of change vary across continents, countries, and communities, no nation in the world can justifiably claim that the quality of life of people who have an intellectual disability is comparable to that of their fellow citizens. In general, people with an intellectual disability, their families, and the staff who work with them are a low priority, compared with other disability groups. Their needs tend to be overlooked, and they are often the last to be considered. Nevertheless, significant advances have been made throughout the world in recognizing the needs and rights of persons with intellectual disabilities. It is the aim of this introductory chapter to highlight some of these changes and to identify challenges for the future.

Summarizing world trends, a number of positive, interactive themes and elements can be identified:

(1) a human rights and values perspective, based on internationally agreed principles, reflected in a range of United Nations (UN) declarations and conventions, as well as UN programs and initiatives;

(2) a reconceptualization and redefinition of intellectual disability not only in terms of the nature and intensity of the supports required by an individual but also ways in which environments and social institutions need to change to remove barriers to learning and participation;

(3) a shift of emphasis from custodial and segregated services to supported living in the community, involving access to mainstream services such as education, health care, employment, housing, social welfare, leisure, and recreation;

(4) an increasingly powerful self-advocacy movement working for choice, self-determination, and autonomy;

(5) a concern for more effective partnership between professionals and parents;

(6) organizations of and for people with intellectual disabilities working alongside other non-governmental organizations at local, national, and international levels.

A. Terminology and Definitions

Issues around terminology are not merely a matter of taxonomic accuracy. The language that we use in discussing people with intellectual disabilities sends out certain signals to the general public whose attitudes and priorities fundamentally affect the prospects for progress.[1] Terminology and definitions, therefore, need to reflect the principles and values of respect for human rights and the dignity and self-respect of the individual. This is not an easy task, since the words used to describe people with intellectual disabilities in popular speech are far removed from the debates of policymakers or those concerned with classification and terminology. Furthermore, the field of terminology is itself beset with confusion and inconsistency.

1. People First Language

There has for some time been a consensus that everyday language used in conversation and in the media should avoid language use that is in any way degrading or that creates or reinforces stereotypes about disabled persons. This has been reflected at a variety of levels. First, this has been reflected by the avoidance of the definite article in phrases such as 'the' intellectually disabled on the grounds that this tends to deny individuality by suggesting that the disability is their main characteristic, rather than their individuality. This has led to the use of phrases such as 'persons (or people) with disabilities'. On the other hand, some self-advocacy organizations reject such usage as patronizing and prefer 'disabled persons', emphasizing that they are disabled by society. Second, this consensus is reflected by the avoidance of degrading terminology such as mongol, idiot, imbecile, moron, or feeble-minded. Similarly, the term 'retardate', which was once regularly used in scientific and professional literature, is now discredited.

The term 'intellectually challenged' is sometimes used as a synonym for intellectual disability but the practice is not widespread. On the other hand 'challenging behavior' is more commonly used to describe people with intellectual disability whose behavior is thought to be a challenge to the system rather than residing in the individual.[2]

2. Terminology for Organizations

In an effort to avoid continuing disputes over appropriate terminology, many national and international organizations have abandoned the use of labels in their titles in favor of a short title that reflects its mission.

For example, the International League of Societies for Persons with Mental Handicap, which initiated debate on this subject some twenty years ago, finally changed its name to Inclusion International in 1994, and is now using 'intellectual disability' in its publications. In the United States, the Association for Retarded Citizens has become The Arc—not as an abbreviation of the former Association of Retarded Citizens but as a noun. The Canadian Association for Mental Retardation became the Canadian Association for Community Living, largely as a result of pressure from its self-advocates, while Australia has statewide voluntary organizations with names such as Challenge, Active, and Endeavor. Fears that the public would not know the goals of these organizations because of their new generic titles and that fund-raising would flounder as a result have fortunately not been born out.

3. Terminology for People

Throughout this chapter, the term 'intellectual disability' has been used in preference to other available terminology, since there is evidence that this is rapidly becoming the preferred terminology for international dialogue,[3] though it is safe to predict that this terminology will follow its predecessors in also becoming unacceptable to service users and professionals. Intellectual disability has long been the accepted terminology in Australia, New Zealand, and Singapore and is in increasing use in the

United Kingdom and in United Nations publications.[4] In keeping with this trend, the International Association for the Scientific Study of Mental Deficiency became the International Association for the Scientific Study of Intellectual Disability, and a number of scientific journals have also changed their names.

Particular exception is taken by people with intellectual disability to the use of the adjective 'mental' because it causes or complicates the confusion that already exists between mental retardation and mental illness[5] and also because it is used as a term of abuse in popular speech. Hence, 'mental retardation' and 'mental handicap' have become unacceptable for this reason alone.

'Mental retardation' is still the official terminology of the World Health Organization (WHO) and of the United States. Ministers in the United Kingdom introduced the term 'learning disabilities' without consultation and for reasons that were never made clear, despite the fact that this terminology is used internationally to describe children with specific problems in acquiring literacy in the setting of average or even above average intelligence. Earlier terms have included 'mental handicap', 'mental subnormality', and 'mental deficiency'.

A few countries still make a distinction between educable and trainable children and use intelligence tests for this purpose. This distinction was abolished in the United Kingdom in 1971 when all children without exception were brought into the education system available to all other children.

4. Revision of the World Health Organization Classification and the Social Model of Disability

For the past ten years, the WHO has been undertaking a radical revision of its classification system known as the International Classification of Impairments, Disabilities and Handicaps (ICIDH).[6] This has been a complex and technical exercise involving worldwide consultation and field trials. The revision process has been strongly influenced by organizations of disabled people who have been concerned to ensure that the revision reflects the social model of disability. The WHO is also in the process of developing clearer and more coherent disability policies across all aspects of its work. Here again, organizations of disabled people, particularly Inclusion International, have worked closely with the WHO in this process.

On the social model of disability, handicap does not reside in the individual but reflects limitations on the individual imposed by society and its institutions through legislation and social attitudes leading to exclusion and marginalization. This includes not only physical barriers but also laws and regulations that exclude disabled people from schooling, employment, leisure and recreation, independent living, as well as discriminatory and oppressive attitudes held by members of the community, including professionals and legislators. People with intellectual disabilities are particularly vulnerable to these negative environmental influences.

In a major report commissioned by the United Nations Educational, Scientific and Cultural Organization (UNESCO) for the World Summit on Social Development, Disability Awareness in Action[7] redefined disability as follows:

The term disability is now used by many disabled people to represent a complex system of social restrictions imposed on people with impairments by a highly discriminatory society. Disability, therefore, is a concept distinct from any particular medical condition. It is a social construct that varies across cultures and through time, in the same way, for example, as gender, class or caste.[8]

The revision of the International Classification of Impairments, Disabilities and Handicaps has now been reissued as ICIDH-2, following a ten-year review period[9] and was submitted to the World Health Assembly in 2001. The former distinctions between impairment, disability, and handicap are being replaced by a more dynamic, interactive model that recognizes that disablement and functioning are outcomes of interactions between health conditions and environmental and contextual factors.

The model distinguishes between the following:

Impairment: a loss or abnormality of body structure or of a physiological or psychological function, eg, loss of a limb or loss of vision;

Activity: the nature and extent of the functioning at the level of the person. Activities may be limited in nature, duration, and quality, eg, taking care of oneself or maintaining a job; and

Participation: the nature and extent of a person's involvement in life situations in relation to impairment, activities, health conditions, and contextual factors. Participation may be restricted in nature, duration, and quality, eg, participation in community activities or obtaining a driving license.

5. *The American Association on Mental Retardation Revised Classification*

The most thorough and comprehensive revision of any classification system has come from the American Association on Mental Retardation (AAMR).[10] The AAMR's 1992 proposals reflected a major paradigm shift, away from a defect model towards one which emphasizes interactions with the environment and includes the nature and intensity of the supports needed by an individual. Ten years later, the definition has been modified again. The 2002 definition is as follows:

Mental Retardation refers to substantial limitations in present functioning. It is characterized by significantly subaverage intellectual functioning, existing concurrently with related limitations in two or more of the following applicable adaptive skill areas: communication, self-care, home living, social skills, community use, self-direction, health and safety, functional academics, leisure, and work. Mental retardation manifests before age 18.

The following four assumptions are essential to the application of the stated definition of mental retardation:

> (1) valid assessment considers cultural and linguistic diversity as well as differences in communication and behavioral factors;
>
> (2) the existence of limitations in adaptive skills occurs within the context of community environments typical of the individual's age peers and is indexed to the person's individualized needs for supports;
>
> (3) specific adaptive limitations often coexist with strengths in other adaptive skills or other personal capabilities; and
>
> (4) with appropriate supports over a sustained period, the life functioning of the person with mental retardation will generally improve.[11]

The 1992 revision contains three steps: diagnosis, classification, and systems of supports. Although the system retains the IQ standard score guidelines of 'approximately 70 to 75 or below' as the upper limit of mental retardation, it departs from previous definitions by specifying that there must also be limitations in at least two out of ten adaptive skills listed.

The four severity grades of mild, moderate, severe, and profound are replaced by levels of intensity, ranging between intermittent, limited, and extensive and pervasive. These are intended to indicate the level of supports or services that an individual needs to function and are applied in four different domains: (1) intellectual functioning and adaptive skills; (2) psychological and emotional considerations; (3) physical health and etiology; and (4) environmental considerations.

Despite extensive consultation, the 1992 definition and classification system have generated considerable controversy.[12] The main criticisms can be summarized as follows:

1. The continued use of IQ boundaries, particularly the setting of 'IQ 70–75' as the upper boundary of intellectual disability, is criticized as 'very imprecise' and affects a large number of individuals whose IQ is likely to fall between 70 and 75.

2. Although adaptive behavior has for some time been recognized (eg, by WHO in 1985) as essential to the definition of intellectual disability, the specific examples listed in the new definition cannot be reliably assessed with known psychometric instruments or scales. Since an individual is to be judged as intellectually disabled on the basis of showing at least two of these ten characteristics, it is essential to ensure that such assessments are reliable and that the risk of misclassification is reduced.

3. Further issues have been raised concerning the applicability of the 1992 revision to preschool children.[13]

II. KEY ISSUES FOR THE FUTURE

Issues concerned with assessment, classification, and terminology directly affect decisions made about individuals and can no longer be considered the exclusive preserve of professionals and policymakers. The voice and views of people with intellectual disabilities themselves must in the future be respected and taken into account.

A. Self-Advocacy

Self-advocacy is the resolute movement of people with intellectual disabilities speaking for themselves, demanding that they be heard, and insisting on their right to make decisions. Self-advocacy is beginning to have a major impact on planners, legislators, professionals, parents, and on society itself. It is a growing voice.[14]

The growth of the self-advocacy movement at local, national, and international levels has been documented from its earliest beginnings[15] to the present day.[16] It is summarized by Dybwad in the following words, 'People with intellectual impairments have—*in my lifetime*—gone from "feebleminded patients" to empowered agents of social change. They work to make the world a better place not just for themselves but for the rest of the world.'[17]

The spirit of this movement is captured in the words of Barb Goode, a Canadian self-advocate and at the time of this speech, an elected member of the executive council of Inclusion International. Speaking to the full General Assembly of the United Nations in the session marking the end of the Decade of Disabled Persons in 1992, Goode declared:

I speak on behalf of persons with mental handicap. We are people first and only secondly do we have a mental handicap.

We want to push our rights forward, and we want to let other people know that we are here. We want to explain to our fellow human beings that we can live and work in our communities. We want to show that we have rights and responsibilities.

Our voice may be a new one to many of you but you had better get used to hearing it. Many of us still have to learn how to speak up. Many of you still have to learn how to listen to understand us. We need people who have faith in us. You have to understand that we, like you, do not want to live in institutions. We want to live and work in our communities. We count on your support to people with mental handicap and their families. We count on your support to ILSMH and its member associations.

Above all, we demand that you give us the right to make choices and decisions rewarding our own lives.[18]

Self-advocates from many countries, working within the framework of Inclusion International, have made some powerful statements.[19] The following are some extracts from their publication.

1. Being a Person First
All people are people first and must be treated with dignity and respect and be accepted.
Don't forget: we have the right.
2. Having our Own Identity
Each person must be recognized as the person they are.
We are all individuals.
3. Making Our Own Decisions
All individuals have the right to make their own decisions and to have those decisions respected.
We must be listened to as we express ourselves.
We have the right to make and learn from our own mistakes.
We must help people who cannot speak for themselves, to have their decisions understood and respected.
4. Believing in My Own Value as a Person
From birth, every human being has the same worth.
We all continue to have worth and must be treated as such.
5. Having Other People Believe in You as a Person
We must not be discriminated against because of our disability.
Other people must learn that we are people and treat us in the same way as everyone else.
We must be able to choose our own friends in our own community.

Inclusion International now sees itself as a human rights and advocacy organization. It directly confronts governments whenever there is evidence of abuse of human rights of people with intellectual disabilities. It has protested to governments on conditions in residential institutions and on the compulsory sterilization of persons with intellectual disabilities and has also influenced the wording of UNESCO's statement on the ethical implications of genetic screening and selective abortion. Together with the other main international non-governmental organizations—such as Disabled Peoples' International, the World Blind Union, the World Federation of the Deaf, and Rehabilitation International—it lobbies governments and United Nations agencies to promote the rights and needs of people with intellectual disabilities.

B. Moving Towards Inclusion

The principle of inclusion follows naturally from self-advocacy and advocacy for human rights. People with intellectual disabilities are demanding the right and the necessary support to participate fully in society and its institutions in the fields of education, housing, employment, public transport, health, and recreation and leisure. Moreover, they want to participate in these activities together with their fellow citizens rather than in or from segregated specialized environments.

Support for individuals in segregated services has traditionally been given within a classical rehabilitation framework. This assumes that the individual needs to be prepared on a graduated, step-by-step basis to function in an integrated setting. Although many adults have been rehabilitated from long-stay residential institutions on this basis, the process is slow and depends on professional judgment concerning the person's 'readiness' to take the next step. This may be affected by a degree of underestimation, as well as by natural caution and a concern not to push the person too fast or too far. A variation of this approach is to place the individual in a series of environments that gradually approximate the demands of everyday environments such as sheltered workshops, halfway residential homes, and special classes in mainstream schools.

A radically different model was developed in the early 1980s in the field of open employment.[20] Instead of step-by-step rehabilitation from segregated institutions into community settings, the individual is placed from the outset in the most integrated and inclusive setting possible but with a high degree of support in the initial stages. This may be expensive at first, but the intensity of the support can be reduced as the individual becomes more independent. The same principle applies when a person with an intellectual disability is placed in an ordinary house or apartment with whatever personal support is needed in the initial stages.

In the same way, children with intellectual disabilities are increasingly placed directly into an ordinary class of a mainstream school but with the individually tailored support of a teacher or classroom assistant.[21]

As Lindqvist points out, a dual approach is needed to make inclusion possible. 'It has become evident that measures to combat social exclusion and bad conditions, to be effective, must be taken in two main areas— support to the individual and measures to create accessibility in the surrounding society.'[22]

To make inclusion possible for people with intellectual disabilities, existing services and the way in which they are delivered will often need to be changed. For example, the curriculum of the ordinary school needs to be made more accessible and relevant for all children, including those with intellectual disabilities or an existing national curriculum made accessible to a wider group of students. (See UNESCO[23] and Ainscow and Sebba[24] for international examples of good inclusive practice in education.)

However well the individual is supported, progress will be limited unless and until changes are also made to the environment in which the person is expected to function. This is well understood at the level of access to the built environment for people with mobility or sensory impairments, resulting in the provision of ramps, widened doors, dropped curbs, and accessible public transport, Braille signs in lifts, auditory traffic signals, etc. Such adaptations are less helpful for people with intellectual disabilities.

Similarly, a variety of changes can be made to the workplace. In some countries, legislation mandates such changes (eg, the Americans with Disabilities Act in the United States and the Disability Discrimination Act in England). Changes can be made to the physical working environment, such as variations in equipment or machinery placement, enlarging instructions, using recorded information, variations in working hours such as flexi-time, and also by providing additional personal support where it is necessary.

An early example was the innovative Pathways to Employment scheme developed in the United Kingdom in the 1970s, which tried to arrange for some degree of informal support from a fellow employee who agreed to 'keep an eye' on his or her colleague without formally being assigned to a training or supervisory role.[25]

1. Problematic Issues in Inclusion

Placement agencies are often too easily satisfied if an individual has somewhere reasonable to live, some work or occupation during the day, and at least access to leisure and recreational opportunities, but such placements are only the starting points for living in more inclusive settings. The work of Schwartz documents the complexity and subtleties of providing support from state agencies and the difficulties involved in professionals supporting a person with an intellectual disability in gaining access to community resources.[26]

Many studies have shown that people with intellectual disabilities are at risk of being marginalized and lonely in community settings; there are studies that document examples of serious victimization and exploitation, especially when housing is provided in areas of high deprivation.[27] Even those who have lived in residential institutions and who would under no circumstances wish to return to them can miss the routines and perhaps the friendships and leisure opportunities provided. Young adults who have never lived in segregated settings may also find themselves bewildered by the demands of everyday living.

Fortunately, many people are resourceful and resilient enough not merely to 'survive' in the community but to become active citizens in every sense. Robert Edgerton's studies in the 1960s showed that the quality of life of people discharged from long-stay institutions depended largely on informal supporters whom they happened to find in the community.[28]

His follow-up studies of this group of individuals provided ample evidence of successful adjustment in quite difficult community settings.[29]

2. Supporting Families

Professionals around the world do not have a good track record in working in partnership with families. A major task for the next century is for families and professionals to evolve new patterns of working together that are based on principles of equality and partnership and that, at the same time, involve the individual with an intellectual disability in discussion and decision making at every turn.

Families around the world have long been dissatisfied with the quality of the support they have received. They are not satisfied with the information made available to them, the attitudes of professionals, and the labels that these professionals often attach to families, such as 'overprotective' or 'rejecting'. Families complain about the absence of partnership and equality in decision making concerning their children and how these decisions affect the family as a whole.

For the past fifty years, families with intellectually disabled members have organized themselves to provide support for one another, to lobby for services and, where these efforts have failed, to establish services themselves.

In recent years, professionals and service providers have become more responsive to the concerns expressed by families. The stereotype of parents racked by guilt, going through a long process of adjustment and always in search of a cure is being replaced by one that sees the family as empowered to demand services and support that meet its needs.[30]

The UN International Year of the Family aimed to stimulate new initiatives at national and local levels and provided an opportunity to draw attention to the needs of families who had a relative with an intellectual disability. Inclusion International set up a task force to raise awareness of family issues in relation to intellectual disability and to make recommendations for a more coordinated approach to support families. This task force consisted of one mother and one father from each of the main regions of the world. It collected stories from families around the world[31] and identified examples of good practice in supporting families.

Reports from different countries suggest that a much broader and richer range of supports is now beginning to be made available. For example, what used to be known as short-term or respite care but is now increasingly being described as shared care, is available on a more flexible and 'as needed' basis. Parents are given vouchers to purchase services, and support is available in their own home rather than in residential hostels or hospitals.[32] More support also comes from other parents and from ordinary health or social services, especially at the time of birth or early identification and sometimes also at transition points such as leaving school and leaving home.

Despite these positive and encouraging trends, only a small minority of people with a family member who has an intellectual disability and might benefit from support services actually has access to them. In some countries, this is largely due to a lack of information. For example, a major study in the United States showed that although forty-six of fifty states provided shared care and other support services, only a minority of families in these states were aware that these services existed. Moreover, even those families who were aware of shared care and other support services had difficulties in obtaining access to these programs.[33]

3. *Community-Based Rehabilitation*

From a global perspective, the vast majority of people with intellectual disabilities are entirely unreached by services of any kind, whether generic or specialized. Varying estimates of the numbers of people unreached by services have been provided by UN agencies, but it is clear that such services as exist are mostly in the larger cities and are commonly far too expensive even for those people who could reach them.

The future for all countries, but particularly for developing countries, would therefore seem to lie in community-based rehabilitation (CBR). CBR is defined in a joint statement by the WHO, the International Labor Organization (ILO), and UNESCO as: '[A] strategy within community development for the rehabilitation, equalization of opportunities and social integration of all people with disabilities. It is implemented through the combined efforts of disabled people themselves, their families and communities and the appropriate health, educational and vocational and social services.'[34]

Ideally, this approach trains and supports ordinary local health workers, teachers, and other community workers in extending their work and their skills to all persons with disabilities and their families. More countries are beginning to experiment with elements of a CBR approach, and there is encouraging evidence of positive results.[35] Examples of countries where CBR initiatives have had a significant impact include China, Ghana, Guyana, India, Laos, the Philippines, and Vietnam.[36] In contrast to earlier developments, more recent CBR initiatives have included and involved people with intellectual disabilities and their families.

Nevertheless, despite a number of well-publicized examples of successful projects, the impact of CBR has been disappointing, so much so that in reviewing the 'first 25 years of CBR', Helander as its main originator now admits that 'for most people with disabilities, the situation can at present be expected to become worse each year'.[37] Writing two years earlier, two key workers in this field characterized CBR as remaining in its infancy and attributed this largely to the fact that models of staff training are still based on institutional models that prepare staff for center-based services.[38]

The fact that developments in the training of teachers to work more inclusively have had relatively greater impact is due in large measure to initiatives taken by UNESCO. The following section therefore reviews the role of UN agencies in initiating change.

III. UNITED NATIONS INITIATIVES

During the last quarter century, the UN has taken an increasingly pro-active role in working for global recognition of the human rights of people with intellectual disability. (See Degener, Chapter 6 of this volume and Herr[39] for an extended discussion. Also, see Lachwitz[40] for a detailed consideration of human rights instruments in relation to persons with intellectual disabilities.)

As early as 1971, the UN adopted the *Declaration on the Rights of Mentally Retarded Persons*.[41] Taken almost verbatim from a declaration made by the International League of Societies for Mental Handicap at its world congress in Jerusalem three years earlier, the Declaration clearly proclaims that persons with 'mental retardation' have 'the same rights as other human beings'. This was followed in 1975 by a *Declaration on the Rights of Disabled Persons* in general, which calls for broad recognition of the social and economic rights of all persons with disabilities.[42]

Some critics argue that the human rights of persons with intellectual disabilities should be assumed to be automatically covered in general human rights declarations such as the *Universal Declaration of Human Rights* and the UN *International Covenant on Economic, Social and Cultural Rights*.[43] Furthermore, some argue that the wording of such statements is too cautious and conservative by today's standards. Inclusion International has itself rejected qualifying phrases such as 'to the maximum extent possible' and has produced strong statements of fundamental principles. For example, 'All people with a mental handicap are citizens of their country, no less entitled than their fellow citizens to consideration, respect and protection under the law.'[44]

Even though the language of the earlier UN declarations now seems dated, other advocates note that it is useful to be able to refer to these declarations when drafting laws or policies at a national level and that in any case general human rights declarations have not been particularly successful in protecting minorities in general or persons with intellectual disabilities in particular. (See Shnit, Chapter 9 of this volume.)

A. International Year of Disabled Persons

The International Year of Disabled Persons (IYDP) in 1981, aimed at the 'full participation and equality of disabled people' and marked a major turning point for disabled people throughout the world. Many governments set up national coordinating committees that were charged with the responsibility of advising or monitoring plans to improve planning and delivery of services and ensuring that generic services such as health, education, and welfare were made accessible to persons with disabilities and their families.

More fundamentally, IYDP was significant for the inclusion of disabled people themselves (sometimes including people with intellectual disabilities) in planning and advising on services and for the establishment in many countries of organizations of, rather than for, disabled persons. At the international level, 1981 saw the birth of Disabled Peoples' International (DPI), with initial financial and organizational support from the UN. DPI has played a major role in lobbying UN agencies and has from the outset been recognized by the UN as an essential source of advice on policy and practice.

Although the UN always emphasized that IYDP and later initiatives were intended to benefit all disabled people, regardless of the nature, severity, or origin of the disability, strong advocacy by Inclusion International and its member associations has been necessary to ensure that the needs of persons with intellectual disabilities and their families were not overlooked. A particular difficulty here is that other disability groups have no difficulty in finding powerful and articulate advocates, whereas self-advocacy by people with intellectual disabilities themselves is still at an early stage.

B. The World Program of Action and the Decade of Disabled Persons

Perhaps the most significant development to come out of International Year of Disabled Persons, however, was the World Program of Action Concerning Disabled Persons and the launching by the UN of the Decade of Disabled Persons (1983–1992) (hereinafter 'Decade'). Adopted by the General Assembly in December 1982, the World Program of Action was concerned not only with prevention and rehabilitation but also emphasized the equalization of opportunities within the framework of the UN goal of a Society for All by 2010.

Equalization of opportunities is defined in the World Program of Action as 'the process through which the general systems of society, such as the physical and cultural environment, housing and transportation, social and health services, educational and work opportunities, cultural and social life, including sport and recreational life, are made accessible to all.'[45]

The principles of the World Program of Action have stood the test of time and are still accepted as the basis for development at national and international levels. Nevertheless, progress in translating these principles into action during the Decade has been disappointingly slow. The work of the Disabled Persons Unit at the UN in Vienna was undermined by lack of resources and was eventually relocated to New York in the course of a major restructuring exercise. Key staff retired and were not replaced because of budgetary constraints, and the unit relied greatly on temporary volunteer help from donor governments or agencies. The annual interagency meetings, to which international non-governmental organizations (INGOs) made an influential contribution, were wound up at the end of the Decade.

Dissatisfaction with the lack of impact of the Decade resulted in a declaration of an Asian Decade of Disabled Persons from 1993 to 2002, and later in the launch of an African Decade. These regional developments have resulted in a number of new initiatives in the form of conferences, workshops, training seminars, and publications.

C. Standard Rules on the Equalization of Opportunities for Persons with Disabilities[46]

Halfway through the Decade, the UN called a conference of governmental and non-governmental organizations in Helsinki, including organizations of disabled persons, such as Disabled Peoples' International, to make recommendations that might lead to greater progress in the second half of the Decade. During the course of this meeting, there was strong support for a UN Convention on the rights of disabled persons that would make it illegal to discriminate on grounds of disability. But despite strong lobbying by a number of governments, particularly Sweden and Italy, it became clear that there was not enough support from national representatives to the UN to enable such a measure to succeed. However, in November 2001, the UN General Assembly supported a resolution proposed by Mexico to set up an ad hoc committee to study proposals for an international Convention to promote the dignity and rights of people with disabilities.[47]

Despite the early failure to secure support for a Convention, work began within the UN on the development of an internationally agreed-upon set of standards for the participation of persons with disabilities in society, based on the principle of full participation and equality of opportunities.

The twenty-two *Standard Rules on the Equalization of Opportunities for Persons with Disabilities* (hereinafter 'Rules') were adopted by the UN General Assembly in December 1993. The purpose of the Rules is 'to ensure that girls, boys, women and men with disabilities, as members of their societies, may exercise the same rights and obligations as others'. In furtherance of this purpose, the Rules identify eight target areas for equal participation (education, employment, access, income maintenance, family life, culture, recreation and sport, and religion) and four preconditions for equal participation (awareness-raising, medical care, rehabilitation, and support services). Although the Rules are not legally binding, 'they imply a strong moral and political commitment on behalf of States to take action for the equalization of opportunities for persons with disabilities', as well as offering a framework for policymaking at the national level.

The UN General Assembly appointed a former Minister of Social Welfare, Bengt Lindqvist, as Special Rapporteur and invited the principal INGOs in the field of disability to appoint a panel to assist him. Since then, every government has received regular requests asking it a number of specific questions addressing implementation plans for the Rules in Member States. The mandate of the Special Rapporteur has subsequently been twice extended, though lack of funding has significantly handicapped the scope of his activity and that of his committee of experts.

Inclusion International, which helped draft the Rules and has two representatives on the panel, is now urging all 200 of its member societies in 180 countries to lobby for the implementation of the Rules at a national level and for governments to commit themselves to targets and timetables to that end. The same policy is being followed by the four other member INGOs—Disabled Peoples' International, World Blind Union, World Federation of the Deaf, and the World Federation of Psychiatric Users.

The *Standard Rules on the Equalization of Opportunities for Persons with Disabilities* differ from other UN initiatives. In the first place, the monitoring process at UN and national levels involves consumers working through NGOs. Second, the Rules differ by virtue of their strong emphasis on human rights, and third, they differ by underlining the responsibility of state governments to remove obstacles to the participation of persons with disabilities in their societies. Evidence that this message is being heard comes from Lindqvist's report of his second global survey, which indicates that most of the responding governments have stated that the Rules have led to rethinking in the disability field. 'Generally, the Rules have been used in the three following ways: to make new legislation; to elaborate national plans of action and to evaluate the situation.' Also noteworthy is that 'organizations of persons with disabilities have been strengthened and that governments are cooperating more systematically with such organizations through coordinating committees or councils'.[48]

On the negative side, Lindqvist reports that few developing countries have shown sustained interest in the Rules or sought the help of the Panel of Experts in implementing them. Nevertheless, it is becoming clear that some developing countries are now taking the lead, particularly in the field of inclusive education.[49]

D. The World Summit on Social Development, Copenhagen, 1995

The World Summit on Social Development took place in Copenhagen in March 1995 and marked one of the largest gatherings of Heads of States. The United States delegation, headed by Hilary Clinton and Vice-President Gore, was particularly supportive of attempts by the disability lobby—which included Inclusion International—to give greater prominence to disability issues in the discussions before, during, and above all, after the Summit.

The three principal themes of the World Summit on Social Development focused on the eradication of poverty, unemployment, and social exclusion. Addressing these issues, the Heads of State entered into ten commitments, including a number that are of direct or indirect relevance to disabled people. For instance, Commitment 6 is a pledge to provide access to both education and health services and to: (1) ensure equal opportunities at all levels for children, youth, and adults with disabilities, in integrated settings, taking full account of individual differences and situations and (2) strive to ensure that persons with disabilities have access to rehabilitation and other independent living services and assistive technology to enable them to maximize their well-being, independence, and full participation in society.

These issues were again taken up by INGOs at the World Summit on Women, held at Beijing in September 1995. The *Beijing Declaration and Platform for Action* referred to the obstacles placed in the way of advancement and empowerment and urged governments to work for equal access to education through measures to eliminate double discrimination based on gender and disability.[50]

E. Implementation

Turning to employment, the ILO has reported that only one-fifth of Member States have fully applied Convention 159 on vocational rehabilitation and the promotion of employment possibilities. Although most countries had introduced measures on anti-discriminatory employment, very few had implemented recommendations concerned with rehabilitation in rural areas, cooperation with organizations of persons with disabilities, or ensuring the availability of qualified staff.

Although it is more than likely that people with intellectual disabilities are the last to gain access to employment opportunities, the ILO has been highly proactive in emphasizing their needs and rights as well as evidence indicating their competence and motivation to work.

It is easy to be cynical about such language and pessimistic to the point of despondency about the gap between the rhetoric and the reality of day-to-day life for people with intellectual disabilities, particularly in countries of the southern hemisphere. But implementation depends on political will and action at the level of national government, and this in turn is affected by public opinion and pressure from national NGOs. This time, the commitments made are more in the public domain and complement the parallel monitoring mechanisms established through the *Standard Rules*. (See Rioux, Chapter 11 of this volume.)

Programs of bilateral or multilateral aid associated with international donors such as the World Bank are being urged to ensure that persons with disabilities are not deliberately or inadvertently excluded from funds allocated for social development. For example, it is important that aid programs do not miss opportunities to remind loan recipients to include children with disabilities in extending schooling to larger numbers of children who have hitherto been excluded. The same principle applies more generally to programs designed to promote employment or social development in general. Performance indicators related to disability are being incorporated into national indices of social and economic development, such as the United Nations Human Development Index and various statistical indicators published through UN and other international agencies.

The most promising recent development relates to new policies to cancel or reduce the crippling burden of debt repayment from many of the poorest countries of the world on condition that the monies thus saved are invested in education and health. Although this policy has been adopted by a small number of governments (notably the UK), implementation has been extremely slow. Nevertheless, Uganda has provided a striking example of the progress that can be made when a country makes a commitment to invest in education. The government has made and is clearly implementing a commitment to provide free primary education for four children in every family. Furthermore, any disabled child in the family is given first priority.

IV. INITIATIVES CONCERNED WITH CHILDREN AND YOUNG PEOPLE

Although there is currently no UN convention specifically recognizing the rights of persons with disabilities in general, Article 23 of the 1989

Convention on the Rights of the Child recognizes the rights of minors with disabilities to 'enjoy a full and decent life' in which 'dignity, self-reliance and active participation are ensured, as well as access to a wide spectrum of education and rehabilitation services and special care'. Several other articles in the Convention are directly relevant to disabled children, including those concerned with the right to free primary education and to active participation in the community.

The Convention on the Rights of the Child was followed a year later by the World Summit on Children and the commitment of the world's leaders to the Education for All initiative expressed in the *Jomtien Declaration*.[51] These initiatives are targeted at the 200 million children worldwide who are not attending school or who are failing to benefit from schooling.

Despite these significant advances, continuing vigilance and advocacy are needed to ensure that children with disabilities, and those with intellectual disabilities in particular, are fully included in national plans. In its evidence to the UN Committee on the Rights of the Child,[52] Inclusion International pointed to many examples of the denial of the rights of children with intellectual disabilities. These include exclusion from schooling, deplorable treatment in psychiatric hospitals and residential institutions, and, most fundamentally, legalized termination of the life of newly born children with severe impairments (so-called 'mercy killings'). Inclusion International has also taken a strong stand against the idea of selective abortion in the context of prenatal diagnosis and has expressed serious reservations about the implications of germ line therapy for the right to life and dignity of children with intellectual disabilities.[53]

A. Education for All (1990) and the Salamanca Declaration and Framework for Action (1994)

In 1990, the world's leaders met at Jomtien, Thailand, and committed themselves to targets to provide four years of primary education, reduce dropout rates and inequalities arising from gender and disability.[54] An official review of these targets held in Dakar, Senegal, ten years later showed that relatively little progress had been made, though individual countries were able to report dramatic progress.[55]

The significance of the *Salamanca Declaration and Framework for Action*[56] was that it provided clear guidance on ways of ensuring that children with disabilities and learning difficulties were fully included in the Education for All Framework. A recent international congress held in Manchester, England, in July 2000, provided many examples of countries whose policy and practice has been directly influenced by Salamanca and by the dissemination of the UN *Standard Rules on the Equalization of Opportunities for Disabled Persons*.[57]

The Special Rapporteur's second report to the UN General Assembly focused on the implementation of Rule 6 (education). He reported that children with special educational needs were still predominantly in separate educational systems and that many were not attending any form of school. In thirty-three out of forty-eight reporting countries, fewer than 1% of pupils are enrolled in special education programs.[58] Nevertheless, a scrutiny of reports from UNESCO reflects marked signs of progress, particularly since the *Salamanca Declaration and Framework for Action*.[59]

In his evidence to the UN Committee on the Rights of the Child, Bengt Lindqvist, emphasized the necessity of a dual approach:

The principles of non-discrimination and the best interests of the child speak strongly in support of integration and mainstreaming, to make it possible for the disabled child to stay in the social context which is natural to him or her. To make this possible, the surrounding society must take the needs of the child into account. It means, amongst many other things, to adapt programs in preschools and schools, to make playgrounds, toys, books and communication facilities accessible and available for disabled children.[60]

Thus, support to the child might take the form of a wheelchair and additional support in the classroom. But the child needs access not only to the playground and the classroom but also to the curriculum of the school. This requires a restructuring of the school curriculum to make it more inclusive and accessible for all pupils—not only those with disabilities but a much wider group of children—who are underachieving or unmotivated and who are not benefiting from school.[61] At the same time, the training of teachers needs to prepare them from the outset to accept responsibility for all children. This aim has been successfully addressed by a UNESCO resource pack, which has now been used in over fifty countries.[62]

V. CONCLUSION

Looking to the future, we can discern a number of positive trends as well as threats. The growth of the self-advocacy movement represents a new consumerism that demands to be heard, but it is a movement that is in tune with the parallel human rights perspective shared by many parents, professionals, and to some extent, by legislators and the general public.

The movement towards inclusion has been strong for some time, particularly in the United States, Italy, Spain, and in Scandinavian countries but is now gaining momentum in some of the poorest countries of the world, such as Uganda, Vietnam, and Laos. It is now clear that much more thought will need to be given to the development of a wider and richer range of informal as well as formal support systems needed by many individuals if they are not merely going to 'survive' in the community but to make an active contribution as local citizens. New thinking is needed on the nature of support for families and how to balance this support with encouragement of self-advocacy. Families need to feel empowered and supported in making real choices for their children while concurrently encouraging their children to become self-advocates and make their own decisions, even though their family may disagree with those decisions.

Efforts to plan or provide better services and to meet the needs of individuals and of families depend on the support of the public and their representatives in decision-making bodies at local, national, and international levels. The education of the public begins with inclusive education, which provides the next generation with the opportunity of learning and living alongside children who have a disability. But much also depends on the way in which intellectually disabled people are presented in the media and the way in which we use language to describe their needs.[63] Family, social, cultural, and attitudinal influences are critical in influencing the learning opportunities made available to persons with intellectual disabilities. We cannot teach individuals with intellectual disabilities without taking full account of the environments in which they are living and learning.

There is a clearer vision of the future we would like to see for the children to be born today and tomorrow and for the families who will care for them for most of their lives. To turn that vision into reality we will need political will, reordered priorities, and appropriate civil rights legislation that is implemented and monitored. In the last analysis, progress depends in large measure on empowered and committed families and above all, on people with intellectual disabilities themselves being afforded equal opportunities to contribute to the communities in which they live.

NOTES

1. J Corbett, *Bad-Mouthing: The Language of Special Needs* (London: Falmer Press, 1996).
2. E Emerson, *Challenging Behaviour: Analysis and Intervention in People with Severe Intellectual Disabilities* (Cambridge: Cambridge University Press, 2001) (2nd edn).
3. P Mittler and R Serpell, 'Services: An International Perspective' in A Clarke, ADB Clarke, and J Berg (eds), *Mental Deficiency: The Changing Outlook* (4th edn, London: Methuen, 1985).
4. eg, E Emerson, C Hatton, J Bromley, and A Caine (eds), *Clinical Psychology and People with Intellectual Disabilities* (Chichester: Wiley, 1998).
5. H Cobb and P Mittler, *Significant Differences between Mental Illness and Mental Retardation* (Revised edn, Brussels: International League of Societies for Persons with Mental Handicap (Inclusion International), 1989).

6. World Health Organization, *International Classification of Impairment, Disability and Handicap* (Geneva: World Health Organization, 1980).

7. Disability Awareness in Action, *Overcoming Obstacles to the Integration of Disabled People*, UNESCO Sponsored Report to World Summit on Social Development (Copenhagen and London: Disability Awareness in Action, 1995).

8. ibid.

9. World Health Organization, *The International Classification of Functioning and Disability—revised edition ICIDH-2* (Geneva: World Health Organization, 1999).

10. American Association on Mental Retardation, *Mental Retardation: Definition, Classification and Systems of Support* (9th Revision, Washington, DC: AAMR, 1992).

11. American Association on Mental Retardation, *Mental Retardation: Definition, Classification and Systems of Support* (10th Revision, Washington, DC: AAMR, 2002).

12. R Luckasson, R Schalock, M Snell, and D Spitalnik, 'The 1992 AAMR Definition and Pre-school Children: From the Committee on Terminology and Classification' (1996) 34/4 *Mental Retardation* 247–253.

13. ibid; S Vig and E Jedrysek, 'Application of the 1992 AAMR Definition: Issues for Preschool Children' (1996) 34/4 *Mental Retardation* 244–246.

14. P Ramcharan, G Roberts, G Grant, and J Borland (eds), *Empowerment in Everyday Life: Learning Disability* (London: Jessica Kingsley, 1997).

15. P Williams and B Shoultz, *We Can Speak for Ourselves: Self Advocacy by Mentally Handicapped People* (London: Souvenir Press, 1982).

16. G Dybwad, 'Setting the Stage Historically' in G Dybwad and H Hersani (eds), *New Voices: Self Advocacy by People with Disabilities* (Boston: Brookline Press, 1996) 1–16; D Whittaker, 'The Fight for Self Advocacy' in P Mittler and V Sinason (eds), *Changing Policy and Practice for People with Learning Disabilities* (London: Cassell, 1996).

17. Dybwad (n 16 above) 16.

18. Quoted in P Mittler 'Preparing for Self Advocacy' in B Carpenter, R Ashdown, and K Bovair (eds), *Enabling Access: Effective Teaching and Learning for Pupils with Learning Difficulties* (2nd edn, London: Fulton, 2001).

19. Inclusion International, *The Beliefs, Values and Principles of Self Advocacy* (London, England: Inclusion International, 1994).

20. GT Bellamy, RH Horner, and DP Inman, *Vocational Rehabilitation of Severely Retarded Adults* (Baltimore: University Park Press, 1979).

21. eg, UNESCO, *Open File on Inclusive Education: Support Materials and Administrators* (Paris: UNESCO, 2001); J Jenkinson, *Mainstreaming or Special? Educating Students with Disabilities in the Mainstream* (London: Routledge, 1997); P Farrell, *Teaching Pupils with Learning Difficulties* (London: Cassell, 1997); P Mittler, 'Educating pupils with intellectual disabilities in England: thirty years on' (2002) 49 *International Journal of Disability, Development and Education* 2, 145–50.

22. B Lindqvist, 'Convention on the Rights of the Child and the Standard Rules' (Address to UN Monitoring Committee on the Rights of the Child, Geneva, 6 October 1997).

23. UNESCO, *Salamanca Declaration and Framework for Action* (Paris: UNESCO, 1994).

24. H Daniels and P Garner (eds), *Inclusive Education: World Yearbook of Education* (London: Kogan Page, 1999); F Armstrong, D Armstrong, and L Barton (eds), *Inclusive Education: Policy, Contexts and Comparative Perspectives* (London: Fulton, 2000).

25. E Whelan and B Speake, *Getting to Work* (London: Souvenir Press, 1981).

26. D Schwartz, *Crossing the River: Creating a Conceptual Revolution in Community and Disability* (Boston: Brookline Press, 1992).

27. M Flynn, *Independent Living for People with Mental Handicap* (London: Cassell, 1984).

28. R Edgerton, *The Cloak of Competence: Stigma in the Lives of the Retarded* (Berkeley: Univ of California Press, 1967).

29. Mittler and Serpell (n 3 above).

30. P Mittler and H Mittler, *Family and Disability*, International Year of the Family Occasional Paper No 10 (Vienna and New York: United Nations, 1994).

31. H Mittler, *Families Speak Out: International Perspectives on Families' Experience of Disability* (Boston: Brookline Press, 1994).

32. Mittler and Mittler (n 30 above).

33. V Bradley, J Knoll, and J Agosta (eds), *Emerging Issues of Family Support* (Washington, DC: AAMR, 1992).

34. International Labour Organisation, *Community Based Rehabilitation for People with Disabilities* (Joint position paper with WHO and UNESCO, Geneva: ILO, 1994).

35. B O'Toole, *Guide to Community Based Rehabilitation Services* (Guides to Special Education, Paris: UNESCO, 1991); E Helander, *Prejudice and Dignity: An Introduction to Community Based Rehabilitation* (Geneva: United Nations Development Fund, 1993).

36. UNESCO, *First Steps: Stories on Inclusion in Early Childhood Education* (Paris: UNESCO, 1996).

37. E Helander, 'The First 25 Years of CBR' (2000) 11/1 *Asia Pacific Disability Rehabilitation Journal* 8–9.

38. B O'Toole and R McConkey, 'A Training Strategy for Personnel Working in Developing Countries' (1998) 21 *International Journal of Rehabilitation Research* 311–321.

39. S Herr, 'Special Education as a Human and Legal Right' in P Mittler, R Brouillette, and D Harris (eds), *World Year Book of Education: Special Needs Education* (London: Kogan Page, 1993).

40. K Lachwitz, *50 Years of Human Rights: A Guide to International Human Rights Instruments for Persons with an Intellectual Disability: 1948–1998* (London, England: Inclusion International, 1998).

41. United Nations, *General Declaration on the Rights of Persons with Mental Retardation* (New York: United Nations, 1971).

42. United Nations, *Declaration on the Rights of Disabled Persons* (New York: United Nations, 1975).

43. eg, Helander (n 35 above).

44. Adopted by Inclusion International General Assembly, New Delhi, Nov. 1994.

45. United Nations, *World Programme of Action in Favour of Persons with Disabilities* (Vienna and New York: United Nations, 1983) para 18.

46. United Nations, *Standard Rules on the Equalisation of Opportunities for Persons with Disabilities* (New York: United Nations, 1993).
47. Inclusion International, 'Working with the United Nations', available at http://www.inclusion-international.org/Documents/Working_with_the_UN/Work_wt_UN.htm (last viewed 6 June 2002).
48. See www.un.org/esa/socdev/enable for overviews of UN activities.
49. eg, D Mitchell and Y Chen, 'Special Education in East and South East Asia' in RI Brown, D Baine, and AH Neufeldt (eds), *Beyond Basic Care: Special Education and Community Rehabilitation in Low Income Countries* (North York, Ont: Captus Press, 1996); P Mittler, 'The Global Context of Inclusion: The Role of the United Nations' in D Mitchell (ed), *Contextualising Inclusive Education* (Routledge Falmer (in press)); see also www.eenet.org.uk and www.isec.org.uk.
50. United Nations, *Report of the Fourth World Conference on Women* (Beijing, 4–15 September 1995).
51. UNESCO, *World Declaration on Education for All and Framework for Action to Meet Basic Learning Needs*, World Conference on Education for All, Jomtien, Thailand (Paris: UNESCO, 1990).
52. Geneva, 6 October 1997.
53. Speech by W Eigner, President Inclusion International to UN High Commission on Human Rights (Geneva, 6 October 1997).
54. UNESCO (n 51 above).
55. K Watkins, *The Oxfam Education Report* (Oxford: Oxfam, 2000).
56. UNESCO, *World Conference on Special Needs Education: Access and Quality* (Paris: UNESCO, 1994).
57. International Special Education Congress, 'Including the Excluded' (Manchester, England, 24–28 July 2000) available at http://www.isec2000.org.uk (last viewed 6 June 2002).
58. United Nations, Review and appraisal of the World Programme of Action concerning Disabled Persons, United Nations report A/52/351 (New York: United Nations, 1997).
59. eg, UNESCO, *Salamanca Five Years On* (UNESCO, 1999) (see also www.unesco/org/education/educprog/sne/publications.html).
60. Lindqvist (n 22 above).
61. UNESCO (n 56 above); P Mittler, 'Special Needs Education: An International Perspective' (1995) 22 *British Journal of Special Education* 3, 105–108; P Mittler, *Working Towards Inclusive Education: Social Contexts* (London: Fulton, 2000).
62. M Ainscow, *Special Needs in the Classroom: A Teacher Education Guide* (London: Jessica Kingsley and Paris: UNESCO, 1994).
63. A Shearer, 'Think Positive! Advice on Presenting People with Mental Handicap' in P Mittler and V Sinason (eds), *Changing Policy and Practice for People with Learning Disabilities* (London: Cassell, 1996).

2
Terminology and Power

RUTH LUCKASSON

This chapter provides an analysis of terminology or naming in mental retardation, which is one aspect of a larger process that includes defining and classifying. Particular attention is given to the power aspects of terminology. The issues of terminology and power are critical to people with intellectual disabilities because of their continuing experience with being named by others, the negative affects of particular names, their historic powerlessness in the naming of mental retardation, and their current attempts to influence, negotiate, or take control of the naming process.

Naming in the field of mental retardation or intellectual disabilities is one aspect of a larger process that includes defining and classifying. Luckasson and Reeve[1] differentiated the three aspects in the following way:

Naming refers to assigning a specific term to something or someone. Naming probably reflects a basic human desire to create order in the world. In order for a name to function in communication and to carry meaning, the name must be commonly accepted as the assigned term....Defining refers to precisely explaining a name or term. The term must be outlined clearly and differentiated from other terms. The purpose of defining is to establish the meaning and boundaries of a term....Classifying refers to dividing into groups what has been included within the boundaries of a name or term. In classifying, one creates subgroups or clusters within the defined group, according to some established criteria.

The American Association on Mental Retardation in its 9th and 10th editions of the mental retardation manual limited its focus to definition and classification.[2] Current questions about naming remain unresolved. The Consortium on Language, Image, and Public Education, an ad hoc group of the major US organizations concerned with the disability, recently concluded that they would focus their attention on the stigma attached to the disability rather than the name.[3]

Naming is not a simple act. The complexities of naming in the field of mental retardation are not yet fully understood, but attempting to understand the complexities should include analyses of social context, personal context, intended meaning, received meaning, ideology, and ownership aspects. Overlaying all of these complexities is power.[4] Whose power is being exerted? On whom? To what effect? Discussions of mental retardation rarely explore issues of power. But naming is an area so saturated with power questions that one cannot ignore it. One may attempt to deny or minimize the power aspects of naming, but one does so at one's peril. Shakespeare's Juliet famously attempted to escape the power of naming, urging Romeo,

> O, be some other name!
> What's in a name? That which we call a rose
> By any other name would smell as sweet;
> So Romeo would, were he not Romeo call'd,
> Retain that dear perfection which he owes
> Without that title. Romeo doff thy name...[5]

But, as we all well know, the lovers' attempts to ignore the power of name ended in tragedy.[6]

Although an extended analysis is beyond the scope of this chapter, culture is also a significant complexity in terminology or naming. Many Native Americans, for example, will not state their true names because of a cultural belief that such knowledge will give the other person too much power. Some African Americans take African names in order to assert ideology or identity. Others invented names that had no previous meaning in order to avoid the limitations of existing social context. In some cultures, people take different names to signify different life stages. Tanno[7] described her use of multiple names to identify herself, including Spanish, Mexican American, Latina, and Chicana. 'Each name reveals a different facet of identity that allows symbolic, historical, cultural, and political connectedness.' The naming of ethnic or cultural groups reflects many of the issues that people with mental retardation face, in terms of social context, personal context, intended meaning, received meaning, ideology, ownership, and power.

I. COMPLEXITIES OF NAMING

The complexities of naming—social context, personal context, intended meaning, received meaning, ideology, ownership, culture, and power—are played out in many everyday naming situations. The act of naming a newborn provides a good case study for viewing the complexities.

We react almost intuitively to the *social context* of names. For example, many names are readily identifiable as representative of particular social contexts, cultures, or even eras. Certain names suggest mainstream family wealth and high status, while others suggest marginalization, foreignness, or cultural or linguistic identity. If one learns that a newborn has been named Eunice, one reacts in a certain way because Eunice is an old-fashioned name more common for an elderly woman named in an earlier era, whereas a baby named Jessica seems to have a modern name more appropriate to the present context.

The usual *personal context* for naming a child is one of joy, love, and caring. Some of us may not like our names in the abstract, but we value them because we know they represent a personal context of love and hope. The child's experience of the name reflects his knowledge and feelings about how he received the name. For most children, their names establish kinship and important ties to people and resources outside of themselves and their nuclear family[8] and thus have a significant lifelong value.

Most parents, it is fair to say, spend a great deal of time deciding on a name for their child. The discussions might peripherally involve the sound or shape of the name but will certainly involve the *meaning intended* by the namers and the likely *meaning received* by others. Sometimes people have spent decades deciding on a name for a future child, for example, people who selected a baby's name while they were still themselves a child. Often, the child's name has been selected after consultation with special books containing hundreds of sample names that contain obscure meanings of each name and references to historical figures who also had the name. A large part of the discussions between the happily anticipating couple and their friends and family typically revolves around the meaning the namers wish to project and the likely meaning received by others. Ultimately, the child's identity is intertwined with his name. Each of us has probably fantasized about assuming a different name but most reject the fantasy because 'that just wouldn't be me'.

Neither is the naming of a newborn free of the possibility of *ideology*. Statements about gender, patriarchy, religion, nature, and politics often enter the naming process. For example, we all know of people who have been given androgynous first names, surnames such as the mother's name, which contrary to societal convention is used to make a statement, or the names of political figures, religious personages, seasons, or royalty. A child who carries the name Luther or Churchill or Jesus also carries a message about ideology.

Which parent actually first proposed the name and what the reaction of the other was becomes the stuff of family legend, partially because of the *power* subtext. Did the mother get to choose the name because the birth was particularly difficult? Did the father get to select the name because the baby was the first boy? Did one or the other insist on a certain name because of some other power prerogative? Pity the interfering relative who tries to make a suggestion or impose a personally favorite name. That will almost always be regarded as an unwarranted intrusion on the 'rights' of parents and an attempted power play.

And pity the poor child who later tries to change her given name, or even assert a nickname. This action may be characterized as an aggressive, rebellious, or disobedient act. Who has *ownership* of the name? Prolonged family discussion will likely ensue, and issues of ownership, power, guilt, and rejection will surely arise. The child may argue that the name and identity belong to her. But it is likely that certain family members will never relinquish ownership and will cling to the original name, even if the child succeeds in publicly renaming herself. 'I refuse to call her X. If I had wanted my daughter to be referred to by a pet's name I would have named her that myself.'

II. SCIENTIFIC ASPECTS OF NAMING IN
MENTAL RETARDATION

Luckasson and Reeve,[9] focusing on the scientific aspects of naming in mental retardation, suggested the following questions to ask when names or terms are considered.

1. Does this term name this and nothing else?

2. Does this term provide consistent nomenclature?

3. Does this term facilitate communication?

4. Does this term incorporate current knowledge, and is it likely to incorporate future knowledge?

5. Does this term meet the purposes for which it is being proposed?

6. Does this term contribute in a desired way to the manner and content of portrayal of people with the disability?

This list of questions, while helpful with some of the complexities of scientific naming, did not address the issues of power inherent in naming.

For example, in the case of terminology and people with mental retardation or intellectual disability, how are social context, personal context, intended meaning, received meaning, ideology, ownership, and power addressed? In what social context are individuals experiencing this name? In what personal context do they feel they received the name? What is the intended meaning of the name? What is the received meaning of the name? What ideologies does the name reflect? Who owns the name? And overarching, what is the place of power in the naming of intellectual disability?

III. COMPLEXITIES IN NAMING AND MENTAL RETARDATION

A. Social Context

In our society, the name 'mental retardation' signifies a problem and a lowered status of having 'less than' the normal amount of intelligence.

Many people with the disability experience a loss of identity, and their individuality becomes overwhelmed by stereotypes and prejudices that attach to the term. There is an incorrect assumption that all people with this name are alike; the heterogeneity and human diversity of people with the disability, identically named, are ignored. While the definition of the term does mean that all people who have the disability share certain attributes, for example significantly subaverage intelligence, other dimensions of their human diversity fall victim to stereotyping. Stigma inherent in the name is widely recognized and many people with the disability try to exert certain defenses such as passing by wearing a 'cloak of competence'[10] or denying that they have the disability.

B. Personal Context

Most people with mental retardation were assigned the name in a clinical setting. It is likely that the family and the child suffered fear and shame during the diagnostic process. The term or its variants have probably been used negatively for teasing, denying access to desired activities such as attending public school or living in neighborhoods, justifying isolation or physical punishments, and limiting citizenship rights such as voting restrictions, removing custody of their children, or involuntary sexual sterilizations. Given these negative consequences of naming, it should not come as a surprise that few people with the disability of mental retardation have positive personal feelings for the name. Some individuals may consider the name part of a Faustian bargain in which they assumed the stigma of the name in trade for eligibility for certain benefits such as social welfare or special education. But beyond eligibility for benefits, the name 'mental retardation', unlike many other names, does not generally help to establish positive personal bonds to others. In fact, the name often distances the person physically, socially, and politically.

C. Intended Meaning

In modern times, most people who use the term 'mental retardation', I am convinced, intend benign consequences. Many people have used it for years and it is intertwined with their education and professional work. To assert that the term is insulting or painful causes them to feel attacked because they do not intend insult or pain. They also express a fear that no matter what term is selected, it will absorb the same negative meaning as the old term; and thus, they conclude, changing terms is a pointless activity that diverts attention from the more pressing problems of stigma and low social status.

But the meaning of words changes over time. Linguists such as Trudgill[11] classify as a myth the idea that the meanings of words should not be allowed to vary or change. He states that '[w]ords do not mean what we as individuals might wish them to mean, but what speakers of the language in general want them to mean....Language change cannot be halted.' Thus, there is no way, really, for a small group to hold fast the line on what a name or term means except as a term of art for that small group. A name or term means exactly what the general users of the language mean.

D. Received Meaning

It is important to differentiate who is receiving the meaning of a term or name. People with mental retardation and their families often express different opinions about the received meaning of the term 'mental retardation'. For example, The Arc[12] reports these examples from a recent poll of parents:

I do not want my lovely daughter referred to as a 'retard', but I have no problem describing her as a young woman with mental retardation. I believe that term describes her physical condition not her persona.

I think that the energies of The Arc would be much better expended to increase services for all who need them than to change definitions.

The dilemma does not lie in the label. We all have them. The dilemma is educating the 'normal', holding the programs to the highest standards. Being proud!

We should not be squeamish with or in any way tiptoe around accurate use of the word 'retarded'. The challenge is learning to say it—to think about it—with love and pride and comfort and worth.

It is my opinion that persons with mental retardation are just that. To use another name/word is like not accepting the son/daughter with mental retardation.

I would rather you stick a knife in my heart than call my child retarded. And I DO take offense when someone labels my child retarded....

Thirty-nine years ago my daughter was born with Down syndrome. Even then, there was a war of words....Spend the time and money that is being used on this subject to better the lives of (our constituents). We have a long way to go!

Continuous usage of 'mental retardation' brings acceptance and understanding. To try to make a change would be to start all over again. We now have 50 years of usage.

Contrast the above comments with the following comments from individuals with intellectual disabilities:

I was a bright child but I was hit on the head with something. It was all my father's fault. Now there's something wrong with my head. I'm sick. I'm epileptic. Sometimes I have trouble thinking right.[13]

I have never really thought of myself as retarded. I never really had that ugly feeling down deep.[14]

The worst word that I have to be called is retarded. That's because I am not retarded.[15]

As can be seen from these examples, stigma can play an enormous role in the lives of people with mental retardation, and their attempts to deal with the stigma, often through passing or denial[16] require a great deal of energy. Others reject the very construct of mental retardation and the system used to classify people.[17] Similarly, the resistance of people with mental retardation to assuming a retarded identity[18] played a role in the very public discussion about whether to refer to a person *as* the disability 'He is a retardate'—compared to using person-first language and referring to the individual as someone *with* a disability—'She is a student *with* retardation.'

Professionals likely also receive yet a different meaning than either individuals with intellectual disability or their families. Over the years, professionals have selected or created many different names for the disability, almost always with benign and scientific motives. But stigma soon follows. As Ferguson[19] noted, 'Tomorrow's playground insults are often foretold by today's professional diagnoses.'

E. Ideology

Many ideologies can be reflected in naming mental retardation. Some names reflect the idea that disability is a trait, basically immutable and inherent in the individual—'She is a Mongolian idiot.' Other names might more reflect a paradigm of social construction, that the person's functioning is a result of the interaction between an individual and a society—'He needs employment supports.' The extended discussion several years ago about whether a disability is something one *is* or something one *has* was essentially an ideological debate about the nature of disability. Writers in the recent symposium, 'What's in a Name?' of the journal *Mental Retardation* represent many different ideologies.[20]

F. Ownership

Historically, the professional community has initially promulgated the terms used for mental retardation. Under an assumption that mental retardation is a scientific study and that professionals are necessary to solving the problem, scientists and professionals have assumed ownership of the term. But that ownership has recently been challenged by people with the disability themselves.

G. Power

Until recently, only rarely have individuals with the disability of mental retardation wielded any significant power. One function of their reduced power has been their relatively minor participation (if any) in the naming process. As Bogdan noted twenty years ago,[21] 'In their struggle not to be called retarded, they are often powerless. In the politics of reality, their competing view of retardation is not treated seriously, not in their own lives, not in the literature on retardation, and not in the way we think about these issues.'

The name 'mental retardation', however, carries tremendous power. It has galvanized advocacy efforts and split coalitions. It has united political groups and divided friends. It has influenced governments and pierced the hearts of children. Because the term carries so much power, ownership has often been claimed by different groups. Groups grab powerful words for their own purposes, and mental retardation and its variants can be used as a strong insult, or a daring characterization, or a sleazy innuendo of the street (or schoolyard) lexicon. If it were not such a powerful word, no one would bother with it.

IV. CONCLUSION

Naming or terminology in intellectual disability are likely to remain problematic for an extended time because although many of the scientific and practice aspects of the term are relatively resolved, the issues of power are only beginning to be understood. Perhaps the power issues cannot be fully understood at this time for several reasons: the disability itself currently interferes with the ability of many people with mental retardation to directly influence, negotiate, or take control of the naming process; the effects of the disability require that many family members, care providers, and others participate and have a stake in the person's daily life; proxies such as families, friends, and professionals can never totally substitute (in a power analysis) for the direct desires of people with the disability; and analysis of the scientific aspects of naming and terminology have a historical head start on the self-advocacy discussions of naming.

Until such time when the power issues are more fully understood and have been resolved, it is critical that any efforts in naming or terminology be sensitive to the issues of power. One interim measure might be for professional organizations and scientific enterprises to limit their naming activities to entities over which they have some claim to power, for example, themselves and their own organizational names, and to resist imposing yet another name change on the individuals whose power it is rightfully to name themselves. At a minimum, proponents of names or terminology to be applied to people with mental retardation should attempt to maximize the participation of all people with the disability in those proposed actions.

NOTES

1. R Luckasson and A Reeve, 'Naming, Defining, and Classifying in Mental Retardation' (2001) 39/1 *Mental Retardation* 47–52.
2. R Luckasson, DL Coulter, EA Polloway, S Reiss, RL Schalock, ME Snell, DM Spitalnik, and JA Stark, *Mental Retardation: Definition, Classification, and Systems of Supports* (9th edn, Washington, DC: AAMR, 1992); R Luckasson, S Borthwick-Duffy, WHE Buntinx, DL Coulter, EM Craig, A Reeve, RL Schalock, ME Snell, DM Spitalnik, S Spreat, and MJ Tasse, *Mental Retardation: Definition, Classification, and Systems of Supports* (10th edn, Washington, DC: AAMR, 2002).
3. RL Schalock and L Sheehan, *The Consortium on Language, Image, and Public Education Phase I (Final Rep.)* (Washington, DC: AAMR, 25 April 2001).
4. FE Stockholder, 'Naming and Renaming Persons with Intellectual Disabilities' in MH Rioux and M Bach (eds), *Disability is not Measles: New Research Paradigms in Disability* (North York, Ont: L'Institut Roeher Institute, 1994) 153–179.
5. W Shakespeare, *Romeo and Juliet* (1595) II 43–47.
6. ibid; R Turnbull, A Turnbull, S Warren, S Eidelman, and P Marchand, 'Shakespeare Redux, or Romeo and Juliet Revisited: Embedding a Terminology and Name Change in a New Agenda for the Field of Mental Retardation' (2002) 40/1 *Mental Retardation* 65–70.
7. DV Tanno, 'Names, Narratives, and the Evolution of Cultural Identity' in A Gonzales, M Houston, and V Chen (eds), *Our Voices: Essays in Culture, Ethnicity, and Communication* (3rd edn, Los Angeles: Roxbury, 2000) 27, 25–28.
8. eg, A Shoumatoff, *The Mountain of Names: A History of the Human Family* (New York: Simon and Schuster, 1985).
9. Luckasson and Reeve (n 1 above).
10. RB Edgerton, *The Cloak of Competence* (Revised and updated, Berkeley: Univ of California, 1993).
11. P Trudgill, 'Myth 1: The Meanings of Words Should Not be Allowed to Vary or Change' in L Bauer and P Trudgill (eds), *Language Myths* (London: Penguin, 1998) 8, 1–8.
12. 'Readers Offer Feedback on Terminology Issue' (2002) 51/4 *The Arc InSight* 8–9.
13. Edgerton (n 10 above) 35.
14. R Bogdan, 'What does It Mean When a Person Says "I am not retarded"?' (1980) 15/1 *Education and Training of the Mentally Retarded* 76, 74–79.
15. ibid.
16. Edgerton (n 10 above).
17. Bogdan (n 14 above).

18. E Goffman, *Stigma: Notes on the Management of Spoiled Identity* (Englewood Cliffs, NJ: Prentice-Hall, 1963).
19. PM Ferguson, *Abandoned to their Fate: Social Policy and Practice Toward Severely Retarded People in America, 1820–1920* (Philadelphia: Temple Univ, 1994) x.
20. 'Symposium: What's in a Name?' (2002) 40/1 *Mental Retardation* 51–80.
21. Bogdan (n 14 above) 77.

3

Cross-Cultural Perceptions of Disability: Policy Implications of Divergent Views

ALISON DUNDES RENTELN

As a matter of fact, one of the most striking facts that emerge from a study of widely varying cultures is the ease with which our abnormals function in other cultures. It does not matter what kind of 'abnormality' we choose for illustration, those which indicate extreme instability, or those which are more in the nature of character traits like sadism or delusions of grandeur or of persecution, there are well-described cultures in which these abnormals function at ease and with honor without danger or difficulty to the society.[1]

I. INTRODUCTION

The existence of persons with varying degrees of abilities is a normal part of all societies in all historical periods.[2] Societies vary as to which particular disabilities matter, the extent to which individuals with those particular traits are stigmatized, and the types of restrictions placed on disabled persons' participation in social life. This chapter is concerned with cross-cultural differences in the manner in which societies interpret disability.[3] Disability encompasses those traits regarded as deviating from a culturally constructed norm.[4] Cross-cultural analysis of disability is liberating because it shows that stigma is not necessarily associated with 'difference' and that different disabilities evoke differing responses depending upon the cultural context.[5] In this chapter, I examine the implications of cultural relativism for theorizing about disability.

I begin with nomenclature, ie, the question of how best to define 'disability'. After discussing the politicized nature of the debate over definitions, I take up the methodological challenges encountered in the cross-cultural study of stigmatized characteristics. Following a consideration of the interpretive issues, I present cases in which cross-cultural differences in the interpretation of disability result in injustices—one involving forced medical treatment of a minor with a 'clubbed foot' and others involving a culture-bound syndrome,[6] namely 'running amok'. The purpose of this chapter is to show that the cultural differences in the understanding of disability can have significant policy implications. The ramifications of culturally divergent perceptions may influence debates not only in national legal systems concerning definitions of disability, but also in international institutions about the best standards to ensure the equalization of opportunities for persons with disabilities.

Although this book is primarily concerned with 'intellectual disabilities', this chapter examines the relationship between disability and multiculturalism more generally.[7] I deal with the hermeneutics of disability because similar biases plague the analyses of both physical and mental disabilities. Moreover, I question the utility of the distinction between mental and physical disabilities, which may reflect a Cartesian epistemological commitment to a mind/body duality—one not found in many other worldviews.[8] Hence, the analysis of culturally specific ideas about disability is of a more general nature. I turn now to definitional matters.

II. DEFINITIONS OF DISABILITY: NOMENCLATURE AND INTERPRETATION

The entire history of the disability rights movements reveals an emphasis on physical disabilities, oftentimes to the exclusion of mental ones. The symbol in the United States of a person in a wheelchair illustrates this tendency. This is unfortunate and misleading, not only because many individuals with disabilities possess mental disabilities, but also because physical and mental conditions are frequently interrelated. For instance, mental illness often has a physical component.

One must tread carefully when selecting terms for the discussion of disability because nomenclature in this arena is hotly contested.[9] Certain words become politically incorrect, eg, 'handicapped' in the US context.[10] There is also cultural variation in the preferred terminology used in different countries. Furthermore, a particular term, eg, the 'deaf', may take on different meanings over time.[11] In addition, sometimes individuals classified under one category are eventually placed under another.[12]

With regard to mental disabilities, naming is a particularly contentious matter, and there are different conventions with respect to terminology. Although 'mental retardation' is the term used historically in the United States, in other countries this has been construed as a pejorative term, and many policymakers and theorists have preferred instead to use 'intellectual disabilities'.[13] In this chapter, I use the term 'mental retardation', though I acknowledge that many dislike it as a major category under the rubric of intellectual disabilities.

Mental illness is another important subcategory under intellectual disabilities and will be considered here. Although mental retardation and mental illness are types of intellectual disabilities, there remains considerable disagreement as to a precise definition of 'intellectual disabilities'.[14]

Those who wish to define disability often begin with the classic definition provided by Nagi: 'an inability or limitation in performing roles and tasks expected of an individual within a social environment'.[15] For the most part, disability, when broadly construed, includes physical, intellectual, and emotional conditions.[16]

The formulation found in the Americans with Disabilities Act (ADA), a law designed to prevent disability discrimination and to promote inclusive policies, is considered to be a reasonably defensible one. The ADA protects persons with disabilities. A person is considered to have a 'disability' if he or she has a physical or mental impairment that substantially limits one or more major life activities, has a record of such an impairment, or is regarded as having such an impairment.

One of the virtues of the ADA is that it includes individuals who suffer discrimination because of perceptions that their conditions affect their capacity to perform whether or not that is actually true. This broadens the scope of protection afforded by the law and, for that reason, is properly regarded as a desirable feature of the definition contained in the law.

Although the ADA definition is a good one, and one that has influenced the development of other legislation,[17] the manner in which the judiciary has interpreted the definition leaves something to be desired.[18] For instance, the US Supreme Court has excluded from coverage individuals whose disabilities can be corrected, eg, with medication or eyeglasses.[19] Moreover, some conditions are excluded from coverage for political reasons. The Americans with Disabilities Act stipulates that a number of conditions, most notably those related to sexual orientation, are not part of the operative definition.[20] So, having a well-formulated definition may be beneficial in the political movement to promote human rights for persons with disabilities, but it is not sufficient to ensure justice for all persons with disabilities.

Various formulations of disability can be found in human rights instruments and the World Health Organization's International Classification of Impairments, Disabilities, and Handicaps (ICIDH).[21] Yet, they are criticized as anachronistic because they are based on the functional limitations approach associated with the now repudiated medical model. With few exceptions, most notably the provision in the Convention on the Rights of the Child (Article 23), international definitions are too flawed to merit consideration.

Some have questioned whether definitions are necessary or desirable. After all, definitions have been used historically to exclude individuals from legal protection. If governments were required to provide basic human rights to all citizens, including adequate housing, health care, education and other social services, there would be little need for any definition of disability. In the real world, though, since governments lack the political will, even if they have the resources, to subsidize economic, social, and cultural rights for all, eligibility criteria for persons with disabilities will be necessary to ensure that the maximum possible number of persons receive basic services.

One of the most profound changes in the understanding of disability is a consequence of the paradigm shift from the so-called medical model to the socio-political model.[22] In the disability rights movement, this has meant challenging the notion that disability is a condition inhering in the individual and accepting that disability is a consequence of the failure of society to make environmental adaptations to ensure the full participation of persons with disabilities. It is not the wheelchair that causes the disability but rather, the stairs serving as the entrance to a building and the absence of a ramp.[23] Hence, this paradigm shift requires changing the responsibility for the lack of access from the individual with the disability to the larger society for failing to remove the barriers to full participation.

The reality is that while the paradigm shift forces a reconsideration of the meaning of disability, the condition remains. That is, the changes made to the environment reflect the disability, eg, curb cuts and ramps suggest limitations in mobility. This means that the definition of disability is, to some extent, implicit in the changes made to the environment.

Insofar as societies differ in the degree to which they empower persons with disabilities, it is useful to take a comparative approach to see cultural variation in the treatment of persons with disabilities. If the extent of limitations is largely a function of the environment, then it is not inevitable that persons with disabilities should experience stigma and exclusion. We now turn our attention at this juncture to existing cross-cultural scholarship on some types of disability.

III. CULTURAL CONCEPTIONS OF DISABILITIES

Even if a satisfactory abstract definition of disability can be identified, the question remains whether it will be possible to apply it cross-culturally, given the wide range of cultural variation that exists across the globe. To determine whether the same characteristics give rise to stigma, one would like to consult existing studies of disabilities in various contexts. Surprisingly, however, relatively little scholarship exists on cross-cultural analyses of disability.[24] What literature can be found consists of articles or collections of essays that focus on one or two groups and their perceptions of one type of disability.[25] To my knowledge, no truly comparative consideration of multiple disabilities has been published.[26]

Some studies on attitudes suggest that there is variation across ethnic groups as to the types of traits that are stigmatized. Westbrook, Legge, and Pennay, summarizing some of the findings in the literature, report that there are:

significant differences in the attitudes held by American, Danish, Chinese, and Greek samples toward people with disabilities, with Americans having the most favorable attitudes and Greeks the most negative. Compared to Americans, the Chinese have been reported to be particularly negative in their attitudes toward people with mental disorders. Research in Israel has demonstrated more negative attitudes toward physical disability among Arabs and Jews from Arab countries than among Jews from western countries.[27]

The authors' own research investigated beliefs among six distinct ethnic communities in Australia. They found what they considered to be 'very different attitudes toward people with a wide range of disabilities':

The German community was significantly more accepting than were Anglo-Australians of people with five disabilities: amputation, stroke, cerebral palsy, psychiatric illness, and mental retardation. Compared to Anglo-Australians, Italians were less accepting of people with five conditions: asthma, amputation, blindness, paraplegia and AIDS. The Greek community was less accepting of people with ten disabilities: asthma, diabetes, heart disease, amputation, cancer, stuttering, blindness, epilepsy, paraplegia and AIDS. The Arabic-speaking respondents reported significantly less acceptance of eleven disabling conditions: asthma, diabetes, heart disease, amputation, cancer, stuttering, blindness, epilepsy, paraplegia, alcoholism and AIDS. The Chinese community was more accepting than the Anglo-Australians of dwarfism and mental retardation, but less accepting of people with nine conditions: asthma, diabetes, heart disease, amputation, cancer, stuttering, blindness, paraplegia, and AIDS.[28]

The analysis by Westbrook, Legge, and Pennay suggests that there is greater stigma in more 'collectivist' Australian ethnic communities. Their data provides more support for theorists who claim greater acceptance exists for persons with disabilities in societies that have a higher standard of living as compared with theorists whose position is that more traditional societies are more accepting.[29]

The data gathered by survey may suffer from limitations. First, the sample size is relatively small and may call into question the generalizability of claims about a particular ethnic group's view of persons with disabilities. It is also possible that respondents may be disinclined to express prejudice via a survey instrument. A more reliable gauge of cultural perceptions is likely to be the folklore of the various societies.

Since scholars have not interpreted images of disability within various cultural communities,[30] the only feasible approach to take for investigating cross-cultural understandings of disability may be to consult the folklore of various groups. The materials reflect social responses to persons who have various disabilities, most commonly persons who are blind,[31] deaf,[32] mentally retarded and mentally ill.[33] This means that despite the paradigm shift from the functional limitations model to a minority rights model, ethnographic studies of disability continue to focus on specific characteristics or 'impairments'.

While some may object to the study of folk texts as a means of gaining insight into societal response to disability, these materials reflect the underlying values of communities.[34] Even though it is extremely difficult to confront hostile attitudes towards persons with disabilities directly, it is necessary to have an accurate idea of social reality before attempting to effect social change.

Because many of the cultural explanations of disability are based on religious beliefs, one must concede that it will be exceedingly difficult to change these entrenched ideas.[35] It is, nevertheless, important to take stock of the belief systems of those whose negative views of persons with disabilities limit their full participation in social life.

Researchers will face methodological challenges when carrying out research projects on disabilities. In some languages there may not exist a term for the category 'disability'. For example, among the Maasai there is no single term that encompasses all types of disability; instead, they use specific terms of particular conditions.[36] For some communities, disability as a concept may apply only to psychological conditions and not to physical impairments.[37]

Because of the stigma associated with persons with disabilities, communities may be reluctant to acknowledge their existence or reveal the manner in which they are treated in their societies. Furthermore, the degree to which a person must experience a loss of function to be regarded by society or himself or herself as 'disabled' may vary. For instance, the research by Lane *et al.* on blind persons in Egypt found that legal definitions of blindness were not universal and that individuals might refuse to accept that they were blind, partly because of the associated stigma.[38] This research provides an example of the difficulty of conducting cross-national research—given the existence of differing legal definitions of specific disabilities—and also raises the further problem of relying on self-definitions of disability.[39]

Another problem that plagues cross-national studies is that of translation, which requires finding equivalent terms for specific conditions in other languages. For instance, the interpretation of 'major depression' led to interpretive difficulties in China.[40]

Ideally, cross-cultural research should involve both the outsider or etic analytic framework with its diagnostic criteria combined with the insider or emic conceptualization of the disability based on the indigenous or folk understandings.[41] Furthermore, persons with the specific disabilities should be part of the research team. More persons with disabilities should have the educational opportunities necessary for them to carry out research of this kind within their own cultural communities.

Failure to take culturally specific concepts into account may lead to distortions. In some cultures, even the concept of the person may differ fundamentally from Western notions.[42]

IV. MENTAL ILLNESS AND CULTURE-BOUND SYNDROMES

Mental illness is subject to considerable stigma, particularly among some communities with Asian cultures.[43] Moreover, as certain types of mental illness are culture-bound syndromes, they are, by definition, not found outside the cultural communities.[44] For instance, the Korean syndrome 'hwa-byung' is characterized as 'a somatic manifestation of suppressed anger or rage'. Brain fag in Nigeria is a common syndrome said to involve 'a sensation of heaviness, or heat in the head associated with the effort of studying and can occur with major depression, anxiety disorders, or adjustment disorders'. In South Asia, the loss of vital essence through semen is believed to cause various physical and psychological symptoms. In India, this is known as the dhat syndrome.[45]

Because of the culturally specific conceptualizations of the disorder, it may be difficult for outsiders to comprehend the nature of the illness, not to mention the stigma associated with it. While culture-bound syndromes remain somewhat controversial in Western, 'cosmopolitan' medicine, their precarious position has changed somewhat with the inclusion of the syndromes in basic medical and psychiatric references such as the *Merck Manual* and the *Diagnostic and Statistical Manual of Mental Disorders* (DSM-IV).[46] In addition to delineating culture-bound syndromes, the DSM-IV also considers how cultural factors influence various disorders. In general, there is growing recognition of the influence of culture on the diagnosis and treatment of mental illness.[47]

V. MENTAL RETARDATION

Of the little scholarship that exists on mental retardation in diverse cultural settings,[48] the seminal work of Robert Edgerton, which assessed the conventional wisdom about the treatment of individuals regarded as mentally retarded in smaller-scale societies, is probably the most significant.[49] His analysis challenges unjustifiable generalizations: 'We must conclude that neither the view that among the primitives all is well with the severely retarded nor the view that all is short and lethal is correct. What happens to the retarded varies among, and moreover, within societies.'[50]

Contrary to the popular view that those with 'mild mental retardation' escape stigma, Edgerton contends that they regularly encounter labeling, though it is not always negative.[51] Indeed, he makes references to societies in which persons with both mild and severe mental retardation are regarded as endowed with special religious powers. However, despite having this status, they may nevertheless be denied the right to marry.[52] Some societies have been known to take a more 'benign' approach to mental retardation. In short, Edgerton's contribution was to demonstrate that the treatment of those designated as 'mentally retarded' was diverse and complex, as one would expect in a pluralistic world.

Although one might expect greater acceptance of persons with disabilities in societies where life is less difficult, Edgerton's discussion, based partly on the behavior of villagers in rural India, suggests that is not necessarily the case.

Edgerton's research, while highly provocative, did not provide a definition of mental retardation that is cross-culturally viable.[53] He is careful to resist the temptation to generalize in the absence of adequate cross-cultural data.

As initially revealed in Edgerton's classic paper, there are many problems with the analysis of mental retardation. First, the measurement tools for evaluating intelligence have been fraught with all manner of biases. The development of the intelligence quotient tests in the United States and other countries substantiates this point.[54] The effect of cultural differences on measurement of cognitive abilities has been noted in Europe as well.

Given the recognition that testing was flawed, the next anthropological move was to shift from the 'mental retardation' formulation to a more general consideration of 'competence'.[55] An important work, Richard Jenkins's *Question of Competence: Culture, Classification and Intellectual Disability* (1998), addresses the question of whether there are cross-cultural criteria for evaluating 'mental retardation', carrying on with the line of enquiry begun by Edgerton.[56] Eschewing definitions associated with the racist pseudoscientific movement of eugenics, Jenkins explains that intellectual or cognitive incompetences are to be preferred because they are broader than mental retardation and learning difficulties. Perhaps most importantly, Jenkins advocates use of local models of understanding competence and incompetence in specific cultural contexts, which is the contribution his collection makes.[57]

One of the most powerful essays in Jenkins's book is Sylvia van Maastrict's 'Work, Opportunity and Culture: (In)competence in Greece and Wales'. According to the study, defining individuals as 'incompetent' may have adverse consequences for them:

In Wales, classification takes place earlier, is more or less permanent, and leads to segregation in many areas of the adult person's life. In Greece, where classification is more ad hoc, segregation is not a direct result, but is, rather, based on individual abilities and circumstances....We thus see, ironically, that in a country where formal interest in and care of, incompetent people is minimal, incompetent people, because of local social and economic structures and a different model of competence, do have a chance to be a part of their society.[58]

It seems counterintuitive that incorporating definitions into social programs turns out to be to the detriment of persons with disabilities. As living independently in the mainstream is a goal of the disability rights movement and reflects the desire of persons with disabilities for greater autonomy, it should give us pause to see the use political authorities make of definitions.

Ultimately, we ought to be concerned with the practical uses of models and categories. Indeed, the central question is how conceptualizations of disability influence the disposition of actual disputes in society. Where groups with differing views of disability exist within the same society, serious difficulties can arise.

VI. CULTURAL CLASHES OVER THE TREATMENT OF DISABILITY

The case of *In re Kou Xiong* involves a clash between two different cultural communities over whether or not to treat a boy's clubbed foot. It demonstrates the practical repercussions of divergent interpretations of a particular disability.[59] A pediatric orthopedic surgeon determined that one of his patients, an 8-year-old Hmong boy by the name of Kou Xiong, would benefit from surgery. When it became clear that his parents were vehemently opposed to having their son undergo the procedure to 'correct' his condition, the doctor sought the help of the Department of Child Protective Services. The department filed a petition in dependency court seeking temporary custody so that it could consent to the medical treatment on behalf of the minor. The Fresno County Social Services Department wanted Kou to have surgery because physicians said that without it he would eventually lose the ability to walk and have to use a wheelchair.[60] The petition stated that he came within the provisions of Welfare and Institutions Code Section 300(b) because his parents had failed to obtain surgery to correct his congenital deformities—a dislocated right hip and clubfeet.

The press reported that the parents initially agreed to allow the surgery to be performed provided they could sacrifice a live chicken in court. According to the account given in the media, this would redirect divine anger against them and direct it toward the Social Services department. Evidently, the parents later changed their mind because they realized that they would nevertheless be considered responsible for allowing the surgical intervention. The court authorized the medical procedure.

The Hmong community was apparently unified in its opposition to the medical treatment. A child born with a disability is thought to have the condition for a reason, namely to atone for the sins of ancestors.[61] To disturb the natural order, they believe, would result in divine retribution. Because of this widely held belief, leaders of all twenty clans signed a petition imploring the Director of Social Services not to force the surgery on the boy over the objections of the family and his community. Despite the strength of their opposition, the court was unwilling to change its judgment on this matter. Although the case went on appeal to Justice O'Connor via an emergency petition, no judge was willing to interfere with the original court's decision to order medical treatment over the family's religious objections.

The case is troubling for several reasons. First, the wishes of the Hmong community were ignored, despite the fact that a consensus existed among the community that the surgery not take place for religious reasons.[62] Second, those with disabilities were deeply offended by the decision, particularly by the presumption that the boy's life would be ruined if he could not walk and had to rely on a chair. The boy had indicated he wanted to be a teacher, a profession that would certainly be possible if he were to use a wheelchair.[63]

There was some question as to whether the surgery was immediately necessary to enable Kou to walk. It seems that it was already considered late to perform the surgery and that the longer he waited to have it, the more radical the medical approach would have to be. But even if it was medically advisable to have the surgery sooner rather than later, it is not at all obvious that the court should authorize surgery over the parents' religious and cultural objections. Kou himself said both that he did not want surgery and that he did not want to be in a wheelchair. He was concerned that were he to have surgery, he might be ostracized afterwards. The psychologist attested to this fear on his part in his description of Kou's playing with dolls.

The family's attorney attempted a series of appeals that reached all the way to Justice O'Connor but lost at every level. Interestingly, however, despite the legal outcome, no doctor was willing to perform the surgery without the parents' cooperation.[64] After all the litigation, the original judge decided to vacate his earlier ruling ordering the surgery. What changed his mind was a psychiatric report that concluded that Kou would be at 'grave psychological risk' if the operation were performed over parental objections. Kou said he was afraid of being separated from his parents if the surgery took place. He was also fearful that something bad would happen to his siblings (and that he would be responsible). Basically, his community would reject him; he would be a social outcast. So, in spite of the protracted litigation, which appeared to disregard the cultural objections for the most part, the Hmong family, in the end, succeeded in avoiding the surgery.

What is striking about this case is that the court ordered the surgery even though the boy's condition was not life threatening. With only a couple of exceptions, courts generally have not intervened in family decision making concerning children in cases that were not life threatening.[65] One can only speculate as to why the court felt the urgent need to depart from the standard doctrinal approach.

It is also important to realize how the disabled community might view the court's treatment of the issue.[66] Although certainly not consciously, the lawyer for Kou implied that life in a wheelchair was unacceptable: 'The parents' right to raise their child in the way they see fit must give way to the child's right to have an opportunity to live a productive and pleasant, or at least bearable life.'[67] In *Xiong*, the explicit presumption was that it is sufficiently important for children to walk that even surgery with uncertain results can be ordered over family objections.

Another Hmong case involved a cultural conflict over the medical treatment of a young girl, Lia Lee, who had epilepsy and was developmentally disabled. Her story is told in a moving account by Anne Fadiman.[68] For the Hmong parents, 'the crisis was the treatment, not the epilepsy.'[69] The parents attributed her grand mal episodes to the medications she took. Her condition was a spiritual matter, not a physical one. The book documents how different cultural interpretations of disability not only interfered with the well-being of the child, but also eventually led a court to remove Lia from her family's home.[70]

Judicial treatment of mental conditions also reflects different understandings of disability, sometimes in the context of disputes involving culture-bound syndromes.[71] In two cases, one from the United States and the other from Canada, judges wrestled with a culture-bound syndrome known as 'running amok'. In such cases, a defendant acts as a result of extreme mental or emotional disturbance, which may only be understandable in a particular cultural context,[72] and the defense depends on the recognition of a culture-bound syndrome.[73] A salient example of an attempt to raise such a defense is the Hawaii Supreme Court case of *People v Ganal*.[74] A Filipino man, Orlando Ganal, shot his relatives and set fire to a home, killing several people. At the trial, he argued that he had 'run amok'.[75] 'Amok' is defined as:

A dissociative episode characterized by a period of brooding followed by an outburst of violent, aggressive, or homicidal behavior directed at people and objects. The episode tends to be precipitated by a perceived slight or insult and seems to be prevalent only among males. The episode is often accompanied by persecutory ideas, automatism, amnesia, exhaustion, and a return to premorbid state following the episode. Some instances of amok may occur during a brief psychotic episode or constitute the onset or an exacerbation of a chronic psychotic process.[76]

In this case, the defense was that Orlando Ganal suffered humiliation in the context of his failing marriage with his wife. Distraught because of his wife's infidelity and her taunting, he was described as experiencing severe emotional distress and depression. This profoundly affected his self-esteem, precipitating his fit of rage.[77] He went on a rampage, killing his wife's parents, and injuring his wife and their son. He also set fire to the home of the brother of his wife's lover, and two young children perished in the flames. Expert witnesses testified about the concept of 'amok' to explain his actions.[78]

Orlando Ganal was convicted of first-degree murder and first-degree attempted murder. On appeal, he challenged his conviction on several grounds, one of which was that the prosecutor made sarcastic comments trivializing the amok defense. The Supreme Court rejected the argument that prosecutorial misconduct required reversal of his conviction.[79]

The use of the 'amok' defense provoked criticism.[80] One criticism was that the defense 'served to spread the erroneous and appalling stereotype that Filipinos are prone to run amok'. Commentators suggested that the defense put the culture on trial.[81] Some denied that it was part of Filipino culture, and that even if the syndrome exists, violent behavior is not condoned in the Philippines.[82] Whether or not the 'amok' defense was properly used in the *Ganal* case, it is clear that culture-bound syndromes are important in some criminal cases.

The amok syndrome was also part of the legal insanity defense in the Canadian case of *R v Hem*.[83] Serey Sonia Hem, a Cambodian man, used a machete to attack Mr. Tray, the father of the Chinese family with whom he was staying. His relationship with the Trays deteriorated after Mrs. Tray's mother fell off the toilet, injuring herself while Hem was taking care of her. The defense psychiatrist, Dr. Lohrasbe, explained 'amok' as a form of psychosis or loss of contact with reality. Dr. Semrau, the Crown's expert, said 'amok' was not a valid psychiatric diagnosis by Western standards, that the defendant's behavior did not fit the diagnostic criteria, and that Hem's was a conscious attack stemming from suppressed anger. The court ultimately rejected the defense of legal insanity.

Although courts have entertained the 'amok defense' in a few cases, some psychiatrists have condemned the recognition of this jurisprudence as a form of what they term 'psychiatric primitivism'. According to this view, amok epitomizes the tendency of Western medicine to represent difference in the 'cultural Other' through projecting 'barbaric stereotypes'.[84]

In some disputes, for instance, *People v Rev. Chung and Rev. Choi*, the victim, rather than the defendant has a culture-bound syndrome.[85]

A Korean woman, Kyung Chung, who was suffering from 'possession by demons', underwent a five-hour spiritual exorcism to rid her of 'evil spirits'. This ritual healing ceremony involved applying pressure to various parts of her body.[86] Unfortunately, the treatment resulted in her death. When her husband and two ministers were prosecuted for murder,[87] they argued that their goal was to exorcise her demons.[88] After a three-week non-jury trial, they were convicted only of involuntary manslaughter; the husband received a two-year sentence and the two ministers the harshest possible, four years each.[89] Evidently, the judge was willing to take the cultural and religious factors into account.[90]

Regardless of whether or not one agrees with the approach taken by the judges in the cases discussed above, they demonstrate the profound ignorance of elites about the meaning of certain disabilities for ethnic minorities and also for the mainstream. In the case of Kou Xiong, whose condition was not life threatening, the bias against a physical disability was so extreme that the legal system violated its own rules governing court-ordered medical treatment over parents' religious objections. In the cases of culture-bound syndromes, judges had trouble even appreciating the nature of the argument. It is hard to see how justice can be done in the absence of information about culturally specific disabilities.[91]

VII. IMPORTANCE OF CULTURAL INFORMATION FOR DISABILITY

There is no question that some forms of disability exist in all societies. It is less clear how different societies around the world conceptualize disabilities and how those perceptions influence community policies. Future research should focus on gaining insight into culturally diverse methods of addressing various kinds of disabilities. Comparative research offers the possibility of finding more humane approaches to social issues such as disability. Cross-cultural studies of disability should be liberating insofar as they reveal the contingent nature of 'normalcy'. To the extent that rules governing participation in social life are based on arbitrary and biased criteria, it should be possible to reconsider the rules of the game. Cross-cultural research will also help demonstrate 'best practices', or exemplary policies that guide the UN in its efforts to promote human rights for persons with disabilities. Should widespread cultural support exist for 'mainstreaming' persons with disabilities, the position of policymakers advocating more inclusionary policies would be strengthened.

NOTES

1. R Benedict, 'Anthropology and the Abnormal' (1940) 10 *Journal of General Psychology* 60.
2. For a study of disability in antiquity, see R Garland, *The Eye of the Beholder: Deformity and Disability in the Graeco-Roman World* (Ithaca, NY: Cornell Univ Press, 1995); T Molleson, 'Archaeological Evidence for Attitudes to Disability in the Past' (1999) 15 *Archaeological Review from Cambridge* 2, 69–77.
3. Surprisingly little scholarship exists on attitudes towards persons with various types of disabilities. Some attitudinal work suggests that there is cultural variation as to the sorts of traits which are disfavored in different places.
4. Ruth Benedict's famous essay 'Anthropology and the Abnormal' contained this insight. Benedict (n 1 above). For a similar argument, see also L Romanucci-Ross and LR Tancredi, 'Psychiatry, the Law and Cultural Determinants of Behavior' (1986) 9 *International Journal of Law and Psychiatry* 265–293.
5. Oddly, even in societies in which persons with disabilities are viewed positively and they are thought to have special religious status, they are nonetheless considered to be simultaneously in a somewhat subordinate position. For commentators referring to their paradoxical position, see, eg, JI Charlton, *Nothing about Us Without Us: Disability Oppression and Empowerment* (Berkeley: Univ of California Press, 1998) 52; and S Akihiro, 'Cultural Analysis of Disability: "Paradox of Blindness" in the Japanese Folk Society' (1990) 54 *Japanese Journal of Ethnology* 4 (in Japanese; English summary 459–463) 461.
6. See the explanation of culture-bound syndromes below.
7. Stan Herr was profoundly concerned about the North American bias in the discussion of disability. For this reason, he asked me to provide a general overview of the challenges multiculturalism poses for the promotion and enforcement of international human rights for persons with disabilities. It was an honor to work with Stan at the UN-sponsored meeting in Hong Kong in December 1999 to assess the status of human rights standards for persons with disabilities.
8. See, eg, CH Ng, 'The Stigma of Mental Illness in Asian Cultures' (1997) 31 *Australian and New Zealand Journal of Psychiatry* 382, 384–385.
9. Unfortunately, many of the words for persons with disabilities have extraordinarily negative connotations, eg, '*invalido*' in Spanish. Other offensive terms for persons with disabilities include '*chirema*', used in Zimbabwe, which means useless; '*pehna*' in Brazil conveys the idea that the affliction is punishment. '*Egbemagbanna*' in Nigeria, among the Edo, means an incomplete person. I Zola, 'Self, Identity, and the Naming Question: Reflections on the Language of Disability' (1993) 36 *Social Science and Medicine* 2, 167–173. See also E Stone, 'Modern Slogan, Ancient Script: Impairment and Disability in the Chinese Language' in M Corker and S French (eds), *Disability Discourse* (Buckingham: Open Univ Press, 1999) 136–170.
10. Some negative terms can only be used by a member of the 'in-group', eg, 'crip' for 'crippled'. This is generally true of minority groups, which may co-opt a negative epithet, eg, 'nigger' and 'queer', as an act of empowerment.

11. Marian Corker explains how the term 'deaf', which originally meant 'wholly or partially without hearing' came to have a broader meaning: 'any person who, regardless of whether they could hear or not, ignored, refused to listen to or comply with something or someone'. M Corker, *Deaf and Disabled, or Deafness Disabled: Towards a Human Rights Perspective* (Buckingham: Open Univ Press, 1997) 60.
12. Jenkins describes how over the past few decades, people with cerebral palsy, previously considered 'retarded' or as having 'learning difficulties' were 'removed from those categories'. R Jenkins (ed), *Questions of Competence: Culture, Classification and Intellectual Disability* (Cambridge: Cambridge Univ Press, 1998) 131.
13. Stan Herr, past president of the American Society for Mental Retardation, did not consider the term objectionable. Personal communication, December 1999. It is somewhat surprising that the term has continued to be used in the US, considering how despised it is elsewhere. See FE Stockholder, 'Naming and Renaming Persons with Intellectual Disabilities' in MH Rioux and M Bach (eds), *Disability Is Not Measles: New Research Paradigms in Disability* (North York, Ont: L'Institut Roeher Institute, 1994) 153–177. Intellectual disabilities usually include learning differences. See also Jenkins (n 12 above) 8.
14. I do not attempt to resolve the debate over the precise meaning of the term 'intellectual disabilities' in this essay.
15. SZ Nagi, 'The Concept and Measurement of Disability' in ED Berkowitz (ed), *Disability Policies and Government Programs* (New York: Praeger, 1979) 1–25.
16. One book emphasizes the importance of having a broad definition of disability including: 'those persons who have physical, intellectual and emotional disabilities, as well as those who have a dual diagnosis'. RP Marinelli and AE Dell Orto (eds), *The Psychological and Social Impact of Disability* (4th edn, New York: Springer, 1999) xix.
17. See, eg, L Waddington, 'Reassessing the Employment of People with Disabilities in Europe: From Quotas to Anti-Discrimination Laws' (1996) 81 *Comparative Labor Law Journal* 62.
18. For an insightful essay analyzing the interpretation of disability under the ADA, see M Crossley, 'The Disability Kaleidoscope' (1999) 74 *Notre Dame Law Review* 621–716.
19. In the *Sutton* case, twin sisters were disqualified from being airline pilots because of their poor vision. Because their vision could be corrected, they were not considered sufficiently disabled for purposes of invoking the ADA. *Sutton v United Air Lines, Inc* 527 US 471 (1999).
20. Crossley summarizes the excluded conditions under the ADA: 'current use of illegal drugs, homosexuality, bisexuality, transvestism, transsexualism, pedophilia, exhibitionism, voyeurism, gender identity disorders not resulting from physical impairments, compulsive gambling, kleptomania, and pyromania'. Crossley (n 18 above) 636. President Bush signed the ADA with the stipulation that these conditions be excluded from coverage.
21. For a background on human rights for persons with disabilities, see T Degener and Y Koster-Dreese (eds), *Human Rights and Disabled Persons: Essays*

and Relevant Human Rights Instruments (Dordrecht: Martinus Nijhoff, 1995). See also the report. The ICIDH was originally completed in 1980. World Health Organization, *International Classification of Impairments, Disabilities, and Handicaps* (Geneva: World Health Organization, 1980). For commentary, see, eg, C Van Stokkom and P Fougeyrollas, *Use and Usefulness of the ICIDH in Maintaining People with Disabilities at Home and in Their Own Community* (Strasbourg: Council of Europe Publishing and Patrick Fougeyrollas, 1998). 'Les Déterminants Environnementaux de la participation sociale des personnes ayant des incapacités: Le Def socio-politique de la revision de la CIDIH' 10 *Canadian Journal of Rehabilitation* 147–160. For a discussion of revisions designed to make the ICIDH methodology valid on a global basis, see RT Trotter, II, B Ustun, S Chatterji, J Rehm, R Room, and J Bichenbach, 'Cross-Cultural Applicability Research on Disablement: Models and Methods for the Revision of an International Classification' (2001) 60 *Human Organization* 1, 13–27; KG Manton, JE Dowd, and MA Woodbury, 'Conceptual and Measurement Issues in Assessing Disability Cross-Nationally: Analysis of a WHO-Sponsored Survey of the Disablement Process in Indonesia' (1986) 1 *Journal of Cross-Cultural Gerontology* 339–362.

22. One of the leading, most eloquent disability theorists, whose scholarship explains the paradigm shift is Harlan Hahn. See, eg, H Hahn, 'The Political Implications of Disability: Definitions and Data' in RP Marinelli and AE Dell Orto (eds), *The Psychological and Social Impact of Disability* (4th edn, New York: Springer, 1999) 3–11 (originally published in (1993) 4 *Journal of Disability Policy Studies* 2, 41–52). For another good critique of the medical model, see M Kalyanpur, 'Special Education Epistemology as a Product of Western Culture: Implications for Non-Western Families of Children with Disabilities' (1999) 22 *International Journal of Rehabilitation Research* 111–118.

23. Taking this argument to its logical conclusion would mean that if the environments were changed sufficiently to accommodate all persons with all disabilities, disability would cease to exist.

24. For a good survey of disability among different ethnic communities within the US, see ML Kuehn, *Cultural Diversity and Disability: An Annotated Bibliography* (Madison: Waisman Center, 1998).

25. See, eg, B Ingstad and SR Whyte (eds), *Disability and Culture* (Berkeley: Univ of California Press, 1995); B Holzer, A Vreede, and G Weight (eds), *Disability in Different Cultures: Reflections on Local Concepts* (New Brunswick: Transaction Publishers, 1999); F Armstrong and L Barton (eds), *Disability, Human Rights, and Education: Cross-Cultural Perspectives* (Buckingham: Open Univ Press, 1999); P Devlieger, 'Disability and Community Action in a Zimbabwean Community: Priorities Based on a Biocultural Approach' (1994) 22 *Journal of the Steward Anthropological Society* 1, 41–57; V Keck, 'Colder than Cool: Disability and Personhood among the Yupno in Papua New Guinea' (1999) 6 *Anthropology and Medicine* 261–283; J Rensel and A Howard, 'The Place of Persons with Disabilities in Rotuman Society' (1997) 30 *Pacific Studies Laie* 3, 19–50.

26. Some regional works exist on particular disabilities. See, eg, J Tossebro, A Gustavsson, and G Dyvendahl (eds), *Intellectual Disability in the Nordic Welfare States: Policies and Everyday Life* (Kristiansand: Norwegian Academic Press, 1999). For a comparative study of epilepsy, see LF Andermann,

'Epilepsy in Developing Countries' (1995) 32 *Transcultural Psychiatric Research Review* 351–384.

27. MT Westbrook, V Legge, and M Pennay, 'Attitudes Towards Disabilities in a Multicultural Society' (1993) 36 *Social Science and Medicine* 5, 615–623.

28. ibid 619–620.

29. ibid 622. For other studies on attitudes towards persons with disabilities, see, eg, V Florian, 'Cross-cultural Differences in Attitudes Towards Disabled Persons' (1982) 6 *International Journal of Intercultural Relations* 291–299; V Florian and S Katz, 'The Impact of Cultural, Ethnic and National Variables on Attitudes Towards the Disabled in Israel: A Review' (1983) 7 *International Journal of Intercultural Relations* 167–179; G Cloerkes and D Neubert, 'Cross-cultural and Historical Variations of the Social Reaction Toward Disabled Persons' (1984) 7 *International Journal of Rehabilitation Research* 339–340; MI Boutte, 'The Stumbling Disease: A Case Study of Stigma among Azorean-Portuguese' (1987) 24 *Social Science and Medicine* 3, 209–217; D Harper, 'Children's Attitudes Toward Physical Disability in Nepal' (1997) 28 *Journal of Cross-Cultural Psychology* 6, 710–729; G Mandel *et al.*, 'The Attitudes of Parents Towards Children with Cerebral Palsy from Different Ethnic Origins in Israel' (1969) 12 *Public Health* 2, 67–73; A Bakheit and V Shanmugalingam, 'A Study of the Attitudes of a Rural Indian Community Toward People with Physical Disabilities' (1997) 11 *Clinical Rehabilitation* 329–334; B Ingstad, 'Coping Behavior of Disabled Persons and Their Families: Cross-cultural Perspectives from Norway and Botswana' (1988) 11 *International Journal of Rehabilitation Research* 4, 351–359; T Sato, 'A Cross-cultural Study of Attitudes Toward Handicapped Individuals in Japan and the US' (MS thesis, California State Univ, Long Beach, 1980) 80.

30. But see Hans-Jorg Uther, *Behinderte in populären Erzählungen: Studien zur historischen und vergleichenden Erzählforschung* (Berlin: Walter de Gruyter, 1981) 172. The title is: *Disabled People in Popular Narratives: Studies in Historical and Comparative Folk Narratives.* For studies of disability in proverbs, see F Loux and P Richard, *Sagesses du corps: La Santé et la maladie dans les proverbes français* (Paris: G-P Maisonneuve et Larose, 1978); RC Lachal, 'Infirmes and Infirmités dans les proverbes italiennes' (1972) 2 *Ethnologie Française* 67–96; *Les Stéréotypés de l'infirme en Italie d'après des proverbs et des livres pour la jeunesse* (Mediterranea No 18) 510. D Neubert and G Cloerkes, *Behinderung und Behinderte in verschiedenen Kulturen: Eine vergleichende Analyse ethnologischer Studien* (Heidelberg: Edition Schindele, 1987). AC Guimbous, *Behinderte in Kenia: Soziale und pädagogische Probleme einer grossen Randgruppe* (Frankfurt: Verlag für Interkulturelle Kommunikation, 1991). F Albrecht and G Weigt (eds), *Behinderte Menschen am Rande der Gesellschaften* (Frankfurt: Verlag für Interkulturelle Kommunikation, 1993).

31. Akihiro (n 5 above); S Deshen, 'Coming of Age among Blind People in Israel' (1987) 2 *Disability, Handicap & Society* 2, 137–149; M Priestley, 'Commonality and Difference in the Movement: An "Association of Blind Asians" in Leeds' (1995) 10 *Disability & Society* 2, 157–169.

32. S Rutherford, *American Deaf Culture* (Bertonville, Md: Linstok Press, 1993).

33. Others have noted this proclivity among researchers, eg, E Kasntiz and RP Shuttleworth, 'Engaging Anthropology in Disability Studies' (1999) 9 *Position Papers in Disability Studies* 1, 7.

34. In Ireland, for instance, the mother claims that a fairy took her child and left in its place, the changeling, ie, the child with the disability. C Haffter, 'The Changeling: History and Psychodynamics of Attitudes to Retarded Children in European Folklore' (1968) 4 *Journal of the History of Behavioural Sciences* 55–61. This might lead to drastic measures. According to Jenkins, 'one recommended treatment for a changeling was to drive the impostor out using fire, another was exposure to the elements.' Jenkins claims these remedies were actually used. Jenkins (n 12 above) 16.

35. Edgerton notes that in many societies mental retardation is 'thought to be a sign of divine displeasure or punishment for past misconduct'. RB Edgerton, 'Mental Retardation in Non-Western Societies: Toward a Cross-cultural Perspective on Incompetence' in HC Haywood (ed), *Socio-cultural Aspects of Mental Retardation* (New York: Appleton-Century-Crofts, 1970) 552. For an excellent study on the meaning of disability in Eastern religions, see M Miles, 'Disability in an Eastern Religious Context: Historical Perspectives' (1995) 10 *Disability & Society* 1, 49–68.

36. A Talle, 'A Child Is a Child: Disability and Equality among the Kenya Maasai' in B Ingstad and SR White (eds), *Disability and Culture* (Berkeley: Univ of California Press, 1995) 56–72; Bernhard Heland's essay 'Disability as Incurable Illness: Health, Process, and Personhood in Southern Somalia', in the same collection, also discusses the absence of a general term for disability in the Somali language.

37. See, eg, M Marshall, 'Problematizing Impairment: Cultural Competence in the Carolines' (1996) 35 *Ethnology* 4, 249–263.

38. Whereas the legal definition of blindness in the US was less than 20/200 in the better eye, the World Health Organization viewed that measure as 'severe visual loss' and designated blindness for those with vision of less than 3/60. Those in an Egyptian community with no light perception whatsoever were considered *ama* or *kafeef* (blind). SD Lane, BI Mikhail, A Rezian, P Courtright, R Marx, and C Dawson, 'Sociocultural Aspects of Blindness in an Egyptian Delta Hamlet: Visual Impairment vs. Visual Disability' (1993) 15 *Medical Anthropology* 245–260.

39. Lane *et al.* offer a few explanations of their data, one of which is: 'cultural beliefs discourage the discussion of disease, since complaining about a condition is equated with questioning the will of God.' The visually impaired valued what vision they had. This was reflected in proverbs: '*iitashash wa la al' ama*' (rather weak vision than complete blindness) and '*nuss al' 'ama, wa la al' ama kull*' (rather half blind, ie, in one eye, than completely blind). ibid.

40. For a somewhat technical discussion of this controversy, see S Lee, 'Cultures in Psychiatric Nosology: The CCMD-2-R and International Classification of Mental Disorders' (1996) 20 *Culture, Medicine, and Psychiatry* 432–433.

41. CH Ng, 'The Stigma of Mental Illness in Asian Cultures' (1997) 31 *Australian and New Zealand Journal of Psychiatry* 3, 382–390.

42. An early classic essay making this point is: RA Shweder and EJ Bourne, 'Does the Concept of the Person Vary Cross-Culturally?' in AJ Marsella and GM White (eds), *Cultural Conceptions of Mental Health and Therapy* (Dordrecht: Holland, 1982) 97–137. Over the past two decades, the discipline of cultural

psychology has attempted to demonstrate subtle differences in reasoning among different ethnic communities.

43. See, eg, Ng (n 41 above); G Canino, R Lewis-Fernandez, and M Bravo, 'Methodological Challenges in Cross-cultural Mental Health Research' (1997) 34 *Transcultural Psychiatry* 2, 163–184.

44. For a good overview, see AC Gaw (ed), *Culture, Ethnicity, and Mental Illness* (Washington, DC: American Psychiatric Press, 1993); CC Hughes and RM Wintrob, 'Culture-Bound Syndromes and the Cultural Context of Clinical Psychiatry' in JM Oldham (ed), *Review of Psychiatry*, 14 (Washington, DC: American Psychiatric Press, 1995) 565–597. For articles on particular groups, see two issues: 'Cross-Cultural Medicine' published in the *Western Journal of Medicine* in 1983 and 1992.

45. These examples are taken from LJ Kirmayer and A Young, 'Culture and Somatization: Clinical, Epidemiological, and Ethnographic Perspectives' (1998) 60 *Psychosomatic Medicine* 420–430. The authors argue that: 'These culture-related syndromes illustrate how ethnophysiological ideas about the body can give rise to culture-specific somatic symptoms and complaints, such as heat in the head, loss of semen in the urine, and specific types of conventional symptoms....Any psychiatric nosology that hopes to have universal applicability must consider these local variations.' ibid 423.

46. R Berkow and AJ Fletcher (eds), *The Merck Manual of Diagnosis and Therapy* (16th edn, Rahway, NJ: Merck Sharp & Dohme Research Laboratories, 1992); *Diagnostic and Statistical Manual of Mental Disorders* (4th edn, Washington, DC: American Psychiatric Association, 1994) [hereinafter DSM-IV]. 'The term *culture-bound syndrome* denotes recurrent, locally-specific patterns of aberrant behavior and troubling experience that may or may not be linked to a particular DSM-IV diagnostic category...[the syndromes] are generally limited to specific societies or culture areas and are localized, folk, diagnostic categories that frame coherent meanings for certain repetitive, patterned, and troubling sets of experiences and observations' DSM-IV 844. For an assessment of the inclusion of cultural material in DSM-IV, see LJ Kirmayer, 'The Fate of Culture in DSM-IV' (1998) 35 *Transcultural Psychiatry* 3, 339–342; C Hughes, 'The Glossary of "Culture-Bound Syndromes" in DSM-IV: A Critique' (1998) 35 *Transcultural Psychiatry* 3, 413–421. For an intriguing analysis of whether the DSM-IV corresponds to the Chinese Classification of Mental Disorders, see S Lee, 'Cultures in Psychiatric Nosology: The CCMD-2-R and International Classification of Mental Disorders' (1996) 20 *Culture, Medicine, and Psychiatry* 421–472.

47. I Al-Issa (ed), *Handbook of Culture and Mental Illness: An International Perspective* (Madison, Conn: International Universities Press, 1996); H Fabrega, 'Cultural Relativism and Psychiatric Illness' (1989) 177 *Journal of Nervous and Mental Disease* 7, 415–430. See also J Leff, *Psychiatry Around the Globe: A Transcultural View* (New York: Marcel Dekker, Inc, 1981).

48. N Groce, 'Disability in Cross-Cultural Perspective: Rethinking Disability' (1999) 354 *The Lancet 9180*, 756–757; J Scheer and N Groce, 'Impairment as a Human Constant: Cross-cultural and Historical Perspectives on Variation' (1988) 44 *Journal of Social Issues* 23–37; ML Manion and HA Bersani, 'Mental Retardation as a Western Sociological Construct: A Cross-cultural Analysis'

(1987) 2 *Disability, Handicap & Society* 3, 231–245; M Miles, 'Concepts of Mental Retardation in Pakistan' (1992) 7 *Disability, Handicap & Society* 3, 235–256.

49. Edgerton (n 35 above) 523–559. For an overview of Edgerton's scholarship, see B Luckin, 'Time, Place, and Competence: Society and History in the Writings of Robert Edgerton' (1986) 1 *Disability, Handicap & Society* 1, 89–102.

50. Edgerton (n 35 above) 530.

51. ibid 532.

52. ibid 535.

53. Edgerton concedes this in the conclusion. ibid 555.

54. SJ Gould, *The Mismeasure of Man* (New York: WW Norton & Co, 1981). Studies have called into question the meaning of performance of children on intelligence tests insofar as the tests fail to take into account differences in environmental background. IC Uzgiris, 'Sociocultural Factors in Cognitive Development' in HC Haywood (ed), *Socio-cultural Aspects of Mental Retardation* (New York: Appleton-Century-Crofts, 1970) 7–58. See also RL Hayman, Jr., *The Smart Culture: Society, Intelligence, and Law* (New York: New York Univ Press, 1998).

55. CB Kidd, 'The Nature of Mental Retardation in Different Settings: Some Problems in Cross-cultural Study' in HC Haywood (ed), *Socio-cultural Aspects of Mental Retardation* (New York: Appleton-Century-Crofts, 1970) 573–604. Scholars have called for a change in thinking about mental retardation that corresponds to the paradigm shift from medical to social models. L St. Claire, 'Mental Retardation: Impairment or Handicap?' (1986) 1 *Disability, Handicap & Society* 3, 233–243.

56. Jenkins (n 12 above). Jenkins's introduction remarks that the edited collection adds to 'the small amount of work that has adopted a comparative perspective on "mental retardation"'. ibid 1.

57. For a superb set of questions about how to conduct cross-cultural research on 'incompetence', see ibid 5–7.

58. S van Maastricht, 'Work, Opportunity, and Culture: (In)competence in Greece and Wales' in Jenkins (n 12 above).

59. For more background on this case, see AD Renteln, 'Is the Cultural Defense Detrimental to the Health of Children?' (1994) 7 *Law and Anthropology* 27–106.

60. Kou's physician, Dr. Brian Shaw, was very much in favor of surgical intervention. Interestingly, his father, Dr. Anthony Shaw, is a member of the Bioethics Committee of the American Academy of Pediatrics. This committee has issued a policy statement calling for the repeal of religious exemptions for parents who rely on faith healing to the detriment of the health of their children (American Academy of Pediatrics, Committee on Bioethics 1988).

61. The Hmong believe that illness is attributable to spiritual causes: 'Aside from natural, organic, and magical sources of illness, it is most widely believed in the Hmong culture that illness can be caused by spirits of ancestors, sky and earth, food and water, sun and moon, or wind. This belief makes up a large system that encompasses virtually every serious illness.' X Thao, 'Southeast Asian Refugees of Rhode Island: The Hmong Perception of Illness' (1984) 67 *Rhode Island Medical Journal* 327, 323–330.

62. One religious belief was that Kou was born with the disability to atone for the sins of ancestors. The other related religious belief was that medical intervention would lead to divine retribution.
63. Testimony in the case reflected an elitist bias. Medical personnel said Kou would be unable to work in a factory if he ended up in a chair.
64. The fact that no physician was willing to perform the surgery, even with the support of the legal system at every level, was proof to the Hmong of the validity of their position. V O'Donovan, Fresno County Counsel, Personal communication (8 April 1992).
65. AG Holder, *Legal Issues in Pediatrics and Adolescent Medicine* (2nd edn, New Haven: Yale Univ Press, 1985); J Goldstein, A Freud, and A Solnit, *Before the Best Interests of the Child* (New York: Free Press, 1979); JE Probst 'The Conflict between Child's Medical Needs and Parents' Religious Beliefs' (1990) 4 *American Journal of Family Law* 175–192; KJ Rampino, 'Power of Court of Other Public Agency to Order Medical Treatment over Parental Religious Objections for Child Whose Life is Not Immediately Endangered' 52 American Law Reported Annotated (3rd) (1973) 1118–1124; Renteln (n 59 above); JC Williams, 'Power of Court or Other Public Agency to Order Medical Treatment for Child Over Parental Objections Not Based on Religious Grounds' (1980) 97 American Law Reports Annotated (3rd) 421–426. The exceptions are discussed in Renteln (n 59 above).
66. See, for instance, RO Salsgiver, 'Editorial on Crippled Hmong Child Draws Dissent' (17 July 1990) *Fresno Bee* B11.
67. Minor's Brief, 9.
68. A Fadiman, *The Spirit Catches You and You Fall Down: A Hmong Child, Her American Doctors, and the Collision of Two Cultures* (New York: Farrar, Straus, and Giroux, 1997). In antiquity, epilepsy was attributed to supernatural causes. ibid 30.
69. ibid 53.
70. 'I have come to believe that her life was ruined not by septic shock or non-compliant parents but by cross-cultural misunderstanding.' ibid 262.
71. Although Western medical experts and legal analysts sometimes discuss culture-bound syndromes under the rubric of insanity, this terminology is likely to be offensive to people whose worldview differs from the dominant one. These syndromes should be considered as a separate category for analysis. King treats the syndromes as mental illness in NA King, 'The Role of Culture in Psychology: A Look at Mental Illness and the "Cultural Defense"' (1999) 7 *Tulsa Journal of Comparative and International Law* 199.
72. H Fabrega, 'Cultural Relativism and Psychiatric Illness' (1989) 177 *Journal of Nervous and Mental Disease* 7, 415–430; G Leong and JA Silva, 'Asian American Forensic Psychiatrists' (December 1989) 19 *Psychiatric Annals* 12, 629–632.
73. For an overview of culture-bound syndromes, see Gaw (n 44 above). They are becoming more accepted within the medical establishment. The DSM-IV (n 46 above) contains a special section, 'ethnic and cultural considerations', and an appendix with a useful glossary. *The Merck Manual* (n 46 above) added a section 275, 'Cross-cultural issues in Medicine (Folk medicine; Ethnomedicine)'.
74. *State of Hawai'i v Ganal* 917 P 2d 370 (Haw 1996).

75. An excellent detailed account can be found in J Li, 'The Nature of the Offense: An Ignored Factor in Determining the Application of the Cultural Defense' (1996) 18 *Univ of Hawaii Law Review* 789–795. Li favors the use of cultural evidence and would leave the determination of the reasonableness of the cultural explanation to the jury.

76. DSM-IV (n 46 above) 845. The description goes on to mention that the original reports of the syndrome came from Malaysia but that similar behavior patterns have been documented in Laos, Philippines, Polynesia (*cafard* or *cathard*), Papua New Guinea, and Puerto Rico (*mal de pelea*) and among the Navajo (*iich'aa*). For more information on 'amok', see JC Spores, *Running Amok: An Historical Inquiry* (Athens, Ohio: Ohio Univ Center for International Studies, 1988). Spores says commentators attributed amok to drug intoxication (opium or hemp), and mentions infections as another cause. ibid 91, 140. European colonial authorities in Malaysia used to capture 'amok runners' and then execute them. ibid 75–89.

77. The concept of self-esteem (*amor proprio*) in the Philippines is based on how one is viewed by one's group or *barkada*. If a man's wife had an affair, this would call into question his maleness or *paglalaki*. Li (n 75 above) 792–793.

78. The experts were Dr. Ricardo Trimillos, Chair of the Asian Studies Program, and Dr. Anthony Marsella, Professor of Psychopathology, both at the Univ of Hawaii at Manoa. Apparently the prosecutors did not make strenuous objections to the introduction of their testimony. ibid 792.

79. The Supreme Court upheld his sentence of life without parole for murder and attempted murder. Subsequently, Mrs. Ganal was held liable in a civil action: if she participated in conduct that caused an unreasonable risk of harm, she could be held responsible. *Touchette v Ganal* 922 P 2d 347 (Haw 1996).

80. Criticisms included: the defense 'served to spread the erroneous and appalling stereotype that Filipinos are prone to run amok'. Anon, 'Ganal Case Jury' (9 April 1993) *Honolulu Star Bulletin* A-10. Another concern was the implication that such crimes would be tolerated in the Philippines. Some charged that the 'amok' defense was 'racist'.

81. B Aquino and V Miarlao, 'Philippine Culture Used as Scapegoat in Ganal Trial' (9 April 1993) *Honolulu Star-Bulletin* A-11.

82. RC Allen, ' "Amok" wasn't Part of Culture' (17 April 1993) *Honolulu Advertiser*.

83. *R v Hem* 72 Criminal Reports (3d) 233 (1990).

84. RH Lucas and RJ Barrett, 'Interpreting Culture and Psychopathology: Primitivist Themes in Cross-cultural Debate' (1995) 19 *Culture, Medicine, and Psychiatry* 238–326.

85. 'This is a murder case that involves the confluence and collision of California criminal law with honestly held Christian religious beliefs overlaid and blended with Korean pre-Christian shamanist practices.' For background provided by one of the expert witnesses, see SY Chin (ND), 'Bearing Witness: Exorcism, Death, and the Law' (unpublished essay).

86. The ritual healing, *ansu kido*, involved 'laying on the hands'. An autopsy revealed 16 broken ribs and 'crushing force' pressed her heart. P Alston, 'Verdicts Expected Today in Deadly Exorcism Case' (16 April 1997) *Daily Breeze* (Santa Monica) B1–B2.

87. KC Kang and M Corwin, '3 Men Charged with Murder in Exorcism Death' (9 July 1996) *Los Angeles Times* B3; Anon, '2 Ministers Sentenced' (25 April 1997). Evidently charismatic beliefs are popular in South Korea, after having been introduced by US missionaries in the 1920s. P Salopek (28 August 1996); 'Korean Exorcism, Bare-Knuckle Style' *Chicago Tribune* 1; M Zane 'Minister in Fatal Exorcism Ordered to Leave U.S.' (6 May 1997) *San Francisco Chronicle* A18.

88. Korean American Christian leaders denied any cultural dimension, claiming that exorcism is 'almost unheard of in their community'. Kang and Corwin (n 87 above).

89. The judge may have been influenced by the husband's demeanor, which was described as 'contrite and tearful' and the pleas of his children for his release. Alston (n 86 above).

90. 'Albracht bucked the current legal trend by recognizing the cultural and religious strains in the case, even welcoming testimony from a cultural anthropologist who appeared as an expert for the defense. Despite a horrifying outcome, Albracht, found, the missionaries acted with the best of intentions.' A O'Neill, '2 Missionaries Guilty in Fatal Exorcism Case' (17 April 1997) *Los Angeles Times* B3.

91. I do not mean to suggest that culture-based arguments should be accepted as valid, but rather that policymakers should take evidence about cultural understandings of disability into account before rendering their decisions. For a study of cultural arguments in legal proceedings, see Alison Dundes Renteln, *The Cultural Defense* (New York: Oxford University Press, 2003).

4

Social Policy Toward Intellectual Disabilities in the Nineteenth and Twentieth Centuries

DAVID L. BRADDOCK AND SUSAN L. PARISH

The purpose of this chapter is to describe the rise over the past two centuries of the asylum model of care for people with intellectual disabilities and the substantial replacement of that model with contemporary family, community, and rights-based models of support. Although the emphasis in this chapter is primarily on developments in North America and Europe, we will also review the recent and widespread adoption of international disability rights initiatives by the United Nations and numerous countries throughout the world. This chapter is based on a more comprehensive history of disability by the present authors, which focused on social policy toward disability generally from antiquity to the enactment of the Americans with Disabilities Act.[1]

Social policy toward people with intellectual disabilities is closely associated with the development and proliferation of asylum care for people with mental illness. Until the twentieth century, in fact, public and private residential care and habilitation for people with intellectual disabilities was primarily provided in psychiatric hospitals.

The first mental hospital established on the North and South American continents was opened in Mexico City two centuries before similar initiatives were undertaken in the United States or Canada. Four decades after the arrival of Cortez, San Hipólito Hospital was established in 1566 near San Hipólito Chapel in Mexico City by the Spanish philanthropist Bernadino Alvarez. Alvarez was joined in the effort by several clergymen from an order that subsequently came to be known as 'Los Hipólitos'. New hospital structures were erected in 1739 and 1777 and the administration of the facility was taken over by the municipal government in 1821. The facility was closed in 1910 when all patients were transferred from this facility, and from a second asylum for women that opened in 1700, to a new institution called La Casteñada Asylum. The women's asylum, 'La Canoa Hospital for Mental Disease', also known as the 'Divino Salvador Hospital', was a product of the efforts of a local carpenter José Sayago and his wife, who provided shelter, food, and care for poor mentally disabled women who were an everyday sight on the streets in the Capitol of the New Spain.[2]

The asylums established in Mexico City were inspired by the asylums previously opened in Spain during the fifteenth and sixteenth centuries.

A psychiatric hospital dedicated exclusively to mental disability was founded by Father Joffre in Valencia in 1409.[3] Other asylums opened in Spain in Zaragoza (1425), Seville (1436),Valladolid (1436), Palma Majorca (1456), Toledo (1480), and Granada (1527). A strong case can be made for Spain as the 'cradle of psychiatry' in the West, even given the early (and more widely publicized in the English language) developments at St. Mary's of Bethlehem Hospital in London in the fifteenth century.[4] The great French psychiatrist Phillippe Pinel specifically cited the excellence of the Zaragoza asylum's program in his noted treatise on mental disability published in 1809.[5]

Asylums did not become common on the American landscape until the Jacksonian era, beginning in the 1820s. At this time, the nation was faced with increasing industrialization, urbanization, and changing demographics that included the first major influx of immigrants. These changing conditions led to social turmoil and institutional solutions for social problems were sought for the first time in the United States. There is disagreement among historians and social scientists as to the reasons for the appearance of institutions in the United States beginning in the 1820s. Rothman[6] contends that it was not inevitable for institutions to develop in the United States, but that they represented an innovative solution to pressing social problems and profound changes in the economic and social structure of the country. He argues that the concurrent development of orphanages, asylums for people with mental disabilities, prisons, almshouses, and reformatories was the result of a nation grappling with tremendous social upheaval and a desire to manage the social order by controlling deviant members. Others have argued that the development of asylums followed the European example and were the product of American interest in solving social problems by adhering to the natural course established by Europe.[7] Clearly, socioeconomic and demographic forces played a major role along with the diffusion of European innovations in asylum care.

The Bishop of Québec erected the first building in Canada exclusively dedicated to the confinement of mentally disabled individuals in 1714.[8] The building was located adjacent to the Québec General Hospital. However, people with mental illness and intellectual disability had been cared for in two general hospitals in Québec since at least 1694.[9] The colonial government of Virginia opened the first mental hospital in the United States exclusively dedicated to mental disability in 1773 in Williamsburg (Eastern State Hospital). The opening of this facility had virtually no impact as a model on other states. The impulse to establish this facility stemmed from Virginia's English colonial governor, Francis Fauquier, who was motivated through a sense of *noblesse oblige* to establish similar institutions abroad.[10] The establishment of this first facility in the Colonies was not preceded by a public campaign as would become the common practice for subsequent American facilities. The Virginia facility's capacity was 24 to 36 persons and the governing authorities 'never publicized the work of the hospital, and thereby reinforced its essentially local character'.[11] The facility shut down for four years beginning in 1782 due to the American Revolution. The State of Maryland then opened the fledgling nation's second state mental institution in 1798—fully twenty-five years after the opening of the first facility in Virginia. The third state institution for people with mental illness opened twenty-five years later, in Kentucky in 1824.[12]

Private initiatives in the northeastern United States led to the creation of several mental hospitals modeled after the York Retreat in England. York was a private facility opened by the Quaker William Tuke in 1792. Between 1817 and 1847, private institutions opened in Philadelphia, Boston, New York, Connecticut, Vermont, and Rhode Island.[13] By the time the Butler Hospital opened in Providence in 1847,[14] however, it had become clear that the exclusiveness and higher costs of private hospitals rendered them inadequate to meet the needs of the poorer classes, particularly the growing populations of urban poor in America's developing cities.[15]

The development of mental asylums accelerated following Dorothea Dix's advocacy beginning in the 1840s.[16] Dix traveled across the country, inspecting conditions of people with mental disabilities kept in prisons, living with their families, and in 'bidded out' contracts. She lobbied individual state legislatures for the construction of asylum facilities for the mentally disabled by writing memorials that described her findings.[17] In her first memorial, written after canvassing conditions in Massachusetts, Dix described: 'The present state of Insane Persons confined within this Commonwealth, in cages, closets, cellars, stalls, pens! Chained, naked, beaten with rods, and lashed into obedience!...Irritation of body, produced by utter filth and exposure, incited [one woman] to the horrid process of tearing off her skin by inches; her face, neck, and person, were thus disfigured to hideousness.'[18]

During the 1840s to 1870s, Dix was involved in the construction or expansion of more than thirty such facilities across the United States and in Britain as well.[19] The asylums were generally designed to house fewer than 300 people and were organized under the leadership of male psychiatrist-superintendents who adhered to the moral treatment method pioneered by Pinel and Tuke.[20] However, the institutions were often marked by specific divisions in the care and treatment of the poor from the privileged classes.[21] This initial segregation within public facilities between the middle class and the poor was the beginning of practices that would eventually become a hallmark of American institutions.[22] During the first half of the nineteenth century, physician-superintendents of the first mental asylums in the United States believed that mental illness was curable.[23] Kirkbride, superintendent of the Pennsylvania asylum, argued that in cases where uncomplicated insanity was 'properly and promptly treated, and having this treatment duly persevered in, may be regarded as curable...80%' of the time.[24]

I. OVERCROWDING AND THE DEMISE OF
THE MORAL TREATMENT

Beginning almost immediately after they were constructed, mental institutions experienced severe overcrowding as prisons sought to release their most dangerous and disturbed inmates to the newly available facilities.[25] Overcrowding and expansion soon made the superintendents' attempts at moral treatment impossible as the management of large facilities became paramount. In the later decades of the 1800s, as treatment gave way to confinement and custodial care in larger facilities, cure rates concomitantly dropped and psychiatrists reported that mental illness was largely incurable.[26]

As populations in these asylums swelled, conditions of overcrowding became serious by the end of the nineteenth century. The sheer number of inmates in most facilities, along with growing administrative responsibilities in increasingly complex institutions, translated into less time with patients for the superintendent. The moral treatment subsequently faded, along with beliefs in the curability of mental illness as custodial functions of the asylums became primary.[27]

By the late 1800s, the earlier optimism of rehabilitating patients with mental illness and sending them back to their home communities had been replaced with a rigid pessimism that decried the possibility of cure and demanded the lifelong custody of patients reported as dangerous to their home communities.[28] Grob[29] argues that superintendents gave way to the inevitability of poor conditions given severe overcrowding and limited contact with patients. Rothman[30] and Scull[31] contend that superintendents used the opportunities presented by expanding demand for mental asylum space to legitimate their own existence and secure their power. Our review of the *American Journal of Insanity* from its 1844 inception to 1900 reveals extensive discussions of the architecture of asylums and the management of such facilities. However, there were fewer than ten articles that dealt with patient treatment or care. This lends credence to Rothman[32] and Scull's[33] claims that superintendents were more interested and absorbed in the management of their facilities than in therapeutic issues.

Growing concern about the number of people with disabilities in the United States resulted in their enumeration by the census. Beginning in

1830, counts were taken of deaf and blind persons, and in 1840, the census began counting people labeled 'idiotic' and 'insane'.[34] The 1840 census reflected pervasive racism. All black residents in some towns were classified as insane.[35] Between 1870 and 1880, the proportion of the population counted as insane rose from 97 to 183 per 100,000, while the proportion of the population counted as intellectually disabled rose from 64 to 153 per 100,000. This dramatic increase can be attributed, at least in part, to the fact that census enumerators received extra compensation in 1880 for each person with mental illness or intellectual disability whom they counted.[36] The rapid increase in the mentally disabled population was seen as evidence that society needed to take drastic measures to address mental disability.[37] These concerns ultimately fueled the agenda of the eugenics movement. The publication and dissemination of the results of such 'scientific inquiry' were widely used in propaganda campaigns to catalyze public support for sterilization and marriage restriction laws.[38] By 1912, numerous states prohibited the marriage of persons with mental disabilities or epilepsy, or allowed such marriages only after age 45.[39]

II. FIRST US INSTITUTION FOR PEOPLE WITH INTELLECTUAL DISABILITIES

Superintendents of asylums for the mentally ill were among the first in the United States to call for separate provisions for people with intellectual disabilities. Reflecting on the path-breaking developments in Europe, the superintendents of the Worcester State Hospital in Massachusetts and New York's Bloomingdale facility both recommended in their 1845 annual reports that their states make a public educational provision for children and youth with intellectual disabilities.[40]

In 1846, the noted reformer and educator of blind students, Samuel Gridley Howe, was appointed to chair an epidemiological committee regarding intellectual disabilities appointed by the Massachusetts legislature. Howe carried out the nation's first investigation of the prevalence of intellectual disabilities and presented recommendations to establish an experimental school. Howe's report is replete with purported connections between the etiology of intellectual disability and the immoral behavior of one's parents.[41] His perspective was indicative of attitudes of the day that disability was a punishment for violating natural law.

The residential school that Howe recommended was opened in October 1848 in South Boston in a wing of the Perkins Institute for the Blind.[42] A few months earlier, in July 1848, Hervey Wilbur had opened a small private school in his own home for the instruction of children with intellectual disabilities in Barre, Massachusetts.[43] A few years later, Wilbur left Barre to superintend the new institution at Syracuse, site of the first institution for people with intellectual disabilities constructed specifically for that purpose in the United States. The Syracuse institution opened in 1855.[44]

It became common for states to initially open experimental schools,[45] and other states followed Massachusetts's and New York's lead. Pennsylvania opened a private school in 1852 that was incorporated in 1853 as the Pennsylvania Training School for Idiotic and Feebleminded Children. In 1855, this school was moved to its present site at Elwyn. Ohio, Connecticut, Kentucky, and Illinois established residential schools in 1857, 1858, 1860, and 1865, respectively.[46] The Illinois school was administered for its first decade under the auspices of the Illinois School for the Deaf. Twenty-six years after Howe opened the United States' first school for ten children, seven states had established publicly operated or assisted institutions for 1,041 residents, and there were two private facilities in Massachusetts.[47] Although the national census of institutions for people with intellectual disabilities was now growing steadily, almshouses housed more people with intellectual disabilities until 1906.[48]

III. FROM TRAINING SCHOOLS TO CUSTODIAL ASYLUMS

Institutions for people with intellectual disabilities, similar to those for people with mental illness, grew rapidly both in size and number following their initial construction in the mid-1800s. Early training efforts were quite successful, and many of the residents with intellectual disabilities were eventually returned to their communities as 'productive workers'.[49] Economic hardship hit the nation following the Civil War, and severe recessions occurred in the 1870s and again in the 1880s. Due to extensive unemployment, it became increasingly difficult for superintendents to discharge trained residents who could not compete for already scarce jobs in their home communities. Superintendents also noted the value of using unpaid resident labor to offset the costs of running the institutions.[50] The exploitation of resident labor, or peonage, prevailed in both institutions for people with mental illness and intellectual disabilities[51] until the 1970s.[52]

By 1880, the training schools envisioned by Howe and Seguin had evolved into custodial asylums with reduced emphasis on educating residents and returning them to community life.[53] The optimism of the 1840–1870 'amelioration' period confronted two difficult realities including negative attitudes toward persons with intellectual disabilities held by the general public and the lack of supportive social services, family support, and work opportunities in the community. Wilbur,[54] at the fifteenth annual gathering of the National Conference of Charities and

Corrections, observed that institutions would offer lifelong protective custodial care. Other professionals in the field joined Wilbur in calling for lifelong institutionalization of people with intellectual disabilities.[55] Samuel Gridley Howe had strongly opposed this trend, arguing in an 1866 speech that people with disabilities 'should be kept diffused among sound and normal persons. Separation, and not congregation, should be the law of their treatment.' The states, he said, should 'gradually dispense with as many [custodial institutions] as possible'.[56]

But the states did not dispense with custodial institutions. They continued to build them, expand them, and stress self-sufficiency and economical management in all aspects of facility operation. In 1900, the census of intellectual disability institutions in the United States was 11,800 persons.[57] Many institutions were located in remote areas and farmed extensive lands. Residents worked laundries, farms, and workshops, not so much to develop skills for community out-placement, but rather to contribute to the self-sustaining economy of the institution. While most superintendents championed the growth of large institutions during this period,[58] Seguin warned against this phenomenon. He wrote, 'let us hope that the State institutions for idiots will escape that evil of excessive growth...in which patients are so numerous that the accomplished physicians who have them in charge cannot remember the name of each.'[59]

At the dawning of the twentieth century, institutions for persons with intellectual disabilities were firmly established in the developed nations of the world. Barr,[60] who wrote the first US textbook on intellectual disabilities, completed an international survey and reported that twenty-one nations were operating 171 institutions for people with intellectual disabilities. There were twenty-five institutions in the United States by 1900.[61] Barr also noted that 'following the experiments worked out in the continental cities and in England, the special classes for backward children opened first in Providence, Rhode Island and [are] now part of the educational systems of New York, Philadelphia, Chicago, and Boston'.[62]

IV. FREAK SHOWS

Institutions were not the only manifestation of society's attitudes toward people with disabilities during the nineteenth century. So-called 'freak shows' displayed people with physical and mental disabilities throughout the nineteenth century in the United States and Europe.[63] People with intellectual disabilities were among those exhibited, their 'abnormal' characteristics exaggerated into caricatures of the grotesque.[64] These exhibits were extremely popular at circuses, fairs, and expositions. People with disabilities who were displayed at freak shows were frequently 'sold' to the show organizers, who maintained the right to display them for the duration of their lives.[65]

In displaying people with disabilities in these shows, exotic stories of wild and far-flung origins of the exhibited people were fabricated by the show organizers.[66] Thomson[67] argues that the exploitation of people with disabilities in the United States served to reinforce average Americans' notions of their own normality, by emphasizing disability and often race as profound and monstrous difference. Freak shows served to institutionalize notions of disability as the ultimate deviance.[68] Freak shows reached the height of their popularity in the United States at the end of the nineteenth century, at a time when eugenic beliefs in the superiority of the white middle class were crystallizing. In the United States, freak shows continued until the 1940s, when competing forms of entertainment, as well as economic hard times, led to their demise.[69]

V. THE EUGENICS ERA

The period from 1880 to the beginning of the Second World War was a time in which persons with intellectual disabilities were viewed as deviant social menaces, and intellectual disability was seen as an incurable disease.[70] The eugenic belief widely held during this period was that intellectual disability was inherited as a Mendelian characteristic that degraded the species.[71] Intellectual disability was linked in numerous studies to criminality, immoral behavior, and pauperism.[72] Intelligence tests, developed shortly after the turn of the century, were employed widely in the major cities of the United States to identify children with intellectual disabilities and place them in segregated special classes. Intelligence tests were also used to support ethnocentric and class biases against immigrants in the United States.[73] Subsequent to the implementation of intelligence testing at ports of entry, deportations for mental deficiency increased 350% in 1913, and 570% in 1914.[74] Rampant abuse existed in the classification of both immigrants and poor Americans as mentally deficient. Workers were 'trained' to classify people as mentally deficient by sight.[75]

Economic problems occurred at the same time that Galton's ideas of social Darwinism were beginning to take hold in the United States and abroad. Superintendents' writings reflect changing attitudes toward their charges as their institutional populations soared; the menace and burden of people with intellectual disabilities was frequently discussed.[76] Society needed protection from these menaces, and institutional care became the way to achieve these goals. Trent[77] argues that the superintendents readily espoused the new social Darwinism and its messages of fear about deviant persons because it offered a way for them to legitimate and consolidate their authority.

The eugenics movement in the United States was accompanied by extensive instances of physicians refusing to treat, and thereby facilitating the death of infants born with disabilities and birth defects.[78] Newspaper accounts publicized the withholding of lifesaving treatment of babies with disabilities during the decade after 1915, and movies propagating the eugenics agenda became quite common.[79]

In England, concern about people termed 'mental defective' led to the 1886 passage of the 'Idiots Act', which called for further clarification of the distinction between 'idiots' and 'lunatics',[80] and preceded the eugenics movement in that country.[81] Passage of the 1899 Education Act led to the growth of institutions for people with intellectual disabilities and epilepsy in England.[82]

In summary, the nineteenth century is best characterized as the century of institutions and interventions. Schools and institutions for persons with intellectual disabilities took root and professionals devised treatment interventions and educational strategies focused on specific impairments. The medical model of defining and classifying disability became thoroughly accepted in this century.

VI. THE TWENTIETH CENTURY

A. Segregation and Expansion of the Institutional Model

At the opening of the twentieth century the eugenics era was gaining momentum, and social reformers sought segregation and prohibitions on marriage and procreation by people with disabilities. Conditions in facilities for people with mental disabilities were deteriorating, and deaf persons were fighting to be able to use sign language in their schools.

In spite of the rapid expansion of institutions for people with mental disabilities after the turn of the century, poorfarms or almshouses were also a significant aspect of state provision for people with intellectual disabilities and mental illness. By the 1920s, poorfarms were 'dumping grounds' for all undesirables, including people with disabilities and the poor. In 1922, Ohio reported that 70% of poorfarm inmates had 'feeble-mindedness'. North Carolina estimated that 85% of inmates were 'mentally abnormal'. Iowa reported that, in 1924, 45% of its poorfarm inmates were mentally ill.[83] In a nationwide study of inmates of poorhouses, 36% were found to be 'feeble-minded, borderline defective, psychopathic, psychoneurotic, epileptic, or suffering from mental disease'.[84]

The sterilization of institutional residents with intellectual disabilities was commonplace in some states.[85] Between 1907 and 1949, there were more than 47,000 recorded sterilizations of people with mental disabilities in thirty states.[86] Of particular interest was the sterilization of people with intellectual disabilities who would eventually be discharged into the community.[87] Sterilization of women with epilepsy and mental illness was also believed by physicians to have therapeutic benefits in spite of empirical evidence to the contrary.[88] In the face of evidence that removal of the ovaries and Fallopian tubes was ineffective, physicians continued to perform such surgery on women with an array of conditions, including hysteria, depression, epilepsy, insanity related to childbirth, and nymphomania. Surgery was also deemed appropriate to 'prevent the prospect of illegitimate and defective children'.[89]

The US Supreme Court's 1927 *Buck v Bell* decision affirmed the states' right to sterilize people with intellectual disabilities and propelled the eugenics movement to further lobby for its agenda.[90] In 1933, using California's program as a model, Nazi Germany enacted its own eugenic sterilization law.[91] This legislation led to the forced sterilization of between 300,000 and 400,000 persons, a majority on the grounds of 'feeblemindedness'. Most were institutional residents. This unprecedented oppression against disabled persons culminated in the murder by euthanasia of between 200,000 and 275,000 individuals with mental and physical disabilities between 1939 and 1945 in Germany. The eugenics movement had reached its zenith.[92] Justification for the killing of people with disabilities in Nazi Germany was made on the basis of utilitarian arguments, and German health professionals and psychiatrists were among those who accommodated themselves to these policies.[93] Psychiatrists, particularly, had been responsible for identifying the pool of potential victims, and in some cases, participated in victim selection and murder.[94]

The United States and Germany were not the only nations to sterilize people with disabilities, however. Denmark had an active program of sterilization between 1930 and 1954, sterilizing at least 8,627 persons over this period. Sweden's program operated throughout the 1930s and 1940s, with 2,278 persons being sterilized in 1948 alone.[95]

Contemporaneous with zealous agitation by eugenicists, evidence began to emerge that questioned the assumptions of deviance in people with intellectual disabilities. In Massachusetts, Fernald's[96] Waverly studies demonstrated that with proper support from their families, individuals with intellectual disabilities could function well in the community. Fernald[97] also concluded that only about 8% of a sample of 5,000 schoolchildren with intellectual disabilities in Massachusetts exhibited behavioral problems of any type. In addition, Wallace[98] presented a compelling paper discrediting the link between intellectual disability and criminality. Also, the 'parole plan', which could lead to permanent institutional discharge, was devised in the first decade of the twentieth century as an early release program for institutional residents with milder impairments. Paroled residents were cared for in the community by relatives, employers, or supportive volunteers.[99]

In 1880, there were 1,382 persons with intellectual disabilities in insane asylums. By 1940, the number of persons with intellectual disabilities living in psychiatric hospitals peaked at nearly 29,000 persons.[100] The census of separate state institutions for people with intellectual disabilities swelled to 55,466 persons by 1926.[101] Switzky *et al.* described several common practices in institutions of this era. Residents were 'patients' who lived on 'wards' in a facility, often called a 'hospital', which was governed by a hierarchical medical structure. Resident programs were termed 'treatments' or 'therapy' (eg, recreational therapy, industrial therapy, and educational therapy). Living units were locked, windows barred, and the institution became increasingly structured 'like a hospital for the care of sick animals rather than as a place for the special education of human children and adults'.[102] Prolonged institutionalization exacted a price from residents by promoting excessive conformity to the institutional culture at the expense of personal spontaneity, excessive fantasizing, fear of new situations, and excessive dependency on the institution.[103]

Because of widespread unemployment and poverty during the Great Depression, families sought institutional care for their relatives with intellectual disabilities in increasing numbers.[104] Institutional facility censuses continued to swell and overcrowding became commonplace.[105] While President Roosevelt's economic recovery programs brought some relief, people with intellectual disabilities were largely excluded. The Social Security Act that passed in 1935 contained benefits for blind persons, but not for people with cognitive disabilities.[106] While Title V of the Social Security Act authorized Crippled Children's Services grants of $2.85 million,[107] minutes of the 1936 Crippled Children's Services National Advisory Committee stated that 'children with incurable blindness, deafness, or mental defect...and those requiring permanent custodial care' were beyond the intended scope of the new program.[108]

The widespread segregation of people with intellectual disabilities in institutions also made them easy targets for medical experiments. At the Wrentham and Fernald facilities in Massachusetts, institutional residents with intellectual disabilities were subjected to tests involving the ingestion of foods with radioactive elements. Neither the individuals with disabilities who served as subjects in these experiments, nor their parents, were apprised of the nature of the foods. This illegal research spanned the period between 1946 and 1973.[109] Residents at the Willowbrook institution in New York were similarly exposed to Hepatitis-B without their knowledge or informed consent.[110] Residents at the Polk facility in Pennsylvania were used as guinea pigs for the testing of the polio vaccine, again without their knowledge or consent, or the consent of their parents.

B. Emergence of Family, Community, and Consumer Models

Although the Depression and the Second World War inhibited innovation in service delivery for people with intellectual disabilities in the United States,[111] some progress was made. New York State, for example, introduced foster family care in the 1930s, authorizing payment for the care of persons with intellectual disabilities in family homes.[112] Research subsequently confirmed the beneficial effects of placement in foster or adoptive homes[113] and the benefits of preschool intervention programs.[114]

Beginning in the 1950s, friends and parents of people with disabilities began organizing for more extensive services for people with disabilities in many parts of the world. At that time, schools and activity centers were established, and ultimately international associations were founded, comprised of national organizations interested in the prevention of disability. Parents of people with intellectual disabilities in Washington State had actually organized to advocate for services for their children as early as the 1930s;[115] however, larger-scale organizing by such groups did not occur until the 1950s. During that decade, local groups of parents from many states joined forces and formed the group that became the National Association for Retarded Children (now The Arc). These families organized to advocate for services for their children including better conditions in institutions and the development of schools and workshops.[116] A similar nationwide organization of families of people with mental illness would not be developed until the 1979 founding of the National Alliance for the Mentally Ill (NAMI).[117]

C. De-institutionalization and the Right to Treatment

The census in public facilities for persons with intellectual disabilities peaked at 194,650 in 1967.[118] More than 20,000 additional persons with intellectual disabilities resided in state and county psychiatric hospitals at the time. The average facility population of institutions for people with intellectual disabilities was 1,422 residents in 1962.[119] Several facilities, such as Willowbrook in New York and Lincoln in Illinois, housed 4,000 to 8,000 residents. In the 1960s, despite growing evidence to the contrary, American society still treated persons with intellectual disabilities as a group that needed to be controlled by segregation, sterilization, and isolation. In light of deplorable conditions in institutions for people with mental illness, discussion began to take shape within the legal community about the right to treatment for people who were incarcerated in these facilities. Morton Birnbaum led this initiative with the 1960 publication of his paper, 'The Right to Treatment'.[120] The first case in which an American court recognized the right to treatment was the landmark 1966 case of

Rouse v Cameron, which held that if an individual was involuntarily committed to a facility, at a minimum, he or she had the right to receive treatment, because the purpose of confinement was treatment and not punishment.[121] Subsequent cases upheld this right, which was extended in the 1970s to include people with intellectual disability as well.[122]

The election of John F. Kennedy to the United States Presidency in 1960 ushered in the modern era of intellectual disability services in the United States and an expanded concern for people with mental illness as well. On 11 October 1961, President Kennedy issued an unprecedented statement regarding the need for a national plan in the field of intellectual disabilities. 'We as a nation', he said, 'have for too long postponed an intensive search for solutions to the problems of the mentally retarded. That failure should be corrected.'[123] Kennedy appointed the President's Panel on Mental Retardation. The Panel's ninety-five recommendations, released in 1962, were broad and far-reaching. They extended from issues of civil rights to the need for scientific research on etiology and prevention. The panel called for a substantial downsizing of institutional facilities, an expansion of community services, and most importantly, it clearly embraced the principle of normalization[124] as a guide to future innovation in service delivery.

Many of the ninety-five recommendations of the President's Panel[125] were enacted into law by the 88th Congress as Public Laws 88-156 and 88-164. Public Law 88-156, the Maternal and Child Health and Mental Retardation Planning Amendments of 1963, doubled the spending ceiling for the existing Maternal and Child Health State Grant Program, and established a new mental retardation planning grant program in the states. The planning effort was unique in the history of the field in that federal legislation required all fifty participating states to produce comprehensive plans for the development of improved residential, community, and preventive services.

The 1970s was a decade of considerable progress in public policy for people with intellectual disabilities in the United States. There were three major, catalytic events: (1) the 1971 passage of the ICF/MR (Intermediate Care Facilities/Mental Retardation) program as part of Title XIX (Medicaid) of the Social Security Act; (2) Judge Frank M. Johnson's landmark 1972 right to treatment ruling in the Alabama case of *Wyatt v Stickney*;[126] and (3) the 1975 passage of the Education of All Handicapped Children Act (now known as IDEA).[127]

The passage of the ICF/MR law in 1971 enabled the states to obtain federal funding for institutional services for people with intellectual disabilities if the care provided met minimal federal standards of treatment and space. Insofar as the federal government would reimburse states for 50% to 78% of the costs of institutional care, states had great incentives to change their services to conform to federal standards. This led to a tremendous push to de-institutionalize as the minimum space requirements were well beyond the overcrowded capacities of nearly all the nation's institutions.[128] Peaking in 1967 at more than 194,000 people, the population of the nation's public institutions for persons with mental retardation and developmental disabilities has declined steadily to 47,415 persons in 2000.[129] Advances in applied behavioral interventions have facilitated community, employment, and social integration.[130]

The *Wyatt v Stickney* decision in regard to people with intellectual disabilities was built upon the principle of right to treatment developed for people with mental illness. Judge Johnson found that people in Alabama's institutions had a constitutional right to treatment.[131] This case began a tidal wave of federal class action cases related to conditions in institutions for people with intellectual disabilities, culminating in more than seventy cases in forty-one states.[132] Similar litigation was also filed on the right to education.[133]

The third watershed civil rights event in the 1970s in the United States was passage of the Education for All Handicapped Children's Act of 1975, which guaranteed children and youth with disabilities the right to a free, appropriate, public education. For the first time in the history of compulsory education in the United States, parents had a federally enforced right to education for their children with disabilities. Beyond the obviously important changes in education for children with disabilities, this legislation also created a generation of parents who believed that their children were entitled to related community services. Many of these parents would become strong advocates for community services and inclusive education. In the 1998–9 school year, 47% of children with disabilities in the United States were educated in regular classroom settings, while the remainder were educated in a combination of other settings including resource rooms, separate classrooms, and separate schools.[134]

In America, states' efforts to 'reform' institutions for people with intellectual disabilities in the 1970s gave way to efforts to reallocate institutional resources to community services activities. States began closing institutions in significant numbers for the first time in the early 1980s.[135] In 1991, New Hampshire closed the Laconia Developmental Center and became the first state in the United States to provide all of its services to people with intellectual disabilities in the community.[136] By 2000, thirty-seven states had closed 125 state institutions for people with intellectual disabilities and four more closures were scheduled to occur by the year 2001. In addition to New Hampshire, all public institutions for people with intellectual disabilities have also been closed in Alaska, the District of Columbia, Hawaii, Minnesota, New Mexico, Rhode Island, Vermont, and West Virginia.[137]

Institutional phase-downs and closures have been accompanied by a growing emphasis on supported community living for individuals with intellectual disabilities. Between 1977 and 2000, the number of persons living in community-based settings for one to six persons expanded from 20,409 to 263,359 persons, a more than twelvefold increase. Much of this tremendous expansion in community services was fueled by the federal–state partnership in the Medicaid Home and Community Based Services (HCBS) Waiver Program.[138]

The reduction in reliance on residential institutions for people with intellectual disabilities occurred in Great Britain and across Western Europe as well.[139] In England, for example, the census of public hospitals for people with intellectual disabilities (those operated by the National Health Service) declined 83%, from 44,400 in 1980 to 7,400 persons in 1996. Similarly significant declines were noted in other UK countries. In Wales, Scotland, and Northern Ireland, census reductions of 70%, 51%, and 48%, respectively, were noted during the same 1980 to 1996 period.[140]

D. Self-Advocacy

Organized self-advocacy is an important manifestation of the emergence of autonomy and self-determination for people with intellectual disability (see Levitz, Chapter 17 of this volume).[141] Membership in local and state-wide self-advocacy groups like People First has grown rapidly. Hayden and Senese[142] identified over 1,000 self-advocacy groups, some in every state. This represented almost a threefold expansion in the number of groups since 1990.[143] In 1995, self-advocacy groups established a national organization called Self Advocates Becoming Empowered (SABE). SABE has developed an advocacy agenda calling for the phase down and closure of all state-operated intellectual disability institutions in the United States.[144]

E. International Disability Rights Initiatives

The 1990 passage of the Americans with Disabilities Act (ADA) in the United States was a watershed event for disability rights on the international stage. This law recognized that discrimination against people with disabilities in the form of purposeful unequal treatment and historical patterns of segregation and isolation was the major problem confronting people with disabilities and not their individual impairments.[145] The ADA also stated that people with disabilities have been relegated to powerless positions based on stereotypical assumptions about their disabilities. As such, the ADA bars discrimination against people with disabilities in employment, public services, public accommodations, and telecommunications.[146]

The ADA was enacted after a concerted effort by a coalition of mental, physical, and sensory disability rights groups to work together to secure its passage.[147] The cross-disability coalition that advocated for enactment of the ADA was built in part on the foundation initially developed by advocates pushing for the enactment and subsequent promulgation of rules for the Vocational Rehabilitation Act Amendments of 1973.[148]

In Britain, a similar law protecting the rights of people with disabilities, the Disability Discrimination Act, was enacted in 1995.[149] This law mandated reasonable adjustments to the policies and physical environments of employers with twenty or more employees, compelling the removal of barriers facing people with disabilities.[150] The law also mandated accessibility in public transportation.[151] While the law has been hailed as an advance in civil rights for people living in Scotland, England, Wales, and Northern Ireland, disability advocates have expressed disappointment that the law did not go as far as it should have in protecting and facilitating enforcement of the rights of people with disabilities.[152]

At the international level, the United Nations General Assembly unanimously adopted in 1994 the *Standard Rules on the Equalization of Opportunities for Persons with Disabilities*.[153] The *Standard Rules* are not legally enforceable internationally, but they do provide basic international standards for programs, laws, and policy on disability. The *Standard Rules* grew out of earlier pressure from international disability interests to promote greater participation by people with disabilities in society. This philosophy was initially expressed in the 1971 *Declaration of the Rights of Mentally Retarded Persons*,[154] the 1975 *Declaration of the Rights of Disabled Persons*,[155] and the more comprehensive statement expressed in the 1982 *World Program of Action Concerning Disabled Persons* (WPA).[156]

The purpose of the WPA is to:

Promote effective measures for prevention of disability, rehabilitation and the realization of the goals of 'full participation' of disabled persons, in social life and development, and of 'equality'. This means opportunities equal to those of the whole population and an equal share in the improvement in living conditions resulting from social and economic development. These concepts should apply with the same scope and with the same urgency to all countries, regardless of their level of development.

The WPA requires member states to plan, organize and finance activities at each level; create, through legislation, the necessary legal bases and authority for measures to achieve the objectives; ensure opportunities by eliminating barriers to full participation; provide rehabilitation services by giving social, nutritional, medical, educational and vocational assistance and technical aids to disabled persons; establish or mobilize relevant public and private organizations; support the establishment and growth of organizations of disabled persons; and prepare and disseminate information relevant to the issues of the World Programme of Action.[157]

The United Nation's 1994 *Standard Rules* was predicated on the principles embodied in the *World Program of Action*, which focuses on the equalization of opportunities for people with disabilities. This commitment to disabled persons goes well beyond traditional international anti-discrimination protections of property, political, and judicial rights by seeking to convey rights to rehabilitation, special education and access to public and private facilities and programs. The European Union[158] has also adopted general disability policies similar to the United Nation's *World Program of Action*.

In addition to Great Britain and the United States, a number of nations adopted legislation in the 1990s prohibiting discrimination against persons with disabilities. Australia adopted the Disability Discrimination Act of 1993, outlawing discrimination on the basis of disability and the constitutions of Germany, Austria, Finland, and Brazil have been similarly amended. Constitutional changes have also been adopted in South Africa, Malawi, Uganda, and the Philippines. These actions are representative of the recent flurry of constitutional and legislative activity on a worldwide basis to promote the rights of people with disabilities.[159]

VII. CONCLUSION

Assertive political activism by people with disabilities and their families is primarily a late twentieth-century phenomenon that, in the United States, draws considerable strength from the example of the civil rights movement for people of color.[160] It is, in fact, an often repeated general truism in the disability field today that prejudicial and exclusionary practices are greater barriers to social participation for disabled people than their particular mental, physical, or sensory impairments.[161]

People with intellectual disabilities have shared a history that has often been oppressive and included abuse, neglect, sterilization, stigma, euthanasia, segregation, and institutionalization. Disabled people, who have survived by relying on tenacity and resourcefulness and on support provided in different measures by family, friends, and local communities, are currently struggling to claim identity[162] and political power.[163] People with intellectual disabilities have only emerged to champion their own interests collectively within the last two decades.

Advocacy by specific, single-disability groups in the United States began to evolve into cross-disability coalition building in the 1970s, 1980s, and 1990s. Cross-disability advocacy, for example, secured passage of the Americans with Disabilities Act.[164] The paternalism of non-disabled nineteenth-century figures such as Howe has been replaced, at least in part, with leadership and self-determination by people with disabilities themselves. Thus, at the dawn of the twenty-first century, the foundation is gradually being established in the West for a new era based on civil rights and social participation. Achieving inclusive societies, however, will require persons with mental, physical, and sensory disabilities to learn more about one another and, on common ground, to construct more powerful community, state, national, and international cross-disability coalitions than have been developed in the past.

The potential strength of cross-disability coalitions should grow as societies age because the prevalence of impairment is directly correlated with aging. Over the course of the next thirty years, the number of persons aged 65 and over will double in the United States, triple in Germany and Japan, and advance rapidly in virtually every developed nation of the world.[165] As more developing countries make significant economic advances, they will experience a concomitant rise in political advocacy by and for people with disabilities. Albrecht and Verbrugge refer to this growing phenomenon of disability across the developed and developing nations of the world as the global emergence of disability. 'With or without anyone's attention,' they argue, 'global disability will be on the rise for many decades to come, fueled by population aging, environmental degradation, and social violence.'[166] The key disability issues for developing societies include controlling infectious diseases, reducing unsafe occupational conditions, managing drought and the environment, limiting ethnic, religious, and regional wars and launching thoughtful innovations in income support, health promotion, special education, rehabilitation, and the promotion of self-determination.[167] By adopting programs that stress consumer, family, and community values, many developing nations will hopefully be able to avoid replicating the developed world's self-destructive preoccupations with segregation, institutionalization, and eugenics.

The principal disability issues currently facing the developed nations in Europe, North America, and Australasia, according to Albrecht and Verbrugge,[168] include fashioning reasonable eligibility standards for income maintenance and service programs for persons with disabilities, advancing civil rights, creating access to employment, public accommodations and society at large and minimizing regional, state, and sub-state differences in public welfare benefits and service programs. To these critically important contemporary issues, we would add that developed nations also must confront (1) ethical and cost-benefit dilemmas accompanying advances in gene therapy, biotechnology, and neuroscience research; (2) the potential for assisted suicide to lead to the widespread euthanasia of persons with disabilities; (3) the continuing segregation of millions of persons with disabilities in nursing homes, institutions, and other segregated settings throughout the world; and (4) developing

productive and reciprocally valued working relationships between consumers with disabilities seeking greater self-determination and political
power and the professionals who provide and study services to people
with disabilities,[169] The United States in particular must also confront the
growing inequality in the distribution of the wealth of its citizenry and the
profound health care and educational disparities between rich and poor.[170]

The disability rights struggle of the first half of the twenty-first century
will fundamentally be a struggle to de-link the enduring and oppressive
relationship between poverty and disability—particularly for people with
intellectual disabilities. Even in the most economically developed nations
of the world today, unemployment rates for disabled persons frequently
approach 80% and average personal income is in the bottom decile. The
number of disabled people in 175 nations of the world today was recently
estimated to range between 235 and 549 million people. The lost Gross
Domestic Product due to unemployment, underemployment and
services/support costs associated with disability was determined to range
between $1.4 and $1.9 trillion per annum in 2000 dollars.[171] Disability
research institutions such as the National Institute on Disability and
Rehabilitation Research (NIDRR) in the United States, and international
development organizations like the World Bank, need to acknowledge the
global emergence of disability by establishing and funding new strategies
for international research leadership and action on disability in the
twenty-first century.

For example, we need to mount a series of rigorous, comparative, recurring empirical studies to monitor the growth of public sector disability-
related financial resources, legislative and policy adoptions, and service
commitments in every country of the world. These recurring studies need
to assess the allocation of resources on a nationwide basis for disability
programs so that all the nations of the world can be held accountable for
their commitments to disabled people and their families. Such studies
would permit the priority that a nation assigns to disability to be evaluated over time and to be compared to other nations with similar levels of
wealth. The information generated in such studies would be useful in
program planning and, by identifying the leaders and the laggards among
the nations of the world, it would be immensely useful to disability
advocates seeking to influence public policy on behalf of their constituen-
cies. Several international organizations should be approached to sponsor
this research including the World Bank, the United Nations, the European
Union, the Pan American Health Organization, and the World Health
Organization. In the United States, the National Institute on Disability
and Rehabilitation Research (NIDRR) should also consider launching one
or more 'International Rehabilitation Research and Training Centers'.
These Centers would focus on significantly expanding educational and

research links on disability between and among the developed and developing nations of the world.

NOTES

1. D Braddock and S Parish, 'An Institutional History of Disability' in G Albrecht, K Seelman, and M Bury (eds), *Handbook of Disability Studies* (New York: Sage, 2001) 11–68.
2. S Ramirez-Moreno, 'History of Psychiatry and Mental Hospitals in Mexico' (1937) 86 *Journal of Nervous and Mental Disease* 5, 513–524; S Ramirez-Moreno, 'History of the First Psychopathic Institution on the American Continent' (1942) 99 *American Journal of Psychiatry* 2, 194–195.
3. RD Rumbaut, 'The First Psychiatric Hospital of the Western World' (1972) 128 *American Journal of Psychiatry* 10, 1305–1309.
4. P Bassoe, 'Spain as the Cradle of Psychiatry' (1945) *American Journal of Psychiatry* 731–738.
5. P Pinel, *Traité médico-philosophique sur l'aliénation mentale* (2nd edn, 1809).
6. DJ Rothman, *The Discovery of the Asylum: Social Order and Disorder in the New Republic* (revised edn, Boston: Little, Brown and Company, 1990).
7. G Mora, 'The History of Psychiatry in the United States: Historiographic and Theoretical Considerations' (1992) 3 *History of Psychiatry* 187–201; GN Grob, 'Marxian Analysis and Mental Illness' (1990) 1 *History of Psychiatry* 223–232.
8. HM Hurd, *A History of Institutional Care of the Insane in the United States and Canada* (Baltimore: Johns Hopkins Univ Press, 1910).
9. JD Griffin, and C Greenland, 'Institutional Care of the Mentally Disordered in Canada: A 17th Century Record' (1981) 26 *Canadian Journal of Psychiatry* 274–278.
10. GN Grob, *Mental Institutions in America: Social Policy to 1875* (New York: Free Press, 1973).
11. ibid.
12. ibid.
13. P Earle, 'Historical and Descriptive Account of the Bloomingdale Asylum for the Insane' (1845) 2 *American Journal of Insanity* 1–13; SW Hamilton, *One Hundred Years of American Psychiatry* (New York: Columbia Univ Press, 1944); T Kirkbride, 'A Sketch of the History, Buildings, and Organization of the Pennsylvania Hospital for the Insane' (1845) 2 *American Journal of Insanity* 97–114; GB Wood, 'History of the Pennsylvania Hospital for the Insane' (1853) 9 *American Journal of Insanity* 209–213.
14. DA Rochefort, 'Three Centuries of Care of the Mentally Disabled in Rhode Island and the Nation, 1650–1950' (1981) 40 *Rhode Island History* 111–132.
15. Grob (n 10 above); Hamilton (n 13 above).
16. Rothman (n 6 above); TJ Brown, *Dorothea Dix: New England Reformer* (Cambridge, Mass: Harvard Univ Press, 1998); GN Grob, *The Mad among Us* (New York: Free Press, 1994).
17. Brown (n 16 above).

18. D Dix, *Memorial: To the Legislature of Massachusetts* (Boston: Munroe & Francis, 1843).
19. Brown (n 16 above).
20. GN Grob, *The State and the Mentally Ill: A History of Worcester State Hospital in Massachusetts, 1830–1920* (Chapel Hill: Univ of North Carolina Press, 1966).
21. S Tuke, *A Letter on Pauper Lunatic Asylums* (London: Winfield and Nicolson, 1815).
22. Rothman (n 6 above); JW Trent, *Inventing the Feeble Mind: A History of Mental Retardation in the United States* (Berkeley: Univ of California Press, 1995).
23. Grob (n 20 above); T Kirkbride, *On the Construction, Organization, and General Arrangements of Hospitals for the Insane* (Berkeley: Univ of California Press, 1973, original work published 1880).
24. Kirkbride (n 23 above).
25. Grob (n 20 above).
26. ibid; Rothman (n 6 above); P Earle, *The Curability of Insanity: A Series of Studies* (Philadelphia: JB Lippincott Co, 1887); A Scull, 'Psychiatry and Social Control in the Nineteenth and Twentieth Centuries' (1991) 2 *History of Psychiatry* 149–169.
27. Rothman (n 6 above); Grob (n 20 above).
28. ibid; Earle (n 26 above).
29. Grob (n 20 above).
30. Rothman (n 6 above).
31. Scull (n 26 above).
32. Rothman (n 6 above).
33. Scull (n 26 above).
34. K Gorwitz, 'Census Enumeration of the Mentally Ill and the Mentally Retarded in the Nineteenth Century' (1974) 89 *Health Services Reports* 180–187.
35. ibid.
36. ibid.
37. GH Knight, 'The Feeble-Minded' (1895) *Proceedings of the Association of Medical Officers of American Institutions for Idiotic and Feeble-Minded Persons* 559–563.
38. MS Pernick, *The Black Stork: Eugenics and the Death of 'Defective' Babies in American Medicine and Motion Pictures since 1915* (New York: Oxford Univ Press, 1996).
39. S Smith, MW Wilkinson, and LC Wagoner, 'A Summary of the Laws of the Several States Governing I. Marriage and Divorce of the Feeble-Minded, the Epileptic, and the Insane. II. Asexualization. III. Institutional Commitment and Discharge of the Feeble-Minded and Epileptic' (1914) 82 *Bulletin of the University of Washington*.
40. A Brigham, *Annual Report of the Bloomingdale Insane Asylum* (Bloomingdale, NY: Bloomingdale Insane Asylum, 1845); S Woodward, *Annual Report of the Worcester State Hospital* (Worcester, Mass: Worcester State Hospital, 1845).
41. SG Howe, *Report Made to the Legislature of Massachusetts upon Idiocy* (1848).
42. SG Howe, 'On Training and Educating Idiots: Second Annual Report to the Massachusetts Legislature' (1851) 8 *American Journal of Insanity* 97–118.
43. Elm Hill Private School and Home, *Elm Hill: Private School and Home* (1911).

44. WE Fernald, 'The History of the Treatment of the Feeble-Minded' (1893) *Proceedings of the National Conference of Social Work* 203–221; JF FitzGerald, 'The Duty of the State towards its Idiotic and Feeble-Minded' (1900) 1 *Proceedings of the New York State Conference of Charities* 172–189.

45. IN Kerlin, 'The Organization of Establishments for the Idiotic and Imbecile Classes' (1877) 3 *Proceedings of the Association of Medical Officers of American Institutions for Idiotic and Feeble-Minded Persons* 19–24.

46. WE Fernald, 'The Growth of Provision for the Feebleminded in the United States' (1917) 1 *Mental Hygiene* 34–59.

47. ibid.

48. US Bureau of the Census, *Insane and Feeble-Minded in Institutions, 1910* (Washington, DC: US Bureau of the Census, 1914).

49. JW Trent, *Inventing the Feeble Mind: A History of Mental Retardation in the United States* (Berkeley: Univ of California Press, 1995); JQA Stewart, 'The Industrial Department of the Kentucky Institution for the Education and Training of Feeble-Minded Children' (1882) *Proceedings of the Association of Medical Officers of American Institutions for Idiotic and Feeble-Minded Persons* 236–239.

50. R Fenton, 'The Pacific Colony Plan' (1932) 16 *Journal of Juvenile Research* 298–303; GH Knight, 'Colony Care for Adult Idiots' (1891) *Proceedings of the National Conference of Social Work* 107–108.

51. ibid; FL Bartlett, 'Institutional Peonage: Our Exploitation of Mental Patients' (1964) 214 *The Atlantic Monthly* 116–119; A Bonsall, 'Discussion on the Care of Imbeciles' (1891) *Proceedings of the National Conference of Social Work* 331–332; A Johnson, 'The Self-Supporting Imbecile' (1899) 4 *Journal of Psycho-Asthenics* 91–99; C MacAndrew and R Edgerton, 'The Everyday Life of Institutionalized "Idiots"' (1964) 23 *Human Organization* 312–318.

52. RC Scheerenberger, *A History of Mental Retardation* (Baltimore: Brookes Publishing, 1983); S Parish, 'Forces Shaping Developmental Disabilities Services in the States: A Comparative Study' in D Braddock (ed), *Disability at the Dawn of the Twenty First Century and the State of the States* (Washington, DC: AAMR, 2002) 351–476.

53. Trent (n 49 above); W Wolfensberger, 'On the Origin of our Institutional Models' in R Kugel and A Shearer (eds), *Changing Patterns in Residential Services for the Mentally Retarded* (rev edn, Washington, DC: President's Committee on Mental Retardation, 1976) 35–82.

54. CT Wilbur, 'Institutions for the Feebleminded' (1888) 17 *Proceedings of the Fifteenth National Conference of Charities and Correction* 106–113.

55. MW Barr, 'The Imbecile and Epileptic Versus the Taxpayer and the Community' (1902) *Proceedings of the National Conference of Social Work* 161–165; E Bicknell, 'Custodial Care of the Adult Feeble-Minded' (1895) 5 *Charities Review* 76–88; WB Fish, 'Custodial Care of Adult Idiots' (1892) 17 *Proceedings of the National Conference of Social Work* 203–218; SJ Fort, 'What Shall be Done with the Imbecile?' (1892) 27 *Maryland Medical Journal* 1057–1063; A Johnson, 'Permanent Custodial Care' (1896) *Proceedings of the National Conference of Social Work* 207–219.

56. Wolfensberger (n 53 above).

57. Fernald (n 46 above).

58. Trent (n 49 above).
59. E Seguin, *New Facts and Remarks Concerning Idiocy, Being a Lecture before the New York Medical Journal Association, October 15, 1869* (New York: William Wood, 1870).
60. MW Barr, *Mental Defectives* (Philadelphia: P Blakiston's Sons & Co, 1904).
61. Fernald (n 46 above).
62. Barr (n 60 above).
63. R Bogdan, *Freak Show: Presenting Human Oddities for Amusement and Profit* (Chicago: Univ of Chicago Press, 1988); N Rothfels, 'Aztecs, Aborigines, and Ape-People: Science and Freaks in Germany, 1850–1900' in RG Thomson (ed), *Freakery: Cultural Spectacles of the Extraordinary Body* (New York: New York Univ Press, 1996) 158–172; RG Thomson, *Freakery: Cultural Spectacles of the Extraordinary Body* (New York: New York Univ Press, 1996); RG Thomson, *Extraordinary Bodies: Figuring Physical Disability in American Culture and Literature* (New York: New York Univ Press, 1997).
64. Bogdan (n 63 above); Thomson, *Extraordinary Bodies* (n 63 above).
65. Bogdan (n 63 above).
66. ibid; Thomson (n 64 above).
67. ibid.
68. ibid.
69. R Bogdan, 'Exhibiting Mentally Retarded People for Amusement and Profit, 1850–1940' (1986) 91 *American Journal of Mental Deficiency* 120–126.
70. Trent (n 49 above); Scheerenberger (n 52 above); Barr (n 55 above); AW Butler, 'The Burden of Feeble-Mindedness' (1907) *Proceedings of the National Conference of Social Work* 1–10; EM East, 'Hidden Feeblemindedness' (1917) 8 *Journal of Heredity* 215–217; WE Fernald, 'State Care of the Insane, Feebleminded, and Epileptic' (1915) *Proceedings of the National Conference of Charities and Correction* 289–297; ES Gosney and P Popenoe, *Sterilization for Human Betterment* (New York: MacMillan, 1929); IN Kerlin, 'Moral Imbecility' (1887) 12 *Proceedings of the Association of Medical Officers of American Institutions for Idiotic and Feeble-Minded Persons* 32–37; W Sloan and HA Stevens, *A Century of Concern: A History of the American Association on Mental Deficiency, 1876–1976* (Washington, DC: American Association on Mental Deficiency, 1976); HN Switzky, M Dudzinski, R Van Acker, and J Gambro, 'Historical Foundations of Out-of-Home Residential Alternatives for Mentally Retarded Persons', in LW Heal, JI Haney, and AR Novak Amado (eds), *Integration of Developmentally Disabled Individuals into the Community* (2nd edn, Baltimore: Paul H Brookes Publishing Co, 1988) 19–35; HM Watkins, 'Selective Sterilization' (1930) *Proceedings and Addresses of the American Association for the Study of the Feeble-Minded* 51–67; CW Winspear, 'The Protection and Training of Feeble-Minded Women' (1895) 20 *Proceedings of the Association of Medical Officers of American Institutions for Idiotic and Feeble-Minded Persons* 160–163.
71. Barr (n 55 above); Fernald (n 70 above); F Galton, *Inquiry into Human Faculty and its Development* (Arlington, Va: Vandamere Press, 1883); NH Rafter, *White Trash: The Eugenic Family Studies, 1877–1919* (Boston: Northeastern Univ Press, 1988); JAF Roberts, 'The Genetics of Mental Deficiency' (1952) 44 *Eugenics Review* 71–83.

72. Fernald (n 70 above); Rafter (n 71 above); RL Dugdale, *The Jukes* (New York: GP Putman & Sons, 1910, original work published 1877); HC Evans, *The American Poorfarm and its Inmates* (Mooseheart, Ill: Loyal Order of Moose, 1926); HH Goddard, *The Kallikak Family: A Study in the Heredity of Feeble-Mindedness* (New York: MacMillan, 1912).

73. Fernald (n 70 above); AB Davenport, 'Selecting Immigrants' (1921) 25 *Proceedings and Addresses of the American Association for the Study of the Feeble-Minded* 178–179.

74. SJ Gould, *The Mismeasure of Man* (New York: Norton, 1981).

75. ibid.

76. ibid; E Bicknell, 'Custodial Care of the Adult Feeble-Minded' (1895) 5 *Charities Review* 76–88; IN Kerlin, 'Moral Imbecility' (1887) 12 *Proceedings of the Association of Medical Officers of American Institutions for Idiotic and Feeble-Minded Persons* 32–37; MW Barr, 'Moral Paranoia' (1895) 20 *Proceedings of the Association of Medical Officers of American Institutions for Idiotic and Feeble-Minded Persons* 522–531; WE Fernald, 'The Burden of Feeble-Mindedness' (1912) 17 *Journal of Psycho-Asthenics* 87–99.

77. Trent (n 49 above).

78. Pernick (n 38 above).

79. ibid.

80. D Gladstone, 'Western Counties Idiot Asylum 1864–1914' in D Wright and A Digby (eds), *From Idiocy to Mental Deficiency: Historical Perspectives on People with Learning Disabilities* (London: Routledge, 1996) 134–160.

81. J Carpenter, 'Rev Harold Nelson Burden and Katherine Mary Burden: Pioneers of Inebriate Reformatories and Mental Deficiency Institutions' (1996) 89 *Journal of the Royal Society of Medicine* 205–209.

82. ibid; S Koven, 'Remembering and Dismemberment: Crippled Children, Wounded Soldiers, and the Great War in Great Britain' (1994) 99 *American Historical Review* 1167–1202.

83. Evans (n 72 above).

84. TH Haines, 'Mental Defect and Poverty' (1925) 30 *Proceedings and Addresses of the American Association for the Study of the Feeble-Minded* 136–145.

85. Watkins (n 70 above); EZ Ferster, 'Eliminating the Unfit: Is Sterilization the Answer?' (1966) 27 *Ohio State Law Journal* 591–633.

86. M Woodside, *Sterilization in North Carolina: A Sociological and Psychological Study* (Chapel Hill: Univ of North Carolina Press, 1950).

87. P Popenoe, 'Success on Parole after Sterilization' (1927) 32 *Proceedings and Addresses of the American Association for the Study of Feeblemindedness* 86–109.

88. A Church, 'Removal of Ovaries and Tubes in the Insane and Neurotic' (1893) 28 *American Journal of Obstetrics and Diseases of Women and Children* 491–498.

89. ibid.

90. DJ Kevles, *In the Name of Eugenics: Genetics and the Uses of Human Heredity* (New York: Alfred A Knopf, 1985); JP Radford, 'Eugenics and the Asylum' (1994) 7 *Journal of Historical Sociology* 462–473; PR Reilly, *The Surgical Solution: A History of Involuntary Sterilization in the United States* (Baltimore: Johns Hopkins Univ Press, 1991).

91. Reilly (n 90 above).

92. ibid; H Friedlander, *The Origins of Nazi Genocide: From Euthanasia to the Final Solution* (Chapel Hill: Univ of North Carolina Press, 1997); HG Gallagher, *By Trust Betrayed: Patients, Physicians, and the License to Kill in the Third Reich* (Rev edn, Arlington, Va: Vandamere Press, 1995); US Holocaust Memorial Museum, *The Mentally and Physically Handicapped Victims of the Nazi Era* (Washington, DC: US Holocaust Memorial Museum, undated); W Wolfensberger, 'The Extermination of Handicapped People in World War II Germany' (1981) 19 *Mental Retardation* 1–7.

93. M Burleigh, 'Psychiatry, German Society, and the Nazi "Euthanasia" Programme' (1994) 7 *Social History of Medicine* 213–228.

94. ibid.

95. S Trombley, *The Right to Reproduce: A History of Coercive Sterilization* (London: Weidenfeld & Nicholson, 1988).

96. WE Fernald, 'A State Program for the Care of the Mentally Defective' (1919) 3 *Mental Hygiene* 566–574.

97. ibid.

98. GL Wallace, 'Are the Feebleminded Criminals?' (1929) 13 *Mental Hygiene* 93–98.

99. C Bernstein 'Self-Sustaining Feeble-Minded' (1917) 22 *Journal of Psycho-Asthenics* 150–161; C Bernstein 'Rehabilitation of the Mentally Defective' (1918) 23 *Journal of Psycho-Asthenics* 92–103; C Bernstein, 'Colony Care for Isolation of Defective and Dependent Cases' (1921) 26 *Proceedings of the American Association on Mental Defect* 43–59; SP Davies, *Social Control of the Mentally Deficient* (New York: Thomas Y Crowell, 1930); WE Fernald, 'The Massachusetts Farm Colony for the Feeble-Minded' (1902) *Proceedings of the National Conference on Charities and Correction* 487–491; ZP Hoakley, 'Extra-Institutional Care for the Feeble-Minded' (1922) 27 *Journal of Psycho-Asthenics* 117–137; JT Mastin, 'The New Colony Plan for the Feeble-Minded' (1916) 21 *Journal of Psycho-Asthenics* 25–35; MA Matthews, 'One Hundred Institutionally Trained Male Defectives in the Community under Supervision' (1921) 26 *Journal of Psycho-Asthenics* 60–70.

100. US Bureau of the Census, *Patients in Mental Institutions* (Washington, DC: US Bureau of the Census, 1939); US Bureau of the Census, *Patients in Mental Institutions* (Washington, DC: US Bureau of the Census, 1940).

101. KC Lakin, *Demographic Studies of Residential Facilities for the Mentally Retarded: An Historical Review of Methodologies and Findings* (Minneapolis: Univ of Minnesota, 1979).

102. HN Switzky, M Dudzinski, R Van Acker, and J Gambro, 'Historical Foundations of Out-of-Home Residential Alternatives for Mentally Retarded Persons' in LW Heal, JI Haney, and AR Novak Amado (eds), *Integration of Developmentally Disabled Individuals into the Community* (2nd edn, Baltimore: Paul H Brookes Publishing Co, 1988) 19–35.

103. SB Sarason and T Gladwin, 'Psychological and Cultural Problems in Mental Subnormality, Part II' in RL Masland, SB Sarason, and T Gladwin (eds), *Mental Subnormality: Biological, Psychological, and Cultural Factors* (New York: Basic Books, Inc, 1958).

104. S Noll, *The Feeble-Minded in Our Midst: Institutions for the Mentally Retarded in the South, 1900–1940* (Chapel Hill: Univ of North Carolina Press, 1996).

105. ibid; Trent (n 49 above); Watkins (n 70 above); PL Tyor and LV Bell, *Caring for the Retarded in America: A History* (Westport, Conn: Greenwood Press, 1984).

106. D Braddock, *Federal Policy toward Mental Retardation* (Baltimore: Paul H Brooks, 1987).

107. D Braddock, 'Federal Assistance for Mental Retardation and Developmental Disabilities I: A Review through 1961' (1986) 24 *Mental Retardation* 175–182.

108. Social Security Board, *Recommendations of the Children's Bureau Advisory Committee on Services to Crippled Children: December 1935 to April 1946* (Washington, DC: Department of Health and Human Services Archives, 1946).

109. J Moreno, *Undue Risk: Secret State Experiments on Humans* (New York: WH Freeman, 1999).

110. DJ Rothman and SM Rothman, *The Willowbrook Wars* (New York: Harper & Row, 1984).

111. Trent (n 49 above); Noll (n 104 above).

112. CL Vaux, 'Family Care of Mental Defectives' (1935) 40 *Journal of Psycho-Asthenics* 168–189.

113. HM Skeels and I Harms, 'Children with Inferior Social Histories: Their Mental Development in Adoptive Homes' (1948) 72 *Journal of Genetic Psychology* 283–294; GS Speer, 'The Intelligence of Foster Children' (1940) 57 *Journal of Genetic Psychology* 49–55.

114. I Lazar and RB Darlington, 'Lasting Effects of Early Education' (1982) 47 *Monographs of the Society for Research in Child Development* 2–3; HM Skeels, R Updegraff, BL Wellman, and HM Williams, 'A Study of Environmental Stimulation, an Orphanage Preschool Project' (1938) 15 *University of Iowa Studies in Child Welfare* 4.

115. LA Jones, *Doing Justice: A History of the Association of Retarded Citizens of Washington* (Olympia, Wash: Arc of Washington, 1987).

116. D Goode, *History of the Association for the Help of Retarded Children of New York City* (New York: AHRC, 1999).

117. GN Grob, *The Mad among Us* (New York: Free Press, 1994); H Lefley, *Family Caregiving in Mental Illness* (Thousand Oaks, Calif: Sage Publications, 1996).

118. US Department of Health, Education, and Welfare, *Mental Retardation Sourcebook of the DHEW* (Washington, DC: US Department of Health, Education, and Welfare, Office of the Secretary, Office of Mental Retardation Coordination, September 1972).

119. Survey and Research Corporation, *Mental Retardation Program Statistics of US—Report to the Department of Health, Education and Welfare Pursuant to Contract PH-86-64-99* (Washington, DC: US Department of Health, Education and Welfare, July 1965).

120. M Birnbaum, 'Some Comments on "the Right to Treatment"' (1965) 13 *Archives of General Psychiatry* 33–45; RM Levy and LS Rubenstein, *The Rights of People with Mental Disabilities: The Authoritative ACLU Guide to the Rights of People with Mental Illness and Mental Retardation* (Carbondale and Edwardsville: Southern Illinois Univ, 1996).

121. Levy and Rubenstein (n 120 above); *Rouse v Cameron* 373 F 2 d 451, 452 (DC Cir 1966).
122. Levy and Rubenstein (n 120 above); J Parry, *Mental Disability Law: A Primer* (5th edn, Washington, DC: American Bar Association, 1995).
123. JF Kennedy, 'Statement by the President regarding the Need for a National Plan in Mental Retardation' in the President's Panel on Mental Retardation, *National Action to Combat Mental Retardation* (Washington, DC: US Government Printing Office, 1961) 196–201.
124. B Nirje, 'The Normalization Principle and its Human Management Implications' in RB Kugel and A Shearer (eds), *Changing Patterns in Residential Services for the Mentally Retarded* (Washington, DC: President's Committee on Mental Retardation, 1976) 231–240; W Wolfensberger, *The Principle of Normalization in Human Services* (Toronto, Ont: National Institute on Mental Retardation, 1972).
125. President's Panel on Mental Retardation, *National Action to Combat Mental Retardation* (Washington, DC: US Government Printing Office, 1962)
126. *Wyatt v Stickney* 325 F Supp 781 (MD Ala 1971), enforced in 334 F Supp 1341 (1971); 344 F Supp 387 (1972); *Wyatt v Aderholt* 503 F 2d 1305 (5th Cir 1974).
127. D Braddock, 'Federal Assistance for Mental Retardation and Developmental Disabilities II: The Modern Era' (1986) 24 *Mental Retardation* 209–218; R Scotch, *From Goodwill to Civil Rights: Transforming Federal Disability Policy* (Philadelphia: Temple Univ Press, 1984).
128. Rothman and Rothman (n 110 above).
129. Scotch (n 127 above).
130. JW Jacobson, SN Burchard, and PJ Carling, *Community Living for People with Developmental and Psychiatric Disabilities* (Baltimore: Johns Hopkins Univ Press, 1992); LK Koegel, RL Koegel, and G Dunlap, *Positive Behavioral Support: Including People with Difficult Behavior in the Community* (Baltimore: Brookes, 1996); T Thompson and J Grabowski (eds), *Behavior Modification of the Mentally Retarded* (2nd edn, New York: Oxford Univ Press, 1977).
131. Levy and Rubenstein (n 120 above); J Parry, *Mental Disability Law: A Primer* (5th edn, Washington, DC: American Bar Association, 1995); *Wyatt v Stickney* 325 F Supp 781 (MD Ala 1971), enforced in 334 F Supp 1341 (1971); 344 F Supp 387 (1972); *Wyatt v Aderholt* 503 F 2d 1305 (5th Cir 1974).
132. Levy and Rubenstein (n 120 above); D Braddock, R Hemp, S Parish, and J Westrich, *The State of the States in Developmental Disabilities* (5th edn, Washington, DC: AAMR, 1998); MF Hayden, 'Class-Action, Civil Rights Litigation for Institutionalized Persons with Mental Retardation and Other Developmental Disabilities' (1997) 21 Mental and Physical Disability Law Reporter 411–423.
133. EW Martin, R Martin, and DL Terman, 'The Legislative and Litigation History of Special Education' (1996) 6 *Special Education for Students with Disabilities* 25–38; *Pennsylvania Ass'n Retarded Child v Commonwealth of Pa* 334 F Supp 1257 (ED Pa, October 8, 1971).
134. US Department of Education, *Twenty-third Annual Report to Congress on the Implementation of the Individuals with Disabilities Education Act* (Washington, DC: US Department of Education, 2001).

135. D Braddock and T Heller, 'The Closure of Mental Retardation Institutions II: Implications' (1985) 23 *Mental Retardation* 222–229.

136. SB Covert, JD MacIntosh, and DL Shumway, 'Closing the Laconia State School and Training Center: A Case Study in System Change' in VJ Bradley, JW Ashbaugh, and BC Blaney (eds), *Creating Individual Supports for People with Developmental Disabilities: A Mandate for Change at Many Levels* (Baltimore: Brookes, 1994) 197–211.

137. D Braddock *et al.*, *The State of the States in Developmental Disabilities: 2000 Study Summary* (Chicago: Univ of Illinois at Chicago, Dept of Disability and Human Development, 2000).

138. ibid; Braddock *et al.* (n 132 above).

139. K Keith and R Schalock, *Cross Cultural Perspectives on Quality of Life* (Washington, DC: AAMR, 2000).

140. E Emerson, J Robertson, N Gregory, C Hatton, S Kessissoglou, A Hallam, M Knapp, Järbrink, PN Walsh, and A Netten, 'Quality and Costs of Community-Based Residential Supports, Village Communities and Residential Campuses in the United Kingdom' (2000) 105/2 *American Journal on Mental Retardation* 81–102.

141. G Dybwad and H Bersani, Jr. (eds), *New Voices: Self-Advocacy by People with Disabilities* (Cambridge, Mass: Brookline Books, 1996); NA Longhurst, *The Self-Advocacy Movement: A Demographic Study and Directory* (Washington, DC: AAMR, 1994).

142. MF Hayden and D Senese, *Self-Advocacy Groups: 1996 Directory for North America* (Minneapolis: Univ of Minnesota, 1996).

143. Longhurst (n 141 above).

144. Dybwad and Bersani (n 141 above).

145. Parry (n 131 above); National Council on Disability, *Equality of Opportunity: The Making of the Americans with Disabilities Act* (Washington, DC: National Council on Disability, 26 July 1997).

146. Parry (n 131 above).

147. National Council on Disability (n 145 above).

148. RK Scotch, 'Politics and Policy in the History of the Disability Rights Movement' (1989) 67/2 *Milbank Quarterly* Suppl 2, 380–400.

149. B Doyle, *Disability Discrimination: The New Law* (Bristol: Jordans, 1996); C Gooding, *Blackstone's Guide to the Disability Discrimination Act 1995* (London: Blackstone Press Limited, 1996).

150. Gooding (n 149 above).

151. ibid; Doyle (n 149 above).

152. ibid.

153. United Nations, *The Standard Rules on the Equalization of Opportunities for Persons with Disabilities* (New York: United Nations, 1994).

154. United Nations General Assembly Resolution 2856 (XXVI), *On the Declaration on the Rights of Mentally Retarded Persons* (New York: United Nations, 1971).

155. United Nations General Assembly Resolution 3447 (XXX), *On the Declaration on the Rights of Disabled Persons* (New York: United Nations, 1975).

156. United Nations, *World Program of Action Concerning Disabled Persons* (New York: United Nations, 1982).

157. RL Metts, *Disability Issues, Trends and Recommendations for the World Bank* (Washington, DC: World Bank, 2000).
158. European Union, *Resolution of the Council and the Representatives of the Governments of the Member States on Equality of Opportunity for People with Disabilities Official Journal C 12, 13.01.1997* (Brussels: European Union, 1996).
159. Metts (n 157 above).
160. J Birnbaum and C Taylor, 'Introduction: Where do We Go from Here?' in J Birnbaum and C Taylor (eds), *Civil Rights since 1787: A Reader on the Black Struggle* (New York: New York Univ Press, 2000).
161. Scotch (n 148 above).
162. RR Anspach, 'From Stigma to Identity Politics: Political Activism among the Physically Disabled and Former Mental Patients' (1979) 13A *Social Science and Medicine* 765–773; CJ Gill, 'Four Types of Integration in Disability Identity Development' (1997) 9 *Journal of Vocational Rehabilitation* 39–46; S Linton, *Claiming Disability: Knowledge and Identity* (New York: New York Univ Press, 1998).
163. H Hahn, 'Disability Policy and the Problem of Discrimination' (1985) 28 *American Behavioral Scientist* 293–318.
164. National Council on Disability (n 145 above).
165. US Bureau of the Census, *International Data Base* (Washington, DC: Bureau of the Census, International Programs Center, Information Resources Branch, 1997); M Janicki and E Ansello, 'Supports for Community Living: Evaluation of an Aging with Lifelong Disabilities Movement' in M Janicki and E Ansello (eds), *Community Supports for Aging Adults with Lifelong Disabilities* (Baltimore: Brookes Publishing Co, 2000) 519–537.
166. GL Albrecht and LM Verbrugge, 'The Global Emergence of Disability' in GL Albrecht, R Fitzpatrick, and SC Scrimshaw (eds), *The Handbook of Social Studies in Health and Medicine* (London: Sage Publications, 2000) 293–307.
167. A Hoffman and S Field, 'Promoting Self-Determination through Effective Curriculum Development' (1995) 30 *Intervention in School and Clinic* 147–156.
168. Albrecht and Verbrugge (n 166 above).
169. C Barnes, 'Disability and the Myth of the Independent Researcher' 11 *Disability & Society* (1996) 107–110; New York: Department of Education for the United States Commission for the Paris Exposition of 1900; JC Humphrey, 'Researching Disability Politics, or, Some Problems with the Social Model in Practice' (2000) 15/1 *Disability & Society* 63–85; M Oliver, 'Changing the Social Relations of Research Production' (1992) 7/2 *Disability, Handicap & Society* 101–114; M Oliver and C Barnes, *Disabled People and Social Policy: From Exclusion to Inclusion* (Chapel Hill: Univ of North Carolina Press, 1999).
170. JK Galbraith, *Created Unequal: The Crisis in American Pay* (New York: Free Press, 1998).
171. Metts (n 157 above).

Part II
The Human Rights Movement: International Norms and Standards

5

From Wrongs to Rights: International Human Rights and Legal Protection

STANLEY S. HERR

I. INTRODUCTION

People with intellectual disabilities are an integral focus of a growing international human rights movement. Although this movement gained momentum after the Second World War, it only made explicit reference to people with intellectual disabilities after the 1968 passage of the *Declaration on the General and Special Rights of Mentally Retarded Persons* in Jerusalem by the International League of Societies for the Mentally Handicapped.[1] There is now growing recognition by scholars and advocates of the applicability of human rights law and UN human rights activities to people with intellectual disabilities and of the increased power that human rights bring to this most vulnerable population.

For persons with intellectual and related disabilities, those objectives are identified in general proclamations and treaties as well as thematic documents on the rights of persons with disabilities. For example, the *UN Declaration on the Rights of Disabled Persons* of 1975 covers some one-half billion persons who have a mental or physical disability.[2] This Declaration, in turn, had its roots in the 1971 United Nations General Assembly adoption of the *Declaration on the Rights of Mentally Retarded Persons*.[3]

Although universal declarations and covenants on human rights apply to persons with mental retardation, they have seldom been invoked on their behalf. As one former institutional superintendent in Connecticut (USA) wrote:

Backward stranger, you have a story to tell without words we can understand. Never thought to possess human needs, your only gifts are isolation and desolation.... *Growing old and inwardly dying each passing day, why can't you accept injustice in silent agony, as we were told you would?* The sands of time create the glass you shatter, and you turn on your own irreplaceable flesh in self-inflicted torture, which no one understands to be your message to the planners: 'I will render my body disfigured and blur my consciousness while you are powerless to stop me. Your conscience can not bear to bind me, and your senses can not tolerate my destruction. When you find the answer and have the means, I will be here to greet my new life; I'm not going anywhere.'[4]

This chapter identifies the history behind human rights law, examines the main principles articulated in international human rights law, suggests some strategies for carrying out those principles, and presents recommendations that will produce further progress and visibility in this crucial area of human rights. It will also consider whether existing human rights statements fit the current understandings of the needs and rights of persons with intellectual disabilities.

There is moral as well as legal authority for the rights articulated in this chapter. Ronald Dworkin, for instance, advances the idea that every human being is sacred, 'commands respect and protection', and that human rights stem in part from this ideology that all people are sacred.[5] This sacredness requires action on both national and international levels. Whether or not human rights are grounded in the religious or philosophical principle that all people are sacred, the idea of human rights is motivated by a larger sense of community. This movement, especially for persons with intellectual disabilities, is based on many concepts such as religion, justice, or self-regard. Yet, current paradigm shifts from charity to rights are heavily influenced by the wrongs that have been committed against those with intellectual and related disabilities.

A. The Wrongs to Be Righted

For centuries people with intellectual disabilities had no rights, and for the residents of the human warehouses, euphemistically named training schools and asylums, 'residents' enjoyed no rights at all well into the twentieth century. Although a few pioneering voices called for recognition of their rights, they tended to be dismissed or ignored. For instance, Samuel Gridley Howe, who created one of the first schools in the United States for this class of persons, declared in 1874, that '[e]ven idiots have rights which should be carefully considered'.[6] Out of fear and convenience, societies committed many wrongs against persons with a variety of labels denoting cognitive limitations. Industrialized nations, including the United States, exiled people called 'retarded' to remote residential institutions; ordered them to be sterilized;[7] denied them schooling; and shamed them and their families for the accident of their birth.

Robert Burt eloquently described the fears of 'mentally normal people' engendered by the image of the 'most profoundly, the most remotely uncommunicative' retarded person: 'The fear that lies behind this image can lead those gripped by it to deny its force in their own minds, to wish they could conquer the fear by banishing the imagined embodiment of that fear. This impulse to isolate and even to abuse the embodied expression of one's own fear can take many forms.'[8]

Commentators and human rights activists have criticized the inhumane conditions of confinement confronting persons with intellectual disabilities in institutions in the United States, Albania, Jamaica, Sweden, Israel, Greece, and elsewhere. They have also deplored the frequency of human rights abuses in so-called natural environments as well as community-based settings, which house anywhere from one to sixteen persons.

Institutional conditions have engendered much criticism and litigation. Starting in the early 1970s, court cases in the United States focused on the rights to treatment (sometimes referred to as habilitation), protections from harm, and transfers of residents to community-based living.[9] At institutions such as Partlow State School in Alabama, Willowbrook in New York, and Pennhurst in Pennsylvania, infamous conditions resulted in the imposition of elaborate judicial remedies and standards. Supervision of these court decrees led to continuing judicial oversight for lengthy periods, in some cases for more than twenty years. In at least thirty additional states, similar class-action suits challenged legal and human rights violations, often resulting in significant internal changes and reductions in institutional populations.[10]

Even after advocates began to speak out, change was often incremental and grudging. As one official British report acknowledged: 'For decades we have known how to put right the appalling conditions to which mentally handicapped people and those who care for them are subjected, and for decades we have allowed those same conditions to survive.'[11] Yet the advocates persisted, demanding change in legislatures, the courts, planning processes, individual placement meetings, blue-ribbon commissions, and in any other forums that promised redress. The historic record revealed even worse horrors. Many of the applicable human rights milestones from 1948 occurred in the face of the Holocaust and the systematic extermination of people based on immutable characteristics of disability. Under the Third Reich, the label 'retarded' or 'useless eater' could mark the individual for forced sterilization or death. The authorities developed mass murder techniques in the 'euthanasia hospitals'. So-called 'wild euthanasia'—the indiscriminate killing of 'welfare wards, asocials, wayward children, healthy Jewish children [and] those of mixed blood'—involved techniques that historian Hugh Gregory Gallagher noted, were 'later utilized against the Jews' and others by the millions.[12]

The modern human rights movement emerged after the Second World War with the UN Charter and its reaffirmation of 'the dignity and worth of the human person' and of 'the equal rights of men and women'.[13] It drew on outraged leadership reactions to human wrongs on a monstrous scale.[14] The perpetrators of those wrongs began by murdering people with disabilities, systematically slaughtering some 270,000 Germans and Austrians deemed mentally retarded, psychiatrically disturbed, or physically deformed after medical doctors rationalized that persons with disabilities led 'lives not worth living'. By applying arguments of cost-benefit, eugenics, and race purity, the Nazi doctors trumped issues of simple decency and respect for life. As a result, the value of all lives were diminished and human rights were rendered meaningless.[15] When the Third Reich crumbled in 1945 and the United Nations was formed, the restoration of decency and the protection of the human rights of the defenseless became central missions of this world body.

Despite the triumph of the idea of human rights and the development of means of rights enforcement,[16] there was often little thought or action given to the human rights of people then known as 'mentally retarded'. Although human rights, as Louis Henkin concluded, 'have now become for everyone, everywhere a "good"', sometimes equated with 'everything good in human life and society',[17] people with intellectual disabilities surely have not had their fair share of human rights protection. If after decades of 'determined international effort, human rights are faring poorly in many countries', Henkin observed, 'and leave at least a little to be desired in every country', then a great deal is still to be desired for people with intellectual disabilities. Scholars have abundantly detailed a litany of wrongs that provoked a remarkable flood of legislative remedies in the United States and other countries.[18]

There are rights to education, habilitation, nondiscrimination, freedom from harm, payment for work, and many more declared rights. There are no grounds for complacency, however. Great wisdom, political will, and economic resources are all required for the proper implementation of those legislative and case rights.

Even today, human rights concerns for people with intellectual disabilities are overshadowed by human rights protections for people with other disabilities. UN documents and publications on human rights addressing issues involving 'mentally ill persons' and 'mental health services' are far more frequent than those referring to 'mentally retarded persons'.[19] The human rights narratives and norms of persons with intellectual disabilities are often linked to wider categories of 'disability', 'disability prevention', 'disabled children', 'disabled persons', and 'disabled women'.[20] At the dawn of the twenty-first century, there are over 180 disability-related UN human rights documents relevant to persons with disabilities.[21]

B. International Human Rights Standards

Since its founding in 1945, the United Nations has promoted human rights as one of its primary purposes. Although the UN Charter and a long line of UN declarations and covenants stress this purpose, the task of publicizing and protecting disability rights through accountability and redress of violations has largely fallen to nongovernmental organizations (NGOs).[22] Inclusion International (formerly known as the International League of Societies for Persons with Mental Handicap), Mental Disability Rights International, and Rehabilitation International have led the way. However, the promotion and protection of rights are interdependent, requiring nongovernmental and governmental sectors to play vital parts in bringing rights into reality.

1. Universal Declaration on Human Rights

In a perfect world, one would need to go no further than the elegant phrases contained in the Universal Declaration of Human Rights (UDHR).[23] Adopted on 10 December 1948, by a vote of forty-eight to zero, the UDHR recognizes 'the equal and inalienable rights of all members of the human family', their inherent dignity and their aspirations to 'freedom from fear and want'.[24] The enumerated rights are inclusive and no distinction in entitlements to those rights and freedoms is drawn on the basis of 'birth or other status'. The term 'disability' is used only once in the entire document, in the context of a right to an adequate living standard and 'the right to security in the event of unemployment, sickness, disability, widowhood, old age or the lack of livelihood in circumstances beyond his control'.[25] These universal rights include the classic negative rights (eg, '[n]o one shall be subjected to…cruel, inhuman or degrading treatment'[26]) and positive rights (eg, '[e]veryone has the right to life, liberty and security of person'[27]). They extend to privacy rights, including freedom from arbitrary interference with family, home, or attacks upon 'honour and reputation',[28] as well as an array of affirmative rights to work, 'equal pay for equal work',[29] education,[30] 'equal access to public service',[31] participation in cultural life,[32] and 'rest and leisure'.[33]

The UDHR, however, is not legally binding. Although it has had an indirect legal effect,[34] many of these social rights, such as the concept that 'everyone has the right…to periodic holidays with pay', have limited reach even in the developed world.[35] More telling is the absence of the application of these principles to persons with intellectual disabilities despite the passage of over fifty years following the UN's adoption of the UDHR. Although the UDHR is often cited in courts around the world (some ninety cases citing the UDHR have been identified), it is rarely aired in cases involving litigants with intellectual disabilities. Even more troubling, governments and the general public rarely take notice of the claims of persons with intellectual disabilities. They rarely apply the UDHR to them, perhaps because of entrenched negative attitudes or the mistaken sense that the general phrases did not really grapple with specific needs and problems of this population.

*2. ILSMH Declaration on the General and Special Rights of
Mentally Retarded Persons*

In the late 1960s, out of frustration with this lack of change or attention,
parents and other allies of persons with intellectual disabilities decided
to act. In 1968, the International League of Societies for the Mentally
Handicapped (ILSMH) met in Jerusalem for their World Congress.
They issued the *Declaration on the General and Special Rights of Mentally
Retarded Persons*. From its initial article, it adopted an egalitarian stance:
'The mentally retarded person has the same basic rights as other citizens
of the same country and the same age.'[36] This NGO declaration then
inspired two UN human rights declarations specifically concerning
disabilities.

3. UN Declaration on the Rights of Mentally Retarded Persons

In 1971, the General Assembly adopted the *UN Declaration on the Rights of
Mentally Retarded Persons*. This declaration was expressed in terms nearly
identical to the ILSMH text. By a vote of 110 to zero and expressed in
seven concise articles, the UN proclaimed that a person with mental
retardation has 'the same rights as other human beings'.[37] They also have
rights to developmental services, 'a decent standard of living', typical
styles of life, protective services, legal protection from 'abuse and
degrading treatment', and other supports to develop their abilities. They
are also entitled to 'proper legal safeguards' when any right is restricted
because of incapacity. In terms influenced by professional principles of
normalization and habilitation, the Declaration's Article 4 accepted
the innovative view that such persons should receive home-based
care, either with natural families or foster families that obtained practical
assistance.

Over three decades, the limitations of this pioneering declaration have
become more glaring. To achieve its unanimous acceptance, this UN
document had to be burdened with a number of caveats. For instance, the
integration of persons of mental retardation was accepted 'as far as possible' in normal life, with no clarification as to whether that belief reflected
views as to the differences of the persons affected, the socio-economic
resources available to serve them, or the cultural readiness of societies to
have such persons living and working in their midst. In terms of residential facilities, the Declaration allowed a loophole in Article 4 when it called
for the person to be served in 'surroundings...as close as possible to those
of normal life'. Here again, in the light of the twenty-first century, phrases
like 'as close as possible' can be interpreted as calls for pragmatism or as
invitations to avoid offering people with intellectual disabilities something less than normal life, perhaps dramatically so. Thus, the 1971
Declaration is both a pioneering set of aspirations and an increasingly
obsolescent expression of where the field currently stands.

4. UN Declaration on the Rights of Disabled Persons

Four years later, the UN turned to broader issues of disability and human rights. As stated in the Preamble of UN Document A/811, the *Declaration on the Rights of Disabled Persons* called for international and national action to protect the rights of all persons with physical and mental disabilities. The Declaration is sweeping in its functional definition of 'the disabled person' and its enumeration of their rights.[38] These rights are granted regardless of the degree, origin, or type of disability. With an emphasis on principles of egalitarianism and normalization, the 1975 Declaration states that persons with disabilities have 'the same fundamental rights as their fellow-citizens of the same age, which implies first and foremost the right to enjoy a decent life, as normal and full as possible'.[39] Other equality provisions set out rights to nondiscrimination, equal civil and political rights, and the broadly stated 'inherent right to respect for their human dignity'.[40]

The Declaration affirms broad social and economic rights. It enumerates rights to treatment, rehabilitation, education, vocational education, training, counseling, aid, placement services, economic security, social security, family living, and participation in recreational and cultural activities to develop 'capabilities and skills to the maximum'. Of great importance, it calls for measures to hasten their 'social integration or reintegration'.[41]

The 1975 Declaration also stresses liberty interests. It prohibits 'all exploitation', discriminatory, abusive or degrading treatment and regulations, and unnecessary 'differential treatment' in residence. Should residence in any essential specialized facility become necessary, it requires living conditions that are 'as close as possible to those of normal life of a person of his or her age'.[42] The Declaration demands that persons with disabilities become as 'self-reliant as possible' and have their 'special needs taken into consideration at all stages of economic and social planning'.[43]

The text recognizes that advocacy and empowerment are critical to meeting its goals. In emphasizing the need for redress and awareness of rights, the declaration requires 'qualified legal aid when such aid proves indispensable' for personal or property protection. It also requires full information to disabled persons and their families on the declared rights.[44] Governments are urged to consult with organizations of disabled persons on all matters regarding their rights.[45] Although this set of standards is impressive, a declaration without powerful advocacy is insufficient for the beneficiaries to realize their rights in fact.

C. International Treaties

1. International Covenants on Human Rights

The *International Covenant on Economic, Social, and Cultural Rights* (ICESCR) and the *International Covenant on Civil and Political Rights*

(ICCPR), both adopted on 16 December 1966, are treaty obligations that are binding on State Parties. Although the language parallels the UDHR, the treaties contain specific protections such as the prohibition of unconsented medical or scientific experimentation on human subjects,[46] and requirements of humane commitment. ('All persons deprived of their liberty shall be treated with humanity and with respect for the inherent dignity of the human person.')[47] It also guarantees the equal protection of the law. This provision includes 'equal and effective protection against discrimination on any ground such as...birth or other status'.[48] Significant social rights include rights to free education (at least through the primary level), the enjoyment of the 'highest attainable standard of physical and mental health' and social security (including social insurance).[49] Promulgating rights and applying them to the specific contexts facing persons with disabilities in countries with varying economic, professional, and disability support resources, are however, two very different exercises.

General Comment 5 of the High Commission for Human Rights underscores the importance and applicability of the ICESCR to the human rights of persons with disabilities. It surveys UN statements such as the Standard Rules and the World Programme of Action Concerning Disabled Persons, as well as the Despouy report on human rights and disability, concluding that persons with disabilities are 'very often denied the opportunity to enjoy the full range of economic, social and cultural rights recognized in the Covenant'.[50] States Parties still give very limited attention in their reports to disability rights issues, and fail to undertake 'decisive concerted measures that would effectively improve the situation' for persons with various disabilities.[51] Comment 5 also criticizes the lack of an internationally accepted definition of disability and the harsh reality that a major policy and program effort for persons with disabilities is required in each country.[52] Indeed, the Comment notes a deterioration in the position of persons with disabilities in the decade from the mid-1980s, which it ascribes to market-based policies.

[C]urrent economic and social deterioration, marked by low-growth rates, high unemployment, reduced public expenditure, current structural adjustment programmes and privatization, have negatively affected programmes and services....If the present negative trends continue, there is the risk that [persons with disabilities] may increasingly be relegated to the margins of society, dependent on ad hoc support.[53]

Although the High Commissioner notes that the absence of an explicit disability rights provision to the Covenant (seen as due to the lack of awareness of the issue at the time of its drafting) the international community has taken subsequent steps to remedy this omission. This includes promulgation of the *African Charter on Human and Peoples' Rights*;[54] the *Additional Protocol to the American Convention on Human Rights as in the Area of Economics, Social and Cultural Rights*;[55] the *World Programme of Action Concerning Disabled Persons*;[56] the *Guidelines for the Establishment and Development of National Coordinating Committees on Disability or Similar Bodies*, adopted in 1990;[57] the *Principles for the Protection of Persons with Mental Illness and for the Improvement of Mental Health Care*, adopted in 1991;[58] and the *Standard Rules on the Equalization of Opportunities for Persons with Disabilities*, (the 'Standard Rules') adopted in 1993, the purpose of which is to ensure that all persons with disabilities 'may exercise the same rights and obligations as others'.[59]

In summary, the UN now recognizes that disability rights are not only covered by the ICESCR, but that it requires domestic disability nondiscrimination laws as well as a host of adjustments and affirmative programs under this treaty to realize these rights in practice.

2. Convention on the Rights of the Child

One group of persons with disabilities has the protection of a human rights treaty based on their age. The UN Convention on the Rights of the Child protects the rights of minors with disabilities,[60] specifying the rights of children with intellectual and physical disabilities to a wide spectrum of rehabilitation services and special care. Article 23 of this treaty is devoted to disability-related issues. It calls for an array of free therapeutic services and educational programs designed to achieve the child's 'fullest possible social integration and individual development'. Article 23 recognizes that such children 'should enjoy a full and decent life', with conditions promoting dignity, self-reliance, and 'active participation in the community'.[61] A vexing question arises as to why a treaty should not be available to persons with disabilities at the other point of the life cycle beyond the age of childhood, which is a topic discussed later in this chapter.

3. Convention on the Elimination of All Forms of Discrimination Against Women

This 1979 thematic treaty, like others of its vintage, does not make explicit reference to disability. It does, however, in Article 11 dealing with employment discrimination, refer to the right to social security in various circumstances, including 'other incapacity to work'.[62] Disability rights activists drew attention to this omission at the Fourth World Conference on Women (discussed below), and have developed an agenda of issues that reflect the disability rights paradigm.

D. Other UN Human Rights Statements

1. UN Standard Rules on the Equalization of Opportunities for People with Disabilities

The world community has developed a comprehensive blueprint for disability rights and policies. On 20 December 1993, the UN General Assembly adopted the *Standard Rules on the Equalization of Opportunities for Persons with Disabilities* ('Standard Rules') as 'an instrument for policy-making and action' for and by persons with disabilities and their representative organizations. Although its framers expressed the aspiration that the Standard Rules would eventually become international customary rules when applied by a sufficient number of nations, they acknowledged that the Rules were neither compulsory nor the equivalent of a binding legal convention.

The Rules, in fact, represent a guiding philosophy. They set out concepts for disability policy, principles for equal participation, and broad outlines for disability programs and policies to support the 'full participation and equality for persons with disabilities'. They also emphasize models, mechanisms and monitoring for rights implementation. Taken together, these approaches intensify the ability of persons with disabilities to achieve 'full and equal enjoyment of human rights and participation in society'.[63] The Rules insist on seeing persons with disabilities and their organizations as central players, 'empowered to exercise their human rights',[64] both involved in decision making on national policies and plans, and assuming greater responsibilities for their own futures.

The Rules break new ground in several areas. These include sexuality (eg, '[p]ersons with disabilities must not be denied the opportunity to experience their sexuality, have sexual relationships and experience parenthood'),[65] employment incentives (eg, systems of social security systems to encourage persons with disabilities to gain income-earning capacity and to seek employment),[66] and employment nondiscrimination.[67]

Despite its commendable breadth, flexibility, and courage, the Standard Rules have several shortcomings. Linguistically, the instrument contains a confusing mix of directives, including the words 'should', 'maybe', 'need', and 'could'. Indeed, the only imperatives couched in 'shall' language pertain to the monitoring mechanism and the duties of the Special Rapporteur. For instance, the Rapporteur is directed to send questionnaires to the States on their plans to implement the Standard Rules, to engage in 'direct dialogue' with States and NGOs on reporting and to provide advisory services on carrying out and monitoring the Standard Rules.[68] In other words, while States have great latitude in what they do under the Standard Rules, this monitoring agent is expected to impose some checks on the various countries. The Rapporteur's final report also summarized UN system activities to implement the Standard Rules.[69]

Not surprisingly, the disability NGOs have urged support for the Special Rapporteur, the distinguished Swedish parliamentarian Bengt Lindqvist, pleading for funds to assist in the global mission of monitoring States. Thus, the NGO's Reykjavik Declaration in Support of the Standard Rules on the Equalization of Opportunities for Persons with Disabilities calls for greater focus on national plans and monitoring.[70]

2. *Vienna Declaration of the World Conference on Human Rights*

In 1993, the World Conference on Human Rights took a large step toward strengthening international disability rights. It made explicit that 'all human rights and fundamental freedoms are universal and thus unreservedly include persons with disabilities'.[71] This statement is designed to close loopholes in earlier declarations by disallowing exceptions to full implementation of the rights of people with intellectual and other disabilities due to lack of economic or technical resources. As a call to action, the Vienna Declaration also requires legislative reform to 'assure access to these and other rights of disabled persons'.[72]

E. The UN Commission on Human Rights

The Commission on Human Rights, as the principal human rights enforcement arm of the UN, remains woefully inattentive to the relevant issues of persons with intellectual disabilities. To remedy this omission, an expert group meeting on disability convened by the UN and held in 1998 by two NGOs urged a number of concrete steps.[73] First, it urged greater coordination between the Commission and the agent promoting the Standard Rules (The Special Rapporteur on Disability of the Commission for Social Development). Second, it proposed a Commission working group to address disability rights violations, with persons with disabilities to be included as its members. Finally, it advocated for the consideration of the rights of persons with disabilities under generic human rights procedures and the thematic Resolutions 1235 and 1503.

In the mental disability field, the UN Commission on Human Rights achieved some success in 1985, when its criticism, along with that of UN Sub-Commission on Prevention of Discrimination and Protection of Minorities, provoked Japan to revise its Mental Hygiene Law. With 300,000 persons confined in mental hospitals under the consent of an immediate relative or other responsible person, the system was assailed by NGOs as lacking effective legal remedies to challenge the lawfulness of institutionalization rates. Under the threat that this system breached Article 9(4) of the *International Covenant on Civil and Political Rights* and after a fact-finding mission by two leading NGOs that concluded that this type of mental confinement violated international law, Japan declared in

August 1985 before the UN Sub-Commission that it would change the offending legislation.[74]

Clearly, comparable violations and UN action scenarios can—and should—arise in the intellectual disabilities context. Despite the long interval since the Japanese case study, the foreword to this book by UN High Commission Mary Robinson raises expectations that persons with intellectual disabilities will receive greater attention in the future.

F. European Convention on Human Rights and Related Human Rights Instruments

Europe has a rich human rights tradition that could offer persons with intellectual and other disabilities assistance. The European Convention on Human Rights[75] is a starting point although one that has shortcomings for persons with disabilities. Article 14, the primary nondiscrimination norm, fails to enumerate disability as one of the protected classes. However, Article 5 dealing with the liberty and security of each person does refer to the lawful detention of 'persons with unsound mind'.[76] In addition, the Convention entitles a detained person with an intellectual disability to speedy court proceedings to determine its legality.[77]

Another article that is relevant to persons with such disabilities prohibits torture or inhuman or degrading treatment or punishment and can be applied to not only persons with disabilities but to non-disabled persons treated as if they were disabled.[78] Finally, there is a right to a 'fair and public hearing within a reasonable time by an independent and impartial tribunal established by law' for anyone seeking a civil rights determination.[79] These latter articles have spawned a robust jurisprudence on the rights of mentally ill patients.[80]

The First Protocol to the Convention, adopted in 1952, declares that '[n]o person should be denied the right to education'.[81] According to a leading commentator, this text has so far failed to protect students with disabilities from educational discrimination, in part because of the timidity of the European Commission and Court on Human Rights and the lack of an appropriate test case strategy by NGOs.[82]

Europe has developed several documents that are relevant to persons with disabilities including the European Social Charter and the Treaty of Amsterdam. Although representative of the old paradigm, the European Social Charter contains a clause on the rights of persons with intellectual or physical disabilities to vocational training and rehabilitation. Thus, the contracting parties are to provide training facilities, 'including, where necessary, specialized institutions' as well as 'measures to encourage employers to admit disabled persons to employment'.[83] This text reflects now dated views that sheltered employment in specialized institutions rather than affirmative measures to include persons with disabilities in the general labor market should be a dominant mode for their workforce participation.[84]

The European Social Charter was revised in 1996, reflecting a paradigm shift from charity and welfare to human rights for persons with disabilities. Thus, persons with disabilities have the declared 'right to independence, social integration, and participation in the life of the community'.[85] Article 15 of the modernized Social Charter calls for more inclusive measures for education and vocational training, access to employment in the ordinary working environment with adjustments to working conditions if necessary, and the promotion of the 'full social integration and the participation in the life of the community' for persons with disabilities.

The Treaty of Amsterdam, which became effective in 1999, amended the Treaty on the European Union. The Conference leading to the Amsterdam Treaty agreed that its institutions shall take account of the needs of persons with disabilities.[86] Here again, this 'Declaration Regarding Persons with a Disability' points to a paradigm shift in approaches to persons with intellectual and other disabilities.

G. UN Specialized Agencies

The specialized agencies of the UN increasingly demonstrate a human rights paradigm shift that can benefit persons with intellectual disabilities. As previously noted, the International Labor Organization (ILO) through Convention No 159,[87] ratified by fifty-six countries, has six articles that correspond to the employment of Rule 7 of the Standard Rules. For example, the ILO Convention calls for policies based on principles of equal opportunity between workers with disabilities and other workers[88] and encourages special positive measures as not being discriminatory against non-disabled workers.[89] Signatories shall also, by law, regulation, or other method, give effect to these and other principles of vocational rehabilitation and employment policies for persons with disabilities.[90] Thus, this Convention can spur the creation of other disability nondiscrimination laws.[91]

The World Health Organization, less tangibly, has entered into discussions between the Disability Rapporteur and its regional rehabilitation advisers resulting in human rights recommendations related to disability. The primary recommendations focus on intensifying anti-discrimination efforts, including disability organizations in all phases of countries' resource programs, offering guiding national policies in developing countries and conducting a broad media campaign linking disability issues and the Standard Rules.

The UN Educational, Scientific and Cultural Organization (UNESCO) has for over thirty years promoted special education, an area that has undergone a rights revolution that has had major impacts on children with intellectual disabilities. Since 1980, it has compiled countrywide practices in this field, publishing a 1996 study on legislation in fifty-two countries. In 1994, it organized the World Conference on Special Needs Education in which ninety countries participated. Held in Salamanca, Spain, the resulting Salamanca Declaration contains numerous clauses that promote the human rights paradigm in disability.

In addition, the UN Children's Fund (UNICEF) has disseminated the Standard Rules, along with the Convention on Rights of the Child and a policy paper on children in need of special protection, to its 150 country and regional offices. These steps offer information that can benefit children with intellectual and other disabilities.

H. The Paradigm Shift in World Conferences

Efforts to place disability rights concerns on the world stage must be intensified to gain parity with other human rights advances. The 1995 World Summit for Social Development in Copenhagen produced modest gains in that respect, but far more needs to be accomplished. The Fourth World Conference on Women, held in Beijing from 4–15 September 1995, also raised the profile of disability rights and sought to devise actions to carry out disability human rights standards. As previously noted, the UN Declaration of Vienna made progress as well by strengthening the recognition of the rights of persons with intellectual disabilities by reaffirming that 'all human rights and fundamental freedoms are universal and thus unreservedly include persons with disabilities'.[92]

I. The Paradigm Shift in Reports and Resolutions

Several UN reports stress rights as a key element in disability-related matters. In 1992, for example, the UN published the comprehensive *Human Rights and Disabled Persons* by Special Rapporteur Leandro Despouy. Reports by UN Special Rapporteur Lindqvist on the implementation of the Standard Rules on the Equalization of Opportunities for Persons with Disabilities have also drawn attention to their human rights. He has chosen to concentrate on six selected Rules, focusing in particular on employment rights, monitoring the International Labor Organization's Convention No 159, and the laws and practices of the fifty-six countries ratifying this convention.

A long series of recommendations and resolutions by the UN and its specialized agencies also manifest a shift from viewing disability as a charitable, medical issue to one of human rights of persons with disabilities. For instance, the World Programme of Action Concerning Disabled Persons, adopted by the General Assembly in 1982,[93] is a comprehensive set of objectives, recommendations, and action steps for implementing the human rights paradigm in the disability field. In 201 paragraphs, it stresses legislation, human rights, and self-advocacy. From an intellectual disabilities perspective, it is advanced in recognizing the heterogeneity of people with disabilities including the different kinds of barriers and the different ways of overcoming them for 'the mentally retarded',[94] including their then embryonic self-advocacy movement.[95]

In conceptual terms, the program has as its objective the goals of 'full participation' and 'equality' for persons with disabilities.[96] As a precursor to the Standard Rules, it defines equalization of opportunities as the accessibility of society to all in spheres such as the physical and cultural environment, educational and work opportunities, and housing.[97] '[H]aving much to learn from the self-advocacy movement of persons with other disabilities', it acknowledges their demands for 'a voice of their own' and their 'right to take part in decision making and discussion'.[98] Once again recognizing differences, the text in all extended discussion of equalization of opportunities refers to the need to cater to people with reduced 'mental faculties' and their need for accommodations in education and employment.[99] For persons with permanent disabilities (such as those with intellectual disabilities), access to community-based supports are to enable them to 'live as normally as possible' at home and in the community.[100]

Legislation is seen as an important tool for remedying many of the problems of exclusion and inaccessibility. Legislative progress is noted in guaranteeing rights to schooling, employment, access to community facilities and nondiscrimination.[101] Although referring to the movement away from institutions, the document recognizes such realities as leper colonies and the unjustified institutionalization of persons with disabilities.[102]

Implementation proposals urge national legislation to eliminate disability discrimination as well as to protect persons with disabilities from inhumane or degrading treatment and to secure their rights to education, work, and social security.[103] This program is designed not only for developed countries, but also for developing countries, including the least developed countries; although, their resource constraints, cultural traditions, and state of socio-economic development may curtail implementation capacities.[104] Thus, this 1982 document, while non-binding, offers a blueprint that could advance the human and legal rights of persons with intellectual disabilities throughout the world.

The Tallinn Guidelines for Action on Resource Development in the Field of Disability has as one of its guiding philosophies that persons with disabilities should 'exercise their rights of full citizenship' and participate as equal partners in decision-making processes in policy and program development since they 'are agents of their own destiny rather than objects of care'.[105]

In 1991, the UN General Assembly adopted the Principles for the Protection of Persons with Mental Illness and the Improvement of Mental

Health Care. Although these principles may affect persons with intellectual disability misdiagnosed as mentally ill or those with dual disabilities, they are clearly limited to those persons receiving 'treatment, care and rehabilitation for a mental illness or suspected mental illness'.[106] From an intellectual disabilities perspective, it is unfortunate that a parallel set of principles have not been adopted, since there are many comparable issues affecting persons with intellectual disabilities, such as nondiscrimination,[107] incapacity,[108] the applicability of the related general human rights idea,[109] limitations on sterilization,[110] and a comprehensive set of human rights protections pertaining to facilities and their admission processes.[111]

J. Implementation of Human Rights Standards

1. Proposed UN Convention on Elimination of Discrimination against Persons with Disabilities

Various NGOs have labored to initiate a UN treaty on disability discrimination. Preparatory work for such an essential 'missing link' in the thematic treaties of the UN occurred at the December 1999 Interregional Seminar and Symposium on International Norms and Standards Relating to Disability, cosponsored by the UN, the Equal Opportunities Commission of Hong Kong, and the Faculty of Law of the University of Hong Kong. This UN Symposium on International Disability Rights recommended that the UN, Member States, and disability NGOs 'should initiate the process for the adoption of an international treaty dealing specifically with the human rights of people with disabilities'.

The NGO Beijing Declaration followed with a similar recommendation. Although initial UN reactions to a disability rights treaty have not been favorable, Ireland and other countries support such a treaty.

2. Inter-American Convention on Elimination of Discrimination by Reason of Disability

Although the campaign for an international human rights convention on disability created by Italy and Sweden faltered in the UN, the idea is gaining momentum. Indeed, a draft InterAmerican Convention on the Elimination of All Forms of Discrimination by Reason of Disability has at least four signatories. The large population of persons with disabilities in the Western Hemisphere has significant human rights concerns. Adoption of such a treaty could raise the visibility of the concern for the rights of persons with disabilities.[112]

The draft convention had its origins in a 1996 working group, and a draft proposal by Panama and cosponsored by Costa Rica.[113] The text defines disability, discrimination by reason of disability and proposes that States Parties prevent and eliminate all forms of discrimination, progressively and in conformity with domestic laws. On 7 June 1999, the Organization of

American States (OAS) in plenary session adopted the InterAmerican Convention and its eventual full promulgation can be expected.

K. Implementation of Human Rights Standards Related to Intellectual Disabilities

Compared to discrimination based on race or gender, disability discrimination has evoked only weak and intermittent international action. Because of their unique vulnerabilities, persons with intellectual disabilities have proved to be the last of the last in realizing the benefit of such action.

1. The Spectrum of Implementation Strategies

The all-too familiar disconnect between UN declarations and treaties and the realities on the ground is especially conspicuous for people with intellectual disabilities. In recent years, the work of specialist disability NGOs, courageous jurists, national legislators and advocates has begun to narrow this gap. This chapter provides an overview of some successful strategies and their impacts.

2. Nongovernmental Organizations

Although there are many useful human rights standards, by and large the intellectual disability community has been uninformed, unengaged, and properly skeptical that human rights talk at the UN Headquarters, in Vienna or Geneva, can translate into real progress on the ground. Although NGOs in the past have sometimes placed disability-related human rights abuses on the world stage, they often focused on such issues as the forced confinement of the sane in institutions for the mentally ill (eg, the Amnesty-backed campaign on the misuse of Soviet-era psychiatric hospitals to imprison political dissidents).[114] The non-treatment, mistreatment, or alleged cruel treatment of people with intellectual disabilities in facilities or in the community has seldom, if ever, received the attention of mainstream human rights groups.[115] Given this history, it remains to be seen whether NGOs will become more assertive in applying international human rights standards and methodologies to people with intellectual disabilities.

Mainstream human rights NGOs need to initiate disability rights projects similar to those now existing in the spheres of women's rights and children's rights.[116] Groups like Inclusion International could collaborate with well-established advocacy groups like Amnesty International or Human Rights Watch. In addition, CAVNET (Communities Against Violence Network), an international group based in the United States, which focuses on violence against people with disabilities, among other issues, has worked collaboratively with Amnesty International to raise consciousness and share information and resources.[117] With a lengthening agenda, the disability NGOs need to draw on additional staff and legal expertise commensurate with the global and extreme problems of abuse they encounter.[118] Mental Disability Rights International, a dynamic organization devoted to increasing human rights awareness and compliance in Central Europe, Latin America, and other parts of the world, is another force for promoting intergovernmental and NGO assistance.

Other international projects on disability rights can assist people with intellectual disabilities. In developing nations and the emerging democracies of Central and Eastern Europe, the Ashoka Foundation has supported 'over 25 Ashoka fellows [who] are showing how even poor societies can bring care to the 95% of their disabled [*sic*] who receive no help now'.[119] Not only do such social entrepreneurs need training in human rights for persons with disabilities, but their example could inspire similar efforts by other nonprofits and governmental development agencies. The Rosemary F. Dybwad International Fellowship also supports short-term study visits and research on human rights that focus on people with intellectual disabilities.

3. Foreign Aid

Wealthier nations can also supply foreign aid to the development of model programs and professional training in the disability field. For instance, the US Agency for International Development (USAID), through the Joint Distribution Committee, created a successful program for community living for persons with intellectual disabilities and developed a cadre of innovative professionals in this field in the Czech Republic. Unfortunately, such efforts may be hard to sustain as short-sighted politics reduce support for such overseas initiatives. In the United States, for example, reduction of foreign aid occurred just at a time when disability aid projects were being created, with cuts of $18.2 billion to $16 billion in one fiscal year and deeper cuts looming in 2002.

4. Case Law

The high water mark for use of the disability declarations in the United States occurred only five months after the General Assembly's 1971 adoption of the Declaration on the Rights of Mentally Retarded Persons. In that year, Federal District Court Judge Frank M. Johnson, Jr. issued the historic right to habilitation decree for the residents of Alabama's Partlow State School and Hospital.[120] As the authority for the proposition that the only constitutional justification for civilly committing a person to an institution is the provision of an 'inviolable constitutional right to habilitation', Judge Johnson cited the 1971 UN Declaration. In his footnote 6 of the *Wyatt* opinion Judge Johnson stated:

It is interesting to note that the Court's decision with regard to the right of the mentally retarded to habilitation is supported not only by applicable legal authority, but also by a resolution adopted on December 27, 1971, by the General Assembly of the United Nations. That resolution, entitled 'Declaration on the Rights of the Mentally Retarded', reads in pertinent part:

'The mentally retarded person has a right to proper medical care and physical therapy and to such education, training, rehabilitation and guidance as will enable him to develop his ability and maximum potential.'

Judge Johnson read this 1971 Declaration in no brief and heard it from no plaintiff or amici counsel. Instead Gunnar Dybwad, the lead expert witness in the *Wyatt* mental retardation hearings, on his own initiative wrote a personal letter to Judge Johnson expressing his sense of appreciation for the court's intervention and attached a copy of the Declaration. Professor Dybwad and other leading national experts exposed the brutalities of institutionalization. In dramatic testimony quoted by the appellate court, he observed that:

The situation which exists and obviously has existed in Partlow for a long time is one of storage, of persons. I am using that word because I would not use care, which involves—has a certain qualitative character, and I would not even use the word, custodial, because custody, in my term, means safekeeping. And, as is visible to the visitor at the present time, employees at Partlow are not in a position to effect safekeeping, considering the number of people they have to take care of; so I would say it is a storage problem at the moment.[121]

Professor Dybwad then concluded with this still unrealized prediction, 'if Partlow has any business in the future, it is to replace itself with a network of small, community-based residential and day programs.'[122]

The *Wyatt* decree with its forty-nine concrete human rights standards, ranging from checks on painful aversive treatments to requirements of least restrictive habilitation settings, is landmark litigation. Described as 'the most significant case in the annals of forensic psychiatry'[123] and as having 'massive influence on the development of state-level' statutory bills of rights, *Wyatt* and its footnote 6 represents a 'seminal decision' on the rights of persons with intellectual disabilities. In the hundreds of residents' rights and other disability rights cases that were to follow, it stirred many refinements and reactions.[124] Indeed, the *Wyatt* case itself is not over. The plaintiffs, allied with the US Justice Department, subsequently applied the Americans with Disabilities Act (ADA) (a comprehensive US civil rights law) as well as other human rights standards to enforce remedies to identify 'individuals who remain inappropriately institutionalized' and to gain 'transfer to community programs for them'.[125]

Although law review articles have stressed the potential uses of UN standards in disability cases, statutes, regulations, and in informing good practices and policies, it is difficult to assess the impact of such human rights standards in this field.[126] In general, US courts have seldom used international human rights law to redress abuses, a reluctance that two recent commentators charge is due to 'unfamiliarity and perhaps a degree of intellectual laziness' as well as 'concerns about institutional competence and deference to the political branches'.[127] However, US courts are more willing now to bring foreign human rights abuses to the dock of justice.[128] Nonetheless, cases, whether involving abuses against persons with intellectual disabilities in the United States or in foreign countries, are still rarities.

In other countries, judges have made strong use of human rights declarations for persons with intellectual disabilities. The European Court has proven less deferential to national determinations.[129] There the Court found that the lack of a criminal sanction for the rape of a 16-year-old girl with an intellectual disability violated her right to be free from the privacy-invading actions of another person. In Canada, *Commission des droits de la personne du Quebec v St-Jean-sur-Richelieu*,[130] upheld an autistic child's right to appropriate education in both special class and regular class settings, using both international and Quebec law. Quebec's Court of Appeals held that the Quebec Charter of Human Rights and Freedoms[131] guarantees that persons with disabilities must be integrated into regular classrooms and that the failure of a school board to adopt such integration policies is violative of Quebec's Charter of Human Rights and Freedoms. In reaching its decision, the court cited the UN Charter, the Universal Declaration of Human Rights, the Convention on the Rights of the Child, the Declaration on the Rights of Mentally Retarded Persons, and the Declaration on the Rights of Disabled Persons, noting that these human rights standards 'have been extended to the domestic legal order applicable to Quebec'. These rights are incorporated through the economic and social rights defined in the Quebec Charter of Human Rights and Freedoms.

Recognizing this body of law as creating 'a *de facto* equality, a tangible equality', the court observed that it 'would be illusory to allow handicapped students free access to adapted educational services within the perspective of integrating them into regular classes in so far as possible if no substantive steps were taken to promote or enhance the exercise of this right'.[132] Because of the school board's failure to integrate this child into a regular classroom, the court held that the board's policy constituted indirect discrimination. It therefore ordered the board to pay for an escort or special education teacher to aid the child's integration into a regular class for reading instruction.

Ireland has also made high-profile use of international law in a disability case. In *O'Donoghue v Minister for Health*,[133] the High Court concluded that the government deprived a child with a disability of a free appropriate education in violation of broad guarantees of a free[134] required education under Ireland's Constitution.[135] The government argued that it did not violate these provisions because the child was 'ineducable', as having Reye's syndrome and being 'helpless'. The judge held that in light of:

the whole momentum, as evidenced in the Declarations emanating from the Vatican, from the United Nations, and in the Protocol of the European Convention on Human Rights...towards the provision for every individual of such education as will enable him (or her)... 'to make the best possible use of his [or her] inherent and potential capacities, physical, mental and moral'...I am unable to accept the contention that the applicant or other children suffering from profound or severe mental handicap are to be regarded as 'ineducable'.[136]

In support of this position, the court cited the Declaration of Rights of Mentally Retarded Persons, specifically Article 2, which upholds 'the rights of all mentally handicapped persons of whatever degree to appropriate educational services'.[137] It also referred to the Declaration on the Rights of Disabled Persons and its provisions on the rights to dignity, education, and measures to foster self-reliance.[138] Finally, the court's opinion refers at length to the Universal Declaration of Human Rights.[139] This scholarly judgment also surveys precedents from the United States, such as *Mills v Board of Education of the District of Columbia*,[140] and its constitutional rationale that the failure to provide education is not excused by a claim of insufficient funds.[141] Thus, the decision rests on Irish constitutional law buttressed by *Pennsylvania Association for Retarded Citizens v Commonwealth of Pennsylvania*,[142] international human rights and the common law of various jurisdictions.

In an involuntary sterilization case, *Department of Health and Community Services v J.W.B. (In re Marion)*,[143] the High Court of Australia severely restricted a guardian's right to authorize the involuntary sterilization of a person with a disability. Judge Brennan's eloquent opinion quotes the UN Declaration on the Rights of Mentally Retarded Persons, and notes '[i]ntellectual disability justifies no impairment of human dignity, no invasion of the right to personal integrity.'[144] In summary, despite these exceptional cases, international human rights standards have not been adequately used in the defense of the rights of persons with intellectual impairments.

5. National Legislation

National laws have also incorporated international treaties and declaration of rights. International standards, however, must be harmonized with national laws, characteristics, and values. For instance, Andrew Clapham has canvassed the issues facing the UK courts in implementing the European Convention on Human Rights through the Human Rights Act.[145] Initially, he notes that mental patients have been among the primary beneficiaries of European Convention on Human Rights (ECHR) judicial decisions emerging from Strasbourg, with their disenfranchisement making

them especially legitimate subjects of judicial review.[146] The UK enactment
of the Human Rights Act 1998 has now resolved the issue of whether
domestic judges can declare the incompatibility of primary domestic legislation with the ECHR and can apply other judicial remedies to incorporate
an international treaty into national law. Because the Human Rights Act
reaches governments' acts of commission, but not those of omission or
those of private actors, it remains to be seen how useful the Act will prove
for persons with intellectual disabilities. Certainly, the Act will help to educate the general public and the judiciary on the fundamental human rights
of these and other UK citizens.[147]

Numerous countries have enacted constitutional and statutory provisions that advance the rights of persons with intellectual and other disabilities. Norway, for instance, has created a provisional Ombudsman
regarding the care of persons with disabilities for the years 1999–2002.
The Ombudsman's main duties are to 'assist people who need the help of
the health and social services authorities and/or their relatives with
complaints relating to this sector, investigate conditions that they find
unsatisfactory, and help to formulate complaints which are then sent to
the appropriate administrative appeals body'.[148] Furthermore, Norway
has established a personal assistant program to aid persons with
disabilities.[149]

One US state has adopted international standards. Tennessee, for
instance, adopted virtually verbatim the ILSMH Declaration on the Rights
of Mentally Retarded Persons. On the federal level the Developmental
Disabilities Assistance and Bill of Rights Act of 2000[150] has enacted six
minimum standards of human rights as a condition for federal funding to
the states for their developmental disabilities programs.[151]

6. National Disability Plans and Recommendations

The international community needs coherent policy making by national
and local governments to ensure that human rights standards result in
changes to existing norms, programs, and practices. Disability services
in industrialized nations consume extraordinary resources, but many of
those funds are used in ways that do not promote independence,
inclusion, empowerment, and human rights.[152] For instance, Bob Williams,
former US Commissioner for the Administration on Developmental
Disabilities has expressed outrage that the United States 'continue[s] to
spend between two and three hundred billion dollars a year keeping
Americans with disabilities economically disenfranchised and, for the
most part, needlessly dependent'.[153] Although the Standard Rules call for
national planning, local planning, and training programs for local staff
with 'manuals or check lists', these broad recommendations need clarification and examples based on practical experience.[154]

One example, in the United States, began in 1994 when the Clinton Administration launched a far-reaching National Disability Policy with high-level White House and interdepartmental representation. It achieved some success in bringing coherence to the bewildering array of benefits programs, service systems, and civil rights policies affecting persons with disabilities. For example, one outcome of this process was the enactment of the Ticket-to-Work and Work Incentives Act,[155] a major step to realizing the Administrations goals of inclusion, independence and empowerment for America's over 53 million citizens with disabilities.

In 1995, the White House Conference on Aging mobilized another important constituency in developing recommendations that aid older persons with disabilities. It recommended changes that will benefit older persons with intellectual and other disabilities, including those dealing with alternatives to guardianship.[156] Some of its resolutions addressed such topics as less restrictive options to guardianship, maintenance of benefits for all legal immigrants, and the provision of strengthened delivery of legal service through 'legal assistance outreach to low-income persons, ethnic and minority persons, persons with disabilities'.[157]

These examples provide meaningful guidance for other national governments to bring disability rights to the forefront of their political and social agendas.

L. Conclusion

This chapter argues that persons with intellectual disabilities, although they have real cognitive differences, wish to be regarded foremost as human beings. Taking this challenge to heart, scholars and activists must continue to think globally and act locally.

The essential proposition is to affirm the universal nature of human rights and their application to persons with intellectual disabilities. On the 'special versus general rights' debate, although persons with intellectual disabilities and related intellectual disabilities have the same universal rights as others, they require additional rights and legal protection to assure reasonable accommodations and the enjoyment of the general rights experienced in their cultures and countries. No one code, no one solution, will fit all countries. But too many wrongs remain, and too many deficiencies prevail to permit the status quo to continue.

One step is to endorse and act on the recommendations set out in the Declaration issued at the Yale Law School's International Symposium on the Rights of People with Mental Retardation.[158] The Declaration defines standards, principles and strategies to promote the full implementation of human rights everywhere.[159] Ethical perspectives also supply rationales for the legal and human rights frameworks for assisting persons with intellectual disabilities and their families. The advancement of those rights is linked to the global burdens of a grotesque history that marked—and in some places still marks—people with such disabilities as second-class citizens.

Within the field of intellectual disabilities the debate on rights has shifted. The issues are no longer whether rights—human and legal—must be respected, but how far and how fast change must come so that individuals with such disabilities can enjoy their present rights. Self-advocates, other consumers, professionals, and policymakers can work together to make rights for present enjoyment, education, habilitation, protection from harm, dignity, and self-determination. Policymakers confronting difficult issues of distributive justice must ensure that persons with disabilities are allocated their fair share of resources.[160] Professionals in the field are now more frequently guided by their clients' basic rights and aspirations. They are prepared to speak out when their clients are exposed to harm. This requires professional action that presupposes some knowledge and training about those rights and basic techniques of advocacy. In these ways, the field can recognize not only human rights but also the practical barriers to narrow gaps to their implementation.

Lawyers, policymakers, and activists must review and apply more creatively the full body of international human rights law. They can use the body of international human rights law in all its forms to prevent existing declarations and standards from simply becoming a record of good intentions. By studying and applying the Universal Declaration of Human Rights of 1948, the UN Declaration on the Rights of Mentally Retarded Persons of 1971, the UN Declaration on the Rights of Disabled Persons of 1975, the Convention on the Rights of Children of 1990, and the UN Standard Rules on the Equalization of Opportunities for People with Disabilities of 1993, advocates and engaged scholars can use these instruments as guides for policy making and action. The citation of such standards in leading disability cases in Australia, Canada, Ireland, the United States, and in other authoritative contexts is an extremely positive development.

Advocacy is the lifeblood of human rights for persons with intellectual disabilities. Because the lives of people with such disabilities are vulnerable when measured by a narrow cost-benefit calculus rather than by legal, religious, and ethical perspectives that offer some protection to the vulnerable, advocates must be forever vigilant. Advocates must also have the persistence and flexibility to adjust their styles from cooperative to adversarial modes, from an intense involvement with an individual to systemic frames of reference. The necessity for qualified legal assistance and for persistent action at national and international levels is recognized in the UN Declaration on the Rights of Disabled Persons. Thus, those who would implement human rights standards must draw on multiple levels of advocacy to mirror the protracted struggles to claim rights and awaken responsibilities.

Members of professional associations increasingly endorse and apply human rights standards. Professional associations are active in the many crucial policy arenas where courts, legislatures, and other opinion makers confront global human rights and challenges. They are also more responsive to the expressed aspirations and wishes of clients. For instance, the American Association on Mental Retardation (AAMR) Policies and Positions on Legal and Social Issues give primacy to basic human rights and urge 'national and international recognition of basic human rights and freedoms for all citizens including those with disabilities'.[161] AAMR further supports 'vigorous, sustained advocacy designed to further such basic rights and freedoms including adequate food, clothing, shelter, education, health care, and economic security; the right to self-determination; and freedoms such as freedom of association, freedom of expression and freedom from torture and oppression'.[162] AAMR and its sister organizations, for instance, are frequent writers of amici briefs to the US Supreme Court and other appellate courts on critical issues to this constituency, such as community-based living, nondiscrimination, and the death penalty and persons with mental retardation.[163]

The interests of persons with intellectual disabilities requires more than episodic attention. Since those interests do not have a strong political power base, their advocates often draw on the prestige of established figures or make common cause with more powerful groups, people with disabilities in general or senior citizens. The Standard Rules also calls for 'national monitoring and evaluation of disability programmes in the implementation of the rules'.[164] This activity also requires national and regional planning to implement rights, desired public policies, and societal outcomes.

Activists must incorporate human rights principles not only in national and local laws but in the customs and ordinary interactions of the people who must apply human rights principles. Human rights and legal protection gain strength when they are not seen as alien or coercively imposed by powers that are distant from people's everyday lives. For instance, laws can enhance opportunities for integration, but they will not keep a schoolchild with disabilities from being shunned by her classmates or an adult in a group home from being treated like an intruder by his neighbors. The human rights paradigm has begun to change those actions and attitudes.

Advocates must first focus on the minimum role of government and enlightened public opinion—to first do no harm to the 'objects of our benevolence'. That caution is a result of the long history of executive, judicial, legislative, and private sector ineffectiveness in preventing or minimizing abuse, discrimination, and degrading treatment. Scholars and advocates must better learn how to protect persons with intellectual disabilities from abuse and how to defend their human rights from callous indifference. Understanding what causes human beings to abuse each other and what rights can remedy—or better yet deter—abuse is an important objective. As the eighteenth-century British statesman Edmund Burke aptly noted, 'The only thing necessary for the triumph of evil is for good men to do nothing.'

Criminal justice concerns are also often overlooked in this field of human rights. People with disabilities are 'more likely than others to be subjected to acts of violence and abuse that are proscribed by criminal and civil law'.[165] They sometimes face treatment practices or actions by others in their environment that are objectively painful to them. The processing of persons with intellectual disabilities as alleged offenders is another context that is fraught with risk of injustice and mistreatment. Individuals with disabilities may be the subject of miscarriages of justice—sometimes well-publicized, sometimes unknown. In the United States, they are even subject to capital punishment.[166]

As societies change, disability approaches have moved from paternalism to empowerment, from dependence to independence, from models of inferior status to models of more egalitarian participation. In this context, people with intellectual disabilities seek supported rather than supplanted decision making. This trend is a growing one. It requires more cross-cultural research to compare the costs and benefits of different legal approaches (eg, mentors, personal assistants, or limited guardians).

Leadership from all points on the spectrum—scholars, self-advocates, family members, intellectual disability professionals, public officials, NGOs, and others with humanitarian values—remains the indispensable ingredient. Leadership from all parts of the world is equally essential. In different voices, such leaders must ask this question: What are the provisions in a civilized society that must be made for the education, treatment, housing, work and recreational opportunities for those with intellectual disabilities? This leadership will require the courage and persistence to believe that human rights can and must become human realities in all parts of the globe.

These leaders must continue to dispel polite fictions that mask human abuse and take risks so that human wrongs are exposed and global rights are given content. That is the permanent work of turning wrongs to rights.

NOTES

1. International League of Societies for the Mentally Handicapped (ILSMH), *Declaration of General and Special Rights of the Mentally Retarded* (Brussels: ILSMH, 1968).

2. SS Herr, 'Rights of Disabled Persons: International Principles and American Experiences' (1980) 12 *Columbia Human Rights L Rev* 1, 2.

3. United Nations, *Declaration on the Rights of Mentally Retarded Persons*, GA Res 2856 (XXVI), 26 UN GAOR Supp (No 29) at 93, UN Doc A/8429 (1971).

4. R MacNamara, frontispiece to B Blatt, *Souls in Extremis: An Anthology on Victims and Victimizers* (Boston: Allyn & Bacon, 1973) 1 (emphasis added).

5. R Dworkin, *Life's Dominion: An Argument about Abortion, Euthanasia, and Individual Freedom* (New York: Vintage Books, 1993) 84.

6. S Howe, *Twenty-Seventh Report of the Superintendent of the Massachusetts School for Idiotic and Feeble-Minded Youth* (1874) 24, quoted in SS Herr, *Rights and Advocacy for Retarded People* (Lexington, Mass: DC Heath, 1983) 28.

7. Courts in several common law countries evince sensitivity to the reproductive rights of persons with retardation. *In re Eve* 31 DLR (4th) 1 (October 23, 1986) (Supreme Court of Canada); *In re B* (A Minor) (Wardship: Sterilization) [1988] 2 WLR 1213; [1987] 2 All ER 206, HL (E); *In re F* (Mental Patient: Sterilization) [1989] 2 WLR, HL; *Wentzel v Montgomery County General Hospital* 447 A 2d 1244 (Md 1982). Those cases are deeply critical of the eugenics approach endorsed in *Buck v Bell* 274 US 200 (1927). There, the US Supreme Court left deep stains on American constitutional jurisprudence when it upheld compulsory sterilization on the pseudo-science grounds that it was necessary in 'order to prevent our being swamped with incompetence. It is better for all the world, if instead of waiting to execute degenerate offspring for crime, or to let them starve for their imbecility, society can prevent those who are manifestly unfit from continuing their kind....Three generations of imbeciles are enough.' ibid. at 207. This ill-informed judicial edict is no longer considered good law or policy. *In re Romero* 790 P 2d 819, 821 (Co 1990); *In re Mental Health of K.G.F.* 29 P 3d 485 (Mt 2001).

8. R Burt, 'Constitutional Rights of Handicapped People and the Teaching of Parables' in SE Lammers and A Verhey (eds), *On Moral Medicine: Theological Perspectives in Medical Ethics* (Grand Rapids, Mich: Eerdmans Publishing Co, 1987) 582, 586. He further adds that the widespread use of isolated residential institutions was a form of abuse, viewing 'this effort to banish retarded people' as 'a kind of warfare with them—often waged with extraordinary brutality, as the history of residential institutions testifies'. ibid.

9. Herr (n 6 above) 107–159.

10. *Halderman v Pennhurst State School and Hospital* 446 F Supp 1295 (ED Pa 1977), *substantially aff'd*, 612 F 2d 84, 113 (3rd Cir 1979) (arguing that residents and parents must be allowed to participate 'in the design of alternative facilities well-suited' to the right to live in the least restrictive environment possible), *cert. granted* 447 US 904 (1980), *and rev'd and rem'd sub nom. Pennhurst State School and Hospital v Halderman* 451 US 1 (1981); *on remand at en banc Halderman v Pennhurst State School & Hospital* 673 F 2d 647 (3rd Cir 1982), *cert. granted* 457 US 1131 (1982), *rev'd and rem'd* 465 US 89 (1984). As of 1993, litigation over Pennhurst State School & Hospital had resulted in over 500 court orders and 28 published court opinions; and the district court was still busy denying 'meritless motions' by the Commonwealth to modify their 'Final Settlement Agreement' entered as a consent decree on 5 April 1985. *Halderman v Pennhurst State School and Hospital* 834 F Supp 757 (ED Pa 1993). The most recent court

order, entered in October 1995, resulted in a 'Quality Assurance Plan' agreed to by both parties and endorsed by Judge Broderick to ensure adequate habilitation in the community through a system of individualized planning and care. [hereinafter *Pennhurst*] 1995 US Dist. LEXIS 15006 (ED Pa 1995).

New York State Association for Retarded Citizens Inc v Rockefeller 357 F Supp 752 (EDNY 1973) (ordering immediate hiring of ward attendants, nurses, physical therapists, physicians, and recreational staff to insure the prevention of the residents' physical deterioration), *aff'd sub nom. New York State Association for Retarded Citizens, Inc v Carey* 596 F 2d 27 (2nd Cir 1979), *cert. denied* 444 US 836 (1979) [hereinafter *Willowbrook*]. The Willowbrook Review Panel established to oversee compliance with the consent judgment effectively ceased to exist in 1980 when the state legislature refused to appropriate funds for its continuance. The litigation, however, continued and in 1983 the State of New York was found to be in non-compliance with the consent judgment. *New York State Association for Retarded Citizens v Carey* 706 F 2d 956 (2nd Cir 1983), *cert. denied* 464 US 915 (1983) later proceeding at 727 F 2d (2nd Cir 1984) affirming order denying motion for injunction.

Wyatt v Stickney 344 F Supp 387 (MD Ala 1972) (establishing minimum constitutional standards for adequate care and habilitation of mentally retarded people and appointing a human rights committee for Partlow State School and Hospital), *aff'd in part, rev'd in part, and rem'd sub nom. Wyatt v Aderholt* 503 F 2d 1305 (5th Cir 1974). *Wyatt v Poundstone* 892 F Supp 1410 (MD Ala 1995) (establishing continuing violations of residents' rights at Alabama institutions.

Welsch v Likins 550 F 2d 1122 (8th Cir 1977); *Massachusetts Ass'n for Retarded Citizens, Inc v King* 668 F 2d 602, 604 (1st Cir 1981) (discussing the unconstitutional conditions in Massachusetts State Hospitals) [Belchertown State School—Massachusetts]; *Ricci v Okin* 823 F Supp 984 (D Mass 1993) (detailing comprehensive order closing the federal court's twenty-one year oversight of five state institutions for the mentally retarded) [Belchertown, Fernald, Monson, Wrentham, and Dever—Massachusetts]; *Garrity v Gallen* 522 F Supp 171 (DNH 1981) (establishing a 26-point order for reforming New Hampshire's habilitation programs for people with mental retardation) [Laconia—New Hampshire]; *United States v Solomon* 563 F 2d 1121 (4th Cir 1977) (finding that the federal government lacked authority to bring suit against a Maryland State Hospital for violating the rights of mentally retarded residents) [Rosewood—Maryland].

In 1980 Congress passed the Civil Rights of Institutionalized Persons Act, PL 96–247 (May 23, 1980), 94 Stat 349, 42 USC §1997 (a)–(j) (2001), to provide the US with such authority to bring pattern and practice violations. The Justice Department then refiled a suit against Rosewood and quickly entered into a consent agreement to improve staffing ratios, reduce the overuse of restraints, and provide programs to treat persons with severe self-injurious or aggressive behavioral problems. This consent decree was the first achieved by the US Department of Justice involving a mental retardation institution in the wake of the 1980 Act. Associated Press, 'Maryland Agrees to Improve Facility for Retarded' (18 January 1985) *Los Angeles Times* 26.

11. Report of the Committee of Enquiry into Mental Handicap Nursing and Care, 1979, Cmnd. 7468-I (Chairman: Peggy Jay, vol I, 1979) 143.

12. HG Gallagher, '"Slapping Up Spastics": The Persistence of Social Attitudes Toward People with Disabilities' (1995) 10 *Issues in Law & Medicine* 401, 402, 404.
13. UN Charter, Preamble.
14. MA Glendon, *A World Made New: Eleanor Roosevelt and the Universal Declaration of Human Rights* (New York: Random House, 2001) 136.
15. They meticulously and officially recorded 70,273 killings under the centralized T-4 *Aktion* operation and killed an additional 200,000 Germans with disabilities through so-called 'wild euthanasia'. Gallagher (n 12 above) 405. The lessons they learned from those appalling acts were soon applied on ever wider scales, until six million Jews, and millions of Russians, gypsies, homosexuals, labor organizers, intellectuals, and other innocents followed them to a tortured end.
16. AH Henkin (ed), *Honoring Human Rights: From Peace to Justice: Recommendations to the International Community* (Washington, DC: Aspen Institute, 1998).
17. L Henkin, *The Rights of Man Today* (Boulder, Colo: Westview Press, 1978) xiii.
18. M Minow, *Making All the Difference: Inclusion, Exclusion and American Law* (Ithaca, NY: Cornell Univ Press, 1990) 116–117, 133–134; ML Perlin, *Law and Mental Disability* (Charlottesville, Va: Michie Co, 1994) 280–281, 638–639; ML Perlin, *Mental Disability Law: Civil and Criminal* (Charlottesville, Va: Michie Co, 1989) §4.07–4.19; Herr (n 6 above) 37–38, 25–29, 107–114; LR Jones and RR Parlour (eds), *Wyatt v Stickney: Retrospect and Prospect* (New York: Grune and Stratton, 1981).
19. Centre for Human Rights, *Human Rights Bibliography: United Nations Documents and Publications 1980–1990* (New York: United Nations, 1993) 1296–1298.
20. ibid vol III, 936–40. The UN's Human Right Biography also lists one entry specifically addressing disability and aging (to wit, the UN Decade of Disabled Persons, E/RES/1989/52).
21. ibid.
22. J Mann, L Gostin, S Gruskin, T Brennan, Z Lazzarini, and HV Fineberg, 'Health and Human Rights' (Fall 1994) 1 *Health & Human Rights* 1, 12.
23. Universal Declaration of Human Rights, UN GA Res 217 A (III), UN Doc A/810 (10 December 1948) art I [hereinafter UDHR].
24. ibid.
25. ibid art 25(1).
26. ibid art 5.
27. ibid art 3.
28. ibid art 12.
29. ibid art 23(2).
30. ibid art 26.
31. ibid art 21(2).
32. ibid art 27(1).
33. ibid art 24.
34. I Brownlie, *Basic Documents on Human Rights* (3rd edn, New York: Oxford Univ Press, 1992) 21.
35. UDHR (n 23 above).
36. ILSMH (n 1 above).
37. GA Res 2856, 26 UN GAOR, Supp (No 29) 99, UN Doc A/8429 (1971).
38. GA Res 3447, 30 UN GAOR, Supp (No 34) 92, UN Doc A/10034 (1975).

'Disabled person' is defined as 'any person unable to ensure by himself or herself wholly or partly the necessities of a normal individual and/or social life, as a result of a deficiency, either congenital or not, in his or her physical or mental capabilities.' ibid art 1.

39. ibid art 3.
40. ibid arts 2, 3, 4. D Shraga, 'Human Rights in Emergency Situations under the European Convention on Human Rights' (1986) 16 *Israel Yearbook Human Rights* 217, 231–232.
41. GA Res 3447 (n 38 above) art 6.
42. ibid.
43. ibid arts 5, 8.
44. ibid arts 11, 13.
45. ibid art 12.
46. ICCPR, art 7.
47. ibid art 10.
48. ibid art 26.
49. ICESCR, arts 9, 12(1), 13(2)a.
50. General comment 5, para 1 (E/1995/22).
51. ibid para 2.
52. ibid paras 3, 8.
53. ibid para 10.
54. Organization of African Unity, *African Charter on Human and Peoples' Rights,* OAU Doc CAB/LEG/67/3 rev 5, 21 ILM 58 (1982), (adopted 27 June 1981, entered into force 21 October 1986) art 18(4).
55. Organization of American States, *Additional Protocol to the American Convention on Human Rights in the Area of Economic, Social and Cultural Rights* 'Protocol of San Salvador', OAS Treaty Series No 69, art 18.
56. United Nations, *World Programme of Action Concerning Disabled Persons,* UN Doc A/37/51 (1983).
57. United Nations, *Guidelines for the Establishment and Development of National Coordinating Committees on Disability or Similar Bodies,* A/C.3/46/4, annex I (1991).
58. United Nations, *Principles for the Protection of Persons with Mental Illness and for the Improvement of Mental Health Care,* GA Res A/RES/46/119 (17 December 1991).
59. United Nations, *Standard Rules on the Equalization of Opportunities for Persons with Disabilities,* GA Res A/RES/48/96 (20 December 1993) [hereinafter Standard Rules].
60. *Opened for signature,* 20 November 1990, *entered into force* 2 September 1990, (1989) 28 ILM 1448, at 1456. UN Doc A/44/25. 'Child' is defined as 'every human being below the age of eighteen years'. Convention on the Rights of the Child, art 1.
61. ibid art 23(1). Ratifying nations recognize the child's right to special care appropriate to the individual's condition and the parental or other caregivers' circumstances. This care and assistance 'shall be designed to ensure that the disabled child has effective access to and receives education, training, health care services, rehabilitation services, preparation for employment and recreation opportunities in a manner conducive to the child's achieving the fullest

possible social integration and individual development....' ibid. Under other relevant articles, States Parties recognize the child's right to periodic review of treatment when placed for purposes of care or treatment of physical or mental problems, right to education, right to health and treatment facilities, and right to the nondiscriminatory enjoyment of declared rights irrespective of the child's disability. ibid arts 24, 25, 28.

62. Convention on the Elimination of All Forms of Discrimination Against Women, art 11(e) (entry into force 3 September 1981) GA Res 34/180 (18 December 1979).
63. Standard Rules (n 59 above) Preamble.
64. ibid R 7.
65. ibid R 9, para 2.
66. ibid R 8, paras 4–5.
67. ibid R 7, para 1 ('Laws and regulations in the employment field must not discriminate against persons with disabilities and must not raise obstacles to their employment').
68. ibid Part IV, para 6.
69. Final Report of the Special Rapporteur of the Commission for Social Development on Monitoring the Implementation of the Standard Rules on the Equalization of Opportunities for Persons with Disabilities, Official Records of the Economic and Social Council, Supp (No 4) E/1995/24, chap 1, sec E (1995); Report on First Mandate of the Special Rapporteur, A/52/56; Report on Second Mandate of the Special Rapporteur, E/CN.5/2000/3.
70. The Reykjavik Declaration in Support of the Standard Rules on the Equalization of Opportunities for Persons with Disabilities, reprinted in *ILSMH News* (1994) 16, 23.
71. Vienna Declaration and Programme for Action, World Conference on Human Rights, Vienna, 14–25 June 1993, UN Doc A/CONF.157/23, II (B) (6) (63).
72. ibid.
73. Report of the UN Consultative Expert Group Meeting on International Norms and Standards Relating to Disability (convened by the UN in cooperation with the Boalt School of Law, Univ of California at Berkeley and the World Institute on Disability, December 1998) available at http://www.independentliving.org.
74. Report of a Mission on Behalf of the International Commission of Tourists and the International Commission of Health Professionals, 'Human Rights and Mental Patients in Japan' (1985).
75. European Convention for the Protection of Human Rights and Fundamental Freedoms, opened for signature 4 November 1959, entered into force 3 September 1953, available at http://www.conventions.coe.int.
76. ibid art 5.1(E).
77. ibid art 5.4.
78. ibid art 3.
79. ibid art 6.
80. LO Gostin, 'Human Rights of Persons with Mental Disabilities: The European Convention of Human Rights' (2000) 23 *Intl J of L and Psychiatry* 125; G Quinn, 'Civil Commitment and the Right to Treatment under the European Convention on Human Rights' (1992) 5 *Harvard Human Rights J* 1.

81. Protocol to the Convention for the Protection of Human Rights and Fundamental Freedoms, art 2 (20 March 1952), available at http://www.conventions.coe.int.
82. G Quinn, 'A Survey of International Comparative and Regional Disability Law Reform: Part 2 Case Study: Using Regional Law as a Catalyst for Change—Towards a "Europeans with Disabilities Act"' in *From Principles to Practice: An International Disability Law and Policy Symposium* (sponsored by US Social Security Administration and presented by Disability Rights Education and Defense Fund) 46.
83. European Social Charter, open for signature 18 October 1961, entered into force 26 February 1965, art 15, available at http://www.conventions.coe.int.
84. L Waddington, 'A European Right to Employment for Disabled People' in T Degener and Y Koster-Drese (eds), *Human Rights and Disabled Persons: Essays and Relevant Human Rights Instruments* (Dordrecht, Boston: M Nijhoff, 1995) 113 (concluding three decades later that European countries still lacked political will to put disability employment policies and rights into practice).
85. European Social Charter (Revised) (1996) art 15.
86. Treaty of Amsterdam, Amending the Treaty on European Union, the Treaties Establishing the European Communities and Certain Related Acts (Cm 3780), signed 2 October 1997, effective 1 May 1999.
87. International Labor Organization, Covenant No 159, Vocational Rehabilitation and Employment (Disabled Persons) Convention, 1983, adopted 20 June 1983.
88. ibid art 4.
89. ibid.
90. ibid art 6.
91. See Herr, Chapter 8 of this volume.
92. Vienna Declaration and Programme for Action (n 71 above).
93. UN GA Doc A/37/51 Supp (No 51) (3 December 1982).
94. ibid para 8.
95. ibid para 29.
96. ibid para 1.
97. ibid para 12.
98. ibid para 29.
99. ibid para 22, the World Programme encourages the use of such accommodations in the ordinary school system and the open employment and housing systems.
100. ibid para 24.
101. ibid para 61.
102. ibid paras 61, 75.
103. ibid paras 109, 111. Based on earlier text, accessibility and nondiscrimination norms should apply to firms, private individuals, NGOs, and governmental agencies. ibid para 23.
104. ibid paras 82, 86. In highlighting the urgency of the problem of persons with disabilities, it is noted that as many as 4 out of 5 of their population of 500,000,000 live in rural areas of developing countries where services are scarcest and poverty is greatest. ibid para 43.
105. UN Human Rights Divisions, GA Res 44/70 (8 December 1989) paras 7–8.

106. Principles for the Protection of Persons with Mental Illness and the Improvement of Mental Health Care, (definitions) GA Res 46/119, 46 UN GOAR Supp (No 49) 189, UN Doc A/46/49 (17 December 1991).

107. ibid Principle 1.4.

108. ibid Principle 1.6.

109. ibid Principles 1.5, 25.

110. ibid Principle 11.12.

111. ibid Principles 13, 15–18.

112. OAS Res AG/RES 112(g), cited in IIHR, Presentation of the Draft InterAmerican Convention on the Elimination of All Forms of Discrimination by Reason of Disability (1994).

113. OAS General Assembly, Panama Commitment to Persons with Disabilities in the American Hemispheres, at AG/RES 1369 (XXVI-0/96).

114. J Power, *Amnesty International: The Human Rights Story* (New York: McGraw-Hill, 1981) 115–118.

115. On the failure to have International Amnesty intercede on behalf of the subjects of extreme forms of aversive treatment, see N Weiss, unpublished paper (1993).

116. Human Rights Watch, 'Human Rights Watch World Report 1995' available at Human Rights Watch, 485 Fifth Ave., New York, NY 10017, summarized in B Crossette, 'Human Rights Organization Urges Stronger Action by the UN' (11 December 1994) *New York Times* 20.

117. Communities Against Violence Network, available at http://www.cavnet.org.

118. J Graeme and S Reid, 'Abuse and Discrimination: An Approach to Guidelines' (ILSMH booklet, 1994); D Sobsey, *Violence and Abuse in the Lives of People with Disabilities: The End of Silent Acceptance?* (Baltimore: PH Brookes Publishing Co, 1994).

119. Ashoka, 'What is a Public Entrepreneur? Ashoka has Defined the Term since 1990' (brochure n.d.).

120. *Wyatt v Stickney* 344 F Supp 387 (MD Ala N Div 1972)

121. *Wyatt v Aderholt* 503 F 2d 1305, 1313 (5th Cir 1974).

122. After a 35-day trial of the *Wyatt* case, and with the Justice Departments Civil Rights Division applying the ADA to de-institutionalization remedies, Gunnar Dybwad's prediction may come close to reality. *Coleman v Zatechka* 824 F Supp 1360, 1372–1373 (D Neb 1993). The Justice Department argued that 'where integrated services have been shown as necessary and appropriate to meet the individual needs of persons with disabilities', then 'integrated services must be provided'. *Wyatt v Hanan*, Plaintiffs' Pre-trial Brief, at 7. They rely in part on ADA commentary notes that 'Integration is fundamental to the purposes of the Americans with Disabilities Act. Provision of segregated accommodations and services relegates persons with disabilities to second-class status.' US Department of Justice Commentary, 28 CFR pt. 35, app. A at 451. *Olmstead v L.C.* 527 US 581 (1999).

123. M Greenblatt, 'Foreword' in Jones and Parlour (eds) (n 18 above).

124. M Perlin, *Law and Mental Disability* (Charlottesville, Va: Michie Co, 1994) 190–194.

125. *Wyatt v Hanan*, CA No 3195-N (MD Ala N Div), 'United States' Response to Defendants' Motion for Judgment on the Pleadings and Plaintiffs' Motion for Summary Judgment on Plaintiffs' Claims under the Americans With Disabilities Act of 1990', at 4: 'Despite the fact that defendants claim to have a significant array of integrated, community-based services in place and a system to identify individuals who remain inappropriately institutionalized, defendants have failed to transfer them to community programs. By failing to serve qualified mentally disabled individuals in the most integrated setting appropriate to their needs, defendants are violating the ADA's prohibition of disability-based discrimination. *Helen L. v. Didario*, 46 F.3d 325 (3rd Cir. 1995). Here, defendants' own judgments indicate that community placement is the only professionally justifiable course of action.'

126. SS Herr, 'Rights into Action: Protecting Human Rights of the Mentally Handicapped' (1977) 26 *Catholic Univ L Rev* 203, 211–215; HR Turnbull, 'Law and the Mentally Retarded Citizen: American Responses to the Declaration of Rights of the United Nations and International League of Societies for the Mentally Handicapped—Where We Have Been, Are, and Are Headed' (1979) 30 *Syracuse L Rev* 1093.

127. A Bayefsky and J Fitzpatrick, 'International Human Rights Law in United States Courts: A Comparative Perspective' (1992) 14 *Michigan J Intl L 1*, 28.

128. *Filartiga v Pena-Irala* 630 F 2d 876 (2d Cir 1980).

129. In *X & Y v the Netherlands*, the Court found that the lack of a criminal sanction for the rape of a 16-year-old mentally retarded girl violated her right to be free from the privacy-invading actions of another person. 91 Eur Ct HR (ser A) (1985), discussed along with art 8 of the European Convention on Human Rights in N Strossen, 'Recent U.S. and International Judicial Protection of Individual Rights: A Comparative Legal Process Analysis and Proposed Synthesis' (1990) 41 *Hastings LJ* 805, 858.

130. 117 DLR (4th) 67 (May 20, 1994).

131. s 40 provides: 'Every person has a right, to the extent and according to the standards provided for by law, to free public education.' s 10 of the Charter guarantees the right of full and equal recognition and exercise of an individual's human rights and freedoms without distinction on the basis of handicap.

132. 117 DLR (4th) at 95.

133. *O'Donoghue v Minister for Health, Minister for Education, Ireland and the Attorney General* [1996] 2 IR 20.

134. 'The State shall provide for free primary education....' art 42.4. Accord *Jamie Sinnott v Minister for Education, Ireland and the Attorney General*, Supreme Court Transcript 12 July 2001 (government must provide free education to age 18).

135. 'The State shall...require in view actual conditions that the children receive a certain minimum education, moral, intellectual and social.' art 42.3.2.

136. *O'Donoghue* (n 133 above).

137. ibid.

138. ibid.

139. ibid.

140. 348 F Supp 866 (DDC 1972)
141. ibid 876. As the trial judge, Joseph Waddy, declared: 'If sufficient funds are not available to finance all of the services and programs that are needed and desirable in the system then the available funds must be expended equitably in such a manner that no child is entirely excluded from a publicly supported education consistent with his needs and ability to benefit therefrom.' ibid.
142. *O'Donoghue* (n 133 above).
143. 106 ALR 385 (High Court of Australia, 6 May 1992)
144. ibid 98. The preceding language bears quotation in full:

   'The inherent dignity of all members of the human family is commonly proclaimed in the preambles to international instruments relating to human rights: see the United Nations Charter, the International Covenant on Civil and Political Rights (which declares "the right to... security of person": Art. 9), the Universal Declaration of Human Rights, the International Covenant on Economic, Social and Cultural Rights and the Convention on the Rights of the Child. The law will protect equally the dignity of the hale and hearty and the dignity of the weak and lame; of the frail baby and the frail aged; of the intellectually able and of the intellectually disabled. Thus municipal law satisfies the requirement of the first paragraph of the 1971 United Nations Declaration on the Rights of Mentally Retarded Persons which reads:
   "The mentally retarded person has, to the maximum degree of feasibility, the same rights as other human beings."
   Our law admits of no discrimination against the weak and disadvantaged in their human dignity.'

145. A Clapham, 'The European Convention on Human Rights in the British Courts: Problems Associated with the Incorporation of International Human Rights' in P Alston (ed), *Promoting Human Rights through Bills of Rights: Comparative Perspectives* (Oxford: Clarendon Press, 1999) 95. Human Rights Act of 1998.
146. ibid 131.
147. ibid 133. Clapham notes that even prior to 1998 the NGO MIND (National Association for Mental Health) resorted to the ECHR as a focus for its advocacy.
148. Norwegian Ministry of Foreign Affairs 2001: 15.
149. ibid 35.
150. PL 106–402, 114 Stat 1678, 42 USC §§15001–09, §109 (2001). The Act identifies numerous rights for individuals with developmental disabilities, including the right to 'appropriate treatment, services, and habitation... designed to maximize the potential of the individual... in the setting that is least restrictive'. ibid at §15009 (a)(1)–(2). The Act also includes provisions on freedom from abuse, neglect, sexual and financial exploitation, violations of legal and human rights, as well as prohibitions on the use of chemical restraints in certain circumstances. ibid at §15009 (a)(3)(B)(i)–(iv).
151. *Pennhurst State School and Hospital v Haldermann*, 451 US 1 (1980). (Court holds that the act is not binding on the state, but only enforceable upon those states that accept federal funds related to the act.)

152. See Braddock and Parish, Chapter 4 of this volume.
153. Address of Bob Williams, Commissioner, Administration for Developmental Disabilities, Administration for Children and Families, US Department of Health and Human Services, 'Assistive Technology Address to RESNA', at 6 (Nashville, Tennessee, 18 June 1994).
154. Standard Rules (n 59 above) R 14, paras 2–5.
155. Ticket to Work and Work Incentives Act of 1999, PL 106–170, 113 Stat 1860, 42 USC 1320 (b)(19)–(22) (2001).
156. See Herr, Chapter 16 of this volume; Dinerstein, Chapter 10 of this volume.
157. The White House Conference on Aging, *Adopted Resolutions* 40, 65, 79 (Washington, DC, 2–5 May 1995).
158. *Should Difference Make a Difference?* (Schell Center for International Human Rights, Yale Law School, 1995).
159. ibid.
160. For instance, US Court of Appeals Judge Skelly Wright's unpublished judicial opinion in 1971 expressed shock that in the capital of the world's richest nation, children with mental retardation and other disabilities had no education. Their neglected rights gave the impetus to the landmark *Mills v Board of Education* case. That 1972 order, in turn, sparked Congress to mandate a right to free and appropriate education, ultimately inspiring countries around the world to re-examine their own laws and educational services. See the Rights to Education for All Handicapped Children, USC (renamed as Individuals with Disabilities Education Act (1990)).
161. American Association on Mental Retardation, *Policies and Positions on Legal and Social Issues* 1 (Washington, DC, 1995) para 11.
162. ibid.
163. *Penry v Johnson* 532 US 782 (2001).
164. Standard Rules (n 59 above) R 20.
165. The Roeher Institute, *Harm's Way: The Many Faces of Violence and Abuse against Persons with Disabilities* (North York, Ont: L'Institut Roeher Institute, 1995) 181.
166. *Penry* 532 US 782.

6

Disability as a Subject of International Human Rights Law and Comparative Discrimination Law

THERESIA DEGENER

I. MEDICAL VS. SOCIAL MODEL OF DISABILITY IN DISABILITY LAW

Disability law has not been a field of legal research and teaching at many universities around the world. As a subject of law in most European countries and in North America, the issue of disability has commonly been included in social security and welfare legislation, health law, or guardianship law. Thus, persons with disabilities were depicted, not as subjects of legal rights, but as objects of welfare, health, and charity programs. The underlying policy has been to segregate and exclude people with disabilities from the mainstream of society and provide them with special schools, sheltered workshops, special housing and transportation—if any services at all. This policy was deemed just because persons with disabilities were believed incapable of coping with society at large and with all or most of the major life activities.

In some countries, when attempts were made to take a more integrative and inclusive approach to disability policy, major legal reforms came along. Attempts to open up employment, education, housing, and goods and services for persons regardless of their disabilities have changed the understanding of disability from a medical to a social category. A key element of this new concept is the recognition that exclusion and segregation of people with disabilities do not logically follow from impairments but rather from political choices based on false assumptions about disability. Inaccessibility problems do not so much result from mobility, visual, or hearing impairments but rather are a corollary of a political decision to build steps but not ramps, to provide information in printed letter version only or to exclude sign language or other forms of communication. Instead of viewing disability as the (individual's) problem, the focus shifted to the environment and society as a whole and to the lack of consideration of human differences. This development of disability policy has been called the shift from the medical to the social model of disability.

The purpose of this chapter is to take a look at how this transformation process is reflected in disability law at national and international levels. As a hypothesis, it is assumed that the shift is most strongly reflected in national discrimination law and international human rights law.

A. Disability as a Human Rights Issue

With the paradigm shift from the medical to the social model,[1] disability was reclassified as a human rights issue. Law reforms are intended to provide equal opportunities for persons with disabilities and to combat their segregation, institutionalization, and exclusion as typical forms of disability-based discrimination. With the evolution of civil rights legislation for persons with disabilities, such as the Americans with Disabilities Act (ADA), the legal paradigm has shifted from welfare law towards civil rights law. This new dimension of disability law has been welcomed as a major milestone toward the eventual recognition of human rights of people with disabilities and more and more governments seem to be willing to follow that path.[2]

Other law reforms tackle the delicate issues of compulsory institutionalization or (medical) treatment of people with disabilities. Countries in all regions of the world have revised their 'mental health' laws in the last decades and applied the rule of law to civil commitment procedures. In a significant number of countries this meant that the legal standards for prisoners were eventually applied to involuntarily institutionalized individuals, including such safeguards as legal representation and judicial review of the commitment decision. One might regard these reforms as a form of equalizing institutionalized persons with prisoners. Another approach would be to recognize these legal developments as a step to apply the human rights values of dignity and autonomy to people with disabilities.

A third field in which disability law reform currently takes place is the traditional area of social welfare law. A number of countries have revised their disability benefit systems to include more community-based services and provisions that support independent living of persons with disabilities. Like disability discrimination laws, these law reforms aim at desegregation and deinstitutionalization of persons with disabilities and thus may be called laws that implement the principle of equality. However, these law reforms are also based on another human rights value, the principle of solidarity. These four human rights values—equality, dignity, autonomy, and solidarity—are the core values that underlie the transformation process of viewing disability as a human rights value.

1. Human Rights Values in the Context of Disability: Equality, Autonomy, Dignity, and Solidarity

While there is consensus about the fundamental nature of the equality principle in domestic as well as in international law, the interpretation of this principle varies. Three main concepts of equality are (1) formal or juridical equality, (2) equality of results, and (3) equal opportunity or structural equality.[3]

First, juridical equality prohibits direct discrimination and aims at shifting the focus of a potential discriminator away from a characteristic such as race, gender, disability, or sexual orientation. Because it is deemed arbitrary to legitimize unequal treatment because of such a characteristic, juridical equality requires ignoring the differences. This concept meets the demands of disability rights activists who try to overcome the medical model of disability, and it underlines the notion that disability is not the problem. But to achieve equality, disability has to be taken into account when it comes to providing access to accommodations such as architectural changes or program adjustments. Granting equal access to all members of societies requires taking a look at the differences that exist among these members. Martha Minow has pointed to the moral policy dilemma of dealing with human differences such as disabilities.[4] To ignore differences helps to prevent stereotypes and stigmatization but at the price of failing to do justice to the reality of difference. Taking difference into account does justice to the reality of difference but at the potential price of perpetuating false assumptions about the nature of difference.

Second, equality of results looks at the end of the spectrum of equal treatment. The concept is based on the human rights theory that all human beings are of equal value and of equal human dignity. This legitimizes the demand for equal allocation of resources. According to this notion, workers with disabilities who receive equal pay but have an unequal burden regarding their personal needs are discriminated against. This view however tackles the question of responsibility. Who is responsible for meeting these needs? Is it the State or the private sector? Equality of results might require a strong welfare state, which may interfere with the ideology of a free market system. At the same time, equality of results may perpetuate injustice because its focus is on results more than on treatment. Segregated education for students with disabilities might be deemed legitimate if special schools for students with disabilities would provide the same educational opportunities and degrees as regular schools. Mainstreaming students with disabilities into regular schools might not be an antidiscrimination goal under this equality concept.

The third concept of equal opportunity is less rigid in that it provides equal chances but not results and thus is more compatible with the market economy. It looks at the history of group discrimination and identifies traditional or classic forms of discrimination. It tackles stereotypes as well as structural barriers as obstacles to inclusion. Disability must be ignored if stereotypes are the basis for action; it must be taken into account if the environment or social life is to be changed in order to grant genuine access and inclusion. The key term for the latter is providing 'reasonable accommodation', which has been developed in the US jurisdiction in the 1970s. Since then it has been adopted—though rephrased in some countries[5]—around the world. The concept of equal opportunity is currently the most frequently applied equality concept in modern disability legislation around the world.

The other three human rights values—dignity, autonomy, and solidarity—have been discussed much less in the context of disability than the principle of equality. The principle of human dignity means that all members of the human family have an 'inherent dignity'.[6] This dignity exists in each human being as a permanent and inseparable attribute. The recognition of human dignity is not dependent on social status, religion, race, gender, genetic makeup, or merit. Every human being is born with dignity and retains dignity until after death. In the context of disability it means that respect for each disabled person's dignity may not be linked to his or her medical condition, functional limitations, or economic and professional performance. That human dignity is an inherent trait of all human beings is all too often forgotten in the discourse on bioethics and particularly in the debate about euthanasia.

Autonomy as a human rights value is based on the assumption that each human being is born free and must not be made the tool of others. It also assumes that every human being is able to decide what kind of life he or she wants to live. The history of human rights shows that the principle of autonomy has often been misunderstood as something that should be reserved for some only, ie, white, nondisabled men. Today it is often misunderstood as a principle that necessitates a certain age or a specific health status in order to be exercised. In the context of disability, the latter misunderstanding is predominant. Persons with disabilities are regarded as being incapable of living as autonomous individuals, which is why nondisabled therapists, guardians, or other experts know better what is in the best interest of the person with a disability. However, this is a perfect example of confusion between the ability to have autonomy and the ability to exercise autonomy in an exclusive and segregating environment. The independent living movement has shown that to live an autonomous life depends not so much on one's physical or mental capacities but rather on the resources a person can utilize.

Solidarity as a human rights value acknowledges the fact that human beings are not living as hermits but as members of a social group. What we think and what we are is to a great extent the result of our communication and interaction with others. The freedom we experience does not exist in a vacuum. It is based on economic and social support. The human rights value of solidarity points to the much debated interrelation, interdependence and indivisibility of both sets of human rights, civil and political on the one hand and economic, social, and cultural rights on the other hand. That both sets of human rights are of equal value and can only be realized together has been emphasized in many documents of the United Nations, most firmly on the World Conference on Human Rights, which took place in Vienna in 1993.[7] The context of disability may be the best example to demonstrate the interrelation. While civil rights laws are necessary to achieve freedom for persons with disabilities, it is clear that they are not enough. It is one thing to abolish barriers and open the gates for every one. The other necessary step is to help everyone get inside.

II. DISABILITY AS A HUMAN RIGHTS ISSUE WITHIN THE UNITED NATIONS

A. Soft Law Developments

Despite being one of the largest minority groups in the world, encompassing 600 million persons (of which two out of three live in developing countries), persons with disabilities were rather ignored during the first three decades of the United Nations' existence. Persons with disabilities as a distinct group, vulnerable to human rights violations, were not thought of when the International Bill of Human Rights was drafted and adopted. The equality clauses of all three instruments of this Bill, the *Universal Declaration of Human Rights* (1948), the *International Covenant on Civil and Political Rights* (1966), and the *International Covenant on Economic, Social and Cultural Rights* (1966), do not mention disability as a covered category. If disability is addressed as a human rights issue in these documents it is in connection with social security and preventive health policy.[8] It was only in the 1970s that persons with disabilities were rendered subjects of human rights declarations in the *Declaration on the Rights of the Mentally Retarded Persons* (1971)[9] and the *Declaration on the Rights of Persons with Disabilities* (1975).[10] Even these early instruments reflect a notion of disability within the medical model, according to which persons with disabilities are primarily seen as persons with medical problems, dependent on social security and welfare and in need of segregated services and institutions. It was also during this time that the General Assembly affirmed that persons with disabilities are covered under the 'other status' phrase of the equality provisions of the *International Bill of Human Rights*.[11]

Throughout the 1970s and the 1980s a number of resolutions were passed by the General Assembly of the United Nations, which led to the 1982 *World Programme of Action concerning Persons with Disabilities* (WPA),[12] which was the guiding instrument for the United Nations Decade of Persons with Disabilities 1982–1993. The first two goals of the WPA, prevention and rehabilitation, reflected a more traditional approach to disability law and policy; the third goal, equalization of opportunities, set the path for change at the international level. Equalization of opportunities was defined as 'the process through which the general system of society, such as the physical and cultural environment, housing and transportation, social and health services, educational and work opportunities, cultural and social life, including sports and recreational facilities are made accessible to all.'[13]

Throughout the decade the equal rights component of disability policy and law became the main target of the emerging international disability rights movement. Other major events that helped to shift the paradigm from a medical to a human rights model of disability were two thematic reports on human rights in the field of mental health and on human rights violations with regard to persons with disabilities prepared by the United Nations Commission on Human Rights.[14] These reports were the first to recognize disability as a thematic subject within the human rights division of the United Nations, and this helped in regarding persons with disabilities not only as recipients of charity measures but as subjects of human rights (and human rights violations). While one report resulted in a non-binding international human rights instrument protecting persons with disabilities in institutions,[15] the outcome of the other has been rather poor. No significant follow-up activities were taken under the auspices of the UN Commission of Human Rights. While other significant guidelines and standards have been adopted during the decade,[16] the proposal for a binding treaty on the human rights protection of persons with disabilities did not find majority support within the Third Committee of the General Assembly in 1987 and again in 1989. As a compensatory alternative, the non-binding UN *Standard Rules on the Equalization of Opportunities for Persons with Disabilities* (StRE) were adopted in 1993.[17] The StRE firmly build on the WPA and clearly accentuates equality, now defined as:

The principle of equal rights implies that the needs of each and every individual are of equal importance, that those needs must be made the basis for the planning of societies and that all resources must be employed in such a way as to ensure that every individual has equal opportunities. Persons with disabilities are members of society and have the right to remain within their local communities. They should receive the support they need within the ordinary structure of education, health, employment and social services.[18]

In contrast with other non-binding international disability instruments, the StRE have a Special Rapporteur and a panel of experts who have the mandate to promote and monitor the implementation of the Rules. The panel of experts consists of ten representatives of the six major international nongovernmental organizations in the disability field.[19] The reports[20] reflect a clear human rights approach in the monitoring performance though the monitoring body is placed under the auspices of the United Nations Commission for Social Development instead of the Commission on Human Rights. Unfortunately, the mandate of the Special Rapporteur, Bengt Lindqvist, ended in 2002 and it seems to be unclear whether there will be a successor.

B. Hard Law Developments: Protection under General Human Rights Instruments

Increasingly, nongovernmental organizations that focus on disability seem to have an impact on how traditional human rights norms are interpreted and implemented as well as on how modern human rights instruments are designed.[21] Currently, there are six international treaties that form the heart of binding international human rights law. The *International Covenant on Civil and Political Rights* (ICCPR) and the *International Covenant on Economic, Social and Cultural Rights* (ICESCR) both were adopted in 1966. The *Convention on the Elimination of All Forms of Racial Discrimination* (CERD) was adopted in 1965, and its counterpart for women, the *Convention on the Elimination of All Forms of Discrimination Against Women* (CEDAW), was adopted in 1979. In the 1980s, the General Assembly of the United Nations adopted two more treaties, the *Convention Against Torture and Other Cruel, Inhuman or Degrading Treatment or Punishment* (CAT) of 1984 and the *Convention on the Rights of the Child* (CRC) of 1989. Only the latter, CRC, contains a provision on the rights of individuals with disabilities (Article 23),[22] while disability was a forgotten category when the other treaties were drafted. However, these treaties are currently interpreted in a way that supports the human rights approach to disability. Such an interpretation process usually takes the form of documents adopted by the respective treaty monitoring body. These UN documents are called general comments or general recommendations.

General Comment No 19 to the ICCPR, which deals with the right to equality (Article 25 ICCPR), is a clear statement that the concept of formal equality does not apply. It affirms that equal treatment does not always mean identical treatment and that states have a duty to take steps to eliminate conditions that perpetuate discrimination.[23] Another General Comment to ICCPR, *General Comment No 25*, specifically addresses persons with disabilities. In three out of twenty-seven paragraphs of the document, persons with disabilities are directly mentioned:

4. Any conditions which apply to the exercise of the right protected by article 25 should be based on objective and reasonable criteria....For example, established mental incapacity may be a ground for denying a person a right to vote or to hold office...

10. It is unreasonable to restrict the right to vote on the ground of physical disability or to impose literacy, educational or property requirements...

20. An independent electoral authority should be established to supervise the electoral process and to ensure that it is conducted fairly, impartially and in accordance with established laws which are compatible with the Covenant...Assistance provided to the disabled, blind or illiterate should be independent. Electors should be fully informed of these guarantees....[24]

These interpretations give significant guidance for including persons with disabilities in electoral processes. The Comment establishes that physical disability may never be a legitimate ground for restricting the right to vote. Neither may any intellectual disability be considered a reason for denying the right to vote or hold office; rather, it must be an established mental incapacity.

Other treaty monitoring bodies have adopted similar documents, which clarify that persons with disabilities are protected by the respective treaty. The Committee on the Elimination of All Forms of Discrimination has adopted General Recommendation No 18, which asks State Parties to include specific information on the status of women with disabilities[25] and has addressed the issue of disability in other thematic recommendations.[26]

The Committee on Economic, Social and Cultural Rights went even further and adopted a whole General Comment on how the ICESCR has to be interpreted and implemented with respect to persons with disabilities.[27] *General Comment No 5*, which was adopted in 1994, is the only legal UN document to date that broadly defines disability-based discrimination:

Both de jure and de facto discrimination against persons with disabilities have a long history and take various forms. They range from invidious discrimination, such as the denial of educational opportunities, to more 'subtle' forms of discrimination such as segregation and isolation achieved through the imposition of physical and social barriers. For the purpose of the Covenant, 'disability-based discrimination' may be defined as including any distinction, exclusion, restriction or preference, or denial of reasonable accommodations based on disability which has the effect of nullifying or impairing the recognition, enjoyment or exercise of economic, social or cultural rights.[28]

The human rights approach to disability is also emphasized by a clear demand for anti-discrimination legislation: 'In order to remedy past and present discrimination, and to deter future discrimination, comprehensive anti-discrimination legislation in relation to disability would seem to be indispensable in virtually all State parties.'[29]

C. Evaluation of the Current Use of the UN Human Rights Instruments in the Context of Disability

While the battle of ideas in international disability policy and law has clearly resulted in a consensus about a human rights approach to disability, the practical results are a different subject. At several UN expert meetings, the issue of human rights implementation for persons with disabilities was critically raised. At the Interregional Seminar and Symposium on International Norms and Standards Relating to Disability, which took place 13–17 December 1999 in Hong Kong (Special Administrative Region), the People's Republic of China led one of the major attempts to create a forum for the critical appraisal of international disability law.[30] The Hong Kong meeting was a follow-up to a smaller meeting that convened a year earlier at the University of California at Berkeley.[31] At both meetings experts expressed the view that the current human rights framework encompasses a new understanding whereby living with a disability is something for society to accept and accommodate. While it was critically recognized that the major part of international disability rights law is 'soft law', with no binding obligations for State Parties to the United Nations, these numerous instruments were deemed significant for the promotion of human rights of persons with disabilities. At the same time, experts acknowledged the need for a disability-specific human rights treaty as a significant advance in creating binding law. By contrast, the current international standards were considered a regime that was little more than a 'toothless tiger' when it comes to actual human rights advocacy. The need for an international disability convention was also stated at two other UN expert meetings, one of which took place at Stockholm, Sweden in November 2000,[32] and the other in New York City in February 2001.[33]

The nongovernmental community has also stressed the idea of a disability convention. A World NGO Summit on Disability was held in March 2000, in Beijing, China. The leading international disability NGOs attended this summit, including Disabled Peoples' International, Inclusion International, Rehabilitation International, the World Blind Union, and the World Federation of the Deaf. As a result of the summit, the *Beijing Declaration on the Rights of People with Disabilities in the New Century,* was adopted, which urges all Heads of States 'to immediately initiate the process for an international convention...'

Finally, in November 2001, the Third Committee of the United Nations General Assembly passed a resolution on a '[c]omprehensive and integral international convention to promote and protect the rights and dignity of persons with disabilities'.[34] The resolution reads in paragraph 1:

Decides to establish an Ad Hoc Committee open to the participation of all Member States and observers to the United Nations, to consider proposals for as comprehensive and integral international convention to protect and promote the rights and dignity of persons with disabilities, based on the holistic approach in the work done in the field of social development, human rights and non-discrimination, taking into account the recommendations of the Commission of Human Rights and the Commission for Social Development.

The resolution also requests that the future ad hoc committee be provided with the outcome of a study undertaken pursuant to Commission on Human Rights resolution 2000/51. This very recent study evaluates the current use and potential of the UN human rights instruments in the context of disability. It was publicly presented by the High Commissioner for Human Rights on 14 January 2002, at the Palais des Nations in Geneva, Switzerland.[35] The study finds that while the treaty-monitoring bodies of the six international human rights treaties have taken significant and laudable efforts to include disability into the mainstream human rights machinery, persons with disabilities remain invisible human rights subjects. Disability is not dealt with in a consistent and coherent manner under the current regime. All too often, the old welfare approach towards disability seems to be the prevailing attitude among State Parties. The study contains several recommendations on how to improve the UN human rights machinery in the context of disability. While the adoption of a disability human rights convention is one of the core proposals, the study emphasizes the need for a twin-track approach. According to such a twin-track approach, the current human rights treaties need to be strengthened with respect to their implementation for persons with disabilities, while a disability convention should be developed at the same time.

D. Conclusions on the Trends in International Human Rights Law

Within the last three decades there has been a clear development towards the eventual recognition of persons with disabilities as deserving protection within international human rights law. Today there are a vast number of soft laws within international human rights law that directly address persons with disabilities and their family members. Most important are the 1993 *Standard Rules on the Equalization of Opportunities for Persons with Disabilities*, which have helped to shift the paradigm from the medical model of disability towards the social model and more precisely, to the human rights model of disability.

With respect to hard international human rights law, the development seems to be promising. Almost all treaty-monitoring bodies of the six main international human rights treaties began to recognize persons with disabilities as human rights subjects under their respective treaties. A number of General Comments interpret these treaties to some extent in the context of disability. However, more work needs to be done to make the UN human rights machinery work better. Treaty bodies need to address the issue of disability more consistently and more comprehensively. The old medical model of disability all too often seems to prevail when it comes to human rights implementation. Too often, persons with disabilities are still invisible citizens in the mainstream human rights machinery of the United Nations. The call for an international disability convention has been heard. In November 2001, the Third Committee of the UN General Assembly initiated the first steps for a drafting process. It is to be hoped that a future convention for persons with disabilities will be a true human rights treaty. In addition, the process of drafting any new treaty should be open, inclusive, and representative of the interests of all persons with disabilities. Persons with disabilities should be principal participants in the drafting of any new treaty at all stages of the drafting process.

III. THE REFORM PROCESS IN COMPARATIVE LAW

At the domestic level, disability law in many countries underwent significant changes during the last few decades. More than 40 out of 189 UN Member States have now adopted some kind of anti-discrimination law for persons with disabilities.[36] To compare and analyze these laws globally is a difficult enterprise for a number of reasons. First, these countries not only have different historic, economic, and political backgrounds, they also belong to different legal systems, notably the common law tradition or the civil law tradition. Since the common law tradition is based on case law, the judiciary plays a different role than in the civil law tradition. Second, disability law as a branch of legal research is a fairly recent development in most countries. Thus, legal literature on disability law and comparative studies on disability laws are still rather rare.[37] Most of the comparative legal literature is focused on European countries.

A. The Template: Using the ADA and Standard Rules as Model Laws Globally

With these reservations in mind, some observations can be made with respect to anti-discrimination laws for persons with disabilities around the world. Most of these anti-discrimination laws were enacted during the last decade, while some countries enacted these laws in the 1980s. Exceptionally early was the United States with the adoption of the Rehabilitation Act of 1973 as one of its first pieces of anti-discrimination legislation for persons with disabilities. The US law has been instrumental in the evolution of disability discrimination law in many countries. Especially, the Americans with Disabilities Act (ADA) of 1990 has had such an enormous impact on foreign law development that one might feel inclined to say that the international impact of this law was larger than its domestic effect.[38] Another incentive to enact disability discrimination legislation came from the UN *Standard Rules for the Equalization of Opportunities* of 1993 (Standard Rules), which states in Rule 15:

States have a responsibility to create the legal basis for measures to achieve the objectives of full participation and equality for persons with disabilities....States must ensure that organizations of persons with disabilities are involved in the development of national legislation concerning the rights of persons with disabilities, as well as in the ongoing evaluation of that legislation....Any discriminatory provisions against persons with disabilities must be eliminated. National legislation should provide for appropriate sanctions in case of violations of the principle of non-discrimination...[39]

The history of disability discrimination law in a number of countries reveals that either the ADA and/or the Standard Rules served as a model law for the domestic legal development. With respect to the legal character of the Standard Rules, this finding is an interesting example for the impact a soft law can have internationally if taken seriously by governments. That these governments took disability seriously as a discrimination issue is the result of the disability movement in each country. Anti-discrimination laws for persons with disabilities are the result of a social movement of organized persons with disabilities and disability advocates around the world. These persons with disabilities demanded human rights instead of pity laws, reflecting the shift in paradigm in disability policy nationally and internationally.

B. A Comparison of Anti-Discrimination Laws Globally

The laws in those forty-two countries that we analyzed[40] differ to a great extent with respect to scope, concept of discrimination and equality, protected groups, enforcement, and other aspects. Some laws define disability-based discrimination and clearly prohibit these acts of discrimination; others leave the question of what constitutes discrimination to the courts or other monitoring bodies. Some laws uphold the principle of equality but entail no clear picture of what needs to be changed in society in order to reach this goal. While these questions are often dealt with in separate regulations amending the act, the language and the structure of the statute may reveal legislative intent. Some laws give the impression that while they contain some anti-discrimination language, they are rather a social welfare law fostering programs that are not necessarily aimed at complete social equality and integration of persons with disabilities.[41] However, it is important to notice that disability discrimination law is truly a new development in disability policy around the world. These laws legally manifest the shift in paradigm from the medical model to the social model of disability. To legally treat disability as a discrimination category implies the recognition that persons with disabilities are persons with rights, not problems.[42] Some of these anti-discrimination laws are strong; others appear to be 'toothless tigers'. Often domestic disability groups fought very hard for equality laws and were not satisfied with the act that was finally passed by their legislators.[43] The history of US discrimination law tells us that the legislative battle for equality is long, and more than one statute needs to be passed by the legislator to reach the goal of comprehensive protection against discrimination. From the first attempts to include disability in the Civil Rights Acts of 1964 until the passage of the ADA in 1990, several decades went by and at least five federal disability discrimination acts[44] were passed by Congress.

1. A Wide Diversity of Different Legal Approaches

Those States that have passed some kind of disability discrimination law today have chosen different legal approaches. Four different legal approaches can be distinguished. Anti-discrimination provisions for the protection of persons with disabilities are regulated in (a) criminal law, (b) in constitutional law, (c) in civil law, and (d) in social welfare laws.

a. Criminal Law

France,[45] Finland,[46] Spain,[47] and Luxembourg[48] prohibit discrimination against persons with disabilities in their criminal laws. The Spanish law prohibits disability-based discrimination as regards recruitment or in the course of employment if the worker with a disability is capable to do the job. Luxembourg and France outlaw disability-based discrimination in employment, business activities, and in the provision of goods and services to the public. The punishment is a maximum of two years' imprisonment or a fine. The Finnish Penal Code punishes employment-related discrimination and discrimination with respect to goods and services for the general public.

Other States that have adopted not criminal but civil or social law statutes regarding disability discrimination also provide for criminal or administrative penalties within these civil or social laws. For instance, the Australian discrimination statute sanctions the incitement of unlawful discrimination or harassment as an offence punishable with six months imprisonment or a fine. Victimization of a person who exercises his or her rights under the act is also declared an offence.[49] Similar provisions are in the Hong Kong *Discrimination Ordinance*. A person who incites hatred towards, serious contempt for, or severe ridicule of persons with disabilities commits a serious offence of vilification and is liable to a fine or two years' imprisonment.[50] The law of Mauritius sanctions certain violations of the anti-discrimination rules with a criminal or administrative fine.[51] The same is true for the respective acts of Israel,[52] the Philippines,[53] Zambia,[54] and Zimbabwe.[55]

While Finland and Spain also have anti-discrimination provisions in other fields of their law system, France and Luxembourg stand out in that they regulate disability-based discrimination exclusively in their criminal codes. That means that disability-based discrimination is prohibited only if it constitutes a criminal offence. That in turn requires that the perpetrator acted with bad intention. In reality, however, disability-based discrimination is often carried out with the best intentions of the perpetrator. The restaurant owner who does not serve wheelchair users because the entrance is inaccessible usually has no hostile feelings towards persons with disabilities. Usually he does not conceive of himself as a discriminator. While we do not have statistical evidence, it seems that criminal anti-discrimination law is rarely executed.

b. Constitutional Law

Several countries have constitutional anti-discrimination provisions that explicitly cover disability. These are: Austria,[56] Brazil,[57] Canada,[58] Finland,[59] Fiji,[60] the Gambia,[61] Ghana,[62] Germany,[63] Malawi,[64] New Zealand,[65] South Africa,[66] Switzerland,[67] and Uganda.[68] These clauses generally prohibit (negative) discrimination of persons with disabilities without defining what exactly constitutes discrimination. Some equality clauses mention direct and indirect forms of discrimination.[69] Exceptionally broad is the equality clause of Fiji's constitution, which covers unfair direct and indirect discrimination and in addition states: 'Every person has the right of access, without discrimination on a prohibited ground [such as disability] to shops, hotels, lodging-houses, public restaurants, places of public entertainment, public transport services, taxis and public places.'[70]

The constitutions of Austria, Brazil, Canada, Germany, Ghana, Malawi, South Africa, Switzerland, and Uganda also enable or entrust the legislature to take affirmative action to combat disability discrimination. Affirmative action means preferential treatment in the form of quotas or other means of positive discrimination. Affirmative action thus targets structural discrimination, which is one of the major obstacles to the equalization of opportunities for persons with disabilities.

In the employment area, many States have introduced quotas for the advancement of persons with disabilities. Employers have a duty to hire a certain percentage of disabled workers in many countries. Initially, these employment quotas, when introduced into disability policy after the Second World War, were classical welfare measures. They were founded on the idea that people with disabilities cannot compete in the real world.

With the rise of civil rights movements in the context of race and gender, quota policies became a new equality related meaning. This in turn has influenced quota schemes in the disability field. In this respect, it is interesting to note that some of the constitutions provide for quota schemes in the field of employment,[71] whereas others provide for quotas in the area of political representation. For example, the constitution of Malawi provides that the Senate, which is a legislative body, shall include representatives of various interest groups, among them disability groups.[72] Similarly, the constitution of Uganda requires that the parliament shall consist of a certain number of representatives of persons with disabilities.[73] Meanwhile, the Ugandan Parliament has five seats reserved for representatives from the disability community, and the first minister for disability (and women and the elderly), Mrs. Florence Nayiga Sekabiro is a person with disability. Based on the affirmative action clause of the constitution, Uganda's legislators passed several acts to increase the representation of people with disabilities in the public sphere. An example is the Local Government Act of 1997, according to which a certain number of seats in elected political bodies at all levels are allocated to people with disabilities. As a result, there are more than 2,000 elected officials who have disabilities at all levels, from the parish to the district level today.[74] Another interesting feature of those constitutions that have been amended to include disability in the prohibition of discrimination is that they recognize the right to use sign language. Finland,[75] South Africa,[76] and Canada[77] have such provisions in their constitutions.

Constitutional anti-discrimination clauses seem to have more effect than criminal anti-discrimination clauses in transforming society. Since in most countries the constitution is the highest law of the land, constitutional amendments receive more public attention and may render lower law unconstitutional and void. Constitutional amendments also have to be followed by the judiciary and thus may lead to reform in disability case law. Yet, there are several reasons why Constitutional disability discrimination law has limited effect.

First, depending on the legal system, some constitutions give no substantive rights to citizens, which means that a person with a disability may not invoke the anti-discrimination clause in court. Second, constitutional rights are applicable only in public or so-called vertical law. Constitutional provisions protect persons with disabilities against discrimination by state entities, not by private employers or private providers of good and services. Finally, constitutional provisions tend to be broad and vague. Neither disability nor discrimination is defined in any of the constitutional provisions except for the constitutional law of New Zealand.[78] This leaves vast discretion to the courts. Court rulings are very much determined by the legal culture.

For example, in Germany, where there is no history of civil rights legislation and litigation, the constitutional anti-discrimination clause has been rendered a toothless tiger by a decision of the Federal Constitutional Court in 1996. In a case filed by a girl who uses a wheelchair and who was denied access to a regular school the Court decided that the constitutional anti-discrimination clause was not violated by the school authorities.[79] The reasoning of the German Federal Constitutional Court is reminiscent of a case that was decided more than 150 years ago by the US Supreme Court and upheld racial segregation in schools. Like the court in *Plessy v Ferguson* in 1896,[80] the German Court reasoned that educational segregation of children with disabilities is not discriminatory because it is separate but equal. The separate but equal clause of *Plessy* was struck down in the United States in 1954 with the groundbreaking decision of *Brown v Board of Education of Topeka*[81] in which the Supreme Court finally acknowledged that separate educational facilities in the context of race are inherently unequal. The German Federal Constitutional Court, however, was very reluctant to consider the exclusion from education in the context of discrimination. While it acknowledged that it would be discriminatory if a student with a disability who did not need any accommodations or special services was denied admission, the Court was unwilling to include students with disabilities who need ramps, lifts, sign language interpreters, alternative reading formats, or any kind of special education services. Thus, the medical model of disability was reinforced by this first decision on the new German anti-discrimination clause for persons with disabilities.

While these shortcomings of constitutional anti-discrimination provisions might lead to the conclusion that constitutional amendments are useless, the example of Ireland proves the opposite. Because the equality clause in the Irish Constitution of 1937 is exceptionally weak, the Irish Supreme Court struck down two pieces of discrimination legislation in 1997, which, among others, also covered disability. The court found that the statutory requirement to engage in reasonable accommodations violated the property rights of employers.[82] The laws had to be redrafted and weakened with respect to disability. Thus, constitutional amendments might serve as an important foundation for statutory anti-discrimination laws.

Finally, a positive example of how to interpret rather vague constitutional equality clauses was given by a 1997 decision of the Supreme Court of Canada. In *Eldridge v British Columbia*,[83] the plaintiffs brought their case before the British Columbia Supreme Court because the province did not provide medical interpretation services to deaf patients. Robin Eldridge had been unable to communicate with her physician, and John and Linda Warren had undergone the ordeal of giving birth to their twins without being able to fully comprehend what their doctors and nurses were telling them. The plaintiffs framed their action under the equality clause (Section 15) of the Charter, claiming that provincial hospitals legislation discriminated against the deaf by failing to provide for sign language interpretive services when effective communication is an inherent and necessary component of the delivery of medical services. While the lower courts rejected their claim, the Supreme Court of Canada found the equality clause violated. By interpreting the equality clause in a way that recognizes that certain groups may need some accommodation in order to enjoy equality, *Eldridge* at least opens the possibility that Section 15 of the Canadian Charter requires governments to take positive and substantive steps to ensure that persons with disabilities and other groups who experience discrimination receive the 'equal protection and equal benefit' of the law. However, despite encouraging comments in *obiter dicta*, the Supreme Court of Canada has continued to leave open the issue of positive obligations under the equality clause.[84]

c. The Enactment of Civil Anti-discrimination Laws

A third approach is to enact civil anti-discrimination laws for persons with disabilities. A number of countries have adopted such laws and more countries are about to follow this path.[85] Countries with a civil rights oriented disability discrimination law are: Australia,[86] Canada,[87] Chile,[88] Costa Rica,[89] Ethiopia,[90] Germany,[91] Ghana,[92] Guatemala,[93] Hong Kong,[94] Hungary,[95] India,[96] Ireland,[97] Israel,[98] Korea,[99] Madagascar,[100] Mauritius,[101] Namibia,[102] Nigeria,[103] the Philippines,[104] South Africa,[105] Spain,[106] Sri Lanka,[107] Sweden,[108] the United Kingdom,[109] the United States,[110] Zambia,[111] and Zimbabwe.[112] With the exception of the law of Chile, all of these statutes cover employment-related discrimination of persons with disabilities. Some laws are labor laws and thus only cover employment discrimination.[113] With respect to other areas, the laws differ to a great extent. The most comprehensive disability discrimination laws are from Australia, Canada, Hong Kong, the Philippines, the United Kingdom, and the United States.

The Australian Disability Discrimination Act of 1992 prohibits discrimination in the areas of work, housing, education, access to premises, clubs, and sports and other facilities, land possession, and the provision of goods and services.[114] The Canadian Human Rights Act of 1985 covers discrimination in the provision of goods, services, facilities or accommodations that are available to the general public (including transportation). Furthermore, it prohibits discrimination in employment, the provision of commercial premises or housing.[115] The 1995 Disability Discrimination Ordinance of Hong Kong covers the areas of employment, education, premises, goods and services, facilities for the general public, barrister chambers, clubs and sports, and government activities.[116] The 1992 Magna Carta for Persons with Disabilities of the Philippines prohibits disability-based discrimination in the fields of employment, transportation, public accommodation, and goods and services.[117] The British Disability Discrimination Act of 1995 covers discrimination in employment, in the provision of goods, facilities, and services and to some degree also covers the area of education and public transportation.[118] Finally, the American with Disabilities Act of 1990 prohibits discrimination in the area of employment, state and local government activities (including education, transportation, social services, etc.) public accommodations (goods and services) and telecommunication.[119]

The civil laws of the other countries are also broad in scope in that the legislation covers a wide range of everyday life areas, but not all of these areas are covered by the anti-discrimination provisions of the law. For instance, the 1996 Act on Equal Opportunities for Persons with Disabilities of Costa Rica covers access to education, employment, public transportation, public services, information and communication, and cultural, sports, and leisure activities. However, discrimination is explicitly prohibited only with respect to employment, public health services, and participation in culture, sports, and leisure activities.[120]

The Indian Persons with Disabilities (Equal Opportunities, Protection of Rights and Full Participation) Act 1995 differs from the other civil rights laws in that it has rather weak non-discrimination provisions but provides for quotas in various areas instead. Non-discrimination provisions cover transportation, roads, built environment, and government employment (excluding the hiring process).[121] Duties to enable access for persons with disabilities apply only *'within the limits of...economic capacity and development'* (emphasis added) and thus are rather easy to evade. A 3% quota scheme relates to government employment, government aided educational institutions, and poverty alleviation schemes.[122] The government employment quota system reserves 1% to persons with certain types of impairments, notably visual, hearing, and physical impairment.[123] Of interest is that any vacancy under the 3% quota scheme in government employment will be carried forward to the next year.[124] Theoretically, this might lead to a situation where a government agency can only hire or promote employees who have disabilities. Many other foreign laws have quota provisions, particularly in the public employment field. As the short excursion into comparative European disability law showed, employment quota schemes have a long tradition and do not necessarily pertain to the anti-discrimination principle.

Compared to criminal and constitutional anti-discrimination laws, civil disability discrimination legislation is more detailed regarding the scope of the law. Most of the laws also provide a definition of what constitutes discriminatory practice or equality. In addition, all the civil disability discrimination laws have provisions on enforcement mechanisms. Both the concepts of discrimination and equality and the different enforcement mechanisms will be discussed below.

d. Social Welfare Laws and Disability

Finally, some countries choose to approach the issue of disability discrimination in traditional social welfare laws for persons with disabilities. These countries are: Bolivia,[125] China,[126] Costa Rica,[127] Finland,[128] Germany,[129] Korea,[130] Nicaragua,[131] Panama,[132] and Spain.[133]

In these laws, anti-discrimination provisions are found next to more traditional provisions on prevention of disability and rehabilitation. Except for the Finnish 1992 Act on the Status and Rights of Patients, which provides that every resident in Finland is entitled to health and medical care without discrimination, the main focus of these laws is social services and integration principles rather than rights-based anti-discrimination provisions. Non-discrimination provisions in social welfare legislation tend to be vague and are limited to one area—eg, public employment or public education. For instance, the Spanish Act on the Social Integration of the Disabled (1982) deals with prevention of disability; diagnosis and assessment; the system of benefits in cash and kind; medical and vocational rehabilitation; and community services and integration at work. The only anti-discrimination provision in the act states that any disability-based discriminatory provision in labor regulations, collective agreements, individual contracts, or unilateral decisions shall be null and void.[134]

The Chinese Law of the People's Republic of China of 1990 contains a general prohibition clause[135] but does not specify what that means for the organization of society. A textual analysis of the law gives the impression that the traditional medical model of disability—institutionalization and segregation—is the framework of the act. For instance, Article 29 stipulates as one guiding principle the rule of concentrated employment for persons with disabilities. This means that employment opportunities are provided in special welfare enterprises and institutions. Within these special institutions, discrimination against persons with disabilities regarding recruitment, employment, promotion, determining professional or technical titles, payment, welfare and other aspects is prohibited.[136] Given that this is the only detailed anti-discrimination provision in the whole act, it seems that the law conveys a rather peculiar concept of equality.

The medical model approach of the law is also displayed by some provisions regarding the obligations of persons with disabilities. According to Article10, Chinese persons with disabilities 'should display an optimistic and enterprising spirit', which implies the notion that disability results in negative attitudes and depression.

Some countries, such as the Philippines, have laws that could be characterized as both social welfare and civil rights laws. The Magna Carta of the Philippines, however, entails a clear statement that manifests the legislature's intent to move from the medical model to the human rights model of disability. Title I, Chapter I, Section 2(b) states that: 'Persons with disabilities' rights must never be perceived as welfare services by the Government.'

The history of US disability discrimination law shows that often states start with anti-discrimination provisions for persons with disabilities in social welfare legislation. This is the area of law where disability law tends to be developed. The United States first prohibited certain forms of discrimination against people with disabilities in the 1973 Rehabilitation Act. The famous Section 504 provides that every entity that receives federal financial assistance or is conducted by any federal agency must not discriminate against an 'otherwise qualified' person with a disability. The 1988 amendment of the Fair Housing Act, which prohibits discrimination in housing matters, was the first step towards including disability in general civil rights legislation in the United States. The final step was taken with the adoption of the Americans with Disabilities Act (ADA). Similarly, Costa Rica and Spain have disability discrimination provisions within social welfare legislation as well as civil laws.

In sum, discrimination provisions in social welfare legislation tend to be less comprehensive and reform-oriented. The paradigm shift from the medical model of disability to the human rights model of disability seems to be less obvious in this kind of legislation.

2. Protected Groups: The Disability-Specific Approach or the Trans-Group Approach

Some of the anti-discrimination laws for persons with disabilities are part of a group law, while other laws focus on disability exclusively. The group law approach protects other minorities or groups that historically have been the targets of discrimination practices, such as women, homosexuals, children, the elderly, linguistic or religious minorities, and others. With the exception of Ghana,[137] all of the constitutional discrimination provisions protect persons with disabilities as a group among others. The same is true for discrimination provisions in employment law as well as criminal laws. Disability discrimination laws that are designed as civil or social laws tend to be exclusively for persons with disabilities.

In addition to protecting persons who presently have a disability, some laws also protect persons who were disabled in the past (Australia, Canada (Human Rights Act), Hong Kong, New Zealand, the Philippines, the United Kingdom, and the United States), may be disabled in the future (Australia, Hong Kong, and Sweden) or who are regarded as being disabled (Australia, Hong Kong, New Zealand, the Philippines, and the United States). Furthermore, some laws also protect family members or otherwise associates of persons with disabilities, (Australia, Hong Kong, New Zealand, the Philippines, and the United States[138]) as well as persons who are victimized because they make a complaint about an act of discrimination or exercise other anti-discrimination rights (Australia, Canada (Human Rights Act), New Zealand, and the United Kingdom).

Most discrimination laws that are civil or social legislation entail a definition of disability. Commonly, the definition is medically oriented in that disability is defined as a physical or mental impairment that results in some significant functional limitations. The issue of disability definitions is discussed in detail by Luckasson in Chapter 2 and Renteln in Chapter 3 of this volume.

3. The Diversity of Equality and Discrimination Concepts at Play

The underlying equality concepts of disability discrimination laws differ under review. Some laws support a more formal equality model in that they guarantee equality rights on the premise that a person with a disability fully adapts to the nondisabled culture and society. Some of the constitutional anti-discrimination clauses can be read this way as shown by the German education case. Other laws explicitly mention that disability may be a legitimate factor for discrimination. For instance, the 1992 Labor Act of Namibia provides that a person shall not be regarded to have been unfairly discriminated against if the person with a disability, because of his or her disability, is unable to perform the job.[139] The 1992 Persons with Disabilities Act of Zimbabwe provides that disability may be a legitimate excuse for employment discrimination,[140] and the denial of any public service or amenity seems to be excused if it is 'motivated by a genuine concern for the safety of the persons with disabilities'.[141] While the Korean Special Education Promotion Law as amended in 1994 prohibits discrimination against students with disabilities in all schools, only special school principals 'should take appropriate measures to provide appropriate convenience for entrance examinations and schooling for children with disabilities based on types and degree of disability.'[142] Thus, principals at regular schools are implicitly limited in their responsibility for discriminatory omissions.

About one-fourth of the laws reviewed here, however, are based on a structural equality concept. This includes a commitment that society has to change in order to guarantee true equal opportunity for persons with disabilities. The key phrase in this respect is 'reasonable accommodations' or 'reasonable adjustments', which have to be undertaken by the employer, the service provider, government, or any other entity under anti-discrimination obligations. The following countries have such a provision in their discrimination laws, even though it does not always apply to all areas covered by the anti-discrimination rule: Australia,[143] Canada,[144] Hong Kong,[145] Hungary,[146] Ireland,[147] Israel,[148] New Zealand,[149] the Philippines,[150] Sweden,[151] the United Kingdom,[152] the United States,[153] and Zimbabwe.[154]

Another indicator for a structural equality concept of the discrimination law may be seen in affirmative action provisions because they imply that positive action has to be taken in order to achieve true equality. Fourteen countries[155] have affirmative action provisions in their laws, most of them relating to quota schemes.

The main focus of the majority of discrimination laws is on employment discrimination. This might be explained by the fact that this is the field where discrimination law relating to groups generally has been developed. Discrimination laws relating to race and gender were first adopted in the employment sector. Thus, it makes sense to follow that path for persons with disabilities. However, it needs to be taken into account that this is the realm of economic, social, and cultural human rights. This is the set of human rights traditionally applied to disability, whereas civil and political rights have usually been neglected in disability policy. In this regard, it is remarkable that some of the disability discrimination statutes explicitly guarantee non-discrimination with respect to civil and political rights for persons with disabilities.[156] Others, however, do not mention civil and political rights explicitly because these rights are covered by the anti-discrimination provisions regarding public premises, services, and accommodations.

The concept of discrimination may be derived from the definition of disability-based discrimination and the areas covered by the discrimination prohibitions. The latter has already been discussed in this chapter; thus, the focus here shall be on the definition of discrimination, which half of the reviewed statutes entail.

The majority of statutes define discrimination as unfavorable treatment on the basis of disability;[157] whereas, a minority define discrimination as unjustified differentiation.[158] Some laws distinguish between direct and indirect forms of discrimination[159]—the latter commonly defined as applying requirements or conditions that persons with disabilities usually have more difficulties complying with. The aforementioned key phrase, 'denial of reasonable accommodations', is entailed in the discrimination concept of twelve statutes.[160] Interestingly, some discrimination acts have provisions on access to public places, buildings and transportation, but inaccessibility is not defined as a discriminatory practice.[161] Particularly if access is not formulated as an individual right, accessibility seems to be given as a welfare service.

Some of the discrimination laws attribute acts of harassment and victimization to the context of prohibited forms of discrimination.[162] The Canadian Human Rights Act additionally outlaws discriminatory public communications, publications, and hate messages.[163] Another interesting finding is that a significant number of discrimination laws also address the issue of exploitation or abuse of persons with disabilities.[164]

While few discrimination laws support the principle of segregated education for students with disabilities,[165] only a minority of the acts convey a clear statement that separate education is inherently unequal and a classic form of disability discrimination.[166] The most comprehensive definitions of disability discrimination can be found in the laws of Australia, Canada, Hong Kong, New Zealand, the Philippines, the United Kingdom, and the United States. These laws define discrimination with respect to every area covered, such as employment, public accommodation, goods and services. With regard to each area, the definitions entail long lists of acts that are considered discriminatory, such as denial of participation, participation under unequal conditions, or separate benefits. In addition to disability, some of the laws explicitly mention auxiliary aids, guide dogs, and interpreters as illegitimate reasons for discriminatory treatment (eg, Australia and Hong Kong).

4. A Variety of Enforcement Mechanisms

Commonly, the enforcement of legislation is the task of public administrative agencies and courts. Legislation that seeks to transform society to some extent, such as human rights and discrimination legislation, usually establishes some kind of special enforcement body. This might be a human rights or an equal opportunity commission, an ombudsperson, a national council, or an agency. Among the disability legislation under review, only the civil or social law statutes include some provisions for enforcement or monitoring of the law.

Thus, the Australian Disability Discrimination Act establishes a Human Rights and Equal Opportunity Commission and a Disability Discrimination Commission.[167] The Canadian Human Rights Act is enforced by a Human Rights Commission and a Human Rights Tribunal.[168] The Equal Rights for Persons with Disabilities Law of Israel entrusts various ministries with the enforcement of the law and additionally establishes a Commission for Equal Rights.[169] In the United Kingdom, a Disability Rights Commission is the watchdog for the Disability Discrimination Act.[170]

A significant number of acts entrust representatives of disability organizations with monitoring the law. For instance, the Law of the People's Republic of China on the Protection of Persons with Disabilities establishes the China Persons with Disabilities' Federation, which has the responsibility to represent and protect the rights and interests of persons with disabilities in China.[171] The Hungarian discrimination act establishes the National Disability Affairs Council in which disability organizations have to be represented.[172] The Indian law established a multi-sector planning and monitoring mechanism. There is a Central Coordination Committee with the Chief Commissioner for Persons with Disabilities and several State Coordination Committees, which are focal points of disability matters at the state level. The law requires that a certain number of seats in each committee be filled by persons with disabilities.[173] The Nigerian discrimination law establishes a National Commission for Persons with Disabilities, whose chairman must be a person with a disability and in which all the major disability groups must be represented.[174] Similarly, the Persons with Disabilities Act of Ghana establishes the National Council on Persons with Disabilities in which six seats are reserved for representatives of disability organizations. The law of Zimbabwe establishes a Disability Board in which half of the seats must be filled by representatives of disability organizations.[175] The same holds true for the Zambian Agency for Persons with Disability, which is the enforcement body of the Zambian discrimination law.[176]

The functions of these monitoring bodies are manifold and vary between advisory and information gathering for the government and over awareness raising in the general public to investigation and complaint filing. The Disability Board in Zimbabwe and the Zambia Agency for Persons with Disabilities also have the mandate to issue 'adjustment orders', requiring specific action from owners whose premises or services are inaccessible to persons with disabilities.

C. Conclusions on the Trends within Comparative Law

Disability discrimination laws around the world take various approaches to the issue. Persons with disabilities may be protected against discrimination in constitutional, criminal, civil, or social law. The most comprehensive legal approach to prevent and to protect against disability-based discrimination seems to be the civil rights path. However, it needs to be kept in mind that the main method of the evaluation of these laws was a textual analysis of a piece of legislation. The few cases cited indicate that the impact an anti-discrimination law may have on society depends to a large extent on the judiciary rather than on the text of the legislation.

Today there is no universal definition of disability-based discrimination and no universal concept of equalization of opportunities for persons with disabilities. Definitions of discrimination rank from unjustified differentiation, over direct or indirect unfavorable treatment, to detailed lists of discriminatory practices. However, it can be concluded that modern disability discrimination laws adhere to the principle of desegregation, de-institutionalization, and the duty to provide reasonable accommodations, which means to actively abolish structural discrimination. In addition to a strong definition of discrimination, the law needs to provide clear and effective enforcement mechanisms in which persons with disabilities individually or as a group need to play a major role.

Not all disability laws that improve the living conditions and integration of persons with disabilities have been analyzed in this chapter. Many countries have laws that afford the integration of persons with disabilities into the community and into public life. Thus, many building laws require that (new) buildings designed for the general public are accessible to persons with disabilities. Education laws often provide that integrated education is a fundamental principle of education policy. Especially in Scandinavia, social welfare laws secure that persons with disabilities have a minimum income. Other countries have strong legal provisions for independent living services for persons with disabilities. Notably, the Finnish Services and Assistance for the Disabled Act of 1987 provides as an individual right benefits to severely disabled persons in Finland to enable them to live independently. These benefits include services such as transportation, housing, interpretation services, and to some extent personal assistance services. Because the act's main purpose is to enable persons with disabilities to live as a member of society on equal footing with others, the act is also called the Disabled Person's Equality Act.[177] However, these disability laws have not been reviewed here because they do not fall within the concept of discrimination laws. Even though these laws aim to establish equal opportunities for persons with disabilities, they do not outlaw inaccessibility, segregation, or denial of independent living as a form of discrimination. Discrimination laws are not the only route to equality for persons with disabilities. They are one rights-based approach taken by many States around the world today. Only disability discrimination laws have been under review here; that should be kept in mind, too.

The global overview of discrimination laws for persons with disabilities gives rise to hope and to concern. The concern is that not every anti-discrimination language in legislation may aim at equal rights for persons with disabilities. Disability organizations need to act as watchdogs so that legislators do not use anti-discrimination language as a pretext to adhere to the medical model of disability policy. But there is also realistic hope that anti-discrimination legislation for persons with disabilities is globally on the rise. There is hope that disability policy will finally adhere to the principle of human rights and structural equality.

IV. CONCLUSIONS

There are strong global and international trends towards discrimination laws and human rights laws for persons with disabilities. The paradigm shift from the medical to the human rights model of disability in disability policy is clearly reflected in comparative and international disability law. Governments worldwide are in the process of drafting, passing, or implementing new disability discrimination laws. The United Nations has just initiated a serious discourse for a future treaty on human rights for persons with disabilities. These promising legal developments require legal expertise. International and comparative disability law is a subject on the rise, which should be taught and researched at many more universities.

NOTES

1. There is a large body of literature on this subject, eg V Finkelstein, *Attitudes and Disabled People: Issues for Discussion* (New York: Rehabilitation Fund, 1980); M Oliver, *The Politics of Disablement* (Basingstoke: Macmillan and St Martin's Press, 1990); M Oliver, *Understanding Disability: From Theory to Practice* (New York: St Martin's Press, 1996); J Morris, *Pride Against Prejudice* (London: Women's Press, 1991).

2. Implementing the World Programme of Action Concerning Persons with Disabilities, Report by the Secretary-General, UN GAOR UN Doc A/54/388 (1999).

3. G Quinn, 'The Human Rights of People with Disabilities under EU Law' in P Alston, M Bustelo, and J Heenan (eds), *The EU and Human Rights* (New York: Oxford Univ Press, 1999) 290. Other equality concepts with respect to disability law have been described by A Hendriks, 'The Significance of Equality and Non-discrimination for the Protection of the Rights and Dignity of Persons with Disabilities' in T Degener and Y Koster-Dreese (eds), *Human Rights and Persons with Disabilities: Essays and Relevant Human Rights Instruments* (Dordrecht, The Netherlands: M Nijhoff, 1995) 40–62; L Waddington, *Disability, Employment and the European Community* (Antwerpen-Apeldoorn, Netherlands: MAKLU, 1995) 53–66.

4. M Minow, *Making all the Difference: Inclusion, Exclusion, and American Law* (Ithaca, NY: Cornell Univ Press, 1990) 19–79.

5. For instance, the term 'adjustments' instead of 'accommodations' is used in UK law.

6. Preamble of the Universal Declaration of Human Rights (1948), which reads in the first sentence: 'Whereas recognition of the inherent dignity and of the equal

and inalienable rights of all members of the human family is the foundation of freedom, justice and peace in the world,...'

7. See para 5 of Vienna Declaration and Programme of Action (1993).
8. See Universal Declaration of Human Rights, art 25, GA Res 217, UN Doc A/8/10, at 71 (1948); International Convention on Economic, Social and Cultural Rights, art 12, GA Res 2200A, UN GAOR, 21st Sess, Supp No 16, at 49, UN Doc A/6316 (1967).
9. GA Res 2856, UN GAOR, 26th Sess, Supp No 29, at 93, UN Doc A/8429 (1972).
10. GA Res 3447, UN GAOR, 30th Sess, Supp No 34, at 88, UN Doc A/10034 (1976).
11. For a more comprehensive analysis, see A Hendriks, 'The Significance of Equality and Non-discrimination for the Protection of the Rights and Dignity of Persons with Disabilities' in T Degener and Y Koster-Dreese (eds), *Human Rights and Persons with Disabilities: Essays and Relevant Human Rights Instruments* (Dordrecht, The Netherlands: M Nijhoff, 1995) 40–62.
12. GA Res 37/52, UN GAOR, 37th Sess, Supp No 51, at 185, UN Doc A/37/51 (1983).
13. *World Programme of Action Concerning Disabled Persons: Report of the Secretary-General*, Addendum at 21, UN GAOR, UN Doc A/37/351/Add 1 (1982).
14. *Principles, Guidelines and Guarantees for the Protection of Persons Detained on Grounds of Mental Ill Health or Suffering from Mental Disorder: Report by the Special Rapporteur, Mrs. Erica-Irene Daes*, UN Sub-Commission on Prevention of Discrimination and Protection of Minorities, UN Doc E/CN.4/Sub.2/1983/17; L Despouy, *Human Rights and Persons with Disabilities* (Human Rights Studies Series, 6) (New York: United Nations, 1993).
15. *The Protection of Persons with Mental Illness and the Improvement of Mental Health Care* (1991), GA Res 46/199, UN GAOR, 46th Sess, Supp No 49 at 188, UN Doc A/46/49 (1992).
16. *The Talline Guidelines for Action on Human Resources Development in the Field of Disability*, GA Res 44/70, UN GAOR, 44th Sess, Supp No 49, Annex, at 196, UN Doc A/44/49 (1990).
17. *Standard Rules on the Equalization of Opportunities for Persons with Disabilities*, GA Res 48/96, UN GAOR, 48th Sess, Supp No 49, at 202, UN Doc A/48/49 (1994). For comment, see T Degener, 'Persons with Disabilities and Human Rights: The Legal Framework' in T Degener and Y Koster-Dreese (eds), *Human Rights and Persons with Disabilities: Essays and Relevant Human Rights Instruments* (Dordrecht, The Netherlands: M Nijhoff, 1995) 9–39; B Lindqvist, 'Standard Rules in the Disability Field—a New United Nations Instrument' in T Degener and Y Koster-Dreese (eds), *Human Rights and Persons with Disabilities: Essays and Relevant Human Rights Instruments* (Dordrecht, The Netherlands: M Nijhoff, 1995) 63–68.
18. *Standard Rules on the Equalization of Opportunities for Persons with Disabilities*, paras 24–27, Introduction, supra.
19. Disabled Peoples' International, Inclusion International, Rehabilitation International, World Blind Union, World Federation of the Deaf, and World Federation of Psychiatric Survivors and Users.
20. *Monitoring the Implementation of the Standard Rules on the Equalization of Opportunities for Persons with Disabilities: Report of the Special Rapporteur of the*

Commission for Social Development, UN GAOR, UN Doc A/50/374, Annex (1995) (first report); *The Implementation of the Standard Rules on the Equalization of Opportunities for Persons with Disabilities: Final Report of the Special Rapporteur of the Commission for Social Development*, UN GAOR, UN Doc A/52/56, Annex (1996) (second report); and *Monitoring the Implementation of the Standard Rules on the Equalization of Opportunities for Persons with Disabilities: Final Report of the Special Rapporteur of the Commission for Social Development on Monitoring the Implementation of the Standard Rules on the Equalization of Opportunities for Persons with Disabilities on His Second Mission, 1997–2000*, UN Economic and Social Council, UN Doc E/CN.5/2000/3 (third report); for comment, see D Michailakis, 'The Standard Rules: A Weak Instrument and a Strong Commitment' in M Jones and LA Basser-Marks (eds), *Disability, Divers-Ability and Legal Change* (The Hague: M Nijhoff, 1999) 117–130.

21. While the focus is here on the human rights division of the UN, it should be mentioned that the Special Agencies such as WHO, ILO, or UNESCO have also taken an equal opportunity approach to disability in recent years. As a strong binding instrument ILO Convention No 159, Convention Concerning Vocational Rehabilitation and Employment (Persons with Disabilities) 1983 is worth mentioning. For an overview on the specialized agencies, see T Degener, 'Persons with Disabilities and Human Rights: The Legal Framework' in T Degener and Y Koster-Dreese (eds), *Human Rights and Persons with Disabilities: Essays and Relevant Human Rights Instruments* (Dordrecht, The Netherlands: M Nijhoff, 1995) 20–33.

22. For a comment, see T Hammarberg, 'The Rights of Disabled Children—the UN Convention on the Rights of the Child' in T Degener and Y Koster-Dreese (eds), *Human Rights and Persons with Disabilities: Essays and Relevant Human Rights Instruments* (Dordrecht, The Netherlands: M Nijhoff, 1995) 147–158.

23. eg, GAOR, 45th Sess, Supp No 40, UN Doc A/45/40 (1990).

24. To be found at http://www.unhcr.ch/tbs/doc.nsf (last viewed 23 October 2001).

25. CEDAW General Recommendation No 18 (x) (1991), UN GAOR, 46th Sess, Supp No 38, UN Doc A/46/38 (1992) 3.

26. CEDAW General Recommendation No 24 (xx) (1999) on 'Women and Health', para 25. available at http://www.unhchr.ch/tbs/doc.nsf/MasterFrameView/3e04c50e8b3399818025681f00531b7a? Opendocument (last viewed 3 April 2000).

27. For a comment, see P Alston, 'Disability and the International Covenant on Economic, Social and Cultural Rights' in T Degener and Y Koster-Dreese (eds), *Human Rights and Persons with Disabilities: Essays and Relevant Human Rights Instruments* (Dordrecht, The Netherlands: M Nijhoff, 1995) 94–105.

28. *General Comment No 5 (1994) Persons with Disabilities*, UN ESCOR, Supp No 2, at 102, UN Doc E/1995/22 para 15.

29. ibid, para 16.

30. T Degener, 'International Disability Law—A New Legal Subject on the Rise' (1999) 18/1 *Berkeley J of Intl L* 180–195.

31. Report available at http://www.un.org/esa/socdev/enable/dpb19991.htm (last viewed 2 March 2002).

32. 'Let the World Know' Report of a Seminar on Human Rights and Disability, Almasa Conference Centre (Stockholm, 5–9 November 2000), available at

http://www.un.org/esa/socdev/enable/stockholmnov2000.htm (last viewed 12 November 2001).

33. *Report: Informal Consultative Meeting on International Norms and Standards for Persons with Disabilities* (New York: United Nations, 9 February 2001), available at http://www.un.org/esa/socdev/enable/consultnyfeb2001.htm (last viewed 2 March 2002).

34. A/C.3/56/L.67/Rev.1 (28 November 2001).

35. G Quinn, T Degener, *et al.*, *Human Rights Are for All: A Study of the Use and Potential of the UN Human Rights Instruments in the Context of Disability* (Geneva: United Nations, OHCHR, 2002) (the study should be available soon at http://www.unhchr.ch/).

36. We have found anti-discrimination laws in the following countries: Australia, Austria, Bolivia, Brazil, Canada, Chile, China, Costa Rica, Ethiopia, Fiji, Finland, France, Gambia, Germany, Ghana, Greece, Guatemala, Hong Kong (SAR), Hungary, India, Ireland, Israel, Korea, Luxembourg, Madagascar, Malawi, Mauritius, Namibia, New Zealand, Nicaragua, Nigeria, Philippines, South Africa, Spain, Sri Lanka, Sweden, Switzerland, Uganda, United Kingdom, United States, Zambia, and Zimbabwe.

37. L Waddington, 'Legislating to Employ People with Disabilities: The European and American Way' (1994) 1 *Maastricht J of European and Comparative L* 4; G Quinn, M McDonagh, and C Kimber, *Disability Discrimination Law in the United States, Australia and Canada* (Dublin: Oak Tree Press, 1993); M Jones and LA Basser-Marks (eds), *Disability, Divers-Ability and Legal Change* (The Hague: M Nijhoff, 1999); M Hauritz, C Sampford, and S Blencowe, *Justice for People with Disabilities: Legal and Institutional Issues* (Sydney: Federation Press, 1998); M Rioux, 'The Place of Judgement in a World of Facts' (April 1997) *J of Intellectual Disability Research* 102–111; P Thornton and N Lunt, *Employment Policies for Disabled People in Eighteen Countries—A Review* (York: Social Policy Research Unit, Univ of York, 1997); M Carley, 'International Equality at Work: Disability, Employment and the Law in Europe—Part One' (December 1994) *Industrial Relations Review* 251; E Besber, 'Employment Legislation for Disabled Individuals: What can France Learn from the American with Disabilities Act?' (1995) 16 *Comparative Labor L J* 399; B Gutow, 'Survey of Rights of Workers with Disabilities: Comparison of the United States with the European Community' (1998) 11/2 *New York International Law Review* 101.

38. Within the US legal literature there is today no consensus whether the ADA has been successful. See the ADA Symposium Issue (2000) 21/1 *Berkeley J of Employment and Labor L*. The Symposium was called: 'Backlash Against the ADA'.

39. GAOR, 45th Sess, Supp No 40, UN Doc A/45/40 (1990).

40. The research was done in preparation of a conference which took place in October 2000 at Washington, DC. 'From Principle to Practice—An International Disability Law and Policy Symposium' was organized by DREDF (Disability Rights Education and Defense Fund). Papers and participants available at http://www.dredf.org/symposium/index.html (last viewed 1 February 2002).

41. eg, the Korean laws. Each statute's prohibition on discrimination takes place in a kind of vacuum. There is no bestowal of individual rights, or any mechanism

that allows persons with disabilities to complain or enforce the prohibition. While the laws contain the potential for actual reform the main legal emphasis is on discretionary and welfare-oriented disability programs that have led to exclusion in the past.

42. G Quinn, 'The Human Rights of People with Disabilities under EU Law' in P Alston (ed), *The EU and Human Rights* (New York: Oxford Univ Press, 1999) 281, 290.

43. In the UK, disability groups had fought for more than a decade to achieve anti-discrimination legislation. They had prepared their own draft, which was rejected by the parliament. When the Disability Discrimination Act was passed in 1995 many disability rights activists were disappointed. BJ Doyle, *Disability Discrimination: The New Law* (Bristol: Jordan, 1995); C Gooding, *Blackstone's Guide to the Disability Discrimination Act 1995* (London: Blackstone Press, 1996).

44. The Architectural Barrier Act of 1968, 42 USCA §§ 4151–4157; The Rehabilitation Act of 1973, 29 USCA §§ 791, 793, 794; The Individuals with Disabilities Education Act (IDEA), 20 USCA §§ 1400–1485 (enacted under another name 'Education for All Handicapped Children Act' in 1975); The Voter Accessibility Act as of 1984 42 USCA §§ 1973ee, 1973ee-1 to 1973ee-6, the Fair Housing Act as amended in 1988 42 USCA §§ 3610–3614, 3614a.

45. Loi 90–602 de 12 Juliet 1990.

46. Penal Code as of 1995, ch 11, s 9 and ch 47 s 3.

47. Law on Infringements and Penalties of a Social Nature 1988.

48. Penal Code of 1997, ss 444 and 453–457.

49. Disability Discrimination Act 1992, ss 42 and 43.

50. Discrimination Ordinance 1995, s 47.

51. The Training and Employment of Disabled Persons Act 1996, s 18.

52. Equal Rights for Persons with Disabilities Law, ss 15 and 19(d).

53. Magna Carta for Disabled Persons 1992, Title IV, s 46.

54. The Persons with Disabilities Act 1996, s 32.

55. Persons with Disabilities Act 1992, s 10(c).

56. Federal Constitutional Law as amended in 1997 (art 7).

57. Constitution of the Federative Republic of Brazil, as of 1993 (art 7).

58. Charter of Human Rights and Freedoms as of 1982 (s 15).

59. Constitution as amended in 1995 and in 2000 (s 6).

60. Constitution as of 1997 (s 38).

61. Draft of a Constitution for the Second Republic of Gambia of 1996 (s 31). It is not certain that the Constitution has been adopted yet. The draft was released for publication in 1997.

62. Constitution as of 1992 (art 29).

63. Basic Law of the Federal Republic of Germany, as amended in 1994 (art 3).

64. Republic of Malawi (Constitution) Act 1994 (s 20).

65. Human Rights Act of 1993 (s 21).

66. Constitution as of 1996 (s 9).

67. Constitution as amended in 1999 (art 8).

68. Constitution of the Republic of Uganda as of 1995 (art 21).

69. Fiji: s 38 (2), South Africa: s 9 (3,4), Gambia: s 33, New Zealand: s 65.

70. s 38 (4).

71. Brazil with respect to public employment, art 37 of the Constitution.
72. s 68 (2)(i).
73. art 78 (1)(c).
74. These numbers were given by Mrs. Nayiga at an international human rights seminar for young disabled women in New York, 1–7 June 2000.
75. s 17. Though Portugal's constitution has no anti-discrimination clause that explicitly includes disability, it should be mentioned here that the right to use sign language was amended in 1997 (art 74).
76. s 6.
77. s 14 entails the right to an interpreter to any deaf party or witness in legal proceedings.
78. Because the Human Rights Act of 1993 is an entire statute dealing with discrimination. The Constitution of New Zealand consists of several legislative acts.
79. Bundesverfassungsgericht, Urteil vom 8. October 1996, Europaeische Grundrechtszeitschrift 1997, S. 586
80. 163 US 537 (1896).
81. 349 US 294 (1955).
82. *In the matter Article 26 of the Constitution of Ireland and in the Matter of the Employment Equality Bill*, Judgement of the Supreme Court, May 1997; Re Article 26 and the Equal Status Bill, judgement of the Supreme Court, May 1997. See G Quinn, *From Charity to Rights—The Evolution of the Rights-Based Approach to Disability: International and Irish Perspectives*, CPI Handbook of Services (Dublin, 2000), available at http://www.enableireland.ie/accesswest/intros/essayindex.html (last viewed 3 March 2002).
83. *Eldridge v British Columbia (Attorney General)* (1997) 151 DLR (4th) 577 (SCC).
84. *Vriend v Alberta* [1998] 1 SCR 493. For more comprehensive analysis, see B Porter, 'Beyond *Andrews*: Substantive Equality and Positive Obligations After *Eldridge* and *Vriend*' (1998) 9/3 *Forum Constitutionnel* 71–82; DM Lepofsky, 'The Charter's Guarantee of Equality to People with Disabilities—How Well Is It Working?' (1998) 16 *Windsor Yearbook of Access to Justice* 155–214; M Jackman, '"Giving real effect to equality": Eldridge v. British Columbia (Attorney General) and Vriend v. Alberta' (1998) 4/2 *Rev of Constitutional Studies* 352–371.
85. eg, Austria, Germany, The Netherlands, Portugal, Switzerland.
86. Disability Discrimination Act 1992.
87. Canadian Human Rights Act, RSC 1985, c. H-6.
88. Act No 19.284 of 1994.
89. Law 7600 for Equalization of Opportunities for Persons with Disabilities (1996).
90. The Rights of Disabled Persons to Employment, Proclamation No 101/1994.
91. Act on the Equalization of Disabled Persons (BGG) in force since 1 May 2002.
92. The Persons with Disabilities Act of 1993.
93. Act for the Protection of Persons with Disabilities, Decree No 135–96 (1996).
94. Disability Discrimination Ordinance 1990.
95. Act No XXVI of 1998 on Provision of the Rights of Persons Living with Disability and their Equality of Opportunity (hereinafter cited as Act No XXVI).

96. The Persons with Disabilities (Equal Opportunities, Protection of Rights and Full Participation) Act 1995.
97. Employment Equality Act of 1998, Equal Status Act of 2000 and National Disability Authority Act (2000).
98. Equal Rights for People with Disabilities Law, 5758–1998 (hereinafter cited as ERPWDL).
99. Act Relating to the Employment Promotion, etc of the Handicapped, Law No 4219 (1990) and The Special Education Promotion Law (1994).
100. Labor Code as of 29 September 1994.
101. The Training and Employment of Disabled Persons Act (Act No 9 of 1996).
102. Labor Act as amended in 1992.
103. Nigerians with Disability Decree 1993.
104. Magna Carta for Disabled Persons 1992.
105. Employment Equity Bill 1998 and Skills Development Bill of 1998.
106. Worker's Charter of 1980.
107. Protection of the Rights of Persons with Disabilities Act, No 28 of 1996.
108. Law on the Prohibition of Discrimination Against Persons with Disabilities in Employment, SFS No 1999—132, 1999.
109. Disability Discrimination Act 1995 and Disability Rights Commission Act 1999.
110. American with Disabilities Act 1990, which needs to be read together with other disability discrimination laws enacted earlier (n 44 above).
111. The Persons with Disabilities Act 1996 (Act No 33 of 1996).
112. Disabled Persons Act 1992.
113. Canada (Employment Equity Act SC 1994–95), Ethiopia, Ireland (Employment Equality Act) Korea (Act Relating to the Employment Promotion, etc) Madagascar, Mauritius, Namibia, South Africa (Employment Equity Bill of 1998) and Sweden.
114. ss 3, 15, 22–30.
115. ss 5–11.
116. ss 11–20, 24, 25–29, 33–37.
117. Title III, chs I–III.
118. ss 4, 19, 22, 29, 30, 32–39, 40–47.
119. Title I–IV.
120. arts 24, 31, and 55.
121. ch VIII, ss 44, 45, 46, and 47.
122. ch VI, ss 33–40.
123. ch VI, s 33(i)–(iii).
124. ch VI, s 36.
125. Act No 1678 on the Person with Disability (1985).
126. Law of the People's Republic of China on the Protection of Disabled Persons (1990).
127. Decree No 119101-S-MEP-TSS- PLAN of 1989.
128. Act on the Status and Rights of Patients (785/1992).
129. Social Law Code (SGB) Ninth Book (IX)—Rehabilitation and Participation of People with Disabilities in force since 1 July 2001.

130. The Welfare Law for Persons with Disabilities, Law No 4179 (1989) and The Special Education Promotion Law as of 1994.
131. Act No 202 Regulations and Politics Regarding Disabled in Nicaragua/Act for the Prevention, Rehabilitation and Equalization of Opportunities for Persons with Disabilities in Nicaragua (1995).
132. Family Law Code, Act No 3 as amended in 1994.
133. Law on the Social Integration of the Disabled (1982).
134. Title VII, s 38(2).
135. ch I, art 3.
136. art 34.
137. The constitutional equality clause (art 17) does not cover disability, which is dealt with by a special provision (art 29).
138. re public accommodations, goods, and services (Title III).
139. s 107 (2) (b).
140. s 9 (2) (b).
141. s 10 (b) (ii).
142. art 13.
143. eg, ss 5(2) and 45.
144. Employment Equity Act, s 5.
145. In various provisions, eg, ss 12, 24–26.
146. ss 5–8.
147. s 16(3)(b) of the Employment Equality Act (1988) and s 4(1) of the Equal Status Act (2000).
148. s 8 (e).
149. eg, ss 29, 35, 43, 56, and 60.
150. Title II, chs 1–7 (ss 5–31).
151. ss 3 and 6.
152. eg, ss 6, 21, 32, etc.
153. eg, s 504 of the Rehabilitation Act, and Title I, s 102, Title II, s 202, and Title III, s 302 of the ADA.
154. ss 7 and 9.
155. Canada (Human Rights Act), Ethiopia (but very weak), Ghana, India, Israel, Mauritius, Nigeria, Philippines, South Africa (Employment Equity Act, but specifically excluding quotas), Spain, Uganda, USA, Zambia, and Korea.
156. The Nigerians with Disability Decree has provisions on the right to vote and the right to information (ss 12 and 13). The Magna Carta of the Philippines has provisions on the rights to vote, to assembly, and to organize (ss 29–31).
157. Australia (s 5), Canada (HRA, ss 5–11), Fiji (art 38), Germany (art 3), Guatemala (arts 35 and 44), Hong Kong (s 6), Ireland (s 16 EEA, s 3 ESA), Namibia (s 107), Mauritius (s 16), New Zealand (ss 22, 37, 42, 53, etc.), Philippines (ss 32), South Africa (s 9), Sweden (s 3), UK (s 5), and Zambia (s 19).
158. France (art 225-1), Luxembourg (art 454), Ethiopia (s 3), Uganda (art 21).
159. Australia (s 6), Fiji (art 38), Namibia (s 107), New Zealand (s 65), the Philippines (s 32), South Africa (s 9), Sweden (ss 3 and 4), and Zambia (s 19).
160. See (n 143 through 154 above).
161. Brazil, China, Costa Rica, Ghana, Guatemala, Israel, and Nicaragua.

162. Australia (ss 35–40), Canada (HRA, s 14) Hong Kong (s 7), Israel (s 10), Sweden (s 9), UK (s 55).

163. ss 12 and 13.

164. Costa Rica (Law on Equal Opportunity, art 4), Ghana (Constitution, art 29) and Panama (art 520).

165. eg, Brazil and Nigeria.

166. In my opinion the laws of the following countries can be read this way: Australia, Canada, Hong Kong, Hungary, the Philippines, USA, and Zambia.

167. ss 67 and 113.

168. ss 26 and 48.

169. ss 20–25.

170. Established by the Disability Rights Commission Act of 1999. This new body replaces the former National Disability Council that was established by the DDA but was much weaker. S Minty, 'Introducing the UK Disability Rights Commission', available at http://www.disabilityworld.org/June-July2000/Governance/UKDisability Rights.htm (last viewed 10 July 2000).

171. art 8.

172. s 24.

173. ss 3, 9, and 13. The disability movement in India is rather disappointed with the slow implementation of these provisions. A Mohit, 'Governance & Legislation: Initiatives of the Government of India to Advance Asia & Pacific Decade of Disabled Persons', available at http://www.disabilityworld.org/April–May2000/Governance/India.htm (last viewed 15 May 2000).

174. s 14.

175. ss 4, 5, and 7.

176. ss 6 and 25.

177. J Korpi, 'Finland, in European Day of Disabled Persons 1995' in *Disabled Persons' Status in the European Treaties: Invisible Citizens* (Brussels: Secretariat of European Day of Disabled People, 1995) 67–70.

7

Liberty, Due Process, and the Pursuit of Happiness

MICHAEL W. SMULL AND LUCIENE PARSLEY

Adults in our society largely determine their own lifestyle. Within the broad boundaries imposed by law, societal customs, and personal resources, how each person lives is up to that person. Each person considers both what is important to and what is important for him or her[1] and makes decisions with the goal of achieving a self-defined positive balance. For people with significant intellectual disabilities this process has been truncated. What is considered and what determines lifestyle choices is what is important *for* the person. For those who receive government-funded services, this decision-making process has been largely vested in a group of paid staff, referred to as an interdisciplinary team.[2] The professionals who serve on these teams have had the burden of not only determining what services a person should receive, but also what his or her life circumstances or lifestyle will be.[3] It is time to revisit these responsibilities.

The past decade has been a time of new learning and of significant changes in how services are configured.[4] The development of techniques that are collectively referred to as 'person centered planning' has provided ways to determine what is important *to* people with significant disabilities as well as what is important *for* them. These techniques allow us to determine what lifestyle preferences will create a balance between what is important *to* the individual and what is important *for* the individual. The development and spread of self-determination has resulted in many people with mild intellectual disabilities having substantial control over how they live and the resources available for their support.[5] For people with more significant intellectual impairments, however, issues of health and safety continue to determine, to a large extent, how and where they live.[6]

This chapter argues that this need not and should not continue. As we move from program services to support services, we have opportunities to support people in their desired lifestyles rather than the lives that we assign to them. This chapter will discuss the moral and ethical obligations of professionals working with persons with intellectual disabilities to discern and act upon the lifestyle preferences of the persons they support and will argue for the creation of a legal duty to so act. Under this new support paradigm, health and safety issues are addressed within the context of the individual's demonstrated statements[7] about what is important to have in his or her life. Since professionals working with people with all levels of intellectual disabilities can now consistently and reliably learn what is important to a person (in addition to what is important for a person), they are obligated to take that information into consideration when determining how he or she is going to live.

I. THE INTERDISCIPLINARY TEAM AND HABILITATION

Traditionally, people with intellectual disabilities are provided 'program services': highly stylized and inflexible training designed to keep a person safe, provide basic care and support to the person, and to teach the person skills that increase independence.[8] Within these services, people are grouped for clinical and administrative convenience.[9] Thus, people who have similar diagnostic labels typically live and spend their days together. The decisions about where people will live and spend their days are referred to as placement decisions. The nature and amounts of services are described in a plan developed by a group of paid staff referred to as the 'team', which considers issues of health and safety and assesses strengths and needs.[10] Typical elements of the plan include not only the hours and type of services provided but also the training goals for the individual. Despite the lack of data demonstrating the benefits of program services, they have persisted as a way to make providers accountable to their funding agency, usually the state or federal government.[11]

In contrast, *support services* recognize a shift in philosophy: as the name suggests, emphasis is placed on flexible services that assist or 'support' the individual with disabilities to live the life he or she wants to have.[12] The services are individualized and designed from the individual's perspective. For those who may not communicate verbally, family, friends, professionals, and others who know the person well come together with the individual with a disability to discern what is important in the person's life and to ensure that the person's services revolve around those important elements.[13]

Program services are guided by the underlying principles of direction through the collective professional judgment of an interdisciplinary team whose goal is to have the individual achieve greater independence through the amelioration of deficits.[14] This process, referred to as habilitation, has a set of standards by which the resulting plans are judged. For example, the 1989 guidebook *Legal Advocacy for Persons with Developmental Disabilities*[15] section on 'Individual habilitation plan review' described five domains that should be present, including (1) functionality (useful objective, age-appropriate, variety of natural environments); (2) community focus (promote community participation and inclusion); (3) technical adequacy (outline observable and measurable sequential steps to annual goals and objectives; specify conditions in which behavior should occur; identify levels of performance to achieve objectives; set deadlines for achievements; specify initiation and review dates; identify criteria for continuing or modifying objectives; name people responsible for writing, implementing, and monitoring objectives); (4) teaching methods (perform task analysis; specify steps of task analysis to be taught; specify adequate frequency and length of learning opportunities; identify clear and detailed teaching methods; provide motivation and reinforcement through teaching; specify prompts and fading); (5) data collection (objective baseline data; specified method for collecting progress data; progress data collected as specified; data evaluated at least monthly).

Under the program services model, at least one professional from each discipline for every area in which the team finds a deficit is included in the decision-making group. The diverse services that these professionals offer clearly need to be coordinated and placed in the context of each individual's life. When each discipline can offer expertise in terms of how to achieve the intellectually disabled individual's goals or preferences, the team approach is at its most useful.

Unfortunately, those professionals who are on the team have been given collective responsibility for determining each individual's lifestyle. Too often, the vocational staff on the team becomes responsible for developing a 'day program' for the individual. Residential staff structure the individual's home life and create goals to address deficits the individual is perceived to have, and the team psychologist is charged with developing a 'behavior plan' for the individual and his or her support staff. This approach is problematic because it parcels out responsibility for the individual to various professionals and does not address the individual as a whole person. It also ignores what is important *to* the person and wholly focuses on what is important *for* the person.

Unfortunately, the concepts underlying the program model have become a new tyranny for many people. We have allowed technology to determine how people spend their time rather than using it to assist people in leading the lives they desire. Thus, despite clear evidence that jobs can be developed for nearly everyone,[16] we continue to segregate those with the most severe cognitive disabilities in 'day programs', put those persons perceived to have some work skills in 'sheltered workshops', and 'allow' individuals with the mildest disabilities to participate in 'supported employment' where they are assisted to hold jobs in their neighborhoods and communities. By congregating people according to their disability labels, we deny them the opportunity to discover how they would like to live their lives. Placed in settings that they have not

chosen, we condemn them to learn the next skill in a prefabricated hierarchy, irrespective of whether this is a skill that they want or need to learn.
At its worst, people spend years being taught skills in areas where they
have no gifts and which would be of marginal utility even if they mas-
tered them. As one who helped develop and now teaches one form of
person-centered planning, one of the authors travels extensively across
the United States. One question that is routinely asked the author during
lectures and consultations is how common are goals that have no utility
for the people with whom plans are created. Consistently this question
draws a strong response as those who have to implement the goals
express their frustration. Recent examples from annual plan goals illustrate the issue. The first was a goal that had been in place for a year that
said: 'Mary will prepare spaghetti every Wednesday night.' In talking
with Mary about her goals, she said that she does not like to cook in general and does not like spaghetti in particular. For Ted, a person with a
more severe disability, the cooking goal was to make tuna fish salad
weekly, although he dislikes it so much that he will not eat it. Goals that
are 'measurable' but not meaningful also abound. In records reviewed by
the author, it is common to find a goal that says the person 'will engage in
a community outing of her own choosing weekly'. While this goal has
superficial appeal, follow-up with the staff indicates that any time the
person goes out they use that as the required activity.

In these consultations and visits, it is not unusual to hear of people with
disabilities who hate to sit still and want an active job to be told that
they must first be successful in doing 'table top' assembly work. In one
instance, the root of trouble between two roommates was that one person
was assembling things using Popsicle sticks while her roommate disas-
sembled what the first person had created. Further, a hallmark of intellectual disabilities is great difficulty transferring skills acquired in one
setting to another. Yet people continue to be taught how to cook and clean
in 'model apartments' that are inside their day service buildings and then
have to be taught the same skills again when they move from their family homes to a place whose layout and appliances are different. The problem is not that there is a system that helps people learn skills, it is that the
system is not required to pay attention to what the person wants to learn,
how they want to learn, and the utility of what they learn. Put simply, the
developmental model has very limited utility.[17]

The innovations that allow us to hear what people are telling us with
their words and behavior are, essentially, a shift in the way we listen to
people with disabilities.[18] The changes can be explained most clearly
using the examples of two groups of people usually considered difficult
to serve in the community: those with labels of 'severe' and 'profound'
disabilities, and persons who challenge the system with their behavior.

Persons with 'severe' or 'profound' intellectual disabilities may not communicate with words; thus, we must rely on their behavior to tell us what they want in their lives. Similarly, individuals with aggressive or unpredictable behavior challenge the system. Traditional programs have focused on strategies to manage behavior.[19] Individuals have often been made to 'earn' what they want in their lives with 'good' behavior.[20] Support services see much of the behavior that is labeled non-compliant or problematic as nonverbal critiques of the services provided.[21]

Previous attempts to develop appropriate programs for persons with intellectual disabilities focused on making the person follow the rules of programs and services. Health and safety concerns were addressed first, but assessments did not explore how these concerns might be addressed in terms of what was important to the person. Where some of what was important to the person had been learned and put in a 'preferences' list, that information was then used to make the person earn what was important to them. Even worse, the direct care staff and family members who spent the most time with the person and knew him or her best were not invited to share their knowledge about the person's lifestyle preferences; that was left to the 'professionals'.

By spending time with individuals, we found another way of listening to them tell us who they are. We realized they had been telling us all along what was important to them, but they were not being listened to and were complaining about it with their behavior. For many of these individuals, there was an unfortunate cycle that began when their complaining behavior was 'targeted' by a behavior plan, developed by team professionals, and the intervention resulted in a louder complaint, followed by more intensive interventions and then a still louder complaint. As this cycle progressed, people were living more and more restrictive lives and 'shouting' with their behavior.

In many ways, beginning to listen to what they were telling us about what was important in their lives not only taught us how these individuals need to be supported, but also showed us what was wrong with the system. By listening to their words and behavior, and by seeking out and listening to those who knew and cared about them, we discovered their desired lifestyle. We found that what they wanted was simple, do-able, affordable, and different from what was typically offered to them. When all of these things were done, the individuals we worked with were successful in staying in their communities and able to live lives that were more fulfilling to them. In addition, the support services we helped put in place were almost always less expensive than the services that were previously provided.

With the alternative 'essential lifestyle approach' to assessment and planning, we start first with asking how the person wants to live. For people with severe disabilities who do not communicate with words, the process uses information from those who have a personal connection with the person. A decade of practice has resulted in the development of questions that consistently determine who has a personal connection with the person for whom the plan is being created. Collecting, comparing, and synthesizing the observations of these individuals, as well as reviewing records, provides the planner with what is known about what is important to the person with whom the plan is being created. What is important in everyday life is described. What is important to the individual then provides the context in which issues of health and safety are addressed. The resulting plan describes what is important to the person and what others need to know or do to support the person. It also offers opportunities for learning that help the person get more of what he or she wants in life.

Within this support model, helping the person have a life in which what is important to him or her is largely present and there is a balance between what is important to and what is important for the person is the beginning of the efforts. As the person's plan is implemented and the person receives support to attain the life he or she wants, support staff (and others close to the person) look for opportunities for the person to spend time in places where he or she is welcomed by others. As the person establishes these community connections, staff and others look for opportunities to establish and nurture relationships. Those people who become a part of the person's life are recruited into a 'circle of support', which serves as a safeguard for the person while describing and helping the person move toward a desirable future. Within this model, one of the key challenges is sharing control with the person while helping him or her have as much positive control over his or her live as possible.

II. RESTRICTING LIBERTY AND SUPPORTING LIFESTYLES

Whenever others determine how another will live, personal liberty is likely to be restricted. When the government restricts a person's liberty interests to a substantial degree, due process may be required.[22] Notwithstanding the degree of one's disability, inherent in the right to substantive due process is the right to a certain amount of autonomy to help direct the services one receives from the State. Now that professionals are able to consistently and reliably learn what is important to a person, that information should be used to ensure that those receiving state-funded services are able to state their preferences and shape their lifestyles.

Due process is required by Section 1 of the Fourteenth Amendment to the US Constitution,[23] which states: 'nor shall any State deprive any person of life, liberty, or property, without due process of law ...' As implied by the text of the Fourteenth Amendment, however, the government's obligation to avoid any action that might limit an individual's rights to life, liberty, or property is not absolute. Constitutional due process analysis balances an individual's interest in freedom against the State's asserted reasons for restraining it.[24] As long as due process has been provided, the government may validly act to limit an individual's rights to life, liberty, or property. The Supreme Court has addressed the individual's right to self-determination in several cases, and has described this right as a 'constitutionally protected' liberty interest.

Since the Supreme Court has not specifically addressed whether there is a fundamental liberty interest in self-determination for persons receiving state-funded disability services, analogies must be drawn from similar cases in creating an argument that such an interest exists. Even though persons with disabilities as a class are subject only to rational basis review, there exists for all persons, including persons with disabilities, a right to basic autonomy that may properly be viewed as part of the 'liberty' guaranteed against state action by the Fourteenth Amendment. The right to give input to the direction of support services should be considered a part of the liberty interest so protected. Thus, a state would need to show a relevant interest that outweighs the individual's liberty interest in basic autonomy, in order to justify its refusal to take the lifestyle preferences of a person receiving services into consideration.

In *Cruzan v Missouri Dept of Health*,[25] the Supreme Court held that a competent person does have a constitutionally protected liberty interest in refusing unwanted medical treatment, and that this right would outweigh any countervailing state interest. Nancy Cruzan suffered severe brain damage in an automobile accident. She remained in a coma in a Missouri state hospital with virtually no chance of ever becoming conscious again. Her parents sued the state on her behalf, asking for a court order requiring the withdrawal of life-sustaining treatment. Nancy's parents claimed she had a Fourteenth Amendment due process right to refuse unwanted medical procedures and that before her accident she told friends that she would not want to be kept alive in a comatose condition. In finding a protected due process right to direct the provision of state-funded medical services, the Court held that a state could limit exercise of the right to cases where there was 'clear and convincing' evidence as to what the person would have wanted.[26] The *Cruzan* court stressed that in the absence of a clearly expressed intent a state may refuse to honor the asserted wishes of the person.[27]

In making an argument that intellectual disability professionals have a legal obligation to consider the wishes of persons with intellectual disabilities in designing their state-funded services, two issues must be considered. The first is whether the individual meets the degree of competency needed to satisfy the court that the person can express 'clear and convincing evidence' of preferences or designation to some other person, such as a family member, to make such decisions for him or her. The second is whether the state has asserted a relevant interest that outweighs the individual's right to basic autonomy.

III. PERSON CENTERED PLANNING ALLOWS FOR ACCURATE AND RELIABLE DETERMINATION OF INDIVIDUAL PREFERENCES

The advent of person centered planning techniques changes the first part of this equation completely, by establishing a degree of competency and clear and convincing evidence of the individual's preferences. Among the general public, competency is widely believed to be a clearly established concept. In reality, competency is measured in degrees; an individual may be competent to make some decisions but not others, may be more or less competent at different times, and may show strengths and weaknesses in the various areas that are measured to evaluate competency. In short, there is no clear dividing line between an individual who is 'competent' and one who is not. Person-centered planning techniques can elicit information about an individual's wishes and preferences that are highly reliable and accurate, and which would therefore provide clear and convincing evidence of the person's competency to make certain decisions by herself, as well as collaborating in the decision-making process with professionals and surrogate decision makers in other decisions.

Recognizing individual preferences in the structure of services is best accomplished using person centered planning techniques. As the most accurate and reliable technology available today, person centered planning is considered 'best practice' in planning services for persons with intellectual disabilities.[28] Person centered planning techniques, when employed by a skilled professional, yield results that are accurate and consistent. Therefore, information about preferences and lifestyle choices made by an individual with an intellectual disability receiving state support services should be considered to meet the 'clear and convincing' standard set forth in *Cruzan*. Likewise, 'clear and convincing evidence' of the person with an intellectual disability's designation of these to allow others who know and care about the person contribute their knowledge about the individual's desires should satisfy the requirement established by *Cruzan*.

In *Youngberg v Romeo*,[29] the Supreme Court ruled that persons receiving state-operated long-term care services had a due process right to be safe and to be free from undue bodily restraint. In determining the structure of services to be provided, the Court emphasized deference to the judgment of qualified professionals working with the individual. Such a professional decision would be presumptively valid, and liability could only be imposed when the judgment of a professional was 'such a substantial departure from accepted professional judgment, practice, or standards as to demonstrate that the person responsible actually did not base the decision on such a judgment'.[30] Since every major professional organization for persons with intellectual disabilities endorses and encourages the use of 'person centered planning' and 'self-determination' principles as best practice by professionals, it can be argued that person centered planning techniques are required to meet the substantive due process guarantees of *Youngberg*.

Further, it can be argued that the implementation of the right to freedom from undue bodily restraint supports the use of person centered planning, since professionals generally agree that having control over one's physical self is meaningless without similar control over other lifestyle preferences the person deems important. This, combined with what is important for the person, results in a decrease in the need for restraints and control struggles.[31] In addition, on a different level, freedom from restraint can be interpreted as freedom from decisions made by others, within the context of professional judgment.

The Fourteenth Amendment's due process protections apply only to state action. About 50% of services provided to people with intellectual disabilities are directly state operated.[32] The other half are provided by private organizations that contract with the state to provide services. The Fourteenth Amendment's due process guarantees probably do not apply to privately run organizations, even when they are heavily subsidized with government funding.[33]

The courts have recognized, however, that recipients of federal financial assistance do have obligations to persons with disabilities under Section 504 of the Rehabilitation Act of 1973 and the Americans with Disabilities Act of 1990. These obligations include the provision of individualized treatment premised on the abilities and potential of each disabled person, rather than upon generalized assumptions about groups of disabled people; the provision of necessary and appropriate auxiliary aids; and the necessity to refrain from providing unnecessarily segregated services for institutionalized persons. Thus, private provider agencies have a legal duty, created by their receipt of federal funds to provide habilitative services that ensure that individuals' services meet their needs. The professional judgment standard, discussed above, requires that this be done by considering the preferences of the individual.

In addition to due process arguments, Section 504 of the Rehabilitation Act and Title II of the Americans with Disabilities Act require state-funded service providers to provide services in the least restrictive environment. Services that are individually developed to support what people want in their lives are the essence of 'least restrictive environment'.[34]

Moreover, providers of support services have an ethical obligation to develop services around the preferences of the individual. When there was no way to determine the chosen lifestyle of an individual with an intellectual disability, a process that simply deferred to professional judgment was accepted. A shifting body of professional opinion determined where and how people with intellectual disabilities lived.

As noted above, today there are reliable techniques to discover the preferred lifestyles of most people with intellectual disabilities. This technology should be considered when balancing the liberty interests of a person with an intellectual disability with governmental interests in restraining that liberty. Persons with intellectual disabilities should not be restricted in their pursuit of a chosen lifestyle any more than is necessary to protect their interests and those of the state. When the government determines the lifestyle of a person with an intellectual disability without considering that person's desires, it has, in effect, deprived that person of liberty without due process of law.

That is not to say that the preferred lifestyle of a person with an intellectual disability is always controlling. A balance is still needed. Many people with intellectual disabilities have health and safety needs that must be addressed. Many are vulnerable to abuse, neglect, or exploitation. The state has a legitimate interest in protecting these individuals. The state also has legitimate concerns regarding the expenditure of its resources. A new balance is therefore needed. One way to strike this balance is through a process that considers: (1) the desired lifestyle of the individual, (2) the health and safety needs of the individual and others, and (3) the resources available to support the individual. Professional judgment remains an integral part of this process. It requires skilled efforts to discover the desired lifestyles of persons with intellectual disabilities. Many individuals cannot speak for themselves. Most do not have sufficient life experiences to clearly determine their preferences, which they may tell us with their words or their behavior. Nearly all of those who do speak for themselves have been trained to suppress their desires and preferences. They tell us what they think we want to hear instead of what they want. Separately and collectively these factors require the counsel of professionals who possess the skills and experience necessary to determine the desired lifestyle.

The distinction between discovering the desired lifestyle of a person with an intellectual disability and actually making it happen is the essential point of departure. Persons with intellectual disabilities should be supported in their desired lifestyles unless there is good and sufficient cause not to. Where such cause exists, individuals should be supported in settings and circumstances that resemble their desired lifestyles as closely as is reasonably possible. The only acceptable reasons for not supporting a person with an intellectual disability in the essential aspects of his or her desired lifestyle are to accommodate resource limitations and health and safety concerns. Even where issues of safety or limitations in resources are raised, however, efforts must still be made to support the essential components of the individual lifestyle.

Issues of health and safety occur in the interactive context of the person's disability and the nature of his or her environment and circumstances. For example, people who have frequent, severe seizures not controlled by medication, which may cause them to fall and injure themselves, may not be able to live alone. Accommodating the physical effects of their disability requires that they have people nearby who can make sure that they do not severely injure themselves. It should be noted, however, that these aides are present to provide assistance during and after the seizure, not to prevent it. Moreover, this accommodation is only an issue where an individual wants to live alone, and even then, it is possible that someone with a severe seizure disorder could live alone with the assistance of appropriate technology (such as the use of a dog trained to detect seizures and summon immediate assistance).

The challenge is to assist people in realizing their desired lifestyles while accommodating their safety needs. Ronald's story is illustrative of how this can typically be done. When individuals working with the author encountered Ronald, they described him as a charming young man who had autism and had not used words to express himself for more than a decade. He was living in a residential school and was referred because he was no longer eligible for educational funding (he had turned 21), and the adult system had contracted with the University of Maryland to return such individuals to their home communities. Part of the original rationale for placing him in the school was that he did not know how to keep himself safe. He has a need to go on walks and wants to take walks whenever he feels the need, not just when they are scheduled. However, he does not recognize that he should stop for oncoming traffic when crossing streets. While in the residential school he was also described as being physically aggressive. It seems that Ronald wanted a tub bath, but the school only had showers. So there were statements in his records regarding 'physical aggression around evening hygiene'.

Because of the severity of his cognitive disability, it is unlikely that Ronald will ever learn to cross streets safely. However, this has not prevented him from achieving his desired lifestyle. Today he lives on five acres in rural Maryland where he can walk without crossing streets. He lives in a house with a tub and bathes without a struggle. (In fact, he has been reported to like long soaks that end only when the water goes from hot to tepid.) He has consequently moved from a very restrictive institutional setting to a setting where his preferences and challenges are accommodated.

Ronald has begun to speak again, but his speech is limited to occasional words and he can neither read nor write. However, his limited verbal communication was not an impediment to determining his desired lifestyle. The author and colleagues have developed techniques that routinely determine the preferences of people who do not use words to speak. The process is one that begins with asking who is in the person's life. Who does the person spend time with? In restrictive settings, a further question is who among those who are paid choose to spend time with the person? These questions tell the planner who to talk to but not who to listen to. Those who know what is important to a person have a personal connection with that person.

The next set of questions is designed to give the planner an indication of the presence of a personal connection. Potential informants are routinely asked what they like and what they admire about the person with whom the plan is being done. Those whose answers suggest that what they like is that the person makes their job easier do not have a personal connection. Those who report on something like a smile that lifts their spirits *do* have that connection. Informants are then asked a structured series of questions that further indicate the nature of the relationship, but more importantly, provide information from which what is important to the person can be abstracted.[35]

Ronald's story is no longer exceptional. Anecdotal reports and written program reviews from other states indicate that these activities are increasingly common. According to Robin Cooper, a policy analyst at the National Association of State Directors of Developmental Disabilities Services, 'Today the vast majority of states are requiring planning that reflects the values and principles of person centered planning in their home and community based waiver and/or in regulation. It is the norm.'[36]

In summary, physical and cognitive disabilities have not proven to be overwhelming obstacles to understanding and realizing the desired lifestyles of persons with disabilities. This does not mean that every person with a disability attains his or her ideal lifestyle. Compromise is part of life. Most of us have desires and preferences that are incompatible with other preferences or desires. But some individuals today are not given the chance to voice or realize any of their preferences. This must change. So the problem now becomes, how do we give a voice to those who have not had a voice?

IV. SUPPORTING ESSENTIAL LIFESTYLE CHOICES

Each of us, consciously or unconsciously, prioritizes our desires and preferences and directs our efforts to assure that we realize the preferences we perceive as essential elements of our lifestyle. By listening to the words and behaviors of persons with intellectual disabilities, we can understand what is most important to them. We can then prioritize our efforts on their behalf to assure that they obtain the essential elements of their desired lifestyles. What continuously impresses people who do this type of planning is how modest the essential aspects of those desired lifestyles are. Although successful efforts may require radical changes in the organization and conceptualization of services, helping people with intellectual disabilities realize their desired lifestyles rarely requires inordinate expenditures of public funds.

The expenditure of any public funds, however, raises concerns about the allocation of limited governmental resources. Our experience has been that for individuals receiving traditional community or institutional residential and day services, current funding is generally adequate to convert the program services to support services for a given individual. While some people require increased funding, others will need less funding. As long as those developing supports are able to manage within budgets for groups of people, they are able to support people within their desired lifestyles. Where this does not occur, the problem is usually that a manager is attempting to 'buy' someone his or her desired lifestyle by adding funding to a program model rather than converting to a support model.

Quality of life is increased and costs are decreased when available resources are used creatively. Supports that are built around the individual to meet the lifestyle choices of the individual are generally cost-effective for two reasons. First, people who are content with their lives require less supervision to address their discontent. Second, the use of generic community resources can reduce the need for public funding while simultaneously enhancing the individual's quality of life.

V. CONCLUSION

We can determine the desired lifestyles of people with intellectual disabilities and assure that the essential elements of their desired lifestyles are present. Typically we can do this while addressing any health or safety issues without increasing costs. Thousands of plans implemented with people with intellectual disabilities in the United States, Canada, and the United Kingdom demonstrate that how they want to live can be discovered and described. The documented preferences are modest and reflect the desire to have an everyday life. These same efforts show that issues of health and safety can be accommodated within the context of providing what is important for people with intellectual disabilities. The learning of the past decade creates an obligation on the part of those who plan services and protect the rights of people with intellectual disabilities. People with intellectual disabilities have the same rights as other citizens, not only in theory, but also in practice.

NOTES

1. MW Smull, 'Helping People Be Happy and Safe: Accounting for Health and Safety in Context of How People Want to Live' in VJ Bradley and M Kimmich (eds), *Quality Enhancement in Development Disabilities: Challenges and Opportunities in a Changing World* (Baltimore: Brookes Publishing Co, 2003) ('Where significant issues of health or safety create boundaries in what the person can do the problem solving is focused on how to help the person have as much of what is important to him as is possible within the boundaries created by issues of health or safety').
2. R Prouty and KC Lakin (eds), *Residential Services for Persons with Developmental Disabilities: Status and Trends through 1999* (Minneapolis: Univ of Minnesota, Research and Training Center on Community Living, Institute on Community Integration, 2000).
3. VJ Bradley, 'Evolution of a New Service Paradigm' in VJ Bradley, JW Ashbaugh, and BC Blaney (eds), *Creating Individual Supports for People with Developmental Disabilities: A Mandate for Change on Many Levels* (Baltimore: Brookes Publishing Co, 1994) 11–34.
4. JA Snow, 'Centering Our Planning on People' (National Program Office on Self-Determination, May 2001) http://www.self-determination.org/publications1251/pcp.html.
5. P Malette, P Mirenda, T Kandborg, P Jones, P Bunz, and S Rogow, 'Application of a Lifestyle Development Process for Persons with Severe Intellectual Disabilities: A Case Study Report' (1992) 17 *Journal of the Association for Persons with Severe Handicaps* 179–191.
6. ibid 181.
7. These 'statements' need not be made verbally, but can be communicated through behavior and previous choices. Many times family, friends, and others who know the person well have a better understanding of his or her preferences than professionals or clinicians.
8. New Hampshire Division of Mental Health and Developmental Services' Training Resource Network, 'A Brief History of Services' in *Enhancing the Lives of Adults with Disabilities* (1996) (on file with the authors).
9. ibid 14.
10. MW Smull, 'Responding to Behavioral Crises by Supporting People in the Lives That They Want' in RH Hanson, NA Wiesler, and KC Lakin (eds), *Crisis Prevention and Response in the Community* (Washington, DC: AAMR, 2002).
11. M Smull and C Lakin, 'Public Policy and Person-Centered Planning' in S Holburn and P Vietze (eds), *Person-Centered Planning: Research Practice and Future Directions* (Baltimore: Brookes Publishing Co, 2002).
12. ibid 5.

13. ibid.
14. ibid 3.
15. Minnesota Disability Law Center, Legal Advocacy for Persons with Developmental Disabilities (1989).
16. M Moon, JM Barcus, V Brookes, K Inge, and P Wehman, *Helping Persons with Severe Mental Retardation Get and Keep Employment: Supported Employment Issues and Strategies* (Baltimore: Brookes Publishing Co, 1990).
17. J O'Brien, 'The Principle of Normalization: A Foundation for Effective Services' in JF Gardener, L Long, D Iagulli, and R Nichols (eds), *Program Issues in Developmental Disabilities: A Resource Manual for Surveyors and Reviewers* (Baltimore: Brookes Publishing Co, 1980).
18. MW Smull, 'Thinking about Support Broker Roles' (Winter 1999/2000) 12/4 *Impact: Feature Issue on Support Coordination and Self-Determination for Persons with Developmental Disabilities* 6.
19. Smull (n 10 above) 3.
20. ibid 2–3.
21. ibid 3.
22. Due process is required by s 1 of the Fourteenth Amendment to the US Constitution, which states '…nor shall any State deprive any person of life, liberty, or property, without due process of law…'
23. US Const amend XIV, § 1.
24. *Kelley v Johnson* 425 US 238 (1976) (regulation of the personal appearance of policemen could be justified so long as the state has a rational connection between the regulation and the promotion of safety).
25. 497 US 261 (1990).
26. ibid 282.
27. ibid.
28. R Cooper, 'From Management to Support: No More Business as Usual' (Winter 1999/2000) 12/4 *Impact: Feature Issue on Support Coordination and Self-Determination for Persons with Developmental Disabilities* 2.
29. 457 US 307 (1982).
30. ibid 321–322.
31. Smull (n 10 above) 7.
32. Prouty and Lakin (n 2 above).
33. See, eg, *Rendell-Baker v Kohn*, 457 US 830 (1982) (private school whose income was derived almost entirely from public funding and which was regulated by public authorities, was not a state actor when it fired employees).
34. MW Smull, 'A Crisis Is Not an Excuse' (1999) 14/1 *Impact: Feature Issue on Behavior Supports for Crisis Prevention and Response* 1.
35. M Smull, B Allen, and ML Bourne, *Families Planning Together* http://www.allenshea.com/familyplan.html (2001) 45–75.
36. Smull and Lakin (n 11 above) 21.

Part III
The Disability Rights Movement: Anti-discrimination Legislation

8

The Potential of Disability Non-discrimination Laws

STANLEY S. HERR

I. INTRODUCTION

Disability discrimination laws can be a potent tool to safeguard the rights and meet the needs of persons with intellectual disabilities. In the United States, the Americans with Disabilities Act of 1990 (ADA) is highly specific and has achieved results for groups and individuals. In Israel, the Equal Rights for Persons with Disabilities Law of 1998 (ERPDL), while relatively untested, combines both non-discrimination and self-determination provisions. Many countries feature disability rights oversight agencies, such as the United Kingdom's Disability Rights Commission (established in conjunction with the Disability Discrimination Act of 1995 (DDA)), or Sweden's Disability Ombudsman that oversees disability non-discrimination laws for the benefit of persons with intellectual and other disabilities.

This chapter analyzes the ways various countries implement laws to remedy discrimination based on disability. These struggles to enforce national disability legislation have also reinforced the campaigns for international treaties on disability rights.[1] National disability non-discrimination laws, however, remain a primary means of human rights progress for people with disabilities.[2]

This chapter focuses on disability non-discrimination laws in the United States, Israel, and the United Kingdom because these three countries have common interests in using alternative dispute resolution methods to minimize, if not eliminate, disability discrimination.

Part II outlines the uses and limitations of disability non-discrimination laws for persons with intellectual disabilities, a group uniquely vulnerable and often limited in their ability to assert their statutory and constitutional rights. Part III explores the origins, provisions, and current status of the ADA, with a critique of the US experience of using the law to foster equality between citizens with and without disabilities. Part IV traces the development of disability anti-discrimination laws in Israel, the United Kingdom, and other countries, along with an overview of disability non-discrimination laws in thirty-eight countries. Part V offers some proposals for reform, while the Conclusion identifies implications for international efforts to combat disability discrimination.

II. USES AND LIMITATIONS OF DISABILITY NON-DISCRIMINATION LAWS

Disability non-discrimination laws have the potential to be of great use to persons with intellectual disabilities in their struggle for equality and integration. This use may come through group litigation more than through individual cases, more through disability rights commissions than through their own initiatives. Despite the obvious barriers, they have allies who are willing to press disability discrimination law to their advantage and have also turned to other non-discrimination laws and constitutional law to win substantial legal victories in their campaign for achieving legal rights.[3]

Although disability non-discrimination laws are becoming a common feature of disability rights laws in many countries, unfortunately, people with intellectual disabilities less frequently take advantage of these laws than people with other disabilities. This result stems from the nature of their disability and current state of advocacy and support services that limits exercise of such laws.

While not true of all persons with intellectual disabilities, many are less assertive, less willing to demand reasonable accommodations, and less able to demand an end to harassment or discriminatory behavior. In addition, they face more pronounced discrimination based on stereotypes. They are also more likely to be unemployed and hence less able to use these laws than those who are already employed. Furthermore, they may face threshold definitional questions of whether they are qualified individuals with disabilities. Employers may argue that they are not 'qualified' because they cannot perform the essential functions of a job, even with accommodations, although there is some work they are able to do.

Furthermore, they often lack advocates or representatives who are knowledgeable about disability non-discrimination laws. Personal care staff are often overworked, underpaid, have high turnover, and are expected to provide a range of services, from basic help with activities of daily living to promotion of independence. Staff often have limited education and receive only basic training to do their job. As a result, staff are not knowledgeable about laws and regulations that would protect the persons they support. Even if they were knowledgeable, they may fear that lodging such complaints might jeopardize the chances of placing future clients in employment. External advocates, such as the government funded Protection and Advocacy offices, formerly exclusively dedicated to enforcing the civil rights of persons with developmental disabilities, now have statutory mandates to provide legal services for all persons with disabilities. As a result, these offices are able to take far fewer individual advocacy cases, preferring to concentrate efforts on litigation and policy that will promote system change.

In general, full enforcement of disability non-discrimination laws is difficult, if not impossible, to achieve. Disability discrimination law, in requiring reasonable accommodations, requires employers to behave in ways that may—or may at least appear—to go against their economic self-interest. Although most studies find the cost of reasonable accommodations to be modest, 'managers will need to be convinced that the risks of liability outweigh the economic costs of compliance with the law.'[4] Thus, some commentators argue that disability discrimination law will not benefit all persons with disabilities, even if fully enforced, because employers are still able to hire any employee without a disability who can do the essential functions of the job marginally better than a person with a disability can, even with reasonable accommodations. Although in law an employer is not permitted to count the cost of the accommodation in considering the marginal superiority or inferiority of the job candidate with a disability, in fact, the candidate will often need to demonstrate superiority to get the job. Such determinations of 'marginal' superiority or inferiority are inherently subjective and may result in discrimination against persons with disabilities. Finally, anti-discrimination measures, which merely attempt to create a level playing field, will be only marginally effective when an individual's disability places actual limits on his or her economic competitiveness[5] as compared to others without disabilities. This proposition may be particularly true for persons with intellectual disabilities, many of whom face challenges in communication, learning, and generalizing knowledge to new situations—skills that are essential to workplace productivity.

Given this plethora of implementation problems, Weber and others argue that there should be a national employment policy for persons with disabilities that would go even further than anti-discrimination laws and affirmative action to a system of prospective set-asides. Under such proposals, private employers and the federal government would be required to participate. They would seek to combat discrimination and competitive disadvantage caused by the disability itself. These commentators opine that legal remedies do not go far enough and that even the best-motivated education and training efforts targeted toward people with disabilities have met with limited success. Thus, they urge new policy and legislative measures to supplement anti-discrimination law to strengthen affirmative action obligations to hire and promote people with disabilities.

III. THE AMERICANS WITH DISABILITIES ACT (ADA)

The ADA shows that progress against exclusionary paradigms toward people with disabilities has only come by struggle.[6] The campaign to bring US citizens with disabilities into the mainstreams of society began in 1973.[7] The Rehabilitation Act of 1973 had terse non-discrimination sections on programs receiving federal assistance, federal contractors, and the federal government. In many respects, the law was ahead of its time and ahead of the political mobilization and education needed to achieve its goals.[8] The ADA was modeled on the Civil Rights Act of 1964, using civil rights remedies to eliminate the marginalization of people with disabilities.[9]

With the support of a powerful coalition of people with disabilities, their families, politicians, and disability professionals, the ADA moved swiftly through Congress.[10] One hundred and eighty national organizations endorsed the bill.[11] These groups represented all the major disabilities, including mental retardation, spinal-cord injuries, and deafness, as well as less familiar ones. On 26 July 1990, President Bush signed the ADA into law on the South Lawn of the White House with great ceremony. He declared, 'Let the shameful wall of exclusion come tumbling down.'[12]

The ADA has achieved only partially successful results in the Supreme Court.[13] Most importantly, the Court has significantly narrowed the definition of persons with disability under the ADA.[14] The Court has also made it difficult, if not impossible, to sue the state for violations of the ADA. In *Board of Trustees of the University of Alabama v Garrett*,[15] the Court held that Congress could not constitutionally make states subject to disability discrimination lawsuits without their consent.[16]

There have, however, been a few consoling victories in the Supreme Court. In 1999, the Court held that persons with asymptomatic HIV infection were persons with disabilities within the meaning of the Act.[17] In the landmark precedent of *Olmstead v L.C.*,[18] a case that will be discussed below, the Court found that isolation of people in state institutions without services was unjustified. Finally, in 2001, the Court with narrow facts and context permitted a professional golfer to use a golf cart as a reasonable accommodation for his painful disability, which affects his legs' circulatory system.[19]

The ADA has been described as a vigorous legal and social enterprise that has helped 'to level a playing field which historically had discriminated against people with disabilities by imposing medicalized stereotypes'.[20] Its effects are visible from curb cuts to sidewalks, Braille signage, and accessible hotel rooms. To ignore the law's requirements is to face the real risks of negative publicity and even the prospects of being named as a defendant in an ADA suit.[21]

The ADA's remedies for discrimination affect many sectors of society, from higher education authorities to most employers (those with fifteen or more employees). Indeed, the ADA has become a central organizing tool for mobilizing and maintaining a cohesive lobby for the civil rights empowerment of America's people with disabilities, estimated to be 52.6 million people.[22] In the United States, as in forty other countries, disability non-discrimination laws are helping to end exclusion.[23]

IV. DISABILITY NON-DISCRIMINATION LAWS IN OTHER COUNTRIES

A. The Equal Rights for Persons with Disabilities Law in Israel (ERPDL)[24]

In 1998, the Equal Rights for Persons with Disabilities Law (ERPDL) was adopted with the twin goals of realizing non-discrimination and achieving equality through a 'legal entitlement to receive adequate support'.[25] However, thus far the law has generated more expectations than action.[26]

The Report of the Public Commission on Comprehensive Legislation concerning the Rights of People with Disabilities (popularly known as the Katz Commission Report) catalogued the grievances of the disability community. Unemployment is rife, with 70% of people with disabilities unemployed and 130,000 people on National Insurance Institute benefits, even though most of them are able to work and want to work.[27] In addition, the systems of residential services are over-reliant on institutionalization, with 5,700 of 7,100 out-of-home placements for people with mental retardation in institutions and 3,530 individuals (more than half) of all people in psychiatric hospitals solely because of the lack of community beds, not because of clinical needs.[28] The Report heavily criticized the inaccessibility of public buildings, public transportation, bomb shelters, and schools, as well as the lack of cognitive accessibility for persons with intellectual disabilities.[29]

In response to the social isolation of people with disabilities, the Commission recommended a statutory duty to provide programs of culture, leisure, and sport, particularly those that would facilitate integration in regular programs.[30] Noting that tens of thousands of children with disabilities do not receive the services mandated under the Special Education Act of 1988 and that several hundred are entirely excluded from school, the Commission called for a right to education that takes into account the needs of persons with disabilities.[31] The Report outlined many other necessary reforms. In the criminal justice context, the Commission urged the adaptation of interrogation and court to protect people with disabilities.[32]

To accommodate special needs, the Commission recommended the rights of people with disabilities to benefits in purchasing special equipment (such as wheelchairs and hearing aids), an expansion of mobility benefits in terms of assistance with car purchases, and the right to professional consultation as a means to minimize the use of guardianship.[33] The Report's centerpiece was the creation of the Equal Rights Commission for Persons with Disabilities to monitor and enforce the proposed legislation.[34]

In passing the ERPDL, the legislature recognized 'the principle of equality and the value of human beings created in the Divine image'.[35] The law protects individual dignity and freedom, enshrines the right to equal and active participation in society in all the major spheres of life, and provides 'an appropriate response to the special needs of a person with a disability, in such a way as to enable the person to live with maximum independence, in privacy and dignity, realizing her/his potential to the full'.[36] The law also contains a strong self-determination mandate: a person with a disability has 'the right to make decisions that pertain to her/his life according to her/his wishes and preferences'.[37] Furthermore, powerful language, absent from the ADA, permits affirmative action in order to correct prior or present discrimination against people with disabilities or to promote their equality.[38]

The movement for non-discrimination for persons with disabilities has spurred a wave of new legislation. For example, Nondiscrimination in the Provision of Goods, Services and Access to Entertainment and Public Accommodations Law, passed on 11 December 2000, furthers egalitarian aims. The Free Education for Sick Children Law (2001), passed on 1 January 2001, gives children (5 years or older) who are absent from school for over twenty-one days, or diagnosed with a condition that prevents them from attending school, a right to at-home schooling. Finally, the Rehabilitation of Persons with Mental Disabilities in the Community Law, passed on 11 July 2000, accommodates mental patients within community-based least restrictive environments. It guarantees their independence, human dignity, and quality of life in the spirit of 'Israel's Basic Law: Human Dignity and Liberty',[39] with individualized personal rehabilitation plans, an oversight committee, and special funding to implement the law's mandate.

Although Israel's special education law is modeled on the Individuals with Disabilities Education Act (IDEA) of the United States, it is neither as comprehensive nor as rights-oriented as its US counterpart.[40] It lacks clear requirements for least restrictive alternatives, remedies for unjustifiably separate schooling, and effective procedural safeguards.[41] As a result, some parents are seeking a law on integration of children with disabilities in the public schools.[42]

The Israeli judiciary is a potential ally for disability rights. Despite deciding only a handful of cases in this field, the leading case,

Botzer v Maccabim-Reut Local Authority, upheld the right of a high school student with physical disabilities to attend a physically accessible school.[43] Writing for the Court, Supreme Court President Barak declared that '[t]he disabled person is a human being who deserves equal rights. Neither outside society nor on its margins, the disabled person is an ordinary member of his society. The purpose of these arrangements is not to improve the quality of his isolation, but rather to integrate him—on occasions using affirmative action—in the regular structure of social life.'[44]

Two years later, in the 1998 decision in *Shtrum v Election Commissioner*, the Court ruled that polling places have to be physically accessible.[45] It interpreted election law to require that at least one polling place be accessible to voters with physical disabilities. Although no voting by mail ballots is permitted, the Minister for the Interior must make arrangements to permit a voter with a disability to vote outside his or her regular polling place in a physically accessible site. A remarkable feature of the *Shtrum* judgment was the Court's threat to postpone nationwide general elections if these access arrangements were not promptly made. The government took the threat seriously and speedily complied.

A recent discrimination case fared less successfully. On 9 September 1999, *Biz'chut* (the Israel Center for Human Rights for Persons with Disabilities) dismissed a case asserting that a pilot with cerebral palsy who used canes for mobility was improperly denied a pilot's license because of unfounded fear and stereotypes. The Israel Civil Aviation Administration had refused to grant him a test flight to demonstrate his abilities. However, a High Court panel of three judges expressed negative views of his chances of prevailing as a matter of law. Facing this explicit warning that the Court would rule against the pilot if pressed to decide, *Biz'chut's* attorney withdrew the claim rather than risk creating an unfavorable precedent.[46]

The judiciary has a role in enforcing non-discrimination disability rights.[47] It finds it easier to enforce rights in circumstances of non-compliance than in those involving the interpretation of ambiguous language. Israeli courts can issue injunctions or declarations of rights in public law cases. They can act when judges find unreasonable delay in the implementation of a law, especially when the law specifies a deadline for issuing regulations. Because the Equal Rights Law contains such a deadline, which expired in January 2000, it appears that the government will be in a legally insupportable position should they face a petition to remedy non-compliance. It can also be expected that the Israeli judiciary will reject an argument that the government lacks the funds to implement a particular law because such an argument has force only before legislation is enacted. This defense is not a good argument for doing nothing and, at best, becomes relevant when there is a choice of means to fulfill the law.

With a number of cases recently filed with promising results, the Israeli disability rights movement is likely to make greater use of the courts. Concepts such as 'the right to dignity', enshrined in one of the country's so-called basic laws, offer a building block for precedent in this field and are consistent with Israeli judicial trends.

Other disability rights claims remain to be filed and explored, but litigation disincentives exist. The lack of regulations renders the statute ambiguous. Some advocates also favor a strategy of quiet negotiations, wishing to avoid a backlash. Furthermore, few lawyers are aware of the ERPDL or willing to test its effectiveness.

The implementation of the ERPDL occurs in the context of a legal and cultural environment that tends to exalt symbol over substance. Like Section 504 of the US Rehabilitation Act, the ERPDL is weaker by being the product of a handful of legally trained activists rather than a strong grassroots disability rights movement. Social legislation generally and employment discrimination laws particularly are notoriously under-enforced in Israel. According to Guy Mundlak of Tel Aviv University's law faculty, 'We have a myriad of laws, with affirmative action, comparable worth for the genders, reasonable adjustments for disabled people. We have it all, everything in the recipe book for remedying unlawful discrimination. But nothing is being done about it.'[48] Mundlak estimates that fewer than ten significant cases have been decided in other fields of employment discrimination. As a result, he is not optimistic that future attempts to remedy disability discrimination through legal means will face better judicial attention.[49]

The success of the ERPDL will require coordination of the efforts of many.[50] In addition to the formation of the statutorily required advisory board, the Commission could accept the proposal for a larger body to be designated the 'Friends for Applying the Equal Rights for Persons with Disabilities Law', a legislative analogy to the role of amici curiae (ie, organizations or individuals who offer expertise to courts).

Disability rights in Israel suffer from a variety of impediments.[51] Several factors are responsible for the limited popular appeal of disability rights in general and the ERPDL in particular: the weakness of civil society,[52] the lack of appropriate and charismatic leadership, the lack of a powerful electorate invested in this issue, and internal dissension and fragmentation among the various groups that could constitute a disability lobby. In the midst of high-stakes concerns about war and peace, it is easy to see why disability rights receive relatively low priority and visibility.

Although Israel likes to think of itself as a compassionate place for people with disabilities, the reality is otherwise, and Israelis with disabilities do not want compassion or pity; they want their rights and the dignity of life in the mainstream. In recent years, the issue of disability is moving from a matter of charity and private misfortune to a matter of rights and public policy. Old notions that intellectual disability should be a basis for exclusion—for being 'put away'—are fading.

B. The UK's Disability Discrimination Act (DDA)

The United Kingdom has developed a comprehensive non-discrimination law—the DDA. A recent 1999 amendment to create the Disability Rights Commission and the Employers' Forum on Disability has structural support for the DDA in general and the corporate community in particular. Yet controversy exists as to whether change is proceeding quickly enough.

English activists sought a disability law to eliminate technical barriers and empower an oppressed minority. Advocates sought a 'Charter of Rights' and civil rights legislation to place more power in their own hands. They viewed barrier removal as not merely the provision of ramps, information in Braille and on tape, and signing on television, but the development of a unique disabled people's perspective on the world and the opportunity to contribute to its future shape.[53] More concretely, they sought civil rights laws to ensure community-based support systems and equal opportunities in employment, education, medical services, housing, recreation, the environment, and information.[54]

English advocates viewed Section 504 of the Federal Rehabilitation Act, and the ADA as significant models for change.[55] The rise of self-help organizations in the disability community and the existence of equal rights laws based on race and gender also fueled demands for a disability discrimination law. However, such efforts repeatedly failed in the 1980s.[56] As of 1991, the Minister for Disabled People was still arguing for persuasion, not legislation, as the way to deal with acknowledged discrimination.[57] The activists viewed such policies of persuasion as bankrupt. 'The American Disability movement', they declared, 'has used (civil rights movement) tactics to good effect in the past 20 years.'[58]

The DDA bans discrimination against disabled persons in four sectors: employment; provision of goods, facilities, and services; purchases or rental of land or real property; and certain forms of transportation. The DDA applies to employers with fifteen or more employees, defining disability discrimination as treating a disabled person 'less favorably' than someone else by reason of the person's disability where the reason: (a) does not, or would not, apply to others; and (b) the treatment cannot be justified.[59] The justification for the deferential treatment must be material and substantial—eg, no adjustment would enable the disabled person to do the job in question or to assume another available position. Like the concept of 'reasonable accommodations' under the ADA, the employer may have to make reasonable adjustments to the disabled person's employment or the premises if the lack of these adjustments substantially disadvantage a disabled person compared to a person who is not disabled.

Part III of the Act prohibits discriminatory practices by establishments that furnish goods and services. These practices include the refusal of services; the provision of services on worse terms or a lower standard of services; the failure to make reasonable adjustments that would allow a disabled person to access a service, provided that in each case the failure to make an adjustment or the treatment subject to complaint cannot be justified.

The Disability Rights Commission (Commission or DRC), which formally replaced the National Disability Council established in 1995,[60] has authority to investigate discrimination and enforce the provisions of the DDA. Launched in 2000, it is intended to avoid 'adversarial' and 'oppressive' approaches and primarily to educate the public and promote good practice.[61] The DRC provides four core services: legal advice to individuals, investigation and resolution of complaints, shaping of policy, and media work. Victims of disability discrimination have won at least four significant monetary settlements under the DDA. However, less than 24% of such applicants (before Employment Tribunals) have prevailed (106 out of 450 cases).[62]

In 1999, the Disability Rights Task Force on Civil Rights for Disabled People recommended numerous changes to strengthen the DDA.[63] The Task Force recommended extension of the DDA to education, strengthening housing protection, and expansion of the definition of disability to cover persons with HIV infection. The Task Force also called for the public sector to promote the equalization of opportunities for disabled people, including the adoption of performance measures to assess the impact of the DDA in the judiciary, local government, and the health and social service sectors.

Yet the DDA remains a law in need of reform, described by a leading commentator as containing many 'flaws' and 'deliberately designed hoops and hurdles which are creating barriers to effective anti-discrimination laws in the field of disability'.[64] The law has been criticized as a half measure that has mollified, but not satisfied, the goal of full-fledged law reform.[65]

The Disability Rights Commission, however, can bolster implementation.[66] It can help to strengthen the requirements for physical alterations by service providers that are due by 2004, and can lobby for statutory and other changes recommended by the Task Force on Civil Rights for Disabled People. It can provoke a useful debate that challenges conventional notions of equality of opportunity as entailing merely the adoption of procedures or the removal of barriers. An intellectually adventuresome DRC can stress the values of human dignity that would lead society to redress disadvantage associated with disability, by improving the individual's ability to compete, giving attention to remedies for cumulative discrimination (eg, combating the problems faced by people of color with disabilities or females with disabilities), and campaigning for positive, affirmative action programs that go further than the narrow legalistic anti-discrimination paradigm.[67]

Vague terms like 'reasonableness' and 'justification' in the DDA made it difficult to prove discrimination and enforce the law. The initial lack of a commission and the status of the National Disability Council as merely an advisory body left the Act without a strong watchdog. The cost of private litigation has limited the number of claims under the Act. Finally, the DDA's wide exemption clauses left many sectors of the English economy and many forms of discrimination outside the reach of the law.[68]

C. An Overview of Disability Non-discrimination Laws in Other Countries

In every continent, countries have enacted disability non-discrimination laws. In forty-one countries, these laws vary from non-discrimination statutes to constitutional non-discrimination provisions, from highly specific protections and prohibitions to more hybrid social welfare laws with some anti-discrimination language, from penal laws to those with civil characteristics, and from generic non-discrimination to disability-specific laws.

1. Analysis of Fifty Disability Laws

Some countries have multiple laws dealing with this subject matter, with half of those fifty laws having been enacted by 1995. The earliest example is found in the United States, with the non-discrimination provisions of the Rehabilitation Act of 1973.[69] Canada and Spain enacted laws in 1982 and 1980, respectively. In 1990, the Americans with Disabilities Act, as the first comprehensive disability non-discrimination law, was followed by forty-seven laws in various countries. The Standard Rules on the Equalization of Opportunities for Persons with Disabilities, declared in 1993, was another inspiration for such laws. The year that witnessed the largest volume of legislation was 1996, with the enactment of eight laws.

The scope of the laws varies from comprehensive protections in employment, public accommodations, education, and government services to general prohibitions against non-discrimination. The most comprehensive laws provide protections in the areas of housing and the provision of goods and services. Only four countries limit coverage to one specific area, such as employment or public access. Eleven countries have a reasonable accommodations requirement in at least one of their non-discrimination laws.

Countries vary widely in their definition of disability. Twenty-seven of the forty-one countries do not define the categories of individuals covered by their law. Countries with a constitutional non-discrimination provision are much more likely to include disability in a list of characteristics against which discrimination is prohibited (eg, race, religion, political beliefs, and disability). The most comprehensive laws include prohibitions against individuals regarded as having a disability and their family members, defining disability to include drug and/or alcohol addiction. One of the most narrowly drafted laws specifically excludes persons with mental illness, alcoholism, and drug addiction.

The most comprehensive non-discrimination laws contain defenses for 'reasonable' discrimination or undue hardship to businesses. In a nod to past paternalistic attitudes, several countries have created a defense for discrimination 'in the best interest' of the person with a disability. In addition, several laws contain a provision allowing the severity of a person's disability to be considered when deciding whether discrimination has occurred. The most comprehensive laws include specific injunctive, declaratory, or judicial remedies, including money damages, although the amount of damages may be limited in some cases.

Nineteen countries have established a commission or ombudsman to mediate claims of disability discrimination or otherwise apply disability laws. The duties of such commissions vary by country, from educational to litigative. The most powerful commissions have the power to promulgate regulations, investigate complaints, and issue injunctions against discrimination. Commissions may also provide mediation or arbitration services, represent an individual with a disability in seeking judicial remedies, and coordinate national disability policy. Other commissions certify workers as 'disabled', or confer tax exemptions on businesses or other organizations providing employment, accommodations, or accessibility to persons with disabilities.

2. *The Swedish Example*

Some countries with a tradition of progressive disability legislation were slow to enact disability non-discrimination laws. For example, Sweden only banned employment discrimination against persons with disabilities in May 1999.[70]

The Swedish anti-discrimination law protects persons with a permanent physical or mental limitation in the ability to function.[71] It covers both direct and indirect discrimination (defining the latter as treating a job applicant or employee less favorably by using a rule, requirement, or procedure that seems neutral but in practice is particularly disfavorable to persons with a particular disability).[72] An innovative feature of the law is to define an action for disability harassment, when an employer who is informed that when an employee considers herself or himself subject to harassment by other employees on the basis of disability. In such situations, employers must investigate the reported harassment and undertake measures reasonably necessary to prevent future harassment.[73]

The law also places duties on the Disability Ombudsman to ensure compliance through persuasive activities in the first instance,[74] or adversarial methods if necessary.[75] This litigation capability resembles powers vested in the US Attorney General under the ADA.[76]

V. PROPOSALS FOR IMPROVING THE ENFORCEMENT OF DISABILITY NON-DISCRIMINATION NORMS

A. Adversarial and Alternative Mechanisms for Dispute Resolution and Compliance

In an era of globalization, scholars and advocates of disability rights glean lessons from the experiences of other countries. The backlash against disability rights and the frequently disappointing outcomes of litigation and administrative remedies in the United States suggest that it is time to explore less adversarial methods. Instead of the hyper-litigation characteristics of the US legal culture, most countries with disability non-discrimination laws are seeking positive outcomes through a mixture of formal and informal ADR strategies, with litigation reserved as a last-ditch strategy for particularly egregious or stubborn misconduct.

This experience can help to fuel the global disability rights movement as well. Instead of over-reliance on lawyers and other highly trained advocates—who may be in short supply (either in absolute numbers or as a result of these professionals' unwillingness to undertake disability rights cases)—the non-litigative approach focuses on methods and approaches grassroots activists can put into practice. Thus, the public protest and civil disobedience that took place in Israel and other bottom-up strategies can empower people with disabilities in both industrialized and non-industrialized nations. Until large numbers of people with disabilities become invested in the implementation of disability non-discrimination laws and other forms of disability rights, there will remain a yawning gap between law on the books and law in reality.

Although disability rights lawyers will continue to play leadership roles in many countries, there is both a pragmatic and a values-centered case for a greater use of political and ADR approaches that other disability rights leaders and allies can more readily employ. For these reasons, a national focal point for the implementation of ADA-type laws and other disability rights, coupled with the use of the full continuum of dispute resolution strategies, offers greater promise of including people with disabilities in the fabric of the social, economic, and cultural lives of their respective countries.

1. *Impact Litigation*

Court cases, by their very nature, focus public attention on a problem by establishing legal precedent or targeting an industry. Litigation establishes a public record and gives future plaintiffs a better understanding of not only the defendant industry and the obstacles to compliance, but a roadmap to effective and sophisticated strategies that advocates can build upon for future cases. Technical assistance providers may also use information acquired through litigation to make their services more useful.[77] Unlike the Alternative Dispute Resolution Movement, where victories are often packaged as compromises and publicity is minimized, litigation attracts attention and can change attitudes within an industry and among the general public about the costs and benefits of compliance. At the appellate level—particularly in the handful of cases that reach a country's highest court—litigation can draw in non-party organizations as amici curiae, thus creating new coalitions and mobilizing a broader array of disability activists.

But litigation is also expensive, time-consuming, and can be administratively burdensome.[78] Political considerations may influence whether meritorious cases are filed. The low rate of success for US plaintiff parties deters private and governmental litigants.[79] In Title I judicial decisions, the employer prevailed in 92% of 760 final merits decisions (1992–1997) and 94.4% of 397 merits decisions in 1998.[80] The public sector has strikingly limited manpower and financial resources for launching cases.[81] In the private sector, there are only a finite number of attorneys with real specialization in ADA law and incentives to bring cases.[82] Finally, the US Supreme Court's recent ADA jurisprudence is controlled by a majority openly skeptical of, if not hostile to, the aims and coverage Congress built into the Act.

2. *Alternative Means of Dispute Resolution*

In the United States, the standard approach to ADA compliance stresses the use of alternative dispute resolution (ADR) techniques. Indeed, the Act itself encourages the use of such techniques.[83] Despite this admonition, there is insufficient discussion and application of these and other creative methods for furthering the sweeping purposes of the ADA.[84]

a. Negotiation

Settlement negotiations generally are employed in all forms of dispute resolution, both in the pre- and post-litigation settings.[85] Good negotiation outcomes may be difficult to obtain for ADA complainants because of sharp disparities in power and knowledge. The complainant may have limited verbal skills, and if a person with intellectual disabilities, may be unable to articulate a persuasive argument.

Negotiation can, however, limit adversarial negativity and backlash. Some defendants who claim to want to 'do the right thing' express surprise and resentment when a lawsuit is filed with no warning or opportunity to correct the problem.

b. Conciliation

In general, 'conciliation' refers to the process of speaking to each party separately, acting as an intermediary, and trying to come to some resolution. A conciliator works with each party to facilitate a meaningful dialogue.[86] Besides offering an amicable remedy, conciliation is arguably a response to the EEOC's often clogged caseload.[87]

c. Arbitration

Arbitration represents a midpoint between mediation and litigation. An arbitrator will conduct a hearing and submit a decision, usually binding, to the parties. Typically, the parties sign an arbitration agreement promising to submit any dispute to arbitration; this is frequently a term of employment or an arrangement made when the complaint arises.[88] In some circumstances arbitration is mandatory.[89]

Compared to litigation, arbitration is generally quick, private, less expensive, and more flexible, all of which avoids damage to the ongoing relationship of parties in a work environment.[90]

Voluntary arbitration may be especially attractive for fact-specific disability rights statutory claims.[91] In the ADA context, such issues include whether the person is a direct threat to himself or others so as to disqualify him for an ADA claim; whether questions asked of the plaintiff are pre-employment medical inquiries that the Act prohibits; and whether health insurance has been denied because of a disability.[92] A reasonable accommodation is another example since changes in the technology such as voice-activated computers and lightweight prostheses demand flexible and timely remedies. In addition, new Internet arrangements that enable more people with disabilities to work at home suggest that a speedy ADR resolution that takes contemporary technology into account is superior to a protracted litigation in which the final decision is rendered moot by the evolving technology.[93]

Furthermore, a party does not forego the substantive rights afforded by the statute; the party merely submits to a resolution in a non-judicial forum.[94] The private nature of the proceedings can also encourage employees to engage in a candid assessment of their disabilities and the required accommodations in a setting that they may perceive as less humiliating and stigmatizing than a public courtroom. Employers may be more inclined to hire workers with intellectual disabilities if a discharge for a legitimate reason will only risk arbitration rather than a costly litigative battle.

Employers also may find that the costs and benefits of providing reasonable accommodations during a period of arbitration allows them to resolve the employment issue quickly without having to screen others for the job or to undertake an expensive reassessment of whether the position should be eliminated altogether. Furthermore, since the ADA involves a case-by-case analysis, there may be little difference in the quality of decision making between a resolution through arbitration or through a courtroom plagued with pressures to resolve claims as quickly as possible. Finally, diverting some ADA claims from congested court dockets or from EEOC backlogs may make eminently good sense.[95] An arbitration decision, however, is usually final or lacks an adequate appeal process. In most cases, a court will not review the decision at all; if review is granted, a court will overturn an arbitrator's decision only under very narrow circumstances.[96]

The lack of a public forum for the dispute deprives the public of knowledge about arbitration awards involving disability discrimination. Because employers are usually repeat players in the process, they can exploit unfair structural advantages over claimants that a public forum might help to neutralize.[97]

d. Mediation

Mediation under the ADA is notable as the 'first civil rights law to affirmatively promote mediation to resolve disputes under its provisions'. The decision to mediate context is completely voluntary.[98] The mediator does not decide who is right or wrong and has no authority to impose a settlement upon the parties. Rather, the mediator helps the parties jointly explore and reconcile their differences. Mediation often takes place early in the grievance process, saving resources by avoiding investigation of a charge, as well as court and attorney costs. In addition, mediation prevents the hardening of positions that can occur during the process of investigation.

In ADA disputes, where the capacity of mediation, with an intellectual disability in question, the individual may need an attorney as well as accommodations or other support helpers to participate effectively. In addition, since the key issue is what constitutes a reasonable accommodation, an 'interactive process' should be used to identify, evaluate, and design alternative disability accommodations.[99] A fair process requires the mediator to ensure that 'the parties have a sufficient understanding of [the parties'] rights and obligations under the ADA, and the implications of any (a) agreement they reach, or (b) decision to reject an offer of settlement.'[100]

Even ADR trade association representatives discourage mediation that is not fully consensual or that involves parties with types of disabilities that inevitably produce tremendous power imbalance.[101] For instance, the Vice President for Governmental Relations of the American Arbitration Association views mediation as inherently unfair to some complainants with intellectual disabilities. As an example, she cites her brother, who has Down's syndrome and who would not be able to fully participate in mediation about what constitutes a reasonable accommodation at work.[102] She also expresses the view that the resolution of disputes involving dyslexia or attention deficit disorder may require the hiring of experts, which may result in a considerable financial hardship for the employee.

B. Other Problem-Solving Approaches

1. *Quasi-Governmental Initiatives*

One critical illustration for people with intellectual disabilities are the efforts to implement the Supreme Court ruling *Olmstead v L.C.* that unnecessary institutionalization of individuals with disabilities is a form of discrimination that violates the ADA.[103] Although the Court held that qualified individuals with disabilities have a right to care and treatment in community-based settings, many critical questions remain unanswered.[104] These questions focus on the funding, the cost of accommodations on the care systems, and the political will to realize the *Olmstead* rights.

Rather than promoting litigation as the tool for resolving the unanswered questions and implementing the Court's mandate, the Department of Health and Human Services established an *Olmstead* working group within the Department. Many different agencies within the Department participated in this work group, whose mission was to lead an effort to identify systemwide solutions that will promote care and treatment in community-based settings.[105] The group's emphasis was on building coalitions within the Department, and with critical stakeholders outside the Department such as states, individuals with disabilities and their families, advocacy organizations, and foundations.[106]

2. *Private Initiatives*

Initiatives by non-profit and other private sector actors are still indispensable for the ADA's proper implementation. The existence of a large, strong and diverse disability coalition was crucial to the enactment of the ADA and remains a vital ingredient for retaining the ADA in its undiluted form. A host of legal, grassroots, and membership organizations continue to give priority to lobbying, litigative, and other creative strategies to transform the ADA's paper rights into real gains for people with disabilities.

Private sector actors have the flexibility, independence, and commitment to press for such changes. Groups like the American Association for People with Disabilities and hundreds of other nonprofits have a real stake in using the ADA, promoting a full array of implementation strategies and developing 'out of the box' ADR solutions to persistent ADA problems. Legal advocates have pressed novel claims that push legal theory to resolve some of the most critical barriers to the implementation of ADA, Section 504 and related disability laws.[107]

Reliance on the private sector, however, has several drawbacks. There is a lack of coordination among the many actors that can produce inefficiency. These actions may have conflicting agendas or represent inconsistent interests. Such organizations are already cash-starved and face numerous demands on their time and resources. In the perennial competition for fund raising and public attention, private actors have to search for 'new and exciting ideas' to fuel their organizations, and therefore may devote less attention to the old, unfinished business under the ADA.

VI. PROPOSALS FOR REFORM

A. Disabilities Rights Commissions

The Israeli experience suggests that strong, independent oversight and enforcement agencies can advance disability non-discrimination law. Indeed, the Equal Rights for Persons with Disabilities Commission is widely viewed as the linchpin for implementing the ERPDL. Government officials seek its advice and consultation on a wide array of disability issues.[108] The Commission is an enforcer, publicist, and politically influential mobilizer of interests to transform the words of the ERPDL into effective action.[109]

Because it is a relatively new entity, the Commission still needs to develop a cohesive strategy, coalition, and set of priorities for its work.[110] The Commission has emerged as a lobbyist for the enactment of a stronger ERPDL and has become a voice for disability rights on governmental committees and public policy issues.[111] The provisional naming of an eleven-person advisory board itself provoked controversy and this entity is likely to be replaced by a larger, more representative body.[112] The Commission can indeed energize the Israeli disability rights movement and stimulate reforms in other countries. Other countries with existing commissions face similar challenges.

B. Creating a White House Office on ADA Implementation and Disability Rights

Reform legislation in Israel, England, and Sweden has important implications for the search for directions for reform and revitalization of the ADA. One promising approach is to create an office for ADA Implementation and Disability Rights in the White House. An analogy for this concept is the White House Office for AIDS/HIV Policy, first instituted by the Clinton Administration and, after some interval of uncertainty, retained by the Bush Administration.[113]

At present, the United States lacks a coherent federal policy on disabilities and a sustained strong central stimulus for disability rights. Given the divided federal responsibilities for ADA enforcement and advisory oversight, an ongoing White House Office can bring visibility and 'political clout' to the complex tasks associated with fully implementing this landmark disability rights legislation. Moreover, the Office can assume other neglected tasks: ensuring that the broad range of federal policies, practices, and budgetary decisions are reviewed for their impact on the approximately 54 million Americans with disabilities by a disability-friendly entity. It can also review the needs for stronger modifications in the ADA itself by closely examining more expansive rights in the non-discrimination laws of other countries.[114] Such an Office would bring to the table important stakeholders outside the federal government and develop better lines of coordination and cooperation with the states, the non-profit sector and other leaders on disability-rights and related disability policies.[115] However, the Office's primary focus should be the ADA and the law's impact on private individuals and on government actors at the federal, state, and local levels. The civil rights provisions of the Rehabilitation Act should receive the Office's attention because they affect federal contractors, federal employees, and recipients of federal assistance.

The formulation of an Office on ADA Implementation and Disability Rights, whether sited in the White House or elsewhere in the federal government, will require careful analysis and a mobilization of interest groups.[116] Its success will depend in large measure on the strength and vigilance of the disability rights movement. Will the Office have sufficient long-term stability to be taken seriously and to ensure continuity of effort? Although in the long term, a statutory body is preferable, the creation of the Office by Executive Order could signal serious purpose, avoid risky congressional debates, and lead to ongoing productive initiatives.[117] Will the tasks that are assigned the Office—and the expectations raised by its creation—overwhelm its capacities? Here again, planning decisions can help meet the objection. Linking the Office to the well-established Domestic Policy Council of the White House also can mitigate the problem.

The prospects for creating a White House Office are enhanced by the likelihood of bipartisan support. In just the second week of his Administration, President George W. Bush announced a $1 billion package for new disability programs and a recommitment to the goals of the ADA. At a White House ceremony on 1 February 2001, he declared, 'Eleven years after the ADA, we are a better country for it.' His statement also recognized shortcomings in compliance, noting that, '[w]e must speed up the day when the last barrier has been removed for full independent lives for every American, with or without disabilities.'[118]

Although some Democratic Congressional leaders were withholding judgment until the details of new programs were released, Senator Tom Harkin, an architect of the ADA, observed that on such disability issues, 'I've never known any partisan debate.'[119]

C. Enhancing the Use of Alternative Means of Implementation and Enforcement

An important insight that flows from the disability rights experience in many countries is the critical role of non-litigation methods. In the United States, Israel, United Kingdom, and other industrialized nations, initial non-adversarial interventions have fostered cooperation and served to minimize backlash from employers and other segments of society.

In England, the Employers' Forum on Disability has demonstrated that employers can be organized to support disability rights and the implementation of non-discrimination laws if positive methods, such as public education, are stressed. UK researchers characterize mediation and arbitration as useful to address 'wider issues than are possible in litigation' with remedies that 'may go well beyond monetary compensation'.[120] Many disability leaders see other avenues for social change that appear more promising (such as, for example, stressing the common interests between employers and workers with disabilities).

D. Developing an Appropriate Test Case Strategy

Advocates will continue to achieve advances through well-chosen litigation. The *Olmstead* case is a good example of the progress that can be achieved through landmark litigation, followed up by problem-solving approaches. Court cases are particularly advantageous when favorable precedent is achieved, when the offending conduct is particularly egregious, or when other methods have or are likely to fail. Particularly in the United States, where the ADA was first enacted in 1990, advocates can make a persuasive argument that employers and other potential defendants have long been on notice of ADA mandates and that litigation is appropriate where a defendant has willfully violated or remained ignorant of the law's requirements.

Political pragmatism, sound social policy, good public relations and, most importantly, the interests of persons with disabilities suggests that a balanced array of implementation options is needed. In the United States, for example, the Bush Administration is likely to make conservative judicial appointments. If the Administration succeeds in this goal, the federal courts and particularly the Supreme Court could become even less receptive to ADA claims than at present.[121] Regardless of the pragmatic considerations, good public policy supports a preference for ADR over litigation where ADR can produce greater satisfaction by disputants or more effective implementation of ADA norms. Public relations also favor a balanced enforcement strategy, since conflicts cast as battles between small, well-meaning commercial establishments and governmental Goliaths can detract from general public and political support for disability rights.

VII. CONCLUSION

As this chapter has shown, the ADA and the laws of Israel, the United Kingdom, and many other countries are tangible manifestations of an international movement for disability rights. They advance recognition of the rights of the world's 500 million people with disabilities. They help governments and the public see and understand the human rights and needs of this huge but largely invisible minority. Such laws can also assist the less assertive and less vocal sectors of this minority—people with intellectual disabilities—to receive the rights and dignity they are due.

The ADA has the potential to play an important role in the Global Disability Rights Movement as an inspiration to countries around the world to enact and apply non-discrimination norms. It can reach persons with intellectual disabilities with a determined push by advocates and concerned scholars. As Justin Dart, Jr. has eloquently written, 'keeping the promise' of the ADA is vital not only for the citizens of this country (US) but is a beacon for the empowerment of 'half a billion people in other nations' who have disabilities.[122] The ADA embodies the international human rights standards on non-discrimination that are identified in Rule 15 of the UN Standard Rules on the Equalization of Opportunities for Persons with Disabilities. Disability non-discrimination laws in forty-one countries attest to this progress and the inspiration provided by the UN Standard Rules and the ADA model. Further study is needed to understand the extent to which these new laws have produced new realities and not merely new expectations. Not only scholars but also disability rights activists will have to be involved in this enterprise. Furthermore, visitors from abroad who come to the United States for study can carry home with them insights and impressions as to whether the ADA represents real progress. Adoption of the reforms proposed in this article can favorably affect those assessments.

Universal disability rights has at least three dimensions: the development of a sense of personal pride and empowerment; the creation of authentic expectations for the rights that people with disabilities should enjoy and the quality of life that should be available to them; and the development of new mechanisms for the implementation of disability non-discrimination laws, such as the Israeli Commission on Equal Rights for Persons with Disabilities, the UK Disability Rights Commission, and the Swedish Disability Ombudsman. Comparative knowledge of disability non-discrimination laws can enrich advocates' and policymakers' understanding of the statutory tools and strategies for advancing equality of opportunities for persons with intellectual disabilities.

Ultimately, laws like the Americans with Disabilities Act, the Israel Equal Rights for People with Disabilities Law, and the UK's Disability Discrimination Act are not panaceas. They constitute benchmarks that the players in the disability rights movement can use to raise public consciousness, change public policies, alter budgetary appropriations, and transform the day-to-day lives of people with disabilities. This process of transformation is measured not only by external criteria but also by shifts in the self-images of adults and children with disabilities as they come to see themselves as talented human beings who have much to contribute to society. The ADA and its counterparts thus act as catalysts for change. The changes have reverberations throughout legal, political, and personal realms.

NOTES

1. SS Herr, 'UN Symposium on International Disability Rights' (Spring/Summer 2000) 7 *Law & Health Care Newsletter* 4; R Jiminéz, 'The Americans with Disabilities Act and its Impact on International and Latin American Law' (2000) 52 *Alabama L Rev* 419, 420; Organization of American States, 'Inter-American Convention on the Elimination of All Forms of Discrimination Against Persons with Disabilities' (7 June 1999) AG/RES, 1608 (XXIX-0199), Argentina, Brazil, Panama, Costa Rica, Mexico, Uruguay, and Chile have ratified the Convention, which entered into force 14 September 2001.
2. I Zitner, 'A Discussion on the Views of Human Rights of People with Disabilities' in E Kemppainen (ed), *Social Commission Report* (1999) 82.
3. *Botzer v Maccabim-Reut Local Authority* HC 7081/93, 50 PD (1) 19, 26 (1993).
4. HC 1759/99; *Avratz v Election Commissioner to the City of Jerusalem* 6790/98 (High Court, Chesin J) (10 October 1998) (petition on comparable issue denied as not timely filed).

5. *Miller v Defense Minister, et al.* 49 PD (IV) 107, 120–121 (1995).
6. N Ziv, 'Disability Law in Israel and the United States—A Comparative Perspective' (1999) 28 *Israeli Yearbook on Human Rights* 171.
7. R Silverstein, 'Emerging Disability Policy Framework: A Guidepost for Analyzing Public Policy' (2000) 85 *Iowa L Rev* 1695.
8. One commentator observed that s 504 was:

> not the result of the efforts of a social movement or of traditional interest group politics but rather the result of a spontaneous impulse by a group of Senate aides who had little experience with or knowledge about the problem of discrimination against disabled people. Seeing an opportunity in a fairly standard piece of legislation, these Senate staff members sought to promote disabled people's participation in employment and other activities by prohibiting discrimination on the basis of handicap in federally supported programs. Because of their strategic role in the legislative process, they were able to do so essentially on their own initiative.

RK Scotch, *From Good Will to Civil Rights: Transforming Federal Disability Policy* (Philadelphia: Temple Univ Press, 1984) 139; *Cherry v Matthews* 419 F Supp 922 (DDC 1976) (requiring HEW to promulgate regulations to enforce s 504); JP Shapiro, *No Pity: People with Disabilities Forging a New Civil Rights Movement* (New York: Times Books, 1994) 64–69 (describing 25-day sit-in that ended when HEW Secretary signed s 504 regulations).
9. RK Scotch, 'Making Change: The ADA as an Instrument of Social Reform' in LP Francis and A Silvers (eds), *Americans with Disabilities: Exploring Implications of the Law for Individuals and Institutions* (New York: Routledge Press, 2000) 276; Shapiro (n 8 above) 114. To address concerns of then Attorney-General Richard Thornburgh and the business community that small business would be disproportionately harmed by the law, the term 'readily achievable' was retained but was defined as meaning 'easily accomplishable and able to be carried out without much difficulty or expense'. 42 USC § 12181(9) (1994). Factors to be considered when determining the ready achievability of accommodations were added, to make clear that the burden on small businesses would be minimal. 42 USC § 12181(9)(a–d) (1994).
10. ibid 126.
11. ibid 127.
12. ibid 140. President Bush further stated that 'every man, woman and child with a disability can pass through once-closed doors into a bright new era of equality, independence and freedom'. A Mayerson and M Diller, 'The Supreme Court's Nearsighted View of the ADA' in LP Francis and A Silvers (eds), *Americans with Disabilities: Exploring Implications of the Law for Individuals and Institutions* (New York: Routledge Press, 2000) 124.
13. Symposium, 'Backlash Against the ADA' (2000) 21 *Berkeley J of Employment & Labor L* 1.
14. *Murphy v United Parcel Service* 527 US 516 (1999); *Sutton v United Air Lines, Inc* 527 US 471 (1999); *Albertson's, Inc v Kirkinburg* 527 US 555 (1999). In reviewing this trilogy of cases, one commentator bemoans the Court's rulings as 'disheartening at best, and abhorrent at worst'; BP Tucker, 'The Supreme Court's

Definition of Disability under the ADA: A Return to the Dark Ages' (2000) 52 *Alabama L Rev* 321, 373.

15. 531 US 356 (2001). The Court did not reach the constitutional issues raised as to whether state employees can sue for damages under the Act's provisions requiring state and local governments to adhere to the norms of non-discrimination, because the issues had not been briefed by the parties and thus that portion of the writ of *certiorari* was dismissed as improvidently granted. ibid 360 n 1.

16. On 11 October 2000, the Supreme Court heard argument in *Board of Trustees of the University of Alabama v Garrett* to determine if Congress acted within its power in enacting the ADA under §5 of the Fourteenth Amendment. Although the State's counsel asserted that there were no challenges to the commerce clause foundations of the ADA, Professor Michael Gottesman for the respondents with disabilities rebutted by noting that there were attempts in other courts to eviscerate the ADA on those grounds as well. The issue, however, is clearly in play as signaled by the concluding line of Justice Breyer's dissent: 'Whether the Commerce Clause does or does not enable Congress to enact this provision,...in my view §5 gives Congress the necessary authority'. ibid 389 (citations omitted).

    The mischief in *Garrett* is not confined to depriving state employees of the effective incentive of monetary damages to compel states to meet their employment disability non-discrimination obligation. Rather, the Court's harsh undermining of Congressional power under §5 to deal with the 'some-what broader swath of conduct' that goes beyond the Fourteenth Amendment text; its imposition on Congress of burdens of proof and strict rules of sufficient evidentiary support for justifying legislative action; and its lack of deference to Congressional competence to legislate in disability rights matters cast a deep cloud over the future of litigation to remedy ADA violations. See Breyer J, dissenting at 376. As the troubled dissenters observe, 'it is difficult to understand why the Court, which applies "minimum 'rational basis' review" to statutes that seek to burden persons with disabilities...subjects to far stricter scrutiny a statute that seeks to help those same individuals'. ibid 387–388.

17. *Bragdon v Abbott* 526 US 1131 (1999).

18. *Olmstead v LC* 527 US 581 (1999).

19. *PGA Tour, Inc v Martin* 532 US 661 (2001).

20. MA Stein, 'Labor Markets, Rationality, and Workers with Disabilities' (2000) 12 *Berkeley J of Employment and Labor L* 314, 331.

21. *Zum Brunnen v Mission Ranch* C97–20668 (SD CA, unpublished jury verdict 29 September 2000). According to a newspaper account, the jury did find two pre-verdict ADA violations (a lack of a ramp and signage for the accessible bathrooms), but since these problems had been remedied and because there were inconsistencies in the plaintiff's account of whether a disability-accessible hotel room was available, the jury ruled in favor of Eastwood. S Lafferty, 'Jury Rejects ADA Claim against Clint Eastwood' (2 October 2000) *The Recorder* (San Francisco) WEST DATABASE LEGALNP.

    Eastwood aggressively responded to the suit by obtaining Congressional sponsors to introduce bills to require a 90-day notice before ADA Title III

litigants can go to court to seek remedies for lack of reasonable accommodations. Disability activists have strongly opposed this delaying tactic,
which would uniquely disadvantage disability rights claimants compared to
other civil rights claimants. The bill titled 'The ADA Notification Act' drew
twenty-three cosponsors to HR 3590 in the prior Congressional session. In
the 107th Congress, 1st Session, it was reintroduced as HR 914 (with 56
cosponsors), with the Senate companion bill, SB 782, having one cosponsor at
this point.

22. US Census Bureau, *Americans with Disabilities: Household Economic Studies:
Current Population Reports 1* (2001) (relying on data from 1997 and including
persons 25–64). Congress found in 1990 that 43 million Americans have a disability. However, it recognized that this number would increase as the population ages. 42 USC §12101 (a)(1).
23. For a list of forty-one countries that have enacted disability non-discrimination
laws and a summary of their main features, see the list maintained by the
Disability Rights Education and Defense Fund at http://www.dredf.org/
symposium/lawindex.html (last viewed 10 April 2002).
24. Equal Rights for Persons with Disabilities Law, 5758–1998.
25. A Golan, 'The Land of Limited Opportunities' (24 May 2000) *Ha'aretz* (English
edition) 5.
26. N Ziv, 'Disability Law in Israel and the United States: A Comparative
Perspective' (1999) 28 *Israel Yearbook on Human Rights* 171.
27. (Israel) *Report of the Public Commission on Comprehensive Legislation Concerning
the Rights of People with Disabilities* (English summary, 1996) [hereinafter Katz
Commission Report].
28. ibid.
29. ibid 8.
30. ibid 7.
31. It also recommended supplemental statutory rights for compensatory education
for children long absent from schools, for schooling from birth to age 3, and for
adaptations to permit entry and study in institutions of higher education. ibid 9.
32. ibid 11.
33. ibid 11–12.
34. ibid 12–13. The Commission specified thirteen functions for the Commission,
including rulemaking, proposed legislative revisions, rights advising, complaint investigation, the filing of suits in the name of the Commission, assistance in helping private parties to file their own suits, and the development of
'mediation, arbitration and other actions designed to settle disputes regarding
the rights of people with disabilities'. ibid 13. These functions were consistent
with my recommendations to the Commission, including giving 'explicit
statutory encouragement to mediation and other means of less formal dispute
resolution' and providing through the Equal Rights Commission 'an administrative remedy for the bulk of the claims under the Act'. Memorandum from
SS Herr to I Katz, 'Invited Submission on Disability Rights Legislation in
Israel' in Katz Commission Report (6 May 1977) 6–7.
35. Equal Rights for People with Disabilities Law of 1998, §1 [hereinafter ERPDL].
The reference to the 'Divine Image' reflects a compromise between legislators

with a religious orientation and those with a secular orientation who wanted to stress equality of opportunity. Such language and the salience of religious issues in the legislature stands in sharp contrast to the US, where principles like 'separation of Church and State' would make such text problematic.

36. ERPDL ch 1 (2).
37. ibid ch 1 (4).
38. ibid ch 1 (3).
39. Basic Law: Human Dignity and Liberty (1992). Z Segal, 'A Constitution Without a Constitution: The Israeli Experience and the American Impact' (1992) 21 *Capital Univ L Rev* 1. This quasi-constitutional law guarantees to all Israeli nationals fundamental rights to privacy, property, and liberty. A 1994 Amendment clarifies that such rights are 'held in the spirit of the principles set forth in the Establishment of the State of Israel'.
40. For a comprehensive review of the IDEA, its 1997 reauthorization, and its strong procedural safeguards and advocacy methods, see SS Herr, 'Special Education Law and Children with Reading and Other Disabilities' (July 1999) 28 *J of L and Education* 337–389.
41. D Mustafi, 'Procedural Justice in Educational Placement of "Exceptional Students" in Israel' (PhD thesis, Bar Ilan Univ, Department of Education) (criticizing failure to carry out reforms in the procedural justice process of placement).
42. The bill referred to as ERPDL would strengthen the integration of children and adults with disabilities in education spheres. For many decades the legal basis for the provision of special education depended on the Compulsory Education Act of 1948, §9. In the late 1980s, the Ministry of Education recognized that 'society's role includes the appropriate legislation, which would enable the special child and his family to function as well as possible, with maximum incorporation into the surrounding society'. Ministry of Education, *Special Education in Israel* (1988) 18; T Rotem, 'The Law is Handicapped' (8 March 2000) *Ha'aretz* 3.
43. REE 5587/97, 51 PD (Iv) 830 (1997).
44. ibid.
45. (1988) 42(ii) PD 661, digested in (1990) 24 *Israel Law Review* 144–148.
46. *Michael Gabay & Biz'chut v The Head of the Civil Aviation Administration* hcj 9207/96 (voluntarily dismissed, 9 September 1999).
47. For discussion of the limited number of Israeli disability law cases in the higher courts, see S Herr, 'Human Rights and Mental Disability: Perspectives on Israel' (1992) 26 *Israel L Rev* 142, 156, 170–173.
48. Interview with Guy Mundlak, Senior Lecturer, Faculty of Law, and the Labor Department in the Faculty of Social Science, Univ of Tel Aviv, in Tel Aviv (April 2001).
49. ibid. Mundlak recounts one case for equal pay under the sex discrimination law of 1964, one for comparable worth under the 1996 law, only two cases of age discrimination, and little more than 'a handful' of cases in other fields.
50. The concept is to use research, advice, and technical assistance to help support the Commissioner and others who would see the concepts of the EPRDL

become a reality. The audience concurred with the view that such international exchange and support is feasible in a world that has grown smaller, and that the problems in Israel have too many counterparts in other lands to reinvent the proverbial wheel in terms of strategies and means to implement non-discrimination laws. For similar views, see Rehabilitation International, 'A Discussion on the Views on Human Rights of People with Disabilities' in E Kemppaninen (ed), *Social Commission Report* (Rehabilitation International, 1999) 9, 10 (collecting information from fourteen countries to 'support the improvement of the opportunities of people with disabilities in different countries' to 'obtain knowledge about the role of human rights in development in the society and about which human rights are the most important').

51. Interview with Ephraim Yuchtman-Yaar, Professor of Sociology, Faculty of Social Sciences, and Head of the Steimentz Center for Peace Research, Tel Aviv Univ, in Tel Aviv (28 March 2000).
52. This refers to a focus on individual pursuits over civil participation, narrow ethnic identities over national solidarity, political divisiveness over shared civil national ends, and security and collective interests over improvement of marginalized groups.
53. V Finklestein, 'Disability: A Social Challenge or Administrative Responsibility?' in J Swain, V Finkelstein, S French, and M Oliver (eds), *Disabling Barriers—Enabling Environment* (London: Sage Publications, 1993) 40–41.
54. ibid 42.
55. M Oliver and C Barnes, 'Discrimination, Disability and Welfare: From Needs to Rights' in M Oliver and C Barnes (eds), *Disabled People and Social Policy: From Exclusion to Inclusion* (Harlow, England: Addison Wesley Longman, 1998) 266, 270.
56. ibid 272.
57. 'Nor would I deny that discrimination exists—of course it does. We have to battle against it, but rather than legislating, the most constructive and productive way forward is through raising awareness in the community as a whole'. Nicholas Scott, Hansard (28 March 1991) 1150, (quoted at ibid 274).
58. ibid 276 (quoting US President George Bush, Sr).
59. Disability Discrimination Act of 1995, c 50 §5 [hereinafter DDA].
60. DDA, Part II. For the first appellate case interpreting justification and remitting an unfavorable decision for a disabled employee to the Employment Tribunal, see *Clark v Novacold* [1999] IRLR 318 (CA) (deeming it unnecessary to identify a non-disabled person in similar circumstances treated more favorably, but only necessary to show that the reason for the less favorable treatment was related to the employee's disability), the Court of Appeals thus reasoned; DDA, Part III; The DRC came into formal operation on 25 April 2000.
61. UK Department for Education and Employment, *From Exclusion to Inclusion: A Report of the Disability Rights Task Force on Civil Rights for Disabled People* (December 1999) 5; Disability Rights Commission Act 1999, c 17.
62. Testimony of Susan Scott-Parker for the Employers' Forum on Disability, House of Commons, Education and Employment Committee (Minutes of Evidence, 10 November 1998) 21.

63. ibid 20.
64. SM Bruyere, Summary of MF Switzer Distinguished Research Fellowship Report, 'A Comparison of the Implementation of the Employment Provision of the Americans with Disabilities Act (ADA) in the United States and the Disability Discrimination Act (DDA) in Great Britain and Northern Ireland' (October 1999). Based on a Switzer fellowship study (#72–05644834F) of over 1,800 US and UK human resources professionals and other employee representatives, legal counsel were deemed the most frequently used and most helpful sources of advice to resolve disputes under disability non-discrimination laws. Bruyere thus concluded that in-house or other counsel must be well informed of the statute, evolving case law, and the practical implications of the workplace adjustments that claimants seek.
65. S Fredman, *A Critical Review of the Concept of Equality in U.K. Anti-discrimination Law* (Univ of Cambridge, Centre for Public Law & Judge Institute of Management Studies, Working Paper No 3 of the Independent Review of the Enforcement of UK Anti-discrimination Legislation, November 1999) 15. Oxford law professor Fredman asserts that direct discrimination 'on grounds of disability should not be justifiable', a position that challenges a premise of the DDA. ibid 17.

    Under the DDA, Employment Tribunals can impose strong remedies: a declaration finding discrimination and requiring employer action (eg, promotion, consideration for a job, or certain training facilities), or compensation, including no monetary limits for injury to feelings. WL Keller *et al.* (eds), *International Labor and Employment Laws*, Vol. 1 (Washington, DC: BNA Books, 1997) 7–78 (noting that the European Court of Justice has imposed this 'no monetary limit' rule and this rule has been followed in *Marshall v Southampton & South West Hampshire Reg'l Health Auth* (No 2) [1993] IRLR 445).
66. B Doyle, *Reform of the Disability Discrimination Act 1* (Univ of Cambridge, Centre for Public Law & Judge Institute of Management Studies, Working Paper No 4 of the Independent Review of the Enforcement of UK Anti-discrimination Legislation, November 1999). Professor (now Judge) Doyle criticized the complexity of the definition of disability as adding to litigation costs, discouraging potential litigants from mounting challenges, and leading to a higher than average rate of settlement and withdrawal in DDA cases. Although he views *Goodwin v The Patent Office* [1999] IRLR 4 as an enlightened approach by the Employment Appeal Tribunal to the handling of medical evidence and the determination of a claimant's disability, he concludes that employers continue to have 'every strategic reason' and encouragement to challenge the status of the claimant as a disabled person. Part III's provisions on goods, facilities, and services are even more problematic than the employment provisions, with their ambiguities and confusion as to whether to apply both a subjective and an objective test for the justification defense to discrimination warranting wholesale reform or at least closer definition. ibid 7.
67. B Doyle, 'Enabling Legislation or Dissembling Law? The Disability Discrimination Act 1995' (January 1997) 60 *Modern L Rev* 64, 78.
68. Despite this formidable agenda of distinctive disability rights issues and concern, there has been some discussion of harmonizing discrimination law in

the UK and bringing race, gender, and disability issues under the purview of a single Equality Commission. However, this seems unlikely to happen, especially given the opposition by disability rights groups that struggled for many years to create the DRC and that fear that gains and concerns will be undermined in a unitary commission by the more powerful lobbies for women and ethnic minorities. B Hepple, M Coussey, and T Choudhury, *Options for Reform: Consultation Paper* (Univ of Cambridge, Centre for Public Law & Judge Institute of Management Studies, Independent Review of the Enforcement of UK Anti-discrimination Legislation, December 1999). Interview with Bob Hepple, Master of Clare College, in Cambridge (3 May 2000) (suggesting, as a matter of logic, that a single commission might be more desirable, but that it is not feasible politically to merge DRC with the two other anti-discrimination commissions when the work of the DRC has just begun, and its tasks are complex and different from those dealing with issues of gender and racial discrimination).

69. 29 USC §794 (2000).
70. 1999:132 (1999). For an unofficial translation of that law, see P Lappalainen, 'Sweden: Separate but Equal Anti-discrimination Laws?' (Paper presented at the 10th anniversary of ADA International Conference, October 2000).
71. 1999:132 (1999) §2.
72. ibid §4.
73. ibid §9. Failure to fulfill this duty can make the employer liable for damages. ibid §15.
74. ibid §17. The Ombudsman must first attempt to convince employers to voluntarily follow the law. The Ombudsman may request and the employer must provide relevant information concerning the employer's activities or the qualifications for a particular job position. A breach of this duty may render the employer liable to a civil fine. This duty is limited by a vague defense that the employer is not to be unnecessarily burdened, and that 'if there are special reasons the employer is not under a duty to provide information'. ibid §18.
75. ibid §§22–23, 25. The Disability Ombudsman can appear before the Board Against Discrimination to impose a civil fine. It can sue under the laws governing trials in labor disputes on behalf of an employee or job applicant, if the individual agrees and the Ombudsman finds that a judgment in the dispute would be important for the application of the law, or there are other special reasons for bringing the case. The Ombudsman may in the same lawsuit also present other claims as the representative of the individual.
76. The United States Attorney General has the power to bring pattern or practice suits or those of 'general public importance'. 42 USC §12188(b)(1)(B). This authority can be compared to the Swedish Disability Ombudsman's standing to pursue certain legally significant claims. But unlike the ADA, a labor union in Sweden may have a superior right to the public official to bring a claim on behalf of the employee. However, the Swedish law does not appear to contemplate class or other group forms of non-discrimination action.
77. Interview with Marc Dubin, Senior Trial Attorney, Disability Rights Section, Civil Rights Division, US Department of Justice, in Baltimore (18 February 2001).

78. Justification memos have to be written; an Executive Order that favors ADR methods has to be considered; and supervisors of line attorneys have to sign off before cases can go forward.

79. 'ABA Judicial and Administrative Complaints' (1998) 22 *Mental and Physical Disability Law Reporter* 403; JW Parry, 'Trend: Employment Decisions under ADA Title I—Survey Update' (1999) 23 *Mental and Physical Disability Law Reporter* 294.

80. ibid. This finding suggests that as few as seventy-nine individuals with disabilities over a seven-year period can be shown by judicial opinion evidence to have obtained a benefit by filing a Title I lawsuit.

81. One positive recent development is the greater involvement of US Attorneys' offices in the various districts of the country to bring their own ADA cases, or to do so in coordination with the Main Justice office in Washington, thus bringing greater litigation resources to bear on the issue. The National Association of Attorneys General (NAAG) also has become active in enforcing state disability discrimination claims.

82. Although many civil rights and other attorneys may hold themselves out as competent to bring ADA cases, the reality may be otherwise. In some states with a strong disability non-discrimination law, such as California, attorneys must first make a sophisticated analysis of whether to elect a state or federal court forum. The hodge-podge of state laws and the resulting complexity of where to file public accommodation (or, to a lesser extent, employment law) claims may further deter inexperienced attorneys from pursuing cases in this field. Furthermore, unlike tort law, ADA cases are not viewed as 'cash cows' especially given that Title III (and Title I (Garrett-type)) claims do not permit damages for private litigants and that attorneys' fees claims may have their own problems. *Board of Trustees of University of Alabama v Garrett* 531 US 356 (2001).

83. 'Where appropriate and to the extent authorized by law, the use of alternative means of dispute resolution, including settlement negotiations, conciliation, facilitation, mediation, fact-finding, mini-trials, and arbitration is encouraged to resolve disputes arising under this Act.' 42 USC §12212.

84. 42 USC §§12101(b)(1), 12101(b)(3). These purposes are also linked to the nationally enunciated goals of assuring 'equality of opportunity, full participation, independent living, and economic self-sufficiency for Americans with disabilities'. ibid §12101(a)(8).

85. G Williams, *Legal Negotiation and Settlement* (St Paul, Minn: West Publishing Co, 1983) (90% rate statistics).

86. Telephone interview with Peter Maida, Executive Director of the Key Bridge Foundation (13 March 2001).

87. According to the EEOC, it received some 80,000 complaints in 2000.

88. Arbitration is generally governed by the Uniform Arbitration Act, which nearly every state has adopted in some form. For the Uniform Arbitration Act and the statutes enacted in each state, see the American Arbitration Association at http://www.adr.org (last viewed 7 April 2001).

89. Arbitration can be court ordered, such as required by the Federal Arbitration Act 9 USC §§1 et seq., or it can be mandated by agreements made prior to any dispute. For example, the 'National Association of Securities Dealers require

members to submit all disputes between them to binding arbitration'. GH Barnes, 'Use of Arbitration Clauses in Commercial Agreements' http://www. hg.org/adrintro2.html (last viewed 7 April 2001).

90. G Cox, 'The Appropriate Arena for ADA Disputes, Arbitration or Mediation?' (1995) 10 *St John's J of Legal Commentary* 591, 594.

91. JW Sturner, 'Arbitration, Labor Contracts and the ADA: The Benefits of Pre-Dispute Arbitration Agreements and an Update on the Conflict between the Duty to Accommodate and Seniority Rights' (1999) 21 *Univ of Arkansas Little Rock L Rev* 455.

92. WD Goren, 'Americans with Disabilities Act: Tips for the Advocate' http://www.mediate.com/articles/adaadr.cfm (last viewed 7 April 2001).

93. Cox (n 90 above) 592.

94. *Circuit City Stores, Inc v Saint Clair Adams* 532 US 105, 123 (2001) (quoting *Gilmer v Interstate/Johnson Lane Corp* 500 US 20, 26 (1991)).

95. H Spragg, 'Enabling the Mentally Disabled Employee: Binding Arbitration under the ADA' (1999) 72 *Southern California L Rev* 929, 954–956; the Supreme Court has recently upheld binding arbitration under the Federal Arbitration Act, exempting only those employment contracts mentioned in §1 of the Act. *Circuit City Stores, Inc v Saint Clair Adams* 532 US 105 (2001).

96. Judges often write that arbitrators are in the best position to make the final determination because of their special knowledge of the subject. Usually the decision will only be overturned if the arbitrator abuses the process of the hearing or his/her powers. GH Barnes, 'Use of Arbitration Clauses in Commercial Agreements' http://www.hg.org/adintro2.html (last viewed 7 April 2001). One reform proposal would provide for a built-in appeals process, especially for statutory claims such as the ADA, to promote fairness in the arbitration decision. Sturner (n 91 above) 455. However, a counter-argument is that such an appeals process would lengthen the time of the dispute, complicate the process, and add cost, all of which arbitration is designed to reduce.

97. M Hansen, 'Contract Disputes: EEOC Reaffirms Policy Favoring Judges over Arbitrators for Workplace and Discrimination Claims' (September 1997) 83 ABAJ 26.

98. BE Myerson, 'Guidelines for Mediation of ADA Claims' (September–November 2000) 5 ADR Currents 3 (Publication of American Arbitration Association).

99. ibid.

100. ibid.

101. ibid.

102. Cox (n 90 above) 595.

103. *Olmstead v L.C. ex rel. Zimring* 527 US 581 (1999).

104. Such questions include the pace of de-institutionalization, and whether the *Olmstead* mandate applies not only to those in institutions but to those at high risk of institutional placement, such as those on waiting lists for services or living with aged or disabled parents. The author gratefully acknowledges the information provided by Tom Perez, former chief of the Office of Civil Rights, US Department of Health & Human Services, who co-chaired the *Olmstead*

working group. Interview with Tom Perez, Director of the Clinical Law Office, Maryland Law School, in Baltimore (3 May 2001).

105. For example, a systemwide solution would address the institutional bias in Medicaid programs.

106. The *Olmstead* working group encompassed an impressively large and diverse set of actors, including approximately a dozen states (which in turn had their own state-level working groups) and thirty advocacy groups ranging from the Voice of the Retarded to more community-oriented organizations.

107. *Sanchez v Johnson* No C 00 1593, ND Cal (filed 4 May 2000) (class action filed by PILCOP, DREDF, and Valarie Vananan, Esq. to enjoin California officials from ADA violations that unnecessarily segregate people in institutions and fail to provide 'even-handedly' for community-based services for those waiting at home and elsewhere because of severe wage disparities between workers in institutions and community-based services, resulting in closures of group homes and chronic inability to hire and retain a qualified and trained workforce that can serve persons with developmental disabilities).

108. Telephone interview with Ariella Auphir, Commissioner of the Equal Rights for Persons with Disabilities Commission (5 May 2001). The ministries making such inquiries include Social Affairs, Interior and Justice; SS Herr, 'Disability Rights: Old Responsibilities, New Challenges' (2001) 21 The Lawyer (Journal of the Israel Bar Association) [in Hebrew].

109. Although the ERPDL gives the Commission the power to litigate, the Commission to date has not filed any cases. Indeed, consistent with the thrust of this article's conclusions, the Commission prefers to use persuasion and other forms of negotiated settlement to resolve disputes. Formal ADR processes have not yet been established, but an influential NGO, the Joint Distribution Committee, is planning a mediation project for and with persons with disabilities to deal with a range of conflicts.

110. The Commission has a staff of five persons: the Commissioner, her deputy, the chief access officer, the policy and information specialist, and the secretary. One of the Commission's early accomplishments is the creation of a hotline on 'equality in employment' to provide advice on a range of employment matters, including supported employment. Auphir interview (n 108 above).

111. Commissioner Auphir sits on many of those committees. She has pressed the National Insurance Institute (the equivalent of the Social Security Administration) to become physically accessible to Israelis with disabilities and to transfer determinations as to degrees of disability for purposes of an individual's disability benefits from the agency's clerks to medical professionals who apply more objective and consistent standards. The Commission also led a campaign for more accessible voting stations, after finding that no voting places were truly accessible by professional standards. It has now advanced reform proposals to the central Elections Commissioner to fix the problems for the next elections. Telephone interview with Dean Arie Rimmerman, Faculty of Social Welfare and Health Sciences, Haifa Univ (2 May 2001).

112. Many of the first group of advisers were professors with disability specialization, one of whom was disabled. The call for a larger body that would include many non-governmental organizations in several respects and

echoes the author's June 2000 proposal for a group to serve as the 'Friends for Applying the Equal Rights for Persons with Disabilities Law'. ibid; Auphir interview (n 108 above).

113. According to the White House website, this office facilitates an Interdepartmental task force on HIV/AIDS, which fosters communication and coordination among the federal agencies involved in HIV/AIDS policy and initiatives. The office was created to 'provide broad policy guidelines and leadership on the Federal government's response to the national and international AIDS pandemic'. Office of National AIDS Policy at http://www.whitehouse.gov/onap (last viewed 3 May 2001). Another example of a high-profile coordinating office is the White House Office of National Drug Control Policy.

114. For example, the ERPDL's provisions on affirmative action to correct discrimination or promote equality of opportunity are worthy of emulation.

115. For a list of 96 major disability-related laws, both generic and disability-specific, enacted from 1956 to 2000, see R Silverstein, 'Emerging Disability Policy Framework: A Guidepost for Analyzing Public Policy' (2000) 85 *Iowa L Rev* 1691, 1785–1801.

116. Early signs in the Bush Administration indicate that civil rights for persons with disabilities will fare better than the rights of other minorities. On the appointment of Cari M. Dominguez as the new EEOC Commission Chair, a *New York Times* profile stated: 'Some analysts suggest that the president may focus on protections for disabled Americans, a result of the main civil rights initiative of his father'. R Abelson, 'A Fighter for Rights but a Conciliator, too' (1 July 2001) *New York Times* § BU 12.

117. An advantage of this approach over legislative enactment is the speed with which the office can be created, and the 'fine tuning' of its mission that can occur over time. In the United States, an office created by the Executive Branch of government has the certainty of an Administration's four-year term of office, an advantage that would not be available under the parliamentary systems of Israel, England, and Sweden.

118. DL Greene, 'President Introduces Programs to Aid People with Disabilities' (2 February 2001) *Baltimore Sun* 3A.

119. In a similar vein, Representative Jim Langevin, the first person with paraplegia to be elected to the US House of Representatives, expressed encouragement at the prospects of continuity with the strong leadership that President Clinton had provided on disability rights issues: 'President Clinton was an outstanding leader. He really gave substance to the issue of breaking down barriers. He did it in legislation, in action and in words. With him leaving the White House, I was concerned. Would there be an erosion of gains? Or would we move forward?' ibid.

120. B Hepple, M Coussey, and T Choudhury (n 68 above) 52. Parties can now settle their cases with the aid of the Advisory, Conciliation and Arbitration Service. Another reason for turning to ADR approaches is that disability cases are prone to experience the longest delays in resolution compared to race and gender discrimination cases, perhaps because of difficult medical issues or issues of disability definition. ibid 44. In the UK, unlike the US, one

expert deems it unlikely that the government will take on the task of providing arbitration or mediation services but will seek instead to privatize this function. Interview with Bob Hepple, Master of Clare College, in Cambridge (3 May 2000).

121. As of May 2001, 94 vacancies existed for the 834 federal appellate and district court judgeships, creating the prospect of sharp conflict between a President committed to appointing 'strict constructionists' (as supported by the Federalist Society which favors limited government) and Democratic senators and their allied civil rights interest groups who fear that conservative and even moderate judicial nominees will undermine affirmative action and other civil rights oriented public policies. DL Greene and T Healy, 'Battle Looms over Judges: Democrats Demand Prominent Role as Bush Prepares Nominations' (6 May 2001) *Baltimore Sun* 1A.

122. J Dart, Jr., 'Introduction: The ADA: A Promise to Keep' in LO Gostin and HA Beyer (eds), *Implementing the Americans with Disabilities Act* (Baltimore: Brookes Publishing, 1993) xvii.

9

When Legislation Should Take Intellectual Disabilities into Account

DAN SHNIT

I. INTRODUCTION

Comparative analysis of legislation on the rights of persons with disabilities in general and on the rights of persons with intellectual disabilities in particular in various developed countries reveals differences in the scope and nature of proposed solutions. It is difficult to single out any country that provides comprehensive solutions for all aspects of the needs and problems of people with intellectual disabilities and the difficulties they encounter. Several countries have outlawed various forms of discrimination against and denial of equal rights to persons with disabilities in general and those with intellectual disabilities in particular.[1] This prohibition refers only to discrimination based on disability and covers employment, public services, and access to services as well as access to public places, public transportation, and communications. The laws in these countries, however, do not include an obligation to provide material assistance and care services tailored to the needs of persons with disabilities. Several countries have enacted legislation acknowledging the right of persons with intellectual disabilities to receive assistance and care services in various spheres of life. Nonetheless, these countries have not outlawed all types of discrimination against persons with intellectual disabilities or all infringements on their right to equal life opportunities.[2]

The rights of persons with intellectual disabilities, as set forth in the United Nations Declaration on the Rights of Mentally Retarded Persons (hereinafter the 'UN Declaration'),[3] are only partially ensured in various countries. As a result, advocacy organizations will have to take diverse forms of long-term action to expand and expedite the integration and implementation of the principles set forth in the UN Declaration into the legislation of each country.

In Israel, legal arrangements concerning the rights of persons with intellectual disabilities are limited in scope and substance. The rights of persons with intellectual disabilities are stipulated in the law only in some contexts.[4] One such area involves protective services provided in cases where the well-being of these individuals is at risk due to negligence on the part of their guardians, lack of suitable treatment, or failure of individuals with intellectual disabilities and their families to cooperate with treatment.

To ensure protection under these circumstances, Israeli law contains regulations that empower the welfare authorities to intervene and provide appropriate assessment and treatment. The law also provides for institutionalization and refers persons with intellectual disabilities to foster families in cases where they need to be protected by society.[5] Israeli law also stipulates an arrangement intended to protect persons with intellectual disabilities who are involved in criminal offenses. According to this arrangement, the court is empowered, in conjunction with a special committee of experts, to absolve offenders with intellectual disabilities of responsibility for their actions in certain cases. In other cases, the law stipulates appropriate treatment that takes into account the best interests of the offender and society.[6]

Sufficient financial support for persons with intellectual disabilities is ensured in a comprehensive arrangement that also applies to persons with mental and physical disabilities. The National Insurance Law grants an income maintenance allowance to persons with all types of disabilities (eg, intellectual, mental, or physical) if the severity of their condition considerably limits their earning capacity.[7]

The Israeli legislature adopted a general arrangement for income maintenance that is intended to ensure that persons with intellectual disabilities as well as other groups of persons with disabilities are able to subsist. Israeli law also provides a general arrangement for appointing guardians for all individuals who are incapable of managing their own affairs.[8]

The need to recognize the right of persons with intellectual disabilities to live in dignity in their community of birth, in the spirit of the principles delineated in the UN Declaration on the Rights of Mentally Retarded Persons, is accepted today in most developed countries. Nonetheless, the considerable discrepancy between the principles set forth in the Declaration and the extent to which they have been enshrined in legislation cannot be ignored.

Another discrepancy, which is no less important, focuses on the clear limitations of implementation and enforcement of non-discrimination laws for populations with disabilities in general and intellectual disabilities in particular. Israel's Equal Rights for Persons with Disabilities Law (ERPDL) does not provide efficient tools to ensure implementation and enforcement in cases of discrimination. In Israel, situations of discrimination and failure to realize the principle of inclusion in employment, education, and access to public services have not generated an appropriate public or legal response. In England, implementation and enforcement of non-discrimination laws for persons with intellectual disabilities are also lacking.[9] The wide gap between principles of such legislation and the low level of implementation and enforcement has led farther away from the goals outlined in the UN Declaration.

Lack of legislative uniformity in various countries raises questions about the efficacy of legislation in attaining its goals. The purpose of this chapter is to examine when and how the needs of persons with intellectual disabilities should be addressed in national legislation. Two main issues will be addressed. In what spheres should countries adopt legislation to secure the rights of the persons with intellectual disability? In order to meet the needs of persons with intellectual disabilities, which kind of legislation is preferable: specific or general?

II. WHERE LEGISLATION IS NEEDED—TOPICS FOR LEGISLATION ACCORDING TO THE UN DECLARATION

The UN Declaration lays the foundation for legislation ensuring the rights and vital interests of persons with intellectual disabilities in every country. The principles underlying the Bill of Rights of the Declaration are grounded in an ideology that emphasizes the need for maximum integration of persons with intellectual disabilities in all types of activities and aspects of community life. Such integration must ensure participation in normal family and community life to the extent possible.

One consequence of this ideology is recognition of the right to live with one's family of origin or with a foster family and to participate in community life in various ways. When circumstances warrant institutionalization of a person with intellectual disabilities, the conditions of the institution must approximate those of the community at large as much as possible.

Another principle of this ideology, which guides the letter and the spirit of the Declaration, is recognition of the right of persons with intellectual disabilities to achieve their maximum potential. This principle involves ensuring that every person, as stated, receives individualized treatment in rehabilitation programs that are adapted to his or her specific limitations and inherent potential.

In the spirit of these principles, the Declaration specifies the domains in which every society should grant rights to persons with intellectual disabilities. The following is a brief list of those domains:

(1) basic rights, equivalent to those enjoyed by the rest of the country's citizens;
(2) the right to economic security, employment, and a reasonable standard of living, as well as the right to treatment, education, rehabilitation,

and guidance that will lead to maximum development of the person's abilities;

(3) the right to protection from exploitation, harm, and restriction or denial of physical or property rights and interests and safeguards to achieve this aim;

(4) the right to legal representation when necessary to protect physical or property interests, including the right to have a guardian appointed when needed.

The drafters of the Declaration were aware that countries differ in their ability to allocate the financial and organizational resources required to implement the Bill of Rights for persons with intellectual disabilities. For this reason, they included a clause stipulating that some countries will not be able to realize all of the rights at this stage because of their present level of development. This chapter will deal only with developed countries that have the financial resources and the social and organizational infrastructure necessary to enact legislation protecting the rights of persons with intellectual disabilities in the above-mentioned fields. The legal situation in developing countries is discussed by Rosenthal and Sundrum in Chapter 18 of this volume.

This chapter will focus on four main issues covered in the UN Declaration: (1) the right to equality in access to services; (2) the right to receive assistance and treatment tailored to the individual's specific needs and circumstances; (3) the right to non-discriminatory legal status, taking into account circumstances that warrant specific attention in the law; and (4) the right to be protected by law from exploitation or harm to physical and property interests.

A. The Right to Equal Access to Services

To ensure maximum integration of persons with intellectual disabilities into normal community life and activity, they must have genuine acceptance and equal opportunities in those legal domains. However, under current economic and social conditions, the opposite is often the case. The economic, physical, and social systems and infrastructure discriminate against persons with intellectual disabilities and limit their access to services intended for the general public as well as their opportunities to participate in occupational or leisure activity. The obstacles and constraints are caused not by the individual's disability but by discrimination and prejudice on the part of society and its institutions. Such discrimination runs counter to the values of justice and equality that would require the law to ensure that persons with intellectual disabilities can enjoy equal opportunities in various aspects of life.

These principles provided the background for the adoption of the Americans with Disabilities Act (ADA) in the United States. This law forbids discrimination against persons with disabilities in employment opportunities and access to public services. Accordingly, it requires that people with disabilities have access to public buildings, public transportation, and telecommunications services.

Similar legislation is included in the Canadian Charter of Rights and Freedoms. In 1994, provisions were also added to the Ontario law to ensure access to post-secondary educational institutions, public transportation, and government publications.[10] This is an example of implementation of the philosophy that maintains that for the persons with disabilities to attain social integration, they must be guaranteed opportunities to participate in all spheres of life—especially in the public sphere.

In 1995, legislation aimed at protecting the rights of persons with disabilities was adopted in the United Kingdom. Like the ADA and Canadian laws, the UK law aims to ensure that persons with disabilities have equal employment opportunities and access to public transportation, telecommunications, and other public services.

Three years after the law was enacted in the United Kingdom, Israel also passed a law, the ERPDL, prohibiting discrimination against persons with disabilities. The Israeli law defines broad goals, as reflected in Section 2:

This law aims to protect the honor and freedom of people with disabilities, and to establish their right to equal and active participation in society in all spheres of life, in addition to providing a suitable response to their special needs in a way that enables them to live as independently and as honorably as possible while maintaining their privacy and fully exercising their abilities.

However, in clear contradiction to the broad-based goal set forth in the law, the practical arrangements stipulated cover only a narrow sphere of life. Specifically, the law formalizes the rights of persons with disabilities only in two spheres of life: prohibiting discrimination in employment and access to public transportation.

The Israeli law reflects a universal approach toward formalizing the rights of persons with disabilities and applies to all types of disabilities without distinguishing between physical, mental or intellectual. Under these conditions, it is not surprising that three years after the law was passed no appreciable change is expected in implementation of the rights of persons with intellectual disabilities in all aspects of employment. The main implications of the law in the future, if and when it is implemented and enforced, will be for persons with physical disabilities and, to a lesser extent, people with intellectual disabilities. It is not expected that the law will be applied to the sphere of employment for persons with intellectual

disabilities (whether or not the disability is accompanied by other physical disabilities). The law has not been applied to discrimination against
persons with intellectual disabilities in other spheres, such as education
and cultural services in the community.

Legislation aimed at preventing discrimination against persons with
disabilities and ensuring equal employment opportunities and access to
public services should include the following elements: (1) clear specification of the target population that will be protected and (2) broad and
explicit specification of the agencies that are obligated to treat persons with
disabilities in an equal and non-discriminatory manner.[11] A more explicit
and comprehensive list of the topics to which the non-discrimination
provisions shall apply is needed. This list should include access to social
and economic services and activities that are vital to normal functioning
and living to the extent that such access does not pose an undue economic
burden on the affected agencies and private entities. Enforcement powers
must be delegated to a strong regulatory agency to provide an effective
deterrent. This agency must be able to bring meaningful sanctions against
institutions and individuals that break the law.

1. The Reasonable Accommodation Requirement

The major issue related to legislation on outlawing discrimination and
ensuring equal opportunities concerns the scope and nature of the anti-
discrimination provisions. Legislation enacted in the United States has
expanded provisions prohibiting on-the-job discrimination by employers.
Accordingly, employers must provide reasonable accommodations for
workers with disabilities and make reasonable adjustments to job responsibilities in a way that enables those employees to integrate into the workplace.[12] Specifically, employers must accommodate all qualified workers.
In an interactive process, employers have discretion to distribute responsibilities reasonably among other employees—ie, tasks that cannot be
performed by workers with disabilities should be delegated to other
workers to maximize integration of persons with disabilities into the
work environment. The goal underlying legislation against on-the-job
discrimination, as in other spheres, is to ensure reasonable physical
changes and accommodations that adapt the work environment to the
constraints of qualified individuals with disabilities.

The primary obstacle to reaching this goal is the difficulty of enforcing
and implementing the reasonable accommodation standard in individual
cases. Notably, the ADA does not set clear rules for accommodations, so
considerable uncertainty and ambiguity exist.

Implementation of employment opportunities is more complex for
persons with intellectual disabilities than for persons with physical
disabilities, owing to the difficulty of assessing the appropriate output to

be expected from those candidates. Notwithstanding this difficulty, the agencies charged with enforcing the law and overseeing its implementation must make sure that persons with intellectual disabilities who have qualifications that meet the standards of a workplace are hired for available positions.

Reasonable accommodations required for job applicants with intellectual disabilities may differ from those required for candidates with physical disabilities. Although this is an issue that warrants separate discussion, it is not enough to simply mention that according to the principle of equal opportunity, employers or service providers must make reasonable accommodations for disabled persons. The law must also include standards that specify which accommodations are reasonable, taking into account the different kinds of disabilities and needs of the business.

B. Assistance and Care Services Tailored to the Needs of Persons with Intellectual Disabilities

The area of assistance and care services includes three distinct subtopics in which assistance and treatment are required: (1) assurance of economic subsistence, (2) universal medical care and education, and (3) individual treatment and services tailored to the special needs of persons with intellectual disabilities.

The laws in most developed countries mandate the provision of basic subsistence for persons with intellectual disabilities. In Israel, as indicated, the law guarantees a monetary allowance for every person aged 18 years and older whose earning capacity has been reduced by at least 50% due to an intellectual disability.[13] This allowance is also allocated to families caring for children with intellectual disabilities who live at home and depend on others for most or all activities of daily living (ADL) due to the severity of their condition.[14] It is a modest benefit intended to provide partial compensation to parents of children with intellectual disabilities for their extra investments of time and money.

The right to an education is also universally guaranteed in developed countries. Just as the laws recognize the right of every child to state education, the laws of many developed countries delineate special provisions regarding education for children with intellectual disabilities.

Israeli law recognizes the right of every child with an intellectual disability who requires special education to enroll free of charge in an appropriate school in his or her area of residence. Persons with intellectual disabilities are entitled to special education from age 3 to 21. The aim of special education is to foster and develop the aptitudes of children with intellectual disabilities and to improve their physical, intellectual, and behavioral functioning. In addition, special education provides the children with knowledge, skills, and habits, which facilitates their integration into the workplace.[15]

The law reflects an ideology that people with intellectual disabilities are different and that it is desirable to help them integrate into society by providing them with special education in a separate system. The Israeli law does not require that the education authorities provide maximum assistance and support for children with intellectual disabilities for the purpose of integrating them into the regular education system. According to the Israeli Special Education Law, integration of children with intellectual disabilities into regular educational frameworks is not the preferred practice.

The right of children with intellectual disabilities or their parents to demand integration into regular schools with appropriate assistance and support for that purpose has not yet been tested by the Israeli courts. The High Court of Justice in Israel ruled that the education system has an obligation to enable maximum integration of children in wheelchairs by making adjustments in the structure of the regular school attended by these children.[16] The court based this ruling on the contention that efforts should be made to integrate children with disabilities into regular social frameworks and in that way, ensure that they have equal opportunities— not 'separate but equal' but 'integrated and equal'.

This liberal decision expressed by the President of the High Court of Justice, Aharon Barak, refers, as mentioned, to the case of a boy with a physical, not an intellectual, disability. The adjustments aimed at integrating the child focused on the physical aspects of the building and did not deal with intervention in the educational and ideological aspects of the argument about integrating children with intellectual disabilities into regular educational frameworks. The Special Education Law in Israel does not declare integration of intellectually disabled children into the regular education system as a priority, but focuses instead on integrating them into a separate system of special education. This in itself reduces the chances that the Supreme Court will adopt an integrative approach that contravenes the aims of the Special Education Law. In any case, Israeli courts have not yet decided whether children with intellectual disabilities have the right to be integrated in the regular education system.

Care and assistance adapted to the individual needs of persons with intellectual disabilities are necessary to enable their integration into their community of residence. Such assistance can be offered in the form of support services and diverse types of care that ensure an appropriate response to the limitations that persons with intellectual disabilities encounter in their daily functioning. Since family members often cannot provide for all of the needs of children with intellectual disabilities, these services ensure that children have a satisfactory quality of life with maximal integration into the community. When a child's condition does not allow for such integration, he or she should be placed in an institutional setting that will provide the best possible quality of life and constitute the closest possible alternative to life in the community. Children with intellectual disabilities who live in the community or in an appropriate institutional setting, must be protected by an established legal provision from abuse by society or infringement on their rights and their physical and material interests.

Until recently, the Israeli law (TRP) mainly protected persons with intellectual disabilities from harm or abuse. In addition, the law granted welfare authorities the power to impose therapeutic frameworks on persons with intellectual disabilities when they did not receive appropriate care from their families.[17] The rights to receive care and services that ensure persons with intellectual disabilities a proper lifestyle in the community or, alternatively, appropriate out-of-home placement are not mandated by Israeli law.

An amendment to the law, passed in June 2000, provides a partial solution to the problem.[18] In Israel, the rights of persons with intellectual disabilities to receive adequate assistance and care—either in the community or in an institutional setting—have not been directly and formally recognized. However, the law indirectly recognizes the rights of persons with intellectual disabilities to out-of-home placement (eg, residential facilities, foster families, or other community housing) or in day care facilities at therapeutic day centers. When the agency authorized by law to deal with the issue (the evaluation committee) decides that a person with an intellectual disability needs out-of-home care in the community or in an institution, the State must bear the cost for implementing that decision. In this way, the law will eliminate the long waiting lists for out-of-home placement, in cases where such arrangements have been approved by authorities but have not been implemented due to insufficient resources.[19]

Recognition of the legal rights of persons with intellectual disabilities to care is subject to several contingencies.[20] First, the public authority designated by the state evaluation committee must determine that there is a need to care for persons with intellectual disabilities in out-of-home settings. Second, the treatment that a person is entitled to is limited to care provided in out-of-home settings: residential facilities, foster families, special community housing, or day centers for persons with intellectual disabilities. Third, executive authorities, such as the Minister of Labor and Social Affairs, may set rules requiring persons with intellectual disabilities or their families to cover part of the cost of treatment. They may also set rules about the location and nature of care provision. Fourth, recognition of the legal rights of persons with intellectual disabilities is subject to the legal obligation to provide these therapeutic services. The law is scheduled to take full effect in 2004. Experience with other social laws for which a target date has been set for full implementation indicates that there is no guarantee that the Israeli legislature will not further postpone implementation on the grounds of budgetary constraints.

Despite the constraints delineated above, there is hope that the rights of persons with intellectual disabilities who have been recognized by the welfare authorities as needing out-of-home care will receive treatment based on financial and other conditions that the Minister of Labor and Social Affairs will delineate in special regulations.

In this context, the case of Sweden is particularly interesting. A law enacted in 1993 entitles persons with intellectual disabilities and autism to required remedial and care services in the community.[21] According to this legislation, any person with an intellectual disability or autism who lives in the community has the right to an individually tailored program that assures quality of life and integration to the extent possible. The care plan must respect the persons' rights to privacy and self-determination and involve them directly in the process of designing their plans.[22] The entitlement includes a diverse array of services, including counseling and assistance in dealing with the problems that persons with intellectual disabilities encounter in daily life. These services include individual therapeutic intervention or financial aid; companion services; housekeeping assistance; payment for brief vacations away from the family; arrangements for people in out-of-home residential settings; and daily activities for unemployed persons of working age.[23] These entitlements provide a model for comprehensive assistance and service in the community, aimed at promoting the well-being of persons with intellectual disabilities and autism in Sweden.

As mentioned, realization of the rights of persons with intellectual disabilities to lead a normal life within the family and in the community, to the extent possible, depends largely on recognition of the legal right to receive individual care and benefit from services tailored to special needs. Treatment and services should be aimed at helping persons with intellectual disabilities live in the community as integral members.

Inadequate legislation in this domain in many developed countries precludes attainment of the goals set forth in the UN Declaration regarding the inclusion of persons with intellectual disabilities into normal community life.

C. Legal Status with Respect to Universal Legislation

The UN Declaration stresses the obligation of countries to enact legislation stipulating that persons with intellectual disabilities enjoy a legal status and civil rights equal to those of the rest of the population. However, provisions of the UN Declaration also indicate that there may be situations in which the law must pay specific attention to the legal status of persons with severe intellectual disabilities. When is it preferable for legislation to relate equally, without discrimination, to all citizens? When is it preferable for legislation to refer specifically to the special limitations of persons with intellectual disabilities? For instance, what should the legal status of persons with intellectual disabilities be with respect to civil contracts? Should they be recognized as having the right to enter civil contracts like anyone else? What is their status as criminal offenders? Should special provisions be applied to them regarding responsibility for criminal acts? When they are recognized as bearing criminal responsibility, should the consequences of failure to meet this responsibility be punitive or therapeutic? These are some examples of the dilemmas involved in establishing the legal status of persons with intellectual disabilities. The following section discusses a few of these concerns from the perspective of Israeli law.

1. Contracts

The Israeli Contracts Law[24] is an example of legislation that is essentially general and universal. The law regulates the contractual obligations of individuals to each other without separate provisions for contracts entered into by intellectually or mentally disabled persons. In the spirit of this universality, the law contains provisions that, under specific conditions, protect parties to a contract who may be exploited on account of their intellectual or mental state. The clauses at issue permit nullification of agreements and compensation for the injured party if an act of deceit,[25] wrongful intent,[26] or abuse through exploitation of the other party's weaknesses has occurred.[27] These provisions place no a priori constraint on the rights of persons with intellectual disabilities to enter into agreements; rather, they are universal provisions that protect persons with intellectual disabilities *post factum*, when the circumstances of the case show that they were exploited by the other party to the agreement, treated in bad faith, or misled by a signatory who enjoyed an overwhelming intellectual advantage.[28] This example of a universal legal arrangement points to a policy that rules out sweeping limitations on the rights of persons with intellectual disabilities to lead normal lives, including the right to enter legal contracts. The law strikes an equilibrium by applying general norms meant to protect people who enter contracts with serious flaws, including flaws that may have been created by or simply not recognized by a person with an intellectual disability. In certain borderline cases, such a legislative policy may lead to situations in which persons with intellectual disabilities without guardians are harmed and cannot be properly compensated under the law. Nonetheless, even if such rare situations are not covered, the law upholds an important principle: recognition of the rights of persons with intellectual disabilities to live in the community on the most normal terms possible without serious limitations on their autonomy.[29]

In some cases, a person's intellectual condition is so severe that his or her ability to perform legal acts must be restricted. Such cases fall into the realm of protective legislation, which enables the court to declare a person with an intellectual disability as legally incompetent[30] and appoint a guardian to represent him or her.

2. *Criminal Responsibility*

Criminal law contains a combination of universal provisions, which establish the principles determining criminal responsibility,[31] and specific provisions, which address the question of responsibility in the case of offenders with intellectual disabilities. The Israeli Penal Law differentiates between two categories of criminals who have been diagnosed as intellectually disabled. The first category includes those whom the court completely absolves of criminal liability because of the seriousness of their condition. For them, the law stipulates the most appropriate care plan under the particular circumstances, which is determined by a special evaluation committee for care of persons with intellectual disabilities.[32] The second category encompasses people whose condition, in the opinion of the courts, is not serious enough to absolve them of criminal responsibility for their actions. In such cases, the court is empowered to determine which course of action is preferable: a care plan recommended by the evaluation committee for persons with intellectual disabilities or a punitive approach that the court deems suitable in view of the gravity and circumstances of the case.[33]

The major test in evaluating universal legislation containing provisions that affect persons with intellectual disabilities is the extent of equilibrium achieved. In striving for equilibrium, unnecessary paternalism and sweeping restrictions must be avoided, while ensuring that the vital interests and needs of persons with intellectual disabilities are taken into account and that these citizens are given suitable protection.

3. *Freedom and Dignity*

In several domains, the courts have not been guided by any clear principles in applying universal legal norms that affect the rights of persons with intellectual disabilities to freedom and dignity. The Basic Law for Human Dignity and Liberty, enacted in 1992, prohibits violation of the individual's freedom and privacy and mandates the protection of his or her body and dignity.[34] However, these rights are not absolute. Thus, under certain circumstances it may be justifiable to violate these basic rights through legislation that upholds the values of the State of Israel as a democratic state, provided that the breach is not greater than necessary.[35]

To date, Israeli courts have not tested the legality of actions taken by governmental or other authorized agencies that may be considered restrictions of the freedom or dignity of persons with intellectual disabilities. Advocacy services are necessary to challenge actions that excessively restrict the freedom and autonomy of persons with intellectual disabilities. Organizations such as Bizkhut, which was founded by the Association for Civil Rights in Israel and deals with advancement of the rights of people with disabilities, may be able to put restrictive actions to a constitutional test. For example, they could bring a case that tests the probity of institutionalizing persons with intellectual disabilities who could be integrated into the community if suitable services were developed. The principle of 'least restrictive measurement'[36] is a guiding value and ethical criterion that may help determine when a solution adopted for an intellectually disabled person is excessive according to the letter and spirit of the Basic Law for Human Dignity and Liberty.

D. Legislation Against Exploitation

Persons with intellectual disabilities are vulnerable to exploitation and harm by others. Hence, protective legislation—which is essentially paternalistic—is needed. It is generally assumed that persons with intellectual disabilities lack the competence to exercise judgment and handle their own affairs, sometimes making it necessary to empower professionals to intervene and act in their best interests. Legislation makes it possible to enforce, under circumstances set forth in law, behavioral patterns or modes of care for persons with intellectual disabilities and their families.

Special legislation in 1969 empowered care-giving authorities to decide, in cases of insufficient cooperation from persons with intellectual disabilities and their families, when to require evaluation and care, including institutionalization.[37] If persons with intellectual disabilities and their families reject the evaluation or care plan stipulated by an interdisciplinary evaluation committee, the court is empowered to enforce compliance by a special order. The order may include auxiliary measures such as placement of a person with an intellectual disability under the supervision of a welfare officer or in a care facility for the purpose of performing necessary tests and providing needed care.

This legislation embodies not only the supremacy of paternalism over recognition of the civil rights of persons with intellectual disabilities but also the supremacy given to professional opinion, without sufficient procedural safeguards and judicial review, to force evaluation and treatment. The evaluation committee is given extensive powers, irrespective of the conditions and rules stipulated in the law, to force specific treatment on a person with an intellectual disability if, in the opinion of the committee members, it is in the person's best interests.

In contrast, the protective power to impose evaluation, hospitalization and treatment of persons with mental illness under the Treatment of Mentally Sick Persons Law, 1991,[38] is characterized by much tighter procedural safeguards for review of the legitimacy of the commitment and treatment. To impose hospitalization or psychiatric treatment, the district psychiatrist must be persuaded that, in the absence of compulsory hospitalization or treatment, the patient may endanger him or herself and others or cause serious property damage.[39] Alternatively, the district psychiatrist must be convinced that a patient seriously threatens the sound existence of others or that his or her ability to provide for his or her own basic needs has been severely diminished.[40]

In practice, there are cases in which petitions against compulsory civil commitment have been submitted to the district court, and some have even reached the supreme court.[41] In contrast, no similar petitions against imposed treatment for persons with intellectual disabilities are known to have reached the courts.

Besides the aforementioned law, which empowers the relevant authorities to enforce treatment and institutionalization of persons with intellectual disabilities, the Safety of Protected Persons Law, 1966,[42] empowers the courts to force adult dependents, including adults with intellectual disabilities, to accept medical or other care intended to prevent serious harm due to inadequate care.[43] This power does not apply to hospitalization and psychiatric treatment of persons with mental illness, which appear only under the provisions of the Treatment of Mentally Sick Persons Law.[44] Furthermore, the juvenile court is empowered to order treatment, hospitalization, or institutionalization of intellectually disabled minors, in cases where they or their parents are unwilling to participate in needed processes voluntarily.

There are three laws that allow care-giving authorities to engage in compulsory protective intervention. Under two of the laws—the Youth (Care and Supervision) Law[45] and the Safety of Protected Persons Law[46]—intervention is implemented by a competent court. The third law—the Treatment of Retarded Persons Law—is administered by the evaluation committee for persons with intellectual disabilities.[47] This orientation reflects a more paternalistic attitude that focuses less on the civil rights and individual liberties of persons with intellectual disabilities in Israel.

III. GENERAL VERSUS SPECIFIC LEGISLATION

A. Guidelines for Categorizing Legislation

Legislation dealing with the rights of persons with intellectual disabilities in various countries can be grouped into the following categories, based on their degree of specificity or universality: (1) specific legislation intended to regulate a specific issue or issues concerning the rights or status of persons with intellectual disabilities;[48] (2) comprehensive legislation intended to regulate an issue or issues concerning the rights of people with a variety of disabilities, including persons with intellectual disabilities;[49] and (3) universal legislation applying to all citizens of the country, which offers solutions applicable to persons with intellectual disabilities in certain cases even though there are no special provisions for that specific population.[50] In addition to these three categories, there may be a negative arrangement in some situations—ie, when a country has no laws at all governing the issue.[51]

Which type of legislation is preferable? On what basis does a country decide whether to adopt specific legislation or to choose comprehensive legislation applying to a range of populations with a broad common denominator such as persons with various types of disabilities?

On the one hand, advocates and scholars are guided by principles that call for maximum social integration of persons with intellectual disabilities within broad, normal community settings.[52] On the other hand, advocates and scholars are guided by principles of individuation, which encourage efforts to realize the full potential of each intellectually disabled individual.[53]

The principles that emphasize integration and normalization ostensibly lead toward integrative legislative solutions that have a broader, more general application. In contrast, the principles that focus on the individual ostensibly lead toward particularistic legislation, reflecting the unique attributes of persons with intellectual disabilities in an attempt to guarantee their rights as effectively as possible. To achieve this goal, the decision regarding the most appropriate type of legislation must take into consideration the various interests and principles underlying the laws in question.

I argue that whenever possible, it is preferable to enact general legislation with a broad application rather than narrow, specific legislation. Several examples of legislation are presented below to indicate how this can be done.

B. Legislation on Equal Opportunities and Accessibility

Legislation dealing with issues such as job discrimination or access to public services and buildings should have a broad application, covering all groups of people with disabilities and not just persons with intellectual disabilities. The ADA in the United States and the ERPDL in Israel are examples of this kind of general legislation vis-à-vis persons with disabilities. This legislation is sufficiently comprehensive to protect all groups of people with physical, intellectual, or mental disabilities. Therefore, separate legislation for each population group is inappropriate. To promote universal adoption of appropriate legislation, an international forum should draft a model code that could be adopted by specific countries, *mutatis mutandis*, in the future.

C. Protective Legislation

Legislation intended to protect persons with intellectual disabilities from neglect or exploitation can be divided into two levels. The first level involves the determination of legal principles, which provide the basis for deciding whether or not compulsory treatment is allowable for protective purposes. The second level is essentially procedural and involves determining how the law should be implemented and applied in specific cases.

In principle, the legislation referred to here empowers people to make paternalistic decisions that limit and infringe on the civil rights and individual liberties of persons with intellectual disabilities. General legislation must stipulate guidelines and procedural safeguards for compulsory treatment and institutionalization that reduce threats to individual freedom and autonomy.

The equilibrium between society's obligation to respect individual freedom and privacy and society's responsibility to protect individuals with severe intellectual and mental disabilities from harming themselves or others should be established in appropriate universal legislation. A particularistic approach—ie, specific protective legislation for persons with intellectual disabilities along the lines of Israeli law[54]—reflects a discriminatory paternalistic attitude. It assumes that persons with intellectual disabilities as a group are inferior to other groups with physical or mental disabilities, and it opens the door for the government to infringe on individual liberties and autonomy.

I argue that the excessively paternalistic orientation of the Israeli law is, *inter alia*, an inevitable result of a specific legislative solution, in contrast to comprehensive legislation that embraces all persons with disabilities who cannot manage their own affairs for whatever reason. In this realm, too, a model code should be drafted that defines balanced principles to guide the rules and procedures that determine whether it is justified to impose care or institutionalization. Procedural issues pertaining to implementation of the model code should be addressed in specific regulations for each population group. In this way, it is possible to ensure that the implementation and application of imposed treatment for persons with intellectual disabilities are tailored to the specific characteristics of this group and are consistent with the structure of services available to them.

D. Legislation Concerning Criminal Responsibility

What should the legislative policy be regarding the extent of criminal responsibility borne by persons with intellectual disabilities? What are the implications of the legislative policy on this issue?

This is a question of legal principle, and the solution should be anchored in general legislation that stipulates the rules determining whether a defendant is fully accountable, partially accountable, or not accountable for a crime committed. The Israeli penal code applies a uniform set of principles to determine whether or not a defendant with a mental or intellectual disability is accountable for a crime.[55]

Israel enacted legislation that delineates procedures for determining the criminal responsibility of a person with an intellectual disability. If it is believed that a criminal suspect is intellectually disabled, the court refers the case to an evaluation committee for persons with intellectual disabilities, which assesses the situation and submits a recommendation. In cases of suspected mental illness, the court refers the case to the district psychiatrist for an expert opinion on the suspect's ability to assume responsibility for his or her actions. These two agencies—the evaluation committee and the district psychiatrist—operate under the provisions of two different laws. The evaluation committee bases its recommendations on the Welfare (Treatment of Retarded Persons) Law 1969,[56] whereas the district psychiatrist follows the Treatment of Mentally Sick Persons Law 1991,[57] to formulate recommendations to the court on matters of criminal responsibility. It is reasonable for two specific laws to govern the decisions made by professionals who evaluate the mental or intellectual state of a criminal suspect. One law focuses on persons with intellectual disabilities, and the other focuses on persons who are mentally ill.

In principle, general legislation is more appropriate for dealing with suspects whose criminal responsibility is in doubt. At the level of implementation, however, specific legislation was enacted in accordance with the organizational context and professional nature of the services that evaluate and treat the population group in question. This functional division in Israeli law seems to be a fair solution, irrespective of one's opinion about the actual principles that determine the criminal responsibility of an intellectually disabled or mentally ill person.

E. Legislation Concerning Competence to Act in Civil Matters

The legal competence of persons with intellectual disabilities to engage in various types of legal action is another sensitive issue. In such instances, a question arises of whether or not specific legislation that stipulates the degree of social and legal control over intellectually disabled persons is needed. A similar question concerns legal actions such as contractual liability and responsibility for damages, marriage, and independent transactions involving money and property. The goal is to strike a balance between the civil right of persons with intellectual disabilities to manage their affairs as independently as possible and the need to protect them from legal actions that may harm them and infringe on their vital interests. The crucial point of equilibrium between these two considerations should be anchored in general legislation covering all persons who are incapable of managing their own affairs. There is no reason to enact special laws for persons with intellectual disabilities, persons with mental illness, or persons with organic brain damage resulting from illness or accident. On this issue, Israeli legislative policy is balanced and universal. The Legal Capacity and Guardianship Law 1962 stipulates that any person is deemed competent to take legal actions as long as this competence is not revoked or limited by law or by the court.[58] The law also defines the rules governing revocation of legal competence in cases where individuals cannot attend to their own affairs because of mental illness or intellectual disability.[59]

   The Contracts Law (General Section) follows this universal approach in stipulating the rules governing nullification of contracts. This refers to the general principles that govern nullification, as opposed to a specific provision referring exclusively to persons with intellectual disabilities. This law is problematic because it does not provide appropriate legal protection for persons who cannot properly manage their own affairs due to an intellectual disability, but whose legal competency has not been formally revoked by a court. Until a court declares these individuals incompetent, they are not legally protected in case of damage to their material interests.[60]

F. Legislation Concerning Income Maintenance Allowance

Generalized legislation is also desirable for ensuring entitlements to benefits and material assistance to the families of persons with intellectual disabilities. Israel's National Insurance Law, like the Swedish law, acknowledges the right of families with disabled children—ie, children who need assistance from others in most activities of daily living—to receive financial benefits.[61] Another National Insurance plan grants general disability allowances to adults (over the age of 18) whose earning capacity has been significantly diminished by a disability.[62] Persons with serious disabilities are entitled to a disability allowance for maintenance purposes and a supplementary benefit for special personal care services.[63]

   Legislation for disability allowances has also generally not differentiated between causes of disability. Persons with intellectual disabilities, like persons who are mentally ill or physically disabled, are recognized and entitled to a general disability allowance in addition to a special services allowance in cases of severe disability. The same rules are applied to everyone for the purposes of examining the functional implications of the disability. Specific criteria stipulating differential entitlements for different types of disabilities are avoided.

G. Legislation Concerning Issues of a Specific Nature

In addition to issues requiring general legislation, as explained earlier, there are also issues that require specific legislation for persons with intellectual disabilities. The common denominator linking these issues is the need to take the special needs of this population group into account. A few examples of issues that inherently call for specific legislation applying exclusively to persons with intellectual disabilities are presented below.

First, legislators must set standards regarding the living conditions of persons with intellectual disabilities who live in institutions or in special community residential settings. Rules governing personnel, care plans, training, and other activities for intellectually disabled persons in institutions must be tailored to the specific needs of this population group. For this reason, the Israeli legislature stipulated specific standards in living conditions for persons with intellectual disabilities living in institutions or community residential settings.[64]

Second, intellectual disability must be evaluated among the target population and specific care plans adapted to the characteristics described in the diagnostic evaluation. The task of evaluating and adapting modes of treatment requires the involvement of experts in the field who follow procedures and rules laid down in specific legislation. Such legislation must take into account the particular needs and characteristics of this population group.[65]

H. Should Difference Make a Difference?

As emphasized above, segregative legislation is not necessarily required for persons with intellectual disabilities. A legislative policy with separate provisions for persons with intellectual disabilities may unnecessarily harm their image and reinforce paternalistic, segregative trends. The social policy of integrating persons with intellectual disabilities as much as possible into open, common social systems should also be expressed in legislation. It is important to adopt a legislative policy that strives to achieve harmony between general legislation aimed at ensuring the civil rights and personal freedoms of persons with intellectual disabilities, and specific legislation aimed at finding solutions for the special needs of those individuals. This integrative approach includes evaluating intellectual disability, pinpointing the proper modes of care and setting appropriate standards for living conditions in residential institutions that accommodate persons with intellectual disabilities.

Balanced integration of general and specific legislation, in accordance with the guidelines outlined above, is a normative goal that should be pursued by the legal system of any country that recognizes its obligations toward persons with intellectual disabilities. Based on these principles, the provisions in a given country regarding the rights of persons with intellectual disabilities should be examined, with emphasis placed on areas that require legislative supplements, modifications, or amendments.

IV. THE NEED TO IMPLEMENT AND ENFORCE LEGISLATION

Failure to implement and enforce legislation following its enactment often occurs, particularly in cases of laws that are intended to ensure rights and equal opportunities to individuals or groups that are unable to stand up for their own rights.

Persons with intellectual disabilities and their families do not have significant clout as a political group. For the most part, they are considered a weak population that has difficulty fighting for the rights of its members, even when those rights are formally protected by the law. Enforcement of the law depends largely on the ability of the affected parties to apply suitable pressure when their lawful rights are not honored. Therefore, it can be assumed that in many cases, the legal entitlements of persons with intellectual disabilities will not be implemented.

In Israel, the disparity between the declared rights of persons with intellectual disabilities and the practical implementation of their entitlements is evidenced in the area of occupational rehabilitation. According to the National Insurance Law, persons with at least 20% medical disability are entitled to occupational rehabilitation tailored to their abilities and competencies, following examination and approval by a rehabilitation committee.[66] Thus, in practical terms, a large proportion of the intellectually disabled do not receive occupational rehabilitation from the National Insurance Institute, even though they meet the criteria set forth in the law. This problem cannot be attributed to the phrasing of the law, which is universal and applies to all disabled population groups, irrespective of their specific type of disability. Rather, it is due to the lack of appropriate provisions ensuring occupational rehabilitation for persons with intellectual disabilities who are capable of and interested in joining the labor force under market or semi-market conditions.[67]

This problem recurs in a different context—ie, the living conditions of persons with intellectual disabilities residing in institutions. In these settings, there is a disparity between the standards prescribed by law[68] and the practical implementation of these standards. Inspection authorities find it difficult to enforce standard of care provisions in institutions that fail to offer legally acceptable care standards and living conditions.

Consequently, in addition to enacting an enlightened set of laws covering various spheres of life that affect the rights and special needs of persons with intellectual disabilities, it is essential to provide tools and conditions for the enforcement and implementation of the statutory provisions. Moreover, petitioning the courts in cases where the rights of persons with intellectual disabilities have been violated—an accepted practice in the United States—is insufficient by itself. It is also important to develop tools and establish organizations whose chief mission is to form a lobby for advancement of the interests of persons with intellectual disabilities to ensure implementation of their statutory rights.

In Israel, there has been some movement in this direction over the past few years. The Association for Civil Rights in Israel, for example, has established an association known as *Bizkhut* (By Right)—the Civil Rights Center for the Disabled, which has been pressing for comprehensive legislation to ensure 'full integration and equal rights for people with disabilities',[69] including intellectually disabled persons. In 2000, the Equal Rights Commission for People with Disabilities was established in Israel under the Equal Rights for People with Disabilities Law (ERPDL).[70] The function of this commission is to promote the goals of the law, to promote equality, to prevent discrimination against people with disabilities, and to encourage their active integration into society. The function of the Israeli commission is similar to that of the Disability Rights Commission (DRC) in England. In April 1999, the DRC was appointed by the British government under the Disability Discrimination Act 1995.

In England, as in Israel, these agencies function in the framework of legislation that aims to combat discrimination and promote equality for persons with disabilities. In both cases, the activities are educational and informative rather than adversarial or oppressive. The purpose of the authority granted to the agencies in England and Israel is to educate the public to promote appropriate practice. However, the Israeli and British commissions lack the powers of enforcement that the American law grants the Equal Employment Opportunities Commission (EEOC), which operates under the Americans with Disabilities Act.[71]

The simultaneous existence of the following three components is essential for concrete implementation of the principles and values of equal rights and social and cultural integration for persons with intellectual and other disabilities. First, comprehensive legislation should be enacted that establishes these principles and values and ensures protection of persons with disabilities against direct or indirect discrimination. Second, agencies should be created with legal powers to enforce the law. These powers will be added to the educational and informative functions granted to these agencies for the purpose of disseminating and assimilating these values and principles among the public at large. Third, public and private nongovernmental organizations (NGOs) that lobby for the rights and interests of people with disabilities should be encouraged. This lobby can serve as a watchdog for implementing the provisions of the law in addition to initiating activities to further the goals and values that the law aims to ensure. Countries that seriously intend to implement the principles of equal rights and social and cultural integration for persons with disabilities in the spirit of the UN Declaration must ensure the simultaneous implementation of the three components defined above. The vulnerability of persons with intellectual disabilities underscores the need for active cooperation with respect to the three components. It is the responsibility of those countries to see that all three components exist and that they will be implemented simultaneously to attain the supreme goals of equal rights and social integration of persons with intellectual disabilities.

NOTES

1. United States: Americans with Disabilities Act, 42 USC §§12101–12213 (supp III 1991) [hereinafter ADA]; Canada: Canadian Charter of Rights and Freedoms, Part I of the Constitution Act 1982, being Schedule B to the Canada Act 1982; United Kingdom: The Disability Discrimination Act (DDA); Israel: Equal Rights for People with Disabilities Law 1998 [hereinafter ERPDL].
2. See, eg, the Swedish law: The Act Concerning Support and Services for Persons with Certain Functional Disabilities (passed on 27 May 1993) and the Assistance Benefit Act 1993.
3. *United Nations Declaration on the Rights of Mentally Retarded Persons*, General Assembly Resolution 2856, adopted 20 December 1971.
4. D Shnit, *The Law, the Individual, and the Social Services: The Legal Basis for Social Work in Israel* (1988) (in Hebrew), 278–324.
5. Welfare Treatment of Retarded Persons Law 1969, 23 LSI, 144 [hereinafter TRP].
6. ibid ss 19b–19g.
7. National Insurance Law (Consolidated Version) 1995, Chapter I, Disability Insurance.
8. Legal Capacity and Guardianship Law 1962, 16 LSI, 106–119.
9. For a comprehensive discussion of the reasons for the limitation in implementing the stipulations outlawing discrimination against persons with disabilities in the legislation of countries such as Israel and England, see SS Herr, Comparative Study of Disability Nondiscrimination Laws and Alternative

Means of Implementation and Enforcement—Final Report for the Mary E. Switzer Distinguished Research Fellowship, 9 June 2001, 27–51.

10. Ontarians with Disabilities Act 1994.
11. Philanthropic, religious, fraternal, and social groups with disabled members are customarily exempted from this requirement.
12. On the application and enforcement of the 'reasonable accommodation' standard as set forth in the ADA, see FS Ravitch, 'Beyond Reasonable Accommodation: The Availability and Structure of a Cause of Action for Workplace Harassment under the Americans with Disabilities Act' (1994) 15/3 *Cardozo Law Review* 1475–1522.
13. National Insurance Law (n 7 above).
14. National Insurance Regulations (Basic Needs Allowance, Assistance with Education, and Arrangements for Children with Disabilities) 1980.
15. The Special Education Law 1988, s 2.
16. HC 7081/93, *Bozer v Maccabim-Reut Local Authority*, 50(1), PD 19, 26.
17. Welfare Law (Treatment of Retarded Persons—TRP), ss 3–12; 16.
18. ibid (Amendment No 4), 2000.
19. Explanations of the bill (Treatment of Retarded Persons) (Amendment 4—Out-of-Home Placement and Day Settings), 2000.
20. ibid (Amendment No 4), 2000, s 7A.
21. n 2 above.
22. ibid s 6.
23. ibid s 9.
24. Contracts (General Part) Law, [1973], 27 LSI, 117.
25. ibid ss 14–15.
26. ibid s 12.
27. ibid s 18.
28. For a discussion of the situation in Israel, see D Shnit, 'Protection in Israel of the Property Interests of the Elderly with Disabled Capacity to Function' (1987) 17 *Israel Yearbook on Human Rights*, 222, 235, 239; regarding the law in New Jersey, see, eg, RD Cotton, 'Agreements of the Mentally Disabled: A Problem of New Jersey Law' (1971) 3 *Rutgers-Camden Law Journal* 241.
29. On the need to maximize autonomy in this context, see SS Herr, 'Maximizing Autonomy: Reforming Personal Support Laws in Sweden and the United States' (1995) 22 *JASH* 213–223.
30. Legal Capacity and Guardianship Law (n 8 above) s 8.
31. Penal Law 1977, s 19, AG Publications Ltd, July 1992.
32. TRP (n 5 above) s 19b.
33. ibid s 19c.
34. Basic Law: Human Dignity and Liberty 1992, 45 LSI, 150.
35. ibid s 8. On the application of this Basic Law in Israel, see A Barak, 'Human Dignity as a Constitutional Right' (1994) 41 *Hapraklit* 291–345 (Hebrew); S Almog, 'Basic Law: Freedom of Occupation; Human Dignity and Liberty' (1992) 1/1 *Mishpat Umimshal* 185–195 (Hebrew).
36. The rights of intellectually disabled people based on the principle of the least restrictive alternative are discussed in DL Chambers, 'The Principle of the Least Restrictive Alternative: The Constitutional Issues' in M Kindred,

TL Shaffer, J Cohen, and D Penrod, (eds), *The Mentally Retarded Citizen and the Law* (New York: Free Press, 1976) 486–499; DL Chambers, 'Alternatives to Civil Commitment of the Mentally Ill: Practical Guides and Constitutional Imperatives' (1972) 70/2 *Michigan Law Review* 1107; D Ferleger and PA Boyd, 'Anti-Institutionalization: The Promise of the Penhurst Case' (1979) 31/1 *Stanford Law Review* 717–752.

37. TRP (n 5 above) ss 5–7.
38. Treatment of Mentally Sick Person Law (1991), LSI 58.
39. ibid ss 6, 7, 9.
40. ibid ss 7(2)(b)–(c), 9.
41. CA (Civil Appeal) 219/79 *Yarmilovitz v Hovav* 35(3) *Piskei Din* (Judgements of the Supreme Court of Israel, hereinafter PD), 766; CA 558/84 *Carmeli v State of Israel* 41(3), PD, 757.
42. Safety of Protected Persons Law 1966, 20 LSI, 48.
43. ibid ss 4–6.
44. ibid s 7.
45. Youth (Care and Supervision) Law 1960, 14 LSI, 44.
46. Safety of Protected Persons Law (n 42 above).
47. TRP (n 5 above) ss 5–7.
48. See, eg, TRP (n 5 above).
49. See, eg, ADA (n 1 above), and Legal Capacity and Guardianship Law (n 8 above).
50. See, eg, Contracts (General Part) Law (n 24 above).
51. eg, there is no law in Israel dealing with compulsory sterilization of intellectually disabled people.
52. For a discussion of the principle of normalization and integration, see, eg, RJ Flynn and KE Nitsch (eds), *Normalization, Social Integration, and Community Services* (Baltimore: University Park Press, 1980) 7–70; Kindred *et al.* (n 36 above) 3, 6, 423–433, 499–450, 499–514; Ferleger and Boyd (n 36 above).
53. RA Kurtz, *Social Aspects of Mental Retardation* (Lexington, Mass: Lexington Books, 1977); On the right to an individualized care plan, see SJ Brakel, J Parry, and BA Weiner (eds), *The Mentally Disabled and the Law* (Chicago: American Bar Foundation, 1985) 352–356.
54. TRP (n 5 above).
55. Penal Law (n 31 above).
56. TRP (n 5 above) ss 19b–19c.
57. Treatment of Mentally Sick Person Law (n 38 above) ss 15–16.
58. Legal Capacity and Guardianship Law (n 8 above) s 2.
59. ibid s 8.
60. I Englard and M Bass, 'The Legal Acts of Persons of Unsound Mind Performed before their being Declared Incompetent: Legislative Proposals' (1979) 9 *Mishpatim* 335 (Hebrew); D Shnit (n 28 above).
61. National Insurance Regulations (n 14 above).
62. National Insurance Law (n 7 above) ss 195–196.
63. ibid s 206.
64. For guidelines on standards in residences for persons with intellectual disabilities in Israel, see Supervision of Residences (Maintenance of Protected

Persons in Residences for persons with intellectual disabilities) Regulations, 1967, 2090 *Kovetz Ha-takkanot* (17 August 1967), 3068.

65. On the power to evaluate under Israeli law, see n 5 above, ss 1, 4–6.
66. National Insurance Law (n 7 above) s 203.
67. See the report of the legislative commission on care of the intellectually disabled (Shnit Commission), June 1995, appointed in 1990 by the Israeli Minister of Labor and Social Affairs, 28–32 (Hebrew).
68. Supervision of Residences Regulations (n 64 above).
69. Bizkhut (By Right), the Civil Rights Center for the Disabled, drafted a comprehensive legislative proposal to ensure complete integration and equal rights for persons with disabilities in Israel. 13 December 1994.
70. ERPDL (n 1 above) ss 20–26.
71. ADA (n 1 above).

10

Statutory Changes in Disability Policy: Types of Legislation, Policies, and Goals

ROBERT SILVERSTEIN

I. INTRODUCTION

In many countries, legislatures have adopted statutory frameworks that reflect a new paradigm in which persons with disabilities, with all of their differences, are socially integrated. As a national example, this chapter focuses on the United States and its federal legislation. These efforts have critical implications regarding the design, implementation, and evaluation of programs and policies that affect persons with all types of disabilities. Persons with intellectual disabilities, as members of this broader class, benefit from the statutory and policy frameworks that all persons with disabilities in their respective countries enjoy, or should enjoy. This chapter emphasizes cross-disability issues, fundamental beliefs, and core policies that vigilant advocacy can realize.

Society has historically imposed attitudinal and institutional barriers that subject persons with intellectual and other disabilities to lives of unjust dependency, segregation, isolation, and exclusion. Attitudinal barriers are characterized by beliefs held by nondisabled persons about persons with disabilities. Institutional barriers include policies, practices, and procedures adopted by entities such as employers, businesses, and public agencies.[1]

Sometimes, these attitudinal and institutional barriers are the result of deep-seated prejudice.[2] At times, these barriers result from decisions to follow the 'old paradigm' of considering people with disabilities as 'defective' and in need of 'fixing'.[3] At other times, these barriers are the result of thoughtlessness, indifference, or lack of understanding.[4]

In response to challenges by persons with disabilities, their families, and other advocates, US policymakers have slowly begun to react over the past quarter of a century. They have begun to recognize the debilitating effects of these barriers on persons with disabilities and have rejected the old paradigm.

A new paradigm of disability has emerged that considers disability as a natural and normal part of the human experience. Rather than focusing on 'fixing' the individual, the new paradigm focuses on taking effective

This chapter is based on portions of a law review article, 85 *Iowa Law Review* 1691 (2000).

and meaningful actions to modify the natural, constructed, cultural, and social environment. In other words, the new paradigm focuses on eliminating the attitudinal and institutional barriers that preclude persons with disabilities from participating fully in society's mainstream.

Aspects of the new paradigm were included in public policies enacted in the early 1970s.[5] Between the 1970s and 1990, lawmakers further defined and society further accepted the new paradigm.[6] In 1990, the 'new paradigm' was explicitly articulated in the landmark American with Disabilities Act (ADA)[7] and further refined in subsequent legislation.[8]

The purpose of this chapter is to provide an emerging disability policy framework consistent with the 'new paradigm' that can be used as a lens or guidepost[9] to design, implement, and evaluate generic,[10] as well as disability-specific, public policies and programs to ensure meaningful inclusion of people with disabilities in mainstream society.

II. CATEGORIES OF LAWS AFFECTING INDIVIDUALS WITH DISABILITIES

Stakeholders who identify legislative solutions to problems affecting persons with disabilities must consider the most appropriate and politically expedient legislation available.

Five general categories of laws affect people with disabilities. These categories are arranged as civil rights statutes, entitlement programs, discretionary grant-in-aid programs, regulatory statutes, and other provisions that include appropriations, tax legislation, and loans.

Entitlement programs, for example, guarantee eligible individuals a specified level of benefits. These laws require that the legislative body appropriate funds sufficient to meet the entitlement. Other laws, such as discretionary grant-in-aid programs, provide benefits only to the extent that the legislative body exercises its discretion to appropriate funds to pay for the benefits.

The type of law stakeholders pursue depends on their purposes and priorities. Persons with disabilities tend to favor legislation that entitles or guarantees them benefits regardless of legislative funding priorities. On the other hand, policymakers who are primarily concerned with budget issues tend to disfavor legislation that offers entitlements and instead prefer grant programs that allow funding discretion.

Some laws cross over into more than one category as both a civil rights statute and discretionary grant-in-aid program. Under Part B of the Individuals with Disabilities Education Act (IDEA), US children with disabilities are entitled to a free appropriate public education consistent with the Equal Protection Clause of the Fourteenth Amendment to the US Constitution. It is thus a civil rights statute and a grant-in-aid program providing financial assistance to the states.

A. Civil Rights Statutes

The first category of laws includes federal civil rights statutes that prohibit covered entities (such as state or local governments and businesses) from discriminating against individuals on the basis of or by reason of disability. These laws are permanent in nature because they do not expire on a certain date. Federal agencies play a key role with respect to the administration of these civil rights statutes, including policy development, complaint resolution, monitoring, and enforcement. Nothing in these federal civil statutes precludes a state or local community from adopting additional or greater protections.[11] Examples include the Americans with Disabilities Act (ADA),[12] Section 504 of the Rehabilitation Act of 1973,[13] the Fair Housing Act of 1968 as amended in 1988,[14] and Part B of the Individuals with Disabilities Education Act (IDEA).[15]

B. Entitlement Programs

The second category of laws affecting people with disabilities involves 'open- and close-ended' entitlement programs.

'Open-ended' entitlement programs guarantee eligible individuals a specified level of benefits. Thus as more people become eligible for the program, costs automatically rise. These programs are often referred to as 'mandatory spending' programs because Congress must appropriate sufficient funds to pay for the benefits. Examples include the Social Security Disability Insurance (SSDI) Program,[16] Supplemental Security Income (SSI) Program,[17] Medicare Program,[18] and Medicaid Program.[19]

A 'close-ended' entitlement program does not create an individual guarantee to assistance; rather, it provides a state or other entity with a fixed allotment of funds over a specified period of time. Unlike mandatory spending programs, individuals receive benefits only to the extent that funds from the fixed allotment are available. Examples include the Vocational Rehabilitation Program under Title I of the Rehabilitation Act of 1973[20] and the Children's Health Insurance Program under Title XXI of the Social Security Act,[21] otherwise known as the State Children's Health Insurance Program (CHIP).

C. Discretionary Grant-in-Aid Programs

Discretionary grant-in-aid programs comprise the third category of laws affecting people with intellectual and other disabilities. These programs provide supplementary federal financial assistance to support specified activities carried out by entities, such as state and local public agencies and private agencies. Some discretionary grant programs are specifically targeted at meeting the needs of persons with disabilities; others are generic and are targeted at specified populations, which include, but are not limited to, meeting the needs of persons with disabilities.

There are two types of discretionary grant-in-aid programs: formula programs and competitive grant programs. Both types of grant programs are subject to annual appropriations by the US Congress. These programs are referred to as 'discretionary' because Congress may appropriate whatever amount of funds it deems necessary or adequate.

1. Formula-Grant Programs

Formula-grant programs support ongoing activities of and foster systemic change by state or local government agencies or nonprofit organizations. A 'formula' is expounded by the legislation and specifies the exact amount of funds each entity will receive.

Examples of formula-grant programs to state and local agencies that are targeted at meeting the specific needs of individuals with disabilities include public education programs provided in Part B of IDEA,[22] early intervention programs provided in Part C of IDEA,[23] employment services provided in Part B of Title VI of the Rehabilitation Act of 1973,[24] independent living services provided in Part B of Title VII of the Rehabilitation Act of 1973,[25] and State Developmental Disabilities Councils provided in Part B of the Developmental Disabilities Assistance and Bill of Rights Act.[26]

Some formula-grant programs allocate a specified amount to a state and then target funds to nonprofit organizations within each state, focusing exclusively on meeting the needs of persons with disabilities. Examples include statewide networks for centers for independent living provided in Part A of Title VII of the Rehabilitation Act of 1973[27] and protection and advocacy systems provided in Part C of the Developmental Disabilities Assistance and Bill of Rights Act.[28] This latter statute was first enacted in 1975 and focused on the rights and needs of the people now referred to as intellectually disabled. Generic formula-grant programs contain specific references to or set-asides for individuals with disabilities. They include job training provided in Title I (Workforce Investment Systems) of the Workforce Investment Act of 1998,[29] school reform provided in school reform legislation (eg, Goals 2000: Educate America Act),[30] early childhood education provided in programs like Head Start,[31] social services provided under Title XX of the Social Security Act,[32] and maternal and child health provided under Title V of the Social Security Act.[33]

2. Competitive Grant Programs

A second category of discretionary grant-in-aid programs involves awards based on competition, rather than on a formula. Typically, a federal agency will announce the existence of a competition and publish requests for proposals. Applicants then submit proposals, which are often subject to peer review by experts in the field, with the federal agency announcing the grant awards.

Competitive grants allow entities to develop a better understanding of a problem, create new knowledge, or train persons to provide necessary services. In addition, the need for further federal assistance can be determined by considering specific information provided in grant applications. One primary example is rehabilitation research funded by the National Institute on Disability and Rehabilitation Research (NIDRR),[34] established under Title II of the Rehabilitation Act of 1973. Other illustrations are the assistive technology program under the Technology-Related Assistance for Individuals with Disabilities Act of 1988,[35] university affiliated programs under Part D of the Developmental Disabilities Assistance and Bill of Rights Act,[36] medical research funded by the National Institute of Health and authorized under Title IV, Part A of the Public Health Services Act,[37] ADA technical assistance,[38] training of educators under Subpart 2 of Part D of IDEA,[39] training of parents under Section 682 of IDEA,[40] and work incentive outreach programs under Section 1149 of the Social Security Act, added by the Ticket to Work and Work Incentives Improvement Act.[41]

Sometimes, programs start on a small scale as competitive grant programs and then become formula grants when the appropriation increases. One example is Section 509 of the Rehabilitation Act of 1973,[42] which provides assistance to support a system in each state to protect the legal and human rights of individuals with disabilities who need services and are ineligible for other programs.

D. Regulatory Statutes

The fourth category of laws affecting people with intellectual and other disabilities includes regulatory legislation that provides minimum protections for a class of persons (including, but not limited to, persons with disabilities). Examples include the National Voter Registration Act of 1993,[43] the Family and Medical Leave Act,[44] and Section 225 of the Telecommunications Act of 1996.[45]

E. Other Laws

The fifth category of laws affecting people with disabilities includes appropriations bills that provide the funding for various programs. Laws on appropriations, tax legislation, and loans often direct various departments and agencies to spend discretionary funds that address the needs of persons with disabilities.

The tax code, for instance, is sometimes used to enhance opportunities for individuals with disabilities directly, or to provide incentives for covered entities to comply with existing responsibilities. Examples include the Disabled Access Tax Credit[46] and the Targeted Jobs Credit.[47]

III. CORE POLICIES

It is critical for stakeholders to specify the core policies that underlie the goals for proposed disability legislation. These core policies are vital because they describe the scope and limitations of the legal protections. In addition, the core policies describe the nature and type of benefits as well as the circumstances under which benefits and services will be provided.

The numerous core policies can best be understood when they are organized under the four goals of disability policy articulated in the ADA: equality of opportunity, full participation (empowerment), independent living, and economic self-sufficiency. Examples are provided below.

A. Equality of Opportunity

The first goal of disability policy articulated in the ADA is equality of opportunity. This goal is accomplished through the following four policies: individualization and interdisciplinary assessments; genuine, effective, and meaningful opportunity; accommodations, program accessibility, and auxiliary aids and services; and modifications of policies and procedures that produce treatment in the most integrated setting appropriate.

1. *Individualization and Interdisciplinary Assessments*

A fundamental concept in disability policy is the importance of focusing on the individual and the individual's unique needs. Decisions must be based on the unique strengths, resources, priorities, concerns, abilities, and capabilities of each person with a disability, including individuals with intellectual disabilities. It is essential that decisions be based on facts relevant to the individual and objective evidence, not on generalizations about all people with disabilities or all people with a particular disability. Decisions cannot be based on fear, stereotypes, or generalizations. Thus, individualized, fact-specific, case-by-case inquiry is a core principle of disability policy.

Similarly, if an individual with a disability and a nondisabled person both require and are eligible for a service, such as child care, the person with a disability should not be denied the services simply because he or she has a disability. People with disabilities must be judged on the basis of objective criteria and facts, not fear, ignorance, prejudice, or stereotypes. In other words, agencies must use definitions and eligibility criteria that result in even-handed treatment between a person with a particular disability and other similarly situated individuals, including nondisabled persons and persons with other disabilities.

Generic programs (such as job training, welfare, child care, and Head Start) must provide universal access, and thereby serve qualified individuals with disabilities instead of simply referring all people with disabilities to disability-specific programs.

Accurate, fact-specific, case-by-case inquiries often require individualized assessments and evaluations. In turn, these assessments and evaluations often require interdisciplinary approaches performed on a timely basis by teams of qualified individuals. To ensure the effectiveness and reliability of these assessments, they must be conducted in 'real' settings where the individual functions as well as in clinical settings. In making these fact-specific decisions, it is necessary to use information provided by the individual with a disability and the person's family or representative. Once the stakeholders identify and agree to the goals, objectives, services, and accountability measures, this agreement is memorialized in an individualized plan.

In the civil rights context, under Section 202 of the ADA and Section 504 of the Rehabilitation Act of 1973, the concept of individualization means that 'no qualified individual with a disability shall, by reason of such disability, be excluded from participation in or denied the benefits of the services, programs, or activities of a public entity, or be subjected to discrimination by any such entity.'[48] In addition, the ADA regulations[49] and the Section 504 coordination regulation[50] specify that a public entity, in providing any aid, benefit, or service, may not, on the basis of disability 'deny a qualified individual with a disability the opportunity to participate in or benefit from the aid, benefit, or service; unequally treat a qualified individual with a disability in participating in or benefiting from the aid, benefit, or service; otherwise limit a qualified individual with a disability in the enjoyment of any right, privilege, advantage or opportunity enjoyed by others receiving the aid, benefit, or service'.[51]

In the employment context, Title I of the Rehabilitation Act of 1973 requires an individualized plan for employment.[52] These plans are jointly agreed to and signed by eligible individuals with disabilities (or their representatives in appropriate situations) and vocational rehabilitation counselors. They are based on assessments performed by qualified personnel and existing data, including data provided by the individual with a disability.

In the educational context, under the IDEA, a team of persons, including the parents of the child and, where appropriate, the child, makes an individualized determination to provide special education and related services to a child with a disability in accordance with an individualized education program.[53] These decisions are based on comprehensive individualized evaluations completed by interdisciplinary teams performed in multiple environments.[54] The evaluation is conducted to determine whether the individual has a disability and is in need of special education and related services as well as to pinpoint the types of services needed.[55]

In the health care context, under the Early and Periodic Screening, Diagnosis, and Treatment Program (EPSDT),[56] states must adopt a comprehensive process through which individual children are screened for health deficiencies and, where appropriate, further diagnosed and treated (to the extent medically necessary services are required to treat the condition). Screening services include, among other things, a comprehensive health and developmental history (including assessment of both physical and mental health development and a comprehensive, unclothed, physical exam).[57]

Another key concept in disability policy is to serve all individuals with disabilities, including individuals with intellectual disabilities, and to give priority to those persons when funds are limited.

Historically, public and private entities excluded persons with the most significant disabilities from receiving services made available to nondisabled persons and persons with moderate disabilities. A prime example was many states' exclusion of children with severe intellectual disabilities from public education. For instance, the State of Maine actually had a policy that authorized the local school superintendent of schools to exclude 'any child whose physical or mental condition make it inexpedient for him to attend'.[58]

In 1975, the IDEA, then titled as the Education for All Handicapped Children Act, was enacted. It included a 'zero reject' policy under which all children with disabilities, including those with the most significant disabilities, are entitled to a free and appropriate public education.[59] Congress adopted this policy to conform to the Equal Protection Clause of the Fourteenth Amendment to the US Constitution, under which all children with disabilities should enjoy the same right to receive a free public education as all nondisabled children. For children with the most significant disabilities, such as intellectual disabilities, public 'education' is defined broadly to include care, treatment, living facilities, and rehabilitation.

The vocational rehabilitation program presumes that all persons with disabilities, including those with intellectual disabilities, can benefit from vocational rehabilitation services in terms of an employment outcome.

To deny services to a person with a disability, a state agency must demonstrate by clear and convincing evidence (the highest standard of proof used in civil actions) that an individual is incapable of benefiting from vocational rehabilitation services.[60] When a state is unable to serve all eligible individuals, it must adopt an 'order of selection' under which it first serves those individuals with the most significant disabilities.[61]

Entitlement programs, such as the SSI program (income support for low-income individuals with disabilities),[62] have always targeted individuals with the most significant disabilities as intended beneficiaries.

2. Effective Opportunity through Accommodations, Program Accessibility, Auxiliary Aids and Services

Eliminating gross exclusions and denials of the same treatment to all individuals is insufficient to assure genuine, effective, and meaningful opportunity for certain individuals with disabilities. For some individuals with disabilities, adjustments to regular programs, separate or different treatment, or the provision of support services may be necessary to ensure that an opportunity is genuine, effective, and meaningful for those individuals. Thus, services may be based on the unique needs of the individual rather than on the basis of the needs of the 'average' person. For instance, a genuine, effective, and meaningful accommodation for a person who is deaf is that the communication is provided with a qualified sign language interpreter.

In the civil rights context, the ADA regulation[63] and the Section 504 coordination regulation[64] generally set forth the concept of effective and meaningful opportunity. A covered entity may not, on the basis of disability, provide a qualified individual with a disability with a benefit or service that is not as effective as that provided to others. When action is necessary to provide qualified individuals with disabilities with benefits or services that are as effective as those provided to others, it is acceptable to provide different or separate treatment.

Specific applications of the 'effective and meaningful' standard are also included in the ADA and Section 504 coordination regulations. For instance, a reasonable accommodation must be provided to employees in order to remove workplace barriers unless it would result in an undue hardship to the employer.[65] Programs in existing facilities must be accessible and new buildings must be readily accessible to and usable by individuals with disabilities.[66]

Appropriate auxiliary aids and services must be provided by covered entities, including communication accessibility and the provision of materials in accessible formats.[67]

In addition, an entity cannot surcharge a particular individual with a disability or any group of individuals with disabilities to cover the cost of measures, such as the provision of reasonable accommodations, auxiliary aids, and services.[68] Furthermore, the regulations include a provision that an individual with a disability is not required to accept an accommodation, aid, service, opportunity, or benefit provided under the ADA.[69]

In the education context, the concept of 'effective and meaningful opportunity' is reflected in the IDEA right of every child with a disability, regardless of the nature or severity of the disability, to receive a free and appropriate public education (FAPE).[70] This right includes, among other things, the right to teachers who possess the skills and knowledge necessary to meet the needs of children with disabilities and the adoption by local school districts of promising practices, materials, and technology to aid children with disabilities.[71]

In the employment context, to ensure 'effective and meaningful opportunity' to benefit from vocational rehabilitation, Title I of the Rehabilitation Act of 1973 describes a broad range of vocational rehabilitation services that a program must provide for an individual with a disability. Examples of services include rehabilitation technology services, interpreter services, and on-the-job or other related personal assistance services provided while an individual with a disability is receiving vocational rehabilitation.[72]

In the health care context, the EPSDT program specifies that a state must guarantee that eligible children receive all medically necessary services required to treat a medical condition.[73] The state may satisfy this obligation directly or through contract or other arrangements with service providers.

3. *Effective Treatment through Modifications of Policies and Procedures*

Public policy in legislation establishes specific rules and procedures of general application to individuals meeting specified criteria. What happens, however, when the rule itself or the application of a rule has the purpose or effect of denying an individual with a disability genuine, effective, and meaningful opportunity to benefit from the program, service, or activity on the basis of the individual's disability?

An important tenet of disability policy is that rules of general applicability must be modified to take into consideration the unique needs of individuals with disabilities (rather than being based on needs of the 'average' person) unless the modification would fundamentally alter the nature of the service, program, or activity. To apply this tenet, it is critical to look behind a rule of general applicability to ascertain its purposes and policy objectives. It is necessary to determine whether a reasonable modification to the rule will enable the individual with a disability to satisfy the underlying purposes, functions, and policy objectives of the rule. It may also include adopting separate or different rules when necessary to ensure genuine, effective, and meaningful opportunity. In other words, it is critical that there be a level playing field for both individuals with disabilities and nondisabled individuals.

In the civil rights context, the ADA regulations[74] and the Section 504 coordination regulation[75] specify that a public entity shall make reasonable modifications to its policies or procedures when the modifications are necessary to avoid discrimination on the basis of disability unless the public entity can demonstrate that making the modifications would fundamentally alter the nature of the service, program, or activity. Thus, an entity might adopt a rule specifying that it will only cash checks for persons who have a valid driver's license. The purpose of the rule is to ascertain that the persons cashing the check are who they purport to be. Since people who are blind and many who have an intellectual disability cannot drive and, therefore, do not have driver's licenses, this rule has the effect of denying them a genuine opportunity to take advantage of the check-cashing service. The ADA and Section 504 require that the entity modify its rule, for example, by accepting a different form of photo identification.

In the educational context, the modification of rules for disciplining children with disabilities must ensure that such children are not inappropriately excluded, segregated, or denied services on the basis of their disabilities.[76] At the same time, the modified rule must ensure that the underlying functions and purposes of these rules (for example, keeping the schools safe and conducive to learning, holding children responsible for their actions, and preventing inappropriate behavior from recurring) are not fundamentally altered.

4. Treatment in the Most Appropriate Integrated Setting

Maximum appropriate integration and inclusion of an individual with a disability consistent with the individual's unique needs is another fundamental tenet of disability policy. In the civil rights context, the ADA statute recognizes that 'historically, society has tended to isolate and segregate individuals with disabilities...and such forms of discrimination against individuals with disabilities continue to be a serious and pervasive social problem'.[77]

The ADA regulation specifies that although special treatment or different programs may be required in some instances in order to ensure genuine opportunity, the provision of unnecessarily separate or different services is discriminatory.[78] For example, a person who can benefit from the generic jobs program (a program providing services to persons with or without disabilities) cannot be sent automatically to the vocational rehabilitation program (a program serving only persons with disabilities) if the individual qualifies for services in the generic program with the provision of reasonable auxiliary aids.

The ADA regulation also specifies that a public entity must administer services, programs, and activities in the 'most integrated setting appropriate' to the needs of qualified individuals with disabilities.[79] The preamble to Title II defines this requirement to mean 'a setting that enables individuals with disabilities to interact with nondisabled persons to the fullest extent possible'.[80] Under Title II, *L.C. v Olmstead*, as more fully described in a prior chapter of this book, has opened more integrated community-based settings for people with intellectual disabilities.[81] The Section 504 coordination regulation includes a provision that is identical to the provision in the ADA regulations.[82] Under the Medicaid program, states may apply for a waiver to allow home and community-based placements in lieu of placement in institutional settings.[83]

In the education context, the IDEA specifies comparable inclusion mandates. It states:

To the maximum extent appropriate, children with disabilities...are educated with children who are not disabled, and special classes, separate schooling, or other removal of children with disabilities from the regular educational environment occurs only when the nature or severity of the disability of a child is such that education in regular classes with the use of supplementary aids and services cannot be achieved satisfactorily.[84]

Furthermore, the IDEA regulations require that services be provided in the least restrictive environment (requiring that a continuum of program options be provided) consistent with the unique needs of the child with a disability.[85]

In the context of intellectual disabilities, the Developmental Disabilities Assistance and Bill of Rights Act defines 'inclusion and integration' to mean:

The use by individuals with developmental disabilities of the same community resources that are used by and available to other citizens; living in homes close to community resources, with regular contact with citizens without disabilities in their communities; the full and active participation by individuals with developmental disabilities in the same community activities and types of employment as citizens without disabilities, living, learning, working and enjoying life in regular contact with citizens without disabilities; and having friendships and relationships with individuals and families of their own choosing.[86]

B. Full Participation through Empowering Individuals and Families

The second goal of disability policy articulated in the ADA is full participation by individuals with disabilities, their families, and their representatives in decisions affecting their lives at the individual and systemic level.

Full participation is achieved by empowering individuals with disabilities and their families. Empowerment includes the concepts of self-determination, self-advocacy, real and informed choice, and active participation in the decision-making process.

At the individual level, full participation includes involvement in decisions concerning, among other things, whether, when, and where to receive services and supports, which services to receive, by whom services should be provided, and which measures of progress should be used.

At the systemic level, the concept of full participation requires various forms of citizen participation in the design, implementation, and evaluation of programs and policies. This includes public hearings, consideration of public comment, and the use of advisory committees and councils. The trend in federal legislation is to provide these advisory committees with more consumer direction and control. Some legislation includes consumer-controlled councils (consisting of a majority of persons with disabilities), which make individuals with disabilities true decision-making partners with professionals and agency officials. They are thus encouraged to take joint responsibility with the government agency for the development of a state plan.

In the vocational rehabilitation program under Title I of the Rehabilitation Act of 1973, the individual with a disability (or the individual's representative as appropriate) and a qualified vocational rehabilitation counselor must jointly agree to and sign an individualized plan for employment.[87] The individual is to have the opportunity to exercise informed choice in selecting an employment outcome, the specific vocational rehabilitation services to be provided under the plan, the entity that will provide the vocational rehabilitation services, and the methods used to procure the services.[88]

Title I of the Rehabilitation Act of 1973 also directs the establishment of a State Rehabilitation Council. The functions of the Council include, in partnership with the designated state unit, developing, agreeing to, and reviewing state goals and priorities, and evaluating the effectiveness of the vocational rehabilitation program and reports of progress.[89] A majority of Council members must be persons with disabilities. Under Title VII of the Rehabilitation Act of 1973, the state vocational rehabilitation director and the chair of the statewide independent living council must jointly develop the state plan relating to independent living services and centers for independent living.[90]

In the social security context, the Ticket to Work and Self-Sufficiency Program Act[91] provides a 'ticket' to specified recipients of the SSDI program and the SSI program to obtain vocational rehabilitation. The recipient with a disability may assign the 'ticket' to any service provider of his/her choice within the employment network that is willing to accept the assignment.[92]

In the educational context, Part B of the IDEA requires that parents become partners in the process of developing their child's individualized education program (IEP) and participate in the child's placement process.[93] Whenever appropriate, the IEP team must also include the participation of the child with a disability.[94] A state may provide for the transfer of rights under the IDEA from parents to children with disabilities when children reach the age of majority.[95] Part B also requires that the state advisory committee consist of a majority of persons with disabilities or parents of children with disabilities.[96]

Under Part C of the IDEA,[97] infants and toddlers and their families are entitled to a family-directed assessment of the resources, priorities, and concerns of the family and the identification of the supports and services necessary to enhance the family's capacity to meet the developmental needs of the infant or toddler. The individualized family service plan must be developed by a multidisciplinary team, including the parents.

Of particular importance to people with intellectual disabilities, the philosophy of self-determination is articulated in the Developmental Disabilities Assistance and Bill of Rights Act.[98] The term 'self-determination' is defined as:

[A]ctivities that result in individuals with developmental disabilities, with appropriate assistance, having:
   The ability and opportunity to communicate and make personal decisions;
   The ability and opportunity to communicate choices and exercise control over the type and intensity of services, supports and other assistance the individuals receive;
   The authority to control resources to obtain needed services, support and other assistance;
   The opportunity to participate in, and contribute to, their communities; and
   Support, including financial support, to advocate for themselves and others, to develop leadership skills, through training in self-advocacy, to participate in coalitions, to educate policy makers, and to play a role in the development of public policies that affect individuals with developmental disabilities.[99]

In the Medicaid program, real choice is still unavailable in many states for those individuals with disabilities who prefer services (such as personal assistance services) in community-based settings rather than in institutions. This statutory flaw is because personal assistance services is an optional benefit under Medicaid and many states do not provide these services at all or do not provide these services on a statewide basis. Most states, however, are increasing choice by taking advantage of the 'home and community-based' waiver option for providing community-based services to targeted groups, often on less than a statewide basis.[100]

C. Independent Living

The goals of 'full participation' and 'independent living' are closely related and overlap to some degree. Full participation, or empowerment, focuses on the role of the individual and the family with respect to the provision of services and supports by public and nonprofit agencies.

The goal of fostering independent living articulated in the ADA includes enabling the individual to live in the community and participate in community activities through support for independent living skills development and specialized planning, support for long-term services and supports, including personal assistance services and supports, and the provision of cash assistance.

The philosophy of independent living includes consumer control, peer support, self-help, self-determination, equal access, and individual and system advocacy.[101]

1. Independent Living Skills Development and Specialized Planning

To enhance opportunities for persons with significant disabilities to live independently in the community and effectively participate in community activities, federal programs provide training, resources, peer counseling, and support. For instance, Title VII of the Rehabilitation Act of 1973 establishes centers for independent living and provides support for state efforts to provide, expand, and improve the provision of independent living services.[102] Independent living services, as defined in the Rehabilitation Act of 1973, include training in individual and systems advocacy; services related to securing housing or shelter, including services related to community group living and adaptive housing services; and mobility training. It also comprises training in the use of assistive technology devices and services and other supportive services, in the management of personal assistance services, in the use of public transportation, and development of skills specifically designed for youth with disabilities to promote self-awareness and esteem, develop self-empowerment skills, and explore career options.[103]

In the education context, the IDEA was amended in 1997 to include preparation for 'independent living' as one of the primary purposes of the legislation.[104] The child's individualized education plan and transition plan must include strategies for preparing children with disabilities for independent living.[105]

The Developmental Disabilities Assistance and Bill of Rights Act sets forth as one of its primary purposes supporting efforts to enhance the 'independence' of persons with developmental disabilities.[106]

2. Long-Term Services and Supports, including
Personal Assistance Services and Supports

Long-term services and supports are necessary to enable certain persons with disabilities to live in the community. Personal assistance services and supports are a significant form of long-term services. 'Personal assistance services' include a range of services, provided by one or more individuals, designed to assist an individual with a disability to perform daily living activities on or off a job, that the individual would typically perform if not for the disability, in order to increase the individual's ability to perform everyday activities.[107]

In the employment context, Title I of the Rehabilitation Act of 1973 authorizes the expenditure of funds to support personal assistance services while the individual is receiving other vocational rehabilitation services.[108]

In the health care context, personal assistance services may be provided as an optional benefit to individuals with disabilities under the Medicaid program,[109] and frequently are included as part of Home and Community Based Services waivers.[110]

3. Cash Assistance and Other Programs of Assistance

The provision of cash assistance under the SSI and SSDI programs is designed, in part, to enable a person to remain in the community rather than live in an institution.[111] Additional examples include housing assistance[112] and Food Stamps.[113]

D. Economic Self-Sufficiency

The fourth ADA goal of disability is to foster economic self-sufficiency, economic security, stability, and productivity of persons with disabilities. Federal legislation accomplishes this goal through such provisions as employment-related skills (education and training), cash assistance programs that include work incentive provisions, and tax policy that provides incentives to employers to hire persons with disabilities (eg, deductions and credits for disability-related expenditures that enable a person with a disability to work).

1. Systems Providing Employment-Related Services and Supports

In the education context, the IDEA was amended in 1997 to include preparing youth with disabilities for 'employment' as one of the primary purposes of the legislation.[114]

In the employment context, Title I of the Rehabilitation Act of 1973 provides assistance to enhance the employability of individuals with disabilities through the provision of vocational rehabilitation services.[115]

Recent amendments to Title I require that the vocational rehabilitation programs are an integral component of a statewide workforce development system under the Workforce Investment Act.[116]

2. Cash Assistance Programs and Other Programs of Assistance that Include Work Incentives

SSI law includes incentives for its beneficiaries with disabilities to work. These incentives include earned income disregards and permission for these individuals to remain eligible for Medicaid (which in some states enables these individuals to continue to receive personal assistance services).[117] The 1997 amendments to the law allow states to increase the income limit for Medicaid coverage of certain SSI beneficiaries (families with income up to 250% of the federal poverty guidelines), and to enable these individuals to 'buy into' Medicaid by paying a portion of premium costs.[118] Under the Ticket to Work and Work Incentives Improvement Act, states may establish one or two new optional Medicaid eligibility categories under which individuals can buy into Medicaid.[119] Under the first option, states may cover individuals who, except for earnings, would be eligible for SSI. If a state provides Medicaid coverage to individuals described in the first option, the state may also provide coverage to employed persons with disabilities (aged 16 to 64) whose medical condition has improved, but who continue to have a severe medically determinable impairment. Under both of these options, states may establish uniform limits on assets, resources, and earned and unearned income (or both) for this group that differ from the federal SSI requirements. In addition, the Ticket to Work and Work Incentives Improvement Act authorizes a state to apply to the Secretary of Health and Human Services for approval of a demonstration project under which a specified maximum number of individuals who are workers with a potentially severe disability can buy into Medicaid.[120]

3. Tax Policy

The Disabled Access Tax Credit provides tax credits to small businesses for expenses incurred in complying with the ADA.[121] The Targeted Jobs Credit[122] provides tax credits for hiring new employees with disabilities referred by vocational rehabilitation and other specified agencies.

IV. CONCLUSION

The human rights oriented paradigm of disability offers substantial promise to individuals with intellectual disabilities. It seeks to eliminate those barriers that have historically excluded persons with disabilities from full participation in mainstream society. The legislation influenced by this paradigm, especially the ADA and IDEA, guarantees that persons with intellectual disabilities receive not only equal protection under the law, but the equal opportunity to both contribute to and benefit from society. This chapter also demonstrates a convergence and harmonization of statutes from many different spheres (eg, non-discrimination, other civil rights, and social services laws) toward the fundamental purpose of taking into account human differences to achieve basic equality. When coupled with the trend toward individualization of service needs, the policy of universal access has also helped to create an environment where persons with intellectual disabilities can obtain meaningful legal assistance.

NOTES

1. See Americans with Disabilities Act of 1990, 2(a), 42 USC §12101(a) (1994) (listing congressional findings regarding Americans with disabilities); see also S Rep No 101-116, at 5–20 (1989). Former Senator Lowell Weicker (R. Conn.) testified before Congress 'that people with disabilities spend a lifetime "overcoming not what God wrought but what man imposed by custom and law"'. ibid at 11 (1989).
2. S Rep No 101-116, at 5–7 (1989).
3. See National Institute on Disability and Rehabilitation Research, 64 Fed Reg 68,576, 68,580 (7 December 1999) (providing notice for the final long-range plan for fiscal years 1999–2003 and explaining that the new paradigm of disability is an expectation for the future).
4. S Rep No 101-116, at 5–7 (1989).
5. See Education for All Handicapped Children Act of 1975, Pub L No 94-142, 89 Stat 773 (adding Part B to the Individuals with Disabilities Education Act, 20 USC ch 33 (1994)). See also Rehabilitation Act of 1973, 29 USC ch 16 (1994).
6. Fair Housing Amendments Act of 1988, Pub L No 100-430, 102 Stat 1619; Developmental Disabilities Assistance and Bill of Rights Act Amendments of 1987, Pub L No 100-146, 101 Stat 840; Air Carrier Access Act of 1986, Pub L No 99-435, 100 Stat 1080; Rehabilitation Act Amendments of 1986, Pub L No 99-506, 100 Stat 1807; Education of the Handicapped Act Amendments of 1986, Pub L No 99-457, 100 Stat 1145.
7. 42 USC ch 126 (1994). President Bush signed the ADA into law on 26 July 1990. ibid. Senator Tom Harkin (D. Iowa), the chief sponsor of the ADA, often refers to the legislation as the '20th century Emancipation Proclamation for persons with disabilities'. 136 Cong Rec S9689 (daily edn 13 July 1990).
8. Ticket to Work and Work Incentives Improvement Act of 1999, Pub L No 106-170, 113 Stat 1860; Individuals with Disabilities Education Act Amendments of 1997, Pub L No 105-17, 111 Stat 37; Developmental Disabilities Assistance and Bill of Rights Act Amendments of 1994, Pub L No 103-230, 108 Stat 284; Rehabilitation Act Amendments of 1992, Pub L No 102-569, 106 Stat 4344.

9. See Re-Charting the Course-First Report of the Presidential Task Force on Employment of Adults with Disabilities (15 November 1998).
10. Generic programs include persons with and without disabilities among the beneficiaries of assistance. An example of a generic program is the recently enacted Workforce Investment Act of 1998, Pub L No 105-220, 112 Stat 936, that establishes an integrated workforce investment preparation and employment system for all job seekers, including individuals with disabilities.
11. See Herr, Chapter 8 of this volume.
12. 42 USC ch 126 (1994).
13. 29 USC §794 (1994) (amended 1998). Pursuant to Executive Order 12250, the Department of Justice is responsible for coordinating the implementation of s 504 by the various federal agencies. 28 CFR §41.1 (1999). The s 504 coordination regulations are set forth in 28 CFR pt 41 (1999). Each federal agency is responsible for promulgating its own regulations implementing s 504. 28 CFR §41.2 (1999). For example, the Department of Health and Human Services s 504 regulations are codified in Part 84 of Title 45 of the Code of Federal Regulations. 45 CFR pt 84 (1999).
14. 42 USC §3604(f) (1994).
15. 20 USC §§1411–1419 (1994) (amended 1997, §1415 amended 1999, §1414a omitted by Individuals with Disabilities Education Act Amendments of 1997, Pub L No 105-17, 111 Stat 37).
16. 42 USC §401 (1994) (amended 1999).
17. 42 USC §§1381–1383c (1994) (§§1382–1382b, 1382d, 1382e, 1383, 1383b amended 1999; §1382c amended 1997; §1383c amended 1996).
18. 42 USC §§1395c–1395ccc (1994).
19. 42 USC §1396 (1994).
20. 29 USC §730 (1994) (amended 1998).
21. Balanced Budget Act of 1997, Pub L No 105-33, 111 Stat 251, 552.
22. 20 USC §§1411–1419 (1994) (amended 1997, §1415 amended 1999, §1414a omitted by Individuals with Disabilities Education Act Amendments of 1997, Pub L No 105-17, 111 Stat 37).
23. 20 USC §§1421–1427 (1994) (repealed by Individuals with Disabilities Education Act Amendments of 1997, Pub L No 105-17, 111 Stat 37, 157).
24. 29 USC §§795i–795q (1994) (amended 1998, §§795o–795q omitted by Workforce Investment Act of 1998, Pub L No 105-220, 112 Stat 931, 1210).
25. 29 USC §§796j–7961 (1994).
26. 42 USC §§6021–6030 (1994 & Supp IV 1998).
27. 29 USC §§796f to 796f-6 (Supp IV 1998).
28. 42 USC §§6041–6043 (1994 & Supp IV 1998).
29. Workforce Investment Act of 1998, Pub L No 105-220, 112 Stat 936.
30. 20 USC §§5801–5802 (Supp IV 1998).
31. 42 USC §§9831–9841 (Supp IV 1998).
32. 42 USC §§1397–1397f (1994 & Supp IV 1998).
33. 42 USC §§701–709 (1994 & Supp IV 1998) (§706 amended 1999).
34. 29 USC §§760–765 (1994 & Supp IV 1998).
35. 29 USC §§2201–2202 (1994) (repealed by Assistive Technology Act of 1998, Pub L No 105-394, 112 Stat 3627, 3661).

36. 42 USC §§6061–6066 (1994 & Supp IV 1998).
37. 42 USC §§281–283f (1994 & Supp IV 1998).
38. ADA §506, 42 USC §12206 (1994).
39. 20 USC §§1461–1474 (Supp IV 1998).
40. 20 USC §1482 (Supp III 1997).
41. Ticket to Work and Work Incentives Improvement Act, Pub L No 106-170, 113 Stat 1860.
42. 29 USC §794e (1994) (amended 1998).
43. Pub L No 103-31, 107 Stat 77.
44. Pub L No 103-3, 107 Stat 6 (codified as 29 USC §§2601–2654 (1994)).
45. Pub L No 104-104, 110 Stat 56.
46. 26 USC §44 (1994).
47. 26 USC §51 (1994) (amended 1999).
48. Rehabilitation Act of 1973 §504, 29 USC §794 (1994) (amended 1998); ADA §202, 42 USC §12132 (1994).
49. 28 CFR §35.130 (1999).
50. 28 CFR §41.51(b)(1) (1999).
51. 28 CFR §35.130(b)(1) (1999); 28 CFR §41.51(b)(1) (1999).
52. Rehabilitation Act of 1973 §102, 29 USC §722(a)(6) (1994).
53. IDEA §614(c), 20 USC §1414(c) (1994) (amended 1997).
54. IDEA §614(a), 20 USC §1414(a) (1994) (amended 1997).
55. ibid.
56. 42 CFR §§441.50–441.62 (1999).
57. 42 CFR §441.56(a)(4) (1999).
58. Me Rev Stat Ann tit 20, §911 (West 1964). The Maine statute was repealed in 1975 to ensure state compliance with IDEA.
59. IDEA §612(a), 20 USC §1412(a)(2)(B) (1994) (amended 1997).
60. Rehabilitation Act of 1973 §102(a)(4)(A), 29 USC §722(a)(4)(A) (1994).
61. Rehabilitation Act of 1973 §101(a)(5)(A), 29 USC §721(a)(5)(A) (1994).
62. See Social Security Act tit XVI, 42 USC §§1381–1383c (1994) (§§1382–1382b, 1382d, 1382e, 1383, 1383b amended 1999; §1382c amended 1997; §1383c amended 1996) (establishing and delineating the Supplemental Security Income Program).
63. 28 CFR §35.130(b)(1)(iv) (1999).
64. 28 CFR §41.51(b)(1)(iv) (1999).
65. 29 CFR §1630.9(a) (1999); 28 CFR §41.53 (1999) (providing examples of reasonable accommodations, including modifying a workplace policy, acquisition or modifications of equipment, the provision of qualified readers and interpreters and appropriate adjustment or modification of examinations).
66. 28 CFR §35.150 (1999); 28 CFR §35.151 (1999); 28 CFR §41.57 (1999).
67. 28 CFR §§35.160–35.164 (1999); 28 CFR §41.51(b), (e) (1999).
68. 28 CFR §35.130(f) (1999).
69. 28 CFR §35.130(e) (1999).
70. IDEA §612(a)(1), 20 USC §1412(a)(1) (1994 & Supp IV 1998).
71. IDEA §612(a)(14), 20 USC §1412(a)(14) (1994 & Supp IV 1998).
72. Rehabilitation Act of 1973 §103, 29 USC §723 (1994 & Supp IV 1998).
73. Social Security Act §1905(r), 42 USC §1396d(r) (1994 & Supp IV 1998).

74. 28 CFR §35.130 (1999).
75. 28 CFR §41.51(b) (1999).
76. IDEA §615(k), 20 USC §1415(k) (1994 & Supp IV 1998) (amended 1999).
77. ADA §2(a)(2), 42 USC §12101(a)(2) (1994 & Supp IV 1998).
78. 28 CFR §35.130(b)(1)(iv) (1999).
79. 28 CFR §35.130(d) (1999).
80. 28 CFR pt 35, app A (1998).
81. See Herr, Chapter 8 of this volume.
82. 28 CFR §41.51(d) (1999).
83. Social Security Act 1915(c), 42 USC §1396n(c) (1994 & Supp IV 1998).
84. IDEA §612(a)(5), 20 USC §1412(a)(5) (1994 & Supp IV 1998).
85. 34 CFR §§300.550–300.551 (1999).
86. Developmental Disabilities Assistance and Bill of Rights Act §102(15), 42 USC §6001(15) (1994 & Supp IV 1998).
87. 29 USC §722(b) (1994 & Supp IV 1998).
88. Rehabilitation Act of 1973 §102, 29 USC §722 (1994 & Supp IV 1998).
89. Rehabilitation Act of 1973 §105, 29 USC §725 (1994 & Supp IV 1998).
90. Rehabilitation Act of 1973 §704(a)(2), 29 USC §796c(a)(2) (1994 & Supp IV 1998).
91. Social Security Act §1148, 42 USC 13206-19 (1994 & Supp IV 1998) (amended 1999).
92. In addition, the Ticket to Work and Work Incentives Improvement Act establishes a Ticket to Work and Work Incentives Advisory Panel. See Social Security Act §1148, 42 USC §13206-19 (1994 & Supp IV 1998) (amended 1999).
93. IDEA §614(d), (f), 20 USC §1414(d), (f) (1994 & Supp IV 1998).
94. IDEA §614(d)(1)(B), 20 USC §1414(d)(1)(B) (1994 & Supp IV 1998).
95. IDEA §615(m), 20 USC §1415(m) (Supp IV 1998).
96. IDEA §612(a)(21), 20 USC §1412(a)(21) (Supp IV 1998).
97. 20 USC §1435(a)(3)–(4) (1994 & Supp IV 1998).
98. See Developmental Disabilities Assistance and Bill of Rights Act §101(a)(2), 42 USC §6000(a)(2) (1994) (stating that disability is a 'natural part of the human experience' and does not diminish the right of independent living and self-determination).
99. Developmental Disabilities Assistance and Bill of Rights Act, S. 1809, 106th Cong §102(2) (1999). In a related context, under the Protection and Advocacy for Mentally Ill Individuals Act: '[F]amily members of individuals with mental illness play a critical role in being advocates for the rights of individuals with mental illness where: (1) the individuals are minors, (2) the individuals are legally competent and choose to involve the family members, and (3) the individuals are legally incompetent and the legal guardians, conservators, or other legal representatives are members of the family.' Protection and Advocacy for Mentally Ill Individuals Act of 1986 §101(2), 42 USC §10801(2) (1994).
100. Social Security Act §1915(c), 42 USC §1396n(c) (1994) (amended 1999).
101. Rehabilitation Act of 1973 §701, 29 USC §796 (1994) (amended 1998).
102. Rehabilitation Act of 1973, 29 USC §§796e–796f (1994) (amended 1998).
103. Rehabilitation Act of 1973 §6(18), 29 USC §705(18) (1994) (amended 1998).
104. IDEA §601(d)(1), 20 USC §1400(d)(1) (Supp IV 1998).

105. IDEA §614, 20 USC §1414 (Supp IV 1998).
106. Developmental Disabilities Assistance and Bill of Rights Act §101(b), 42 USC §6000(b) (1994).
107. Rehabilitation Act of 1973 §6(28), 29 USC §705(28) (1994); Developmental Disabilities Assistance and Bill of Rights Act §102(18), 42 USC §6001(18) (1994).
108. Rehabilitation Act of 1973 §103(a)(9), 29 USC §723(a)(9) (Supp IV 1998).
109. 42 USC §1396d (1994) (amended 1999).
110. Social Security Act §1915(c), 42 USC §1396n(c) (Supp IV 1998). Additional categories of long-term services and supports may be provided under the Waiver program.
111. See Social Security Act, 42 USC §§1381–1383c (1994) (§§1382–1382b, 1382d, 1382e, 1383, 1383b, amended 1999; §1382c amended 1997; §1383c amended 1996); see also Social Security Act, 42 USC §§401–434 (1994 & Supp IV 1998) (amended 1999) (providing 'Federal Old-Age and Survivors' with disability insurance benefits).
112. See Housing Act of 1937 §8, 42 USC §1437f(o) (1994) (providing rental vouchers for low-income families).
113. Food Stamp Act of 1977, 7 USC §§2011–2036 (1994 & Supp IV 1998).
114. IDEA §601(d)(1), 20 USC §1400(d)(1) (Supp IV 1998).
115. 29 USC §§720–753a (1994 & Supp IV 1998).
116. Rehabilitation Act of 1973 §100(a)(2)(A), 29 USC §720(a)(2)(A) (1994 & Supp IV 1998).
117. Pub L No 99-643 (1986) codified s 1619 of the Social Security Act, 42 USC §1382h (1994). See Social Security Act §1905(q), 42 USC §1396d(q) (1994) (defining 'qualified severely impaired individual').
118. Balanced Budget Act of 1997, Pub L No 105-33, 111 Stat 251.
119. Pub L No 106-170, 113 Stat 1860. These options are authorized under s 201 of Pub L No 106-170, which adds ss 1902(a)(10)(A)(ii)(XV) & (XVI) to the Social Security Act.
120. Pub L No 106-170 §204 (1999).
121. 26 USC §44 (1994 & Supp IV 1998).
122. 26 USC §51 (1994 & Supp IV 1998) (amended 1999).

Part IV
Equality and Difference: Social Policy Perspectives

11

On Second Thought: Constructing Knowledge, Law, Disability, and Inequality

MARCIA H. RIOUX

I. INTRODUCTION

People with disabilities provide us with a means to understand the way in which social life can be organized to be fair, to be just, to be humanitarian, and to be equal. They provide us an opportunity to go beyond finding the roots of charity and to look instead for the roots of justice. Equality and nondiscrimination, which are the very basics of human rights law, can be brought into clear focus by reflecting on the place of people with disabilities in our societies.

A human rights and social justice approach enables the use of various categories of rights and recognizes how rights have to be a concern in thinking about approaches to disability and social policy that enhance, rather than diminish, the status of those with disabilities. These include political and civil rights, such as the right to life, freedom of opinion, a fair trial, and protection from torture and violence. These are the rights that are the most common concern of nations, particularly in the North and West. Human rights also include economic, social and cultural rights such as the right to work, social protection, an adequate standard of living, the highest possible standards of physical and mental health, education, and enjoyment of the benefits of cultural freedom and scientific progress. Finally, human rights include the right of nations to development, economic autonomy, and security of their citizens.

Civil, political, social, and economic rights are reflected in such international agreements on human rights and disability as the:

- UN Universal Declaration of Human Rights (1948)
- UN Declaration on Disabled Persons (1975)
- UN International Year of Disabled Persons (1981)
- UN World Program of Action concerning Disabled Persons (1983)
- UN Decade of Disabled Persons (1983–1992)
- UN Convention on the Rights of the Child (1989)
- UN Standard Rules on the Equalization of Opportunities for People with Disabilities (1993)

- Social Development Accord (Copenhagen 1995)
- Beijing World Conference on Women (1996)
- UN Human Rights Commission Resolutions 2000/51 (2000)

Despite these international norms and standards there is persistent social and legal exclusion of people with disabilities throughout the world. It is important to take a closer look at why people with disabilities continue to be subject to infringements and contravention of their human rights. This is revealed in two ways. One can be found in the way in which the norms and standards are constructed—the content of the instruments themselves. The other is found in the manner in which nations meet their commitments to the standards that are set down.

Masked behind both the content of norms and standards and the treatment of people with disabilities are differing understandings of the concepts of disability and equality themselves. This article will unpack prevailing notions of disability and theoretical understandings of equality and examine how these differing notions have inherent, built-in biases towards particular standards of policy, program, and legal status. This has an effect on whether the human rights of people with disabilities are respected or abridged.

The scientific and social justifications for political action related to disability at both the national and international levels are traceable to identifiable and shifting ideological frameworks. The article will begin by exploring these social and scientific formulations of disability which underpin social policy and their reflections in the current dominant paradigms—one which is centralizing and homogenizing and one which is based on difference and diversity. These discrepant formulations of disability underlie the kinds of policy and programs that are found in most nations of the world, suggesting that knowledge in this field is created internationally, not nationally.

Shifting legal and philosophical standards of equality that further complicate the impact of the various formulations of disability will then be explored. Assumptions arising from the changing conceptual development of the notions of disability and equality that form the basis for many state policies, programs, and services, have made the many different and, at times, contradictory ways of treating people with disabilities arguably just and fair. They have provided a foundation for keeping people with disabilities in the status of second-class citizens both within nation states and as world citizens. These assumptions have also influenced the meaning and parameters of quality of life evaluations and have arguably limited the goals of rehabilitation and of human rights protections.

To study the case of disability is, therefore, to reflect upon the struggle for social justice and the political obligation to relieve inequality.[1] There is within the disability movements in many nations a resurging discussion of some fundamental principles about how all people should be treated and the economic, social, and political rights to which they are entitled. Questions are being asked about the quality of the care being received by people with disabilities and whether it meets even minimal notions of what is fair and just. People with disabilities and their advocates are recognizing the need to put these questions within the broader context of principles of justice, fairness, and equality as they recognize that the way society treats people and the share of the national funding allocations they receive reflects other, more fundamental inequalities in society.[2] It is these more generalized inequalities that will have to be addressed if people with disabilities are to be full participants in their societies.

Disability provides insight into the interplay between national and international declarations of rights and rehabilitation systems and the way these have contributed to, and result in, differential treatment. The case of disability affords a way to tease out how the conceptualization and measurement of disability supports and reinforces limiting both the state and professional obligations to people with disabilities. Assumptions about equality raise some fundamentally different assumptions about disability itself, about whether disability is a private or a public responsibility and about the legal and social status of persons with disabilities. Understanding of disability and disability policy, therefore, finds its roots in particular theoretical and scientific constructs of both disability and of equality and of the interplay between the two.

II. SOCIAL AND SCIENTIFIC CHANGE IN HOW DISABILITY IS PERCEIVED, DIAGNOSED, AND TREATED[3]

How disability is perceived, diagnosed, and treated, scientifically and socially, is reflected in assumptions about the social responsibility towards people with disabilities as a group. The assumptions or postulates about disability are neither mutually exclusive nor temporally chronological. Some disciplines have clung tenaciously to the characterization of disability as either solely a medical condition or a personal deficit, while others have adopted either the framework of disability as a social and political condition or some hybrid of these two major schools of thought. Consequently, policy and programming, both within the professional sphere and coming from government, reflects attempts to accommodate these shifting understandings of disability as a status.

Marcia H. Rioux

III. SOCIAL AND SCIENTIFIC FORMULATIONS AND TREATMENT OF DISABILITY

There are four identifiable social and scientific formulations of disability reflected in the treatment of persons with disability in law, policy, programs, and rights instruments. Two of them emanate from theories of disability coming from individual pathology and two from disability coming from a social pathology.

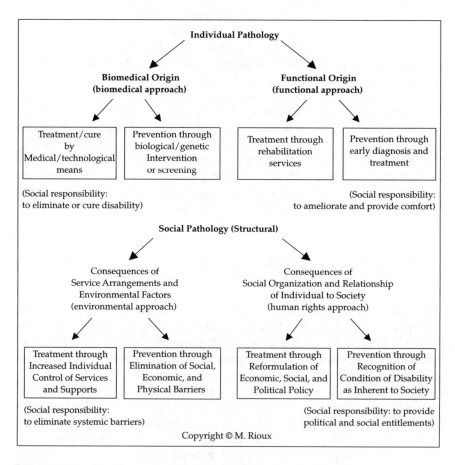

FIGURE 11.1. Social and scientific formulations and treatment of disability

A. Formulations of Disability Based on Individual Pathology

There are two identifiable formulations of disability that arise from an assumption that disability is an individual pathology. One is grounded in a biomedical approach and the other is grounded in a functional approach. The two have a number of common characteristics. They:

(1) approach disability as a field of professional expertise;
(2) primarily use a positivist paradigm;
(3) emphasize primary prevention including biological and environmental conditions;
(4) characterize disability as incapacity in relation to nondisabled persons (a comparative incapacity);
(5) distinguish disability and its attached costs as an anomaly and social burden;
(6) portray the inclusion of people with disabilities as a private responsibility;
(7) use the individual as the unit of analysis for research and policy purposes; and
(8) depict the individual condition as the primary point of intervention.

1. The Biomedical Approach

Of formulations of disability that arise from individual pathology, the first emphasizes its biomedical origin. The biomedical approach has been a powerful influence in establishing disability policy and practice and the pre-eminence of biological science as the basis for diagnosing disability, influencing treatments, and guiding access to disability benefits.[4] From the perspective of biology and the attendant biomedical approach, it is assumed that disability is caused by a mental or physical condition that can be prevented or ameliorated through medical, biological, or genetic intervention. Such a characterization of disability makes the condition itself the focus of attention. The aim of the professional or the researcher is to decrease the prevalence of the condition in the general population. Treatment and prevention occur through biological intervention and critical care, including surgery, drug therapy, prenatal screening, and genetic intervention. Commonly, the individual or fetus is viewed as sick, afflicted, or injured.

With the rise of institutional facilities and public benefits, medical science became established as the mechanism for gate keeping for determining those who are to be legitimately considered disabled. Assessments extend to various aspects of an individual's range of disability such as employability; capacity for learning and being educated; fine motor skills and hand–eye coordination; the need for financial benefits and mobility aids and devices; as well as the need for treatment services.

The biomedical model, with a focus on altering the biological condition, places secondary emphasis on the role society plays in limiting and enabling people. The public responsibility is restricted to the custodial and medical care that is characterized as beneficial within the parameters of a biomedical approach.

The social obligation attached to such characterizations of disability is limited to medical diagnosis and treatment, including medically directed therapeutic interventions. For those who cannot be cured or rehabilitated, institutions, other segregated housing, and all encompassing service provision centers have been the conventional models of care. Until quite recently (because people with disabilities were expected to make no con-tribution to society, were in many cases considered a danger to society,[5] and were characterized as without potential), families were encouraged to place their children in institutions where they would receive the basic necessities of food, shelter, and clothing. The alternative was to keep them at home where they would have familial contact and care, but the State was under little obligation to provide services, supports, or the financial resources to acquire those. Quality of life within such a framework is meas-ured within a set of parameters limited to the provision of basic needs.

Rights entitlements are restricted to their feasibility within the context of individual incapacity and to the extent of independence in exercising them. For example, individuals are entitled to an education in the neigh-borhood school if they can access the school and are able to learn in the classroom as it is structured. The onus is on individuals to fit within the institutions as they are structured and participation is a right only to the extent that that is possible.

2. *The Functional Approach*

The second of the two formulations of disability as an individual pathology is a functional approach. Like the biomedical approach, the underlying presumption is that the deficit stems from an individual condition or pathology. The feature that distinguishes this approach from the biomed-ical approach is that the way of understanding the condition is the impact it has on functional capacity. The ways of treating or addressing the func-tional incapacity are broader and include both ameliorating the condition and developing ways to enable people to develop their own potential.

Within the functional approach, the problems experienced by people with disabilities are interpreted as a result of a functional incapacity resulting from an individual impairment. To treat this functional incapacity, services are made available to enable the individual to become as socially functional as possible. For example, the goal of rehabilitation is to increase an individual's range of skills and abilities to function more independ-ently and to become a productive member of society. A program's success is measured by how closely people who use services can approximate the lives of 'normal' people and to what extent they can achieve the skills of able-bodied persons.[6]

Services developed from a functional approach (eg, physiotherapy, occupational therapy, nursing, and health visiting) have gone beyond therapeutic programs associated with the biomedical approach to include life skills training, prevocational training, functional assessments, counseling, and job training, as well as skills for independent living. They are usually publicly funded to the extent they are considered effective in normalizing, often through rehabilitation programs.

Society's responsibility in dealing with disability is to ameliorate and reduce the negative effects and provide comfort of some kind. This approach develops systems of assessment, habilitation, and measures to improve self-care and social skills. This responsibility derives principally from a sense of charity and benevolence (and in some cases, a reduction of the social cost that attaches to being dependent in society). The definition of the hierarchy of needs to ameliorate the functional inability is left to professionals, who are attributed with the skills and knowledge to determine what is in the best interests of the individual and what will be most beneficial to the individual. Success in meeting the social and professional obligation (to ensure the individual's quality of life) is measured by how closely people with disabilities who use services can approximate 'normal' people.

Placing the focus on the individual makes the interplay of environmental and situational factors with individual functional capacity a secondary, although not necessarily irrelevant, consideration in diagnosing and addressing the means to normalize a person's life opportunities. Targeting the individual for change places professionals and public programs using a functional approach at risk of operating on assumptions about the person's 'best interests' that may not always coincide with what a person wants for him or herself.

In both formulations of disability originating in an individual pathology, labeling or diagnosing the physiological or psychological state is important to determine the individual pathology or functional disabilities and as a basis for undertaking curative or remedial treatment. Given the medicalization of disability, many instruments have been developed for the purpose of diagnosis such as the International Classification of Impairment, Disability and Handicap (ICIDH), now revised as the Diagnostic Statistical Manual (DSM), the International Classification of Disease (ICD), and various IQ tests. On the basis of such diagnostic tools, medical, or alternatively rehabilitation, therapy is initiated to address the diagnosed problem. The outcome for the treatment is to enable the individual to function as independently as possible within the social and economic environments, as they are currently structured. Where environmental modifications are made, they have tended to be limited to the personal or immediate sphere, not the macro or systems level of social and economic organization.

B. Formulations Grounded in Social Pathology

In contrast to the two approaches to disability based on individual pathology, there are two identifiable approaches that recognize disability as a consequence of social pathology. They both start from a perspective that assumes that disability is not inherent to the individual. Rather, they assume that the disability is inherent to the social structure. It is a structural model rather than an individual model. The pathology is that there is something wrong with the society that has to be fixed rather than something wrong with the individual that needs fixing.[7]

These approaches have a number of identifiable characteristics. They:

(1) assume that disability is not inherent to the individual independent of the social structure;
(2) give priority to political, social, and built environment;
(3) emphasize secondary prevention rather than primary treatment;
(4) recognize disability as difference rather than as an anomaly;
(5) portray the inclusion of people with disabilities as a public responsibility;
(6) use the social structure as the unit of analysis for research and policy purposes; and
(7) depict the social, environmental, and economic structures as the primary point of intervention.

1. The Environmental Approach

Advances in knowledge based on an understanding of disability as a social pathology show that personal abilities and limitations are the result not only of factors residing in the individual, but also of the interaction between individuals and their environments. Increasingly, researchers demonstrate that the impacts of disability are exacerbated by the failure of ordinary environments to accommodate people's differences.

An environmental perspective on disability places the policy and program focus on the way the environments are arranged. For example, the absence of ramps into an office building creates an employment handicap for someone who relies on a wheelchair for mobility. The lack of an ergonomically adapted workspace makes it impossible for a person with limited upper body movement to perform job tasks. Similarly, many policy studies have shown that the lack of proactive hiring and employment retention policies creates disadvantages for individuals who require time away from work because of fatigue and other conditions caused by disability.[8] An educational service disadvantages persons with a speech impairment where it fails to provide the opportunity to learn an alternative method of communication, for example, through bliss symbolics or sign language instruction.

Increasingly, there is evidence in policy research that the impact of disability can be lessened, as environments are adapted to enable participation. Policy research demonstrates that building codes, principles of barrier free design, adapted curricula, targeted policy and funding commitments are useful mechanisms to reduce discrimination and increase equal participation. These mechanisms enable modifications and supports to be made in home, school, work, and leisure environments, and increase the participation of people with disabilities in society while limiting the disadvantages they would otherwise face.

Disability is handled from this approach by identifying the barriers in society that restrict the participation in economic and social life of people with impairments or disabilities including criteria or program parameters that restrict individual determination of needs and individual control of services and supports. Structural barriers to independent living or community living become the site of 'therapy' or modification.[9] Prevention, then, is through the elimination of social, economic, and political barriers. Elimination of physical barriers, for example, building ramps or adoption of employment equity or affirmative action policies, is a method of prevention from the perspective of this approach to disability.

2. The Rights Outcome Approach

Another approach to disability is the notion that disability has social causes. It is a consequence of how society is organized and the relationship of the individual to society at large.[10] Research, policy, and law from a rights outcome approach looks beyond particular environments to focus on broad systemic factors that keep some groups of people from participating as equals in society.

This approach identifies wide variations in cognitive, sensory, and motor ability as inherent to the human condition, and consequently, the variations should not limit the potential to contribute to society. It draws from a variety of disciplines (eg, anthropology, sociology, economics, and law), but it frames disability issues through the lens of human rights principles. It assumes that public policy and programs should aim to reduce civic inequalities and address social and economic disadvantage. It presumes that some people will need supports (eg, personal services, aids, and devices) in order to gain access to, participate in and exercise self-determination as equals in society.

This is a much more expansive theoretical framework than the other approaches. Policy from a rights outcome approach constructs an analysis of how society marginalizes people and how society can be adjusted to respond more effectively to the presence and needs of those who have been systemically marginalized. Treating the disadvantage is postulated as being the reformulation of social and political policy. Prevention is effected through recognizing the condition of disability as inherent to society. It is presumed that people with disabilities are an inherent part of society, not some kind of anomaly to normalcy.

From this perspective disability is regarded as a predetermined and a 'normal', inevitable part of the population, not a deviant condition. The quality of life indicator theorized from this perspective is the degree to which civic inequalities have been reduced, that is, the degree to which social and economic disadvantages have been addressed. Recognition of social and political entitlements is based on humanity rather than economic contribution and rights are equated with those of all others in society. Society is obliged to provide supports and aids and devices to enable social and economic integration, self-determination, legal and social rights, focusing on the disabling aspects of society, supporting human diversity and empowering disadvantaged individuals.

These social and scientific formulations of disability provide a means to recognize how scientific ideology has justified the kinds of political policies and programs and the kinds of treatment and treatment modalities that are in place. They are significantly important in the lives of people with disabilities—in the allocation of national and international research funds in the field, in medical and social decision making, in treatment and care, in legal decisions about entitlements and capacities, in housing and welfare arrangements, and in the protections of human rights of people with disabilities.

IV. CHANGES IN UNDERSTANDING THE CONCEPT OF EQUALITY[11]

While there have been changes in how disability is perceived, a concurrent shift in the theoretical constructs of equality is occurring. These constructs fit generally into three categories. One is the formal theory of equality, that is, the equal-treatment model.[12] The second is the liberal theory of equality,[13] incorporating both the ideals of equality of opportunity and special treatment. The third is the equality of well-being, or equality of resources model.[14]

Each of these models makes different claims to the meaning of equality. The choice of model has importance for people with disabilities, particularly in light of the ways in which disability is perceived. For example, take the case where the social, economic, and political organization in place is assumed to be necessary for society to function, and differences are defined as intrinsic to the individual. Those defined as different, who might make a claim for greater equality with others in society, will, in those circumstances, have no grounds on which to challenge their unequal status and benefits. They will be denied on the basis of their inherent differences and the need to maintain the status quo for the good of society.

Assumptions about the meaning and content of equality can be identified in the mechanisms for distributive justice applied to disability. The premises on which distributive justice is argued may vary significantly depending on which meaning of equality is adopted. This is not a new dilemma. Political and professional tensions about distributive criteria have shaped and are shaped by the understandings and approaches to disability, including criteria concerning appropriate recipients of social assistance or support.

What will constitute equality generally and which model of equality is most likely to ensure a just distribution of goods, services, and support to individuals in achieving equality is yet to be resolved. The resolution of this debate is particularly significant for persons with disabilities because of the nature of their differences. Their differences tend to stem from those characteristics on which participation in the social structure and determination of equal status have been determined. Implicit in the notion of participation is the notion of who will not participate, and that makes up the content of difference on which entitlement to participation is limited. The traditional assumption is that, having limited abilities considered intrinsic to citizenship or exercising legal rights in the conventional social, legal, and economic environment, people with disabilities have had no basis for a claim to equality. It is often the case that they establish such a claim only to the extent they can approximate other citizens.

The implications of a priori assumptions about the genesis and relative value of human characteristics are decisive in ensuring equality. The elements understood to comprise equality are as important.

A. Equal Treatment

If equality depends on sameness (the equal treatment model) and being *similarly situated* (in the same circumstances), the concept of equality requires that likes be treated alike and presumes the impartial enforcement of legal and social rights. Because difference warrants unequal treatment, there is no utility in clarifying what makes people equal in particular circumstances or for particular purposes. The principle simply establishes the generally accepted rule of law that procedural fairness must be applied for law to be legitimate.[15] Neutrality in the application of the law and the absence of different treatment are presumed to result in equality. The differential impact of the law or the treatment has no consequence on whether equality has been achieved. Individual difference justifies limiting claims to entitlement, while still meeting the standard of equality.

The equal treatment standard of equality can be relatively easily met. If the social and scientific perception of disability rests in an individual deficit (as when it is characterized as a biomedical or functional problem), the equal treatment standard can be met even in the face of significantly different social and economic entitlements and outcomes. Failure to provide education or the same standard of education for people with disabilities has been justified on this basis. The restriction on immigration of people with intellectual disabilities to Canada has not yet been stricken down as an infringement of equality rights under an equal treatment standard of equality. Therapeutic interventions, for example, prevocational training and sheltered workshops, have met this standard of equality based on the reasoning that segregating people or failing to provide access to usually provided public programs is legitimate in the case that a person has a capacity that can be differentiated from the norm.

For example, people who cannot fill out forms may be denied the right to vote, while others who can read and write are afforded that right. The law is equally applied to all those who cannot supply the information in the administratively specified method. Therefore, the fact that it may have a differential impact on those with some disabilities is deemed insignificant, as are the extraneous causes for such lack of ability. Neither the legal exclusion of some groups of people with disabilities from the regular school system nor the means of eliciting the information, which is in a mode of communication less accessible to them than to others, are taken into account in determining which distinctions are justified and unjustified.

This standard of equality justifies many predominantly used measures of quality of life that are based upon notions of diminished capacity, competence, and exercise of social life, as determined by some objective standard. For example, legal decisions deny babies with serious physical and mental disabilities medical interventions because their predicted 'quality-of-life' will be limited.[16] The standard of 'quality of life' in those instances is based on a particular set of definitions normally attributed by those without disabilities. It fails to recognize that the benchmarks for 'quality' may vary from the subjective perspective of those living with disabilities. Thus, they assume a standard that cannot be shown to be empirically objective and universal.

B. Equality of Opportunity

Much recent discourse on equality has addressed the inherent problems of such a limited notion of equality. The literature draws attention to the substantive inequality between disadvantaged groups and advantaged groups in society.[17] Equality of opportunity addresses some of the limitations of formal equality by taking into account and redressing historical conditions of inequality. It removes the necessity for the disadvantaged group to prove they are the same with the same skills and abilities as others. Equality of opportunity recognizes that there may be prejudices and barriers to participation (eg, in education or the labor market) that have disadvantaged some groups of people unfairly. They, therefore, have a legitimate claim to compensation—in such forms as affirmative action and employment equity—to enable them to start in a relatively similar position as others.

The dilemma for enabling equality for people with disabilities using this model is that their differences are not solely the result of historic circumstances, and there is no obligation to address disadvantage inherent to the structure of social standards. Lynn Smith, a University of British Columbia legal scholar, argues that the equal opportunity model fits well in cases such as race, where physical differences can be legitimately argued to be legally irrelevant. However, she observes that:

[T]here are physical differences between the sexes in relation to child-bearing and breast feeding which make identical treatment of the sexes unequal in some contexts. Running the race from the same starting line does not solve the problem of maternity along the way. Classifications based on sex may be legally relevant. Similarly there are differences between the able-bodied and the disabled and between young, middle-aged, and old people which can make identical treatment unequal. Simple equality of opportunity cannot conceivably produce equality of results in many of these situations. Such issues do not arise as squarely with respect to racial discrimination.[18]

In most cases, people with disabilities cannot overcome natural characteristics and become like the 'norm', even if given equality of opportunity. This is because equality of opportunity is based on the assumption that the objective is to provide access to the competitive, individualistic market, not to such non-comparable goods as minimal nutrition and medical support. The basis for the claim to equality of people with disabilities can be made only on their citizenship, their humanness or on a general egalitarian value assumption—for example, that all people should be accorded equal respect by their government because they are persons,[19] not because of their ability to compete. Their claim on resources is to enable participation, even though in some cases they will unlikely be competitive (within the existing social and economic climate) without some degree of ongoing support. The claim is not for support to redress past discrimination or to overcome particular barriers to participation (equality of opportunity). Instead, the claim of people with disabilities is for redistribution of state resources and ongoing systemic support to allow them to exercise the same rights as others. This claim is not premised on the measurable social benefits, such as economic efficiency and effectiveness, foreseen as achievable in exchange for additional state costs or support.

The unarticulated premises of the equality of opportunity model, homogeneity and interchangeability, combined with a perception of disability as an individual deficit rather than a structural or systemic problem, limit equal outcomes. The individual is expected to integrate within social and economic structures that are based on substantively male nondisabled standards, making no long-term allowances for the individual's inherent differences.

C. Equality of Well-Being

A model of equality based on well-being as an outcome incorporates the premise that all humans—in spite of their differences—are entitled to consideration and respect as equals, and have the right to participate in the social and economic life of society. Unlike the other models of equality, it would take into account the conditions and means of participation that may vary for each individual, entailing special accommodation to make this possible. Although the outcome—equality of well-being—should be universal, the programs or means to ensure equality should justifiably be targeted to enable support on a temporary or long-term basis for those least able to achieve well-being. Difference would be both acknowledged and accommodated in ensuring the outcome. Political and legal decisions would have to take differences in the achievement of well-being into account in the distributive paradigm of social justice.

Well-being has a number of components including equal achievement of self-determination, participation and inclusion in social life through democratization, and the exercise of fundamental citizenship rights.[20] Equality itself would be an end, not a means, to meeting other social goals. Alternatively, equal treatment and equal opportunity in most formulations treat equality as a means to ensure fairness in achieving some other end. Thus, in the latter case, people of equal need and ability should have equal opportunity to obtain desired scarce resources. Equality of well-being recognizes that while people are not equal in talent, social usefulness, or willingness to serve the community, they are entitled to make choices about how to live and what constitutes the good life for them as long as they operate within the framework of mutual recognition of others' self-determination. Quality of life is measured by neither an exclusively objective nor an exclusively subjective standard. It becomes the interpretation and the personal and collective realization of generally accepted social values and goals.

Equality, defined as the inclusion and participation of all groups in social positions, makes clear the onus to include even those people who cannot meet the standards of economic self-sufficiency. Equality as inclusion and participation shifts the basis for distributive justice away from economic contribution as the primary factor of entitlement to other forms of participation.[21] The reproduction of material and ideological conditions that benefit only one segment of the population is no longer the primary rationale of social institutions, law, and policy. Rather, their rationale is to support the outcome of equality of well-being for all citizens.

V. THE INTERSECTION OF THESE TWO TRENDS

The intersection of these two major trends—the shifting formulations of the meaning of disability and the philosophical and practical formulations of the concept of equality—provide a schemata for deriving new structures and policies, programs and treatment modalities. The interaction of these two trends also provides a means for explaining the incongruous decisions in case law and policy involving disability as well as the discrepancies in international instruments affecting the rights of persons with disabilities. As with any schemata, this one has a certain degree of subjectivity. It is presented as a way of making some order out of the various claims formulated about disability and uncovers the arbitrary nature of the subject matter itself.

In practice, the diverse ways of perceiving, diagnosing, and treating disability combined with the differing models of equality lead to identifiable legal, clinical, and service treatment modalities and differing standards and measures of quality of life and entitlements to human rights. There is evidence of each of these models in existing national policies and programs and in international standards. They reflect the adoption of one or another of the approaches to disability and a preference for one model of equality over another. Some distinguishable typologies of disability emerge from the concepts explored. They include policy and legal entitlements based on the status of civil disability;[22] the status of compensatory privilege; and entitlement based on well-being. Although these models provide a general guideline to begin exploring services, laws, and ethical standards in place, the mosaic is more complicated because of combinations and variations. There are no hard and fast lines between the typologies, and their overlap can be seen in Figure 11.2.

This schema suggests a progression from a view of disability as a biological condition or a functional anomaly that would justify a standard of equality that differentiates people on the basis of their objective deviation from the norm (the civil disability model), leading to a dissimilar social

Concepts of Equality	Formulation of Concept of Disability			
	INDIVIDUAL PATHOLOGY		SOCIAL PATHOLOGY	
	Bio-Medical Approach	Functional Approach	Environmental Approach	Rights Outcome Approach
Equal Treatment	*Civil Disability*			
Equal Opportunity		*Compensatory Privilege*		
Equal Outcome				*Well-Being Status*

FIGURE 11.2. Impact of these two major trends

responsibility, legal treatment, and ethical standards. The schema moves to a characterization of disability as a functional differentiation from the norm that may emanate from a biological condition, or the interaction of biological with existing environmental conditions. This is coupled with a model of equality that poses recognition of difference as a basis for entitlement to the extent that the difference is shown to be based on unjustifiable discrimination. This approach still maintains the essence of the existing meritocracy. The third typology consolidates a characterization of disability as a result of social and political conditions with a substantive notion of equality that presumes the participation and inclusion of all groups in the social and economic standard of living to which States entitle their citizens and a consequent redistribution of resources. Difference, in this typology, becomes the source of entitlement rather than disentitlement.

Each of the three identified typologies has a distinguishable standard of social responsibility, an inherent ethical foundation, and a justification of individual rights and opportunities.

A. Civil Disability

A social responsibility to protect individuals with disabilities, both legally and socially, flows from the presumption that disability is the consequence of an individual's largely unchanging pathology coupled with equality premised on equal treatment. Similar to the status of children and people who are sick, people with disabilities are given a distinct status: a status traditionally entitling them to protections by the State (both negative and

GOAL:	To protect society and individuals from ill effects of disability
MEASURES:	Extent to which a person is protected from harm to self and others
RIGHTS GUARANTEE:	Guarantees or assures protection and security for people with disabilities

**EXAMPLES IN CLINICAL AND SERVICE TREATMENT
AND GOVERNMENT POLICY:**

- Total care institutions
- Involuntary sterilization (including both surgical and chemical means)
- Prohibitions on immigration
- Non-consensual treatments (eg, aversive therapies and drug regimes as therapeutic protocols)
- Imposition of 'parens patriae'
- Legal determination of incompetence
- Refusal of treatment for newborns

FIGURE 11.3. Civil disability standard (civil status which assumes equal treatment and individual pathology)

positive) to which others, who do not have that status, are not entitled. The State is responsible to protect such individuals from the ill-effects and limitations of disability and to provide at least minimal assistance. The protection may include both entitlements to minimal material goods such as welfare and to the limitations of rights normally accorded citizens.

State protection is based on a positivist social premise, premised on some clearly identifiable and distinguishable characteristics inherent to the individual on whom a distinction can be made and legitimated as a basis for differentiation. For instance, the World Health Organization has defined this as an impairment.[23] The objectivity of the classification, grounded in scientific identification of disability as inherent to the individual, enables law and policy to be designed to exclude or treat differently those designated and still meets the test of equality (based on the equal treatment model). The implicit assumption is that there is something both abnormal and negative (ie, deviant) about those identified characteristics, warranting both the protection of the individual from society and the protection of society from the individual with such characteristics.

The negative value placed on such characteristics has led to a widespread, arguably universal, presumption that preventing such characteristics is a social good. As a result, significant scientific and social activity is directed to the elimination, cure, or amelioration of the characteristics, including such diverse practices as social segregation, genetic research, genetic screening, facial surgery for Down syndrome, and involuntary sterilization of those identified with intellectual disabilities.

The ideal of impartiality on which the normative difference is premised justifies a legal and social status that both entitles and disentitles individuals, giving over to the State, or the provider of entitlements, decision-making authority in a complicated interaction. Authority is given over to those who claim the scientific knowledge to determine capacity and competence. This differentiation includes the power to suspend citizenship rights and to formalize the dependent relationship of the individual to the State through legislation that provides unequal social and economic entitlements. It legitimates the imposition of care, treatment, service, and legal status that is not imposed on others without the disability. The individual deficit provides the basis for the differential and unequal treatment. This translates in practice to paternalistic decision making, policies, programs, and services including, for example, institutional living, segregated education, sheltered workshops, services based on professional classification schemes, and rehabilitative protocols. Basic social rights are, then, traded for the charity that is provided by the State and others. The person with a disability is forced to surrender private judgment in return for such concrete benefits as medical care, housing, welfare, and therapeutic services. This has been the basis for statuses, such as unemployability and ineducability, that limit usual responsibilities both of the State and of the individual. For example, if an individual is determined to be uneducable, he or she has no responsibility to attend school. On the other hand, there is no requirement on the State to ensure that schools can accommodate such a student or to put in place alternative learning models.

The state of disability has also been used to limit access to medical procedures including such procedures as organ transplants and life-saving surgeries for newborns. It has also led to widespread counseling for selective abortion and euthanasia. These procedures tie into predictive notions of quality of life that use indicators held to be objective and which do not incorporate the subjective knowledge of the disabling condition. The cultural authority of the medical decision maker or genetic counselor is premised on a notion of disability as an individual's undesirable pathology, thereby legitimating a different standard of medical and ethical care. The treatment may have two elements: (1) to suspend the usual rights and responsibilities of the individual and (2) to give the authority to the professional to deviate from the usual norms, both legal and social, and substitute his or her authority.

There are also legal consequences. Legal distinctions are drawn based on determinations made within a framework of so-called objective, value-neutral, positivist scientific criteria. Disability has provided a social, legal, and ethical justification for curtailing legal status through legislation establishing, for example, legal incompetence and prohibitions on marriage, immigration, and democratic rights such as voting. Legal declarations of incompetence relieve the requirement for individual consent and justify substituted legal consents, either by the State or by a guardian.

Restrictions on the exercise of human rights, lifestyle choices and self-determination are legitimated both because of the portrayal of disability as a characteristic particular to the individual and because the individual is then differentiated from others in ways that are portrayed as material to access to rights and social goods.

B. Compensatory Privilege

There is a long history of providing care and treatment to people with disabilities as a charitable act. The *compensatory privilege* that can be claimed, using this standard, is based on benevolence and compassion and on forms of paternalism. The social responsibility arises from the acknowledgement that while there is a functional incapacity inherent to the individual, the physical and social environment may exacerbate it. Therefore, equal opportunity should be provided to the extent that the disability is a consequence of external factors. It is recognized that if it can be shown that the way in which services have been delivered and the environment structured has resulted in discrimination, independent of the disability, the individual, and even the class of individuals, may be entitled to redress of those historical injustices.[24] The argument, in such a circumstance, is that the historical injustices are socially caused. It is not binding on the State to provide the same outcome as other citizens, however, because difference can be attributed to the individual.

To the extent that an individual is able and can show abilities to exercise rights in the manner of other citizens and function in society as others, he or she is entitled to equitable treatment and rights. Where the cause of the individual functional incapacity can be attributed to social, economic, and physical barriers, there is a social responsibility to provide the additional resources to enable individuals to exercise their rights.

Using this standard, people with disabilities may trade rights for charity.[25] Generally, third parties and professional gatekeepers make decisions with respect to the extent of disability attributable to individual incapacity and the extent attributable to environmental barriers. In other words, reflected in clinical, social service, and legal practice is control exercised through medical decision making and expert judgment. Statutory human rights commissions are commonly charged with the authority to make decisions about what is 'reasonable accommodation' and what is 'undue hardship' and thus, what discrimination is justified.

GOAL:	Control and benefit exercised through expert judgment of medical professionals, caregivers, and bureaucrats to ensure fair and equitable distributive process
MEASURES:	Extent to which an individual is able to achieve potential within the framework of externally defined criteria
RIGHTS GUARANTEE:	Political obligation, based on notion of 'desert' and assumption of inherent difference, guarantees 'best interests' as standard for decisions

EXAMPLES IN CLINICAL AND SERVICE TREATMENT AND GOVERNMENT POLICY:

- Treatment modalities based on objective standards
- Structure of welfare programs, including enhanced permanent benefits
- Learning methods grounded in normalized pedagogy
- Employment equity and affirmative action
- Service provided based on standardized testing and classification

FIGURE 11.4. Compensatory privilege standard (treatment based on benevolence, compassion, and forms of paternalism protecting equal opportunity, based on functional capacity in pre-existing social conditions or on environmental adaptation)

The means of dealing with identified dependency is to provide an opportunity for the individual to overcome the dependency through affirmative action and to demonstrate the capacity for equal participation in school, labor markets, and other social arrangements. Otherwise, society provides compassionate care under the direction of the experts in the field. Social responsibility and political obligation towards people with disabilities derives from the notion of 'desert' based on a presumption of intrinsic dependency and an assumption that others will have the knowledge to determine what constitutes the person's 'best interests'. This has resulted in policies based on professional paternalism, that is, the *quid pro quo* for benefits (or enhanced benefits) in exchange for possible future reduction of social costs. Social segregation and limiting entitlements to social benefits and rights is justified where social dependency has little or no probability of being ameliorated.

Rights and benefits providing income and employment for people with disabilities are meted out according to individual potential for self-reliance. A marked preference and concern for those seen to have the greatest potential for independent functioning is inherent to goals of prevention and amelioration. However, for the residue, the 'worthy poor' who need some form of permanent care and financial support, benefits are provided as a humanitarian gesture rather than as an entitlement based on enabling them to achieve the benefits of society available to those without disabilities. Quality of life in this context involves situational-specific conditions measured by external and professionally designed criteria.

Two of the key international human rights instruments designed to provide rights to people with disabilities reflect a *compensatory privilege* standard of entitlement. In the *UN Declaration on the Rights of Mentally Retarded Persons* of 1971, the rights delineated are programmatic benefits such as, for example, habilitation, medical care, physical therapy, rather than the types of universal outcome rights, which are recognized in the *UN Universal Declaration on Human Rights* of 1948. In the 1948 Declaration, rights such as the following are recognized: 'recognition everywhere as a person', 'freedom of movement', and 'a standard of living adequate for health and well-being'. Similarly, programmatic rights are delineated in the *UN Declaration on the Rights of Disabled Persons* 1975. In both disability declarations a clause limits the state responsibility to integration within the ability of the State (in terms of capacity and resources) to meet the obligations under the declarations. Further, there are clauses which qualify and limit the responsibility of the State to integrate the individual to the capacity of the individual to exercise the delineated rights (ie, 'The mentally retarded person has, to the *maximum degree of feasibility*, the same rights as other human beings'; and 'Whenever mentally retarded persons are *unable, because of the severity of their handicap*, to exercise all these rights....'). The implications of these clauses which qualify the extent to which the State is obliged to guarantee rights (for reasons of the State's incapacity or of the individual's incapacity) are enormous, because they limit the claims that can justifiably be made relating to the allocation of resources. It is therefore possible to justify the protection of the rights of some people but not of those with disabilities and meet the standard set in the very instruments designed to protect their specific rights.

The legitimate limiting of the rights of people with disabilities within the context of compensatory privilege is reflected in these and other international instruments and in national policies. Programmatic benefits, rather than rights, are laid out, but even those are restricted, dependent on the extent to which the individual deficit can substantiate the abridgement of those entitlements. Equality of opportunity is thus circumscribed by the extent to which an individual will be able to exercise the opportunity.

C. Well-Being

An emerging standard is treatment, care, and the allocation of resources based on entitlement to citizenship rights and *equal outcome* for people with disabilities (equality of well-being). Society's responsibility is to provide political and social entitlements that are equal in outcome to those of other citizens and is built on the acknowledgement that disability is a consequence of social, economic, and political organization, not individual pathology. It takes into account the historical disadvantages that people with disabilities have faced, the current structure of society, which maintains systemic discrimination, and the reformulation of non-disability specific policy, programs, and services. The disability itself is less the focus of attention, rather it is evidence of lack of entitlement or the limitation of the exercise of fundamental human rights and freedoms. The quality of the act rather than the quality of the actor is the core of the standard and it is the nature of the activity itself, including policies, social programs, and services, that comes under scrutiny.

This standard—ensuring human rights, citizenship, and equality of well-being—does not assume that everyone starts in the same position or that the removal of formal barriers, both systemic and individual, will leave everyone in the same position. Rather, it argues that formal barriers have placed groups in substantively different social positions, ie, that differences are sources of social disadvantage. Consequently, removing the barriers without also redressing associated disadvantages does not result in significant change.

This standard recognizes the limitations of the traditional legal justifications for excluding people legally, socially, and economically. It also addresses the limitations of the law in ensuring equality by taking into account the fallacy of the assumption that existing distributions of power and wealth are a product of individual initiative rather than state action. Entitlement is based on a comprehensive notion of human rights and citizenship not on an individual's status as a member of a class of deserving poor or on inequality in talent or social usefulness. Resource redistribution necessary to ensure equality of well-being requires both the redistribution necessary to enable equal opportunity as well as the redistribution necessary to take into account unequal needs because of physical and mental differences. In other words, differences must be accommodated in order to neutralize them as barriers to entitlement and participation.

This could mean, as it did in a 1997 decision of the Supreme Court in Canada, that adverse effects of policies or programs, faced by an individual, are not simply the result of an imposition of a burden not faced by nondisabled people in the population. Adverse effects result from the failure to ensure that people with disabilities benefit equally from a service offered to everyone. In that particular case,[26] three individuals, born deaf and preferring sign language as their form of communication, contended that the absence of interpreters impaired their ability to communicate with their doctors and other health care providers and thereby increased the risk of misdiagnosis and ineffective treatment. Medical care, in their province of British Columbia, is delivered primarily through two mechanisms, neither of which pays for sign language interpretation. Sign language interpretation has traditionally been paid for as a personal service through welfare or a service delivery mechanism. Hospital services are funded by the government under the Hospital Insurance Act,[27] which reimburses hospitals for the medically required services provided to the public. The province's Medical Services Plan provides funding for medically related services delivered by doctors and other health care practitioners. Arguing that a government is required to take special measures to ensure that members of disadvantaged groups are able to benefit equally from government services, and that discrimination can accrue from a failure to take positive steps, the court held that government must provide interpreters for deaf persons as a medically required service, to meet the constitutional equality rights set out in the *Charter of Rights and Freedoms*.[28]

A question that arises with the standard of equality of well-being is how to acknowledge difference (pluralism) without resulting in inequitable or unfair practices, while at the same time ensuring the benefits of integration (assimilation) into the economic and social structure. Assimilation has to be achieved without overlooking the unique needs and differences faced by disadvantaged individuals and groups that must be addressed to realize those benefits, including the expression of self-determination, inclusion in social life through democratization and the exercise of fundamental citizenship rights. At issue is the conventional framing of equality and difference as mutually exclusive terms, a framing that misrepresents their relationship.[29] Placing equality and difference in an antithetical relationship denies the way difference has figured in political notions of equality, presuming in the case of disability that the pathology is traceable to the individual.

Equality, within a political theory of rights, depends on the recognition of a group of people as different. The issue, therefore, is to find a notion of equality predicated not on sameness but on difference. Albie Sachs, the South African jurist, argued against the usual presumption that the right to be the same and the right to be different are competing rights: On the contrary, the right to be the same in terms of fundamental civil, political, legal, and social rights, provided the foundation for the expression of difference through choice in the sphere of culture, lifestyle, and personal priorities. In other words, provided that difference was not used to maintain inequality, subordination, injustice, and marginalization, it represents a positive value in human society.[30]

Internationally, the importance of different treatment as a means to achieving equality is being recognized. The UN Human Rights Committee issued a General Comment in 1989, stating that 'The enjoyment of rights and freedoms on an equal footing, however, does not mean identical treatment in every instance.'[31]

GOAL:	Equal outcome in expression of self-determination, inclusion in social life (through democratization), and exercise of fundamental citizenship rights
MEASURES:	Extent to which equality of access to social, economic, and legal opportunities/variables is achieved
RIGHTS GUARANTEE:	Guarantee of social, economic, democratic, political, and legal rights accorded to others in nation state (and in international agreements)

EXAMPLES IN CLINICAL AND SERVICE TREATMENT AND GOVERNMENT POLICY:

- Equitable access to social and economic opportunities
- Opportunity for inclusion in non-segregated activities
- Human rights legislation with anti-discrimination prohibition based on mental and physical disability
- Physical and program adaptations to generic facilities, institutions, services
- Individual control of service program, financing, and staff
- Income programs based on need and individualized funding

FIGURE 11.5. Equality of well-being standard (standard which protects equality of outcome and rights based on difference; defines disability as a political condition)

Some examples, specific to disability, should prove helpful. In Canada, under the Canadian Charter of Rights and Freedoms,[32] individuals are protected both before and under the law and are entitled to the equal protection and equal benefit of the law. A 1989 decision by the Supreme Court of Canada has suggested how extensively this is to be interpreted.[33] Although the legal decision did not concern an individual with a disability, it has a significant impact because of the interpretation provided of what equality means under the Charter. The Supreme Court extended the concept of equality to recognize that 'every difference in treatment between individuals under the law will not necessarily result in inequality and, further, that identical treatment may frequently reproduce serious inequality'. As the Court held, 'In fact, the interests of true equality may well require differentiation in treatment.'[34] If equality implies an even distribution of and access to justice, then the accommodation of differences is a substantial part of the essence of equality. The Court also held in that case that 'distinctions based on personal characteristics attributed to an individual solely on the basis of association with a group will rarely escape the charge of discrimination, while those based on an individual's merits and capacities will rarely be so classed'.[35]

A Canadian education decision applied this legal standard of equality to a case involving education in the local school for a student with an intellectual disability.[36] The court held that education in a special school or class is not a question of pedagogical theories but is 'one of determining the legal framework within which that choice is made'. Acknowledging the obvious difference in ability of Emily Eaton and other children of her age, and the obvious application of the best interest principle for Emily, the judge maintained that the issue in question was not the right to education but the right to equality. She held that the Charter 'requires that, regardless of its perceived pedagogical merit, a non-consensual exclusionary placement be recognized as discriminatory and not be resorted to unless alternatives are proven inadequate'.[37] She went further to place education in its social context: 'When a measure is offered to a disabled person, allegedly in order to provide that person with her true equality entitlement, and that measure is one of exclusion, segregation, and isolation from the mainstream, that measure, in its broad social and historical context, is properly labeled a burden or a disadvantage.'[38] She concluded: 'There may be ongoing pedagogical debate as to what is best for Emily's education. There can be no doubt, however, that as a person with disabilities, it is not against her best interest to assert her equality right.'

This case was subsequently overturned by the Supreme Court of Canada[39] in a decision that turned on whether Emily Eaton experienced a burden or disadvantage from the denial of access to inclusive education. Arguing that since she was not denied equality under Section 15 of the Charter, there was no need to get to a discrimination inquiry. The Court, by arguing that: 'Integration can be either a benefit or a burden depending on whether the individual can profit from the advantages that integration provides',[40] changed the equality issue into one of pedagogy and then argued that since it was in the best interests of Emily to attend a segregated school, it could not be discriminatory. Using the best interests argument had been explicitly rejected by Madame Justice Arbour at the Appeals Court level where she argued that to apply such a test obscures the right to equal benefit and protection of the law.

This case shows how amorphous the line is between the various legal notions of equality and disability as a category. While the decision at the Ontario Appeal Court was clearly argued from the perspective of equality as equal outcome and a formulation of disability as constructed from systemic conditions that lead to the disentitlement to rights, the Supreme Court went back to a standard of 'best interests', one that even precluded the family as an authority on deciding best interests and reflected a civil disability standard. Further it privatized the notion of disability and medicalized the educational needs of children with disabilities. There remain, however, in the decision some important conclusions about disability equality. The Court recognized that Section 15's equality guarantee has

two aims: first, to eliminate discrimination that attributes untrue characteristics to a person based on stereotyping attitudes about a person's
immutable characteristics and second, to establish that equality requires
structural and societal changes. The Court ruled that 'exclusion from the
mainstream of society results from the construction of a society based
solely on 'mainstream' attributes to which the disabled person will never be
able to gain access'.[41] Equality requires changes be made so that society's
'structures and assumptions do not result in the relegation and banish-
ment of disabled persons from participation'.[42]

Analysts[43] have predicted that the Court's holding that integration is a
starting point for the placement of children with a disability, requiring
school boards to justify exclusion and that there is a prerequisite for a
child and his or her parents to have a meaningful role in decisions about
the child's placement suggest that the equality provisions will likely be
upheld in future cases, even in the face of this case. And the emphasis of
the Court on the importance of removing barriers facing people with disabilities to ensure full participation in society suggests that the direction
of future courts, and particularly in circumstances that do not include the
complication of involving a child, will likely tend towards an equality of
well-being standard of law.

VI. CONCLUSION

Monitoring the exercise of human rights of people with disabilities according to a standard of well-being involves the unmasking of the structural
and systemic context of people with disabilities. This is because it is a standard that recognizes disability as a consequence of social organization and
the relationship of the individual to society, coupled with an understanding
of equality as equality of outcome. To monitor human rights by this standard, the following would be open to analysis: the equitable access to social
and economic opportunities that are available to citizens in general and the
structural conditions that facilitate or inhibit access to those opportunities
(including legal, financial, and service opportunities). Well-being is measured according to the equality of access and the exercise of human rights
and citizenship. Such a standard questions the legally and socially constructed barriers individuals face in access to those outcomes.

In recognizing the social and scientific formulations on which treatment
and care of people with disabilities has been constructed and the way in
which this interacts with theories of equality to determine entitlement to
citizenship rights, the basis for fair, non-discriminatory social policy
becomes clearer and more transparent. Understanding the rationale for
a social policy of exclusion raises questions of the most appropriate

method of addressing rights. Does society continue to confine the rights analysis to individualistic needs of those with disabilities? Or does society begin to recognize the inequalities inherent in the institutional structures and put the onus on the State and on international bodies to begin to develop provisions based on principles that include the rights of all people to participate freely and adjust achievement measures?

The human rights of people with disabilities leads to examining the various categories of human rights, recognizing the interdependence of civil and political rights and economic, social, and cultural rights. One of the major innovations of the Convention on the Rights of the Child[44] is that its provisions are the first in a treaty to integrate fully the two broad classifications of rights: civil and political, and economic, social, and cultural. As Toope concluded: 'The world community spent almost twenty years attempting to codify in the form of one binding treaty the provisions of the Universal Declaration of Human Rights. It never succeeded, largely because of the failure to agree on the interrelationship between civil and political rights and economic, social and cultural rights. It became necessary to conclude two[45] separate treaties.'[46]

The drafters of the Children's Convention were able to agree upon a text that treats the broad classifications of rights as interdependent and morally equivalent. This equivalency will open up arguments that both categories of rights are equally binding. Before the Children's Convention, it was possible to argue that whereas civil and political rights were binding here and now, economic, social, and political rights were mere statements of aspiration, requiring only the efforts of States to promote 'progressive implementation' of the rights where circumstances permitted. States could divorce the two types of rights because they were physically divorced in the key international conventions. Significantly, the Children's treaty contains specific provisions for children with disabilities.[47]

The equivalency of the two sets of rights is important in the field of disability. The assumption, made by many governments, particularly Western governments, that the achievement of civil and political rights will ultimately lead to a democratic polity ensuring that people will be treated equitably in relation to their economic, social, and cultural rights, has not proved to be true for people with disabilities. Political and civil rights of people with disabilities have not guaranteed that their needs are met. This is a result of the construction of legal and social inequality and exclusion using standards of civil disability and of compensatory privilege. Social and economic rights are, not infrequently, seen as optional and dependent on the economy of the state government. That the roots of discrimination against people with disabilities are grounded in expenditures that excluded them from social participation, and consequently from the exercise of their rights, is not considered. The argument is made that if disability is an individual pathology and equality implies equal treatment or equality of opportunity, then denial of rights can be justified.

These arguments and others suggest the importance of reviewing international agreements, particularly those related to disability, to ensure that they do not have inherent biases that legitimize segregation and the denial of rights of people with disabilities. If we wish to work towards societies that are distinguished by a culture of justice, recognition of difference and the public ownership of private disadvantage, scholars and citizens have to find a framework that takes into account and struggles to include all people, including those who do not fit conventional norms. This deconstruction of inequality will have to be addressed by concerted, coherent action.

The recognition of rights as greater than simply the individualistic indicators inherent in the deficit model of disability and in equal treatment frameworks of equality, places accountability on social, political, and economic structures. They have to be organized in a manner that enables individuals to participate in decision making. They have to permit the development of a human rights model and indicators of compliance that incorporate both structural and individual properties.

Patterns of injustice throughout the world have prevented people with disabilities from participating in the same way as those without disabilities. Science, medicine, economics, and government policy—in both the national and international sphere—have rationalized and justified selective participation, entitlement, and rights. In every nation of the world a system of social discrimination disentitles and restricts the opportunities of people with disabilities to participate equally in society. Despite the facts we now know about the many abilities of people with disabilities, people with disabilities continue to experience the general injustice of disregard, disrespect, isolation, and discrimination. The injustice of having a double standard—one standard for those without disabilities and one for those with disabilities—in allocating resources and in developing criteria for participation in society—has to be addressed. By redressing the denial of human rights, fundamental freedoms and the restriction of participation in society, governments must deliver on their promise to their citizens, both those with and without disabilities.

NOTES

1. Commission on Social Justice, *Social Justice in a Changing World* (London: Institute for Public Policy Research, 1993); Roeher Institute, *Social Well-Being: A Paradigm for Reform* (Toronto: Roeher Institute, 1993); G Drover and P Kerans, *New Approaches to Welfare Theory* (Aldershot, Hants: Edgar Elgar Publishing Ltd, 1993); A Yalnizyan, *Defining Social Security, Defining Ourselves: Why We Need to Change Our Thinking Before It's Too Late* (Ottawa: Canadian Centre for Policy Alternatives, 1993).

2. S Goudry, Y Peters, and R Currie, 'Income Security Reform from a Disability Equality Perspective: Proposals for an Analytic Framework' (Winnipeg: Canadian Disability Rights Council, 1994); L Barton, 'The Struggle for Citizenship: The Case of Disabled People' (1993) 8 *Disability, Handicap & Society* 235–248; Canada, 'Pathway to Integration: Mainstream 1992' (Report to Ministers of Social Services on the Federal/Provincial/Territorial Review of Services Affecting Canadians with Disabilities; Ottawa: Government Printing Office, 1993); M Oliver, *The Politics of Disablement* (London: McMillan, 1990); R Leal Ocampo, 'Stronger Families—Stronger Societies' in Roeher Institute (ed), *As If Children Mattered: Perspectives on Children, Rights and Disability* (Toronto: Roeher Institute, 1995).

3. This section has been adapted from an earlier published article, MH Rioux, 'Disability: The Place of Judgement in a World of Fact' (April 1997) 41 *Journal of Intellectual Disability Research* 102–111.

4. P Starr, *The Social Transformation of American Medicine* (New York: Basic Books, 1982).

5. Canada, 'Pathway to Integration: Mainstream 1992' (n 2); S Cohen and A Scull, *Social Control and the State* (Oxford: Martin Robertson, 1983); N Sutherland, *Children in English-Canadian Society* (Toronto: Univ of Toronto Press, 1976); S Cohen, *Visions of Social Control: Crime, Punishment and Classification* (Cambridge, Mass: Polity Press, 1985).

6. LH Meyer, CA Peck, and L Brown, *Critical Issues in the Lives of People with Severe Disabilities* (Baltimore: Paul H Brookes, 1990); W Wolfensberger, *Normalization: The Principle of Normalization in Human Services* (Toronto: National Institute on Mental Retardation, 1972).

7. World Health Organization, *International Classification of Impairments, Disabilities and Handicaps* (Geneva: World Health Organization, 1980).

8. National Institute for Disability Management and Research, 'Code of Practice for Disability Management' (Port Alberni, BC: National Institute for Disability Management and Research, 2000); Job Accommodation Network, Website: Job Accommodation Network, 2001 available at http://www.jan.wvu.edu; *VandeZande v State of Wis Dept of Admin* 44 F 3d 538 (7th Cir 1995).

9. Canadian Association of Independent Living Centres, *A Time for Change/ The Time for Choices: A Proposal for Improving Social Security Arrangements for Canadians with Disabilities* (Ottawa: Canadian Association of Independent Living Centres, 1994); Roeher Institute, *Income Insecurity: The Disability Income in Canada* (North York, Ont: Roeher, 1988).

10. W Roth, 'Disability as a Social Construct' (1983) 20 *Society* 56–61; P Beresford and J Campbell, 'Disabled People, Service Users, User Involvement and Representation' (1994) 9 *Disability and Society* 315–325; MH Rioux and M Bach (eds), *Disability is not Measles: New Research Paradigms in Disability* (North York, Ont: Roeher, 1994); Roeher Institute, *Social Well-Being: A Paradigm for Reform* (Toronto: Roeher Institute, 1993); Canadian Society for ICIDH, 'The Handicap Creation Process' (1991) 4 *ICIDH International Network*; M Oliver, *The Politics of Disablement* (London: McMillan, 1990).

11. Parts of this section have been adapted from an earlier published article, MH Rioux, 'Towards a Concept of Equality of Well-Being: Overcoming the

Social and Legal Construction of Inequality' (January 1994) 7 *Canadian Journal of Law and Jurisprudence* 1.

12. Aristotle, 'The Varieties of Justice' in J Sturba (ed), *Justice: Alternative Political Perspectives* (Belmont: Wadsworth Publishing Company, 1980); R Nozick, *Anarchy, State and Utopia* (New York: Basic Books Inc, 1974).

13. R Dworkin, *Taking Rights Seriously* (Cambridge, Mass: Harvard Univ Press, 1977); J Rawls, *A Theory of Justice* (Cambridge, Mass: Belknap Press of Harvard Univ Press, 1971); B Williams, 'The Idea of Equality' in PR Laslett and WB Runciman (eds), *Philosophy, Politics and Society* (Oxford: Basil Blackwell, 1962); J Rawls and E Kelly, *Justice as Fairness: A Restatement* (Cambridge, Mass: Harvard Univ Press, 2001).

14. R Veatch, *The Foundations of Justice: Why the Retarded and the Rest of Us have Claims to Equality* (Oxford: Oxford Univ Press, 1986); R Dworkin, 'What is Equality: Part 1, Equality of Welfare' (1981) 10 *Philosophy & Public Affairs* 185–246; R Dworkin, 'What is Equality: Part 2, Equality of Resources' (1981) 10 *Philosophy & Public Affairs* 283–345; CE Baker, 'Outcome Quality or Equality of Respect: The Substantive Content of Equal Protection' (1983) 131 *Univ of Pennsylvania L Rev* 933.

15. WS Tarnopolsky, *The Equality Rights* (Toronto: Carswell, 1982); W Tarnopolsky and WF Pentney, *Discrimination and the Law* (Don Mills: Richard De Boo Publishers, 1989).

16. *Re S.D.* 3 WWR 597 (BC Provincial Court, 1983); 3 WWR 618 (BC Supreme Court, 1983.

17. A Sachs, 'Human Rights in the Twenty First Century: Real Dichotomies, False Antagonism' in TA Cromwell *et al.* (eds), *Human Rights in the 21st Century* (Ottawa: Canadian Institute for the Administration of Justice, 1996); M Minow, *Making All the Difference: Inclusion, Exclusion and American Law* (Ithaca, NY: Cornell Univ Press, 1990); K Greenawalt, 'How Empty is the Idea of Equality' (1983) 83 *Columbia L Rev* 1167–1185.

18. L Smith, 'A New Paradigm for Equality Rights' in L Smith *et al.* (eds), *Righting the Balance: Canada's New Equality Rights* (Saskatoon: Canadian Human Rights Reporter, Inc, 1986) 365.

19. K Greenawalt, 'How Empty is the Idea of Equality' (1983) 83 *Columbia L Rev* 1167–1185.

20. Roeher Institute, *Social Well-being: A Paradigm for Reform* (Toronto: Roeher Institute, 1993).

21. IR Young, *Justice and the Politics of Difference* (Princeton: Princeton Univ Press, 1990).

22. S Herr, 'Rights into Action: Implementing the Human Rights of the Mentally Handicapped' (1977) 26 *Catholic Univ L Rev* 203–318.

23. Canadian Society for ICIDH, 'The Handicap Creation Process' (1991) 4 *ICIDH International Network*.

24. JC Livingston, *Fair Game? Inequality and Affirmative Action* (San Francisco: WH Freeman & Co, 1979).

25. M Rioux, 'Exchanging Charity for Rights: The Challenge for the Next Decade' (1993) 89 *British Institute of Learning Disabilities*.

26. *Eldridge v British Columbia (Attorney-General)* [1997] 141 DLR 577.

27. Hospital Insurance Act of British Columbia.
28. Canada, *Constitution Act, Part 1—Canadian Charter of Rights and Freedoms* (1982).
29. M Minow, *Making All the Difference: Inclusion, Exclusion and American Law* (Ithaca, NY: Cornell Univ Press, 1990); JW Scott, 'Deconstructing Equality-Versus Difference: or, The Uses of Poststructural Theory for Feminism' (1988) 14 *Feminist Studies*.
30. A Sachs, 'Human Rights in the Twenty First Century: Real Dichotomies, False Antagonism' in TA Cromwell *et al.* (eds), *Human Rights in the 21st Century* (Ottawa: Canadian Institute for the Administration of Justice, 1996).
31. UN Committee on Human Rights, 'General Comment No. 18' (1989) Supplement No 40, UN Official Records, 173–175.
32. Canada, *Constitution Act, Part 1—Canadian Charter of Rights and Freedoms* (1982).
33. *Andrews v Law Society of British Columbia* [1989] 1 SCR 143.
34. ibid.
35. ibid.
36. *Eaton v Brant (County) Board of Education* [1995] 123 DLR (4th) 43.
37. ibid.
38. ibid 59.
39. *Eaton v Brant (County) Board of Education* [1997] 1 SCR 241.
40. ibid 274.
41. *Eaton v Brant (County) Board of Education* [1995] 123 DLR (4th) 43, 405–406.
42. ibid 406.
43. M David Lepovsky, 'A Report Card on the Charter's Guarantee of Equality of Persons with Disabilities after 10 Years—What Progress? What Prospects?' (1997) 7 *National J of Constitutional L* 3, 263–431; J Mosoff and I Grant, 'Intellectual Disability and the Supreme Court: The Implications of the *Charter* for People who have a Disability' (Report prepared for the Canadian Association for Community Living, Toronto, 1999).
44. UN Convention 1991.
45. UN, *International Covenant on Civil and Political Rights*, 1967; UN, *International Covenant on Economic, Social and Cultural Rights*, 1967.
46. S Toope, *The Convention on the Rights of the Child: Implications for Canada* (Toronto: Child, Youth and Family Policy Research Centre, 1992).
47. UN, *UN Convention on the Rights of the Child*, art 23.

12

Respecting Persons with Disabilities and Preventing Disability: Is there a Conflict?

ADRIENNE ASCH, LAWRENCE O. GOSTIN, AND
DIANN M. JOHNSON

I feel so cheated.
You were so perfect, my little one
the small life inside of me
my tummy still flat, I knew you were growing
the first flutter
then a kick
A boy or a girl? we wondered.
But never would you be right
the whole time you grew
from pinpoint tiny to person-sized
you were never right
never perfect
We rejoiced and planned
we raised glasses to toast and
cried tears of joy
through autumn, then winter
You kicked and stretched
my tummy swelled
But even then you were different
even then
you didn't look like us
or think like us
Precious as you were, a life we created
you weren't the baby we waited for
The showers, the painting, the preparation
the excitement and anticipation
we waited to meet and love
the person we had already loved
and dreamed of
for months while you grew
But all the time you were different
not the normal, healthy child we prayed for
and felt sure was coming

This article was written by Diann Johnson in her private capacity. No official support or endorsement by Department of Health and Human Services, Office of Inspector General is intended or should be inferred.

Then you arrived
so early and so quickly
Your daddy helped me breathe
and I cried out when it hurt
and the nurse said "hold on"
"the reward is your baby"
I feel so cheated.[1]

Attitudes toward congenital disability per se have not changed markedly. Both premodern as well as contemporary societies have regarded disability as undesirable and to be avoided. Not only have parents recognized the birth of a disabled child as a potentially divisive, destructive force in the family unit, but the larger society has seen disability as unfortunate....Our society still does not countenance the elimination of diseased/disabled people; but it does urge the termination of diseased/disabled fetuses. The urging is not explicit, but implicit.[2]

I. INTRODUCTION

The field of public health faces a dilemma in the area of disability prevention. The mandate of public health has traditionally been read to embrace the prevention of disabilities. However, this mandate also includes a duty to enhance the well-being of persons with disabilities. Essential to this latter duty is increasing the respect of society for persons with disabilities as contributing to their families, communities, and the world in which we live. This chapter attempts to address the problems that can arise when public health simultaneously tries to prevent disability and elevate the status of persons with disabilities within our society.

We argue that most forms of public health activities that seek to promote health and well-being and to prevent injury or illness do not in themselves compromise the goal of promoting the equality and dignity of persons with disabilities, but that certain primary prevention activities have been conducted and supported in ways that potentially undercut the goals of equality and full inclusion of people with disabilities.

II. CONTRASTING VIEWS OF DISABILITY

Two major social and legislative enterprises in the late twentieth century illustrate the potential conflict between public health prevention and respect for persons with disabilities and demonstrate very different understandings of the difficulties posed by physical, sensory, and cognitive impairment. In 1988, Congress launched an almost unprecedented commitment to basic and applied science when it appropriated funding for the first year of an estimated fifteen-year project known as the Human Genome Initiative.[3] Two years later, Congress enacted civil rights legislation aimed at ending the second-class status of people with disabilities.[4] The anticipated fruits of the Human Genome Initiative include learning the effect of each gene on all other genes; discovering genetic mutations for particular characteristics; and developing diagnostic procedures for carriers of, and treatments for, genetic disorders.[5] The Human Genome Project located the problem of disability as inherent in the atypical bodies of individuals. It proposed medical resolutions of those problems by treatments of affected individuals or by diagnostic tests that could alert prospective parents to any health problems in embryos or fetuses and permit such prospective parents to prevent future births of people affected by diagnosed health problems. The purpose of the Americans with Disabilities Act is to end the exclusion and discrimination that have denied persons with disabilities access to jobs, schools, public accommodations, public transportation, public services, and telecommunications. Sometimes full access will be achieved only through substantial alterations of physical structure and institutional practices or the provision of reasonable accommodations.[6]

The Human Genome Initiative and the Americans with Disabilities Act capture sharp contrasts in our society's understanding of what it means to have a disability. Each embodies very different objectives: the former preventing diminution of health; the latter seeking to maximize opportunities for those with and without disabilities, and promote the comfortable incorporation of diversity into society. Taken separately, these goals are laudable; however, they can express tensions when examined together. We begin this chapter with an examination of historical perceptions of and attitudes toward disability and then focus on the impact of prevention activities on disability equality.

One need only examine the language and culture of disability to understand the profound negative connotations of the word 'disability'. Disability—and such other related terms as chronic illness, 'birth defect', 'deformity', 'impairment', 'handicap'—is something that 'disqualifies a person',[7] a 'deprivation or lack especially of physical, intellectual, or emotional capacity or fitness', or a 'particular weakness or inadequacy'.[8] To 'disable' a person is to 'deprive of some ability, to make unfit or useless'. To be disabled is to become 'incapacitated'.[9] A 'handicap' 'lessens one's chance of success or makes progress difficult'.[10] Thus, the social understanding of disability focuses almost entirely on its perceived burdensome and undesirable qualities—inadequate capacity to function and perform, lack of capacity or qualification to achieve, and deviation from the 'normal'. Historically, but persisting into the twenty-first century, people with mental impairments have been especially feared, stigmatized, and ostracized. Discussing trends in attitudes toward people with disabilities, contributors to the *Handbook of Disability Studies* write: '[P]eople with physical disabilities were more often absorbed into the community, even though infanticide and abandonment were common in some cultures and historical periods. On the other hand, people with mental conditions were more probably institutionalized or separated from the community in some other way.'[11] From antiquity, then, there has been a pervasiveness of the concept of the separateness of those labeled 'intellectually disabled' from full personhood.[12]

From *Richard III*, to George in *Of Mice and Men*, Tiny Tim in *A Christmas Carol*, or Rochester's mad wife in *Jane Eyre*, persons with disabilities have historically been portrayed as villains, undesirables, objects of pity, and burdens to family and society. The editors of the above-mentioned volume ask: 'Why are so many depictions of disability in art and literature negative in character, portraying disabled people as dependent, "nonhuman," "freaks," marginal, or even dangerous?' They then review a considerable body of research on representations of disability and summarize their results as follows: 'positive visual and verbal imagery of disability is practically nonexistent.'[13] Only in the late twentieth century did we begin to see examples of persons with disabilities functioning as accepted members of society in television programs such as 'Life Goes On' and 'L.A. Law', or movies such as 'Children of a Lesser God'. Even so, the villain with either mental or physical disabilities is a common feature of many modern thrillers or horror films.

Popular language, culture, and medicine, then, often perceive disability in negative terms, as a barrier or impediment to achievement, a disadvantage or limitation in life's struggle, an affliction or a source of distress and torment for the person, and a burden for the family and others. Given these attitudes, disability is something to be avoided, and scientific intervention to prevent or ameliorate disabling conditions is to be prized.

In many ways, the deeply negative social construction of disability is puzzling, given how ubiquitous it is. To be sure, the dominant perception of disability is that of the unwanted 'other'. Many people without disabilities, particularly the young and the strong, cannot conceive of themselves as being disabled; their response to disability ranges from loathing and fear to pity. Unfortunately, the dominant view of having an illness or disability attributes any non-medical problems faced by people with such conditions to the conditions themselves. This view of disability presumes that impaired mobility, physical deformity, sensory deficit, atypical learning style or speed, or departures from what is customary in energy, stamina, or flexibility is the reason why people with disabilities are less educated, less likely to be working, often in poverty, and more socially isolated than people who do not have impairments. Operating within the medical framework and the worldview of bioethics, health is prized because 'impairments of normal species functioning reduce the range of opportunity open to the individual...[to] construct [a] "plan of life" or "conception of the good." '[14]

By contrast, recent scholarship and strands of social policy and legislation contend that it is both inaccurate and socially dangerous to regard people with disabilities as 'other' and to base social policy on the belief that impairment is not a part of common human experience. As Irving Kenneth Zola reminds us in his classic essay, 'The Sleeping Giant in Our Midst', we are all likely to experience disability and this reality ought to fundamentally alter our response:

What may have looked initially like a methodological debate—what is the 'real' number of people with disabilities—has become one that goes to the heart of current policy formulation. The latter has been built on the notion of people with disabilities being another oppressed statistical minority like people of differing racial, ethnic, and gender backgrounds. I am arguing that people with disabilities do not represent a statistical minority. It is not merely, as the cliche states, that everyone is only a slip away. The empirical reality is that everyone, unless they experience sudden death, will in fact acquire one or more disabilities with all their consequences. This is the reality on which future conceptualization, measurement, and policy must be based—truly the sleeping giant in our midst.[15]

By including people who have a disability, have a record of disability, or are regarded as having a disability, the Americans with Disabilities Act of 1990 is one of the most significant embodiments of the view that disability is part of the human experience and that people with disabilities are a part of the community to be included when formulating public policy. The last two decades of disability scholarship and activism contend that if a disabled person experiences isolation, powerlessness, poverty, unemployment, or low social status, these are not inevitable consequences of biological limitation. The culprit is not biological, psychic, or cognitive equipment but the social, institutional, and physical world in which people with impairments must function—a world designed with the characteristics and needs of the nondisabled in mind. As physical, social, and institutional environments change to better include the millions of people with impairments of all ages, many of the negative social and economic consequences now linked to disability will be eradicated, and conceivably disability might become a characteristic of human diversity that does not occasion fear, loathing, revulsion, or unremitting grief.

III. PREVENTING DISABILITY

Those disability scholars and activists who support public policy changes that promote the respect for and inclusion of people with disabilities in society have confronted the potential conflict between such respect for people with disabilities and the desire to promote health and avert or ameliorate impairment and disability whenever possible. Prevention strategies in medicine and public health are highly regarded and have achieved considerable success in reducing morbidity and premature mortality. Diseases like diphtheria, scarlet fever, small pox, and polio, once regarded as deadly scourges, have been virtually eliminated in this country through successful public health initiatives. Traditional public health approaches seek to identify causes of disease and then to intervene medically, behaviorally, nutritionally, or environmentally to ameliorate ill-health and avert the spread of disease. Public health programs to prevent disability are held in high esteem. This reflects both the negative pervasive perception of disability and the scientific imperative to better the conditions of living. Numerous federal (eg, the Centers of Disease Control and Prevention (CDC) and National Institutes of Health (NIH)) and state (eg, public health departments) agencies are established precisely to fund and coordinate research, screening, and treatment aimed toward prevention and amelioration of disability. Much of the health care system, including managed care, exists to provide clinical prevention services such as prenatal testing, mammograms, pap smears, and vaccinations. As a nation we spend billions of dollars annually to prevent morbidity and premature mortality, and our government has a concerted strategy to achieve this objective.[16] The federal 'public health genetics' project vividly illustrates this view of disability by conceiving systematic approaches to preventing and reducing ill-health and disability in the population.

Prevention strategies are further categorized as primary and secondary prevention. Primary prevention is designed to avoid the birth of persons with various disabilities, while secondary prevention is designed to ameliorate existing disabilities or avert additional disabilities in the population. Primary prevention can occur at an earlier stage, before conception for instance by changes in diet and the environment. Science is rapidly developing the capacity to diagnose genetic carrier states in prospective parents. For example, it is possible to identify carriers of such diseases as cystic fibrosis, sickle cell, Tay Sachs, and fragile X syndrome.[17] Indeed, society has frequently discussed, and sometimes implemented, mass screening programs for carrier status. A number of states implemented mass screening for sickle cell in the 1970s,[18] and public health authorities have discussed and, in part, implemented cystic fibrosis screening in certain populations.[19] Science is on the verge of identifying genetic factors that may facilitate screening in a broad range of complex, chronic diseases such as cardiovascular disease, neoplasms, schizophrenia, and manic depressive psychosis.

Primary prevention, of course, does not rely only on genetic testing and screening. Mothers, for example, may transmit infection to the fetus or infant in utero, during delivery, or through breast-feeding. The CDC recommends routine HIV screening for all pregnant women, and for those found to be HIV positive, an arduous regimen of anti-viral medication to reduce the risk of perinatal transmission of HIV.[20] Similarly, interventions to reduce drinking alcoholic beverages or smoking cigarettes during pregnancy are designed to avert fetal alcohol syndrome or the health effects of tobacco use such as low birth weight.

Secondary prevention strategies are designed to avert disabilities within the population and to minimize the severity of those which are not averted. An influential definition of public health illuminates our understanding of secondary prevention. 'Public health is what we, as a society, do collectively to assure the conditions for people to be healthy. This requires that continuing and emerging threats to the health of the public be successfully countered.'[21] These threats include disease epidemics, injuries, chronic illness, and the toxic byproducts of a modern economy, transmitted through air, water, soil, or food. The US Government's 'Healthy People 2010' initiative sets targets for increased health, reduced disease and disability, and longer life expectancy. It seeks to achieve its goals through increased access to medical care, improved diet, nutrition and exercise, more advanced sanitation and sewage, better disease surveillance, and cleaner water, air, and environmental conditions.[22]

In general there is no special conflict between respecting the dignity, equality, and worth of persons with disabilities and valuing strategies that promote health and treat or cure disease and disability. As with nondisabled people, many who have disabilities take steps to stay healthy, and they support societal activities that improve the environments of homes, cities, and workplaces. We are confident that no proponent of the social or minority group model of disability out of which we write possibly endorses the outcome of recent research that led to brain damage and developmental disability in children living in homes containing dangerous levels of lead.[23] Similarly, people from within the disability rights movement wholeheartedly support worldwide activities to improve nutrition, remove environmental toxins, make workplaces and travel safer, and educate the population about the consequences of sexually transmitted diseases. Although deploring campaigns of health promotion that inaccurately depict the tragedy of disability, we laud efforts to help people retain typical capacities of learning, moving, communicating, and taking in the world. Most primary and secondary prevention strategies, then, need not reflect negatively upon living as a person with a disability.

IV. QUESTIONING FORMS OF PRIMARY PREVENTION

One form of primary prevention would avert the births of people with disabilities by promoting prenatal testing and selective abortion of fetuses determined to have disabling traits, and this practice has occasioned considerable concern and apprehension from many quarters within the disability rights movement; it is to this form of disability prevention that we devote the remainder of this chapter. Critics contend that social endorsement of this practice differs from endorsing other actions that prevent disability. Prenatal testing and selective abortion should not be compared with prenatal care for women, vaccinations for children, or health promotion for everyone. Selective abortion prevents disability not in an existing human being or in a fetus likely to come to term; instead, it prevents disability by preventing the fetus from becoming a person with a disability. It implies that it may be better for the child not to be born at all rather than to be born with a disability. Advocacy for this form of primary prevention, then, appears to disvalue and disrespect persons living with similar disabling conditions, sending them the message that they are mistakes that society would eliminate if it had the technological capacity. It connotes that if people do not meet a certain health standard, they should not be welcomed into the family or the world.[24]

Primary prevention begins with identification of women or men who are likely to have children with disabilities or fetuses that could have a disability. Science has long sought the capacity to make reliable prenatal diagnoses of the fetus. Prenatal diagnosis offers the promise of some effective intervention to treat or cure the disabling condition. Emerging technologies to intervene surgically or genetically in utero may enable the birth of an infant without specific disabilities. For example, fetal therapy, including fetal gene therapy, may in the future provide cost-effective methods for curing or treating the fetal condition before birth.[25] At present, however, science usually offers identification of the fetal abnormality often without the realistic possibility of intervention.

Developed in the late 1960s and early 1970s, amniocentesis enabled medicine to offer mothers second-trimester testing for chromosomal abnormalities such as Down syndrome. The availability of amniotic fluid, and later maternal serum, permitted the development of biochemical assays of not only the fluid, such as alpha-fetoprotein determination, but also the cells contained in this fluid. This technology allowed identification of dozens of fetal conditions such as neural tube defects, anencephaly, and Turner's syndrome. Refinements in ultrasound technology also led to a wide variety of prenatal diagnoses such as hydrocephalus, pleural effusion, atrial and ventricular septal defects, and limb abnormalities. More recent developments in ultrasound technology may permit the diagnosis of Down syndrome and facial deformities.[26] During the last two decades, many other techniques for prenatal diagnosis have been introduced, the most important of which is DNA analysis. Genetic testing can now identify hundreds of conditions in the fetus such as hereditary spastic paraplegia, prelingual deafness, and Huntington's disease.[27] The Human Genome Initiative will certainly produce many additional tests for diseases with a genetic component.[28]

This public health prevention strategy, however, potentially conflicts with at least two central ideas that have equal power in modern society—respect for the dignity and integrity of persons with disabilities, and social diversity that values people of many different abilities, races, and forms. The civil rights movement, which includes persons with disabilities, espouses pride in the individual human being. Each person—irrespective of his or her race, sex, sexual orientation, or health status—is entitled to respect and dignity.[29] Along with others who criticize the current enthusiasm for and practice of prenatal testing followed by selective abortion, we urge social reflection and reform that would reduce an apparent conflict between respect for people with disability and efforts to prevent the births of those who might have the same disabling traits.

As described by Eric Parens and Adrienne Asch, the central points in a disability critique of prenatal diagnosis can be summarized as follows:

Rather than improving the medical or social situation of today's or tomorrow's disabled citizens, prenatal diagnosis reinforces the medical model that disability itself, not societal discrimination against people with disabilities, is the problem to be solved.... In rejecting an otherwise desired child because they believe that the child's disability will diminish their parental experience, parents suggest that they are unwilling to accept any significant departure from the parental dreams that a child's characteristics might occasion.... When prospective parents select against a fetus because of predicted disability, they are making an unfortunate, often misinformed decision that a disabled child will not fulfill what most people seek in child rearing.[30]

This critique reflects the links of the disability rights movement with the historic civil rights movements of racial minorities, women, and gays and lesbians. The civil rights movement is also built on the central idea of diversity. Rather than seeking uniformity and consistency in the population, civil rights supporters applaud difference. They believe there exists an intrinsic value to having a varied population along a number of dimensions—eg, different races, cultures, and religions. While disability is not the same as race and sex, human diversity certainly includes persons with many different mental and physical strengths, weakness, and forms. Persons with disabilities are an integral and contributing part of the community. The unabashed social commitment to this form of public health prevention should make us ponder anew what type and how much variation in humanity we can tolerate and appreciate.

Examining prenatal testing also raises the moral dilemmas faced by parents in deciding whether to have a child that will probably be born with a disability. There is no simple answer to these complex questions. Throughout this chapter, we maintain that women and families should remain free to make these informed decisions, without professional or governmental pressures to continue or to terminate pregnancies. With this in mind, we examine a number of potential trends that could interfere with this freedom and suggest ways to protect choice in a changing healthcare environment.

Prenatal identification of disability, without an intervention that will change the health of the developing fetus, creates a moral dilemma for the mother. She can choose to continue with the pregnancy, given prevailing perceptions of the burdens on the child, society, and family, or she can terminate the fetus solely because the child will be born with a disability.

Think of the pain exhibited by the woman in the poem, 'I feel so cheated', with which we begin this chapter. The shattered dreams portrayed in the poem make clear societal expectations of the 'normal' or 'desirable' child—one who has no physical or intellectual impediment to socially desired achievement. Even beyond the absence of disability, the 'ideal' child in much of today's United States is perceived as brilliant, good-looking, a high academic achiever, and with aptitudes for the arts or sports or both. The perception of being cheated is reinforced by prominent members of the medical profession. One medical textbook describes the dilemma of parents facing decisions about prenatal testing and abortion; these parents are affected by the 'burden of having defective children...If they elect to continue the pregnancy, they face five or more months of agonized waiting and a defective child at the end...In the end they must reconcile themselves to the disappointment of having had a defective fetus or child, and the unfulfilled hope for a normal child.'[31]

Abortion stirs much debate, but quite different questions are involved about the morality and legality of abortion itself that need not be addressed here. From within our pro-choice perspective, and that shared by many other disability rights advocates, the central issue is whether women should have unrestricted choice in reproductive decisions. Like other pro-choice advocates, we argue that at least within the first two trimesters of pregnancy, women should have the unfettered discretion to terminate the pregnancy for any reason. What is absent from the typical debate is a deeper question—is selective abortion based solely on a likely future disability of the child morally defensible?

Consider the following conversation that took place with one of the authors (LG) at a national conference on mental retardation. A young man with Down syndrome had just given a highly articulate speech to a group of professionals in which he thoughtfully demonstrated the importance of inclusion of all persons with disabilities in public life. 'You must be very proud of your son,' the mother was asked at lunchtime. She replied: 'I have great pride in my son, and I gain much joy from him.' The mother was asked about a hypothetical reproductive decision if she were again pregnant and prenatal testing showed the child would be born with Down syndrome. After a long pause she replied, 'I believe I would have an abortion.' 'How would your son feel about that decision?' 'He would be devastated.'

It must be an extraordinarily difficult moment for a mother to hear that her baby will be born with a significant disability. Yet this mother is already aware of the rewarding life of her son and receives great joy from him. Why would a deeply compassionate and caring mother make a conscious choice not to have a second child with Down syndrome? Her considerations may focus on the perceived quality of life of the child, the ridicule and stigma he or she may face in society, the personal and economic hardships on the family, or the wish for a child who would feel more like the nondisabled parent. Perhaps, despite the mother's appreciation of her son, she, too, feels 'cheated' of some kind of life experience and parental dream. Irrespective of the reasons for the mother's decision, the message inferred by her son with Down syndrome and other individuals with mental retardation is one the mother recognizes to be distressing. On a personal level, the child may feel that he or she is a burden, or a disappointment, and the family or society may be ridding itself of future disappointment and burden. The person with a disability might reasonably observe that this 'burden' is 'my life', and might wonder whether he or she can be accepted for who he or she is.

Feminist theory is largely divided on the issue of prenatal testing and selective abortion.[32] Some feminist theorists see emerging trends in prenatal testing as a means to further subordinate women,[33] while others argue that women have an obligation not to knowingly bring a child with a disability into the world.[34] Self-determination has always been highly prized by feminist theory.[35] If the woman has an entitlement to true unfettered choice, it is not for others to judge the moral sufficiency of her reasons for making that choice.[36] The US Constitution also requires that the state not impose an undue burden on a woman's reproductive decisions.[37] This certainly means that government could not ban abortions during the first two trimesters of pregnancy, and courts might bristle at the notion that the government could pick and choose among the reasons women give for their decisions.

The question arises, if women can choose abortion for _any_ reason and can abort _any_ fetus, does it necessarily follow that they can choose for a morally troubling reason having to do with the characteristics of a particular fetus? What is the moral consequence if a woman chooses to abort a fetus solely because of a single characteristic of the fetus, such as its likely sex, intelligence, appearance, or physical prowess? Imagine a world where prenatal screening informed parents, not only about the sex of the child, but also whether she is likely to be excessively shy, short in stature, obese, or whether she might be depressed or develop physical and cognitive deficits. Put in more concrete terms, if a woman aborts a fetus for no reason other than a prenatal diagnosis that the child may be born blind, deaf, intellectually disabled, or infected with HIV, should such a decision be subjected to moral scrutiny? If so, what moral differences would there be regarding preferences for boys rather than girls or for the nondisabled rather than the disabled? If disability matters, what level of disability becomes morally relevant? If women's decisions should not be subjected to moral scrutiny, would a selective abortion decision based on preferences for _enhanced_ physical or mental attributes, such as higher intelligence or stronger physical capacity, matter? Should we 'draw lines' around permissible and impermissible prenatal tests that could be developed or offered as standard components of prenatal care?[38]

It may be because these moral judgments are so hard to make that society must place trust in a woman to make individual choices with her family and physician. Even if we disagreed with her choice we might decide not to compel a woman to have, or not to have, an abortion. For those who agree with this position, and even those who would themselves choose to abort a fetus diagnosed with a disabling condition, there remains something disturbing about a world where such decisions are made absent any rules of professional practice or moral guidance. Set aside for a moment visions of a world peopled by a genetically flawless, homogenous super race, or even a world without disability, to consider some of the possible, or even likely, outcomes for families, people who have disabilities, and efforts at social inclusion of all human beings with their diverse attributes.

V. ECONOMIC AND COMMERCIAL INFLUENCES ON PARENTAL AND PHYSICIAN DECISIONS

Already, women face pressure from both family members and society not to bring a child with a disability into this world, and these pressures are only likely to increase in the future. As tests designed to screen for fetal impairments become less expensive and more widely available, health insurance or managed care organizations may perceive a new opportunity to reduce health care costs. By mandating testing as a condition of insurance coverage and/or refusing to pay for the birth or health care costs of a child born with a disability, these organizations could further pressure women to make reproductive choices that are already morally troubling. Theoretically, the choice would remain with the woman or couple, but their decision will necessarily be influenced by the increased financial pressure that denial of coverage would mean.

Consider also the practices of pharmaceutical companies marketing prenatal tests, which may serve to increase societal pressure to avoid the birth of a child with a disability. Increasingly, pharmaceutical companies are trying to target the ultimate consumer of pharmaceutical products and services—the patient. This is done largely through direct advertising in television, radio, and print media. This raises concern because such advertising may influence popular attitudes and because the role of the physician is minimized. Again, the ability of a woman or couple to make a well-reasoned moral judgment may be influenced by outside forces. This is particularly disconcerting as we improve our ability to detect conditions that were previously considered minor. It is possible that we will someday be able to tell which children will be uncoordinated or have severe adolescent acne. If pharmaceutical companies can convince us that we should test and abort for these characteristics, there will inevitably be those who make the decision to avoid the birth of a child with such conditions.[39]

We have previously said that the role of the physician should be neutral, but this too may change. Physicians are susceptible to cost-cutting pressures in an environment of intense economic competition. Managed care organizations have a strong incentive to reduce the number of infants born with costly acute or chronic conditions. These organizations may develop practice guidelines that encourage physicians to offer prenatal testing and directive reproductive counseling. A physician's income, for example, may be linked to the number of patients in her practice who are tested and counseled. Because physicians have considerable influence over patient decisions, their potential loss of neutrality will likely influence the reproductive decisions of individuals. Rather than the ideal situation in which a physician helps her patient make a decision about whether to conceive or carry a fetus to term, we may increasingly see physicians subtly shaping decisions. We are already familiar with research on genetic counseling that indicates the biases genetic counselors bring to their work in terms of the information they give to prospective parents about raising children with particular disabling traits.[40]

Physician behavior may also be influenced by the threat of 'wrongful birth' or 'wrongful life' suits. In a wrongful birth suit the parents of a child born with a disability sue the physician in charge of prenatal care for failing to offer preconception or prenatal tests that could have alerted them to the potential disability. In a wrongful life suit, lawyers bring suit on behalf of the child herself, alleging that the physician's failure to offer testing or warn of the 'risk' of disability caused her to be born into a 'life of suffering'.[41] While the courts are split on the issue of whether wrongful birth or wrongful life is even a recognizable claim[42] and some states have banned such suits,[43] there are courts which have gone so far as to permit recovery for the full cost of raising a child with a disability and the emotional damages suffered from giving birth to the child.[44] Implicit in both wrongful birth and wrongful life suits is the idea that the parents would have chosen to abort the affected fetus. In a wrongful life suit the alleged wrong is literally the existence of the child bringing the suit. While courts are reluctant to announce that being born with a disability is worse than not being born at all, their rhetoric may still be harsh, describing the birth of a 'severely deformed baby' as 'an unpleasant and aversive event'.[45] The communication about the disaster of and distaste for a child with a disability is powerful, and the cost of litigation is high. To avoid such suits physicians may more frequently offer testing and may emphasize the negative aspects of having a child with a disability.[46]

VI. PROFESSIONAL, SOCIETAL, AND GOVERNMENTAL INFLUENCES ON PARENTAL AND PHYSICIAN DECISIONS

Health care professionals and the government possess many ways, both subtle and blatant, to influence the reproductive decisions of parents. These range from public health practices, policies, guidelines, and funding decisions to coercion about screening, reproductive counseling, sterilization, and abortion. The US Public Health Service, state health departments, and professional organizations (eg, the American Medical Association or the American Academy of Pediatrics) can strongly affect physician and patient behavior by issuing recommendations under the rubric of public health prevention or sound clinical practice. Health authorities may recommend routine offering of prenatal tests to all patients in certain settings (eg, acute care hospitals or maternity wards), in select populations (eg, testing for Tay Sachs among Ashkenazi Jews or sickle cell among African-Americans) or more generally (eg, cystic fibrosis among couples planning a pregnancy).[47] If testing is recommended in the absence of therapeutic interventions, government and or medicine appear to condone, and even encourage, families to avoid the birth of infants with specific disabilities. Decisions of public health authorities to recommend or make available prenatal screening to a broad population send powerful messages about the disutility of those with disabilities.

Governmental or professional recommendations may also focus on reproductive counseling. Reproductive counseling can be seen merely as the right of prospective parents to know the probabilities that their child would be born with discrete genetic or other conditions. An implicit component of carrier testing is that it enables individuals to avoid conception and the birth of infants with disabilities. Reproductive counseling can be neutral, allowing each couple to make decisions for themselves, or it can be directive, emphasizing the burdens of a child with a disability. The more that government or professional societies recommend directive reproductive counseling, the more systematically society will 'screen out' children with disabilities. Significant reform of prenatal testing and counseling procedures is discussed in many statements by disability groups and by recent bioethics working groups that have examined the disability rights critique of prenatal testing, and we support the spirit of these recommendations.[48]

Governmental or professional influences on sterilization and abortion decisions are, of course, more controversial, and personal decisions of these kinds are constitutionally protected.[49] Yet, professional advice to women and governmental funding decisions can affect even the most intimate and personal decisions. A friend of one of the authors (DJ), when pregnant with her first child, was advised to undergo amniocentesis after an AFP test indicated the possibility that the child might be born with Down syndrome. This woman refused testing because she knew the results would not alter her decision to continue the pregnancy; however, she felt pressured by state health care personnel not only to undergo testing, but also to terminate the pregnancy if this condition was diagnosed, and she believed that other women in the same circumstances might easily succumb to such pressure. This story is corroborated by some empirical research on parents' experiences of contact with professionals after a diagnosis of fetal impairment.[50] Even more troublesome, it would not be difficult to envisage Medicaid or welfare benefits being conditioned on reproductive decisions of women. Already, laws have been adopted to limit welfare payments to teen mothers or women who continue to have children.[51] Women might in the future lose certain benefits if they decide to refuse prenatal diagnosis and selective abortion or they knowingly give birth to an infant with a disability.

Explicitly coercive powers over reproductive freedom are even less tolerated—constitutionally and ethically. As the public, legislatures, and the courts continue to struggle over the morality and legality of abortion, there may be calls to limit the practice except in such instances as avoiding the births of 'defective' children; or, the time limits for legal abortions might be cut back with exceptions given for selective abortions. We agree with other commentators that tolerating more leeway in abortions to avoid giving birth to children with disabilities than exists for abortion decisions for other reasons would indeed discriminate against people with disability and could be seen to directly contravene the purposes of the Americans with Disabilities Act.[52] Yet government could theoretically introduce compulsory prenatal testing or even forced sterilization. Instances of compulsory screening and sterilization, although rare, have been implemented in the name of improving the human condition.[53] The eugenicists backing compulsory sterilization laws in the early twentieth century believed strongly that undesirable traits had a genetic etiology and hoped to eradicate criminals, 'dependents', the feeble minded, the insane, and almost every category of disability then known.[54] They successfully enacted laws that resulted in the sterilization of tens of thousands of individuals characterized as mentally retarded or mentally ill.[55] Some countries continue in their use of compulsion to reduce the number of infants born with disabilities. China, for example enacted a law on maternal and infant health care that included a compulsory premarital medical examination designed to detect serious genetic diseases and a variety of mental disorders. Those couples that test positive for one of these diseases or disorders must refrain from marrying or undergo compulsory long-term contraception or sterilization. Prenatal testing is also compulsory and couples may be forced to terminate a pregnancy when one of the prohibited disorders is detected.[56]

VII. DIVERSITY IN HUMAN POPULATIONS AND RESPECT FOR PERSONS WITH DISABILITY

Studies in the United States do show a decrease in the prevalence at birth of certain disorders since the introduction of prenatal screening. The CDC reports that the prevalence of spina bifida was reduced by as much as 30% between 1985 and 1994 in some states,[57] and there has been a significant decrease in the prevalence of Down syndrome in infants born to mothers over the age of 35.[58] Similar decreases have been reported in other countries as well. In Australia, increases in AFP screening and amniocentesis resulted in a 60% decrease in Down syndrome; in Cuba, AFP screening and ultrasound monitoring have resulted in a 90% decrease in the prevalence of neural tube defects; and in Montreal, Canada, carrier screening for Tay Sachs and betathalassemia has resulted in a 90% to 95% decrease in the incidence of these two diseases.[59] While some of these decreases may be attributable to new knowledge about the dietary needs of pregnant women, specifically the use of folic acid to reduce neural tube defects, at least part of the decrease is attributable to genetic testing and pregnancy termination. In a study in Edinburgh, Scotland, screening for cystic fibrosis resulted in the termination of all eight identified affected fetuses, and a Russian study reported that all twenty-five fetuses diagnosed with lysosomal storage diseases were aborted.[60] It is not difficult to conceive of substantial reductions in the prevalence of an array of preventable disabilities in the future. Given the scientific and social imperative to prevent disease and disability, it is important to ask what effect significant reductions in the prevalence of persons with disability would have on humanity. We recognize that our observations are speculative and not based on empirical research.

Is there inherent importance in maintaining diversity in physical and mental capacities in society? Diversity has no agreed upon social meaning, and there are likely to be sharp differences of opinion as to the value of, say, persons with lower than average intelligence and the ability to learn. To some, diversity evokes Darwinian principles of evolution that operated to generate the species: variation, competition, and selection. Those who hold this view may see no social advantage to continued thriving of all persons with disability. We disagree with this 'Darwinian' view. Society should respect diversity in all forms and value the experiences and contributions of all its members. Society may not *need* disability; it can regret that disability occurs, while respecting people with disabilities and valuing the contributions they make to society. They make such contributions neither because of, nor in spite of having disabilities, but simply because they have other human qualities of importance.

A substantial reduction in the number of people with disabilities could adversely affect persons with disabilities themselves as well as wider society. Persons with disabilities might reasonably feel their political position threatened by the pressure put on prospective parents to avert disability. Decisions to avoid the birth of an infant *because* of possible disability appear to rank their lives lower than those of nondisabled children because they are different from the majority; the disabled population and their supporters may fear that society will reduce its commitment to meeting the goals of inclusion embodied in the Americans with Disabilities Act, the Work Incentives Improvement Act, and the recently renewed laws mandating public education for children with disabilities. Society, moreover, gives a mixed message if, on the one hand, it proscribes disability discrimination and, on the other, tolerates or encourages, the birth of fewer persons with disability. The positive self-image of persons with disabilities may be hard to maintain in a world where they know that science and social policy urge women to end pregnancies based on diagnosis of a disabling trait. Such people as are born with or acquire disabilities may find greater difficulties of social acceptance, toleration, and accommodation.

Along with these concerns for everyone with a disability is yet another frightening possibility: a change in the demographics of disability. Prenatal screening is expensive, and many Americans do not have health insurance to cover such a service. These individuals are effectively unable to make the same reproductive decisions that people with insurance make, and consequently, they have a higher likelihood of giving birth to a child with a disability. The long-term effects of this may be an increasing number of persons with disabilities born into poverty. In addition to the fact that poverty can increase the adverse consequences of disability for children and their families, greater proportions of the disabled population who are poor, or who are people of color, could mean the loss of political power and economic support that has come to the aid of the disabled population based on the celebrity status of an individual or family member who uses wealth and access to power to improve life for others with disabilities.

On a global scale the change may be much greater. Eighty percent of the world's population lives in resource-poor countries. The majority of people in these countries have little access to basic health care services let alone sophisticated prenatal testing, and those who do are almost certainly among the elite minority. Lack of basic nutrition and health care have already caused an increasing number of persons with disabilities to be born in the developing world. China, for instance, is facing an epidemic of cretinism caused by a lack of iodine in the diet.[61] Prevention of this condition seems relatively simple—add trace amounts of iodine to table salt, but in a large developing country like China, even this is a major undertaking which has not yet been fully successful. To make matters worse, the same problems that make it difficult to implement this relatively simple prevention also make it difficult to provide adequate care for the people impaired by iodine deficiency. As women in developed countries increasingly utilize prenatal testing and base their reproductive decisions on the result, an increasing proportion of the world's disabled persons are likely to be born in developing countries that are ill-equipped to accommodate their needs.

Reduction in the number of persons with disabilities has not raised a substantial amount of ethical debate, especially where individuals are not compelled to make reproductive decisions. The probable explanation for this lack of concern is that the majority sees no moral problem in prevention of disability because physical and mental deficits are thought to be marked disadvantages. In fact, influential voices in the medical and genetics professions, and architects of the Human Genome Project acknowledge just such goals:

Human mating that proceeds without the use of genetic data about the risks of transmitting diseases will produce greater mortality and medical costs than if carriers of potentially deleterious genes are alerted to their carrier status and *encouraged* to mate with non-carriers or to use other reproductive strategies [emphasis added].[62]

Although some would argue that the success of the program should be judged solely by the effectiveness of the educational programs (ie, whether screenees understood the information), it is clear that prevention of [cystic fibrosis] is also, at some level, a measure of a screening program, since few would advocate expanding the substantial resources involved if very few families wish to avoid the disease.[63]

[W]e place most of our hopes for genetics on the use of antenatal diagnostic procedures, which increasingly will let us know whether a fetus is carrying a mutant gene that will seriously proscribe [*sic*] its eventual development into a functional human being. By terminating such pregnancies, the threat of horrific disease genes contributing to blight many families' prospects for future success can be erased.[64]

What if it were possible to prevent the conception or birth of a child with a characteristic that is, or ought to be regarded, as value neutral? Consider the practice of sex selection common in several parts of the world, particularly in countries like China and India with strong social and economic incentives to have male children, and likely to become increasingly common throughout the world with the introduction of techniques that permit sex selection prior to conception.[65] Although the ratio of male to female births is normally 105/100, sex selective practices in India and China have led to ratios as high as 140/100 in some regions.[66] This contributes both directly and indirectly to the oppression of women; male children continue to be favored and a decline in the number of women available for marriage leads to an increase in the abduction and sale of women for marriage.[67]

If we decide that sex selection is morally troublesome, why do we feel less morally concerned about selective reproductive decisions on the basis of disability? Perhaps it is, as we have just said, that society feels that disability always presents a hardship, while gender does not. One scholar told one of the authors (LG) that she did not see how averting additional disability in the population through prenatal or carrier screening was any different than achieving the same result by fortifying bread with iodine. We remain convinced that terminating an otherwise wanted pregnancy because of disability, or refusing to reproduce to avoid future disability, differs from other prevention strategies discussed throughout this article because it is these strategies that select *against* disability rather than promote health. Some health professionals fear that the increased use of genetic testing will lead to an increasing demand for 'quality control' and diminished tolerance of difference.[68] What if the adverse selection were made on grounds of perceived disabilities that had virtually no effect on the physical and mental functioning of the individual? Consider a social policy that militated strongly against the birth of persons of short stature caused, for example, by dwarfism. These individuals may have no significant physical or mental impairments apart from the social reaction to their physical appearance. Yet decisions might be taken at the individual or societal level not to give birth to infants 'at risk' for this condition. Here, society in general, and its medical professionals in particular, demonstrate no particular desire to morally challenge prospective parents who do not conceive or who terminate pregnancies because of the possibility of a child of short stature. It is worth asking what this moral vacuum means about the way society values persons with disabilities.

Indeed, many people that society has labeled disabled do not consider themselves disadvantaged at all. Consider the cultural meanings of the absence of hearing in the Deaf community. 'Deaf culture' is a sometimes controversial label for a segment of the Deaf community who conceive of deafness as a cultural difference rather than a disability. They see their use of sign language as merely a linguistic difference and believe that their inability to hear is no different than the average American's inability to comprehend Portuguese or Hungarian.[69] Members of Deaf culture are protective of what they see as their exclusive culture, and they are hurt by what they perceive as efforts to destroy this culture through integrated education or cochlear implants.[70] So strong is this sense of deafness as a culture rather than a disability that some deaf couples would prefer the birth of a deaf child and would make reproductive decisions accordingly.[71] Most hearing people would be shocked at the idea of rejecting a 'normal' child in favor of a deaf child, but is this preference to have a 'child like me' any different for a deaf couple than for a hearing couple?[72] We take no stand on whether deafness should be seen as a culture instead of a disability, or on whether parents should withhold interventions from children that could provide the ability to hear, but we do feel that true reproductive choice must tolerate selecting for, as well as against disability; nonetheless, we argue that basing reproductive decisions upon the presence of disability, using disability as a reason to have a child as well as not to have one, makes disability more defining of identity than we see as desirable.[73]

VIII. COST CONSIDERATIONS IN PREVENTION AND THE IMPLICATIONS FOR PERSONS WITH DISABILITIES

Cost considerations in the health care setting are charged with controversy. To some, taking account of cost in health care decisions is tantamount to health care rationing. Others may object to any balancing of the productivity of the life to be preserved with the social and economic costs of the treatment; the assumption that the value of a human life can be quantified is anathema.

But while many, including the authors of this chapter, balk at the idea of commodifying human beings, this does not obviate the need to include economic factors in our decision-making calculus. Every day businesses, government agencies, charitable institutions, and individuals—whether they are aware of it or not—make decisions based in part on cost considerations. We therefore discuss when and how cost considerations should figure into disability prevention.

Health care is a scarce resource; there is not enough of it for everyone to have all they want or need. This scarcity has driven up the price of health care. Americans spend approximately $1 trillion on health care each year. In the United States, health care expenditures now account for roughly 15% of GNP.[74] While health care systems differ among countries, providing quality health care is an expensive proposition under any system, and everyone is looking for a way to reduce health care costs. One of the fundamental justifications for preventive medicine is the idea that it is more cost effective to prevent diseases or disabilities than it is to treat them after they occur. But because health care resources are so scarce, decisions must be made as to how they will be allocated between prevention and treatment. Furthermore, within either of these categories, decisions must be made among different projects, methods, and strategies. All of these decisions are based on cost. There is nothing inherently wrong with this, but caution must be exercised in determining how the costs and benefits involved in a decision are quantified. Fundamental to this discussion is the idea that one human being cannot be treated as more valuable than another because of the absence or presence of a particular disability or personal trait.

There are few moral issues raised by cost-effectiveness considerations in secondary prevention programs, provided these programs make no assumptions about the quality or value of an individual life. If secondary prevention is designed to improve the functioning of and opportunities available to people, its value ought to be self-evident. Of course, the decision of whether or not to accept treatment deemed cost effective must still be left up to the individual. We believe diversity should be accommodated and even embraced when it occurs.

Primary prevention presents more vexing questions. Prenatal diagnosis followed by selective abortion is highly cost effective. For example, consider that amniocentesis costs between $1,000 and $3,000 and may enable a woman to avoid the birth of a child with spina bifida whose medical costs may be more than $100,000 for the first year of life alone.[75] On an individual basis, when a woman or couple has to make the decision whether to undergo amniocentesis or to abort a fetus diagnosed with spina bifida, cost alone provides a distorted guide. Missing from the calculus is the social, familial, and eventual economic contribution of the person who will have spina bifida. However, cost-effectiveness analysts frequently fail to include this value in their calculations; they include only the economic costs associated with the averted birth of an affected child, failing to recognize the value of that child's life.[76] When decisions are made not on an individual basis, but rather by profit driven administrators, or even those truly seeking to maximize the greatest good for the greatest number, cost frequently becomes the driving factor, materially guiding many of the decisions discussed in this chapter.

The looming specter of genetic enhancement also raises economic issues that should be included in this discussion. In the United States, where healthcare is viewed as a commodity, genetic testing, selective abortion, and fetal gene therapy could all be used someday to create a profitable market for the 'designer child'.[77] The concern here is that scare health care resources will be diverted from those most in need,[78] while tolerance for those same individuals will be decreased.

IX. CONCLUSION

This chapter has examined the issues surrounding disability prevention, especially primary prevention, and the potential impact that it may have on persons with disabilities and on society as a whole. There is no easy solution to guarantee that disability prevention does not alter society and the role of persons with disabilities within society. The decision whether or not to give birth to a child with a disability is complex, and we respect the rights and needs of women to make such decisions based on assessments of their own situations. But these decisions are not value-neutral, and society ought to think rigorously about the moral dimensions of selective abortion. Certainly, a woman's choice should be informed by balanced information about the opportunities, potential, and joys of children and adults with disabilities.

Currently, a woman's reproductive decisions are influenced by a number of subtle and not so subtle pressures. These pressures may manifest themselves in the form of moral arguments, aesthetic preferences, or economic constraints. They may come from a woman's family, society, her physician, or the government. Given that these pressures exist, how then do we ensure that a woman's choice is her own—a choice based on deliberate moral reasoning and not a concession to those who create these pressures?

There are no guarantees, but we, as a society, can try to insulate these decisions from outside pressures. For instance, by ensuring that government policies and professional guidelines remain neutral, expressing neither a preference for nor discouraging selective abortion, we remove some pressure. We can also try to provide women with balanced information on the realities of having a family member with a disability. This may help to alleviate some of the misconceptions and stereotypes which enter into the decision-making process. Finally, we can continue to integrate persons with disabilities into mainstream society. In a society that is more accepting of persons with disabilities we would expect more respect for the contributions each person makes and more empathy for the societal changes that will ease their full inclusion and maximize their contributions. If this is true, reproductive decisions may not be any easier to make, but they may be a truer product of deliberative moral reasoning rather than choices dictated by others.

NOTES

1. JWS, 'I feel so cheated...', in J Finnegan, *Shattered Dreams, Lonely Choices: Birthparents of Babies with Disabilities Talk about Adoption* (Westport, Conn: Bergin & Garvey, 1993) 9, 10.
2. J Retsinas, 'Impact of Prenatal Technology on Attitudes Towards Disabled Infants' in D Wertz (ed), *Research in the Sociology of Healthcare* (Westport, Conn: JAI Press, 1991) 89, 90.
3. RM Cook-Deegan, 'The Genesis of the Human Genome Project' [1991] *Molecular Genetic Medicine* 1, 1–75.
4. Americans with Disabilities Act 1990, Pub L No 101-336.
5. W Gilbert, 'A Vision of the Grail' in DJ Kevles and L Hood (eds), *The Code of Codes: Scientific and Social Issues in the Human Genome Project* (Cambridge, Mass: Harvard Univ Press, 1992); L Hood, 'Biology and Medicine in the Twenty-first Century' in *The Code of Codes*; R Hubbard and E Wald, *Exploding the Gene Myth* (Boston: Beacon Press, 1993).
6. J West (ed), *The Americans with Disabilities Act: From Policy to Practice* (New York: Milbank Memorial Fund, 1991); LO Gostin and HA Beyer, *Implementing the Americans with Disabilities Act: Rights and Responsibilities of All Americans* (Baltimore, London: Paul H Brookes, 1993).
7. E Goffman, *Stigma: Notes on the Management of Spoiled Identity* (Anglewood Cliffs, NJ: Prentice-Hall Press, 1963).
8. *Websters' Third New International Dictionary, Unabridged* (1986) 642.
9. ibid.
10. *Oxford American Dictionary* (1980) 295.
11. GL Albrecht, KD Seelman, and M Bury, 'Introduction: The Formation of Disability Studies' in GL Albrecht, KD Seelman, and M Bury (eds), *Handbook of Disability Studies* (Thousand Oaks, Calif: Sage Publications, Inc, 2001) 5.
12. TR Parmenter, 'Intellectual Disabilities—*Quo Vadis?*' in GL Albrecht, KD Seelman, and M Bury (eds), *Handbook of Disability Studies* (Thousand Oaks, Calif: Sage Publications, Inc, 2001) 270–271.
13. Albrecht, Seelman, and Bury (n 11 above) 3, 4.
14. NL Daniels, *Just Health Care: Studies in Philosophy and Health Policy* (Cambridge: Cambridge Univ Press, 1985) 27.

15. IK Zola, 'The Sleeping Giant in Our Midst: Redefining "Persons with Disabilities"' in LO Gostin and HA Beyer (eds), *Implementing the Americans with Disabilities Act: Rights and Responsibilities of All Americans* (Baltimore, London: Paul H Brookes, 1993) xix.

16. US Department of Health and Human Services, *Healthy People 2010* (Washington, DC, 2000).

17. PE Taschner, N de Vos, and MH Breuning, 'Rapid Detection of the Major Deletion in the Batten Disease Gene CLN3 by Allele Specific PCR' (Nov 1997) 34 *Journal of Medical Genetics* 11, 955–956; SA Rowland, A Dodd, AL Roche, S Manilal, MA Kennedy, DM Becroft, S Tonkin, C Chapman, and DR Love, 'DNA-Based Diagnostics for Adrenoleukodystrophy in a Large New Zealand Family' (Aug 1996) *New Zealand Medical Journal* 109, 312–315; H Kakinoki, K Kobayashi, H Terazono, Y Nagata, and T Saheki, 'Mutations and DNA Diagnoses of Classical Citrullinemia' (1997) 9 *Human Mutation* 3, 250–259; CM Eng, C Schechter, J Robinowitz, G Fulop, T Burgert, B Levy, R Zinberg, and RJ Desnick, 'Prenatal Genetic Carrier Testing Using Triple Disease Screening' (Oct 1997) 278 *Journal of the American Medical Association* 15, 1268–1272.

18. T Powledge, 'Genetic Screening as a Political and Social Development' in D Bergsma (ed), *Ethical, Social and Legal Dimensions of Screening for Human Genetic Disease* (Miami: Symposia Specialists, 1974) 25–26; CF Whitten, 'Sickle-Cell Programming: An Imperiled Promise' (1973) *New England Journal of Medicine* 288, 316–319.

19. American Society of Human Genetics Ad Hoc Committee on Cystic Fibrosis Carrier Screening, 'Statement of the American Society of Human Genetics on Cystic Fibrosis Screening' (1992) *American Journal of Human Genetics* 51, 1443; DJ Brock, 'Prenatal Screening for Cystic Fibrosis: 5 Years' Experience Reviewed' (1996) 347 *Lancet* 8995, 148–150.

20. 'CDC: Provide HIV Counseling and Voluntary Testing to all Pregnant Women' (5 September 1995) *Hospital Health Network* 69, 8.

21. Institute of Medicine, *The Future of Public Health* (Washington, DC, 1988).

22. US Department of Health and Human Services (n 16 above).

23. M Roig-Franzia, '"My Kids Were Used as Guinea Pigs": Lead Paint Study Adds to Debate on Research' (25 August 2001) *The Washington Post* A01.

24. A Asch, 'Reproductive Technology and Disability' in S Cohen and N Taub (eds), *Reproductive Laws for the 1990s* (Clifton, NJ: Humana Press, 1989) 69–124; A Asch, 'Prenatal Diagnosis and Selective Abortion: A Challenge to Practice and Policy' (Nov 1999) 89/11 *American Journal of Public Health* 1649–1657; C Borthwick, *Prevention of Disablement* (Melbourne: Collins Dove, 1994); C Newell, 'The Social Nature of Disability, Disease, and Genetics: A Response to Gillam, Persson, Holtug, Draper and Chadwick' (1999) 25 *Journal of Medical Ethics* 172–175.

25. BK Zimmerman, 'Human Germline Therapy: The Case for its Development and Use' (Dec 1991) 16/6 *Journal of Medical Philosophy* 593–612.

26. S Squires, 'For Sonograms, An Added Dimension: Composite Fetal Images Wow Parents with Their Startling Clarity' *Washington Post* (11 September 2001) HE-1.

27. C Powell, 'The Current State of Prenatal Genetic Testing in the United States' in E Parens and A Asch (eds), *Prenatal Testing and Disability Rights*

(Washington, DC: Georgetown University Press, 2000) 44–53; P Hedera, JA Williamson, S Rainer, D Alvarado, T Tukel, M Apak, and J Fink, 'Prenatal Diagnosis of Hereditary Spastic Paraplegia' (2001) 21 *Prenatal Diagnosis* 202–206; T Antoniadi, A Pampanos, and MB Petersen, 'Prenatal Diagnosis of Prelingual Deafness: Carrier Testing and Prenatal Diagnosis of the Common GJB2 35delG Mutation' (2001) 21 *Prenatal Diagnosis* 10–13; JL Tolmie, HR Davidson, HM May, K McIntosh, JS Paterson, and B Smith, 'The Prenatal Exclusion Test for Huntington's Disease: Experience in the West of Scotland, 1986–1993' (Feb 1995) 32 *Journal of Medical Genetics* 97–101.

28. A Rosenzweig, H Watkins, DS Hwang, M Miri, W McKenna, TA Traill, JG Seidman, and E Seidman, 'Preclinical Diagnosis of Familial Hypertrophic Cardiomyopathy by Genetic Analysis of Blood Lymphocytes' (19 Dec 1991) 325 *New England Journal of Medicine* 1753–1760; MA Nance, EA Sevenich, and LJ Schut, 'Knowledge of Genetics and Attitudes toward Genetic Testing in Two Hereditary Ataxia (SCA 1) Kindreds' (15 Sept 1994) 54 *American Journal of Medical Genetics* 242–248; H Shimuzu, H Niizeki, R Aozaki, R Kawaguchi, K Hikiji, and T Nishikawa, 'Prenatal Diagnosis of Oculocutaneous Albinism by Analysis of the Fetal Tyrosinase Gene' (July 1994) 103 *Journal of Investigative Dermatology* 104–106; Committee on Genetics, 'Prenatal Genetic Diagnosis for Pediatricians' (1994) 93 *Pediatrics* 1015; JL Tolmie, HR Davidson, HM May, K McIntosh, JS Paterson, and B Smith, 'The Prenatal Exclusion Test for Huntington's Disease: Experience in the West of Scotland, 1986–1993' (Feb 1995) 32 *Journal of Medical Genetics* 97–101; M Levy, Y Pirson, P Simon, B Boudailliez, H Nivet, N Rance, A Moynot, M Broyer, and JP Grunfeld, 'Evaluation in Patients with Alport Syndrome of Knowledge of the Disease and Attitudes toward Prenatal Diagnosis' (Oct 1994) 42 *Clinical Nephrology* 211–220; T Furu, H Kaariainen, EM Sankila, and R Norio, 'Attitudes towards Prenatal Diagnosis and Selective Abortion among Patients with Retinitis Pigmentosa or Choroideremia as well as among their Relatives' (Mar 1993) 43 *Clinical Genetics* 160–165; as of the year 2000, up-to-date information about capacity of prenatal testing can be found in CM Powell, 'The Current State of Prenatal Genetic Testing in the United States' in E Parens and A Asch (eds), (n 27 above), 44–53.

29. United Nations, *Universal Declaration of Human Rights*, GA Res 217A, 3d Sess, UN Doc No A/810 Preamble (1948).

30. E Parens and A Asch, 'The Disability Rights Critique of Prenatal Genetic Testing: Reflections and Recommendations' (Sept–Oct 1999) 29/5 *Hastings Center Report* S1–S22, S2.

31. DD Weaver, *Catalog of Prenatally Diagnosed Conditions* (Baltimore: Johns Hopkins, 1989) xvi.

32. KH Rothenberg and EJ Thomson (eds), *Women and Prenatal Testing: Facing the Challenges of Genetic Technology* (Columbus: Ohio State Univ Press, 1994); A Asch and G Geller, 'Feminism, Bioethics, and Genetics' in SM Wolf (ed), *Feminism and Bioethics: Beyond Reproduction* (New York: Oxford Univ Press, 1996) 318–350.

33. EE Culpepper, 'Uncovering Patriarchal Agendas and Exploring Women Oriented Values' in HB Holmes, BB Hoskins, and M Gross (eds), *The Custom Made Child? Women-Centered Perspectives* (Clifton, NJ: Humana Press, 1981) 301.

34. LM Purdy, 'Genetic Disease: Can Having Children Be Immoral?' in JD Arras and NK Rhoden (eds), *Ethical Issues in Modern Medicine* (3rd edn, Mountain View, Calif: Mayfield Publishing Co, 1989).

35. SR Peterson, 'The Politics of Prenatal Diagnosis: A Feminist Ethical Analysis' in HB Holmes, BB Hoskins, and M Gross (eds), *The Custom Made Child? Women-Centered Perspectives* (Clifton, NJ: Humana Press, 1981) 101.

36. Asch and Geller (n 32 above) 318–350; MB Mahowald, *Genes, Women, Equality* (New York: Oxford Univ Press, 2000); Rothenberg and Thompson (eds) (n 32 above).

37. *Planned Parenthood v Casey* 505 US 833 (1992).

38. JR Botkin, 'Line Drawing: Developing Professional Standards for Prenatal Diagnostic Services' in E Parens and A Asch (eds), *Prenatal Testing and Disability Rights* (Washington, DC: Georgetown University Press, 2000) 288–307.

39. Contrasting views on the wisdom of drawing lines between permissible and impermissible prenatal tests can be found throughout the book *Prenatal Testing and Disability Rights* and are summarized in E Parens and A Asch, 'The Disability Rights Critique of Prenatal Genetic Testing: Reflections and Recommendations' in E Parens and A Asch (eds), (n 38 above), 3–43.

40. A Lippman and B Wilfond, 'Twice-told Tales: Stories about Genetic Disorders' (1992) 51 *American Journal of Human Genetics* 936–937; DC Wertz, 'Medical Genetics: Ethical and Social Issues' in WT Reich (ed), *Encyclopedia of Bioethics* (New York: Macmillan, 1995) 1652–1656.

41. PN Ossorio, 'Prenatal Testing and the Courts' in E Parens and A Asch (eds), (n 38 above), 308–333.

42. MG Kelly, 'The Rightful Position in "Wrongful Life" Actions' (1991) 40 *Hastings LJ* 505–590.

43. Minn Stat Ann §145.424(2) (West 1989) (eliminating wrongful life and birth claims).

44. *Greco v United States* 893 P2d 345 (Nev 1995) (The mother of a child with Spina Bifida, paraplegia, and mental retardation was permitted to recover for the full cost of raising her child with no offset for the emotional benefit of the child's birth.)

45. ibid.

46. Ossario (n 41 above) 308–333.

47. 'Genetic Testing for Cystic Fibrosis' (14–16 April 1997) 15/4 NIH Consensus Statement Online 1-37 at http://odp.od.nih.gov/consensus/cons/106/106_intro.htm (accessed 8 May 2002).

48. National Down Syndrome Congress, 'Position Statement on Prenatal Testing and Eugenics: Families' Rights and Needs' (1994) at http://members.carol.net/~ndsc/eugenics.html (accessed 20 September 2001); Little People of America, 'Position Statement on Genetic Discoveries in Dwarfism' (1995) at http://www2.shore.net/~dkennedy/dwarfism_genetics.html (accessed 20 September 2001); Disabled Peoples' International, 'The Right to Live and to Be Different' paper presented at the DPI Conference on Disabled People, Bioethics and Human Rights (Solihull, UK, 2000); Parens and Asch (n 38 above) 3–43.

49. *Roe v Wade* 410 US 113 (1973); *Bellotti v Baird* 428 US 132 (1976); *Downs v Sawtelle* 574 F2d 1 (1st Cir 1978); *Avery v County of Burke* 660 F2d 111 (4th Cir 1981).

50. Parens and Asch (n 38 above) 3–43; N Press, 'Assessing the Expressive Character of Prenatal Testing: The Choices Made or the Choices Made Available?' in E Parens and A Asch (eds), (n 38 above), 214–233.

51. Personal Responsibility and Work Opportunity Reconciliation Act of 1996, Pub L No 104-193, 1996 HR 3734, s 103(a)(2)(A)–(D). Although the Act does not specifically mandate reduced payment to out-of-wedlock mothers, it conditions state receipt of bonuses on such a reduction.

52. MA Field, 'Killing "the Handicapped"—Before and After Birth' (1993) 16 *Harvard Women's LJ* 79–138.

53. *Buck v Bell* 130 SE 516 (Va 1925).

54. PA Lombardo, 'Medicine, Eugenics, and the Supreme Court: From Coercive Sterilization to Reproductive Freedom' (1996) 13 *J of Contemporary Health L and Policy* 1–25.

55. NM Glover and SJ Glover, 'Ethical and Legal Issues Regarding Selective Abortion of Fetuses with Down Syndrome' (Aug 1996) 34 *Mental Retardation* 207–214.

56. US Department of State, 'China Human Rights Practices, 1995' (1996) *Department of State Dispatch*.

57. JD Cragan, HE Roberts, LD Edmonds, and MJ Khoury, 'Surveillance for Anencephaly and Spina Bifida and the Impact of Prenatal Diagnosis—United States, 1985–1994' (1995) 44 *Morbidity and Mortality Report Weekly* SS-4, 1–13.

58. Centers for Disease Control and Prevention, 'Down Syndrome Prevalence at Birth—United States, 1983–1990' (1994) 43 *Morbidity and Mortality Report Weekly* 617–622.

59. T Cheffins, A Chan, EA Haan, E Ranieri, RG Ryall, RJ Keane, R Byron-Scott, H Scott, EM Gjerde, AM Nguyen, JH Ford, and S Sykes, 'The Impact of Maternal Serum Screening on the Birth Prevalence of Down's Syndrome and the Use of Amniocentesis and Chorionic Villus Sampling in South Australia' (Dec 2000) 107 *British Journal of Obstetrics and Gynaecology* 1453–1459; L Rodriguez, R Sanchez, J Hernandez, L Carrillo, J Oliva, and L Heredero, 'Results of 12 Years' Combined Maternal Serum Alpha-fetoprotein Screening and Ultrasound Fetal Monitoring for Prenatal Detection of Fetal Malformations in Havana City, Cuba' (Apr 1997) 17 *Prenatal Diagnosis* 301–304; JJ Mitchell, A Capua, C Clow, and CR Scrivner, 'Twenty-Year Outcome Analysis of Genetic Screening Programs for Tay-Sachs and Beta-thalassemia Disease Carriers in High Schools' (Oct 1996) 59 *American Journal of Human Genetics* 793–798.

60. DJ Brock, 'Prenatal Screening for Cystic Fibrosis: 5 Years' Experience Reviewed' (Jan 1996) 347 *Lancet* 148–150; XD Krasnopolskaya, TV Mirenburg, VS Akhunov, and EY Voskoboeva, 'Postnatal and Prenatal Diagnosis of Lysosomal Storage Diseases in the Former Soviet Union' (Feb 1997) 1093 *Wien Klin Wochenschr* 74–80.

61. PE Tyler, 'China Confronts Retardation of Millions Deficient in Iodine' (4 June 1996) *New York Times* A1.

62. US Congress, Office of Technology Assessment, *Mapping Our Genes* (1988) 84.

63. AL Beaudet, 'Carrier Screening for Cystic Fibrosis' (1990) 47 *American Journal of Human Genetics* 603.
64. JD Watson, 'President's Essay: Genes and Politics' (1996) *Annual Report Cold Spring Harbor* 19.
65. M Wadman, 'So You Want A Girl?' (19 February 2001) *Fortune* 174–182.
66. CW Dugger, 'Abortions in India Spurred by Sex Test Skew the Ratio against Girls' (22 April 2001) *New York Times*; J Pomfret, 'In China's Countryside, "It's a Boy!" Too Often' (29 May 2001) *Washington Post* A-1.
67. H Chu, 'In China, 7 Brides for 14 Brothers; A Male-Centered Tradition and a "One-Child" Policy have Created a Huge Demographic Imbalance. Trafficking in Women Is a Brisk Business' (14 February 2001) *Los Angeles Times* A-1.
68. B Rothman, 'Reproductive Technology and the Commodification of Life' in EH Baruch, J Seager, and AF D'Adamo (eds), *Embryos, Ethics and Women's Rights* (New York: Haworth Press, Inc, 1988) 95–100.
69. E Dolnick, 'Deafness as Culture' (Sept 1993) 272 *The Atlantic* 37–51.
70. C Milstone, 'Sound and Fury; Controversy over Cochlear Implants' (Mar 1996) 111 *Saturday Night* 2, 25(3).
71. TH Murray and E Livny, 'The Human Genome Project: Ethical and Social Implications' (Jan 1995) 83 *Bulletin of the Medical Librarian Association* 14–21; 'UK Couple "Choose" to Have Deaf Baby' (8 April 2002) BBC at http://news.bbc.co.uk/hi/english/health/newsid_1916000/1916462.stm (accessed 8 May 2002).
72. DS Davis, 'Genetic Dilemmas and the Child's Right to an Open Future' (1997) 27 *Hastings Center Report* 2, 7–15.
73. DS Davis, 'Cochlear Implants and the Claims of Culture? A Response to Lane and Grodin' (1997) 7/3 *Kennedy Institute of Ethics Journal* 253–258; for a discussion of disability as a component of identity, see A Asch, 'Why I Haven't Changed My Mind about Prenatal Diagnosis: Reflections and Refinements' in E Parens and A Asch (eds), *Prenatal Testing and Disability Rights* (Washington, DC: Georgetown University Press, 2000) 234–258.
74. PA Gorski, 'Caring Relationships: An Investment in Health?' (1 March 2000) *Public Health Reports* 144–150.
75. DT Morris, 'Cost Containment and Reproductive Autonomy: Prenatal Genetic Screening and the American Health Security Act of 1993' (1994) 20 *American Journal of Law and Medicine* 295–316.
76. TG Ganiats, 'Justifying Prenatal Screening and Genetic Amniocentesis Programs by Cost-Effectiveness Analyses: A Re-evaluation' (Jan 1996) 16 *Medical Decision Making* 45–50.
77. JC Fletcher and G Richter, 'Human Fetal Gene Therapy: Moral and Ethical Questions' (Aug 1996) 7 *Human Gene Therapy* 1605–1614.
78. JC Fletcher and G Richter, 'Ethical Issues of Perinatal Human Gene Therapy' (1996) 5 *Journal of Maternal-Fetal Medicine* 232–244.

13

Studying the Emerging Workforce

PETER BLANCK AND HELEN A. SCHARTZ

I. INTRODUCTION

Although there is great diversity of definitions, causes, conditions, and consequences of discrimination against persons with disabilities in employment and other aspects of daily life, there are fundamental themes that unite countries in their pursuit of policies to improve the social and economic status of persons with disabilities. The premise of this chapter is that comparative research is crucial to identifying individual, organizational, cultural, attitudinal, and legal themes necessary for the effective development of disability employment policies.

In the later part of the twentieth century, international initiatives such as the 1993 United Nations (UN) Resolution 48/96 established standards for the equalization of employment opportunities for persons with disabilities.[1] Prior to the 1993 Resolution, the 1971 and 1975 UN Resolutions regarding the rights of persons with intellectual disabilities helped to frame then emerging issues facing persons with disabilities in all parts of the world and at different economic and social levels in society.

In 1996, UN Resolution 50/144 further urged Member States to consider and study the legal, administrative, and policy measures required to implement prior standards recommended by the UN.[2] The pursuit of standards in disability policy reflected a new moral and political commitment by Member States toward equal opportunity for persons with disabilities throughout the world in the areas of employment, housing, transportation, and individual rights.[3]

The views herein reflect only those of the authors and not of any funding agency. This research was in part funded by grants to the first author from: US Department of Education, National Institute on Disability and Rehabilitation Research (1) Rehabilitation Research and Training Center (RRTC) on Workforce Investment and Employment Policy for Persons with Disabilities, Grant No H133B980042-99, (2) 'IT Works', Grant No H133A011803, and (3) 'Technology for Independence: A Community-Based Resource Center', Grant No H133A021801; and the University of Iowa College of Law Foundation. For related projects, see The Law, Health Policy and Disability Center website at http://www.its.uiowa.edu/law. For their helpful comments, we thank the editors of this chapter, and Lisa Clay and James Schmeling.

This chapter asserts that comparative analysis and research has played, and will increasingly assume, a significant role in informing policymakers and citizens of issues central to the development of national disability employment policies. Among the major preconditions for the equal participation in society of persons with disabilities as recognized by the UN is raising awareness about the rights, needs, and employment potential of persons with disabilities.[4]

To a large extent, there exists a lack of systematic comparative study of the complex issues surrounding disability employment policy formulation, implementation, and evaluation. Countries implementing antidiscrimination disability employment policies, such as the Americans with Disabilities Act in the United States, are at the forefront to examine and document the effects of this new generation of civil and human rights laws. This examination, whether based in economics, psychology, sociology, medicine, or law, will help to uncover central issues in designing, implementing, and improving disability employment policy.

In the United States presently, critical questions are being examined from multiple disciplinary perspectives about the composition, quality, and competitiveness of the American work force. What types of work skills will be needed for American employers to remain competitive in the United States and abroad? Will America's increasingly diversified and aging workforce include millions of persons with disabilities? What will be the characteristics and qualifications of the American workforce of persons with disabilities? What types of job training, technology, and accommodations will be available to that workforce? And, how will the changes that have occurred in the last quarter of the twentieth century in American disability, welfare, and health care policy affect that workforce?

These questions reflect a dramatic shift in emphasis over the past twenty-five years in American disability laws and policies, from a model of charity and compensation, to medical oversight, and then to civil rights.[5] The civil rights model that first began to influence American government policy toward disabilities in the 1970s conceptualized the disabled as a minority group entitled to the same hard-won legal protections for equality that emerged from the struggles of African Americans and women. Proposing disability as a social and cultural construct, the civil rights model focuses on the laws and practices that subordinate disabled persons.

The new civil rights model insists that government secure the equality of disabled persons by eliminating the legal, physical, economic, and social barriers that preclude their full involvement in society. Contemporary American employment policies and laws are focused on increasing the labor force participation of qualified persons with disabilities and reducing their dependence on government entitlement programs. American federal laws, such as the Workforce Investment Act of 1998 (WIA), the Ticket to Work and Work Incentives Improvement Act of 1999 (TWWIIA), and the Americans with Disabilities Act of 1990 (ADA), illustrate support for enhancing employment opportunities for working age adults with disabilities and preventing disability discrimination in the workplace.[6]

TWWIIA, for instance, expands the availability of health care coverage for individuals with disabilities so that US states may allow their disabled citizens with incomes over 250% of poverty level to 'buy into' governmental Medicaid health insurance programs if they are otherwise eligible for the Supplemental Security Income (SSI) program. In addition, TWWIIA established the Ticket to Work and Self-Sufficiency Program (TWSSP), in which participants use a 'ticket' or voucher to obtain employment services from employment networks ('ENs'). The goal of the ticket program is to give participants greater choice and control over the type of employment service and to foster competition and innovation among employment service providers. With similar goals of employment in mind, WIA establishes 'one stop' employment and job training centers across the country that ideally provide employment and other services to all individuals, including those with disabilities.

In American, as in comparative examinations, the primary way to assess whether disability employment laws and policies, such as the ADA or TWWIIA, are economically and socially beneficial is through assessment of information regarding their impact on persons with disabilities, and their families and employers.[7] Although researchers approach this question from distinct perspectives, policymakers, employers, and disabled individuals will gain a more complete perspective about the effects of these policies if information is gathered using a range of approaches from a variety of sources. In addition to providing breadth of information, assembling research from multiple disciplinary and comparative sources highlights different perspectives and assumptions in ways to reconcile apparently conflicting outcomes.

II. THE ROLE OF COMPARATIVE STUDY

To illustrate the importance of comparative study to the implementation of disability policy, this chapter presents findings from an investigation of employment of individuals with intellectual disabilities, conducted during early implementation of the Americans with Disabilities Act (ADA).[8] Begun in 1989,[9] the investigation follows the lives of more than 5,000 adults and children in Oklahoma with intellectual disabilities (primarily mental retardation) by collecting information on individual, economic, health, and legal measures from 1990 to 1999.[10]

Although dramatic changes in the United States and abroad have occurred in attitudes and behaviors toward individuals with disabilities in employment, governmental services, telecommunications, and public accommodations,[11] as mentioned, these changes have not been documented adequately. The documentation of these changes is necessary to determine if the integration and inclusion promises of laws like the ADA and TWWIIA have been fulfilled.[12] There is no denying that these initiatives warrant attention; they are comprehensive American laws addressing potential employment discrimination against one-fifth of the American population.[13] The ADA is the most significant US federal anti-discrimination law since the Civil Rights Act of 1964 outlawed racial discrimination.[14]

Those critical of the impact of the ADA and other disability employment laws and policies on the US labor market argue that there is little evidence that such initiatives have resulted in larger numbers of qualified persons with disabilities participating in the labor force.[15] Critics focus, for instance, on the costs of litigation associated with the ADA, and they point to the Act as the reason for the rise in complaints filed with the Equal Employment Opportunity Commission (EEOC), the federal agency responsible for enforcing the law.[16] Business failures and job losses were predicted to result from application of the ADA to small employers.[17]

Much may be learned about our society and its laws through study of the principles underlying the ADA. Moreover, identifying the ADA's strengths and weaknesses informs other nations as they implement similar legislation securing equal employment opportunity for persons with disabilities. But not only is communicating employment information about people with disabilities critical to ADA implementation, it is central to the study of broader employment policy issues facing persons with disabilities throughout the world.[18] Certainly, the ADA offers only one model for defining the rights and remedies necessary for achieving non-discrimination in employment and other aspects of daily life.[19] Documenting ADA implementation, however, will inform policymakers in other countries who are designing related initiatives about the advantages, disadvantages, and practical issues of implementing such initiatives.[20]

A. Purpose of the US Investigation

The purpose of the investigation presented in this chapter is threefold: first, to foster a dialogue about American disability law and policy; second, to raise awareness about the lives and capabilities of people with intellectual disabilities; and third, to foster comparative study of disability initiatives by providing an information base to improve communication.[21] These goals are consistent with ones established by the UN to ensure that persons with disabilities hold an equal place in society.

Comparative research raises other questions that promote the development of disability employment policy.[22] In the present investigation, such questions include:

- How does a society define a disability (both legally and socially)?
- How does a society define the importance of work for all persons?
- For purposes of disability law and policy, what constitutes a limitation on the ability to work?
- How do different types of disabilities affect an individual's ability to work or perform daily life tasks?
- How do the living environments (eg, physical, programmatic, and technological aspects) of individuals with disabilities support or limit the ability to attain and retain work?
- In what ways do individual empowerment strategies, such as self-advocacy, enhance workplace rights and social advancement for people with disabilities?
- How will structural labor market forces and an increasingly global economy affect employment integration and the labor force participation of persons with disabilities in countries around the world?

B. Overview of the Oklahoma Investigation

The findings from the analysis of information collected during the years 1990 to 1999 help to address the questions posed above. A theoretical model or research framework for the empirical study of employment integration has been developed and presented elsewhere in detail.[23] The model identifies measures to be studied to achieve an understanding of employment integration and economic opportunity. Examination of similar measures in other countries, the topic discussed in Part III of this chapter, may inform policymakers of the economic and social progress of their citizens with disabilities.

Several assumptions guide the research model.[24] First, descriptions of legal and social conceptions of disability (and of physical or mental impairments) require interdisciplinary analysis. Second, disability is conceived as a function of limitations in skills or capabilities that must be defined in the context of the living environment and level of support from that environment. Third, for all people, disabilities coexist with individual strengths and capabilities, and with appropriate supports, the functioning of persons with disabilities improves. Fourth, disability is a natural part of the human experience.[25]

By focusing on individual strengths and capabilities, on environments, and on access to supports and services as underlying assumptions, the present investigation reflects emerging views and research about the interplay of disability and society.[26] As an empirical matter, the model allows for analysis: (1) over time, (2) on cross-sectional and longitudinal information collected annually, (3) from an interdisciplinary perspective, and (4) in ways consistent with the major goals of US disability policy (ie, focus on exploration of equality and opportunity, full participation, independent living, and economic self-sufficiency).[27]

There are two major types of outcome measures in the model. The first is a measure of employment integration, assessed by employment category and by changes in employment category from over time (ie, employment movement).[28] The second dependent measure, economic opportunity, is defined by measures of earned and gross income and by changes in income over time (ie, economic growth).

1. Employment Integration

Four categories of employment type are defined and arranged from less to more integrated as follows:[29] (1) no employment—no employment and minimal employment training, (2) sheltered employment—work or training in a nonintegrated group setting with wages less than the required minimum wage,[30] (3) supported employment—supported with services of a job coach and with at least minimum wage, and (4) competitive employment—without the services of a job coach.[31]

2. Economic Opportunity and Changes in Income

US census data from 1991 to 1992, collected prior to the effective date of ADA Title I, show that persons with disabilities have lower incomes when compared to their nondisabled peers.[32] The current research examines changes in the participants' monthly incomes over time and relates them to other independent variables.[33] This design enables the analysis of economic growth and opportunity over time, as well as of the relationship between income levels and other measures in the model, such as individual job skills and qualifications.[34]

3. Personal Background Measures

Personal background variables (other than disability) refer to the participants' age, gender, ethnicity, and minority status. The model describes the relationship between the background variables and employment integration and economic opportunity. Personal background variables alone should not predict employment integration or economic opportunity for qualified persons with disabilities. Prior studies, however, point to the relationship of gender, race, and disability to workforce participation and advancement.[35]

4. Capabilities and Qualifications

Individual capabilities and job qualifications are defined as the interaction among intellectual, physical, and social demands of the environment.[36] In the investigation, two measures comprise the job capabilities and qualifications composite factor—job skill scores and health status.[37] These two measures reflect one working definition of the term a 'qualified' worker, for instance, within the legal meaning of ADA Title I. Although central to most legal disputes involving the ADA, there is little prospective research devoted to examining individual job qualifications.[38] To date, the common approach has been to define qualifications retroactively on a case-by-case basis.[39]

The job skill measure assesses an individual's functioning and developmental growth.[40] The health status measure assesses the medical needs of the participants.[41] For persons with intellectual disabilities, health status often relates to the need for supports and services and the opportunity for integrated work.[42] A third limited measure of adaptive equipment (eg, workplace accommodation) needs has been included as an exploratory measure.[43]

5. Inclusion Factors

Full inclusion into society for persons with disabilities is a primary goal of recent American policy initiatives. Inclusion in employment brings economic opportunity and social participation.[44] The model measures inclusion by degree of integration and independence in living arrangement (ie, the integration aspect) and by reported satisfaction and choice with employment and daily living (ie, the consumer measure).

Integrated and independent living is central to civil rights for people with disabilities.[45] People with intellectual disabilities who live in integrated settings show significant advancements in job capabilities and participation in society.[46] The four categories of living type range from less to more integrated (ie, from custodial to independent) and include the following: institutional residences, family homes, group homes, and independent or supported living homes.[47]

The second inclusion component, the consumer measure, is based on participants' views of their employment, daily needs, and opportunities, and is obtained from a subset of persons responding directly to the research interviewers.[48] The study examines the relationship of satisfaction and choice in work and daily life to subsequent employment integration and economic opportunity. Prior research shows that inclusion into society results in enhanced personal satisfaction and perceptions of choice and control in life.[49]

6. Empowerment Factors

Three measures explore the concept of self-empowerment. The self-advocacy measure reflects contact and participation with self-advocacy programs.[50] Self-advocacy is 'teaching people with a disability how to advocate for themselves and to learn how to speak out for what they believe in'.[51] Self-advocacy in the field of intellectual disabilities is a crucial means for ensuring full participation in society.[52] The research examines the amount of contact these participants have with self-advocacy organizations (eg, involvement with 'People First').

In addition to self-advocacy, family and governmental supports are assessed. Studies show that the use of cost-effective and natural supports in homes, employment, and communities empower persons with disabilities.[53] Appropriate supports improve the job capabilities and functioning of persons with intellectual disabilities.[54] Family and governmental supports are crucial to employment opportunity because they provide a natural and ongoing means for enhancing independence and community integration. Additionally, vocational education and job training are becoming increasingly individualized and coordinated across disciplines for persons with disabilities and these factors are assessed in the model.

7. Legal Factors

These measures examine perceptions of access to employment and daily life.[55] The areas examined include access to employment, education, transportation, and physical access to buildings. The investigation solicits participants' views of employment accessibility (eg, ADA Title I issues).[56] Participants are asked about their access to educational and governmental training services, to public transportation (ADA Title II issues),[57] and to public accommodations (ADA Title III issues).[58]

C. The Investigation's Core Findings

Five core findings emerge from the investigation. The findings reveal positive change and chronic stagnation in the employment and economic status of persons with intellectual disabilities from 1990 to 1999.

1. Employment Integration

With regard to employment integration, the findings reveal that from 1990 to 1999 almost half (42%) of the participants did not change their employment status. During the period, however, almost half of the participants (46%) did move to more integrated employment settings, such as into competitive and supported employment. Moreover, by 1999, four times as many participants were engaged in competitive or supported employment, as compared to 1990 (24% versus 6%, respectively).

From 1990 to 1999, relative unemployment levels for all participants declined dramatically—cut by half, from 43% in 1990 to 22% in 1999. However, approximately one-tenth (11%) of the participants regressed into less integrated employment settings, moving from integrated settings to sheltered workshops or unemployment. These findings were evidenced regardless of the gender and race of the participant.

Individuals with better job skills and capabilities (eg, with higher adaptive behavior scores or better health status), more involved in self-advocacy activities, and having greater independence in living are the most likely to attain and remain in integrated employment. Yet many individuals in competitive work reported limitations and discrimination in employment. This suggests that there may be differences in what policymakers and researchers know about the implementation of disability legislation and what may be perceived by the disability community.

2. Economic Opportunity

From 1990 to 1999, the incomes of the participants increased substantially. Older, relative to younger, participants show substantial increases in earned income and in attainment of competitive employment. The strongest independent predictor of employment advancement and earned income is job skill level. However, social inclusion measures (eg, independence in living) and empowerment factors (eg, self-advocacy involvement) contribute to predictions of employment advancement and higher earned income levels. The findings support the view that employment and income are central factors affecting life satisfaction and quality of life for persons with disabilities.[59] Yet prior research shows significant wage disparities between people with and without disabilities in comparable jobs.[60] Over time, these wage disparities often act as disincentives to work for qualified individuals with disabilities.

3. Individual Growth

The personal growth of participants from 1990 to 1999 is measured in several ways. These include improvements in job capabilities and qualifications, level of inclusion and empowerment in society, and degree of accessibility to society. Several findings emerge. First, the proportion of participants involved in self-advocacy increases substantially, from 17% in 1990 to 28% in 1999. Second, reported accessibility to, and satisfaction with, work and daily life shows improvement. Third, the reported health status of the participants improves. Finally, the proportion of participants living in integrated community settings (ie, as opposed to larger congregate care facilities) rises dramatically, from 2% in 1990, to 50% in 1999. The trends suggest improvement in areas central to equal opportunity, access to, and involvement in society, and increased satisfaction with work and daily life.

4. The Black Hole Effect

Although progress is evident, troubling results emerge. More than three-quarters (78%) of the participants who were unemployed or in non-integrated sheltered workshops in 1990 remained in the black hole of these non-integrated settings in 1999. Moreover, movement from noninte-grated employment settings to integrated employment is limited for all persons, regardless of their level of disability.[61] Nevertheless, almost half (49%) of individuals who were in competitive and supported employment in 1990 remain in these settings in 1999.

5. Perceptions of Rights and ADA Implementation

Perceptions of rights and ADA implementation varied over time. During the years 1990 to 1992, the period that the ADA was signed until the effect-ive date of Title I, participants reported an increasing level of effectiveness of the law and its principles. High expectations for a new and emerging era were apparent.

From 1992 to 1994, a different picture developed. Perceptions of ADA effectiveness and self-reported access to society dropped, in absolute terms, to levels almost comparable to those evidenced in 1990. From 1994 to 1999, however, perceptions of rights and access to society again rose, but remained lower than the earlier enthusiastic levels. The findings sug-gest that upon passage of the ADA, disabled Americans' expectations for the rights and the law were high. However, the reality of implementation may not yet have achieved its full promise. Although it is too early to make any definitive conclusions about this trend, researchers must address expectations of and promises for full inclusion, empowerment, and equal opportunity to work for qualified individuals.

III. IMPLICATIONS

A. Overview

The findings of the present investigation illustrate that assessing employ-ment integration is a monumental task. No anti-discrimination law or policy alone is the reason for social change. Policymakers must assess whether change is occurring or whether there is merely an appearance of change. Researchers need to address how social change is to be defined under subsequent disability policy initiatives for persons with physical and intellectual impairments. The answers to these questions depend not only on the type of disabilities covered by the law, but also on varying cultural perspectives of disability.[62]

This part examines how the research questions identified in the investigation described above may be addressed through empirical study in the United States and abroad. A word of caution is in order. To effectively assess the impact of the emerging national employment policy, researchers must examine a range of outcomes, in addition to traditional measures of competitive employment, income, and education rates. Although competitive employment should lead to economic self-sufficiency and provide sufficient income for independence, it is the case that millions of Americans with disabilities continue to live in poverty. Without true inclusion, integration, and attitudinal changes, individuals with disabilities will not have access to competitive employment to approach self-sufficiency.

Prompted by the UN proclamation of the Decade of Disabled Persons (1983–1992), the UN's recommendations, and the implementation of the ADA, some comparative study has been undertaken on the status of people with disabilities, in employment and other aspects of daily life.[63] The UN has developed its Disability Statistics Data Base (DISTAT) to gather disability-related statistics. According to DISTAT, for instance, in 1986, Canada had a 13% disability rate,[64] while Australia had an 18% rate.[65] Yet, the unemployment rate of people with disabilities in Canada has been estimated at more than 50%.[66]

Eurostat, the European database on disability prevalence, found in 1992 that more than 12% of adults in Great Britain are disabled.[67] A 1995 Eurostat report compiled data on Member States of the European Community and international organizations addressing the socio-economic status of disabled persons. The report found that Germans with disabilities comprise roughly 13% of the population.[68] Studies show that the unemployment rate for Germans with disabilities is more than double that of the unemployment for persons without disabilities.[69]

Another Eurostat study demonstrates that the United Kingdom's unemployment rate for the general population is 7%, whereas the unemployment rate for persons with disabilities is more than 30%.[70] Though comprehensive statistics for Ireland have not been compiled, some data suggest that the unemployment rate of its people with disabilities is 70% or higher.[71]

Additional studies from DISTAT suggest that in many countries people with disabilities are unemployed and underemployed because they lack access to adequate job training and work skill development programs. As discussed in the next section, these supports are crucial for persons with disabilities to attain and retain meaningful employment. Some countries, such as Canada, have governmentally enforced employment programs that require the employment of disabled people in proportion to the percentage of people with disabilities available to work in the entire population.[72]

One limitation of this approach has been that people with disabilities are placed in employment without adequate job training. The result has been that the work quality and long-term career potential of disabled persons are limited. In the United States, systematic study is addressing the role of the private staffing industry and of public programs sponsored by the states (eg, through the Workforce Investment Act described earlier, or through state-sponsored entrepreneurial development programs) in support of the employment training and career development of persons with disabilities. Two such illustrative studies we have conducted are presented next.

B. Bridges from Welfare to Work

1. *The Private Staffing Industry: The Manpower Study*

In 1997, my colleagues and I began a case study of Manpower, Inc, the world's largest staffing employer.[73] Manpower annually has provided temporary employment opportunities to more than 800,000 people in the United States and more than 1,500,000 people worldwide, maintaining 2,500 offices in forty-three countries.

The Manpower study examines emerging employment opportunities available to persons with disabilities within the private staffing industry. The study explores the importance of these opportunities to reform strategies that provide a bridge to full-time employment. Interviews with Manpower employees suggest that a critical element of the company's success in hiring and retaining workers with disabilities has been its investment in individualized training, worker assessment, and job-matching tools.

In the United States alone, the size of the contingent workforce—including self-employed, temporary, and part-time workers—has been estimated to range from 34 million to 42 million individuals, roughly 25% to 31% of the American labor force in 1996.[74] From 1980 to 1996, the contingent workforce grew faster than the US economy as a whole.[75] The US Bureau of Labor Statistics estimates that between the years 1994 and 2005, temporary employment opportunities will grow by 55%.[76]

Manpower's business mix is approximately 40% light industrial, 40% office, and 20% technical or professional assignments. The company provides workers with opportunities in positions at different skill levels. Manpower has expanded its services to include the provision of an onsite job coach to support a client company's staffing needs. Other services include job training, programs that assist workers in finding permanent jobs, skills assessment, and career training services.

Manpower's role as a provider of temporary workers has evolved into sophisticated human resources functions. The role serves as a bridge for qualified workers with disabilities seeking to enter the labor force. The Manpower study identifies aspects of its corporate culture that foster employment of persons with disabilities, including a belief that there are no unskilled workers, that every individual has skills and aptitudes that can be measured, and that every job may be broken down into essential tasks. Job training is focused on what workers can do and on identifying several jobs for each employee.

The Manpower study identifies the ways the staffing industry supports the employment of workers with disabilities, illustrating that (1) individualized training and job placement are available; (2) above minimum wages and health insurance benefits are provided; (3) there is opportunity for career advancement; (4) there is opportunity for transition to full-time competitive employment; and (5) there are opportunities for self-advancement and self-learning.

In making job placements, Manpower assesses its customers' job needs and work environment. Examination is made of customer expectations, physical details of the work area, work pace, hours, breaks, safety issues, parking, and accessibility issues. Assessments of workers' skills are individualized. Intake begins with an interview that gathers information on work history, job skills, and preferences. Applicants describe their preferred work environment and job responsibilities. Applicants complete job skills assessments selected according to their abilities and interests. The assessments use work samples to provide workers a preview of the job and measure their job skills and accommodation needs.

In addition to job skill assessment, Manpower offers its employees skill enhancement through work training programs. Skills training is individualized depending on the employee's job abilities and interests. When the skills assessment and training process is complete, Manpower uses its databases of customer needs and employee information to make a match.

Manpower serves as a bridge to the workforce for qualified workers. Increasingly, US businesses view their supplemental workforce as a source of candidates for permanent positions. More than 40% of Manpower's workforce accepts permanent jobs offered to them as a result of Manpower assignments.

2. State-Sponsored Initiatives: Entrepreneurs with Disabilities Study

True employment inclusion and integration require access to a range of workplace and non-workplace activities. Traditional economic outcome measures, such as those studied in the longitudinal Oklahoma investigation, need to be augmented by examining a range of employment activities, including self-employment, entrepreneurial activities and temporary employment (eg, as illustrated by the Manpower study above). Recent US policy initiatives have sought to increase the range of employment opportunities available to persons with disabilities, including providing training and assistance for persons with disabilities interested in self-employment and entrepreneurial activities.

One question worthy of study, for instance, is how government policies, like TWWIIA and WIA will assist disabled individuals to pursue non-traditional employment options (ie, jobs outside of large corporate settings)? And, how these non-traditional activities can serve as foundations for individuals with disabilities to become self-sufficient?

To begin to address such questions, we conducted a case study of Iowa's state-supported Entrepreneurs with Disabilities (EWD) program. The EWD program was established as a partnership among the Iowa Department of Economic Development, the Iowa Department of Education's Division of Vocational Rehabilitation Services, and the Iowa Department for the Blind. The EWD program provides technical and financial assistance, and business development grants to qualified individuals with disabilities to establish or expand small businesses with the goal of becoming self-sufficient.

Our preliminary study of Iowa's EWD program describes how participants with disabilities progress through the program, as well as the characteristics of successful participants.[77] We examined the public–private partnership approach used by the program and analyzed demographic information to paint a portrait of entrepreneurs at the time they applied to the EWD program, using factors such as applicants' age, gender, education, source of income support, disability, and prior earnings and hours worked. We fashioned a portrait of a sub-sample of thirty program participants in terms of their business success, their quality of life, knowledge of laws and policies affecting persons with disabilities (eg, ADA, WIA, and TWWIA), and the barriers they face in everyday life.

We found that EWD applicants are twice as likely to be men than women (67% vs 33%). EWD applicants are usually in their mid-forties (mean age of 46), with a range in age from 21 to 69 years old. Roughly half of the EWD applicants are married (52%). As compared to individuals with disabilities generally, the sample of EWD applicants is highly educated; about half of the applicants are high school graduates (49%), more than one-third have at least some college experience (39%), and about 10% have less than a high school education.

Almost half of EWD applicants (47%) report orthopedic impairments as their primary disability. After orthopedic impairments, the next most frequently reported disabilities are mental and emotional conditions. Roughly one in five (19.8%) EWD applicants report a mental or emotional condition as their primary disability. Mental and emotional disorders include neurotic and psychotic conditions, schizophrenia, post-traumatic stress disorder, and other mental and emotional disorders.

More than one-third (40%) of EWD applicants report financial assistance from family and friends as their primary means of support. More than half (54%) of EWD applicants proposed business ventures in the service sector, and these applicants proved to be particularly successful in their business ventures. Data were available on thirteen participants' earned weekly income at the time of their EWD application and at their case closure. At case closure, an average increase of $230 per week in income was reported, with a median increase in weekly income of $150, and a wide range in increased income from $124 to $868.

The ability to obtain and afford health care and insurance was the major concern for the entrepreneurs with disabilities. Less than one-quarter (23%) of EWD participants interviewed about health insurance had health insurance coverage with their existing businesses. Most of these participants (71%) had private health insurance before becoming self-employed. Yet more than half (58%) responded that they lost private health insurance coverage when they began their own business. In many cases, EWD participants receive private health insurance coverage under a spouse's policy.

Lastly, the majority of participants interviewed indicated that they encountered employment discrimination after they became disabled. Of the thirty-five people who answered questions related to discrimination, nineteen people (54%) indicated that they experienced employment discrimination, which they attributed to their disability. For many participants, more than three-quarters (76%) of those interviewed, it was this discrimination (actual or perceived) that motivated them to start their own businesses. In other cases, entrepreneurs pursued self-employment to 'self-accommodate' their workplace needs, which often were not accommodated in prior competitive employment.

We have illustrated in the case study of Iowa entrepreneurs that outcome research need not be limited to traditional competitive employment status and income growth. For self-employment, for instance, independence may mean job choice, self-determination, flexibility in work schedules and tasks, and self-accommodating for workplace accessibility. In this line of study, we emphasize a broader view of outcome analysis, using multiple indicators including the ways employees work and how work is essential to other aspects of daily life.

In addition, one of the expected benefits of the new generation of American employment policy initiatives—the ADA, TWWIIA, WIA, Medicaid Buy-In—is a reduction in disabled individuals' long-term dependence on governmental supports and health benefits. The study of labor supply decisions—such as the decision to pursue self-employment—would help to isolate whether changes in nonwork sources of income help explain the employment patterns of persons with disabilities.

To the extent that disabled entrepreneurs place importance on access to health care in their decisions regarding labor force participation, changes in the provision of health care, in regulations regarding health care coverage, and in public assistance programs could be considered as alternative explanations for patterns in existing studies. As illustrated by the Manpower study, the effects of private initiatives, such as changes in the nature of job training, need to be further assessed.

In light of the prior illustrations, the following sections review disability policy and job training initiatives in select countries and regions. Much of the development of law and policy to date understandably has focused on the unemployment problem facing people with physical disabilities. However, analysis has prompted comparative questions regarding implementation of national disability policy, governmental responsibility to initiate policy, and the role of private sector employers.

C. Implications in the United States

In the United States, the problems of chronic unemployment and underemployment faced by qualified persons with disabilities are evident. For persons with intellectual disabilities in the various investigations described above—Oklahoma, Manpower, and EWD studies—successful long-term employment is a function of experience in and attempts at competitive work. Yet the 'black hole' stagnation facing persons with disabilities points to the need for job-training strategies to assist thousands of persons to enter the workforce. Placement services and job retention and advancement strategies are needed to help individuals with disabilities not only get jobs but to maintain their employment and achieve their potential.

Many economic and social benefits associated with the new disability laws and policies remain to be discovered and documented. The findings presented in this chapter highlight an emerging workforce of persons who experienced mainstreamed education and whose families have advocated for their rights.[78] Adequate economic data examining the effect on the US economy of the population of young persons with disabilities entering the workforce is not yet available.[79]

Evidence suggests that ADA implementation has coincided with larger numbers of persons with severe disabilities entering the US labor force. In 1996, the US Census Bureau released data showing that the employment to population ratio for persons with severe disabilities has increased from roughly 23% in 1991 to 26% in 1994, reflecting an increase of approximately 800,000 additional people with severe disabilities in the workforce.[80] Other studies suggest that from the years 1970 to 1992 there has been no significant change in the US labor force participation rate among persons with disabilities.

More recent studies show that employment rates rise substantially when different definitions of disability (eg, varying measures of functional limitations) are used in the analysis of other national data sets.[81] Defining disability in different ways, therefore, can have a substantial effect on the conclusions that researchers and policymakers draw about the employment rates of individuals with disabilities.[82]

However, even when they are employed, Americans with disabilities work fewer hours and earn less per hour than their nondisabled colleagues. The 1998 Current Population Survey found that employees with disabilities with full-time, year-round employment had average annual earnings of $29,513, more than $8,000 less than the $37,961 average annual earnings of their nondisabled coworkers.[83] Although 82% of nondisabled employees held full-time jobs, only 64% of individuals with disabilities who were employed reported full-time employment.

Empirical information is emerging on the economic value of disability and ADA compliance practices by employers. This information provides feedback to employers and employees about ADA implementation in different business sectors.[84] In a longitudinal study conducted on the ADA practices of Sears, Roebuck & Co, a company with 300,000 employees, 20,000 of whom are persons with impairments, the average direct cost of providing accommodations to qualified workers with disabilities was less than $50.[85] The economic benefits to Sears (eg, avoiding turnover costs) of employing workers with disabilities far exceeded the costs of accommodations.

Analysis is needed of workplace accommodation strategies affecting job applicants and employees without disabilities, such as those geared toward employee wellness programs, flexible hours for workers with young children, employer-sponsored child care centers, job sharing strategies for workers with limited time availability, or employee assistance programs. US companies expend large sums of money accommodating workers without disabilities, which in the aggregate may be substantially greater than the costs associated with accommodations for workers with disabilities.[86] Analysis of these strategies show that they complement accommodations required by workers with disabilities.

Other studies show that accommodation strategies enhance the productivity and job tenure of workers without disabilities who are injured on the job or who may become impaired in the future. In an eight-year study of Coors Brewing Company's health screening program covering almost 4,000 employees, the company realized direct savings of roughly $2.5 million in terms of saved payments in short-term disability, temporary worker replacement, and direct medical costs.[87] Given a conservative estimate of even a $100 average cost per employee for accommodations based on the Sears findings described earlier, the savings generated by the Coors study could fund accommodations for 25,000 qualified workers.

These and other findings suggest the huge economic implications associated with accommodation strategies designed to prevent workplace injury and to help retain the increasing numbers of employees with disabilities. Considering that by the year 2000, the costs to employers associated with back injuries alone in the American workplace approached $40 billion, examination of the savings related to accommodation strategies, injury prevention and wellness programs is well warranted. The educational side effects associated with accommodation strategies also enhance employee morale and lead to positive attitudes about qualified coworkers with disabilities.[88]

Creating economic opportunity, improving access to job training services, and raising awareness are concerns not limited to the United States. For many nations, these concerns are increasingly important, as reflected in UN initiatives. Deciding what type of change is required, who should initiate and implement change, the role of the private and public sector employers, and other related issues will depend on varying cultural, political, and economic factors.

Although the answers to these questions differ from nation to nation, countries developing disability policies learn from the experience of other nations. At a minimum, approaches to common issues may be shared and evaluated.[89] More broadly, a systematic method of evaluating implementation may emerge. By identifying the preconditions for equal participation of persons with disabilities in the workplace (eg, awareness-raising, appropriate health care and support services, and empowerment strategies), the UN is clarifying areas requiring future study.

Countries have varying forms of disability policy. Policy initiatives range from those developed in response to decades of political action (eg, in the United States, United Kingdom, Israel, Hungary, and Germany) to efforts addressing emerging problems (eg, in India and Latin America). Comparative study is needed to establish a unified approach for assessing rights of persons with disabilities throughout the world.

The next section illustrates varying national approaches to disability law and policy and their implications for the employment of persons with disabilities.[90] Common themes identified and requiring study include analysis of (1) cultural and legal definitions of disability, (2) the importance of work to effective disability policy, (3) worker empowerment strategies, (4) the means for providing support for independent living and adequate health care, and (5) the effects of structural labor market and global economic forces on disability policy.

D. Initiatives in Canada

The Canadian Health and Activity Limitation Survey (HALS) defines disability as an impairment in the activities of daily living.[91] The definition does not include people who, through the use of assistive technology, mitigate their limitations.[92] Canada's Employment Equity Regulations define disability as encompassing people who have an impairment, who consider themselves impaired, or who are considered by others as impaired.[93]

Canada has a governmental program to support the employment of people with disabilities.[94] The Employment Equity Act (EEA) of 1996 ensures that people with disabilities are represented in the Canadian workforce.[95] The EEA requires a proportion of people with disabilities in a workplace equivalent to the percentage of disabled people in the Canadian workforce or a segment of the workforce from which an employer would reasonably draw upon for staffing purposes.[96]

The EEA covers firms with one hundred or more workers.[97] In contrast to its predecessor, the Employment Equity Act of 1986, EEA requires employers to submit reports indicating the number of employees covered by the law and charges the Canadian Human Rights Commission with ensuring compliance for private and public sector employers.[98] If an employer's proportion of disabled employees is below the percentage of workers available and the Commission has been unable to negotiate a written agreement with the employer as to specific measures to remedy the non-compliance, the Commission can issue a direction for the employer to comply or request a review by the Employment Equity Review Tribunal.[99] The revision of the EEA in 1996 provides the opportunity to assess whether compliance measures have an effect on employment rates of individuals with disabilities, providing relevant information for policymakers.[100]

In Canada, as in the United States, sheltered work options for people with disabilities have generated considerable discussion.[101] Some Canadians suggest that the sheltered work system fails to provide meaningful work opportunity due to the restricted types of jobs that people with disabilities are encouraged to pursue (an analogous argument supported by the 'black hole' trends illustrated above).[102] Policy changes have been proposed that focus on governmental funding for supported employment schemes.[103] Governmental funds are allocated for post-employment placement activities, such as job coaching. Support is needed for job planning and career development, such as identified by the Manpower study described above.[104]

E. Initiatives in the European Community

The Commission of the European Communities estimates that approximately 38 million Europeans have a disability.[105] The European Community action program in support of persons with disabilities is a comprehensive initiative.[106] Established in 1988, HELIOS (The Handicapped People in the European Community Living Independently in an Open Society) was a program to ensure the integration of persons with disabilities into society.[107] In 1991, the European Commission proposed HELIOS II. This program, adopted by the European Council in early 1993, remained in effect through 1996.[108]

HELIOS II covers functional rehabilitation, educational integration, vocational training, employment rehabilitation programs, and promotes economic, social integration and independent living for persons with disabilities.[109] HELIOS II encourages cooperation among European non-governmental organizations (NGOs) and Member State NGOs to provide employment opportunities and analysis of job training and empowerment strategies for persons with disabilities. To achieve its policy goals, HELIOS II seeks to (1) improve information collection and exchange; (2) provide information on technical aids through a computerized information system (called 'Handynet') to people with disabilities; (3) stimulate participation of persons with disabilities in European Union programs on job training, technology, mobility, and youth exchanges; and (4) improve public information and awareness.[110]

Several bodies advise the European Commission on HELIOS II implementation. Advisory groups include the European Disability Forum, a group of European NGOs and representatives from employer's organizations and trade unions, and a liaison group consisting of one representative per Member State and 12 members of the Forum. The Commission receives guidance from an advisory committee composed of officials from Member States and a Commission representative.[111]

A central component of HELIOS and HELIOS II is the Handynet system. Under HELIOS II, the European Commission will expand the Handynet system to promote the exchange and study of information on disability statistics. Support of this initiative is provided by the Commission, including financial support for the Handynet computerized information and documentation system and the support of projects to raise public awareness.[112] Handynet is a tool for future comparative study of issues related to the development of disability policy.

Other European initiatives address the employment of persons with disabilities. In 1990, the European Commission proposed the HORIZON program, designed to integrate persons with disabilities into the labor market by improving their job skills and training. The HORIZON program creates small and medium-sized enterprises in the form of cooperatives.[113] The program addresses the impact of labor market forces and global competition on persons with disabilities.

Additional initiatives identified by the European Union Council of Ministers are designed to enhance access to the workplace by persons with disabilities. One resolution requests that the Commission formulate a community action program to provide access to public transportation for persons with reduced mobility.[114] This resolution recognizes that barriers in the living environments of persons with disabilities limit objectives of disability policy initiatives. A related initiative is the TIDE program, which focuses on technological applications for persons with disabilities.[115] The program seeks to create an affordable and cost-effective market in assistive technology.[116]

During the year 2000, the European Union Council of Ministers adopted an anti-discrimination policy, including a directive that prohibits employment discrimination on all grounds.[117] According to the directive, European Union Member States must adopt laws to prohibit employment discrimination against individuals with disabilities by 2006.[118] This anti-discrimination legislation must prohibit direct and indirect discriminatory actions and harassment, and require employers to make reasonable accommodations that do not pose a disproportionate burden on the employer.[119] This directive provides an opportunity for comparative, longitudinal research to assess the affects of initiating anti-discrimination policies in different cultures.

F. Initiatives in Ireland, Germany, and the United Kingdom

Ireland

It is estimated that more than 10% of the Irish population have disabilities. In 1993, the Commission on the Status of People with Disabilities was established by the Irish Minister of Equality of Law Reform. In preparing its report, the Commission received suggestions from individuals with disabilities, their families, and organizations representing people with disabilities.[120] The Commission's report reflects a commitment to disability policy that is consistent with UN recommendations for support of persons with disabilities in the areas of economic rights, education, housing, and transportation.

The Commission concluded that disability must be considered as part of Ireland's social and cultural context. Prior to the Commission report, disability issues received little attention in Ireland and there were no official statistics on the national prevalence of disability.[121] At the time the Commission issued its report, there was no national anti-discrimination policy protecting people with disabilities in Ireland.

In 1999, Ireland enacted the National Disability Authority Act, establishing the National Disability Authority. The Authority is charged with developing and advising the Ministry on disability policy. The Authority's focus is solely on individuals with disabilities. It has the power to review and make recommendations about a broad range of policies that affect persons with disabilities, including related social welfare initiatives.[122]

Ireland has in place an Employment Support Scheme to enhance the wages of people with disabilities. Under this scheme, employers receive grants from the National Board's Workplace Equipment Adaptation Grant Scheme to provide workplace accommodations. The Disability Commission has advocated that discrimination against a person with a disability be prohibited where the individual is capable of performing job functions with accommodations. The Commission recommended that the government provide information to employers to encourage the recruitment of people with disabilities and that governmental funds be provided to enhance job training and support. In 1997, the Irish government introduced a 3% quota of public service jobs for people with disabilities. The quota requirement recently was met in civil service jobs and has not been met by private employers.

In response to the failure of private employers to meet their quota requirements, the Government of Ireland is instituting a public awareness campaign to promote employment of individuals with disabilities.[123] The campaign's focus is to dispel myths and stereotypes by making employers aware of the employment potential of individuals with disabilities.[124] It is estimated that the Government of Ireland will spend 700,000 Irish pounds on the campaign.[125]

Germany

In recent years, Germany has extended workplace protections for persons with disabilities.[126] One central policy theme has been to eliminate employment discrimination and prejudices against persons with disabilities and promote employment opportunities. A 1992 study by the European Centre for the Development of Vocational Training examined the ways in which people with disabilities may be integrated into the German labor market. The authors concluded that sheltered employment in Germany has failed to transition participants to competitive employment.[127] Consistent with the 'black hole' findings described earlier, more than three-quarters of the individuals who transition into the labor market between the years 1980 and 1983 were not employed by 1984.[128]

The Germany disability statute, the *Schwerbehindertengesetz*, is designed to enhance work opportunities for people with disabilities.[129] The statute contains provisions affecting employers and persons with disabilities. The legislation defines an employer's duty to assess its workplace for the hiring of workers with disabilities whenever positions are vacant.[130] The German system uses quotas to mandate the employment of workers with disabilities.[131] The employment quotas are enforced by monetary sanctions and a levy is paid for each month that a covered position is not filled by an individual with a disability. The proceeds from the levy are used to provide assistance to people with disabilities.[132] The cost of accommodations, including payment for structural changes to the environment or the purchase of aids, are reimbursed by the government.[133] Wage subsidies are available for workers with disabilities.

United Kingdom

In contrast to the German scheme, in 1995, the United Kingdom adopted the Disability Discrimination Act (DDA).[134] Under the DDA, it is illegal to discriminate against a person on the basis of disability.[135] The DDA repealed the prior quota system and the reserved occupation system.[136] The DDA does not prohibit employers from adopting systems to create targets for the employment of persons with disabilities or prohibit preferential treatment in favor of workers with disabilities.[137]

During the first thirteen months of DDA implementation, 1,198 complaints were filed under the law.[138] The majority of complaints (59%) were allegations of wrongful employee dismissal, 18% for failure to make reasonable accommodations, 10% for discrimination in job applications, and 13% for other detriments including harassment, employee benefits, pay, and promotion.[139] These findings are similar to experiences in the United States following the enactment of the ADA.[140] Comparative analysis of disability legislation provides policymakers with insights as to what to expect if they initiate similar disability reforms.

Recently, the United Kingdom has set out a new agenda of legislative reform.[141] The agenda calls for, among other things, removing the small employer exemption from DDA, expanding the definition of disability to include people with HIV or cancer from the point of diagnosis, and removing exemptions for certain public employees.[142] The economic and social costs and benefits of these changes in policies are areas worthy of future study.[143] Research on the effects of removing the small employer exemption from DDA, which is scheduled to go into effect in 2004, may provide valuable information on the necessity for such an exemption and the economic consequences of this policy change.[144]

G. Initiatives in Non-union Europe

Disability policy initiatives have been undertaken by non-union countries in Europe. Economic opportunities for persons with disabilities have been addressed in Bulgaria and Hungary. Since 1993, persons with disabilities in Bulgaria have participated in subsidized and self-governed cooperatives.[145] In 1998, Hungary passed its first anti-discrimination law on the basis of disability. The Hungarian Equal Opportunities Law establishes civil and economic rights of persons with disabilities. The law is modeled on aspects of the ADA.

Economic opportunity, access, and job training programs have been addressed in non-union countries. In Bulgaria, indirect benefits to persons with disabilities have resulted from various economic incentive programs. Initiatives include incentives for companies to employ up to 60% of their workforce with workers with disabilities, a state rehabilitation fund that provides subsidized loans,[146] reduced social security contribution requirements for companies employing persons with disabilities,[147] and pensions to retiring persons who care for individuals with disabilities.

H. Initiatives in Israel

In 1998, the Israeli Equal Rights for People with Disabilities Law was enacted to protect the civil rights of persons with disabilities. Persons with disabilities comprise more than 10% of Israel's population.[148] The Equal Rights Law acknowledges the rights of people with disabilities and the necessity of equality in work. The law defines disability in ways similar to the ADA, covering individuals with physical, emotional, and intellectual disabilities who are substantially limited in major spheres of life. Protected individuals are those with a record of a disability and regarded as having a disability, as well as relatives of people with disabilities.

The Israeli law prohibits discrimination in employment and covers private employers with twenty-five or more workers. Discrimination includes the failure to provide workplace accommodations that do not impose undue burdens on employers. Governmental programs created by the law include development of rehabilitation and job placement programs. The Israeli law, like the 1998 Hungarian law mentioned above, provides an opportunity for study and comparison of a new generation of disability anti-discrimination laws.

I. Initiatives in Latin America

Spurred by the First Central American Seminar on disability in 1995, disability initiatives have been undertaken in Latin America.[149] The *Partnerships in Community Living Project* examines policies and programs related to children and young adults with disabilities in the Americas. The Partnership Project examines disability policies in their cultural and legal context.[150] The Project has identified policies affecting persons with disabilities and those that assist in providing opportunity to youths with disabilities. Similar to the initiatives in Europe, the Project recognizes that issues of employment integration, independent living, and empowerment strategies for persons with disabilities must be evaluated through comparative study.

Analysis of information collected by the Partnership Project demonstrates a concern for individual rights and freedoms, protection from discrimination, citizenship and voting, social rights, and protection from deprivation of property. In addition to identifying the need for comparative study of disability policy, the Project recommended study of international agreements governing disability policy, such as study of the UN Declarations on Human Rights, the Rights of People with Disabilities, the Rights of People with Mental Retardation, and the Universal Convention on the Rights of the Child.[151] Although the Partnership Project has identified a preliminary model for comparative analysis, the endeavor reflects an important effort to improve long-term global knowledge of disability policy.

J. Initiatives in Asia and the Pacific

At its forty-eighth session in 1992 in Beijing, the Economic and Social Commission for Asia and the Pacific announced that the period 1993–2002 would be the Asian and Pacific Decade of Disabled Persons.[152] Related advances for persons with disabilities have been made in the past ten years and provide opportunity for study of disability employment policy developments.

China

In 1990, the government enacted the Law of the People's Republic of China on the Protection of Disabled Persons to protect more than 60 million of its citizens with disabilities.[153] The law makes it illegal to discriminate against persons on the basis of disability. Local governments have adopted measures to implement the law.[154] Similar to nations described above, China supports a quota system in the hiring of workers with disabilities. The government funds job training for persons with disabilities by establishing vocational education programs. The implementation of welfare enterprises involves the employment of persons with disabilities.[155] These enterprises are provided economic incentives to employ persons with disabilities, such as business tax exemptions, depending on the numbers of employees with disabilities employed.[156] Welfare enterprises are maintained by state and local committees or by individuals with disabilities.[157]

Other nations may learn from research on China's initiative to address the prejudices and attitudinal barriers that individuals with disabilities face. The China Disabled Persons Federation (CDPF) was established by the Chinese government in 1988.[158] The Federation is, in part, credited with cultural changes. For example, the common term used to describe individuals with disabilities has changed from 'canfei', a word which implies worthlessness, to 'canji', which means disabled.[159] In addition, stories of individuals with disabilities have been made into Chinese movies.[160] To better understand the effects of government policy, researchers need to consider a broad range of effects from multidisciplinary perspectives.

Japan

There are an estimated five million persons with disabilities in Japan.[161] Japan does not have a comprehensive anti-discrimination law that protects the rights of its citizens with disabilities.[162] Japan's Law to Promote the Employment of the Handicapped was amended in 1988 to include persons with intellectual disabilities.[163]

Japan uses a quota and levy program to support the employment of workers with disabilities.[164] Japan's Ministry of Labor's Deliberation Panel on the Employment of the Handicapped regulates quotas of workers with disabilities, with required quotas approximately at 2% in the private and public employment sectors.[165] Levies are collected from employers that do not meet the required quotas. The Japanese government uses these funds to support vocational rehabilitation and job assistance for persons with disabilities.[166]

One study by the Japanese Ministry of Labor finds that the employment of disabled persons has increased from the years of 1986 to 1994 in public and private sectors. Despite advances, many employers pay the levy for not employing the required quota of persons with disabilities.[167]

In 1995, the Japanese government established the Government Action Plan for Persons with Disabilities.[168] The plan spans fiscal years 1996 to 2002 and establishes implementation goals for the equal employment of persons with disabilities.[169] The goals include providing job training, employment and housing, promoting independence, creating a barrier-free society, eliminating prejudice and discrimination through the eradication of attitudinal and cultural barriers, and increasing opportunities for comparative study.[170]

Australia

In 1992, Australia passed the Disability Discrimination Act (DDA) covering one-quarter of its population.[171] Under the DDA, it is illegal to discriminate in employment on the basis of disability.[172] The DDA applies to public and private sector employers.[173]

The Australian Commonwealth Government's Disability Strategy, adopted in 1994, monitors DDA implementation.[174] The *Commonwealth Disability Strategy First Progress Report 1995* provides a basis from which to compare changes reported in the *Second Progress Report of 1997*. Comparisons show advances in employment, transportation, telecommunications, education, assistive devices, and public attitudes.[175] Findings show that 80% of government organizations increased the number of employees with disabilities.[176]

In addition to efforts to increase the representation of persons with disabilities in employment, Australian workplaces have become more accessible. Related initiatives include support for home employment, permanent part-time employment, flexible hours, and job sharing.[177] Employers have provided job information in accessible formats to persons with disabilities through computer programs and adaptive equipment.[178]

Australia has established national councils to equalize employment opportunities for persons with disabilities. The National Disability Advisory Council was created in 1996 to provide communication between persons with disabilities and the government.[179] Like Canada, employment of individuals with disabilities in sheltered workshops has become a controversial issue in Australia.[180] As various countries face similar difficulties, policymakers and researchers need to open a dialogue about ways to integrate individuals with disabilities into employment settings, and the use of economic incentives and disincentives, as well as legal reforms. In this way, policymakers may make informed choices, based on a growing wealth of information.

India

In 1996, India passed the Persons with Disabilities Act.[181] This law defines the government's obligation in areas of disability prevention, anti-discrimination rights, the provision of adequate health care, employment rehabilitation, education, and job training services.[182] The purpose of the law is to create a barrier-free society and to integrate persons with disabilities.[183] Independent of the law, the government reserves 3% of public employment positions for persons with visual, hearing, or physical disabilities.[184] Studies of Indian disability policy suggest that there exists a lack of support for effective implementation, a constrained definition of persons with disabilities, and insufficient assessment capabilities due to a lack of national data on disability.[185]

IV. CONCLUSION

This chapter has described common issues that nations must address in studying and developing national employment disability laws and policies. Many possibilities remain for comparative study. In the United States, study must assess the relationship among severity and type of disability, levels of inclusion and empowerment in society, the types and quality of jobs sought, attained, and retained, and the resolution of employment disputes.

The definition of disability and the identification of those who have a disability are critical to any policy or research addressing relative employment levels of individuals with disabilities. If the purpose of the policy or research is to enhance labor demand and supply of those with disabilities relative to those without disabilities, use of a measure that asks individuals whether they are disabled, or whether they have a disability that prevents or limits the work they can do would possibly be sufficient.[186] However, such an approach, for instance, in the United States taken without regard to the ADA's language, likely will not yield valid conclusions if the purpose of the research is to assess the effects of the ADA.

An understanding of comparative approaches to the definition of disability not only may help avoid and resolve disputes, but also may aid policymakers in gauging the effectiveness of national disability legislation. This information is needed at a time when dramatic policy reforms are occurring in welfare, rehabilitation and health care, and health insurance law, affecting employment opportunities for millions of workers with disabilities.[187] In the United States, and in other countries, analysis is needed of the relation among welfare reform, governmental entitlement program regulations, anti-discrimination laws, and changes in the labor force participation of persons with disabilities. Policymakers need to coordinate programs that enable workers with disabilities to maintain adequate health insurance coverage, receive workplace accommodations and job training. Job coaching, vocational training, workplace accommodation strategies, and new technologies enable persons with physical and intellectual disabilities to achieve self-sufficiency and attain and retain quality employment in large traditional and smaller entrepreneurial and microenterprise settings.[188]

In 1995, the European Commission articulated a goal of full employment and solidarity as the basis for future European social policy.[189] The Commission concluded that European disability policy serves these interests of the Union as a whole.[190] The Commission determined that substantial effort must be directed at combating disability discrimination.[191] The findings presented in this chapter, from the United States and other countries, support the objective of developing policies to enhance the equal employment of persons with disabilities.[192]

The findings foreshadow the need for study of law and policy implementation to support economic opportunity throughout the world for persons with disabilities. Comparative information will help to defuse myths and unwarranted fears that the implementation of disability employment policy is costly and burdensome. Understanding the economic opportunities and barriers to employment in the United States and abroad is one step toward fulfilling the spirit of UN initiatives that support participation by persons with disabilities in employment as equal citizens of the world.

NOTES

1. General Assembly of the United Nations, Resolution Adopted by the General Assembly A/RES/48/96, Standard Rules on the Equalization of Opportunities for Persons with Disabilities (20 December 1993).
2. General Assembly of the United Nations, Resolution Adopted by the General Assembly A/RES/50/144, Towards Full Integration of Persons with Disabilities in Society: Implementation of the Standard Rules on the Equalization of Opportunities for Persons with Disabilities and of the Long-Term Strategy to Implement the World Programme of Action Concerning Disabled Persons to the Year 2000 and Beyond (30 January 1996).
3. Standard Rules on the Equalization of Opportunities for Persons with Disabilities (n 1 above).
4. ibid.
5. PD Blanck, 'Civil War Pensions and Disability' (2001) 62 *Ohio State LJ* 109; PD Blanck and M Millender, 'Before Disability Civil Rights: Civil War Pensions and the Politics of Disability in America' (2000) 52 *Alabama L Rev* 1. For a study illustrating the relation of nationality and politics to these developments, see PD Blanck and C Song, 'With Malice toward None; with Charity toward All: Civil War Pensions for Native and Foreign-born Union Army Veterans' (2001) 11 *Journal of Transnational Law and Contemporary Problems* 1; PD Blanck and C Song, 'Civil War Pension Attorneys and Disability Politics' (2001–2002) 35 *Michigan J of L Reform* 1.
6. For a review of disability employment law and policies, see PD Blanck and HA Schartz, 'Towards Researching a National Employment Policy for Persons with Disabilities' in LR McConnell (ed), *Switzer Monograph Series* (National Rehabilitation Assoc, July 2001); P Blanck, L Clay, J Schmeling, M Morris, and H Ritchie, 'Applicability of the ADA to "Ticket to Work" Employment Networks' (2002) 20 *Behavioral Sciences and the Law* 621–636.
7. S Schwochau and PD Blanck, 'The Economics of the Americans with Disabilities Act: Part III—Does the ADA Disable the Disabled?' (2000) 21 *Berkeley J of Employment and Labor L* 271–313; S Schwochau and PD Blanck, 'Does the ADA Disable the Disabled?: More Comments' (2002) 42 *Industrial Relations* 67–77; FC Collignon, 'Is the ADA Successful? Indicators for Tracking Gains' (January 1997) 549 *The ANNALS of the American Academy of Political and Social Science* 129–147. See also P Blanck, H Ritchie, JA Schmeling, and D Klein, 'Technology for Independence: A Community-Based Resource Center' (2003) 21 *Behavioral Sciences and the Law* 51–62.
8. PD Blanck, *The Americans with Disabilities Act and the Emerging Workforce* (Washington, DC: AAMR, 1998); PD Blanck, 'Employment Integration, Economic Opportunity, and the Americans with Disabilities Act: Empirical Study from 1990–1993' (1994) 79 *Iowa L Rev* 853 [hereinafter Empirical Study]; B Dole, 'Are We Keeping America's Promise to People with Disabilities?—Commentary on Blanck' (1994) 79 *Iowa L Rev* 925; T Harkin, 'The Americans with Disabilities Act: Four years Later—Commentary on Blanck' (1994) 79 *Iowa L Rev* 935.

9. Earlier parts of this series are: PD Blanck, 'The Americans with Disabilities Act: Putting the Employment Provisions to Work' (1993) White Paper of the Annenberg Washington Program [hereinafter Annenberg White Paper] (discussing need for communication to effectuate ADA implementation); PD Blanck, 'Empirical Study of the Employment Provisions of the Americans with Disabilities Act: Methods, Preliminary Findings and Implications' (1992) 22 *New Mexico L Rev* 119 (discussing findings and methodological issues); PD Blanck, 'On Integrating Persons with Mental Retardation: The ADA and ADR' (1992) 22 *New Mexico L Rev* 259 (discussing alternative dispute resolution and the ADA); PD Blanck, 'The Emerging Work Force: Empirical Study of the Americans with Disabilities Act' (1991) 16 *J Corporate Law* 693 (discussing findings and Civil Rights Act of 1991).

10. Empirical Study (n 8 above) 869–886 (study's time interval encompasses a two-year period prior to the passage of the ADA in 1990, and a period subsequent to the effective date of Title I of the Act in 1992).

11. Annenberg White Paper (n 9 above); PD Blanck, 'Communications Technology for Everyone: Implications for the Classroom and Beyond' White Paper and CD-ROM of the Annenberg Washington Program (1994).

12. JM McNeil, 'Current Population Reports, Americans with Disabilities: 1991–1992, Data from the Survey of Income and Program Participation 5', Pub No P70–33 (US Bureau of the Census, 1993) (presenting data on the disability status of noninstitutionalized persons in the United States).

13. The 1964 Civil Rights Act does not address discrimination on the basis of a disability. The Rehabilitation Act of 1973 prohibits discrimination against persons with disabilities but applies only to federal contractors and recipients of federal grants. EC Morin, 'Americans with Disabilities 1990: Social Integration through Employment' (1990) 40 *Catholic U L Rev* 189, 201–202 (comparing the ADA with other legislation).

14. HH Perritt, Jr., *Americans with Disabilities Handbook 1* (New York: John Wiley & Sons, 1990) 1 (Title I is the most significant labor and employment legislation in a decade); BP Tucker, 'The Americans with Disabilities Act: An Overview' (1989) *U Illinois L Rev* 923, 923 (quoting Senator Harkin that the ADA is the 'Emancipation Proclamation' for Americans with disabilities).

15. S Rosen, 'Disability Accommodation and the Labor Market' in CL Weaver (ed), *Disability and Work: Incentives, Rights, and Opportunities* (Washington, DC: AEI Press, 1991) 18, 22.

16. 'A Disability Deluge: Told You So, Editorial' (19 July 1994) *Colorado Springs Gazette Telegraph* B4.

17. Max Schulz, 'Commentary: Disability Rules Moving in on Smaller Businesses' (28 August 1994) *Washington Times* B3.

18. McNeil (n 12 above) 3 (estimating the number of people with disabilities to be 48.9 million, or 19.4% of the total US population of 251.8 million); PD Blanck, 'The Americans with Disabilities Act and Health Care Reform—Access and Partnerships' Presentation to the President's Committee on Mental Retardation (24 April 1994).

19. SS Herr, 'The ADA in International and Developmental Disabilities Perspectives' in LO Gostin and HA Beyer (eds), *Implementing the Americans*

with Disabilities Act (Baltimore: Paul H Brookes Publishing Co, 1993) 229–230. Herr offers five reasons, including: (1) the assertion that the ADA is consistent with international human rights standards and provides legal protection for the equal rights of persons with disabilities, (2) the ADA reflects a political statement by a leading nation, (3) the ADA's principles have extraterritorial effects, (4) foreign visitors and trainees observe US practices and carry the ADA's message abroad, and (5) the ADA may be improved by knowledge of other countries' laws.

20. In the United States, studies reveal a mixed picture of the benefits of equal employment and affirmative action law. LB Edelman, 'Legal Ambiguity and Symbolic Structure—Organizational Mediation of Civil-Rights Law' (1992) 97 *American J of Sociology* 1531, 1533.

21. Annenberg White Paper (n 9 above) 23; ABA Commission on Mental and Physical Disability Law and Commission on Legal Problems of the Elderly, *Targeting Disability Needs: A Guide to the Americans with Disabilities Act for Dispute Resolution Programs* 3 (Washington, DC: American Bar Association, 1994).

22. PD Blanck, 'Assessing Five Years of Employment Integration and Economic Opportunity under the Americans with Disabilities Act' (1995) 19 *Mental & Physical Disability L Reporter* 385–393 (describing 1994 findings).

23. Empirical Study (n 8 above) 857–859.

24. These principles are derived from the American Association on Mental Retardation (AAMR), *Mental Retardation: Definition, Classification, and Systems of Support* (Washington, DC: AAMR, 1992) 1.

25. Harkin (n 8 above) 936.

26. AAMR (n 24 above) 135; L Rowitz, 'Prologue' in L Rowitz (ed), *Mental Retardation in the Year 2000* (New York: Springer-Verlag, 1992) 5 (discussing the changing paradigms of disability).

27. 'ADA Watch Year One: A Report to the President and the Congress on Progress' in *National Council on Disability, Implementing the Americans with Disabilities Act* (National Council on Disability, 1993) 3, 7.

28. PD Blanck, HA Schartz, and KM Schartz, 'Labor Force Participation and Income of Individuals with Disabilities in Sheltered and Competitive Employment: Cross-Sectional and Longitudinal Analyses from Seven States during the 1980s and 1990s' The President's Task Force on Employment of Persons with Disabilities (2003) (reviewing and analyzing updated information on the present investigation); B Altman and PJ Cunningham, 'Dynamic Process of Movement in Residential Settings' (1993) 98 *American J Mental Retardation* 304, 304 (finding mobility among living settings for persons with mental retardation and citing studies emphasizing quality of the movement and long-term outcomes); P Wehman and J Kregel, 'Supported Employment: Growth and Impact', in P Wehman, P Sale, and W Parent (eds), *Supported Employment: Strategies for Integration of Workers with Disabilities* (Boston: Andover Medical Publishers, 1992) 3–6 (reviewing supported employment programs for persons with disabilities).

29. Empirical Study (n 8 above) 870–874 (describing the four levels of employment involvement); The State Supported Employment Services Program, 34 CFR §§252, 254 (1991) (integrated settings involve job sites where co-workers

are not disabled and individuals with disabilities are not part of a group of other individuals with disabilities).

30. cf JP Shapiro, *No Pity: People with Disabilities Forging a New Civil Rights Movement* (New York: Times Books, 1994) 4, 143 (the absence of nondisabled co-workers in a sheltered workshop is confirmation of a prejudiced opinion that people with disabilities cannot work).

31. FR Rusch and C Hughes, 'Overview of Supported Employment' (1989) 122 *J Applied Behavior Analysis* 351, 352 (competitive work occurs when an individual averages at least 20 hours per week for each pay period); MS Shafer, J Hill, J Seyfarth, and P Wehman, 'Competitive Employment and Workers with Mental Retardation: Analysis of Employers Perceptions and Experiences' (1987) 92 *American J Mental Retardation* 304, 304–311 (competitive and supported employment are effective means for workers with mental retardation).

32. McNeil (n 12 above) 11.

33. The EEOC estimates that positive economic effects are likely to result from Title I in the form of minimal costs to employers for reasonable accommodations, increased productivity gains and tax revenues, and decreased support and social welfare payments. 56 Fed Reg 8583, 8581 (1991) (real wages of employees with disabilities are only 71% of non-disabled employees with a comparable education).

34. The group with the highest monthly gross and earned incomes is comprised of participants who reside in integrated settings and are competitively employed. DL Braddock, R Hemp, L Bachelder, and G Fujiura, *The State of the States in Developmental Disabilities* (Washington, DC: AAMR, 1995).

35. WJ Hanna and E Rogovsky, 'On the Situation of African-American Women with Physical Disabilities' (1992) 23 *J Applied Rehab Counseling* 39–45 (25% of black women with disabilities employed full time, as compared to 77% of white men, 44% of white women, and 57% black men with disabilities); McNeil (n 12 above) 10 (data from 1991 to 1992 showing differences among races and ethnicity groups in disability prevalence).

36. AAMR (n 24 above) 11.

37. cf Empirical Study (n 8 above) 876–877.

38. TH Barnard, 'The Americans with Disabilities Act: Nightmare for Employers and Dream for Lawyers?' (1990) 64 *St John's L Rev* 229, 242–245 (ADA will result in litigation as to who is 'qualified'); KF Ebert and JM Perkins, 'New Era in Employment Litigation: Overview of Americans with Disabilities Act' (1991) 34 *Res Gestae* 318, 319–320 (ADA invites litigation over definition of 'qualified').

39. 29 CFR §1630.5 (1991); LA Lavelle, 'The Duty to Accommodate: Will Title I of the Americans with Disabilities Act Emancipate Individuals with Disabilities Only to Disable Small Businesses?' (1991) 66 *Notre Dame L Rev* 1135, 1142.

40. Empirical Study (n 8 above) 876–878; AAMR (n 24 above) 38 (analysis of intellectual functioning and of adaptive behavior must proceed with caution and consider factors related to degree of mental retardation).

41. The needs assessed include: general urgency of medical care, prior contact with medical personnel, and difficulty in receiving medical services. Empirical Study (n 8 above) 878.

42. ibid 878–879 (the 1990 findings showed a positive relationship between health status and employment integration).
43. Empirical Study (n 8 above) 879 (more sophisticated measures are warranted, and insufficient attention paid to assessing accommodation needs and employment integration).
44. n 9 above (citing studies).
45. JE Heumann, 'Building Our Own Boats: A Personal Perspective on Disability Policy' in LO Gostin and HA Beyer (eds), *Implementation of the Americans with Disabilities Act* (Baltimore: Paul H Brookes Publishing Co, 1993) 257 (force behind policy toward persons with disabilities is independent living movement).
46. Empirical Study (n 8 above) 892–894; AAMR (n 24 above) 114.
47. Empirical Study (n 8 above) 879–883; Altman and Cunningham (n 28 above) 304–305 (study of movement from less to more independent living settings).
48. Empirical Study (n 8 above) 882–883 (methodological and ethical issues when interviewing consumers of the ADA).
49. W Parent, 'Quality of Life and Consumer Choice' in P Wehman (ed), *The ADA Mandate for Social Change* (Baltimore: Paul H Brookes Publishing Co, 1993) 19–20 (choices and participation in life decisions improve quality and positively influences sense of self-worth, and independence).
50. Empirical Study (n 8 above) 883–885 ('People First' is a self-advocacy group present in almost every state).
51. D Braddock, 'Responding to the Self-Advocacy Movement' (July/August 1993) *AAMR News & Notes* 2.
52. Blanck (n 8 above) (discussing empowerment issues for persons with mental retardation).
53. Empirical Study (n 8 above) 884 (natural supports assist the person to attain independence and productivity and facilitates community integration); AAMR (n 24 above) 101.
54. AAMR (n 24 above) 101–103 (this belief is exemplified by emphasis on supported employment programs).
55. Empirical Study (n 8 above) 885–886.
56. ibid 885.
57. Title II of the ADA covers state and local agency services, and public transportation services. 42 USC §§12131–12165 (Supp IV 1992). Lack of access to education and transportation often forecloses the possibility of employment for people with disabilities; ibid.
58. 28 CFR §36 (1993) (Title III requires public accommodations to make reasonable modifications so that they may be accessible to persons with disabilities).
59. L Harris and Assocs, *Survey of Americans with Disabilities* (1994) 37, 108 (adults with disabilities perceive as problems insufficient finances (67%), lack of full social life (51%), and inadequate health insurance (26%)).
60. Empirical Study (n 8 above) 874–875.
61. ibid.
62. Definition of 'change' may include debate about the diverse methods of determining the scope of persons covered by the law and penalties for non-compliance. CA Rasnic, 'A Comparative Analysis of Federal Statutes for the

Disabled Worker in the Federal Republic of Germany and the United States' (1992) 9 *Arizona J of Intl and Comparative L* 283, 332.

63. L Despouy, *Human Rights and Disabled Persons* (New York: United Nations Publication, 1993) 1.
64. Y Yu, 'The Demography of Disability' (1991) 30 *Population Bulletin of the UN* 61, 63.
65. Australian Institute of Health and Wealth, *Australia's Health 1996*, available at http://www.aihw.gov.au/publication/health/ah96/index.html (last viewed 7 December 2001).
66. Despouy (n 63 above) 26.
67. Eurostat, *Disabled People: Statistics*, published under Theme 3: Population and Social Conditions, Series D: Studies and Analysis, 2 (1992).
68. Eurostat, *Disabled Persons: Statistical Data*, published under Theme 3: Population and Social Conditions, Series D: Studies and Analysis, 2 (1995).
69. Eurostat (n 67 above) 8.
70. ibid.
71. Commission on the Status of People with Disabilities, *Commission on the Status of People with Disabilities, A Strategy for Equality* (1996) 135.
72. C Raskin, 'Employment Equity for the Disabled in Canada' (1994) 133 *Intl Labour Rev* 75.
73. PD Blanck and P Steele, *Communicating the Americans with Disabilities Act: The Role of the Staffing Industry in the Employment of Persons with Disabilities—A Case Report on Manpower, Inc* (Iowa City: Iowa CEO and Law, Health Policy and Disability Center, 1998).
74. RS Belous, 'The Rise of the Contingent Workforce: Growth of Temporary, Part-Time, and Subcontracted Employment' (1997) 19 *Looking Ahead* 1, 2–24; R Belous, 'The Rise of the Contingent Workforce' in D Lewin, DJB Mitchell, and MA Zaidi (eds), *The Human Resource Management Handbook*, Part II (Stamford, Conn: JAI Press, 1997) 3–19.
75. ibid.
76. 'Contingent Workers Said to Comprise 25% of U.S. Workforce' (22 August 1997) 8 *Staffing Industry Report* 9–10.
77. PD Blanck, LA Sandler, JL Schmeling, and HA Schartz, 'The Emerging Workforce of Entrepreneurs with Disabilities: Preliminary Study of Entrepreneurship in Iowa' (2000) 85 *Iowa L Rev* 1583–1670.
78. Shapiro (n 30 above) 4 (effects of the emerging workforce comprised of young people with disabilities).
79. PD Blanck, 'Empirical Study of the Americans with Disabilities Act: Employment Issues from 1990 to 1994' (1995) 14 *Behavioral Science & L* 5–27 (providing data on emerging workforce of young adults with disabilities).
80. Blanck (n 8 above) (1998).
81. D Kruse and L Schur, 'Employment of People with Disabilities' (2002) 42 *Industrial Relations* 31–66 (reporting increased employment rates from 1990 to 1994 when using functional definition of disability in analysis of Survey of Income and Program Participation (SIPP) data set).
82. CC Zwerling, PS Whitten, NL Sprince, *et al.*, 'Workforce Participation by Persons with Disabilities: The National Health Interview Survey Disability Supplement, 1994–5' (2002) 44/2 *J of Occupational and Environmental Medicine* 358–364.

83. S Schwochau and P Blanck, 'The Economics of the Americans with Disabilities Act: Part III—Does the ADA Disable the Disabled?' (2000) 21 *Berkeley J Employment & Labor L* 271–313.
84. PD Blanck, 'The Economics of the Employment Provisions of the Americans with Disabilities Act: Part I—Workplace Accommodations' (1997) 46 *DePaul L Rev* 877–914; PD Blanck, 'Attitudes, Behavior and the Employment Provisions of the Americans with Disabilities Act' (1997) 42 *Villanova L Rev* 345–408. cf Edelman (n 20 above) 1539 (under Title VII, weak enforcement mechanisms and ambiguous terms provide inadequate feedback to covered entities about compliance with the law).
85. PD Blanck, 'Communicating the Americans with Disabilities Act: Transcending Compliance: A Case Report of Sears Roebuck and Co' Annenberg Washington Program Report (Washington, DC, 1994); PD Blanck, 'Communicating the Americans with Disabilities Act, Transcending Compliance: 1996 Follow-Up Report on Sears, Roebuck & Co' The Annenberg Washington Program Reports (Washington, DC, 1996).
86. Blanck (n 8 above) (1998); K Schartz, HA Schartz, and P Blanck, 'Employment of Persons with Disabilities in Information Technology Jobs: Literature Review for "IT Works"' (2002) 20 *Behavioral Sciences and the Law* 637–657.
87. HJ Greenwood, 'Coorscreen—A Low Cost, On-site Mammography Screening-Program' (1996) 10 *American J Health Promotion* 364–370.
88. AI Batavia, 'Ideology and Independent Living: Will Conservatism Harm People with Disabilities?' (January 1997) 549 *Annals, AAPSS* 10–23.
89. cf PD Blanck, 'Communications Policy Issues in Disaster Relief and Mitigation for Persons with Disabilities' Annenberg Washington Report (Washington, DC, 1995).
90. This discussion is not comprehensive and illustrates disability policy initiatives, from cooperative efforts in the European Union, to long-established policies in Germany, to emerging efforts in Bulgaria, Israel, Hungary, and Latin America. Other important initiatives may be identified and studied. 'Doing Business in Poland' (27 October 1994) European Union, European Update; 'The Woes of China' (25 January 1990) *Wall Street J* A10.
91. Raskin (n 72 above) 76.
92. ibid; PD Blanck and JL Schmeling, 'Americans with Disabilities Act: Recent and Pending US Supreme Court Decisions and Implications for Spine Professionals' (2002) 27/4 *Spine* 439–443 (discussing US Supreme Court rulings that, under the ADA, courts are to take into account an individual's mitigating measures, in defining disability under the law).
93. Raskin (n 72 above) 76.
94. ibid 77–78.
95. Treasury Board of Canada Secretariat, Overview of the Employment Equity Act (1996) from a public Service Perspective, available at http://www.tbs-sct.gc.ca/pubs_pol/hrpubs/tb_852/over_e.html (last viewed 19 December 2001).
96. ibid.
97. ibid.
98. ibid.

99. ibid.
100. GCM Wallace and GM Currie, 'Employment of Persons with Disabilities: The Employment Equity Act 1986 to 1996' (Autumn 1996) 1/3 *The Expert Witness Newsletter*, available at www.economica.ca/ew13p2.htm (last viewed 19 December 2001).
101. J Sowers, P Cotton, and J Malloy, 'Expanding the Job and Career Options for People with Significant Disabilities' (1994) 22 *Developmental Disabilities Bulletin* 53.
102. ibid 54.
103. ibid 55.
104. ibid.
105. Commission of the European Communities, Proposal for a Council Decision on the European Year of People with Disabilities 2003, Brussels (29 May 2001) 2.
106. The European Community will be referred to as the European Union hereinafter, with one exception; if a program was enacted under the European Community and is referred to as such in the original title of the law.
107. European Union, Social Policy, European Update, §8.1.2 (27 October 1994) (WESTLAW, 1991 WL 11753 (DRT) Eurupdate, 345).
108. OJ Eur Comm (L56) (1993). A minor corrigendum was published in OJ Eur Comm (L234) (1993). European Union, Social Policy, European Update, §8.1.2 (27 October 1994) (WESTLAW, 1991 WL 11753 (DRT), Eurupdate, 345).
109. European Union, Social Policy, European Update, §8.1.2 (27 October 1994) (WESTLAW, 1991 WL 11753 (DRT), Eurupdate, 345).
110. ibid (program has a budget of ECU 37 million over a four-year period).
111. ibid.
112. ibid.
113. This program is allotted 180 million ECU from the European Union's structural funds.
114. OJ Eur Comm (C18) (1992); European Union, Social Policy, European Update, §8.1.4 (27 October 1994) (WESTLAW, 1991 WL 11753 (DRT)).
115. European Union, Social Policy, European Update, §8.1.4 (27 October 1994) (WESTLAW, 1991 WL 11753 (DRT)); OJ Eur Comm (L240) (1993); European Union, Social Policy, European Update, §8.1.4 (27 October 1994) (WESTLAW, 1991 WL 11753 (DRT)).
116. Projects assisting in this goal have been allocated ECU 30 million with the expected benefits of such a program going to 60 to 80 million European citizens. European Union, Social Policy, European Update, §8.1.5 (27 October 1994) (WESTLAW, 1991 WL 11753 (DRT)).
117. OJ Eur Comm (L 303) (2000); Commission of the European Communities, 'Proposal for a Council Decision on the European Year of People with Disabilities 2003' (2001) 3.
118. L Waddington and M Diller, 'Tensions and Coherence in Disability Policy: The Uneasy Relationship between Social Welfare and Civil Rights Models of Disability in American, European and International Employment Law' presented at *From Principles to Practice: An International Disability Law and Policy Symposium* (October 2000).
119. ibid.

120. Commission on the Status of People with Disabilities (n 71 above) iii.
121. ibid 7.
122. H Murdoch, 'Barrister Reviews Recent Irish Legislation' (2001) 9 *Disability World*.
123. Irish Campaign to Promote Employment Opportunities (2001) 10 *Disability World*, available at http://www.disabilityworld.org/09–10_01/employment/ briefly.shtml (last viewed 18 February 2002).
124. ibid.
125. ibid.
126. CD Rasnic, 'A Comparative Analysis of Federal Statutes for the Disabled Worker in the Federal Republic of Germany and the United States' (1992) 9 *Arizona Intl & Comparative L* 283.
127. E Seyfried, *Requirements for the Successful Integration of Disabled People into Working Life* (CEDEFOP Document, Berlin: European Centre for the Development of Vocational Training, 1992) 40.
128. ibid 40.
129. Rasnic (n 126 above) 298–300.
130. ibid 322–325.
131. Seyfried (n 127 above) 13–18.
132. ibid 13–14.
133. ibid 16.
134. C Bourn and J Whitmore, *Anti-Discrimination Law in Britain* (London: Sweet & Maxwell, 1996) 13.
135. B Doyle, 'Enabling Legislation or Dissembling Law? The Disability Discrimination Act 1995' (1997) 60 *Modern L Rev* 64, 69–70.
136. BJ Doyle, *Disability Discrimination: The New Law* (Bristol: Jordan Publishing Ltd, 1996) 43; BJ Doyle, 'Disabled Workers' Rights, the Disability Discrimination Act and the UN Standard Rules' (1996) 25 *Industrial LJ* 1.
137. BJ Doyle, 'Disabled Workers' Rights, the Disability Discrimination Act and the UN Standard Rules' (1996) 25 *Industrial LJ* 1, 10–11.
138. UK Employers' Forum on Disability, available at http://www.employers-forum.co.uk/www/index.htm (last viewed 12 December 2001) (discussing DDA and other disability policy initiatives in the UK).
139. European Union, 'Doing Business in Bulgaria' European Update 4.4 (14 October 1993); 1992 WL 22707 (DRT) 90.
140. C Gooding, 'The DDA—How Is It Shaping Up?' (Spring 1998) 1 *Legal Update* 3.
141. ibid.
142. ibid 3–4 (reporting that under the ADA from 1992 to 1996 in the US, 51.9% of claims alleged wrongful dismissals, 28.1% lack of reasonable accommodations, 12% harassment, and 9.8% discrimination in recruitment).
143. 'Timetable: Government Response to Task Force Recommendations' (Summer 2001) 6 Legal Update 1.
144. ibid 1–2.
145. ibid.
146. ibid 1.
147. ibid.

Peter Blanck and Helen A. Schartz

148. CG Gregorio and XE Iannino, 'Identification of Policies Concerning Persons with Disabilities and Their Families' Working Document, First Central-American Seminar (24–29 January 1995).
149. ibid.
150. Information was gathered at the 1993 International Seminar, in Managua, Nicaragua, 'Towards a New Model for the Development of Social Policies for Children and Youth with Disabilities and Their Families' (23 November–3 December 1993).
151. ibid.
152. Commission Resolution 48/3 on the Asian and Decade of Disabled Persons, 1993–2002, available at http://www.dpa.org.sg./DPA/ESCAP.reso.htm (last viewed 7 December 2001).
153. US Department of State, *China Report on Human Rights Practices for 1997*, available at www.state.gov/www/global/human_rights/1997_hrp_report/china.htm (last viewed 7 December 2001).
154. US Department of State, *China Report on Human Rights Practices for 1996*, available at www.state.gov/www/global/human_rights/1996_hrp_report/china.htm (last viewed 7 December 2001).
155. RS Pandey and L Advani, *Perspectives in Disability and Rehabilitation* (New Delhi: Vikas Publishing House Private Ltd, 1995) 111.
156. ibid.
157. ibid.
158. N Young, 'Disability and Civil Society' (2001) 19 *China Review*.
159. ibid.
160. ibid.
161. Ministry of Health and Welfare, *White Paper: Annual Report on Health and Welfare*, available at www.mhlw.go.jp/English/wp/wp-hw/index.html (last viewed 7 December 2001).
162. US Department of State, *Japan Report on Human Rights Practices for 1996*, available at http://www.usis.usemb.se/human/human96/japan.html (last viewed 21 April 1998).
163. US Department of State, *Japan Report on Human Rights Practices for 1997*, available at www.state.gov/www/global/human_rights/1997_hrp_report/japan.html (last viewed 7 December 2001).
164. Ministry of Labour, *For Persons with Disabilities and Other Persons in Need of Special Consideration*, available at www2.mhlw.go.jp/english/outline/07–1.htm (last viewed 7 December 2001).
165. *Japan Report on Human Rights Practices for 1997* (n 163 above).
166. ibid.
167. K Onoue, 'Dignity [a]nd Freedom, Not Protection or Charity: A Critique Based on the Reality of Discrimination [a]gainst Disabled Persons in Japan' in *Human Rights in Japan from the Perspective of the International Covenant on Civil and Political Rights* (1993) 67.
168. *Japan Report on Human Rights Practices for 1997* (n 163 above); *White Paper* (n 162 above).
169. *White Paper* (n 162 above).
170. ibid.

171. *Australia's Health 1996* (n 65 above).
172. B Doyle, *Disability, Discrimination and Equal Opportunities: A Comparative Study of the Employment Rights of Disabled Persons* (New York: Mansell Publishing, 1995) 130.
173. ibid.
174. Health and Family Services, *Commonwealth Disability Strategy: Second Progress Report 1997* (1997) iii.
175. ibid.
176. ibid 24.
177. ibid 25.
178. ibid 26.
179. Health and Family Services (n 154 above) 1.
180. A Dean, 'It's a Shame about the Pay' (8 August 2001) *Melbourne Times* 8, available at http://www.dice.org.au/employment/melbournetimes.html (last viewed 18 February 2002).
181. MPA Kumar, 'India's New Rights Law Foundering' (December 1997) *New Mobility: Disability Culture & Lifestyle* 39.
182. ibid.
183. ibid.
184. US Department of State, *India Report on Human Rights Practices for 1997*, available at http://www.state.gov/www/global/human_rights/1997_hrp_report/india.html (last viewed 7 December 2001).
185. MPA Kumar (n 181 above).
186. TW Hale, 'The Lack of a Disability Measure in Today's Current Population Survey' (2001) 124 *Monthly Labor Rev* 38–40.
187. Executive Order 13078 (13 March 1998) (establishing the Presidential Task Force).
188. PD Blanck (ed), *Employment, Disability, and the Americans with Disabilities Act: Issues in Law, Public Policy, and Research* (Evanston, Ill: Northwestern Univ Press, 2002); PD Blanck and LA Sandler, 'ADA Title III and the Internet: Technology and Civil Rights' (2000) 24/5 *Mental & Physical Disability L Rep* 855–859.
189. Social Policy: Commission Unveils White Paper for Employment and Solidarity (9 September 1994) Multinational Service (WESTLAW, 1994 WL 2724323).
190. ibid.
191. ibid.
192. 'United States: The Halt, the Blind, the Dyslexic—Has the Americans with Disabilities Act Gone Too Far, or not Far Enough?' (23 April 1998) *The Economist* 25–26 (discussing future trends in disability policy).

14

The Economics of Equality: An Exploration of Country Differences

JOHN H. NOBLE, JR.

I. INTRODUCTION

Adopted 20 December 1971, General Assembly Resolution 2856 (XXVI) proclaims the United Nations (UN) Declaration on the Rights of Mentally Retarded Persons and reaffirms 'faith...in the principles of peace, of the dignity and worth of the human person and of social justice....' Calling for national and international action to secure the same rights as other human beings, 'to the maximum degree of feasibility', among other things, the Resolution champions 'a right to proper medical care and physical therapy and to such education, training, rehabilitation and guidance as will enable' persons with mental retardation to realize their maximum potential.[1]

For people living in the United States, a country with one of the highest per capita Gross Domestic Products in the world—an estimated $36,200 in the year 2001—Resolution 2856 simply restates what is held as a matter of fundamental values and belief. However, in the United States there have been many serious compromises of the UN Declaration that are difficult to tolerate or understand. After all, the United States has witnessed unprecedented real growth in spending for the wide range of supports and services that are called for by the UN Declaration on the Rights of Mentally Retarded Persons. Indeed, one study by Braddock[2] indicates that from 1977 to 1992, public spending for mental retardation and other developmental disabilities grew 124%, adjusted for inflation.

Efforts in the United States to assist persons with mental retardation are directed not only to meeting the remediation and habilitation needs of persons with mental retardation but also value attainment. Each year advocates and service providers in the United States strive to improve the performance and delivery of support services to persons with mental retardation and invest many millions of dollars each year in research and development and the training of professionals, paraprofessionals, and lay persons. These efforts indicate a national commitment to the notion that progress will continue as long as the government spends more money and/or reallocates current spending for evolving state of the art services.

At root, the UN Declaration prescribes the economics of equality for all countries and peoples to follow in responding to the special needs of persons with mental retardation.

II. THE ECONOMICS OF EQUALITY

Economists studying the 'social cost' of mental illness and mental retardation typically have distinguished between 'direct' and 'indirect' costs when estimating the amount by which the well being of society is reduced by mental illness or mental retardation.[3] In this usage, 'indirect costs' denote the reduced states of individual and social well-being whereas 'direct costs' specify the resources that are spent to achieve well-being. For example, direct costs generally refer to the costs of providing persons with developmental disabilities custodial, remedial, habilitative, educational, and other special services over what would have been expended if the affected persons were not disabled.[4] Indirect costs alternatively refer to those ways in which mental illness or mental retardation interferes with a person's normal functioning and reduces the person's well-being as well as the well-being of his or her friends, family, teachers, and associates. Indirect costs include: (1) the loss of output that society incurs because some people with mental illness or mental retardation do not work or produce less than would be expected of a non-disabled person of similar age and sex; (2) loss of homemaking services; (3) loss of other unpaid, volunteer work at home and in the community; (4) an increase in undesirable events and behavior, eg, crime and delinquency; and (5) other socially disruptive effects on people's lives, eg, frustration, insecurity, bitterness, marital instability, inferior child care, unwise decisions, etc.

Laws that create and fund programs providing medical, remediative, and habilitative services for persons with mental retardation seek to minimize overall social costs by increasing the direct costs of providing services in order to reduce the indirect costs of the condition. In terms of cost-benefit analysis, funding programs assisting persons with mental retardation are the 'costs' and the reductions of indirect costs of the condition are the 'benefits'. Under a utilitarian model, so long as the marginal increase in benefits exceeds costs, funding these programs is justified because overall social costs are reduced.[5]

A useful way to think about the direct and indirect costs of developmental disabilities and the economics of equality is to consider the situation of infants with disabilities. Infants born with a congenital defect that leads to mental retardation or other developmental disability are born unequal in their capacity to function as a 'normal' person. Indeed, they may have unequal chances for survival—especially if born with the combination of mental and physical defects, eg, Down syndrome and duodenal or esophageal atresia, or if born in a country which condones direct killing or selective non-treatment of disabled infants. Those who survive and continue to live often require life-long special care and accommodation from family, friends, and the community in order to offset, to the extent possible, their unequal capacity to function. Spending to offset or reduce the inequalities that persons with mental retardation experience at birth and throughout their lives defines the economics of equality.

In the United States, every state and the District of Columbia have established major programs that seek to reduce these inequalities.[6] The extent to which these programs succeed in achieving their goal of reducing the indirect costs of mental retardation and other developmental disabilities is the subject of a very large and expanding literature.

III. SOCIAL DISCRIMINATION AND INEQUALITY

Insofar as reducing the inequalities experienced by persons with mental retardation is dependent on society's decisions to allocate resources, it is necessary to address the issue of social discrimination and its effects. Ideally, government spending is determined by political processes that translate the individual values of citizens into social choices that seek to maximize society's social utility or welfare. Social choices depend on the values that individuals ascribe to different sets of alternatives.[7] To the extent that spending for one purpose represents an opportunity cost to spend for a different purpose, social choice inevitably requires the ranking of priorities. The perceived value of the objects of beneficence as well as technological and resource constraints figure prominently in the ranking of priorities subject to social choice.

There are historical and contemporary reasons to believe that the life of a person with mental retardation has not had, and still does not have, the same value for everyone everywhere. Even in an affluent society, moral perspectives and self-interest often decide who lives and who dies; who receives available resources and who is left without—who, in effect, is allowed to join the moral community of humanity in which equality of opportunities is held forth as the normative ideal.[8]

The advent of the hospital neonatal intensive care unit (NICU) is illustrative. In communities affluent enough to afford them, access to NICUs has provoked legal battles about the proper care and treatment of disabled newborns. It has likewise spawned a whole literature relating to the rights and duties of parents, physicians, nurses, and hospitals in reaching selective non-treatment decisions—including the right of the severely disabled child to later sue and recover damages based on a negligence theory of 'wrongful life'.[9]

Multiple congenital impairments causing mental retardation are typically implicated in NICU selective non-treatment cases, eg, Down syndrome plus duodenal or esophageal atresia or congenital heart disease, or Trisomy 18 plus congenital heart disease, and the like. In these cases, the decision not to perform corrective surgery often involves judgments about future prospects for suffering and the 'quality of life' of the neonate and other family members. The reasoning of a sampling of ethicists in this regard provides insight into the 'gut' value judgments that lead individuals and sometimes the broader community to discriminate against persons with mental retardation.

Ethicists are of no single mind about the value that should be ascribed to the lives of neonates with severe congenital defects, and their value judgments are reflected in the diverse criteria they advocate for reaching morally defensible decisions to treat, let die, or terminate life. Ethicists rooted in the Judeo-Christian tradition[10] believe that all *non-dying* neonates should be treated because there is no moral basis for choosing 'that some live and others die, when the medical indications for treatment are the same'.[11] Regardless of the neonate's state or condition, these ethicists further argue that the 'equality of life principle' should govern over considerations of the individual's future quality of life, impact on parents and siblings, possible contributions to society, and the like. Jewish law likewise takes the position that 'the title to life is absolute and equal to that of any other person, from the moment of birth,' and even if born with 'teeth and tail like an animal', the innocent life deserves protection regardless of condition.[12]

Conversely other ethicists[13] argue that the properties of 'personhood' rather than status as a human being convey the right to life. There is no right to life, these ethicists maintain, unless the individual is a 'continuing subject of experiences and other mental states that can envisage a future for itself and have desires about the future'.[14] Thus, fetuses and very young neonates with no prospect of cognitive lives are considered nonpersons, and killing them 'is morally permissible in most cases where it is otherwise desirable'.[15]

Taking the middle ground, some ethicists[16] emphasize the right of parents to 'avoid severe and unnecessary familial burdens' in a *small* number of cases. Under this view, the decision to treat, let die, or terminate life should be based on the parent's knowledge, their attitudes toward defects, the extent of risk for future harm, the family's economic resources, the welfare of other children involved, and the parent's physical and emotional capacity to cope.

Most ethicists outside the Judeo-Christian tradition express the views and values of moral relativism. This ethic tends to confer less value on the lives of neonates whose impairments cause mental retardation as compared to neonates with other kinds of impairments. In this regard, the views and moral reasoning of ethicists about selective non-treatment undoubtedly reflect the values and behavioral tendencies of broader society. After all, can the thinking and actions that take place in the isolation of the hospital NICU be much different than what goes on outside?

What is the heritage of broader society? Until recent times infanticide was commonly practiced throughout the world. According to anthropologist Laila Williamson,[17] infanticide 'rather than being an exception has been the rule' on every continent at every level of civilization throughout history. The reasons for infanticide fall into three categories: (1) maintaining a balance between population size and economic resources; (2) eliminating defective newborns; and (3) socio-cultural, eg, protecting genealogical purity, minimizing the dowries for females and avoiding the shame of illegitimacy or miscegenation.[18]

In places such as Benin and Côte D'Ivoire, amidst a mixture of traditional practices, beliefs and superstitions overt infanticide is still practiced in cases of serious birth disabilities.[19] In other countries, evidence of a lower threshold for infanticide in general is found in reports that female infanticide is a factor contributing to lower than expected female birth rates in some areas of China and India. In South Korea, consistent with the conservative Confucian tradition that subordinates women socially, economically, and legally, an estimated 400,000 surplus bachelors is predicted in the next generation because of fetal sex testing and abortion.

Although not discussed openly, the covert practice of infanticide through selective non-treatment is probably very widespread throughout the world, and the results are reported in each country's infant mortality rates. In this context, the UN Declaration on the Rights of Mentally Retarded Persons is, therefore, an important and necessary reminder to everyone everywhere that individuals with mental retardation *are* human persons deserving of full participation in the moral community of mankind, including access to supports and services that will enable them to realize their fullest potential as human beings. The qualifying phrase, 'to the maximum degree of feasibility', however, raises some question about how the economics of equality will be operationalized in different countries. Will cultures subscribing to the Judeo-Christian religious tradition try harder to reduce inequalities—regardless of the nation's level of development and resource availability? Or is the economics of equality really contingent on resource availability and national development?

What about countries that reject Western views of human rights and the Western-influenced human rights pronouncements of international organizations such as the United Nations? According to the US Department of State,[20] Iranian government officials insist that Iran should be judged by Islamic law rather than Western human rights principles. Likewise, in Saudi Arabia, international definitions of human rights are ignored in favor of Islamic law. Some commentators, like Huntington,[21] would interpret this as evidence of grounds for the new post-Cold War pattern of conflicts within and between countries along the fault lines of civilizations and cultures.

Other commentators, however, are critical of the perceived selective application of Western standards. For instance, responding to Huntington, Mahbubani[22] points to then recent events in Bosnia-Herzegovina and argues that 'the dramatic passivity of powerful European nations as genocide is committed on their doorstep has torn away the thin veil of moral authority that the West has spun around itself as a legacy of its recent benign era'. Citing structural weaknesses in the West's core value systems and institutions, these commentators consequently question why 85% of the world's population should accept decrees legislated by 15%.

I have undertaken an exploratory analysis of available statistics to clarify one of these issues: the influence of culture as compared to economics in explaining inequalities in the treatment of persons with physical and mental disabilities among different countries. Do cultural differences—as manifested by predominant religion—more than economic means—as indicated by per capita Gross Domestic Product—account for the inequalities among countries in the treatment of persons with physical and mental disabilities? Competing explanations for any cultural differences that may be revealed include: the type of government, political stability, and the impact of Western medical technology, as signified by the number of physicians per 100,000 population providing general health care.

IV. METHODS

A. Proxy Variables

Our measurement model for comparing and explaining the inequalities that affect the lives and opportunities of persons with mental and physical disabilities living in different countries relies on a number of proxy variables. These proxy variables are *assumed* to represent different kinds and levels of inequality, the model's dependent variables, and several independent variables that explain or predict variation in the dependent variables.

1. Infant Mortality Rate

The first and most basic dependent variable is the infant mortality rate. The infant mortality rate captures an estimated 6% of neonatal deaths that would almost inevitably result from premature birth and a variety of congenital anomalies if not treated by high technology medicine in a hospital neonatal intensive care unit (NICU).[23] Thus, the infant mortality rate represents the inequality faced by those disabled persons who at birth do not have access to high technology medicine and therefore do not have an equal opportunity for life.

2. Support Services

After birth, survivors with congenital abnormalities often suffer lifelong physical and mental impairments. Such persons and others whose disabilities occur later in life are unequal in their ability to function in society's expected roles unless accommodated and assisted by family, kin, and neighbors as well as by governmental and/or charitable organizations. Often unaccepted and unassisted, they encounter overt as well as more subtle forms of discrimination and stigma.

The provision of informal and formal services is one sign of societal acceptance. Likewise, the level of government-funded disability services and the extent to which accessibility laws are implemented are two indicators of societal efforts to accommodate and reduce the inequalities that prevent persons with disabilities from functioning in society's expected roles.

Although this phenomenon was not quantified, we believe that government-funded disability services are typically provided hierarchically—first for persons with physical and sensory disabilities, followed as resources allow, by provisions for persons with mental retardation, and then, lagging still further behind, provisions for persons suffering from the highly stigmatized conditions of severe mental illnesses and substance abuse.[24] The latter conditions contain an imputed element of personal responsibility and blame.

3. Religion

Religion is considered one, if not the most important, of the determinants of culture. Hence, the country's predominant religion is used as the proxy for culture in determining the relative importance of the independent variables—culture, income, type of government and government stability—used to explain variation in the dependent variables.

4. Income

Income as measured by per capita Gross Domestic Product (GDP)—essentially the US dollar denominated value of a country's total production of goods and services divided by population size—represents the extent of a country's economic means to provide for the needs of its citizens, including varying levels of health care, economic assistance, and services and accommodations to meet the needs of persons with disabilities. As previously mentioned, to the extent that a country chooses to spend a portion of its available income to offset the indirect costs of disability on individuals, families, and the community, it seeks to reduce the inequality suffered by its citizens with disabilities.

5. Government Stability

Our analytic model postulates government stability both as a necessary condition for a society to reach abiding decisions about laws and provisions that offset the indirect costs of disability and as a determinant of the available income that could be used for this purpose. Unstable regimes are generally unwise places for financial institutions and investors to put their money with an expectation of a return on capital!

6. Type of Government

Type of government represents hypothesized propensities of different kinds of government to reflect the desires and priorities of citizens in its laws and practice. The model assumes that democratic governments through free elections, majority rule, and the separation of powers, are more capable than other forms of government in transforming individual values into binding social choices of law and practice.[25] This is not, however, to deny the beneficence of some traditional monarchs or religious leaders in decisions that are of importance to them.[26]

Democratic forms of government are also believed to promote stability because they are attentive to the preferences of their citizens—a belief only partially sustained by our data. Applying our definition of stability, 90% or more of the communist regimes, parliamentary democracies, constitutional monarchies, traditional monarchies, and federal republics were characterized as stable.

7. Western Medical Technology

Last, as a proxy for Western medical technology, the number of physicians per 100,000 population providing general health care, was introduced to test a competing explanation for why one or more Western religions or one or more Western forms of government might account for lower infant mortality in poorer countries. Our analytic model postulates that religion represents differences in cultural values among countries, and that some religious values and practices might account for variations in infant mortality. But could it be that religion is really a proxy for infant mortality reducing Western medical technology that was introduced by foreign missionaries? Could it also be that different types of government and how they respond to the individual values of citizens to reach binding social choices of law and practice are actually a proxy for certain Western forms of government that promote adoption of infant mortality reducing medical technology?

B. Data Sources

Information on disability services and building accessibility laws, as well as the extent of government instability, in 193 countries was obtained from the *1994 Human Rights Reports*.[27] The Country Reports[28] convey to the US Congress 'a full and complete report regarding the status of internationally recognized human rights', as defined in the Universal Declaration of Human Rights of the United Nations, in countries that either receive US foreign aid or are members of the United Nations.[29]

Officials of the Department of State, Foreign Service, and other US government agencies prepare initial drafts of the Country Reports based on information gathered from 'a variety of sources across the political spectrum, including government officials, jurists, military sources, journalists, human rights monitors, academics, and labor activists'.[30] These drafts, in turn, are reviewed by the Bureau of Democracy, Human Rights, and Labor, in cooperation with 'other State Department offices, US and other human rights groups, foreign government officials, representatives from the United Nations and other international and regional organizations and institutions, and experts from academia and the media.'[31] The Country Reports cover individual, civil, political, and labor rights—and, for the second consecutive year, indicate the extent of discrimination against persons with disabilities, focusing on laws, regulations, or state practices that are inconsistent with equal access to housing, employment, education, health care, or other government benefits.

Available estimates of infant mortality (rate per 1,000 live births) and income (per capita GDP) for 1992 and 2001, respectively, were gleaned from the *UN 1992 Demographic Yearbook*,[32] the *UN Statistical Yearbook*,[33] and the CIA *World Factbook*.[34] The number of physicians per 100,000 population was derived from the WHO *Statistical Information System Estimates of Health Personnel*.[35] Information on the type of government and the distribution of religions within each country was gathered from the *World Almanac and Book of Facts*,[36] the *Political Handbook of the World*,[37] and *The Statesman's Year Book, 2002*.[38] No one source provided complete information in the desired form for every country.[39]

Information on persons with disabilities contained in the Country Reports was read and coded twice to assure consistency of interpretation, and decision rules were adopted for resolving ambiguous reports.[40] Unfortunately, the Country Reports' treatment of persons with disabilities focused primarily on building access laws and the extent of their implementation.

Among their shortcomings, the Country Reports neither distinguished between persons with physical disabilities and persons with mental disabilities nor addressed their differing needs for services and accommodation throughout the range of normal living roles and activities. In fact, the phrase 'physical and mental disabilities' was rarely encountered in the Country Reports, indicating the prevailing insensitivity among international monitors of human rights to the existence of people with mental disabilities and their need for accommodations beyond physical access to buildings. Regrettably, some of this insensitivity may be the result of the cultural bias of US Department of State officials in rendering observations overseas.[41]

Given the purpose and context of the Country Reports, the task of operationalizing and coding government stability from information contained therein unavoidably involves elements of subjectivity. Twenty-three percent of the countries were characterized as 'unstable' in 1994 and 19% in 2001. Undoubtedly, our sensibilities about civility and order influenced judgments about specific countries. Rather than try to defend these judgments, decision rules and examples are provided to clarify the meanings ascribed by the author to government 'instability'.[42] Table 14.1 lists the unstable countries in 1994 and 2001 along with the sources of their instability.

TABLE 14.1. *Unstable Countries by Source of Instability, 1994 and 2001*[a]

Country	Source
Afghanistan	1994—Civil war and widespread lawlessness
	2001—US military pursuing remnants of Al Qaeda and Taliban amidst widespread land mines and factions competing for control of central government and regions
Algeria	1994—Transitional government ruled under state of emergency
	2001—After amnesty disbanding of Islamic Salvation Army, residual fighting continues
Angola	1994—Civil war and no implementation of Lusaka peace accord
	2001—After national unity government installed in 1997, serious fighting continues rendering hundreds of thousands of people homeless
Armenia	1994—Legislature unable to approve a constitution or pass an election law
	2001—Armenia–Azerbaijan conflict continues with economies of both sides hurt by inability to reach peace
Azerbaijan	1994—Overthrow of democratic government and widespread rights abuses
	2001—Armenia–Azerbaijan conflict continues resulting in 750,000 refugees and internally displaced persons and widespread corruption

TABLE 14.1. *(continued)*

Country	Source
Bosnia-Herzegovina	1994—Civil war and ethnic purging of Muslims by Serbs 2001—Occupying NATO-led stabilization force (SFOR) of 21,000 troops deters renewed hostilities
Burkina Faso	1994—Abuse and extrajudicial killings by government with little opposition 2001—President Compaore faces an increasingly well-coordinated opposition after 1998 assassination of newspaper editor by member of Presidential Guard
Burma	1994—SLORC attacked winning parties with intimidation, detention, and house arrest 2001—Followers of Nobel Peace Prize recipient in house detention are routinely harassed or jailed
Burundi	1994—Assassinations of President and President and VP of National Assembly 2001—Widespread, often intense ethnic violence continues between Hutu and Tutsi factions with tens of thousands dead
Chad	1994—Transitional government ruled with little achieved in first year 2001—New rebellion in northern Chad continues to escalate and northern ethnic oligarchy retains power despite multiparty presidential and National Assembly elections
Colombia	1994—Rights abuses by police, armed forces and widespread drug trafficking 2001—Large parts of countryside are under guerrilla control and neighboring countries worry about violence spilling over their borders
Comoros	1994—Rights abuses, killings by security forces, and interference in last elections 2001—Colonel Azali seized power in 1999 and the Organization of African Unity has yet to recognize the 2000 Fomboni Accord to resolve secessionist crisis
Croatia	1994—One-quarter of land occupied by rebel Serbs despite UN peacekeeping force 2001—Stability apparently restored with last Serb-held enclave under UN supervision returned to Croatia in 1998
Djibouti	1994—FRUD insurgency with scattered attacks on government troops 2001—Stability apparently restored by late 1994 peace accord ending three-year uprising
Ecuador	1994—Inflation at 25% and arbitrary arrests by police, extrajudicial killings

TABLE 14.1. *(continued)*

Country	Source
	2001—Military-indigenous coup toppling democratically elected president in January 2000 is expected to complete remainder of former president's term to 2003
Equatorial Guinea	1994—DPEG controls judiciary and legislature, the latter through fraudulent elections
	2001—1991 presidential and 1999 legislative elections are widely seen as flawed
Eritrea	1994—New government faces sporadic terrorist attacks by Eritrean Islamic Jihad
	2001—Stability apparently restored in December 2000 with ending under UN auspices of 1998 border war with Ethiopia
Ethiopia	1994—Transition government favors Tigreans over Amharas, the traditional power
	2001—Stability apparently restored in December 2000 with ending under UN auspices of 1998 border war with Eritrea
Gambia	1994—Gambia National Army by *coup d'état* deposed elected government and parliament
	2001—Stability apparently restored in 1996 with new constitution and presidential elections and 1997 parliamentary balloting and nominal return to civilian rule
Georgia	1994—Abkhazia declared independence; presence of UN peacekeeping force
	2001—Russian troops remain garrisoned at four military bases as peacekeepers in separatist regions of Abkhazia and South Ossetia
Ghana	1994—Transitional government; claims by four opposition parties of massive electoral fraud
	2001—Stability apparently restored with election of President John Kufuor in 2000, despite rising discontent over inflation, currency depreciation, deficits, and austerity measures
Guinea	1994—Government through Ministry of Security controlled election of president
	2001—Unrest in Sierra Leone has spilled over into Guinea creating a humanitarian emergency
Guinea-Bissau	1994—No report of instability
	2001—Still recovering from 1998 bloody civil war, crippled economy, and military meddling in civilian government
Haiti	1994—Illegal military regime ousted by US occupational forces; Aristide restored
	2001—Following 2000 legislative elections fraught with irregularities, US and EU suspended almost all aid to Haiti, where 80% of population lives in abject poverty

TABLE 14.1. *(continued)*

Country	Source
India	1994—Abuses, killings generated by intense social tensions, violent secessionists
	2001—Continuing dispute with Pakistan over Kashmir, massive overpopulation, environmental degradation, extensive poverty, and ethnic strife
Iraq	1994—Ethnic divisions resulting in civil uprisings in the north and the south
	2001—UN trade sanctions remain in effect due to incomplete Iraqi compliance with relevant UN Security Council resolutions; ongoing threat of US intervention
Kenya	1994—Large internal security force harasses opposition politicians and critics
	2001—Country faces political uncertainty because constitution requires President Moi to step down at the next elections in early 2003
Lebanon	1994—Syrian, Israeli military forces, and armed Palestinians control much of Lebanon
	2001—Lebanese armed forces extend central government over two-thirds of country, while radical Hizballah party retains weapons and Syria occupies the Bekaa Valley
Liberia	1994—Divided factionally and geographically, despite end of civil war in December
	2001—Years of fighting, flight of most businesses, and unsettled domestic security disrupt rebuilding the social and economic structure war-torn country
Macedonia	1994—Severe shortages due to regional conflict and sanctions on Serbia-Montenegro
	2001—Stability apparently restored with lifting of Greek trade blockade in 1995, despite continuing ethnic tension from a large Albanian minority seeking regional autonomy
Malawi	1994—Severe shortages, rapid depreciation of currency, high inflation, and drought
	2001—Stability apparently restored by successful national multiparty elections in 1999 and approval for relief under the Heavily Indebted Poor Countries (HIPC) program
Mozambique	1994—After decades of war and first free election, political tensions resurfacing
	2001—Stability apparently restored by popular vote for five-year term of President Chissano and abatement of inflation and favorable foreign-assisted economic growth
Nepal	1994—No report of instability
	2001—Six-year Communist guerrilla insurgency to oust the constitutional monarchy continues

TABLE 14.1. *(continued)*

Country	Source
Niger	1994—Tuareg insurgency in the north, killing both soldiers and noncombatants
	2001—1995 peace accord ended Tuareg insurgency, but coups in 1996 and 1999, but transition in1999 to civilian rule under National Reconciliation Council is unsettled
Nigeria	1994—Military coup in 1993 and continuing suspension of 1979 Constitution
	2001—Civilian government under new 1999 constitution faces daunting task of defusing long-standing ethnic and religious tensions and rebuilding economy
Occupied Territories, a.k.a. Palestine West Bank	1994—Unrest and numerous terrorist attacks despite 1993 Declaration of Principles
	2001—September 2000 intifada causing widespread violence in the West Bank, Gaza Strip, and Israel continues to escalate with hundreds killed on both sides
Pakistan	1994—Arbitrary arrest and detention, torture, and repression of Sindh-based MQM
	2001—US military pursuing remnants of Al Qaeda and Taliban fleeing from Afghanistan; ongoing dispute and nuclear bomb threats against India over Kashmir
Rwanda	1994—Ethnic genocide of one-half million Tutsi and four months of renewed civil war
	2001—Recovery challenged by massive population displacement, nagging Hutu extremist insurgency, and two wars in four years in neighboring Congo (formerly Zaire)
Serbia-Montenegro	1994—US and international community do not recognize the brutal FRY regime
	2001—Stationing of NATO and Russian peacekeepers in Kosovo stabilizes the regime of President Vojislav Kostunica who replaced former President Milošović
Sierra Leone	1994—Military junta continues to fight rebel RUF forces and renegade RSLMF soldiers
	2001—Despite a cease-fire, 13,000 UN peacekeepers protect the capital and key towns in the south and a UK force of 750 help to reinforce security and train the army
Somalia	1994—Civil war since 1988 led to UN intervention in 1992 and now withdrawal
	2001—Transitional National Government created in 2000 cannot reunite unstable regions in the south where numerous warlords and factions still fight for Mogadishu
Sri Lanka	1994—Conflict continues between government and Liberation Tigers of Tamil Eelam

TABLE 14.1. *(continued)*

Country	Source
	2001—Ethnic war continues with tens of thousands killed since mid-1980s
Sudan	1994—NIF restricts most civil liberties and continues suspension of 1985 Constitution
	2001—Civil war pitting Christians and animists in the south against Arab-Muslims in the north causes 1.5 million deaths and displacement of millions of others
Togo	1994—Togo's government is too weak and fragile to ensure practical democracy
	2001—Under fire from international human rights organizations for abuses and plagued by political unrest, most bilateral and multilateral aid remains frozen
West Sahara	1994—Sovereignty remains in dispute between Morocco and the Polisario
	2001—Repeatedly postponed referendum on final status of Rabat's sovereignty is not expected to occur until at least 2002
Yemen	1994—Civil war between north and south Yemen; secessionists defeated
	2001—Stability apparently restored by unification of north and south and by 2000 Saudi Arabia–Yemen agreement on their mutual borders
Zaire, now Democratic Republic of Congo	1994—Transitional government; UDPS and others refuse to accept Kengo's election
	2001—Cease-fire signed in July 1999 but sporadic fighting continues; President Laurent Kabila was assassinated in January 2001 and his son Joseph replaced him

[a] In the seven-year span, according to the *CIA World Factbook* (2001), stability was restored in Croatia, Djibouti, Eritrea, Ethiopia, Gambia, Ghana, Macedonia, Malawi, Mozambique, and Yemen. Stable in 1994, the Communist insurgency in Nepal has destabilized that country, and Guinea-Bissau is still struggling to recover from its bloody 1998 civil war. In the statistical analyses, countries in 2001 are coded as either stable (0) or unstable (1).

C. Statistical Analyses

Descriptive statistics and regression tree analysis were used to explore and describe various facets of the analytic model.[43] The dependent variables—per capita GDP and the infant mortality rate—are clearly ratio scales. Extent of disability services (coded '0', '1', or '2') and building access law implementation (coded '0', '1', or '2') are ordinal scales with considerable quantitative variability in categories '1' and '2'. The latter dependent variables were treated as interval scales when estimating the effects of the model's independent variables.

V. FINDINGS

The median per capita GDP in 1992 among the 193 countries sampled was $1,740, ranging from $115 to $23,400. In 2001, the median had risen to $4,000, ranging from $510 to $36,400. The median infant mortality rate in 1992 was 36.5 per 1,000 live births, ranging from 3.9 to 156. In 2001, the median had dropped to 29.0, ranging from 1.5 to 193.7. Twenty-three percent of the countries had unstable governments in 1994. Almost 10% of the countries had transitional governments; another 3% were ruled by the military. In 2001, the situation had changed for the better with only 19% of the countries deemed unstable.

In both 1994 and 2001, the most common form of government was the republic (45%), followed by parliamentary democracy (17%), parliamentary republic (7%), constitutional monarchy (11%), federal republic (6%), traditional monarchy (4%), Islamic republic (2%), communist state (3%), and not elsewhere classified others (2%), such as Macau, Hong Kong, and the United Arab Emirates. The predominant religions practiced in the various countries were: Roman Catholic (31%), Muslim (26%), Protestant (22%), indigenous religions (7%), Buddhist (7%), Orthodox Christian (5%), atheist (1%), Hindu (2%), and Jewish (Israel).[44]

Government funding of disability services was as follows: Minimal funding (51%), more extensive funding (27%), and no apparent funding (22%).[45] The existence and implementation of building access laws were as follows: no law (74%), law with little or no implementation (16%), and law with more extensive implementation (10%).[46] Worldwide, the median number of physicians was 103.6 per 100,000 population. The country distribution, ranging from 1.8 to 664 per 100,000 population, indicates how unequal and skewed is the availability of Western medical technology among nations.

Regression tree analysis was used to test the hypothesis that culture, as represented by predominant religion, more than per capita income level, government stability, or general health care coverage, as measured by the number of physicians per 100,000 population, determined both the extent of government funding of disability services and implementation of building access laws. Regression tree analysis was also used to test the hypothesis that type of government more than per capita income level, government stability, or general health care coverage determined the extent of government funding of disability services and implementation of building access laws. As shown by Figures 14.1 and 14.2, the per capita income level was the dominant explanation in both cases. Type of government had no effect in either case. Protestant religion interacting with per capita income level predicted 8% of the total 44% explained variance among countries in the case of building access law implementation.

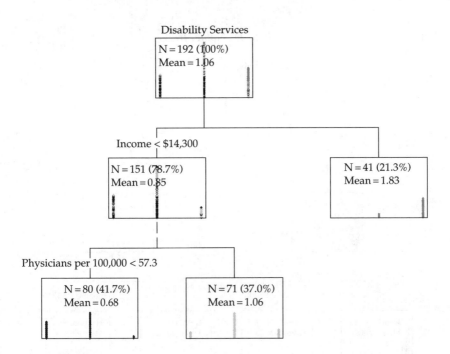

FIGURE 14.1. Regression tree for country disability service estimates, 1994 (PRE = 0.39)

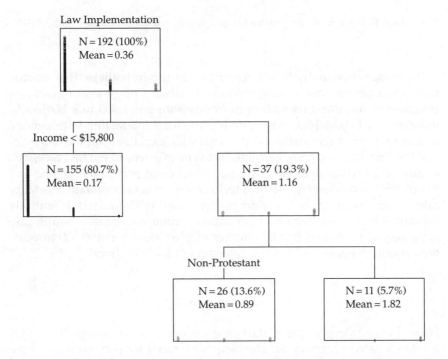

FIGURE 14.2. Regression tree for country accessibility law implementation, 1994 (PRE = 0.44)

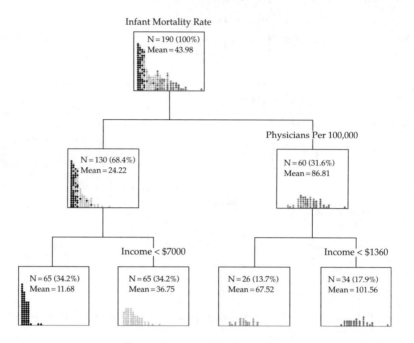

FIGURE 14.3. Regression tree for country infant mortality rate estimates, 2001 (PRE = 0.71)

Regression tree analysis was used to test the hypothesis that culture more than per income level, government stability, or general health care coverage determined the infant mortality rate per 1,000 live births. As indicated by Figure 14.3, per capita income level interacting with general health care coverage predicted the total 71% explained infant mortality variance among countries. Religion and type of government had no effect. Figure 14.4 further demonstrates the influence of per capita income and the provision of Western medical technology on country infant mortality rates. The infant mortality rate *change* from 1992 to 2001 is entirely explained by the interaction of per capita income and general health care coverage, as measured by the number of physicians per 100,000 population. Again, religion and type of government had no effect.

VI. DISCUSSION

How do we interpret these statistical findings? If we accept the infant mortality rate as a proxy for the inequality faced by persons with physical and mental disabilities at birth for having an opportunity for life, then

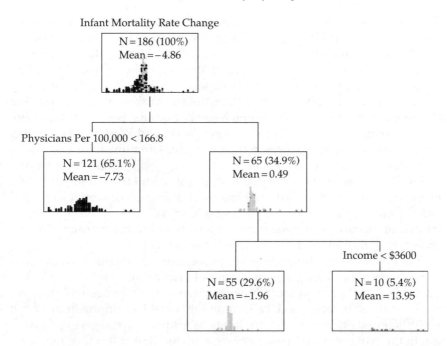

Infant Mortality Rate Change

N = 186 (100%)
Mean = −4.86

Physicians Per 100,000 < 166.8

N = 121 (65.1%)
Mean = −7.73

N = 65 (34.9%)
Mean = 0.49

Income < $3600

N = 55 (29.6%)
Mean = −1.96

N = 10 (5.4%)
Mean = 13.95

FIGURE 14.4. Regression tree for country infant mortality rate change, 1992–2001 (PRE = 0.13)

it follows that economic means, as measured by a country's per capita GDP, more than any alternative explanatory factor determines inequalities for life itself. That is, economic means more than any alternative explanatory factor determines the extent to which a society can provide disability services in order to reduce the indirect cost burden of disability on individuals, families, and the community. Notwithstanding Huntington's contention that cultural conflicts—the 'clash of civilizations'—rather than economic competition over scarce resources will dominate the post-Cold War world, available statistical evidence points to differences in economic means rather than cultural differences among countries as the best explanation for the inequalities faced by people born with a physical or mental impairment.

Available statistical evidence also suggests that culture as manifested by a country's predominant religion may shape at margin the way economic resources are allocated to accommodate people with disabilities. In countries with per capita incomes equal to or greater than $15,800, predominant Protestant religious belief appears to account for more extensive implementation of building access laws. But in Huntington's broader, more dynamic view, there is no doubt that statistical evidence from unstable countries embroiled in conflict—Afghanistan, Algeria, Angola, Armenia, Azerbaijan, Bosnia-Herzegovina, Burkina Faso, Burma, Burundi, Chad, Columbia, Comoros, Congo Democratic Republic (formerly Zaire), Ecuador, Georgia, Guinea, Guinea-Bissau, Haiti, Indian-Pakistan, Iraq, Kenya, Lebanon, Liberia, the Palestinian Authority (formerly the Occupied Territories), Nepal, Niger, Nigeria, Ruanda, Serbia-Montenegro, Sierra Leone, Somalia, Sri Lanka, Sudan, Togo, and West Sahara—points to the inevitable consequences of future conflicts. Outbreaks of violence in countries that now enjoy stable governments will surely increase the inequalities faced by people born with physical and mental impairments in these countries. Wars kill and maim and disrupt economic activities and thus reduce available income and add to the stock of misery and the burden of care for survivors, many of whom will have acquired physical and mental disabilities in the course of the conflict.

There may be, as Huntington conjectures, future conflicts within and between countries along the fault lines of civilizations and cultures. The available data do not suggest, however, that religion per se will provoke these conflicts. Indeed, the UN Summit for Social Development in March 1995[47] suggests that conflicts are likely to erupt over staggering disparities in the economic well-being among nations—not cultural differences.

VII. CONCLUSIONS

Where do we go with these findings in the next ten years knowing that they are based on the exploration of very limited statistical data? Do we send money or missionaries, or both, to the underdeveloped countries? If missionaries, should they preach traditional religious values or the secular value of democracy as the means of expressing the will of the people and promoting political stability? If we act on the basis of the explanatory power of available statistics and other relevant information, the proper policy mix would be the combination of money for economic development and debt-forgiveness based on either religious belief or secular humanism and political pragmatism. The worldwide reduction in infant mortality rates from 1992 to 2001 that accompanied the increase in per capita GDP during that period argues strongly for adoption of such a policy by the richer nations of the world.

There is increasing recognition that relief from debt is a necessary condition for the salvation of individual countries as well as the reform of global society.[48] Soros has argued for an open global civil society to counter the excesses of globalization.[49] An international coalition of economic activists, known as the Jubilee Movement, has succeeded in obtaining debt relief for more than twenty of the poorest nations.[50] Further restructuring of International Monetary Fund (IMF) and Work Bank policies and larger spending by the richer nations on international health and economic development are seen as the key to the advancement of global society. Soros's recommendation that 'standstills', ie, moratoriums on debt repayment, would be more productive than current policy of lending massive amounts of new money to repay the debt of bankrupt nations and maintain their overvalued exchange rates.[51] According to Soros, the ultimate challenge of globalization is to make the most of the interdependence it imposes on individual nations through collective action to provide global public goods, including law and order. He appeals to the ultimate pragmatism of abandoning narrow self-interest in favor a vision of a better world accompanied by action to combat poverty, ignorance, and repression.

In this vein, more developed countries with money and technical assistance to offer could well set aside and link a portion of support for economic infrastructure development to the creation or expansion of services for persons with disabilities, including mental retardation. The United States, for example, spends millions of dollars each year on research and development and training to improve the delivery of services to persons with mental retardation and other developmental disabilities. Would it cost that much to share the results of this effort with the less developed countries of the world?

The US government will use the Department of State's *1994 Human Rights Reports* as a resource for 'shaping policy, conducting diplomacy, and making assistance, training, and other resource allocations and as a basis for the US Government's cooperation with private groups to promote the observance of internationally recognized human rights'.[52] Subject to the approval of the US Congress, the Department of State could easily begin with the information already in its possession to implement the proposed modification of its international assistance programs. Working cooperatively with the UN and other non-governmental organizations would increase the leverage and impact of this enterprise. Debt forgiveness under the Highly Indebted Poor Countries (HPIC) initiative, approved in 1996 by the International Monetary Fund, the World Bank, and the G-7 group of leading industrialized nations, if linked to explicit plans to prevent disabilities and to habilitate and rehabilitate citizens who acquire one, would provide a strong incentive for countries to do so. At the same time, the United States by itself could make use of its existing authority under Titles II and III of PL 480, the Agricultural Trade Development and Assistance Act of 1954, as amended, and related laws to encourage needy countries to develop and implement plans to benefit persons with disabilities.[53]

Last, US Department of State officials responsible for compiling the *Human Rights Reports* as well as members of Amnesty International, Human Rights Watch, and other organizations that monitor human rights abuses throughout the world should be sensitized to the dimensions of the problem as it relates to persons with mental as well as physical disabilities. They already do an excellent job of flagging highly visible abuses of persons with physical disabilities.[54] The reporting of less obvious matters is not taking place.

Much more needs to be done in reporting the conditions under which persons with mental retardation and other mental disabilities live throughout the world. Simply citing the existence and extent of implementation of building access laws as evidence of non-discrimination is insufficient and misleading. The job of educating officials of the US Department of State and the international human rights community about what to look for could easily be undertaken by The Arc of the United States, Mental Disability Rights International, Rehabilitation International, or other interested advocates. It is a job well worth doing and one that could eventually benefit millions of persons with mental retardation and other mental disabilities throughout the world.

NOTES

1. United Nations, *Declaration on the Rights of Mentally Retarded Persons*, General Assembly Resolution 2856 (XXVI) (New York: United Nations, 20 December 1971).
2. D Braddock, R Hemp, L Bachelder, and G Fujiura, *The State of the States in Developmental Disabilities: An Overview* (4th edn, Chicago: Univ of Illinois at Chicago Institute on Disability and Human Development, 1995).
3. eg, R Fein, *Economics of Mental Illness* (New York: Basic Books, 1958); D Rice, 'Estimating the Cost of Illness' *Health Economics Series No 5*, Public Health Service Publication No 947–6 (Washington, DC: Government Printing Office, 1996); RW Conley, *The Economics of Mental Retardation* (Baltimore: Johns Hopkins Univ Press, 1973); DS Levine and DR Levine, 'The Cost of Mental Illness' *Mental Health Statistical Series B No 7*, NIMH (Washington, DC: Government Printing Office, 1975).
4. JH Noble and RW Conley, 'Fact and Conjecture in the Policy of Deinstitutionalization' (1981) *Health Policy Quarterly* 1/2, 99–124.
5. JH Noble, RW Conley, F Laski, and MA Noble, 'Issues and Problems in the Treatment of Traumatic Brain Injury' (1990) *Journal of Disability Policy Studies* 1/2, 19–45.
6. Braddock *et al.* (n 2 above).
7. KJ Arrow, *Social Choice and Individual Values* (2nd edn, New Haven: Yale Univ Press, 1963).
8. RF Weir, *Selective Nontreatment of Handicapped Newborns: Moral Dilemmas in Neonatal Medicine* (New York: Oxford Univ Press, 1984).
9. *Curlender v Bio-Science Laboratories* 106 Cal App 3d 811; 165 Cal Rptr 477, 479, 480, 488–489 (1980).

10. Islamic religious teaching is the same. The child in Islam has an inalienable right to life and equal life chances. According to the Qur'an (6:151, cf 17:23), the third commandment in Islam is preservation of the child's life. H Abdalati, *Islam in Focus* (Indianapolis: American Trust Publications, 1975) 120. My thanks to Mohammad Totonji, Imam/Campus Minister, George Mason University, for this reference and clarification of its meaning in Muslim belief and practice.

11. P Ramsey, *Ethics at the Edges of Life* (New Haven: Yale Univ Press, 1978).

12. I Jakobovits, 'Jewish Views on Infanticide' in M Kohl (ed), *Infanticide and the Value of Life* (Buffalo, NY: Prometheus Books 1978) 23–31.

13. eg, M Tooley, 'Decisions to Terminate Life and the Concept of Person' in J Ladd (ed), *Ethical Issues Relating to Life and Death* (New York: Oxford Univ Press, 1979) 62–93.

14. ibid.

15. Weir (n 8 above), quoting M Tooley, 'In Defense of Abortion and Infanticide' in J Feinberg (ed), *The Problem of Abortion* (2nd edn, Belmont, Calif: Wadsworth, 1984) 120–134.

16. eg, MJ Garland, 'Care of the Newborn: The Decision Not to Treat' (1988) *Perinatology/Neonatology* 1/2, 14–21, 43–44; J Fletcher, 'Moral Aspects of Decision-Making' in TD Moore (ed), *Report of the Sixty-Fifth Ross Conference on Pediatric Research: Ethical Dilemmas in Current Obstetric and Newborn Care* (Columbus, Ohio: Ross Laboratories, 1976).

17. L Williamson, 'Infanticide: An Anthropological Analysis' in M Kohl (ed), *Infanticide and the Value of Life* (Buffalo, NY: Prometheus Books, 1978) 61–75.

18. EE Shelp, *Born to Die?* (New York: Free Press, 1986).

19. US Department of State, *1994 Human Rights Reports* (Washington, DC: US Department of State, 1995).

20. ibid.

21. SP Huntington, 'The Clash of Civilizations?' (1993) *Foreign Affairs* 72/4, 22–49.

22. K Mahbubani, 'The Dangers of Decadence: What the Rest Can Teach the West' (1994) *Foreign Affairs* 72/4, 10–14.

23. RF Weir, *Selective Nontreatment of Handicapped Newborns: Moral Dilemmas in Neonatal Medicine* (New York: Oxford Univ Press, 1984) 38.

24. This hypothesis is somewhat supported by the finding of a cross-sectional spending pattern for MR/DD community services among the states that depart from the more typical pattern for corrections, natural resources, and education. Braddock *et al.* (n 2 above). Our precise hypothesis as it relates to different countries is that spending for disability services increases as a function of economic means—with indeterminate time lags between sending first for persons with physical and sensory disabilities, then for persons with mental retardation and developmental disabilities, and last for the most stigmatized conditions such as severe mental illness and substance abuse.

25. KJ Arrow, *Social Choice and Individual Values* (2nd edn, New Haven: Yale Univ Press, 1963).

26. Consider the following examples. According to the 1994 Human Rights Reports, education of children with special needs has long been a priority of the Queen of Tonga. Members of the Jordanian royal family promote

programs to educate and rehabilitate their subjects with disabilities. In Bahrain, ruled since the late 18th century by the Al-khalifa family, 'a variety of government, quasi-government and religious institutions are mandated to protect disabled persons'. US Department of State (n 19 above).

27. The Country Reports were submitted to Congress by the US Department of State pursuant to ss 116(d) and 502(b) of the Foreign Assistance Act of 1961, as amended, and s 505(c) of the Trade Act of 1974, as amended.

28. US Department of State (n 19 above) Preface, 1.

29. In 1994, there were several exceptions involving countries that neither received US Foreign Aid nor were members of the United Nations, eg, the Israeli Occupied Territories, Western Sahara whose sovereignty was disputed by Morocco and the Polisario Front, and Serbia-Montenegro, which neither the United States nor the international community recognized. As of 15 May 2002, the situation had somewhat changed. The Occupied Territories were now recognized as the Palestine Authority and received some US foreign aid; Western Sahara still awaited a referendum on its final status after the Polisario Front guerrilla war ended; and Serbia-Montenegro, also known as the Federal Republic of Yugoslavia, replaced former President Slobodan Milošović with President Vojislav Kostunica in an October 2000 election accompanied by massive demonstrations and strikes.

30. US Department of State (n 19 above) Preface, 3.

31. ibid.

32. United Nations, *1992 Demographic Yearbook* (New York: United Nations, 1994).

33. United Nations, *Statistical Yearbook, 39th Issue* (New York: United Nations, 1994).

34. Central Intelligence Agency, *World Factbook* (Washington, DC: Government Printing Office, 2001), available at http://www.odci.gov/cia/publications/factbook (last viewed 15 May 2002).

35. World Health Organization, *Statistical Information System Estimates of Health Personnel* (Geneva: World Health Organization, 2002) available at http://www3.who.int/whosis/health_personnel/health_personnel.cfm?path=whosis,health_personnel (last viewed 15 May 2002).

36. *World Almanac and Book of Facts* (Mahwah, NJ: Funk and Wagnalls, 2002).

37. *Political Handbook of the World* (New York: McGraw-Hill, 1999).

38. *The Statesman's Year Book* (New York: Palgrave, 2002).

39. In 2002, the CIA World Factbook provided purchasing power parity per capita income for all countries except Western Sahara as well as infant mortality rates for all countries except Micronesia and Western Sahara. Statistics of the type needed for calculating the number of physicians per 100,000 population could be cobbled together from various sources for all countries except Western Sahara. Central Intelligence Agency (n 34 above).

40. For example, where the Country Reports did not mention the extent of services beyond the statement that people with disabilities were not subject to discrimination in the use of available government services the report was coded as 'minimal'. In those countries where the Country Reports made no mention of any services provided the report was coded as 'none'.

41. A slight digression and interpretation is appropriate here. A national survey of state vocational rehabilitation and mental health service agencies, conducted by the National Alliance for the Mentally Ill, found that with the exception of four state vocational rehabilitation agencies located in Illinois, Massachusetts, Minnesota, and Pennsylvania, the states and the District of Columbia made no mention of accommodations for persons with mental disabilities, including mental illnesses or mental retardation and other developmental disabilities, in the Self-Evaluation Reports or Plans for Correction which they had prepared pursuant to the requirements of the Americans with Disabilities Act (ADA) of 1990 and s 504 of the Rehabilitation Services Act of 1974, as amended. JH Noble, RS Honberg, LL Hall, and LM Flynn, *A Legacy of Failure: The Inability of the Federal–State Vocational Rehabilitation System to Serve People with Severe Mental Illnesses* (Arlington, Va: National Alliance for the Mentally Ill, 1997).

42. All governments described in the Country Reports as 'transitional' were coded 'unstable', as were instances of civil war, abuse, and extrajudicial killing of political opponents by government forces, insurgency movements, *coup d'état*, presence of UN peacekeeping force intervention, US intervention, control of major territory by non-government forces, major unrest and terrorist attacks, ethnic genocide or purging, government suspension of constitutional rights and restriction of civil liberties, severe economic problems arising from regional conflict and sanctions or the combination of rapid depreciation of currency, high inflation, and drought.

43. SPSS, Inc, *SYSTAT 10 Statistics I* (Chicago: SPSS, Inc, 2000).

44. **Country predominant religions** are: **Roman Catholic:** Andorra, Argentina, Austria, Belgium, Belize, Bolivia, Brazil, Burundi, Canada, Cape Verde, Central Africa, Chile, Colombia, Congo Democratic Republic (formerly Zaire), Congo Republic, Costa Rica, Croatia, Cuba, Czech Republic, Dominica, Dominican Republic, Ecuador, El Salvador, Equatorial Guinea, France, Grenada, Guatemala, Haiti, Honduras, Hungary, Ireland, Italy, Kenya, Kiribati, Liechtenstein, Lithuania, Luxembourg, Malta, Mexico, Monaco, Netherlands, Nicaragua, Panama, Paraguay, Peru, Philippines, Poland, Portugal, Rwanda, San Marino, São Tomé, Seychelles, Slovak Republic, Slovenia, Spain, St. Lucia, Switzerland, Trinidad, Uruguay, and Venezuela. **Muslim:** Afghanistan, Albania, Algeria, Azerbaijan, Bahrain, Bangladesh, Bosnia-Herzegovina, Brunei, Chad, Comoros, Djibouti, Egypt, Eritrea, Ethiopia, Gambia, Guinea, Indonesia, Iran, Iraq, Jordan, Kazakhstan, Kuwait, Kyrgyzstan, Lebanon, Libya, Malaysia, Maldives, Mali, Mauritania, Morocco, Niger, Nigeria, Occupied Territories (now Palestinian Authority), Oman, Pakistan, Qatar, Saudi Arabia, Senegal, Sierra Leone, Somalia, Sudan, Syria, Tajikistan, Tunisia, Turkey, Turkmenistan, United Arab Emirates, Uzbekistan, West Sahara, and Yemen. **Protestant:** Antigua, Australia, Bahamas, Barbados, Denmark, Estonia, Fiji, Finland, Gabon, Germany, Guyana, Iceland, Jamaica, Korea Republic, Latvia, Lesotho, Malawi, Marshall Islands, Micronesia, Namibia, Nauru, New Zealand, Norway, Papua New Guinea, Solomon Islands, South Africa, St. Kitts, St. Vincent, Suriname, Swaziland, Sweden,

Tanzania, Tonga, Tuvalu, Uganda, UK-Northern Ireland, USA, Vanuatu, West Samoa, and Zambia. **Indigenous:** Angola, Benin, Botswana, Burkina Faso, Cameroon, Côte D'Ivoire, Ghana, Guinea-Bissau, Liberia, Madagascar, Mozambique, Togo, and Zimbabwe. **Buddhist:** Bhutan, Burma, Cambodia, Hong Kong, Japan, Laos, Macau, Mongolia, Singapore, Sri Lanka, Taiwan, Thailand, and Vietnam. **Orthodox Christian:** Armenia, Belarus, Bulgaria, Georgia, Greece, Macedonia, Moldova, Romania, Serbia-Montenegro, and Ukraine. **Hindu:** India, Mauritius, and Nepal. **Atheist:** China, North Korea, and Russia. **Jewish:** Israel.

45. Country disability services funding was: **No apparent funding:** Bhutan, Bolivia, Bosnia-Herzegovina, Botswana, Burundi, Cambodia, Cameroon, Chad, Congo Democratic Republic (formerly Zaire), Dominica, Ecuador, Equatorial Guinea, Gambia, Haiti, Indonesia, Iran, Iraq, Kyrgyzstan, Lebanon, Libya, Macedonia, Malawi, Morocco, Nepal, Nigeria, North Korea, Pakistan, Paraguay, Rwanda, São Tomé, Senegal, Solomon Islands, Somalia, Sudan, Swaziland, Vanuatu, Vietnam, West Sahara, West Samoa, and Yemen. **Minimal funding:** Afghanistan, Albania, Angola, Antigua, Argentina, Armenia, Azerbaijan, Bangladesh, Barbados, Belarus, Benin, Brazil, Burkina Faso, Burma, Cape Verde, Central African Republic, Chile, China, Colombia, Comoros, Congo Republic, Costa Rica, Côte D'Ivoire, Cuba, Czech Republic, Dominican Republic, Djibouti, Eritrea, Estonia, Ethiopia, Fiji, Gabon, Ghana, Grenada, Guatemala, Guinea, Guinea-Bissau, Guyana, Honduras, Hong Kong, Hungary, India, Ireland, Jamaica, Japan, Jordan, Kazakhstan, Kenya, Kiribati, Laos, Latvia, Lesotho, Liberia, Liechtenstein, Lithuania, Macau, Madagascar, Malaysia, Mali, Marshall Islands, Mauritania, Mauritius, Mexico, Micronesia, Moldova, Mozambique, Namibia, Niger, Occupied Territories (now Palestinian Authority), Panama, Papua New Guinea, Peru, Philippines, Poland, Romania, Serbia-Montenegro, Seychelles, Sierra Leone, Slovak Republic, Slovenia, South Africa, South Korea, St. Kitts, St. Lucia, St. Vincent, Suriname, Syria, Tajikistan, Tanzania, Thailand, Togo, Trinidad, Turkey, Tuvalu, Uganda, Ukraine, Uruguay, Venezuela, Zambia, and Zimbabwe. **More extensive funding:** Algeria, Andorra, Australia, Austria, Bahamas, Bahrain, Belgium, Belize, Brunei, Bulgaria, Canada, Croatia, Denmark, Egypt, El Salvador, Finland, France, Georgia, Germany, Greece, Iceland, Israel, Italy, Kuwait, Luxembourg, Malawi, Maldives, Malta, Monaco, Mongolia, Nauru, Netherlands, New Zealand, Nicaragua, Norway, Oman, Portugal, Qatar, Russia, San Marino, Saudi Arabia, Singapore, Spain, Sri Lanka, Sweden, Switzerland, Taiwan, Tonga, Tunisia, Turkmenistan, UK-Northern Ireland, United Arab Emirates, USA, and Uzbekistan.

46. Country building access law status was: **No law:** Afghanistan, Albania, Algeria, Angola, Antigua, Armenia, Austria, Azerbaijan, Bangladesh, Barbados, Belize, Benin, Bhutan, Bolivia, Bosnia-Herzegovina, Botswana, Brunei, Bulgaria, Burkina Faso, Burma, Burundi, Cambodia, Cameroon, Cape Verde, Central African Republic, Chad, Chile, Colombia, Comoros, Congo Democratic Republic (formerly Zaire), Costa Rica, Côte D'Ivoire, Croatia, Cuba, Czech Republic, Djibouti, Dominica, Ecuador, Egypt, El Salvador, Equatorial Guinea, Eritrea, Estonia, Ethiopia, Fiji, Gabon, Gambia, Georgia,

Ghana, Grenada, Guinea, Guatemala, Guinea-Bissau, Guyana, Haiti, Honduras, Hong Kong, Hungary, India, Indonesia, Iran, Iraq, Ireland, Jamaica, Japan, Kazakhstan, Kenya, Kiribati, Kuwait, Kyrgyzstan, Laos, Lebanon, Lesotho, Liberia, Libya, Liechtenstein, Lithuania, Luxembourg, Macau, Macedonia, Madagascar, Malawi, Malaysia, Maldives, Mali, Marshall Islands, Mauritania, Mauritius, Mexico, Micronesia, Moldova, Morocco, Mozambique, Namibia, Nepal, Nicaragua, Nigeria, North Korea, Occupied Territories (now Palestinian Authority), Oman, Pakistan, Panama, Papua New Guinea, Paraguay, Peru, Poland, Qatar, Romania, Rwanda, São Tomé, Saudi Arabia, Senegal, Seychelles, Sierra Leone, Solomon Islands, Somalia, Sri Lanka, St. Kitts, St. Lucia, St. Vincent, Sudan, Suriname, Swaziland, Switzerland, Syria, Tajikistan, Tanzania, Thailand, Togo, Tonga, Trinidad, Turkey, Tuvalu, Uganda, Ukraine, United Arab Emirates, Uruguay, Uzbekistan, Vanuatu, Vietnam, West Sahara, West Samoa, Yemen, and Zambia. **Law with little or no implementation:** Argentina, Bahamas, Belarus, Brazil, China, Congo Republic, Dominican Republic, France, Greece, Israel, Italy, Jordan, Latvia, Malta, Mongolia, Niger, Norway, Philippines, South Korea, San Marino, Serbia-Montenegro, Slovak Republic, Slovenia, South Africa, Spain, Taiwan, Turkmenistan, Venezuela, and Zimbabwe. **Law with more extensive implementation:** Andorra, Australia, Bahrain, Belgium, Canada, Denmark, Finland, Germany, Iceland, Monaco, Nauru, Netherlands, New Zealand, Portugal, Singapore, Sweden, Tunisia, UK-Ireland, and USA.

47. W Drozdiak, 'Rich, Poor Meet at Summit, and Go Their Separate Ways' (12 March 1995) *Washington Post* A14.
48. JH Noble and FL Ahearn, 'Critical Assumptions in Providing Aid to Forced and Voluntary Migrants in Managua, Nicaragua' (2001) *Journal of Social Work Research and Evaluation* 2/2, 125–141; G Soros, *On Globalization* (New York: Public Affairs, 2002); JE Stiglitz, 'Argentina, Shortchanged: Why the Nation that Followed the Rules Fell to Pieces' (12 May 2002) *Washington Post, Outlook* B1, B5; JE Stiglitz, 'A Fair Deal for the World' (23 May 2002) *New York Review of Books* available at http://www.nybooks.com/articles/15403 (last viewed 14 May 2002).
49. G Soros, *Open Society: Reforming Global Capitalism* (New York: Public Affairs, 2000).
50. Stiglitz (n 48 above); see also JE Stiglitz, *Globalization and Its Discontents* (New York: Norton, 2002).
51. Soros (n 49 above).
52. US Department of State (n 19 above) Preface, 4.
53. The major authorities for grant and concessional credit food aid are the Agricultural Trade Development and Assistance Act of 1954 as amended (PL 480), the Food for Progress Act of 1985, and s 416(b) of the Agricultural Act of 1949. Amendments to these authorities are contained in Title XV of the Food, Agriculture, Conservation, and Trade Act of 1990 (FACT Act). Title II of PL 480 provides for donation of US agricultural commodities to meet humanitarian food needs in foreign countries. Title III provides for government-to-government grants to support long-term economic development in least developed countries. Donated commodities are sold on the domestic market in the recipient countries

and the revenue generated from these sales is used to support programs of economic development.

54. eg, the Country Reports noted that '[h]andicapped persons, other than war veterans, are reportedly not allowed within the city limits of Pyongyang (North Korea)...[and that] authorities check every 2 to 3 years in the capital for persons with deformities and relocate them to special facilities in the countryside'. Similarly, the Country Reports concluded that 'misdiagnosis, inadequate medical care, pariah status, and abandonment remain the norm for China's disabled population'.

15

Out-of-Home Placement of Children with Intellectual Disabilities: The Need for a Family Support Policy

ARIE RIMMERMAN

I. INTRODUCTION

Families of children with severe intellectual disabilities are at highest risk for out-of-home placement. Despite policies discouraging institutional placement of children with severe disabilities and dramatic reductions in the number of children in institutions, admissions to large state facilities is growing faster than discharges from them.[1] Although most of the children with severe intellectual disabilities will spend their childhoods in their own homes,[2] many will not. According to Meyer,[3] up to 40% of children with severe and profound intellectual disabilities in the United States may no longer be living out-of-home. Parents of these children are caught in the dilemma of whether to place them out-of-home or rear them at home until they reach adulthood.

During the past thirty years, researchers have studied the motives of parents seeking out-of-home placement for their children with intellectual disabilities.[4] In the late 1950s and early 1960s, out-of-home placement was viewed as a desirable option for parents of children with disabilities.[5] Since the early 1970s, however, in many parts of the developed world the policy has changed toward supporting families raising the child at home until he or she reaches adulthood.[6]

In analyzing parental applications for placement, professionals tend to differentiate between two types of placement: planned and unplanned.[7] Planned placement occurs when an adult with intellectual disability reaches adulthood, as a result of rational parental planning. Unplanned placement is made before the child has reached adulthood and is often associated with parental stress and the inability to care for the disabled child at home.[8]

The research on parental placement also reflects a shift in societal values and human rights. Until recently, most researchers shared the view that parental application for placement is a function of stress and the lack of resources to cope with it.[9] Parents who applied for placement were described as experiencing high levels of stress related to child and family problems and unable to utilize their internal and social resources. The author[10] has offered a different perspective that views the parental placement decision as the end of a process rather than a separate and distinct final act. Most parents of children with intellectual disabilities consider possible placement, some intend to place, but only a few actually apply for it. Some researchers assumed that changes in parental consideration of placement are brought about by the child's growth and changes that occur within the family cycle.

The research on placement can help shape social policy and implementation of human rights for families of children with intellectual disabilities. One core aspect of the research is that parental perception of placement reflects their degree of coping with the family life cycle.

This chapter has two main purposes: (a) to update the research on out-of-home placement and (b) to present implications for family support policy and human rights.

A. Research Review

Until the 1980s researchers looked for factors associated with parental application for out-of-home placement. The common factors were: (a) *child characteristics*, such as low level of functioning;[11] lack of adaptive behavior and the existence of behavioral disorders;[12] (b) *family characteristics*, such as parental aging, and one-parent families;[13] and (c) *the burden of care and the lack of family support programs.*[14]

Bromely and Blacher[15] offered a new formulation for the study of placement. They reported that stressful events and daily altercations experienced by the parents were associated with the parental tendency to place children out of the home. Secondary motives were: the child's low functioning, the existence of behavior disorders, and the negative impact on other members of the family. The most surprising finding was that formal support was moderately associated with parental application for placement.

Blacher,[16] a central researcher on out-of-home placement, offered a developmental approach to the study of out-of-home placement. She thought that the key buffer against unplanned placement is the mother–child relationship. When the relationship is reciprocal and responsive, the mother perceives her role as rewarding. Conversely, when the quality of contact is characterized by an ambivalent or negative relationship, the mother will lean toward unplanned placement. In verifying the importance of the mother–child relationship, Bromely and Blacher[17] found that parents reported that attachment and guilt related to separation from the child were the key variables associated with the prevention of early placement.

Cole[18] offered a comprehensive model for studying motives for out-of-home placement. He viewed parental application for placement as a function of family maladaptation (eg, stressful events related to the child's disability, prior stressful life events, and the accumulation of ongoing crises). The existence of personal and family resources and the ability to discover new coping resources are critical, however, for parental adjustment and the rejection of out-of-home placement. Testing this model, Cole and Meyer[19] found that the occurrence of stressful life events before the child reached the age of 21 were not related to out-of-home placement. However, when these events recurred after age 21 they were associated with parental application for out-of-home placement. In confirming their model, the researchers found that parents with personal resources were not interested in pre-termed placement. Furthermore, among parents of children under 21 years of age, social support moderated their inclination to apply for out-of-home placement. Crnic, Friedrich, and Greenberg proposed a similar conceptualization of testing placement as a function of parental coping resources.[20] They found that application for pre-termed placement was based on the existence of parental and family problems, parental pessimism about the child's future, and their perception of the child's physical incapacitation.

Most of the research on placement made a retrospective comparison between parents who placed with those who did not place.[21] Rimmerman[22] proposed a different approach, defining placement as a process rather than a single outcome. In his opinion, parental application for out-of-home placement is the result of a process containing thought, arrival at intention and culmination in the decision itself. Parents differ in their thoughts, their intentions, and decisions regarding placement in different stages of the family life cycle. Therefore, the consideration of placement is related to parental stressful life events and two intervening factors: internal resources such as locus of control, hardiness, sense of coherence, and external resources such as social support, family cohesion, and adaptation.

II. INTENTION AND DECISION ABOUT PLACEMENT

A central question raised by policymakers is whether it is possible to predict parental need for out-of-home placement. Bromely and Blacher[23] provided a predictive approach examining motives rather than correlates of placement. They asked parents who had already placed their child why they had not done so sooner. The parents' response was that they had given thought to out-of-home placement at an earlier stage in their child's life. However, they reported that earlier separation from the child instilled in them an enormous sense of guilt that erased any intention to apply for out-of-home placement.

Blacher and Hanneman[24] studied attitudes, raising the question of whether parental positive or negative attitudes toward placement would predict application for out-of-home placement. They studied the intention to apply for placement among 100 parents of children and adolescents with severe intellectual disability at four intervals of time over a period of six years. These findings showed that parental intentions regarding placement were predictable over the short run. They also confirmed that the decision for out-of-home placement should be the result of a process of consideration as to the wisdom of the step. Indeed parental intention toward placement may change over time in response to family life events. Therefore, it is important to examine the relationship between the child's age and the time of parental application for placement.

A. Child's Age Related to Time of Parental Application

Another research perspective is to examine parental placement in relation to the child's age. Based on 1990 data from California, Rosey, Blacher, and Hanneman[25] reported that the highest placement rate was during the child's first year of life. These rates were the highest among parents of children with severe and profound intellectual disability. Parental application time is related to the child's age and the family life cycle. Thus, when the child is young, parents are concerned about the family as a whole and either tend toward or fear isolation. At this stage parents think about placement but tend to postpone any decision.[26] When the child grows older, parents face a greater burden of care and express more inclination to apply for family support services. At this stage, out-of-home placement is considered a more acceptable decision that arouses a lesser degree of guilt feelings.[27]

Several researchers examined the relationship between the child's age and parental readiness for out-of-home placement. Tausig[28] distinguished between parental motives before and after the age of 21. Parental motives under age 21 were related to problems within the family while after age 21 they were often associated with parental health status.

B. Out-of-Home Placement among Parents of Children with Intellectual Disabilities in Israel: Research Review

The research on out-of-home placement among Israeli parents of children with intellectual disabilities is relatively new. Since 1991, the author and his associates have carried out six studies related to parental perception of out-of-home placement. The latest interest in this research reflects changes in societal values and government policy toward families of children with intellectual disabilities. First, the media exposed the tragedy of parents abandoning their newborn children with Down syndrome in hospitals. Second, the Minister of Labor and Welfare stated that all families who made application for out-of-home placement would be responded to during 1994–1995. Third, parents' organizations demonstrated the need to expand the number of community residences. At present, several non-profit organizations are involved in the expansion of community residences for adults with intellectual disabilities.

Israeli studies reflect the new research approach to study intention and application for out-of-home placement in relation to child's age. The summary of the six studies on parental out-of-home placement is presented in Table 15.1. Five studies focus on parental perspective about out-of-home placement.[29] One study deals with parental involvement in the transition process of their children moving from institutions to residence in community facilities.[30]

In a study on out-of-home placement by parents of young children with intellectual disabilities, Raif and Rimmerman[31] tested placement as a function of stress, sense of coherence, and social support. Parental sense of coherence, reflecting the ability to comprehend, manage, and give meaning to their social support, moderated their stress levels and intention to apply for out-of-home placement.

Other studies have been done on children and adolescents with severe intellectual disability. Rimmerman[32] compared two groups of parents regarding their intention to apply for out-of-home placement. Parents who intended to make placement did not differ in their levels of stress from their counterparts, parents who prefer to raise their children at home. Surprisingly, parents who intended to apply had higher commitment to normalization than to parents who preferred to raise their children at home.

In an additional study, Rimmerman[33] examined whether two resources, parental locus of control and social support, moderated stress and parental application for out-of-home placement. The findings were that parents who applied for placement had external locus of control, characterized by passivity and inability to cope with stress, lacked social support and had high stress levels. Conversely, parents who preferred to raise their children at home had internal locus of control, expressed by the ability to master their own lives, sufficient social support, and low stress levels. The findings support the hypothesis raised in the previous review of the literature, that locus of control (internal resource) and social support (external support) served as moderators of stress and the parental application for out-of-home placement.

Another study carried out in 1994 and published in 1996 by Rimmerman and Duvdevany[34] examined out-of-home placement applications of

TABLE 15.1. *Summary of Israeli studies on out-of-home placement*

Authors	Subjects	Core findings
Rimmerman (1991a)	112 parents of children and adolescents with severe mental retardation	No differences have been found in coping resources between parents who intend and do not intend to place. Those who intend to place were more committed to normalization
Rimmerman (1991b)	86 parents of adolescents with severe mental retardation	Parents who applied to placement were less educated, had higher levels of stress, external locus of control, and less social support compared to parents who did not apply
Raif and Rimmerman (1993)	61 parents of young children with developmental disabilities	Parental sense of coherence and informal social support serve as moderators of their intention to apply for out-of-home placement
Rimmerman and Muraver (1993)	112 parents whose children live in institutions	Young parents, married, educated, and less pessimistic about their children had more intention to be involved in their transition to community residences
Rimmerman and Duvdevany (1996)	88 parents of children and adolescents with severe mental retardation	Parental stress (high), social support (less), attitudes toward normalization (favorable), family environment or climate (low), and children age (adolescents) were predictors in multiple regression analysis. However, only the first three (stress, social support, and attitudes toward normalization) contributed to the model of prediction of placement
Rimmerman (1995)	36 parents of young adults with moderate mental retardation	Parents who participated in the transition program for community residence gained more support and readiness for the possible placement compared to the control group

Sources: A Rimmerman, 'Parents of Adolescents with Severe Intellectual Disability: Resources, Stress, and the Application for Out-of-Home Placement' (1991a) 17 *Australia and New Zealand Journal of Intellectual Disabilities* 45–53.

A Rimmerman, 'Parents of Children and Adolescents with Severe Mental Retardation: Factors Related to the Consideration of Out-of-Home Placement' (1991b) 11 *Society & Welfare* 109–116.

R Raif and A Rimmerman, 'Parental Attitudes to Out-of-Home Placement of Young Children with Development Disabilities' (1993) 16 *International Journal of Rehabilitation Research* 97–105.

A Rimmerman and M Muraver, 'Making the Move to Community Residences: Parental Involvement in the Transition Process of their Adult Children with Mental Retardation' (Research report, School of Social Work, Bar Ilan University: Ramat Gan, Israel, 1993).

A Rimmerman and I Duvdevany, 'Parents of Children and Adolescents with Severe Mental Retardation: Stress, Family Resources, Normalization and their Application for Out-of-Home Placement' (1996) 17 *Research in Developmental Disabilities* 487–494.

A Rimmerman, 'Readiness for Community Residence: The AKIM-Jerusalem Demonstration Project' (1995) 18 *International Journal of Rehabilitation Research* 86–90.

88 Israeli parents who had younger children and adolescents with severe intellectual disability. It looked at the question of whether parental application for placement is a function of their marital status; level of education; child's age; parental stress; family environment (climate); social support and attitudes toward normalization. Multiple regression analysis showed that five predictors had significant correlation with parental application: parental stress (high); social support (less); attitudes toward normalization (favorable); family environment or climate (low); and children's age (adolescents). However, only the first three predictors (stress, social support, and attitudes toward normalization) contributed to the explanation of placement.

Although former studies focused on parental perspectives toward placement, a study by Rimmerman[35] tested whether the readiness program that was provided to parents and their children changed their attitude toward placement. The program consisted of an individualized program for the young adults including their experience of out-of-home overnight stay and support group for the parents. The main results were that parents who participated in this program reported greater social support and more willingness to place their children out-of-home compared to non-participants. Parental stress levels, however, did not change after the readiness program.

The author also studied parents of children who resided in institutions and their intention to be involved in their child's transition to community residences.[36] The basic assumption was that parents who placed their children in institutions would be concerned about their possible transition to community residences. The findings were that younger parents, married with a high level of formal education and low pessimism toward the child with intellectual disability, had a greater desire to be involved in their children's transition to community residences. Conversely, older parents, and single-parent families with a low level of formal education and high pessimism toward the child with intellectual disability had a lesser desire to be involved in the transition process. Surprisingly, findings were that parental locus of control and family cohesion and adaptation, and child's characteristics were not related to parental involvement in the possible transition to community residence.

The findings of all six studies can be summarized as follows: parents intending to place their children with intellectual disability expressed high levels of stress related to their burden of care on the family as a whole; parental intention to apply for out-of-home placement is a function of their internal resources; parents with external locus of control are passive and are skeptical about their ability to raise the child at home; parents with a low sense of coherence have less ability to understand and manage any crisis and therefore will consider placement; parental intention to apply for out-of-home placement is a function of their external (social) support; the child's age is not related to parental application rates for out-of-home placement. However, compared to parents of young children, parents of adolescents are more aware about normalization, integration, inclusion, and their implication on habilitation program. Parents can benefit from readiness programs that can prepare them for their children's transition to community residence. Finally, elderly parents and one-parent families with a low level of formal education whose children live in institutions and are candidates for transition to community residence are pessimistic about this move and show less interest in being involved in the possible transition.

C. Implications for Social Policy

As in most developed countries, the family is the main caregiver of habilitation services in Israel.[37] Of the estimated 18,000 Israeli individuals with intellectual disability, two-thirds live with their families and about one-third in out-of-home placement facilities. Nevertheless, the 1993 budget was allocated only 10% to community support services. An additional indicator of the lack of daily support services is the delay in the implementation of *The Special Education Law of 1988*. This law provides day treatment services and extends the hours of special education. Due to the lack of family and other support services some parents considered placement earlier than they had planned.

This chapter identifies the parents who apply for placement as lacking internal and/or external resources. This lack of resources is critical during the first year of life when children are at greatest risk of placement. Parental burden of care increases during childhood and adolescence but so does the parents' attachment to the growing child. Parents of young adults are aware of the need for placement but express emotional difficulties in separating themselves from their children. Researchers and service providers are united in their belief that the provision of family support services may prevent premature placement. It is later in life that parents of young adults need guidance and training for their possible transition to community residence.[38]

To reduce premature or unplanned application rates for out-of-home placement, the government should expand social support services at the local level. The following programs are recommended:

1. Respite care services, including daily, weekly, and weekend periods, to ease the parental burden of care. These services are given at home when the child is young and out-of-home when the child gets older.[39] Respite care is subsidized by the government and is provided to families according to their demonstrated need and socio-economic status. Respite care programs

are limited in scope and only modestly supported by the Israeli government.

2. Extended hours in schools to let parents work and live a normal life. This need for extended hours is especially acute for persons with severe and profound intellectual disabilities.

3. Recreation program for adolescents and adults to enhance their social skills and to also enable their parents to have leisure time for themselves. This program should be integrated in the community.

4. Individual and group support services for families in crisis.

5. Training and guidance programs for parents. These programs provide parents with coping skills and the ability to plan transitions for their children from childhood to adolescence and from adolescence to adulthood. Such programs require special attention for the establishment of transitional programs for parents and their adult children to prepare both for the transitions from home to community residences and from school to work. An innovative readiness program for the transition from home to community residences by AKIM-Jerusalem demonstrated the importance of such programs.[40]

The Ministry of Labor and Welfare in Israel should learn from the above research and foster the re-examination of their policy regarding out-of-home placement. Instead of looking at the parental application for placement as an isolated outcome, the policy has to look at parents as partners and who are interested in their children's well-being. Therefore, if the Government is to reduce premature placement, it should provide support services to all families of children with intellectual disabilities and not only those who apply formally for placement. Without social support policy for all families, the current policy to reduce the waiting list for out-of-home placement may fail to address future applications for placement.

D. Placement Policy: An American Perspective

Israel and other developed countries can learn a great deal from the history of placement policy in the United States. In the past, parents were urged to place their children with intellectual disabilities in specialized residences, whether they wanted to or not. Bergman and Singer[41] outlined three major shifts in services for people with intellectual disabilities over the past fifty years. The parents' movement originated in the 1950s and brought a shift from custodial institutional care to deinstitutionalization and public education. A second shift occurred in the development of specialized community programs and habilitation programs referred to as a services paradigm. A third shift now underway is described as the emergence of a support paradigm. At its core, family support is the core development and it focuses on natural settings. It envisions the provision of a family support policy to enable children with intellectual disabilities to live within their own families. The first two movements concentrated attention on the individual with a disability. The third movement focuses on the social context, especially on the family of young children as the unit to be supported.

Blacher[42] described the prevailing professional presumption in the 1980s and 1990s as minimizing out-of-home placement. She believes in permanency planning and family support policies that all children, regardless of disability, belonged to families and therefore they must be supported in every way to keep the child at home. She cited Birenbaum and Cohen,[43] who called for broadening the definition of medical and health care needs and also including social support services. Non-medical services, including respite care as well as others, are essential to encourage parents of children with severe disabilities to nurture them at home.

In most states in the United States, family support programs have two major goals: (1) to support families caring for their children and dependents with intellectual disabilities; and (2) to reduce costly out-of-home placements. In some states, the availability of family supports has encouraged a family to bring a member home from out-of-home placement. Over twenty-five states across the United States offer social support programs. There is a wide variation in the types of services and there are several different ways the family support money can be spent. According to Braddock, Hemp, Parish, and Rizzolo,[44] family support has grown dramatically in the past decade. (See the discussion by Braddock and Parish in Chapter 4 of this volume.) Between 1993 and 1998, funding for family support increased 93%. In 1998 over 327,000 families were served at total expenditures of $736 million.

In general, states spend family support resources in a combination of three methods: direct payment to the provider of the deeded service, reimbursement to the family upon receipt of appropriate documentation, and provision to the family of a direct cash subsidy. The funding for these services usually comes from state general funds and federal funds such as Medicaid, although some programs rely extensively on United Way donations.

Blacher[45] raised questions about the validity of the above policy. She discovered that, contrary to some of the literature, the more support services that parents and children received, the more likely they were to consider out-of-home placement.[46] She viewed two interpretations of this paradoxical finding. The first was that families who received many types of support have children at high risk of placement to begin with, or they had already begun to give placement some thought. A second interpretation was that parents who used formal support services, such as respite care, could adapt to the child's temporary absence and become gradually more accepting toward longer and ultimately more complete placement.

Due to the lack of research on the impact of social support policy on placement, the field can expect two possible outcomes: family support can prevent institutionalization, or it may only postpone the need for an out-of-home placement. The family's ability to gain access to needed supports depends a great deal on the local disability services.

E. Implications for Human Rights

The research on out-of-home placement has great relevance to human rights. The right of a child with an intellectual disability to live with his natural parents may conflict with the parents' right to obtain placement in order to maintain their well-being. Professionals are often puzzled by the question of at what costs do they attempt to preserve the family–child bond. Parents and other family members, for example, may face a loss of opportunity costs when they provide care under stress and difficult circumstances.[47] It is not easy for parents to make placement decisions when the current view is family preservation at all cost. However, when parents reach an informed placement decision after receiving the appropriate support services society has to offer them, they may be able to reconcile their human rights with those of their children.

As the main caregiver, the Israeli family has the right to receive family support services for their child from birth to adulthood. Under existing Israeli legislation, parents have the right to apply for out-of-home placement but their right to receive family support services is not expressed in law. Thus, paradoxically, it is easier for parents to apply for out-of-home placement than to receive ongoing family support services. As in many countries, Israeli legislation should mandate parents' right to receive family support services from their child's birth to adulthood.

In this context of legislative reform, there is a need to re-examine the rights of parents. These rights include, but are not limited to, the right to services for their children with disabilities.

NOTES

1. R Hemp, 'State of the States Developmental Disabilities Project' (Unpublished preliminary data, Department of Disability and Human Development, Univ of Illinois at Chicago, 2000).
2. CE Meyer and J Blacher, 'Parents' Perception of Schooling for Severely Handicapped Children: Home and Family Variables' (1987) 53 *Exceptional Children* 449.

3. CE Meyer, SA Barthwick, and RK Eyman, 'Place of Residence by Age, Ethnicity, and Level of Retardation of the Mentally Retarded/Developmentally Disabled Population in California' (1985) 90 *American Journal of Mental Deficiency* 266–270.

4. B Farber, 'Effects of Severely Mentally Retarded Child on Family Integration' (1959) *Monographs of the Society for Research in Child Development* 24 (2, Serial no 71).

5. RM Moroney, 'Family Care: Toward a Responsive Society' in PR Dokecki and RM Zaner (eds), *Ethics of Dealing with Persons with Severe Handicaps* (Baltimore: Brookes, 1986).

6. A Rimmerman, 'Readiness for Community Residence: The AKIM-Jerusalem Demonstration Project' (1995) 18 *International Journal of Rehabilitation Research* 86–90.

7. A Rimmerman, 'Parents of Adolescents with Severe Intellectual Disability: Resources, Stress, and the Application for Out-of-Home Placement' (1991) 17 *Australia and New Zealand Journal of Intellectual Disabilities* 45–53.

8. R Raif and A Rimmerman, 'Parental Attitudes to Out-of-Home Placement of Young Children with Development Disabilities' (1993) 16 *International Journal of Rehabilitation Research* 97–105; DA Cole, 'Out-of-Home Child Placement and Family Adaptation: A Theoretical Framework' (1986) 91 *American Journal on Intellectual Disability* 226–236.

9. MM Seltzer and MW Krauss, 'Placement Alternatives for Retarded Children' in J Blacher (ed), *Severely Handicapped Young Children and their Families: Research in Review* (Orlando: Academic Press, 1984) 143–175.

10. A Rimmerman, 'Parents of Children and Adolescents with Severe Intellectual Disability: Factors Related to the Consideration of Out-of-Home Placement' (1991) 11 *Society & Welfare* 109–116.

11. RB Sherman, 'Predictors of the Decision to Place Developmentally Disabled Family Members in Residential Care' (1988) 92 *American Journal on Intellectual Disability* 344–351.

12. ML German and AA Maisto, 'The Relationship of a Perceived Family Support System to the Institutional Placement of Mentally Retarded Children' (1982) 17 *Education and Training of the Mentally Retarded* 17–23.

13. MM Suelzle and V Keenan, 'Changes in Family Support Networks over the Life Cycle of Mentally Retarded Persons' (1981) 86 *American Journal on Mental Deficiency* 267–274.

14. DA Cole and LH Meyer, 'Impact of Needs and Resources on Family Plans to Seek Out-of-Home Placement' (1989) 93 *American Journal on Intellectual Disability* 380–387; B Bromely and J Blacher, 'Out-of-Home Placement of Children with Severe Handicaps: Factors Delaying Placement' (1989) 94 *American Journal on Intellectual Disability* 284–291.

15. B Bromely and J Blacher, 'Parental Reasons for Out-of-Home Placement of Children with Severe Handicaps' (1991) 29 *Intellectual Disability* 275–280.

16. J Blacher, K Nihira, and CE Meyers, 'Characteristics of Home Environment of Families with Mentally Retarded Children: Comparison across Levels of Retardation' (January 1987) 91/4 *American Journal on Mental Deficiency* 313–320.

17. Bromely and Blacher (n 14 above).

18. Cole (n 8 above).
19. Cole and Meyer (n 14 above).
20. KA Crnic, WN Friedrich, and MT Greenberg, 'Adaptation of Families with Mentally Retarded Children: A Model of Stress, Coping, and Family Ecology' (1983) 88 *American Journal on Mental Deficiency* 125–138.
21. Rimmerman (n 6 above).
22. Rimmerman (n 10 above).
23. Bromely and Blacher (n 14 above).
24. J Blacher and R Hanneman, 'Out-of-Home Placement of Children and Adolescents with Severe Handicaps: Behavioral Intentions and Behavior' (1993) 14 *Research in Intellectual Disabilities* 145–160.
25. AM Rosey, J Blacher, and R Hanneman, 'Predictors of Out-of-Home Placement of Children with Severe Handicaps: A Cross-Sectional Analysis' (1990) 94 *American Journal on Intellectual Disability* 522–531.
26. HR Turnbull, AP Turnbull, GJ Bronicki, JA Summers, and C Roeder-Gordon, *Disability and the Family: A Guide to Decisions for Adulthood* (Baltimore: Brookes, 1989).
27. Rimmerman (n 7 above).
28. M Tausig, 'Factors in Family Decision-Making about Placement for Developmentally Disabled Individuals' (1985) 89 *American Journal of Mental Deficiency* 352–361.
29. Rimmerman (n 7 above); Rimmerman (n 10 above); Raif and Rimmerman (n 8 above); Rimmerman (n 6 above); A Rimmerman and I Duvdevany, 'Parents of Children and Adolescents with Severe Intellectual Disability: Stress, Family Resources, Normalization and their Application for Out-of-Home Placement' (1996) 17 *Research in Intellectual Disabilities* 6, 487–494.
30. A Rimmerman and M Muraver, 'Making the Move to Community Residences: Parental Involvement in the Transition Process of their Adult Children with Intellectual Disability' (Research report, School of Social Work, Bar Ilan Univ: Ramat Gan, Israel, 1993).
31. Raif and Rimmerman (n 8 above).
32. Rimmerman (n 7 above).
33. Rimmerman (n 10 above).
34. Rimmerman and Duvdevany (n 29 above) 487–494.
35. Rimmerman (n 6 above).
36. Rimmerman and Muraver (n 30 above).
37. Rimmerman (n 7 above).
38. Rimmerman (n 6 above).
39. Rimmerman (n 7 above).
40. Rimmerman (n 6 above).
41. AI Bergman and GH Singer, 'The Thinking behind the New Public Policy' in GHS Singer, LE Powers, and AL Olson (eds), *Redefining Family Support: Innovations in Public–Private Partnership* (Baltimore: Brookes, 1996) 435–460.
42. J Blacher, 'Attachment between Severely Impaired Children and their Mothers: Conceptual and Methodological Concerns' (Paper presented at the meeting of the Society for Research in Child Development, Baltimore 1994).

43. A Birenbaum and HJ Cohen, 'On the Importance of Helping Families: Policy Implications from National Study' (1993) 31 *Intellectual Disability* 67–74.
44. D Braddock, R Hemp, S Parish, and MC Rizzolo, 'The State of the States in Intellectual Disabilities: 2000 Study Summary' (Department of Disability and Human Development, Univ of Illinois at Chicago, 2000).
45. Blacher (n 42 above).
46. ibid; Blacher and Hanneman (n 24 above).
47. Blacher (n 42 above).

16

Self-Determination, Autonomy, and Alternatives for Guardianship

STANLEY S. HERR

I. INTRODUCTION

Self-determination involves the struggle for control and a voice in the key personal decisions that affect the life of an individual with intellectual disabilities. On its face, guardianship seems antithetical to self-determination, as it shifts the locus of control from the affected individual to a legally empowered agent, the guardian. In recent years, a number of countries have adopted new legislation to minimize the use of guardianship and to introduce less restrictive alternatives. This chapter outlines these developments as well as related legal reforms that enable persons with intellectual and other disabilities to obtain companionship for personal support and other forms of assistance.

The imposition of guardianship poses important ethical, legal, and practical problems for the disability rights community. Those problems also arise for elderly and other 'vulnerable' persons, however they are labeled, whose right to make their own decisions is challenged.

Paternalism, beneficence, and the power relationships between guardian and ward are all implicated in the search for better answers; policymakers and other leaders seek to devise new modes for self-determined personal support through which the individual with a disability, with the assistance

The author acknowledges the research support provided by Dean Karen H. Rothenberg through the University of Maryland School of Law Summer Research Program; the National Program Office on Self-Determination, a program of the Robert Wood Johnson Foundation, the University of New Hampshire, Institute on Disability; the University of Haifa Faculty of Social Welfare and Health Sciences; the Trump International Institute for Continuing Education in Developmental Disabilities; and the Switzer Fellowship program of the National Institute on Disability and Rehabilitation Research. The views expressed herein are solely those of the author, and not necessarily those of any supporting organization. An earlier and partial version of this chapter appears in a monograph of the National Program Office on Self-Determination, of the University of New Hampshire, Institute on Disability: Stanley S. Herr, 'Maximizing Autonomy: Reforming Personal Support Laws in Sweden and the United States' (1995) 22/2 JASH 213–223. The kind permission of TASH, an organization focusing on disability advocacy worldwide, to republish in part is appreciated. [Eds Note: Prof. Herr passed away before completing this chapter. For additional data and reference support, see his monograph cited above.]

of a personal agent and others the individual invites to participate, has the authority to plan for his or her own future and oversee the implementation of those plans.[1]

This chapter views ways to minimize the use of guardianship through a comparative law perspective. It explores alternatives to both maximize the individual's autonomy and to offer community-support services that aid the individual to participate in society's decision-making processes. Those processes include medical, financial, rehabilitative, and other surrogate-based protective service systems.

Community-support problems become more acute as institutions are downsized or eliminated. Nursing homes and other congregate care facilities, once described as the 'poor man's guardianship' by virtue of their exercise of plenary authority over residents, are now under federal (US) legal mandates to counsel residents and their families on proxy decision making. Unfortunately, such mandates may lead to even more persons being placed under guardianship as a matter of administrative or medical convenience.

In the United States, guardianship is an overused legal institution in danger of collapse. It is a blunt device for managing the property or personal affairs of an allegedly incompetent person. In too many cases, the guardian may assume total control over the individual's personal and financial decision making. The legal and scientific literature is critical of the practice of involuntary guardianships over persons with intellectual or physical disabilities. Guardianship intrudes on fundamental liberties and privacy rights, employs vague criteria, fails to tailor the scope of the guardian's authority, denies procedural safeguards, and lacks adequate monitoring and review.

Despite these shortcomings, more people with disabilities are subject to guardianship proceedings, most often due to their inability to consent to medical care. Because informed consent to treatment is a requirement in the United States and other common law countries as well as a mandate of the US Nursing Home Reform Act of 1987, healthcare providers are concerned when a patient appears to lack the capacity to provide direct consent. In part due to their lack of familiarity with the alternatives, service producers often propose guardianship when less restrictive solutions would suffice. Such problems are not only widespread in the United States, but also arise in other industrialized countries.

There is a global search for personal support solutions that are empowering rather than disenfranchising. In noting the self-determination movement's focus on empowerment, Nerney *et al.* point out that adults 'develop their own capacity and competency for self-determination'. However, they do not gain that knowledge, skill, and experience by themselves; some require personalized supports to enhance their self-determined options. It is the task of humane twenty-first century societies to recognize that the capacities of persons with disabilities are not static, that they may learn and grow and, if offered support commensurate with their needs and aspirations, live autonomously.

More societies should listen to people with disabilities rather than dictate to them based on the presumed superiority of the experts. Such societies would reallocate resources so that, instead of proffering only restrictive options, the law would provide self-determination and cost-efficient support options.

II. THE US POSITION: ON THE EDGE OF REFORM

Consumer and professional groups are concerned about both under-protective and over-protective approaches to meeting protective service and community-support needs. The issues are legally, ethically, and politically sensitive as well as technically complex because some individuals have authentic needs for assistance.

The US legal position is not one approach, but fifty-one varying approaches. The laws of any state may offer many alternatives to plenary guardianship (eg, limited guardianship, temporary guardianship, health care proxy decision makers, representative payees for income maintenance benefits, supported training for self-advocacy, and other options). Moreover, the lack of training and resulting confusion about which options maximize autonomy can lead to the unnecessary disempowerment of some persons with disabilities. Other problems include the cost and delay of overly legalistic models and the inability of professionals to search vigorously for available less restrictive alternatives.

Despite these difficulties, the field of intellectual disabilities is poised for reform. The reasons for this confidence include: (1) the growing professional and academic interest in making self-determination a reality for all people with disabilities; (2) a vigorous advocacy movement that seeks to change overly protective or discriminatory laws, policies, and practices; (3) a system of federalism in which states, in Justice Louis Brandeis's memorable phrase, can be 'laboratories for innovation'; and (4) increasingly popular communitarian ideas stressing the importance of interdependence in social relations and complementing individual rights approaches.

III. THE SWEDISH POSITION: OFFERING SUPPORT OPTIONS

Sweden has replaced guardianship with two forms of support. The primary and less restrictive is 'the god man' (translated into English as 'good man' or 'mentor'). The *god man* is a helping and supportive aide, far from the coercive authority figure some guardians become. It is statutory-based and publicly funded. The Swedish experience with the *god man* on legal, programmatic, and personal levels has proved very positive. Thus, Sweden is one of the most advanced countries in developing legal techniques to reinforce rather than disregard a person's capacity for self-determination. The second form of assistance is the *Forvaltare*, which Swedish legal authorities translate as administrator or trustee.

A. Legal Background

Sweden's progress in disability policies and programs is anchored in its national law. The mental retardation law of 1967 produced rapid gains in community-based habilitation and individualized services by creating broad entitlements to services for even the most severely disabled individuals. In 1985, the Swedish government enacted a law phasing out all special hospitals and institutions, prohibiting new admissions, and mandating a variety of guidance and support measures, including the services of a 'contact person'. In January 1994, the mental retardation law was replaced by a broader law on support and services for certain persons with disabilities (hereinafter LSS). The LSS provides comprehensive entitlements for persons with severe physical or intellectual disabilities, estimated to number 100,000 persons in the national population of over eight million people.

Not all services that benefit persons with disabilities are covered by the LSS. For instance, the 'parent law' (*Foraidrabalken*) regulates guardianship and some of the less restrictive alternatives in the field of parent–child obligations and relationships. In a 1989 amendment to this law, the Parliament (*Riksdag*) restricted guardianship to minors under the age of 18. Sweden thus became a pioneering country in abolishing guardianship for adults with disabilities.

Disability services in Sweden are highly decentralized. Although the national government legislates, regulates, and offers guidance on the provision of disability services, responsibility for their implementation has devolved from the county to the municipality (*kommune*). Each of Sweden's 270 municipalities has an office of public trusteeship administration, formerly known as offices of the 'Chief Guardian', charged with oversight of *god men* and trustees. The National government subsidizes the local governments, supplying resources for group homes and other community living arrangements for persons leaving institutions.

Swedish law also liberally provides the right of appeal to the courts. Thus, a person aggrieved by a determination of his or her need for personal assistance or other LSS provision can proceed through three levels of the court system: district court (*Lansratt*), appeals court (*Kammaratt*), and the Supreme Court (*Regeringsratt*). Furthermore, the political parties are generally supportive of disability policies. The legal reforms of the past two decades have been marked by a high degree of consensus among politicians, professionals, consumer activists, administrators, and the public.

B. *God Man* (Mentor)

Mentorship is now the preferred, predominant method of support service in Sweden. According to the Swedish National Board for Judicial Administration, in 1992, 28,000 Swedes had mentors and 4,000 had administrators. By December 1999, the numbers of persons with mentors had swelled to about 40,000 while the numbers of Swedes with administrators had declined to 3,500. The law requires that mentors be appointed instead of administrators whenever possible.[2]

As previously noted, guardianship has now been eliminated except for minors. This change was fueled by concern over the individual's marginalization: loss of voting rights and the imposition of other legal limitations that stigmatized the individual and heightened his or her sense of social inferiority. In contrast, the appointment of a *god man* does not alter the civil rights enjoyed by a person with a disability. The *god man* is to act only with the consent of the person and has rights and duties that roughly correspond to the authority of a person acting as a power of attorney.[3] However, in contrast to a power of attorney, a *god man* can be appointed for a person incapable of giving consent.

In appointing *god men*, the district court may tailor the relationship to the needs of the individual. He or she may represent the individual in making an application for special services, supervising financial matters, or attending to the person's other needs for support and guidance. The law emphasizes acting with the person's volition. Indeed, the person has legal remedies against the mentor who acts outside of his or her authority or who attempts a transaction where the person 'would have been able to give his consent but did not do so'.[4]

Mentors may be appointed for persons whose intellectual disability, illness, or deteriorated health places them in need of help with their legal, financial, or personal affairs. Mentors can also tend to the affairs of refugees, missing persons, or Swedes living abroad. For persons with disabilities, most appointments are by consent. For those persons incapable of giving consent, the court may appoint a *god man* upon a medical certification of the person's incapacity to consent.

Application procedures for appointment are relatively informal, fast, and free for the applicant. The person with a disability, a close relative, or the public trustees can apply. Since most cases are based on direct consent and a review of the documents by the court, no personal appearance or hearing is necessary. In routine cases, the appointment process takes only two to three weeks to complete with the judge writing the court order in about ten minutes.

God men, including those who are relatives of the person with a disability, are paid for their services.[5] Although professionals, such as lawyers, accountants, or social workers, sometimes have a caseload of ten to twenty wards, the more common practice is a one-to-one relationship. In addition to parents and siblings, *god men* are often recruited from the ranks of the police, retired teachers, social workers, bank employees, and politicians who wish to display their civic-mindedness. If the individual with a disability lacks funds, the municipality will bear the expenses of the *god man*.

In the Stockholm office, most users of adult protective services are elderly. As of December 1999, 375 had administrators and 4,995 had mentors. In 1992, the respective numbers were 163 administrators and 3,324 mentors, a trend suggesting greater use of both types of supports. These support persons are to exercise powers no more invasive than necessary. In 1999, Henrik Hoogland, head of the Stockholm Public Trustees Administration, estimated that 30% of the administratorships and 25% of the Mentorships in Stockholm were limited. The most common form of limitation focuses on economic and financial matters (*forvallaegevloan*), as distinguished from matters pertaining to legal rights (*bevakaratt*) or custody of the person (*forj a for personen*).

Recruitment of the right type of person to be a *god man* can pose a problem. The Swedish Association for Persons with Mental Retardation (FTJB) asserts that most adults with a severe intellectual disability should have a *god man*. (The Swedish definition commonly limits this category to some 30,000 persons, based on definitions of severity of disability far lower than in the United States.) FTJB representatives believe that municipalities are largely passive and do not take active measures to identify and supply persons needing such appointments. Many *god men* now lack the training, information, and motivation to fulfill the role to its fullest potential. *God men* should receive more systematic training and orientation on the rights of persons with disabilities and their responsibilities in helping them to realize those rights. The passage of the LSS offers an opportunity to provide that orientation to *god men*, staff, consumers, and their families.

Additional suggestions for improving Sweden's mentorship arrangements include:

(1) greater attention to the personal support provided by the mentors as distinguished from the current emphasis on financial aspects;

(2) closer oversight by Offices of the Public Trustee of the non-financial aspects of the mentor's responsibilities;
(3) replacement of mentors who fail to discharge their duties or who act in a way contrary to their ward's interests;
(4) coordination between welfare authorities and offices of the public trustee to encourage greater use of the mentor as an agent to help persons with disabilities to understand the changing network of services and legal entitlements, to move from institutions to apartments, and to cope with the variety of choices posed by living in Swedish mainstreams;
(5) motivation of mentors who lack enthusiasm or who perpetuate the old model of guardianship authority in dealing with individuals with disabilities;
(6) realization of the principles of human dignity and the least-restrictive alternative that are central to the premises of modern Swedish law.

Despite such shortcomings, Swedes express considerable satisfaction in the theory and implementation of *god men* and *forvaltare* laws. Critiques of these laws are also healthy signs of the disability system's desire for continuing improvement.

C. *Forvaltare* (Administrator or Trustee)

The *forvaltare* is now the device of last resort when other forms of assistance are insufficient, such as when the person with a disability objects to the decisions or appointment of a *god man* and property or personal interests would otherwise be seriously jeopardized. Unlike the *god man*, who must act in consultation with the person, the administrator may make substitute decisions. This legal role resembles that of the guardian, except that person retains the right to vote in general elections.

Sweden's universal protection of the franchise is an extraordinary expression of the dignity of persons with intellectual disabilities. No Swede is a second-class citizen barred from political participation on account of a disability. In the United States, by contrast, forty-two states and three territories bar at least some individuals with intellectual disabilities from voting.[6] In eliminating such exclusions, Sweden even permits persons with disabilities to receive assistance in exercising their right to vote.

Even though persons with a *forvaltare* have such civil rights, they have significant legal protections from their own seriously improvident acts. For instance, a person who has an administrator with unlimited authority and who attempts an economic transaction that he or she is not entitled to undertake will be fully protected. The administrator cannot only have the transaction canceled, but also can reclaim any monies spent, and the person with a disability has no duty to compensate the merchant for any loss. Courts, however, often limit the reach of the *forvaltare* financial authority to only some of the person's affairs—managing a particular bank account, for instance, or only those transactions involving credit cards, expensive installment-payment arrangements, or the sale of valuable real estate.

Given the serious consequences of such appointments and the power of the administrator to act without the individual's assent, such cases are subject to greater judicial scrutiny. Unlike *god man* proceedings, a lawyer is often appointed to represent the individual with an alleged disability.

D. *Kontakt* Person (Contact Person)

In contrast to the preceding roles, contact persons have no economic power or legal status to conduct the affairs of another. Instead, their role is to provide companionship activities for a person who would otherwise be isolated or inactive. Under the LSS, the provision of a 'contact person' is a service entitlement for those with disabilities. Thus, a person who might otherwise languish in an insular setting receives opportunities for leisure activities and social contacts.

Some Swedes question the philosophy that underlies this apparent benevolence—the idea of a paid friend—yet they also recognize the merit of offering social relationships to persons who lack friends or family members to engage them in stimulating activities. It is a mark of the comprehensiveness of Sweden's disability services that this need for recreation and emotional outlets is identified as a matter of right. In many other countries, persons who are institutionalized or severely disabled too often lead extremely isolated lives. Volunteer services, while worthwhile, do not fill the void. Sweden, in marked contrast, is tackling the human dimensions of this problem in a systematic and structured way.

E. Personal Assistant

A key means of maximizing autonomy is the use of personal assistants, hired and, if necessary, fired by the person with a disability acting as an employer. Government funding of personal assistants was discretionary: the LSS made it an entitlement as of January 1994. Activists and officials expressed national pride in the new law showpiece feature: free personal assistant services according to the individual's needs.

Section 2 of the LSS makes the personal assistant a mandated support service that can either be provided directly by the government or by a cash allowance to the person with a disability. This measure and the entire

LSS passed the Parliament with little debate. The lack of opposition may be attributed to the Swedish political consensus on disability policy.

The law contains certain limitations on eligibility. To keep the costs within limits, the users must be under the age of 65. Persons in institutions or group homes are also outside this program's reach. The person must need more than twenty hours of service per week to receive funding from the national government. (For those with fewer hours of service needs, the municipality remains the source of funding.) The Social Insurance Office administers the national program, but unlike other insurance programs, it is funded entirely from the national budget, not from employers' contributions.

Persons with disabilities would also need training and counseling to make appropriate use of personal assistants. They would need to be 'good supervisors' and not treat personal assistants 'like servants', noting that people who had so long been oppressed—'who couldn't choose more than the type of sandwich to eat' in formerly restrictive living environments— would have to become fair and reasonable employers. Although most members of centers for independent living have physical disabilities, anyone can join, and some members have Down syndrome or other intellectual disabilities. Although the personal assistant concept was first conceived as an aid for persons with mobility limitations, the law makes personal assistance available to persons with physical or intellectual disabilities. According to the Report of the Disability Commission (1989), a special parliamentary commission appointed by the government stressed the inclusive nature of personal assistance:

We feel that the availability of [personal] assistance must be reinforced, so as to improve freedom of choice, autonomy and continuity in the personal living situation. We therefore recommend that [the] LSS...include entitlement to a personal assistant for everybody who can be deemed to need such a measure and who is included in the population to which Ethel LSS refers. The personal assistant input also implies that the individual decides or does a great deal to influence who is employed as an assistant, and also that the individual must exert a great deal of influence on the time of help. Improved availability of personal assistance will also augment the possibilities of coordinating the personal support now provided in homes, at work and in schools. We also take the view that the introduction of entitlement to a personal assistant will facilitate the resettlement of intellectually handicapped persons and long-term mental patients, for example, away from institutions.[7]

In summary, Sweden has undertaken a legal reform that deserves worldwide attention. Further study is needed to determine if the implementation experience under the LSS avoids manipulation of determined hours of need—and thus costs—to municipalities. User and cost may prove unreliable. Persons with severe intellectual disabilities will need sufficient training and orientation to make appropriate use of this service. As of 1998, the statistics were encouraging. Some 8,350 Swedes with disabilities received over twenty hours per week of personal assistance. Another 4,000 people received aid under other components of the LSS. As of 2000, an estimated 25,000 personal assistants provide this service because some people with disabilities require more than one personal assistant. With personal assistance provided as a matter of right, Sweden made a dramatic step forward in the field of disability rights and policies.

F. Escort Person

The LSS also created an entitlement to the services of an 'escort person'. Listed as one of the ten statutory support services, this support was formerly limited to blind persons who needed help to attend some special event. This program, however, was considered ineffective. Under the new law, a person who did not have a personal assistant but who was eligible for LSS services can arrange for an escort to accompany him or her to the cinema, a sporting event, or other visit to a leisure-time activity. The person receiving this service contacts the municipality and can plan regular trips or can schedule special events more flexibly. Here again the national government assumes the excess costs beyond the existing escort services provided by municipalities.

G. Implementation of the Law on Support and Services for Certain Persons with Disabilities

The LSS was planned during the early 1990s at a time when the economy was booming and social service expectations were high. Two English language summaries of the work of the 1989 Commission on Policies for the Disabled, *Disability, Welfare, Justice*, presented in May 1991,[8] and *A Society for All: Summary*, the Commission's final report issued in 1992,[9] capture that spirit. The Commission criticized the existing 'patchwork quilt' of individualized measures, and called for simultaneous, right-based efforts 'to assure disabled persons of basic opportunities of social participation'. Sweden sought 'to develop and guarantee general accessibility and distinct assumption of responsibility in every social sector, with regard to matters affecting the disabled'.[10] These objectives aimed at equality and participation, including the right to accessible (1) basic public information, (2) local government activities, (3) housing and environment design, (4) culture, media, and teaching materials, (5) travel facilities, (6) basic telecommunications, (7) opportunities in the employment sector, and (8) legal protection against discrimination in the private sector. Although the Commission proposed an amendment to the Swedish Constitution prohibiting discrimination based on disability,[11] it was not until 1999 that a statutory bar to such prohibition was enacted. With these documents— based on six reports—Sweden has a detailed blueprint, with actual funding and implementation priorities that permit persons with severe disabilities 'to share, on the same terms as other members of the community, in the growth of national prosperity'. With some of these costs and adjustments spread out for periods of as long as fifteen years, the Commission estimated a 'total annual cost of only about 0.1 per cent of GDP (gross domestic product), resulting in expenditures in societal sectors described as 'a very modest scale'.

The LSS has many innovative features. The definition of 'certain disabled people' includes persons with mental retardation, autism or autistic-like conditions, persons who became severely brain-damaged as adults, and (a new category under Swedish disability law) other persons with physical or psychiatric disabilities (not a result of old age) that manifest severe difficulties in daily living. The Act lists ten support services, only the last of which is unavailable to persons in this new category: (1) counseling and other personal support services (eg, habilitation, psychological, and social work services); (2) personal assistants; (3) escort services; (4) contact persons; (5) respite care in the parent's home; (6) respite care outside the parent's home; (7) after-school recreation program for children over age 12; (8) housing in special apartments for adults; (9) housing for children who cannot live in their own homes and require a 'family home'; and (10) daily activity centers.[12]

The LSS provides a broad right of appeal from any denial of such services. For example, local government officials determine the number of hours of personal assistance an individual 'needs for daily living'.[13] An aggrieved individual can appeal to a special board of the Social Insurance Office. If still dissatisfied, the person with a disability may appeal to the courts through as many as three levels of the judiciary.

The Swedish model is based on offering multiple forms of support. In theory, an individual can have a *god man* and a personal assistant or a *god man* and a contact person. Thus, measures are tailored to the unique needs of the individual. Thus, the LSS promises the most sweeping and progressive changes in Sweden's policies on disabilities.

H. Evaluation of Swedish Legal Reforms to Increase Autonomy and Integration

Sweden has made steady progress in moving persons with intellectual and other disabilities into the mainstream. Legal reforms and legal institutions have played significant parts in those advances.

Those reforms embody several characteristics. First, Sweden has replaced a law that focused on mental retardation with one (the LSS) that encompasses the full range of severe disabilities. Second, by effectively abolishing guardianship, there is a continuum of supportive services, none of which disenfranchise adults with disabilities, regardless of their degree of impairment. Services once offered on a discretionary basis are now legal entitlements, such as personal assistants and escort persons. Finally, access to the courts ensures that remedies are available at administrative and judicial levels. The courts have proved willing to ensure that disability laws are observed by local governments despite occasional opposition from officials and funding scarcities.

The *god man* concept offers an unobtrusive form of decision-making support. It is a flexible, free, and relatively simple method of securing a mentor for persons who in other countries or eras might face restrictive guardianships. Refinements in mentorship and administratorship arrangements, however, could stress greater attention to the personal, non-financial aspects of those roles, and the provision of better training and orientation for mentors.

By law, residential institutions are being closed and replaced with support services and living arrangements that are community based. Since the first legislation in the field of intellectual disabilities in 1968, steady legal pressure has helped to create group homes and other community-based living arrangements. The process of de-institutionalization has moved quickly and without real opposition. For example, in Gothenburg, over 600 persons have moved from institutions in this region, with more than 100 institutionalized persons moving in 1992, mostly to single-person flats in rehabilitated buildings housing a total of five to seven persons. Because of good personal supports to these residents and largely positive publicity, adverse reactions from neighbors are rare. Throughout Sweden, moratoriums on new admission and legal mandates to phase-out institutions are being implemented.

The closure of institutions and the end of guardianship reflect national commitments to least restrictive alternatives and greater autonomy for persons with disabilities. A strong national consensus in favor of this position is expressed in law, policy, and budgetary decisions. Strong parliamentary support and unified public opinion in favor of greater independence and self-determination for persons with disabilities supports these developments.

Mentorship arrangements and other protective services that do not legally disable the individual can be realized in other countries. Although the mechanics, procedures, and nomenclature will vary from country to country, these concepts are certainly 'exportable'.

The principle of the least restrictive alternative is being vigorously applied in the theory and practice of Swedish disability law. Although Sweden did not enact an anti-discrimination law such as the ADA until 1999 and lacks the tools for large-scale legal intervention such as the civil rights class action in the United States, its leaders found other effective means to advance the rights of persons with disabilities that are articulated in international human rights standards. In the words of the 1989 Disability Commission, 'we have also attached very great importance to strengthening individual opportunities of autonomy and influence with regard to measures of personal support and service.'[14] All this is in keeping with the Swedish pledge of 'A Society for All' that aims to distribute the opportunities for the good life to all persons, disabled and nondisabled alike.

IV. THE GERMAN POSITION: REFORMING A TRADITIONAL GUARDIANSHIP LAW

Germany has similarly undertaken a thorough reform of its guardianship law. In 1992 the Parliament replaced the procedures of interdiction ('legal incapacitation'), guardianship, and curatorship with one flexible measure. The German term for this measure is *Betreuung*, the law is called *Betreuungsgesetz*, and the agent performing this role is a *Betreuer*. The law permits flexible measures that are sensitive to principles of the least restrictive alternative and procedural justice.[15]

A. Guiding Principles for the Preservation of Rights

Several principles reinforce the German law's shift from the denial of rights to the preservation of liberty. These features include:

The principle of necessity: which bars appointment if the person can manage independently or with the support of other social services;

The principle of flexibility: which limits the scope of the *betreuer's* authority in order to conform to the constitutional principle of the least-restrictive alternative, because the *betreuer* is to 'follow the wishes of the supported individual as long as the well-being of the handicapped person is not likely to be impaired', and recognizes that the person's well-being includes 'the possibility to lead a self-determined life to the highest possible degree';

The principle of self-determination: which permits a durable power of attorney as a substitute for a *betreuer*;

The principle of rights preservation: expressed in 'the principle of subsidizing sufficient practical support' and the 'avoidance of formal legal incapacitation' with the result that, unlike the old law, the appointment of a *betreuer* does not automatically deprive the person with an intellectual disability of such fundamental rights as the rights to vote, to marry, and to make a will.

This statutory protection for self-determination and in particular, the express recognition of the importance of 'helping people to lead a self-determined life', are significant legal advances. Realizing these noble aspirations poses significant challenges for the future.

B. Procedural Safeguards

The new law has added procedural rights to safeguard the individual's liberties and interests. These checks include:

(1) a personal interview by the judge of the Guardianship Court with the person with the disability, generally at the person's permanent residence;

(2) the power of the person to bring appeals from a guardianship and to participate fully in the proceedings, regardless of legal capability;

(3) the certificate of an expert that describes the person's medical, social, and psychological condition and offers recommendations regarding the tasks and duration of the *betreuer's* role;

(4) the requirement of a 'final conversation' between the judge and the individual to explain the investigation's results, the expert's findings, and the *betreuer's* identity and scope of authority; and

(5) a durational limit of no more than five years for the *betreuer's* appointment.

C. Protecting Zones of Autonomy and Limiting the Substituted Decision Maker's Powers

The German law attempts to preserve zones of autonomy for the person with a disability by limiting the authority of the *betreuer*. For instance, rather than imposing plenary authority over all of the affairs of the supported person, the appointment can be restricted to personal or financial matters. Only if the person's decisions would seriously jeopardize his or her personal well-being or finances will the Guardianship Court issue a special decree that authorizes the *betreuer* to consent to specific personal decisions. In general, the appointment of a *betreuer* does not affect the legal capacity of the person to make decisions of a personal nature. These legal reforms have led to the following rules:

(1) medical examination or treatment is permitted only with the patient's informed consent, unless the *betreuer* has the court's authorization for substituted consent;

(2) medical treatment that has a high risk of death or of causing severe and permanent impairment requires the Guardianship Court's additional declaration of consent;

(3) sterilization by substituted consent requires the Court's additional declaration of consent, the appointment of a special *betreuer* and compliance with strict criteria (no opposition by the person of any kind, permanent incapacity to consent, high risk of pregnancy, no practicable contraceptive alternative, the concern that any pregnancy would be life-threatening or 'cause a severe physical or mental impairment of the pregnant woman that could not otherwise be prevented, and the method of sterilization employed must leave the highest chance of reversibility');[16] and

(4) additional safeguards against coercive measures, such as the Guardianship Court's additional declaration of consent before an individual can be placed in a closed institution, or be subjected to mechanical measures or medication that will limit the individual's liberty or freedom of movement.

In selecting a *betreuer*, the Guardianship Court must abide by the individual's choice. If the individual has not expressed such a wish, the Court should give priority to relatives or other persons with a close relationship to the individual, consistent with the individual's well-being and the avoidance of possible conflicts of interest. An individual selected for this task must be able to give personal support to the person with a disability. If no such person is available, the Court may select legal entities such as private social service associations or public authorities. The preference for the individual *betreuer*, however, is so strong that these legal entities are under a statutory duty to recruit, train, and support such individual *betreuers* and to notify the Court whenever the appointment can be transferred to such an individual.

D. Strengthening the Consumer's Rights in Practice

Full implementation of these reforms will take new resources and time. An estimated 350,000 persons were under some form of guardianship before the law's enactment in 1992. Applying these new legal standards requires significant financial and professional commitments. For instance, the German *betreuers* complain that, with the workload of guardianship judges nearly doubling as a result of the new procedural safeguards, costs are higher than expected. Additional court staff and payments for expenses and salaries of *betreuers*, also contribute to those costs.[17]

Provisions in the sixteen German provinces remain quite uneven. Under the *Betreuungsgesetz*, private, non-profit advocacy organizations (called *Betreuungsverein*) are to be created in each city and county to recruit, orient, train, and advise volunteer *betreuers*. The professional staff of these advocacy organizations will also accept appointments that cannot be handled by volunteers. However, the federal law only entitles those professionals who have assumed appointments to be paid by the government. Most of the supported persons are poor, and for those with bank accounts of less than 4,500 DM (approximately US $2,700) the services of a *betreuer* are to be free of charge.

Unfortunately, with mounting caseloads, especially within Public Guardianship Authorities, the law's benevolent intentions and its ideal of individualized advocacy are undermined. Even before the 1992 law, a 1989 survey documented that the average public guardian staggered under a caseload of 107 persons. The problems may now be even worse, as German reunification[18] and a 'steady increase of absolute numbers' of people under legal protection orders increased the service demands on public and private organizations in this field.

Other factors also undermine the voices and rights of consumers. Old attitudes may persist as part of the legacy of 'the traditional, paternalistic guardianship-system' that pre-dated the 1992 legal change. In addition, consumers tend not to exert a sufficient self-advocacy presence and check on these processes. Germany lacks a sufficient disability rights movement to pressure for change. One positive step, however, is the mandate under legal regulations to organize 'committees for participation in decision-making in residential facilities and sheltered workshops'. However, according to legal expert Hellmann, the absence of a self-advocacy group's presence to support independent life planning undermines the proper application of the 1992 law. He states that 'a very important element in the network of *Betreuung* that could contribute very effectively to a successful implementation of the *Betreuungsgesetz* with its guiding "Principle of Necessity," is still missing.'

In summary, the effectiveness of the German reform remains to be studied. Although the law itself outlines many substantive and procedural advances, it requires stronger public support and financing to effectuate those gains. Excessive paternalism may be difficult to avoid, even under a reformed guardianship law. The energy of many committed judges, advocates, advocacy associations, and *betreuers*, however, promises progress. The High Civil Court of Berlin has already applied the new law to withhold the judiciary's consent for the use of potent drugs for the treatment of mental illness that would result in unwanted changes in the patient's personality and mentation. Such a precedent suggests that the self-determination philosophy underlying the 1992 law is indeed being taken seriously.

V. GUARDIANSHIP LAWS IN OTHER COUNTRIES

Other industrialized nations are also reforming their existing guardianship laws and stressing self-determination. Some examples are outlined below.

A. Israel

In 1999, Israel created the Equal Rights for Persons with Disabilities Law. The law both reforms personal supports and prohibits discrimination based on disability. A striking feature of this enactment is its clear focus on self-determination. To this end, Section 4 states that '[a] person with a disability has the right to make decisions that pertain to her/his life according to her/his wishes and preferences; this right shall be exercised in conformity with the law'. The prominent placement of this provision in the law's opening chapter on basic principles signals that individual autonomy is a major purpose of Israeli disability legislation.

Other purposes include the protection of the individual's dignity and freedom. The law also enshrines the right to 'equal and active participation in all the major spheres of life', and the right to an appropriate response to the individual's needs, in such a way as to 'enable her/him to live with maximum independence, in privacy and in dignity, realizing her/his potential to the full'.[19] These provisions apply to a broadly defined group of people with disabilities, including those with severe physical, emotional, or mental disabilities, including intellectual disabilities that substantially limit the person in one or more major spheres of life. Although inspired by the Americans with Disabilities Act (ADA), the law promises to advance wider aims than the ADA, committing Israeli society to strengthen disability rights based on 'the principle of equality and the value of human beings created in the Divine Image'.

B. Austria

In Austria, legal reforms in 1984 led to the development of limited guardianships. As of 1981, some 27,000 persons were under a form of plenary guardianship. Although the 1984 law was expected to lead to a marked decrease in guardianships after an initial decline the number of persons under guardianship climbed to about 23,000. Three professionally staffed organizations provide guardianship services as well. Under a new commitment law, patient advocates are also appointed for each committed mental health patient.

The Austrian law on guardianship has also been credited with influencing the reforms in Germany. One of the main goals of the 1984 law was to destigmatize the provision of protective services.

C. The Netherlands

After long deliberations, the Netherlands enacted an important law on mentorship. For over three decades, activists criticized the existing law on guardianship of property (*curatele*) for its formality, expense, and failure to address the personal needs of its subjects.[20] Finally, on 1 January 1995, a government bill on mentorship entered into force. The bill has several innovative features, including provisions for (1) payment to mentors, even if they are relatives; (2) giving preference for the appointment of relatives; (3) considering the wishes of the person with a disability as to the choice of mentor; (4) requiring periodic review and limits on the duration of appointments; and (5) permitting flexibility to limit the appointment to financial or personal matters.

Under the principle of the least restrictive alternative, a local magistrate could authorize a mentorship for personal matters or limited guardianship for only financial matters. In contrast, a plenary guardianship (*onder curatele stelling*) can only be ordered by a federal judge, presumably with greater formalities and procedural safeguards. These measures offer the Dutch a wider continuum of supportive options.

Under this law, some 2,000 mentorships are established each year. In addition, limited guardianships are established in approximately 6,500 cases, and full guardianships in only about 540 cases. Mentorship has achieved more flexible results, and although often combined with limited guardianship over financial matters produces a good blend of adequate protection from financial exploitation with preservation of the individual's important personal liberty interests.

D. Spain

In 1983 Spain modified its guardianship laws. The range of supports now include forms of temporary guardianship (*guarda de hecho*), and a guardianship limited to representation in a specific legal proceeding (*defensor judicial*). There are also proceedings for 'prolonged minority' (*prolongacion patriae potestar*), guardianship of property (*curatela*); and total or plenary guardianship (*tutela*).

E. New Zealand

New Zealand's law on guardianship is noteworthy for its comprehensiveness and its emphasis on tailoring measures for the least intrusion into the affairs of the person with a disability.

As this concise discussion reveals, countries from different regions and legal cultures are embracing newer models of support. They are diversifying the measures that fulfill the universal needs for support for people with intellectual disabilities who have difficulty making informed, voluntary decisions for themselves.

VI. CONCLUSION

Around the world, the movement for enhanced self-determination is gaining momentum. It is expressed in international human rights documents such as the Inter-American Convention on the Elimination of All Forms of Discrimination Against Persons with Disabilities[21] and the European Union's statement on principles of legal protection.[22] (See Herr, Chapter 5 of this volume.) It is reflected in the rise of self-advocacy groups and in a variety of legal reforms. This chapter has sketched some of those reforms, especially in the development of mentorship arrangements and other support services that free persons with disabilities from disenfranchisement. The lessons that can be learned from the Swedish, German, and Israeli experiences, and that of other reforming nations need to be widely disseminated and carefully assessed. The Swedish *god men* (mentors), the German incorporation of self-determination principles in new guardianship laws, and the consumer preferences embodied in the Israel Equal Rights for Persons with Disabilities Law all bear close inspection as activists in various countries explore paths to progress and true partnerships.

A thorough review of guardianship and alternative personal supports in the fifty states and other jurisdictions of the United States is long overdue. For too many people with disabilities, disempowering plenary guardianships are in place when less intrusive and more consensual forms of support will suffice. Self-advocates and scholars demand such reforms that will replace the paternalism of the past with authentic partnerships for the future. As cases such as the US Supreme Court's *Olmstead v L.C.* decision fuel the drive for de-institutionalization, and consumers face the prospect of more self-determined personal decisions and options, the urgency of reform is ever more apparent.[23]

Leading NGOs in the field have long recognized this need. Three decades ago, the International League of Societies for the Mentally Handicapped (now Inclusion International) sharply criticized custodialism and outmoded forms of guardianship as 'an ancient institution which is in urgent need of revitalization to meet the needs of this century'.[24] The League concluded that institutions were 'conducted at best on paternalistic lines, and at worst as an oligarchy in which the disenfranchised residents have no individual or collective voice in their affairs, no control over their environment and no way of changing, protesting, or appealing against conditions under which they might be living, whether benign or harmful'.[25] In many parts of the world, those words remain true in the twenty-first century.

The American Association on Mental Retardation has lent its prestige to the drive toward full recognition of the right to self-determination.

In a 1999 position paper, it defined this term as 'the right to act as the primary causal agent in one's life, to pursue self-defined goals and to participate fully in society'. The Association thus urged service providers to protect the rights of individuals to 'make fundamental life choices, to enhance their authority to act in accordance with those choices and to build the capacity of communities to embrace the active participation of all community members'.

By helping to develop mentorship and other non-coercive support arrangements, engaged scholars and professionals can realize these aims. In this way, guardianship can be minimized and reserved for situations of absolute necessity. The problem with guardianship, after all, is that it lets the courts into the lives of people with disabilities. It can also have a number of negative consequences that may reduce the rights of the individual with intellectual disabilities to a level of civil rights that is even lower than that of even convicted felons.[26]

Finally, through a comprehensive disability rights movement, people with disabilities have created grass-roots pressure for change. Justin Dart, Jr., a senior statesman and the 1998 recipient of the US Presidential Medal of Freedom, articulated the need for an empowerment revolution, changes in support services identified in this chapter:

Our present social programs have reached their limits. We need a clarified vision. Persons with or without disabilities will never fully achieve any of their legitimate goals until there is a revolution of empowerment, a revolution to eliminate primitive practices and stereotypes and to establish a culture that focuses the full force of science and democracy on the individual's potential for self-determination, productivity, and quality of life.[27]

Around the globe this empowerment revolution is stirring. Its impact on primitive or overprotective legal measures is now being felt. Sweden and Israel have already decoupled guardianship and loss of civil rights. Today the citizens of those countries can exercise the right to vote regardless of any protected status. With ingenuity, political will, and legal reforms, more citizens with intellectual disabilities are being emancipated from avoidable guardianships. As people gain in decision-making skills and capabilities, guardianship is being replaced by less intrusive and formalistic measures. The movement for self-determination is a force for such long overdue changes.

NOTES

1. T Nerney, RF Crowley, B Kappel, *et al.* 'An Affirmation of Community: A Revolution of Vision and Goals' (Center for Self-Determination Position Paper, 1994) 14.

2. SS Herr, 'Law and Mental Retardation: International Trends and Reforms' (1987) 38 *International Digest of Health Legislation* 849, 858.
3. A Everett, 'The New Sweden Guardianship Law' (7 June 1989) (unpublished paper).
4. ibid 2.
5. Parents acting as the mutual guardians of their minor children are not eligible for guardianship fees.
6. B Sales, *et al.*, *Disabled Persons and the Law: State Legislative Issues* (New York: Plenum Press, 1982) 100–104.
7. Report of the 1989 Disability Commission, Disability, Welfare, Justice: Summary 22 (SOU 1991:46).
8. Report of the 1989 Disability Commission, 'Disability, Welfare, Justice: Summary 22' (SOU 1991:46).
9. SOU 1992:52.
10. ibid 9.
11. Proposed s 16a to the Constitution Act, SOU 1992:52 at p. 63 (Swedish-language version).
12. This type of day care is limited to persons with mental retardation, autism, autistic-like condition, or brain damage. The reason for this narrowed eligibility was described as simply a compromise driven by cost factors.
13. The local authorities are also responsible for determining an individual's needs for housekeeping services, which is distinguished from the personal assistant who attends to more intimate help such as dressing, toileting, and bathing.
14. SOU 1991:46 (n 8 above).
15. This section draws on interviews with Ulrich Hellmann, and his informative paper presented at XIX International Congress of the International Academy of Law and Mental Health, at the panel on 'Minimizing Guardianship, Maximizing Autonomy: Least Restrictive Alternatives in Surrogate Decision-Making' in Lisbon, Portugal, 14 June 1993.
16. As an indication of the hesitation of the Parliament to approve any such non-consensual sterilization in light of the Nazi history, the Parliament required the federal government to report every four years on the practical results of implementing this aspect of the law.
17. In the Bavarian state, the costs for voluntary and private professional *betreuers* alone are estimated at 22 million German marks (DM, roughly equivalent to US $13 million). Volunteers can receive their expenses, while private professionals (usually lawyers or social workers) are paid on an hourly basis.
18. The former East German law, dating from 1961 and providing for curatorship under the Family Law, was rarely invoked due to the citizen's fear of state involvement in their lives. Hence a pent-up need for legal measures may lead to an increase in legal proceedings in regions of the former East Germany.
19. Equal Rights for People with Disabilities Law, 5758–1998, s 2 [Israel].
20. SS Herr, 'Rights into Action: Protecting Human Rights of the Mentally Handicapped' (1976) 26 *Catholic Univ Law Rev* 203, 276–278, 286–287.
21. Open for signature by members of the Organization of American States as of 8 June 1999. Article V calls for the governments to promote participation by persons with disabilities and their organizations in developing measures to

implement this human rights treaty. Article I clarifies that a 'necessary and appropriate' declaration of legal incompetence does not constitute discrimination under this treaty. Some human rights experts have urged that States adopt a 'reservation' [amendment] striking this clause.

22. European Union Principles Concerning the Legal Protection of Incapable Adults: Recommendation No R (99) 4 and Explanatory Memorandum (1999).

23. See *Tommy Olmstead, Commissioner, Georgia Department of Human Resources v L.C.* 527 US 581 (1999).

24. International League of Societies for the Mentally Handicapped, 'Symposium on Guardianship of the Mentally Retarded' (Brussels, author, May 1969) 10.

25. ibid 29.

26. See J O'Sullivan, 'Adult Guardianship for the Disabled—A Serious Matter' (Fall 1999) 1 *Advances in Aging* 3, 7 (Univ of Maryland at Baltimore Geriatrics and Gerontology Education and Research Program) (quoting Claude Pepper, the late US Representative and champion of older Americans, who wrote: 'The typical ward has fewer rights than the typical convicted felon—they no longer receive money or pay their bills. They cannot marry or divorce…It is, in one short sentence, the most punitive civil penalty that can be levied against an American citizen, with the exception…of the death penalty.').

27. J Dart Jr., speech presented at ABA conference 'In Pursuit…A Blueprint for Disability Law and Policy' in American Bar Association Commission on Mental and Physical Disability Law, (1999) *Disability Law and Policy: A Collective Vision* 1.

Part V
Future Goals and Aspirations

17

Voices of Self-Advocates

MITCHELL LEVITZ

Each of us has the right to dream and the right to try to make our dreams come true. This chapter is an account of some of my dreams and the challenges that I have faced as a person living with an intellectual disability making these dreams come true. Although the chapter largely discusses my personal challenges and some of the lessons I have learned along the way, I hope that the reader will consider how my life experiences can be applied to other people with similar kinds of challenges. I encourage you to use examples of my experiences to help erase negative stereotypes and improve public attitudes about persons with intellectual disabilities. I likewise hope that my thoughts and ideas will serve as a framework for advocates and policymakers around the world to improve the quality of life of people with intellectual disabilities.

I. BEING INDEPENDENT

Since I was young, I have dreamed of having a job, wearing a jacket and tie to work, carrying a brief case, and most importantly, being fully independent! Now that I am 31 years old, to a large degree, I have realized my dream of living independently. After graduating from high school, I lived in a transitional apartment about 75 miles from my parents' home in Peekskill, New York. There, I learned to cook, clean, do laundry, shop, budget my money, and go places by myself or with a friend. I also had a job and took the train to work. So, just like my sisters who, at this same time, went off to college, I had the opportunity to live away from home and develop skills to be independent. One and a half years later, when I moved back to Peekskill, I returned as an adult and got a job in an office where I wore a jacket and tie to work and carried a brief case. I lived by myself in a small house near my parents for the next two years and was generally self-sufficient.

I continued to gain skills to be more independent and demonstrated that I could make good decisions. So, when I was recruited for an exciting employment opportunity in Ohio, a long distance away from my family and hometown, I felt confident in myself and ready to make this major career and life change. With the support of my family, I accepted this position and made the move to a new community. For the past six years I lived by myself, on my own, in a one bedroom apartment in Hyde Park, a suburb of Cincinnati. I recently moved back to my hometown to help my family at a time of need. I am assisting with the family business and, in addition to this work, I am beginning a new position that continues my career in the disability field.

The location where someone lives is the key to just how independent he or she really can be. I use public transportation, and I don't drive. But, I live in a townhouse within walking distance to a bus route, so I can get to work and many other places on my own. I can also walk to a nearby retail shopping center, supermarkets, restaurants, bank, barber, pharmacy, cleaners, tailor, synagogue, doctors' offices, and the dentist. This means I am less dependent on other people for my daily activities. You can see how important public transportation is for me. Without access to public transportation, people like me are limited in their ability to be independent. However, there are times when I need to either call a taxi or someone that I know to drive me places that I cannot get to by public transportation such as to the airport, bus station, and to various evening meetings. That is when it is important for me to reach out to people in the community. A strategy I use is to ask if anyone attending a meeting or event is driving there from my neighborhood. I have been successful in making the necessary arrangements and this has enabled me to serve on the boards of directors and committees of community organizations and take advantage of opportunities to participate in social activities. It does not mean I am less independent, it just acknowledges the importance of interdependence and that I am part of a community.

To some extent, my dream of living independently has been contingent upon my access to public services and the support of my family, friends, co-workers, and people in the community. However, just like everyone else, adults with intellectual disabilities must have choices about where we live and work, whom we live with, and how we spend our leisure time. It is critical to develop appropriate services, supports, and resources so that we, too, can have the dignity of making choices about our daily lives.

'The concept of *Independent Living* was born in the mid-1960s when a group of students with disabilities at the University of California, Berkeley obtained a federal grant to provide housing designed to enable people with severe disabilities to live self-sufficiently. This project lead to the formation of the Berkeley Center for Independent Living, Inc and set in motion a nationwide self-help/self-advocacy group movement in rehabilitation.'[1]

Support does not mean control. In their efforts to shield us from harm, parents, friends, advocates, and service providers must be careful not to be over-protective. They should recognize our need for privacy and give us time for ourselves. We should be encouraged to take risks and try new things on our own, but we should also have a safety net should we occasionally stumble. Sometimes this safety net is simply a network of people. For those of us who need extra help, it is important that we have people in our lives that we can depend upon—not to do things for us, but rather to help us to do things for ourselves. A *Circle of Support* is a good example.

'A Circle of Friends, also referred to as a Circle of Support, is a planning process that emphasizes the interdependent nature of relationships among individuals with disabilities, their families and friends, close acquaintances in the community, and paid professionals. The process focuses on the development of community connections that provide the support an individual needs to live in the community, feel like a valued member of that community, and maintain lasting friendships.'[2]

In my life, I have been very fortunate to have a network of family, friends, and associates to support and encourage me. A lot was accomplished when I, along with my parents, educators, and people in my community pooled our resources and worked together to help prepare me for my dream of living independently.

Being independent also means having responsibilities and taking these responsibilities seriously. For example, taking good care of oneself and one's home, being a reliable employee, supporting oneself financially, and keeping one's promises.

To be responsible and make good choices, we need information that is written or explained to us in a way that we can understand so that we will be able to make the best decisions. It is also important for us to be aware of the kinds of decisions we are capable of making completely on our own and the kinds of decisions we should ask others for help in making. For example, I do not need help in deciding what to cook for dinner, what suit to wear, how to style my hair, or with whom I want to get together. Yet, when it comes to making money and financial decisions, signing contracts, and dealing with medical problems, I am learning every day that I need to ask for advice. It is also important for me to identify the particular people who I trust and can give me good advice regarding these kinds of questions and decisions. Even though the decisions should be mine to make, it is necessary that I get appropriate advice first. Otherwise, the consequences for me could be very serious and difficult to fix if I make poor decisions. In addition, if I do not make informed decisions about serious matters, my parents and colleagues may lose confidence in my ability to have this level of independence and control. My feeling of independence has continued to grow over time as I have been successful in good decision making. It is also sometimes hard for me to recognize that there may be certain areas where I will always need some assistance, but I understand this more clearly with each new experience.

II. MAKING MONEY AND FINDING A CAREER

From an early age, students should have both volunteer and paying jobs. Jobs are important to help us develop skills and find our talents. Having a job teaches you about being punctual, following instructions, working independently, being flexible, getting along with others, and about earning, saving, and managing money.

A good career matches each person's likes, interests, and preferences with his or her unique capabilities. Each of us can learn to do some kind of job well and gain satisfaction from doing it as long as we have the necessary support and accommodations.[3] For some of us, this may include employment counseling, job development, assistive technology, job coaching, and job sharing. Being employed leads to careers that we can enjoy and find meaningful and can enable us to feel and be productive and independent citizens.

While in high school, I volunteered as an intern for my local legislator, George Pataki, who is now the Governor of the State of New York. This was an important experience for me. I found out that I like working in an office, being politically active, and helping the public. The job gave me a sense of direction for my future career.

After my internship, I worked as a bulk teller handling the coin counting at a bank where I learned how to interact with customers. It was exciting for me to have this work experience featured in the award winning film, *Employability: Integrating People with Developmental Disabilities into the Workplace*, which was distributed in videocassette form to business leaders, members of Congress, governors, and developmental disabilities professionals.[4]

A few years later, I worked as an office assistant at our local Chamber of Commerce. There I gained the skills that I needed to work in a modern office such as using multi-line telephones, fax machines, copiers, and computers. Sometimes, in pursuing our own career goals we create opportunities for others. My job at the Chamber of Commerce, for example, was partially funded through a federal on-the-job training program. While working in this position, I helped develop a survey to find out from member businesses if they would consider hiring persons with disabilities. We received many favorable responses.[5] This led to a contract, between the Chamber of Commerce and the New York State Office of Vocational and Educational Services for Individuals with Disabilities (VESID), for the local Chamber of Commerce to do job development for people with disabilities in the business community. I am proud that this model is now being used statewide and has helped many other people with disabilities get jobs in their own communities. The lesson we learned is that businesses can and will be good partners in creating job and career opportunities but only if we reach out to them to join our team.

My next job was working as a paid intern with the Westchester Arc. My job involved community education, legislative advocacy, quality assurance, and self-advocacy. As part of my job as the Consumer Ombudsman, I helped develop and facilitate a self-advocacy group. Many people who participated had never been part of a peer support group before, had never shared their feelings, or talked about things in their lives that they wanted to change. Soon, they began asking one another questions. They started to understand that they did have choices. Over time, some became more outspoken. They encouraged one another to talk to their families and to the program staff that might help them achieve some of these changes. This opportunity for sharing helped build their capacity and self-confidence to speak out on their own behalf. A few became the group leaders and are helping other self-advocates by speaking to legislators and attending meetings. The Westchester Arc revised its bylaws to assure that self-advocates would be represented on its Board of Directors.

I also worked with the Quality Assurance Department in developing a survey that was sent to community residence managers to determine how consumer empowerment was being promoted within the agency's programs. How organizations evaluate quality assurance and consumer choice is becoming more individualized and focused on what has been achieved in making each person's life better. 'The Council on Quality and Leadership in Supports for People with Disabilities (The Council), formerly known as The Accreditation Council, altered its definition of *quality* from "compliance with organizational process" to "responsiveness to people"...The Council has identified three dimensions (experience, support, and creativity) that interact to make choice meaningful.'[6]

While employed with the Westchester Arc, I was recruited to work for a new non-profit organization called Capabilities Unlimited Inc (CUI) as the Self-Advocacy Coordinator. I moved to Cincinnati, where I lived for the past six years. The goal of this organization is to enable people with developmental disabilities to be part of their community by learning to advocate for themselves by strengthening their individual capabilities and maximizing their self-advocacy skills. I believe that more self-advocates should be employed by local, state, and national disability organizations or actively volunteer on boards and committees. As part of my work with CUI, we developed and implemented a leadership training program that included peer support. At this same time, CUI helped community organizations learn how to recruit and support self-advocates as employees and volunteers. I was also editor-in-chief and, along with my co-editors, was responsible for publishing our national newsletter,

Community Advocacy Press, written by and for people with developmental disabilities across the country.

During that period of time, I was working for The Arc of Ohio on a statewide grant, called CHOICES, funded by the Ohio Developmental Disabilities Planning Council. This project helps people with disabilities make informed choices about where they want to live and if they want to move out of institutions, nursing homes, or large congregant Intermediate Care Facilities for Mental Retardation and Developmental Disabilities (ICF/MRDD). I was one of two team leaders that match volunteer self-advocates, one-to-one, with individuals who want to experience what life is like for someone with a developmental disability who lives in the community. If the person decides to move into a smaller living arrangement in the community, the CHOICES teams helps by linking them to supports, services, and resources. My new position is with the Consumer Resource Center at the Westchester Institute for Human Development, a University Center of Excellence in Disabilities in Valhalla, New York. I will be assisting with peer-to-peer support, health promotion, technology research projects, self-determination initiatives, training professionals, and other activities.

III. MAKING OUR OWN DECISIONS

Being able to make informed decisions about employment opportunities and other life experiences comes from having knowledge, experience, and practice. I feel that students who need more time and different job experiences should have these opportunities as part of a school educational program that prepares students for life as adults. In the United States, transition planning is now mandated under the Individuals with Disabilities Education Act to help students ages 15 and older prepare for life after high school.[7] However, this is not being fully implemented for most students. This kind of planning activity should be promoted. It is an important way to help young people move smoothly from school to the workplace, helping them reach their dreams and have fulfilling lives.

'If transition is to be effective, it must be based on assessment of the student's needs, preferences, and interests, using a variety of methods. Such assessment should be an ongoing process that assists students with disabilities and their families define goals, monitor progress toward those goals, and make appropriate adjustments while preparing for future adult roles. Young adults will go on to post-secondary education or training or employment and will develop meaningful personal and social relationships.'[8]

Transition planning should include all areas of life experience, such as continuing education, employment, community participation, living arrangements, budgeting and managing money, social relationships, fun and leisure time, personal hygiene and keeping fit, building support systems such as guardianship and other legal arrangements, and health care. What is most important is that planning must include setting goals that are based upon each student's personal dreams! This can be effectively accomplished through a group planning process called person-centered planning. *'Person-centered planning* is a term used to describe a group of approaches intended to organize and guide the efforts of an individual with a disability, his or her family members, friends, and service providers, as they work collectively to assist the individual in pursuing his or her interests, desires, and goals.'[9]

Our schools should be planning with us, not for us, so that we will feel a personal responsibility and commitment to carrying out the choices we identify. As a secondary school student, I found that attending my Individualized Education Program (IEP) meetings helped me learn to listen, speak-up for myself, work with other people, determine my preferences, explore options, and make choices.[10] I believe that students must be involved in any planning that impacts their lives. The fact that we might not be able to make some decisions without help is no reason to exclude us from making any decisions at all.

Historically, however, that is just how society has treated people like me. In the United States and around the world, I know people with intellectual disabilities who have never been asked to make choices. They are just told what to do. Indeed, some people have never been informed that they have the same rights to make choices as everyone else. It is our responsibility to ensure that people with disabilities have the right to *self-determination*—that is, having control of our own lives.

'When a person acquires more control to direct his or her life, it will have consequences at several levels. The meaning of *self-determination* may best be regarded as the sum total of these changes: people's actual control over the conduct of their lives and their sense of being in control of their lives, identity, and future. People should have a network of relationships and be involved in the community. This will result in greater inclusion and a feeling of full citizenship.'[11]

IV. BEING INCLUDED

People with intellectual disabilities can lead full and active lives. Through the years, in my free time, I have enjoyed water skiing, downhill skiing, tennis, biking, kayaking, ping-pong, and I am a big sports fan. Everyday I read the newspaper and watch the news so that I know what is going on in the world. Perhaps we all have more in common with one another than you might have expected. Many people with intellectual disabilities are talented and accomplished in diverse ways. Often, however, we are never given the chance to develop our talents.

For example, when I traveled across country participating in conferences, I met many young people who never learned to read and write because people assumed they could not learn, so no one had ever bothered to teach them. We must promote each person's potential for achievements and accomplishments. Without the opportunity to learn all kinds of new information we will never know our true potential.

Students with intellectual disabilities should attend their neighborhood schools, make friends, and have the opportunity to be included in activities with their peers without disabilities. I attended my local schools and benefited from special education and speech and language services. Upon reflection, while in school I was very motivated to work hard and keep up with other students even though I did not learn as quickly. In 1991, I graduated with a regular academic high school diploma.

Fortunately for me, my parents, who know me best, made sure that they were always part of any decision-making team. They fought for what they believed I needed, and this opened doors that had previously been closed to students like me. I was the first student in my neighborhood schools with Down syndrome or other intellectual disabilities. I attended school with my sisters and my neighborhood friends, and they became an important support for me. In looking back, I know that they gained as much as I did from our relationships.

Even though I was successful in school, there were some times when peer pressure and teasing from other students made school life more challenging. While in school I developed some effective strategies for handling this type of treatment—valuable strategies that remain with me today such as walking away, ignoring comments, and talking to a counselor. I think that being in a regular school prepared me for the real world where everyone is not always so understanding, open minded, or accepting of differences.

In addition to attending a regular school, my parents encouraged me to participate in activities with children without disabilities, such as scouts, competitive soccer, camps, and religious education. They felt that I should not be deprived of these exciting opportunities because of the preconceptions and often times limited expectations of others. They also believed that other students needed to understand and accept me for who I am, because someday as adults, we might work together, be neighbors, or participate in the same community activities.

Based on my own experiences growing up, I believe that people with intellectual disabilities should, if they wish, have the same opportunities to receive religious education and training, and to be involved in community synagogue, temple, or church activities, and practice their personal beliefs.

It is important for congregations to reach out so that each one of us will experience a sense of belonging and a connection to our heritage, culture, and traditions.

V. PARTICIPATING IN OUR COMMUNITIES

With inclusion comes the responsibility to be an active member of our community. Each of us can make a difference and should try to have our voices heard by participating and contributing to make our communities a better place for everyone. There is an important place in our society for volunteerism and that should include people with disabilities. It is a good feeling to be the one to give help rather than always being the recipient of help. We can let people know that we want to participate side by side with our families and neighbors in such activities as joining community service clubs, assisting with fund-raising events, and volunteering at places where assistance is needed such as food pantries and homeless shelters.

There is also an important place for leadership in our society. 'People with cognitive disabilities have, time and time again, assumed and excelled in roles of leadership.'[12] Some friends and colleagues and I participated in the *Next Generation Leadership Symposiums* and *Leadership Academies* that made public policy recommendations to the *President's Committee on Mental Retardation*. We also attended *Partners in Policy Making* training programs in our own states. Through this 'empowerment' training program, created by Colleen Wieck, Executive Director of the Minnesota Governor's Planning Council, we heard national speakers talk about best practices in developmental disability issues. We learned how to effectively advocate for systems change. 'Partners in Policymaking was designed to provide information, training, and skill building in the area of developmental disabilities to individuals with disabilities, parents and guardians so that they may obtain appropriate, state of the art services for themselves and others, develop their leadership potential, and impact public policy development.'[13] Many of the graduates now serve on important policy boards such as State Developmental Disabilities Councils.

Self-advocacy leaders must continually learn about the issues, prepare and deliver reports, and make decisions about funding allocations. Leadership training opportunities and experiences increase our knowledge and expand our ability to contribute. An area of training should include preparing individuals with intellectual disabilities to serve on local, state, and federal grant review panels. I participated in such training sponsored by the US Office of Special Education and Rehabilitation Services for self-advocates and our individual support persons, who we personally identified for this pilot project.

The project resulted from concerns raised by some in the disability community that individuals with cognitive disabilities, specifically mental retardation, were not included among the potential reviewers who might be used to evaluate applications. They believe there is a cadre of self-advocates active at the state and federal levels who have the skills and experience to be good reviewers. The evaluation found that people with cognitive disabilities, categorized by the disability systems as having mental retardation, can be effective reviewers of grant applications submitted in response to OSERS competitions.[14]

Leadership training on how to be effective on an advisory board, task force, or committee is essential in order for individuals with intellectual disabilities to meaningfully contribute and make a difference. We need to have information and materials presented in a format that is understandable. Other people need to have patience and be mentors to support us as we learn. Individuals with disabilities must become registered voters, learn the issues, and support political candidates who understand and will act upon our concerns. People with disabilities and our families are a large constituency in numbers of potential votes, but we must become more politically active. I learned a lot by helping with some local and state political campaigns. Presenting congressional testimony for funding for research and supportive employment and for the reauthorization of IDEA, participating in national governmental affairs seminars and developing legislative platforms, and attending events and rallies in Washington, DC, have all played a role in motivating me to pursue my interest in advocacy and public policy.

I have volunteered my time to be involved with an Employment Consortium, an Inclusion Taskforce and other initiatives. I received a scholarship to participate in the United Way Leadership Training for community members to learn all about serving effectively on not-for-profit boards. A follow-up requirement of this training is to select and join such a board. I became a member of the Board of Directors of the *Greater Cincinnati Down Syndrome Association*, and after three years and experience on their Executive Committee, I then served as a Vice President. I also volunteered my time with the local Arc as a member of the Board of Directors and participated in their public policy initiatives. For example, working with the city and metro to ensure that people with physical disabilities have access to taxi cabs.

Throughout the years, I have been appointed to numerous state committees and local policy and planning councils because I contacted public officials and offered to volunteer my time. Although an increasing number of self-advocates like me are now being asked to serve on advisory boards and policy councils, more needs to be done in this area. Greater efforts, for example, need to be made to recruit, train, and support people with learning challenges to be contributing members of our communities.

Many of my peers are making valuable contributions to their communities. Jason is very active with the Self-Advocacy Association in his State. Alan participated in his high school leadership class and now is involved with community theater projects and continues to serve as a church alter boy. Brian participated in a club that reports weather conditions for the local radio station and has worked as an intern for the town clerk. Gary and Ralph are members of their local volunteer fire department. Annie serves on the President's Committee on Mental Retardation and has a company that sells disability-theme items that has raised thousands of dollars for the National Down Syndrome Congress. Mia is a licensed trainer to teach self-advocates about leadership, takes courses at a nearby college, and serves on the Board of Directors of the National Down Syndrome Society. Tia is a public speaker on self-determination and participates in peer review teams for University Centers of Excellence for Developmental Disabilities Education, Research and Services. James was president of a national People First organization called Self-Advocates Becoming Empowered. Liz serves on the Board of Directors of AAMR. Marvin and his brother Leon, who was placed in a nursing home years ago, are now living together in the community as roommates after being separated for many years.

VI. ADVOCATING FOR EACH OTHER

Being an advocate means speaking out for oneself and others on issues that affect our lives—issues such as human rights, equal opportunities and discrimination, health care, individual and family supports, early intervention, quality education and inclusion, employment opportunities, and full integration into society. Often, the first step in becoming a successful advocate is being a successful self-advocate.

Young people will only learn to advocate for themselves if they are asked and encouraged to make choices and decisions. Making wise choices, however, requires knowledge. Consequently, in school, in the community, and at home, students need to understand and learn how to share information and express their ideas through discussions and meetings.

Talking about having a disability may be difficult. But, in whatever way we are able to communicate, we need to express ourselves instead of keeping it inside. Only then will others begin to understand how we feel about the problems, obstacles, and challenges we face and be able to help us find strategies to solve these problems. At the same time, we want people to focus on our abilities, not our disabilities. People should think of us first as individuals and second that we happen to have some special challenges.

'In its most basic form, *People First Language* puts the person before the disability. In addition, *People First Language* uses words to describe what a person "has", not what a person "is". But it is much, much more; *People First Language* is about dignity and respect. Many people take politically correct language to extremes, but some politically correct terminology is valuable and appropriate when it helps promote equality and fairness.'[15]

VII. CONCLUSION

My friend Jason Kingsley and I had our book *Count Us In: Growing Up with Down Syndrome* published in 1994.[16] While promoting the book, we had the opportunity to travel all across the United States speaking with people with disabilities and their families, friends, and supporters. Through radio, television, newspapers, and magazines, we were able to spread our message and improve public attitudes towards persons with intellectual disabilities. Other people with special challenges have told us that hearing about our book encouraged them to also share their personal stories and experiences. *Count Us In* is on the recommended reading lists in many schools, libraries, and college curricula in human services and education. Improving public attitudes about people with disabilities is very rewarding and meaningful. I have had the opportunity to visit with students in schools and universities in many different states. I talked to the students about my experiences, disability awareness, and how to be effective leaders in their schools and communities.

In *Count Us In*, Jason describes how people with disabilities have the same hopes, dreams, goals, and feelings as everyone else; that we each have our own opinions, beliefs, interests, tastes, and personalities. I believe that there can be many opportunities to succeed in life but only if we take advantage of these opportunities. And, where opportunities do not exist, we must work together to see that opportunities are created. With high expectations and positive thinking, and with the love of our families and the support of our friends and communities, more people can be successful in achieving their dreams, just as I am achieving my dreams. Each of us is important in our own way—so Count Us In! Count Everyone In!

NOTES

1. P Browning, *Transition-in-Action for Youth and Young Adults with Disabilities* (Montgomery, Ala: Wells Printing, 1997).
2. J Kregel, 'Developing a Career Path: Application of Person-Centered Planning' in P Wehman and J Kregel (eds), *More Than a Job: Securing Satisfying Careers for People with Disabilities* (Baltimore: Paul H Brookes Publishing, 1998) 71–91.

3. The Americans with Disabilities Act specifically uses the term 'reasonable accommodation' to describe job supports that may need to be provided to assist people with disabilities in performing related job duties. According to the Act, it may mean 'making existing facilities...readily accessible to and useable by individuals with disabilities', modifying employment schedules, or providing necessary equipment or devises. Americans with Disabilities Act 1, 42 USC 12102 (1995).

4. EP Kingsley and B Levitz (writers), Northern Light Productions (producers/ directors), *Employability: Integrating People with Developmental Disabilities into the Workplace* (New York: Woolworth Corp, 1993).

5. M Levitz *et al.*, 'Three Minute Survey' unpublished (1993).

6. J Gardner, S Nudler, and M Chapman, 'Personal Outcomes as Measures of Quality' (1997) 35/4 *Mental Retardation* 295–305.

7. Individuals with Disabilities Education Act (IDEA), 20 USC 1400 (Supp 1995). Congress enacted IDEA 'to assure that all children with disabilities have available to them...a free and appropriate public education which emphasizes special education and related services to meet their unique needs to assure that the rights of children with disabilities and their parents or guardians are protected, to assist States and localities to provide for the education of all children with disabilities, and to assess and assure the effectiveness of efforts to educate children with disabilities.' ibid.

8. PL Sitlington and DS Neubert, 'Transition Assessment: Methods and Processes to Determine Student Needs, Preferences, and Interests' in M Wehmeyer and D Sands (eds), *Making It Happen: Student Involvement in Education Planning, Decision Making, and Instruction* (Baltimore: Paul H Brookes Publishing, 1998) 75–98.

9. Kregel (n 2 above) 71–91.

10. The IEP is a 'written statement' which outlines the student's educational program. It includes categories such as 'annual goals,...short-term instructional objectives,...specific educational services' and determines a timeframe for accomplishing these tasks. Each year, members of the committee on special education (CSE) meet with the teachers, parents or guardians and in some cases, the student, to draft this plan that is approved by the local school board. 42 USC 1401 (a) (19) (1990).

11. S Dowson and B Salibury, *Foundations for Freedom: International Perspectives on Self-Determination and Individualized Funding* (Baltimore: TASH, 2001).

12. M Wehmeyer and R Berkobien, 'The Legacy of Self-Advocacy' in G Dybwad and H Bersani (eds), *New Voices: Self-Advocacy by People with Disabilities* (Cambridge, Mass: Brookline Books, 1996) 245–257.

13. TJ Zirpoli, D Hanox, C Wieck, and ER Skarnulis, 'Partners in Policymaking: Empowering People' (1989) 14/2 *JASH* 163–167.

14. GS Bonham, *Evaluation of OSERS Grant Review Pilot to Use Reviewers with Mental Retardation* (Baltimore: Bonham Research, 2001).

15. K Snow, *Disability is Natural: Revolutionary Common Sense for Raising Successful Children with Disabilities* (Woodland Park, Colo: Braveheart Press, 2001).

16. J Kingsley and M Levitz, *Count Us In: Growing Up with Down Syndrome* (San Diego, Calif: Harcourt Brace, 1994).

18

Recognizing Existing Rights and Crafting New Ones: Tools for Drafting Human Rights Instruments for People with Mental Disabilities

ERIC ROSENTHAL AND CLARENCE J. SUNDRAM

After years of neglect, there is now a growing interest in drafting new domestic and international human rights laws to protect the rights of people with intellectual and other disabilities.[1] In April 2000, the UN Human Rights Commission adopted Resolution 2000/51 calling for increased international attention to the rights of people with disabilities.[2] The resolution called on governments to improve their own reporting to the UN oversight bodies on the enforcement of rights under current UN human rights conventions,[3] and it called for more active monitoring by UN agencies. On 19 December 2001, the UN General Assembly adopted Resolution 56/168.[4] This historical resolution initiated a formal UN process for drafting a specialized convention on the rights of people with disabilities. Resolution 56/168 did not commit governments to supporting a new convention, but it created an *Ad Hoc Committee* 'to consider proposals' for a convention 'to promote and protect the rights and dignity of persons with disabilities'.[5] The General Assembly also asked the *Ad Hoc Committee* to consider the results of a forthcoming study examining the effectiveness of existing human rights conventions and treaty-monitoring bodies in protecting the rights of people with disabilities.[6]

The Human Rights Commission released the findings of the study 'Human Rights are for All: A Study on the Current Use and Future Potential of the United Nations Human Rights Instruments in the Context of Disability,' in February 2002.[7] The authors of the study, Professors Gerard Quinn and Theresia Degener, found that existing human rights conventions and 'United Nations human rights treaty bodies have considerable potential in this field but have generally been underused so far in advancing the rights of persons with disabilities.'[8] Thus, the study recommends that treaty-based monitoring bodies 'adopt General Comments on the nature of State obligations under the respective treaties

The authors acknowledge the support of the World Health Organization. The WHO monograph cited here represents the views of the authors and has not been finalized by WHO.

in the context of disability'.[9] The study also recommends a number of actions the treaty-monitoring bodies and the Commission on Human Rights can take to educate the public and focus the attention of governments on the requirements of existing human rights conventions.[10]

In addition to improving the use of existing conventions, the report strongly backs the need to adopt a new convention on the rights of people with disabilities. The authors 'conclude that such a convention is necessary and would underpin—and not undermine—the existing instruments in the field of disability'.[11] In April 2002, the UN Human Rights Commission 'welcomed' the findings of this study and recommended the consideration of its findings by the *Ad Hoc Committee*.[12] Like the General Assembly, the UN Human Rights Commission has not yet endorsed the need for a human rights instrument and it emphasizes the need to maintain 'consistency with the high quality of existing international standards'.[13]

The UN *Ad Hoc Committee* met in New York during the summer of 2002 without a firm decision by the international community to endorse a new human rights instrument, yet the governments, legal experts, and activists threw themselves into the process of drafting a new instrument. The government of Mexico, which sponsored by resolution in the Third Committee of the General Assembly that led to the adoption of Resolution 56/168, submitted a draft to the *Ad Hoc Committee* for consideration.[14] The Mexican delegation expressed their commitment to advancing the drafting process as quickly as possible. A leader of the Mexican delegation confided that the drafting process would be the best way to engage governments and gain their support for the idea of a new convention.[15] The 2002 *Ad Hoc Committee* ended without any further decision by participating governments to back the convention, but the drafting process for the convention is now actively underway. The *Ad Hoc Committee* has agreed to meet again in May or June 2003.

While the United Nations has not yet committed itself to the adoption of a new convention, there is a growing consensus in favor of a convention among the major world organizations representing people with disabilities.[16] One of the forces driving the new organizing efforts to back a convention is the recognition that, while existing human rights protections are potentially valuable, discrimination and abuse of people with disabilities is widespread. Three United Nations Special Rapporteurs have identified this problem, calling for major improvements in international human rights law.[17] Over the last ten years, independent organizations, such as Mental Disability Rights International (MDRI), have identified the particular vulnerabilities of people with intellectual disabilities who are detained in institutions for people with intellectual disabilities, psychiatric hospitals, orphanages, social care homes, prisons and jails.[18] In Russia, there are half a million children in institutions.[19] Children with the most severe intellectual disabilities are often placed in the worst conditions, in 'lying down rooms' where they are placed in cribs and receive almost no form of human contact other than the feeding necessary to keep them alive. Behind the closed doors of children's and adult facilities, MDRI identified extensive problems of inhuman and degrading treatment. In Mexico, Uruguay, and Hungary, MDRI found that powerful and potentially dangerous psychotropic medications are often misused, creating dangers for patients. In Bulgaria, psychiatric institutions continue to use unmodified electro convulsive therapy, which creates a grave risk of harm to patients. In Hungary and Bulgaria, MDRI found people detained for prolonged periods of time in cages in which they sometimes could not stand upright. In Mexico, Uruguay, and other countries, MDRI investigators observed children and adults left tied to wheelchairs and bed frames in a state of total neglect.

In the thirteen countries of Latin America and Central and Eastern Europe investigated by MDRI, one of the primary reasons people with intellectual disabilities were placed in institutions was a lack of social services and support systems that would allow them to live in the community. The lack of effective human rights oversight and enforceable legal protections permits abuses to go on unchecked. Due process protections that might prevent arbitrary or improper institutionalization are lacking in most of the countries investigated by MDRI. The lack of protection against discrimination makes it difficult for people who avoid institutionalization to succeed in the community.

MDRI has found that UN staff and programs serving people with mental disabilities may be oblivious to human rights issues facing this population. MDRI's report, *Not on the Agenda: Human Rights of People with Mental Disabilities in Kosovo*, released in August 2002, found inhuman and degrading conditions of confinement and a lack of protections against physical and sexual abuses in institutions administered by the UN Mission in Kosovo (UNMIK).[20] Despite extensive international funding for civil society programs in Kosovo, MDRI found that donor organizations provided no targeted support for human rights work by or for people with mental disabilities. UNMIK created a 'Disability Task Force' to promote participation in public policy by people with disabilities. In the absence of any organization representing individuals with intellectual or psychiatric disabilities, UNMIK selected the chief social worker at the psychiatric ward of Prishtina General Hospital to represent people with mental disabilities. According to this social worker, patients on the ward are 'ill and not disabled' and have no place on the Disability Task Force.[21]

MDRI's report on Kosovo demonstrates the lack of attention to the rights of people with mental disabilities by some UN agencies and the international development organizations that fund and implement programs. In Kosovo, according to MDRI, these organizations contributed to reinforcing a segregated service system for people with intellectual disabilities. UNMIK used funds and technical assistance from the Norwegian Red Cross and the Dutch Government to rebuild Shtime, an institution for people with intellectual disabilities, and proceeded with this program despite the fact that international experts and professionals at the facility found that the majority of people at Shtime had no need for institutionalization. As of May 2002, UNMIK had planned no community-based alternatives for people with intellectual disabilities. After MDRI's report brought world press attention to the human rights abuses in Kosovo's institutions,[22] the Dutch and Norwegian governments agreed to begin funding community placements for people with intellectual disabilities.

MDRI's findings in Kosovo underscore the importance of UN Human Rights Commission Resolution 2002/61, which called on the UN Secretary-General to report on the progress of UN agencies to take action to enforce human rights within their own programs. MDRI's findings are consistent with the frustrations of international disability rights organizations concerning the lack of enforcement of existing human rights law for people with disabilities. The inhumane treatment and arbitrary detention documented by MDRI in Kosovo—and other countries—is prohibited by existing international conventions. Yet governments, UN technical agencies, and international development organizations have not been held accountable to these laws. As this chapter describes, the prohibition against discrimination in the International Covenant on Economic, Social, and Cultural Rights (ICESCR) has been interpreted to prohibit unnecessary segregation from society of people with disabilities. In the absence of a convention that spells out the prohibition against segregation in detail, the implications for the structure of mental health and social service systems is not yet clear.

This chapter describes a number of tools that can be used by the drafters of new human rights instruments (or domestic laws) to provide clearer and stronger protections for people with mental disabilities. These tools are relevant to domestic legislators and to the work of the UN *Ad Hoc Committee* as it drafts a new UN human rights convention. While there is an urgent need for a new convention, there is also a need for the drafters of any new disability rights instrument to proceed with caution. Given the long awaited and potentially limited opportunity for the United Nations to act to draft and adopt a new convention, there is enormous political pressure on disability rights organizations to back a new draft convention. In the interest of adopting valuable new international instruments, disability groups and governments will inevitably be forced to make compromises. This chapter will describe how a number of pitfalls in drafting undermined previous international disability rights. In some cases, these instruments have weakened protections in existing mainstream human rights law. In other cases, terminology laden with dated, discriminatory, or disempowering language has rendered otherwise valuable instruments politically unacceptable to the very individuals they were intended to protect.

The United Nations General Assembly has adopted a valuable set of guidelines for '[s]etting international standards in the field of human rights' that should be taken into consideration by legislative drafters from the outset.[23] These include the recommendations that any new instrument:

(a) Be consistent with the existing body of international human rights law;
(b) Be of fundamental character and derive from the inherent dignity and worth of the human person;
(c) Be sufficiently precise to give rise to identifiable and practicable rights and obligations;
(d) Provide, where appropriate, realistic and effective implementation machinery, including reporting systems; and
(e) Attract broad international support.[24]

This chapter examines two valuable sources of guidance for applying these general principles to the rights of people with disabilities, particularly to people with intellectual disabilities. The first is the product of an international conference among legal experts, disability service professionals, educators, and disability activists, inspired and organized by Professor Stan Herr, at Yale University in 1995. The outcome of this international gathering among experts in such diverse fields was a resolution, eponymously named by Professor Herr, 'The Yale Declaration'. (See Appendix.) In its vision for international action and for the development of international human rights law, the Yale Declaration was well ahead of its time. Among its insights, the Yale Declaration warns about the dangers of new legal instruments that do not reflect the binding nature of human rights law relating to people with disabilities. In the absence of a binding disability rights convention, the many non-binding UN human rights resolutions can reinforce the widespread misconception that disability rights are matters that are ultimately left to the domestic discretion of governments. One of the main arguments that has been made for a specialized convention on the rights of people with intellectual or other disabilities is to make clear to the world a fundamental point that is widely misunderstood: that existing international human rights law creates binding obligations on governments that protect the rights of people with disabilities.

This chapter also examines a second tool that can be used by drafters of a new human rights convention, the study by Eric Rosenthal and Clarence

Sundram commissioned in 2001 by the World Health Organization (WHO), 'The Role of International Human Rights in Domestic Mental Health Legislation'.[25] As the Yale Declaration gives policy guidance to legislative drafters to help them build on lessons learned from the intellectual disability rights movement, the WHO study is intended to assist legislators on the domestic level to understand current protections under international human rights law. The WHO study describes the core minimum *obligations* on governments under existing human rights covenants to protect the rights of people with intellectual disabilities. This chapter suggests that the WHO study is just as relevant to the international community as it is to legislators working at the domestic level. By clarifying the current obligations on governments in existing conventions, the WHO monograph helps to establish a baseline for the protections that new human rights convention should include.

The Yale Declaration links the concept of human rights protection with that of community integration. It calls on governments and international development programs to promote 'best practices' of service in the most integrated settings possible in order to reform service systems. Without bringing an end to the segregation of people with intellectual disabilities in closed institutions, it may be difficult to provide them any meaningful rights protection. By adopting 'best practices', reformers build on the lessons of the intellectual disability rights movement in other countries and avoid repeating their mistakes. As community integration is recognized as a right in and of itself, the development of best and most integrated service systems becomes a human rights prerogative. This chapter includes selections of the WHO study on the right to health and the right to protection against discrimination. These selections show that the right to community integration has been recognized under international law as part of both the protection against discrimination and the right to the highest attainable standard of physical and mental health.

I. THE YALE DECLARATION AS A GUIDE TO DRAFTING NEW INTERNATIONAL HUMAN RIGHTS INSTRUMENTS

Participants at the Yale Conference, titled 'Should *difference* make a difference?' grappled with the dual challenge of (1) making the best use of mainstream international human rights conventions—which protect all people but make almost no mention of disability—and (2) calling for a specialized new international law that would define and draw attention to the rights of people with intellectual disabilities. At the time the Yale Declaration was drafted, the United Nations had explicitly rejected the idea of a disability rights convention despite years of effort by disability activists in the 1980s.[26] Thus, the Yale Declaration outlines a strategy for making the best use of existing human rights law while boldly calling for renewed efforts to gain support for a disability rights convention:[27] 'People with mental retardation [and other disabilities] currently lack the protection of a binding, international convention devoted especially to their rights. Treaties have been recently adopted to protect the rights of women, children, and racial minorities, and people with mental retardation and other disabilities deserve no less.'[28]

Seven years after the Yale Declaration, the international community is just beginning to catch up to the vision set forth in this document. UN General Assembly Resolution 56/168 has now created an *Ad Hoc Committee* 'to consider proposals for a comprehensive and integral international convention to protect and promote the rights and dignity of persons with disabilities'.[29] Encouraged by 'the increasing interest of the international community in the promotion and protection of the rights and dignity of persons with disabilities', the United Nations General Assembly acted out of concern for the 'disadvantaged and vulnerable situation faced by six hundred million persons with disabilities around the world'. Thus, the General Assembly's action responds to 'the need to advance in the elaboration of an international instrument'.[30]

The government of Mexico has promised to proceed quickly with the drafting process, and presented a draft convention to the first meeting of the *Ad Hoc Committee* in July 2002.[31] If other convention drafting processes are any indication, however, the process of drafting the new UN Disability Rights Convention could take years. Once a new convention is drafted, the UN General Assembly must adopt the convention and send it to governments to seek ratification. While the drafting of the Disability Convention may well proceed quickly, it will take some time before governments ratify the convention and the instrument enters into force as binding international law.

As governments, legal experts, and disability rights activists gather to work on a convention, there are a few recommendations—and a warning—in the Yale Declaration that deserve particular attention. Until such time as a new UN Disability Rights Convention is adopted and enters into force, the Yale Declaration calls for the full enforcement of existing human rights law. The Yale Declaration cites the Declaration of Vienna, adopted by the World Conference on Human Rights in 1993, for its affirmation that, despite the lack of explicit language on disability rights in existing conventions, 'all human rights and fundamental freedoms are universal and thus unreservedly include persons with disabilities'.[32] Thus, the Yale Declaration states '[a]ll States must immediately begin a process of reforming their laws and public policies to achieve or exceed international standards'. The Yale Declaration calls for 'full protection' of human rights for people with mental disabilities 'consistent with the requirements of the International Covenant on Civil and Political Rights [ICCPR] and the International Covenant on Economic, Social, and Cultural Rights [ICESCR]'.[33] As a guiding principle for action, the Yale Declaration cites the UN General Assembly's Standard Rules on Equalization of Opportunities for People with Disabilities ('Standard Rules'),[34] which would require every country to begin a national planning process to reform laws and bring them into conformity with international human rights law. The Standard Rules specifically recognize that this process must be inclusive and that people with intellectual as well as physical disabilities should be involved in drafting new legislation on matters that affect them.[35] Token representation of an individual with a disability does not meet the requirements of the Standard Rules, which states in Rule 15 that '[s]tates must ensure that organizations of persons with disabilities are involved in the development of national legislation concerning the rights of persons with disabilities'.

The Yale Declaration provides valuable advice to the drafters of new human rights instruments. As any new instruments are drafted, such as a new UN Convention on Disability, the Yale Declaration advises that: 'International laws and standards should be set at the highest level for the treatment of people with mental retardation, even if full enforcement is not possible immediately in all countries. Where objective constraints on resources exist, immediate and verifiable efforts to enforce human rights to the maximum of available resources should be required.'[36] The Yale Declaration goes on to caution against drafters of new instruments promoting laws or standards that provide *fewer* protections than now exist under binding and enforceable human rights conventions: 'New international laws should not include limitations on rights characteristic of early U.N. formulations that may be interpreted to permit any nation to postpone action on human rights enforcement. New Laws should set forth rights that are universal, fair, clearly defined, and enforceable.'[37]

The prime example of a new instrument that weakens existing human rights law is the Inter-American Convention on the Elimination of All Forms of Discrimination on the Basis of Disability (referred to here as the Inter-American Convention on Disability).[38] The Inter-American Convention on Disability entered into force in September 2001, and as of January 2003, nine countries in the Americas had ratified the convention.[39] The Inter-American Convention on Disability codifies many extremely valuable principles, including the elimination of 'all forms of discrimination against persons with disabilities' and the promotion of their 'full integration into society'.[40] The link established in the Inter-American Convention between the protection against discrimination and the right to community integration is important and represents the first such explicit language in a human rights convention. Article III of the Convention speaks of an obligation of governments to take action to end discrimination and promote community integration: 'To achieve the objectives of this Convention, the states parties undertake...(1) [t]o adopt the legislative social, educational, labor-related, or any other measures needed to eliminate discrimination against persons with disabilities and to promote their full integration into society.'

Unfortunately, just as the Yale Declaration warned, the specific language of Article III undercuts the potential for enforceability. Article III (1) finishes by stating that governments may meet their obligations by taking action, 'including but not limited to measures to eliminate discrimination *gradually*' [emphasis added]. The term 'gradually' is never defined. While the Convention is still new, and it is possible that the language of Article III will be interpreted in the spirit of the legal obligations set forth in its opening, there is great danger that the term 'gradually' could be used by governments as an escape from the requirement that they take immediate action to ban discrimination or bring about community integration.

The Inter-American Convention on Disability would have been much stronger if the drafters had imported the language of enforceability from existing human rights conventions, such as the International Covenant on Civil and Political Rights (ICCPR) and the International Covenant on Economic, Social and Cultural Rights (ICESCR) (known collectively, along with the Universal Declaration of Human Rights (UDHR), as the 'International Bill of Rights'). Article 2(1) of the ICCPR requires governments to 'respect and ensure' rights, creating an immediate obligation on governments to bring about full enforcement of the rights protected in the covenant.[41] Within the realm of laws considered to be 'economic and social rights', as protected by the ICESCR, there is an obligation of 'progressive enforcement'.[42] Article 2(1) of the ICESCR requires that governments 'undertake to take steps...with a view to achieving progressively the full realization of the rights recognized in the present Covenant'. While the ICESCR has been criticized for giving governments too much room to postpone reform, there is an extensive body of jurisprudence and comment interpreting the obligation to 'take steps' as an immediate obligation on governments to work toward the full realization of rights.[43]

In addition to the lack of truly enforceable language in the Inter-American Convention on Disability, there is a provision on the regulation of guardianship that is particularly dangerous for people with intellectual disabilities. The concern is so serious that a UN Panel of Experts recommended that any country ratifying the convention do so with a reservation with regard to this provision.[44] The definition of disability includes the statement that: 'If, under a state's internal law, a person can be declared legally incompetent, when necessary and appropriate for his or her well-being, such a declaration does not constitute discrimination.' As people

with intellectual disabilities have experienced around the world, guardianship laws in domestic legislation, while almost always created with the
stated purpose of promoting the 'well-being' of people with disabilities, in
practice, may improperly strip people of their right to make some of the
most important and basic decisions about their lives.[45] It is a common
practice in many countries for individuals with a psychiatric diagnosis or
mental retardation to be considered 'mentally incompetent' without any
form of legal process. Where legal process is used, an individual with limited disabilities (as well as many practical abilities) may be placed under
'plenary guardianship'—and stripped of all rights to make choices about
his or her life. In some countries, guardianship procedures have been used
to circumvent laws that would protect against improper involuntary
detention in a psychiatric facility. Once a family member or the director of
a psychiatric facility is declared an individual's guardian, he or she may
'voluntarily' commit a person to a psychiatric facility—without ever asking
that person what he or she really wants and, in fact, over the active objection
of the person. Without due process protections for the review of that decision,
guardianship is commonly used to commit a person to an institution for life.
It is arguable that many provisions of domestic legislation on guardianship
are, on their face, violations of the anti-discrimination provisions of the
ICCPR and the ICESCR.[46] Thus, the Yale Declaration advises governments to
'explore alternatives to the use of guardianships, such as mentors and citizen
advocates....The legal principle of substitute decision making should be
replaced, wherever possible, by supported decision making.'[47]

   Despite the flaws of the Inter-American Convention on Disability, many
activists in the Americas have observed that, in countries that now have
few domestic legal protections for people with disabilities, the Inter-
American Convention on Disability is a step forward as a matter of law,
as a statement of principle, and as a form of public education. The Yale
Declaration recognizes that one of the greatest values of a new convention
is just this form of public education: 'The process of ratification allows
countries the opportunity to adopt international standards through their
own political processes and helps develop world consensus for the recognition and enforcement of the rights of people with mental retardation.'[48]
While recognizing the value of the Inter-American Convention, there are
also real risks to the ratification of this covenant or any new international
instrument with similar limitations. In international law, more specific
instruments are frequently used to interpret more general protections of
existing conventions. When the more specific instrument contains fewer
rights, it can result in the erosion of rights that might be recognized under
the more general convention. Section II of this chapter will demonstrate
the methodology that international oversight and enforcement bodies
have used to interpret the general protections of existing general human

rights conventions with regard to disability rights. This analysis underscores the dangers of using language in a new disability rights convention (such as obligations to take action 'gradually') that can undercut enforceable rights created by such conventions as the ICCPR and the ICESCR. To the credit of its drafters, Article VII of the Inter-American Convention creates a limitation clause intended to prevent the weakening of rights ('[n]o provision of this convention shall be interpreted as restricting, or permitting the restriction by states parties of the enjoyment of the rights of persons with disabilities recognized by customary international law or the international instruments by which a particular state party is bound'). While the explicit limitation of rights is clearly prohibited, there are many situations where rights under the general language of mainstream conventions are not as well defined as they should be and remain open to new interpretation. There are some very promising new interpretations of the ICCPR and the ICESCR that could be undercut by a disability rights convention that establishes lower standards or creates escape clauses with regard to governments' obligations toward people with disabilities.

The fact that the Yale Declaration recognizes the ICCPR and ICESCR as meaningful protections for people with intellectual disabilities is important—and not a view as widely shared as it should be. Since the International Bill of Rights does not refer specifically to people with mental or physical disabilities, there is a widespread tendency to overlook these instruments as binding sources of law.[49] As Gerard Quinn and Theresia Degener found in their study for the UN Human Rights Commission, while most nongovernmental disability rights organizations recognize that people with disabilities *should* be protected under international human rights law, the study finds that these groups have yet to make use of international human rights oversight bodies.[50] These groups have filed few complaints with UN oversight bodies and have rarely submitted 'shadow reports' that can provide the UN bodies the facts needed to find governments in violation of international human rights law.[51] Since most human rights instruments referring specifically to people with disabilities are non-binding UN General Assembly Resolutions, many governments and activists may be left with the impression that international human rights law leaves the protection of rights for people with intellectual disabilities to the discretion of domestic policymakers.

The drafters of the new UN Convention on Disability should not make the mistakes made in the Inter-American Convention on Disability. Any new instrument should use, as a starting point, the protections that now exist under international human rights law. In drafting new human rights instruments, or in developing new domestic intellectual disability legislation, governments and activists may need practical guidance as to what protections are now provided by the mainstream human rights conventions.

II. THE WHO MONOGRAPH ON INTERNATIONAL
HUMAN RIGHTS LAW

By commissioning the monograph by Rosenthal and Sundram, 'The Role of International Human Rights in Domestic Mental Health Legislation,' the World Health Organization (WHO) has created a useful tool that will assist governments and disability activists in understanding the requirements of the mainstream conventions.[52] The WHO monograph examines some of the most important convention-based protections for people with intellectual disabilities under the International Bill of Rights. The monograph is designed to show how domestic legislation can be drafted to ensure compliance with international human rights obligations. WHO is currently translating the monograph into six languages, and it will be published on the web and as a monograph. The WHO monograph is not intended to be comprehensive, but it demonstrates a methodology that can be used to interpret broad language of the mainstream conventions. The monograph demonstrates how the detailed language of non-binding UN General Assembly resolutions can be used as a guide to more general provisions of conventions. The monograph examines the way case law from regionally based human rights commissions and courts in Europe and the Americas can provide persuasive interpretations of general treaty provisions. The monograph cites the most important General Comments that have been adopted by treaty-based committees that provide non-binding but official interpretations of the protections in the conventions.

The WHO monograph includes an analysis of the following series of rights:

(1) the right to the highest attainable standard of physical and mental health under Article 12 of the ICESCR;
(2) protections against discrimination on the basis of disability under Article 26 of the ICCPR and Article 2(2) of the ICESCR;
(3) protections against inhuman and degrading treatment under Article 7 of the ICCPR;
(4) the right to liberty and security of the person under Article 9 of the ICCPR;
(5) safeguards required to protect convention-based rights under both the ICCPR and the ICESCR.

Two international principles are essential to ensure the human rights of persons with disabilities: (1) the right to the highest attainable standard of health (often referred to as the 'right to health') and (2) the right to protection from discrimination. The section on the right to health demonstrates that even for 'economic and social' type rights that may be dependent on the infusion of resources, governments have a series of immediate obligations. This includes an obligation to take steps toward reforming service systems necessary to promote the community integration of people with intellectual disabilities. The section on the protection against discrimination demonstrates that the very general terms of the ICESCR and the ICCPR, which do not even mention the protection against discrimination for people with disabilities, have been interpreted to provide significant and enforceable protections for people with disabilities. The right to community integration for people with disabilities has been recognized as an outgrowth of the protection against discrimination. This analysis also shows how domestic laws on guardianship may violate the ICCPR or the ICESCR.

The emphasis in this chapter on the right to health is not intended to suggest that economic and social type rights under the ICESCR are more important than the civil and political rights protected by the ICCPR. Indeed, the ICCPR creates immediate obligations on governments. Protections against inhuman and degrading treatment under the ICCPR are among the most important and the most strictly protected rights established under the convention. These rights have great relevance to people with intellectual disabilities and drafters of domestic legislation or new international instruments are strongly encouraged to refer to the WHO monograph to examine the protections provided by the ICCPR.

A. Right to the Highest Attainable Standard of Physical and Mental Health

Article 12 of the ICESCR establishes 'the right of everyone to the enjoyment of the highest attainable standard of physical and mental health'. The Constitution of the World Health Organization (WHO), adopted in 1946, first enunciated a right to health and mandated WHO to promote that right.[53] The language of Article 12 mirrors the language of WHO's constitution: 'The enjoyment of the highest attainable standard of health is one of the fundamental rights of every human being without distinction of race, religion, political belief, economic or social conditions.'

While Article 12 is often referred to conveniently as the 'right to health', the 'word "attainable" makes clear that States Parties are not required to guarantee that all citizens be healthy—an absurd proposition.'[54] Instead, Article 12 has been interpreted as an obligation on governments to take specific steps to protect and promote health.[55] The right to health can be viewed both as a 'positive' right to government action or services necessary to maximize health and as a 'negative' right to protection against unhealthy or dangerous conditions.[56] General Comment 14, adopted by the Committee on Economic, Social and Cultural Rights (CESC) states as follows:

The right to health contains both freedoms and entitlements. The freedoms include the right to control one's health and body, including sexual and reproductive freedom, and the right to be free from interference such as the right to be free from torture, non-consensual treatment and experimentation. By contrast, the entitlements include the right to a system of health protection which provides equality of opportunity for people to enjoy the highest attainable level of health.[57]

General Comment 14 also establishes that the right to health is 'related to and dependent upon the realization of other human rights as contained in the International Bill of Rights'.[58] Thus, while this document examines rights under the ICCPR in different sections, it is important to recognize that implementation of the full range of human rights is essential in order to guarantee the right to health.

The right to health care also extends to the right of access to the 'underlying determinants of health'.[59] This includes access to: 'adequate sanitation, an adequate supply of safe food, nutrition, housing, healthy occupational and environmental conditions, and access to health-related education and information, including sexual and reproductive health. A further important aspect is the participation of the population in all health-related decision-making at the community, national and international levels.'[60]

For further elaboration of the ICESCR's requirements, General Comment 14 recognizes the 'Principles for the Protection of Persons with Mental Illness and for the Improvement of Mental Health Care' (the MI Principles)[61] as a guide to State obligations under the convention, particularly with respect to protections against improper coercive treatment.[62] While the MI Principles were drafted primarily to define the rights of people with psychiatric disabilities, they provide rights to 'all persons who are admitted to a mental health facility'.[63] In many countries, people with intellectual disabilities are frequently detained in mental health facilities. Thus, the protections established under the MI Principles are directly relevant to all people with mental disabilities.

In 1996, the Committee on Economic, Social, and Cultural Rights adopted General Comment 5,[64] detailing the application of the International Covenant on Economic, Social, and Cultural Rights (ICESCR) with regard to people with intellectual and physical disabilities.[65] General Comment 5 of the Economic, Social and Cultural Rights Committee states that UN human rights standards can be used for guidance in interpreting relevant portions of the covenant. General Comment 5 specifically mentions that the MI Principles and the Standard Rules can be used for guidance. Indeed, General Comment 5 makes clear that under Article 12 of the ICESCR, governments are required to provide health care services 'in such a way that the persons concerned are able to maintain full respect for their rights and dignity'.[66]

The concept of 'progressive realization' under the ICESCR, as described above, recognizes that resources are not limitless, and governments cannot be expected to do more than to make the best of available resources. However, certain elements of the right to health are immediate, including the obligation to guarantee protections against discrimination.[67]

1. Access to Appropriate and Professional Services

The right to the highest attainable standard of mental health under Article 12 entails a right on the part of people with intellectual disabilities to services that are (a) available, (b) accessible, (c) acceptable, and of (d) appropriate and good quality.[68] To be appropriately available, services must be provided in 'sufficient quantity' by 'trained medical and professional personnel'.[69] The concept of accessibility goes beyond physical access; it also requires that services be affordable and available in a non-discriminatory manner.[70] The requirement that services be 'acceptable' means that they must be provided in a manner that is culturally appropriate and respectful of medical ethics.[71] For services to be of appropriate quality, they must also be culturally acceptable, medically appropriate, and provided in a safe and clean environment.[72]

General Comment 5 adds some specific content to the right to health, specifying that it includes a right of access to rehabilitation services.[73] The MI Principles elaborate extensively on the availability, accessibility, acceptability, and quality of services, providing an example of internationally accepted standards. Under the MI Principles, '[a]ll persons have the right to the best available mental health care, which shall be part of the health and social care system.'[74] MI Principle 14 requires qualified staff in sufficient numbers.

Principle 4 requires that 'a determination that a person has a mental illness shall be made in accordance with internationally accepted medical standards'. Thus, domestic legislation will need to incorporate standardized diagnostic systems such as those contained in the Diagnostic and Statistical Manual of the American Psychiatric Association[75] or the International Classification of Diseases[76] as well as address the qualifications of persons who make a determination of mental illness. These Principles implicate the relatively brief and informal process of evaluation of patients that exists in many countries, which results in the diagnosis of mental illness or intellectual disability that can have severe and lasting consequences for the individual's health and liberty.

Principle 13 provides for rights and conditions in mental health facilities to enable them to meet the needs of patients, while Principle 14 provides specifically for resources including:

(a) qualified medical and other appropriate professional staff in sufficient numbers and with adequate space to provide each patient with privacy and a program of appropriate and active therapy;
(b) diagnostic and therapeutic equipment for the patient;
(c) appropriate professional care; and
(d) adequate, regular and comprehensive treatment including supplies of medication.

General Comment 14 on the ICESCR, paragraph 43, makes it clear that the core obligations of States include the provision of essential drugs, as determined from time to time under the WHO Action Programme on Essential Drugs.[77]

a. Right to Individualized Treatment

The principle that people with intellectual disabilities have a right to individualized treatment is emphasized throughout the MI Principles. Principle 9(2) states that '[t]he treatment and care of every patient shall be based on an individually prescribed plan discussed with the patient, reviewed regularly, revised as necessary and provided by professional staff'. MI Principle 8 recognizes that, within health care systems, a person with intellectual disabilities 'shall have the right to receive such health and social care as is appropriate to his or her health needs'. Medication 'shall meet the best health needs of the patient'.[78] In addition to treatment that is individualized to meet a particular person's health needs, the treatment of every person must also be 'suited to his or her cultural background'.[79]

The right to individualized treatment entails governments' obligation to provide professional services tailored to individual needs (1) in the best judgment of professionals but also (2) respecting the preferences of the individual receiving services. Thus, one of the goals and requirements of individualized treatment is respect for individual choice in treatment. This is a key principle underlying the right to informed consent to treatment as established in Principle 11.

These principles address issues that are commonly found in institutions for people with intellectual disabilities. Due to shortages of professional staff and other resources, institutions may not be able to provide any treatment at all or may be reduced to providing the same treatment or medications to all patients regardless of their diagnosis or individual need.

b. Right to Rehabilitation and Treatment that Enhances Autonomy

In 1971 the UN General Assembly adopted the 'Declaration on the Rights of Mentally Retarded Persons' (the MR Declaration).[80] Both the MR

Declaration and the MI Principles recognize that all treatment must be directed toward the enhancement of the autonomy and skills of each individual. The MR declaration recognizes a right of each person to the medical care, therapy, education, and training 'as will enable him to develop his ability and maximum potential' and 'to care and treatment in accordance with the same standards as other ill persons'.[81] MI Principle 9(4) recognizes that '[t]he treatment of every patient shall be directed towards preserving and enhancing personal autonomy'. The more generic UN Declaration of the Rights of Disabled Persons adopted in 1975[82] also recognizes the importance of self-reliance and social integration.[83]

The profound importance of this principle—and the fact that it applies to 'every patient'—cannot be overemphasized. Throughout the world, people are placed in custodial facilities where the mental health or social services system functions to keep a person alive but essentially gives up on the hope that a person has any potential to develop his or her skills or return to the community. This danger is particularly great for people with the most severe intellectual disabilities, who are often relegated to the 'back wards' of psychiatric institutions or mental health facilities. Sociologists have observed that, over time, individuals placed in institutions who are not challenged to use the social skills that they have upon placement inevitably lose those skills and establish an 'institutionalized' mentality. By recognizing a right of every person to treatment that preserves or enhances his or her skills or develops maximum potential, the MI Principles and the MR Declaration raise expectations to a level that cannot be met by custodial care alone.

General Comment 5 makes clear that these rights are core principles under the ICESCR. The UN Economic, Social and Cultural Rights Committee interprets the right to health under the ICESCR to place great emphasis on promoting individual independence and social integration. General Comment 5 states that 'the right to physical and mental health...implies the right to have access to, and benefit from, those medical and social services...which enable persons with disabilities to become independent, prevent further disabilities and support their social integration'.[84]

Thus, in providing rehabilitation, General Comment 5 quotes the Standard Rules to state that rehabilitation services should be designed to enable individuals 'to reach and sustain their optimum level of independence and functioning'.[85]

2. Right to Independence and Social Integration

The rights to independence and social integration do not stop at the walls of the institution but clearly suggest the right to assistance in becoming free of reliance on mental health services. The right to social services that promote independence and social integration has major implications regarding the way mental health systems are structured—clearly favoring community-based services over services within the closed environment of institutions. The MI Principles elaborate on both these concepts of independence.

a. Right to Least Restrictive Services

The MI Principles have a number of provisions that promote the right to individual independence and autonomy within mental health care treatment. Under MI Principle 9(1), every individual 'shall have the right to be treated in the least restrictive environment and with the least restrictive or intrusive treatment appropriate to the patient's health needs and the need to protect the physical safety of others'. The right to treatment in the least restrictive environment is reinforced by the Principle 9(4) requirement that '[t]he treatment of every patient shall be directed towards preserving and enhancing personal autonomy'.

The principle that treatment should be the least restrictive possible is built into protections against such practices as physical restraints or involuntary seclusion. Principle 11(11) states that such practices should be used 'only when it is the only means available to prevent immediate or imminent harm to the patient or others'. Principle 11(11) contains a number of procedural safeguards against abuse, such as the requirement that each use of restraints or seclusion be recorded in the patient's record, along with an explanation of the 'reasons for them and their nature and extent'. The 'personal representative' of the patient should be informed promptly of any use of physical restraint or seclusion.

Consistent with the philosophy that each recipient of services deserves individually tailored treatment, the Principles require that any decision to use restraint or seclusion must also be individualized. Thus, such procedures cannot be a condition of confinement applicable to all residents of a ward.

Recognition of the right to the least restrictive services is also built into the MI Principles' commitment standards. The MI Principles permit involuntary detention to prevent against 'serious deterioration' in a person's medical condition. However, involuntary treatment for this purpose can only be justified if 'appropriate treatment...can only be given by admission to a mental health facility in accordance with the principle of the least restrictive alternative'.[86] Thus, if a person can receive appropriate treatment in the community, involuntary commitment could not be justified on these grounds.

b. Right to Community-Based Services

In addition to recognizing the right to independence within mental health services, MI Principle 3 recognizes that '[e]very person with a mental illness shall have the right to live and work, as far as possible, in the community'. It is important to note that MI Principle 3 is a right to community integration (or 'social independence') that is not linked to whether or not a person receives mental health treatment. The MI Principles also recognize the right to community-based services and support systems necessary to promote this right. MI Principle 7(1) states '[e]very patient shall have the right to be treated and cared for, as far as possible, in the community in which he or she lives.'

In many countries, the absence of adequate community programs and services for persons with mental illness leads to an unnecessary reliance on institutions to provide care and treatment. Admission to these facilities is usually necessitated not so much by the clinical condition of the patient but by the absence of any other alternative. Once in the institution, the same lack of community alternatives serves to retain patients in the institution long after their psychiatric condition has stabilized and they could function in the community if adequate services and supports were available. In some institutions, long-term patients for whom there are no bona fide diagnoses of mental illness are confined and remain simply due to an absence of other alternatives. This common condition, in which patients who no longer clinically require this level of service occupy institutional beds, also makes mental health care inaccessible to many who need it because the available beds are full. The doctrine of the least restrictive environment is meaningless unless States take affirmative steps to create less restrictive alternatives in the community to meet a range of needs that can be predicted. As General Comment 14 to the ICESCR recognizes, States can address the need for a range of community services needed to serve people with intellectual disabilities in their planning and budget development processes. 'Such steps must be deliberate, concrete and targeted towards the full realization of the right to health.'[87]

B. The Right to Protection Against Discrimination

A fundamental human rights obligation that cuts across all areas of mental health legislation is the protection against discrimination. This right, which is recognized both in the UN Charter itself (Articles 55–56) and the Universal Declaration of Human Rights, which protects 'everyone', is further protected under the ICESCR and the ICCPR and it is recognized by the major UN human rights standards concerning people with intellectual or physical disabilities.

The concept of non-discrimination is closely linked with the concept of equality stated in Article 1 of the Universal Declaration of Human Rights: 'All human beings are born free and equal in dignity and rights.'[88] The protection against discrimination is, first and foremost, a promise that people with disabilities will enjoy the same legal rights as all other individuals.[89] Article 26 of the ICCPR establishes that: 'All persons are equal

before the law and are entitled without any discrimination to equal protection from the law. In this respect, the law shall prohibit any discrimination and guarantee to all persons equal and effective protection against
discrimination on any ground such as race, color, sex...or other status.'[90]
As the Vienna Declaration makes clear, 'or other status' includes intellectual or physical disabilities. The United Nations Committee on Economic,
Social, and Cultural Rights has made it clear that the protection against
discrimination on the basis of 'other status' under Article 2(2) of the ICE-
SCR 'clearly applies to discrimination on the grounds of disability'.[91]
Unlike many of the 'positive rights' created by the ICESCR, which are
subject to 'progressive realization', non-discrimination on the basis of disability is an obligation that is effective immediately.[92] In the context of
health care, the Human Rights Committee has emphasized a positive
right to access services.[93] Examples of the negative right to protections
against discrimination include protections against restrictions on marriage and raising children, forced sterilization,[94] exclusion from employment, using mental illness as grounds for divorce, limitations on voting
rights, and other limitations on civil rights.

Some conventions, such as the European Convention on Human
Rights, protect only against discrimination in the exercise of rights guaranteed under the convention itself.[95] Article 26 of the ICCPR protects
against discrimination in any area of law.[96] The UN Human Rights
Committee, established by the ICCPR to assist in the interpretation of the
convention, defines discrimination as 'any distinction, exclusion, restriction, or preference...which has the *purpose or effect* of nullifying or impairing the recognition or enjoyment or exercise by all persons on an equal
footing, of all rights and freedoms'.[97]

Thus, protections against discrimination under international law go
much further than simply outlawing laws that explicitly or purposefully
exclude or deny opportunities to people with disabilities. Legislation that
has the *effect* of denying rights and freedoms is discriminatory, as well. As
the UN Committee on Economic, Social, and Cultural Rights has
observed, the problem of discrimination goes well beyond that:

Both *de jure* and *de facto* discrimination against persons with disabilities have a
long history and take various forms. They range from invidious discrimination,
such as the denial of educational opportunities, to more 'subtle' forms of discrimination, such as segregation and isolation achieved through the imposition of physical and social barriers....The effects of disability-based discrimination have been
particularly severe in the fields of education, employment, housing, transport,
cultural life, and access to public places and services.[98]

Thus, the Committee states that '[i]n order to remedy past and present
discrimination, and to deter future discrimination, comprehensive

anti-discrimination legislation in relation to disability would seem to be indispensable in virtually all States Parties'.[99]

1. *Affirmative Action and Reasonable Accommodation*

Both the ICCPR and the ICESCR have been interpreted to require more than equality under the law; they require special efforts to ensure that individuals can enjoy the benefits of equal protections.[100] As described below, both the ICCPR and the ICESCR have been officially interpreted by UN oversight bodies to require 'affirmative action'. The Economic and Social Committee has gone even further than the Human Rights Committee by including in its definition of discrimination under the ICESCR the 'denial of *reasonable accommodation* based on disability which has the effect of nullifying or impairing the recognition, enjoyment or exercise of economic, social or cultural rights'.[101]

a. Affirmative Action

For people with intellectual or physical disabilities, the protection against discrimination would be of limited value if it only meant that people situated similarly are treated equally.[102] In addition to outlawing explicit discrimination, domestic mental health law is an important tool needed to bring about the equality guaranteed by the ICCPR. The UN Human Rights Committee makes clear that Article 14 'does not mean identical treatment in every instance'.[103] Under the ICCPR, special protections or 'affirmative action' is permissible—and at times required—to bring about equal protection under the law.[104] The MI Principles also affirm that, in the context of mental health care, '[s]pecial measures to protect the rights, or secure the advancement, of persons with mental illness shall not be deemed discriminatory.'[105] The Standard Rules also support the idea that resources may be needed in order to protect equal rights: 'The principle of equal rights implies that the needs of each and every individual are of equal importance, that those needs must be made the basis for the planning of societies and that all resources must be employed in such a way as to ensure that every individual has equal opportunities for participation.'[106]

b. Reasonable Accommodation

While General Comment 5 recognizes the right to reasonable accommodation under the ICESCR, it does not provide further definition of this right. The principle of reasonable accommodation was established as part of United States anti-discrimination law in the Rehabilitation Act of 1973, and it is now incorporated into the Americans with Disabilities Act.[107] The concept has had great influence on the development of legislation in other countries.[108] Reasonable accommodation has been defined in US law as 'providing or modifying devices, services, or facilities, or changing practices or procedures in order to match a particular person with a particular program or activity'.[109]

In the employment context, a person with an intellectual disability could, for example, receive reasonable accommodation by being allowed to adjust his or her work schedule to take time off to see a psychotherapist or to arrive late in the morning and make up the time later in the day. The accommodation would only be required if it still allows the individual to perform the 'essential functions' of his or her job. An accommodation would not be considered 'reasonable' if it places 'undue financial and administrative burden' on an employer or if it requires 'a fundamental alteration in the nature' of a program.[110] US law is obviously not an authoritative interpretation of the ICESCR's protection of the right to reasonable accommodation, but the growing jurisprudence in the countries that have adopted similar legislation provides extensive guidance that can be used to develop effective protections.[111]

International human rights law creates direct legal obligation only on governments and not on private actors although governments can be required to adopt legislation that protects vulnerable populations even in the private sphere.[112] Thus, the right to reasonable accommodation under the ICESCR is at its strongest in the area of public accommodations, particularly where they impact on the right to health. Public programs that allow non-disabled people to live in the community and avoid institutionalization may, for example, need to be crafted so that they meet the needs of individuals with intellectual disabilities. If a government creates a foster care program for all children, a child with an intellectual disability could make a claim for reasonable accommodation to ensure that he or she could benefit from the program. For example, reasonable accommodation might mean the provision of counseling to the parents on the needs of a child with an intellectual disability or an additional payment to a family to cover respite care.

2. Rule of Proportionality and Due Process Protections

International human rights law has developed rules to determine which distinctions are legitimate and which constitute unlawful discrimination. The UN Human Rights Committee has stated that a distinction is justified 'if the criteria for…differentiation are *reasonable and objective* and if the aim is to achieve a purpose which is *legitimate*'.[113]

Even though Article 14 of the European Convention contains a more limited scope of protections than Article 26 of the ICCPR, the case law under the European Convention provides useful guidance in the further interpretation of the convention's requirements. In the *Belgian Linguistic* case, the European Court pointed out that '[a] difference of treatment in the exercise of a right…must not only pursue a legitimate aim: Article 14 is likewise violated when it is clearly established that there is no reasonable relationship of proportionality between the means employed and the aim sought to be realized'.[114] A restriction is not considered proportionate if a less restrictive alternative can be shown to be equally effective.[115] When a right must be restricted, the principle of proportionality may require governments to use appropriate due process.[116] This may include judicial safeguards, such as a hearing or a guarantee of independent and impartial decision making.[117]

The principle of proportionality is similar to the approach taken in the Siracusa Principles for the derogation of rights. The Siracusa Principles create the outside parameters for the protection against discrimination—setting forth a rule for the extreme cases where the right to protection against discrimination can be derogated. The Siracusa Principles would permit a derogation of the protection against discrimination if the limitation were 'strictly necessary' for a legitimate objective of public interest—provided that there were no less restrictive way for that objective to be met.

3. Applications of Protection Against Discrimination in Mental Health Law

Protections against discrimination impact all areas of government practice. As the Human Rights Committee has stated, '[t]he impact of the right contained in Article 26 may extend also to any legislative measure in domestic law.'[118] While protections against discrimination in education, employment, housing, or access to public services may be the most common areas where anti-discrimination laws are needed, it is also important to examine the implications of anti-discrimination law for areas of mental health practice in which people with intellectual disabilities are treated differently from other individuals.

a. The Right to Community Integration

The protection against discrimination has major implications for the broadest legal framework in which mental health and social service systems operate. Throughout the world, outmoded mental health systems provide services within the segregated environment of closed institutional wards for people with intellectual disabilities who would be capable of living in the community if services and support systems were located there. General Comment No 5 recognizes that the right to community integration—including the right to medical and social services to permit people to participate fully in the community—is needed to protect people with disabilities against discrimination under the ICESCR. While there is no specific language about this in the general comments of the ICCPR, the identification of segregated services as a form of discrimination under the ICESCR may indicate that the ICCPR provides similar protections.[119]

This is an area in which law is continuing to evolve, and US anti-discrimination law may serve as a model in other countries. In *Olmstead v L.C.*,[120] the United States Supreme Court interpreted the Americans with Disabilities Act of 1990[121] and its implementing regulations, which oblige states to administer services, programs, and activities 'in the most integrated setting appropriate to the needs of qualified individuals with disabilities'.[122] In doing so, the Supreme Court ruled that it is discrimination to deny people with disabilities services in the most appropriate integrated setting.

The Court stated that '[u]njustified isolation...is properly regarded as discrimination based on disability'. It observed first, 'institutional placement of persons who can handle and benefit from community settings perpetuates unwarranted assumptions that persons so isolated are incapable or unworthy of participating in community life.' Second, the Court found that institutional confinement severely curtails opportunities for participation in everyday activities, such as family and social activities, work and educational options, economic independence and cultural enrichment. To remedy this type of discrimination, the Court stated that the ADA requires states to serve individuals with disabilities in community settings rather than in segregated institutions when this is appropriate and reasonable in light of certain factors.

If the reasoning of the US Supreme Court were to be adopted in interpreting the non-discrimination provisions of the ICESCR and ICCPR, there would be major implications for the tens of thousands of people with intellectual disabilities who are confined in institutions throughout the world without a current clinical justification for their segregation from society. The disability rights experts convened by UN Special Rapporteur Bengt Lindqvist in November 2000 discussed this matter and supported this principle.[123] The experts concluded that mental health services provided in an exclusively segregated environment are 'inherently suspect as a form of discrimination' under international human rights law.

b. Improper Guardianship as Discrimination

MI Principle 1, which protects against discrimination on the basis of mental illness, specifies that:

Any decision that, by reason of his or her mental illness, a person lacks legal capacity, and any decision that, in consequence of such incapacity, a personal representative shall be appointed, shall be made only after a fair hearing by an *independent and impartial tribunal established by domestic law*. The person whose capacity is at issue shall be entitled to be represented by counsel. MI Principle 1(6) (italics added)

In addition to providing a right to legal counsel, MI Principle 1(6) provides detailed provisions to ensure that these rights are effective, including the right to payment for such counsel if an individual lacks resources. MI Principle 1(6) requires there be protections against a conflict of interest between the individual and the mental health facility or its personnel. Thus, 'counsel shall not in the same proceedings represent a mental health facility or its personnel and shall not also represent a member of the family of the person whose capacity is at issue....' MI Principle 1(6) also provides a right to the periodic review of any decision regarding capacity 'at reasonable intervals prescribed by domestic law' and provides a right to appeal this decision to a higher court.

There are many safeguards to protect against the improper use of guardianship developed under the domestic laws of many countries that the MI Principles do not mention. The lack of any mention in the MI Principles does not mean that human rights law does not create additional obligations in this area. In many countries, courts are required to limit the power of guardians to only those subjects or areas in which a person is shown to truly lack legal competence. These laws strive to enable individuals with intellectual disabilities, who cannot necessarily make all decisions about themselves, to nevertheless retain the opportunity to make most decisions. This matter has not yet been tested by international courts, but the principle of 'proportionality' under international discrimination law would seem to require a close relationship between any limitation on a person's legal rights and his or her actual ability to make decisions about himself or herself with regard to a specific activity.

III. CONCLUSIONS: TOWARD A UNITED NATIONS CONVENTION ON DISABILITY RIGHTS

While the WHO monograph by Rosenthal and Sundram demonstrates that a broad array of international human rights protections do exist under existing international human rights conventions, a new disability rights convention that spells out these rights in detail would greatly aid compliance by clearly notifying governments as to their international obligations. A disability rights convention could also assist legislators or activists seeking to draft new domestic legislation that conforms to the full requirements of existing international human rights law—if the disability rights convention is well drafted and reflects the core minimum of rights now protected by international law. The new disability rights convention would most likely create a new UN treaty monitoring body, establishing a mechanism for continued oversight of governmental performance in respecting the rights of persons with intellectual and physical disabilities who have long been excluded from the protection of international law as a matter of practice.

One of the most important principles included in the Yale Declaration is that government reformers, even in developing nations, should promote new service systems that represent 'best practices'. This principle can be extended to the drafting process for new international human rights instruments. To be fully effective, any new human rights convention should represent the best practice in legislative drafting—including the recognition of the highest level of protection now recognized in international human rights law. The convention can also draw on models from domestic legislation in countries where rights protections have proven successful.

As a practical matter, a new human rights convention that represents best practices is most likely to gain the support of the people it is intended to protect—people with intellectual and other disabilities. Once a convention is drafted, it will be a major challenge to bring about the political support necessary to get governments to ratify a new convention. Even after a new convention enters into force, there will be a further challenge to pressure governments to implement the new requirements it establishes.

Drafters of a convention should note the difficulties currently experienced in bringing about the implementation of the two of the most important UN General Assembly resolutions on the rights of people with intellectual disabilities—the MR Declaration and the MI Principles. Political support for the application of these instruments has been limited by the fact that the organized movement of people with intellectual disabilities does not look to these instruments as representing best practices.[124] The MR Declaration refers to the protected population and people with 'mental retardation', a term that is dated and considered derogatory today by many people with intellectual disabilities. The MI Principles refer to its protected population as 'patients', a medical categorization that seems to define people by their limitations and not by their basic humanity. International organizations, such as the World Network of Users and Survivors of Psychiatry also object to the lack of recognition of some very important rights under the MI Principles, such as the right to refuse treatment—a right that is widely if unevenly recognized in domestic legislation.

Drafters of a new human rights convention may choose to avoid some of the difficult and controversial rights by framing a convention in general language. Activists who are fighting for a ban on coercive treatment, for example, may find it impossible to gain political support for language of this kind. Instead, they could seek a strong right to refuse treatment coupled with broad anti-discrimination language that might be interpreted to find coercive care institutions to be discriminatory. Drafters of a convention will have to make a political calculation as to how much support they will gain from the mainstream and how much support they may lose from committed activists whose motivating issues are not detailed fully in the convention.

The drafters of a new convention should consult and collaborate closely with the disability rights community as they consider these political trade-offs. A convention that is both practical and enforceable and that represents the aspirations of the disability rights community is most likely to gain the political support necessary to gain widespread ratification and have a chance for effective implementation. Activists should be open and willing to make practical compromises to gain political support for a convention that will be adopted by the United Nations and widely ratified. As described in this chapter, however, they should be careful not to compromise on rights now recognized under international human rights law. The strategies outlined in the Yale Declaration and the WHO monograph outlining current human rights protections will assist the framers of a new human rights convention in making the informed decisions they need to succeed in their task.

NOTES

1. See eg Interregional Seminar and Symposium on International Norms and Standards Relating to Disability (Hong Kong, Special Administrative Region of China, 13–17 December 1999), 15 July 2000, UN Doc A/AC.265/CRP.3, at 6.
2. Human Rights Commission, E/CN.4/RES/2000/51, para 13.
3. In the resolution, the Commission 'urges Governments to cover fully the question of the human rights of persons with disabilities in complying with the reporting obligations under the relevant United Nations instruments.'
4. Comprehensive and integral international convention to promote and protect the rights and dignity of persons with disabilities, GA Res 168, UN GAOR, 56th Sess, Agenda Item 119(b), UN Doc A/RES/56/168 (2001).
5. ibid para 1.
6. ibid para 5.
7. Human rights of persons with disabilities, Note by the Office of the United Nations High Commissioner for Human Rights, Report of the United Nations High Commissioner for Human Rights and Follow-up to the World Conference on Human Rights, UN Doc E/CN.4/2002/18/Add.1, 12 February 2002 (the Executive Summary of the report is attached as an Annex). The full report is 'Human Rights are for All: A Study on the Current Use and Future Potential of the United Nations Human Rights Instruments in the Context of Disability' (Gerard Quinn and Theresia Degener (eds), Office of the UN High Commissioner for Human Rights, February, Geneva 2002).
8. Executive Summary at 5.
9. ibid at 9.
10. The report recommends that treaty-monitoring bodies set aside a thematic day to focus on the rights of people with disabilities and suggests that 'the List of Issues sent to States parties by those treaty-monitoring bodies that issue such documents should more regularly request information on the enjoyment

of human rights by persons with disabilities in keeping with the thematic priorities to be set in General Comments.' ibid. The report recommends that the Commission on Human Rights disseminate information about the rights of people with disabilities and 'after consultation with the stakeholders a series of more focused thematic studies and practical manuals on subjects such as the human rights of institutionalized persons, the right to education for disabled children...and the human rights issues connected with intellectual disability.' ibid at 10. The report recommends that at least one staff member at the Commission be dedicated full time to the rights of people with disabilities. ibid.

11. ibid at 12.
12. Res 2002/61, UN GAOR, Hum Rts Comm, 55th mtg, UN Doc E/2002/23-E/CN.4/2002/200, chap XIV (2002), para 7.
13. ibid para 1.
14. Comprehensive and integral international convention to promote the rights and dignity of persons with disabilities, working paper submitted by Mexico, 12 July 2002, UN Doc A/AC/265/WP1.
15. Personal discussion with Victor Hugo Flors, adviser to the Government of Mexico on Disability (9 April 2002).
16. The convention has been endorsed, for example, by the International Disability Alliance, a coalition of the six major international disability organizations including Disabled Peoples' International, Inclusion International, Rehabilitation International, World Blind Union, World Federation of the Deaf, World Federation of the Deafblind, and the World Network of Users and Survivors of Psychiatry.
17. The current Special Rapporteur on Disability is Bengt Lindqvist, appointed by the Economic and Social Council to monitor the implementation of the United Nations Standard Rules on Equalization of Opportunities for Persons with Disabilities. UN Economic and Social Council Resolution 2000/10, UN Doc No E/RES/2000/10, 27 July 2001. Lindqvist's report is available on the web at http://www.un.org/esa/socdev/enable/dismsre1.htm. As part of the Decade for Disabled Persons from 1983 to 1992, the UN Human Rights Commission appointed two special rapporteurs, Leandro Despouy and Erica-Irene Daes. United Nations, Economic and Social Council, Commission on Human Rights, Sub-Commission on Prevention of Discrimination and Protection of Minorities, 'Human Rights and Disability' UN Doc E/CN.4/Sub.2/1991/31 (prepared by Leandro Despouy) [hereinafter Despouy Report]. United Nations, Economic and Social Council, Commission on Human Rights, Sub-Commission on Prevention of Discrimination and Protection of Minorities, 'Principles, Guidelines, and Guarantees for the Protection of Persons Detained on Grounds of Mental Ill-Health or Suffering from Mental Disorder' UN Doc E/CN.4/Sub.2/1983/17 (prepared by Erica-Irene Daes) [hereinafter Daes Report]. Independent non-governmental organizations have also documented human rights abuses in a number of countries.
18. Mental Disability Rights International, 'Human Rights & Mental Health: Mexico' (2000); Mental Disability Rights International, 'Children in Russia's Institutions: Human Rights and Opportunities for Reform' (1999); Mental Disability Rights International, 'Human Rights & Mental Health: Hungary'

(1997); Mental Disability Rights International, 'Human Rights & Mental Health: Uruguay' (1995); Amnesty International, 'Amnesty International Urgent Action on Bulgaria' at http://www.amnesty.org; R Jimenez, 'Los Derechos Humanos de Las Personas con Discapacidad' (1996).

19. MDRI, 'Children in Russia's Institutions: Human Rights and Opportunities for Reform' (n 18 above); Human Rights Watch, 'Abandoned to the State: Cruelty and Neglect in Russian Orphanages' (1998).
20. This report is available through MDRI. The full text is posted on MDRI's website at http://www.MDRI.org.
21. ibid at 22.
22. See eg *Washington Post* editorial, 18 August 2002, at B6.
23. GA Res 120, UN GAOR, 41st Sess, UN Doc A/Res/41/120 (1986).
24. ibid s 4.
25. E Rosenthal and C Sundram, 'The Role of International Human Rights in Domestic Mental Health Legislation' (2002) 21 *NYL Sch J Int'l & Comp L*. This article appears in full on MDRI's website http://www.MDRI.org. The WHO study by Rosenthal and Sundram should be distinguished from a manual on mental health legislation also being drafted by WHO. At the time of this writing, the WHO manual was not yet complete.
26. UN Doc A/C.3/42/SR.13 (1987). T Degener, 'Human Rights and Disabled Persons' in T Degener and Y Koster-Dreese (eds), *Human Rights and Disabled Persons: Essays and Relevant Human Rights Instruments* (Dordrecht, Boston: M Nijhoff, 1995).
27. The terms 'convention' and 'treaty' have approximately the same meaning and are used interchangeably in this article.
28. Yale Declaration, Part VI A.
29. GA Res 56/119, 28 November 2001, UN Doc A/C.3/56/L.67/Rev.1, para 1.
30. ibid preamble.
31. Comprehensive and integral international convention to promote and protect the rights and dignity of persons with disabilities. Working paper by Mexico, 15 July 2002. UN Doc A/AC.265/WP.1.
32. Vienna Declaration, s II(B)(6)(63).
33. Yale Declaration, Part VI (B).
34. *Standard Rules on the Equalization of Opportunities for Persons with Disabilities*, UN Doc A/48/96 [GA Res 48/96 (1993)].
35. Yale Declaration, Part I (B).
36. ibid Part VI (C).
37. ibid Part VI (B).
38. AG/RES 1608 (XXIX-0/99), 29th Sess of the General Assembly; opened for signature 7 June 1999, entered into force 14 September 2001 [not published]. For the full text and most recent list of countries that have ratified the convention, visit the official Inter-American Commission on Human Rights website at http://www.cidh.org (last viewed 30 April 2002).
39. As of January 2003, the countries that have ratified the Inter-American Convention on Disability include: Argentina (10 January 2001); Brazil (15 August 2001); Chile (26 February 2002); Costa Rica (8 February 2000); El Salvador (8 March 2002); Mexico (25 January 2001); Panama (16 February 2001);

Peru (30 August 2001); Uruguay (20 July 2001). The website of the Inter-American commission of human rights has an updated list of ratifications at http://www.cidh.org/Basicos/disabi.rat.htm.

40. Inter-American Convention on Disability, art II.

41. O Schachter, 'The Obligation to Implement the Covenant in Domestic Law' in L Henkin (ed), *The International Bill of Rights* (New York: Columbia Univ Press, 1981) 311.

42. Art 2(1) of the ICESCR states that '[e]ach State Party to the present Covenant undertakes to take steps, individually and through international assistance and co-operation, especially economic and technical, to the maximum of its available resources, with a view to achieving progressively the full realization of the rights recognized in the present Covenant by all appropriate means, including particularly the adoption of legislative measures.'

43. P Alston and G Quinn, 'The Nature and Scope of States Parties' Obligations under the International Covenant on Economic, Social and Cultural Rights' (1987) 9 *Human Rights Q* 156, 159 (describing the immediate obligations created under art 2(1) of the ICESCR).

44. One of the core recommendations of the UN committee of experts meeting in Hong Kong at the 'Interregional Seminar and Symposium on International Norms and Standards Relating to Disability' in December 1999 is for governments in the Americas to ratify the Inter-American Convention on Disability. Despite this, the experts committee recommended that governments ratify the convention with a reservation as to art I (2)(b) on the issue of guardianship. Interregional Seminar and Symposium on International Norms and Standards Relating to Disability (Hong Kong, Special Administrative Region of China, 13–17 December 1999), 15 July 2000, UN Doc A/AC.265/CRP.3, at 7, recommendation 4 and note 3.

45. MDRI, Human Rights & Mental Health: Hungary (n 18 above) 58; MDRI, Human Rights & Mental Health: Mexico (n 18 above) 34.

46. See discussion in Rosenthal and Sundram, The Role of International Human Rights in Domestic Mental Health Legislation (n 25 above), in text accompanying and following n 184.

47. Yale Declaration, Part II (B) 4–5.

48. ibid Part VI (E).

49. E Rosenthal, 'International Human Rights Protections for Institutionalized People with Disabilities: An Agenda for International Action' in M Rioux (ed), *Let the World Know: A Report of a Seminar on Human Rights and Disability* (Almasa, Sweden: 5–9 November 2000) 68, 7071.

50. G Quinn and T Degener (eds), *Human Rights for All: A Study on the Current Use and Future Potential of the UN Human Rights Instruments in the Context of Disability* (Geneva: Office of the UN High Commissioner for Human Rights, February 2002).

51. ibid.

52. n 25 above.

53. World Health Organization, *Twenty-five Questions and Answers on Health and Human Rights* (November 2001) 10.

54. VA Leary, 'Implications of a Right to Health' in KE Mahoney and P Mahoney (eds), *Human Rights in the Twenty-first Century: A Global Challenge* (Dordrecht, Boston: M Nijhoff, 1993) 485.

55. As stated by the UN High Commissioner on Human Rights, Mary Robinson, 'The right to health does not mean the right to be healthy, nor does it mean that poor governments must put in place expensive health services for which they have no resources. But it does require governments and public health authorities to put in place policies and action plans which will lead to available and accessible health care for all in the shortest possible time. To ensure that this happens is the challenge facing both the human rights community and public health professionals.' World Health Organization (n 53 above) 12.

56. Leary (n 54 above) 486.

57. General Comment No 14 (2000)(E/C.12/2000/4) on the right to the highest attainable standard of health (art 12 of the ICESCR), adopted by the Committee on Economic, Social and Cultural Rights at its twenty-second session in April/May 2000, para 8.

58. ibid para 3.

59. ibid para 11; World Health Organization (n 53 above) 10.

60. CESC General Comment 14, para 11.

61. *Principles for the Protection of Persons with Mental Illness and for the Improvement of Mental Health Care*, GA Res 119, UN GAOR, 46th Sess, Supp No 49, Annex at 188, UN Doc A/46/49 (1992) [hereinafter the MI Principles].

62. CESC General Comment 14, para 34.

63. ibid, Definitions, s (f).

64. Committee on Economic, Social, and Cultural Rights (Eleventh session, 1994), *Persons with Disabilities*, 9 December 1994, General Comment 5, para 34.

65. For a background on the development of General Comment 5, see P Alston, 'Disability and the International Covenant on Economic, Social and Cultural Rights' in T Degener and Y Koster-Dreese (eds), *Human Rights and Disabled Persons: Essays and Relevant Human Rights Instruments* (Dordrecht, Boston: M Nijhoff, 1995) 100–102.

66. General Comment 5 (n 64 above) para 34.

67. General Comment 14 (n 57 above) para 30.

68. ibid para 12.

69. ibid para 12(a).

70. ibid para 12(b).

71. ibid para 12(c).

72. ibid para 12(d).

73. General Comment 5 (n 64 above) para 34.

74. In 1991, the UN General Assembly adopted the 'Principles for the Protection of Persons with Mental Illness and for the Improvement of Mental Health Care' (the MI Principles) (n 61 above).

75. American Psychiatric Association, *Diagnostic and Statistical Manual of Mental Disorders, DSM-IV* (1994).

76. World Health Organization, *ICD-10 Classification of Mental and Behavioral Disorders: Clinical Descriptions and Diagnostic Guidelines* (1993).

77. General Comment 14 (n 57 above) para 47.
78. ibid; MI Principles (n 61 above) 10(1).
79. General Comment 14 (n 57 above) para 47; MI Principles (n 61 above) 7(3).
80. GA Res 2856 (XXVI), 26 UN GAOR Supp No 29 at 99, UN Doc A/8429 (1971) (MR Declaration); SS Herr, 'Rights of Disabled Persons: International Principles and American Experiences' (1980) 12 *Columbia Rights Rev* 1 (reviewing content and implications of the MR Declaration).
81. MR Declaration (n 80 above) para 2.
82. GA Res 3447 (XXX), 30 UN GAOR Supp (No 34) at 88, UN Doc A/10034 (1975).
83. ibid.
84. General Comment 5 (n 64 above) para 34.
85. ibid, citing StRE, Rule 3.
86. MI Principles (n 61 above) 16(1)(b).
87. General Comment 14 (n 57 above) para 30.
88. The link between equality and non-discrimination has been described as 'the dominant single theme of the Covenant [on Civil and Political Rights]'. BG Ramcharan, 'Equality and Non-Discrimination' in L Henkin (ed), *The International Bill of Rights* (New York: Columbia Univ Press, 1981) 246–269; A Hendriks, 'The Significance of Equality and Non-discrimination for the Protection of the Rights and Dignity of Disabled Persons' in T Degener and Y Koster-Dreese (eds), *Human Rights and Disabled Persons: Essays and Relevant Human Rights Instruments* (Dordrecht, Boston: M Nijhoff, 1995) 45–53 (discussing the difference between 'formal' and 'material' equality and non-discrimination).
89. ibid 254.
90. Universal Declaration of Human Rights, UN GA Res 217A(III) (1948) arts 2 and 7.
91. General Comment 5 (n 64 above) para 5.
92. General Comment 14 (n 57 above) para 30 provides:
'While the Covenant provides for progressive realization and acknowledges the constraints due to the limits of available resources, it also imposes on States parties various obligations which are of immediate effect. States parties have immediate obligations in relation to the right to health, such as the guarantee that the right will be exercised without discrimination of any kind (art. 2.2) and the obligation to take steps (art. 2.1) towards the full realization of article 12. Such steps must be deliberate, concrete and targeted towards the full realization of the right to health.'
93. As part of the right to access health services, the principle of non-discrimination means that 'health facilities, goods and services must be accessible to all, especially the most vulnerable or marginalized sections of the population, in law and in fact, without discrimination on any of the prohibited grounds'. ibid para 12(b).
94. Principle 11 provides that '[s]terilization shall never be carried out as a treatment for mental illness'.
95. Art 14 of the European Convention provides that '[t]he enjoyment of the rights and freedoms *set forth in this Convention* shall be secured without

discrimination on any ground...' (italics added). Art 2(1) of the ICCPR and art 2(2) of the ICESCR have similar protections.

96. UN Office of the High Commissioner for Human Rights, *Manual on Human Rights Reporting* (1997) 197, HR/PUB 91/1 (Rev1), para 7, 253, 255.

97. UN Human Rights Committee, General Comment No 18, para 7 (emphasis added). Note that the MI Principles incorporate almost the exact words of this definition of discrimination into Principle 1(4). This is one indication that the drafters of the MI Principles intended Principle 1 to help interpret art 26 of the ICCPR. General Comment 5 of the UN Committee on Economic, Social, and Cultural Rights uses almost the same definition, but also includes language that creates even broader rights, such as the right to reasonable accommodation. General Comment 5 (n 64 above) para 15.

98. General Comment 5 (n 64 above) para 15.

99. ibid para 16.

100. Hendriks (n 88 above) 56.

101. General Comment 5 (n 64 above) para 15.

102. Hendriks (n 88 above) 40.

103. General Comment 18(37), para 8, in *Manual on Human Rights Reporting* (n 96 above) 253.

104. The Human Rights Committee states that 'affirmative action' may at times be required under the convention:
    'The Committee also wishes to point out that the principle of equality sometimes requires States Parties to take affirmative action in order to diminish or eliminate conditions which cause or help perpetuate discrimination prohibited by the Covenant. For example, in a State where the general conditions of a certain part of the population prevent or impair their enjoyment of human rights, the State should take specific action to correct those conditions. Such action may involve granting for a time to the part of the population concerned certain preferential treatment in specific matters as compared with the rest of the population. However, as long as such action is needed to correct discrimination in fact, it is a case of legitimate differentiation under the Covenant.' ibid para 10, 253–254.

105. MI Principles (n 61 above) 1(4).

106. Standard Rules (n 34 above) para 25.

107. ADA Title I, s 12111(B) states that '[t]he term "reasonable accommodation" may include (A) making existing facilities used by employees readily accessible to and usable by individuals with disabilities and (B) job restructuring, part-time or modified work schedules, reassignment to a vacant position, acquisition or modification of equipment or devices, appropriate adjustment of modifications of examinations, training materials or policies, the provision of qualified readers or interpreters, and other similar accommodations for individuals with disabilities.'

108. Hendriks (n 88 above) 58.

109. R Burgdorf, 'Accommodating the Spectrum of Individual Abilities' (1983) 122 *United States Commission on Civil Rights*, Pub No 81.

110. *Southeastern Community College v Davis* 442 US 379 (1979).

111. For a practical discussion on the right to reasonable accommodations for people with mental disabilities, see RM Levy and LS Rubenstein, *The Rights*

of People with Mental Disabilities: The Authoritative ACLU Guide to the Rights of People with Mental Illness and Mental Retardation (Carbondale: Southern Illinois Univ Press, 1996) 159.

112. Ramcharan (n 88 above) 261–263. One member of the Human Rights Committee observed that 'article 26 could not be interpreted as referring only to public acts. It must cover the internal system of a country and the authorities who decided who could work, occupy land, and so forth. If the State owned all housing and was the sole employer then its provisions applied to the State. In a different system, however, with private housing and numerous private employers, it was the latter who must be prevented from practicing discrimination.' Tarnopolsky, UN Doc CCPR/C/SR.170, para 82 (1979), as cited in Ramcharan (n 88 above) 262. In General Comment 14 on the right to health, 'the Committee stresses the need to ensure that not only the public health sector but also private providers of health services and facilities comply with the principle of non-discrimination in relation to persons with disabilities.' General Comment 14 (n 57 above) para 26. World Health Organization (n 53 above) 18 (describing governmental obligations in relation to non-state actors).

113. General Comment No 18, para 13 (emphasis added).

114. *Belgian Linguistics Case* (1979–80) 1 EHRR 241.

115. *Campbell v UK* (1993) 14 EHRR 137.

116. *W. v UK* (1988) 10 EHRR 29.

117. K Starmer, *European Human Rights Law: The Human Rights Act 1998 and the European Convention on Human Rights* (London: Legal Action Group, 1999) 147, 175.

118. General Comment 18(37) in *Manual on Human Rights Reporting* (n 96 above) 255.

119. G Quinn, 'The International Covenant on Civil and Political Rights and Disability: A Conceptual Framework' in T Degener and Y Koster-Dreese (eds), *Human Rights and Disabled Persons: Essays and Relevant Human Rights Instruments* (Dordrecht, Boston: M Nijhoff, 1995) 84.

120. 527 US 581 (1999).

121. 42 USC §12101 (2000).

122. 28 CFR §35.130(d) (2000).

123. M Rioux (ed), *Report of a Seminar on Human Rights and Disability Held at Almasa Conference Centre* (Stockholm, Sweden, 2000). While this meeting included representatives of the six major international disability groups, this group of experts should not be confused with the UN Panel of Experts authorized by the UN General Assembly to advise the Special Rapporteur. The report of the conference does not make specific reference to the resolution adopted by the experts at the meeting.

124. Rosenthal and Sundram (n 25 above). For a detailed analysis and critique of the right to refuse treatment under the MI Principles, see C Gendrau, 'The Rights of Psychiatric Patients in the Light of the Principles Announced by the United Nations: A Recognition of the Right to Consent to Treatment?' (1997) *20 Int J of L and Psychiatry* 259, 267 (suggesting that MI Principle 11 creates more limitations on individual rights than protections). One of the main concerns raised by Disabled People's International (DPI) on the draft of the MI

Principles was the lack of stronger protection of the right to refuse treatment. As DPI pointed out, even the World Health Organization had recommended the explicit recognition of the right to refuse treatment. (Written statement submitted by Disabled People's International, citing E/CN.4/Sub.2/ 1988/66.) The World Network of Users and Survivors of Psychiatry has also singled out Principle 11 as the source of its major concerns about the MI Principles. 'The World Network of Users and Survivors of Psychiatry (WNUSP) supports most of the Principles but has grave concerns about Principle 16—Involuntary Admission and Principle 11, paragraphs 6 to 16— Consent to treatment.' World Network of Users and Survivors of Psychiatry, *Preliminary Statement on the United Nations Principles for the Protection of Persons with Mental Illness to the UN Commission on Human Rights*, unpublished statement submitted to the UN Commission on Human Rights, 9 February 2000. Copies of statements by the WNUSP can be obtained by contacting the organization directly at law.dk@get2net.dk.

19

Recommendations for the United Nations and International NGOs

RONALD C. SLYE

I. INTRODUCTION

At the conclusion of the conference, Should Difference Make a Difference (Yale Law School 1995, see Preface), participants from all corners of the globe recommended courses of action to improve the awareness, protection, and promotion of the rights of persons with intellectual disabilities. Recommendations were created out of three working groups focused respectively on developed countries, developing countries, and the United Nations ('UN') and international non-governmental organizations ('NGOs'). Eric Rosenthal and Clarence Sundram outline the recommendations for developing countries (see Chapter 18 of this volume). Here, I briefly highlight the recommendations that were made to the UN and international NGOs. These recommendations were made in March 1995. Since that time, some progress has been made on a few of them, while others still require much more work.

The recommendations can be divided into five basic categories: (1) collection and dissemination of information; (2) monitoring; (3) advocacy; (4) standard setting; and (5) incorporation into international development programs and other planning processes.

II. COLLECTION AND DISSEMINATION OF INFORMATION

Many of the recommendations for international organizations concern the Standard Rules on the Equalization of Opportunities for Persons with Disabilities ('Standard Rules') and efforts to use the Standard Rules as a guide for local, national, and international action. Those recommendations include:

• Use the Standard Rules as a guide to creating an inclusive process for the reform of the laws and policies of state governments

I want to thank Amy Borden Michael, who provided extensive research help in preparing this chapter.

- Disseminate the Standard Rules, and collect and disseminate 'best practices' of state legislation and policies
- Place the Standard Rules and 'best practices' on-line in a way that is accessible
- Draft and distribute 'plain language' versions of the Standard Rules
- Increase the legitimacy of the Standard Rules through endorsements by professional and human rights organizations
- Foster the exchange of information among consumers and advocates by the United Nations and international non-governmental organizations
- Train all UN staff with responsibilities in areas that affect persons with intellectual disabilities in current standards and techniques for enhancing the rights of persons with intellectual disabilities
- Increase staff and resources of the United Nations dedicated to affecting persons with intellectual disabilities

The United Nation's Standard Rules is the most recent comprehensive pronouncement by the UN on the rights of persons with disabilities. A UN Declaration specifically focused on the rights of persons with intellectual disabilities was passed in 1971.[1] There have been subsequent pronouncements of 'soft law' since then, but none have focused on the rights of persons with intellectual disabilities, and some have focused on the very different concerns raised by persons with mental illness, or the concerns of persons with general disabilities.[2] Many of these early UN pronouncements adopted less of a rights-oriented approach, instead viewing persons with disabilities as individuals with special medical and social welfare assistance needs.[3]

While there have been some recent efforts to increase international standard-setting in this area (see below concerning the recommendations on standard setting), in lieu of new declarations the United Nations has created a Special Rapporteur on Disabilities.[4] The office of the Special Rapporteur has consolidated UN activities with respect to persons with disabilities, and acts as a clearinghouse on state practice with respect to disability laws and policy and the use of the Standard Rules. The results of many of his activities can be found on the Special Rapporteur's website. A much more extensive collection of information is collected on the UN website's 'Persons with Disabilities' homepage.[5] This last website includes an extensive collection of international treaties and other declarations and standards that apply to persons with disabilities. On neither the main UN disabilities website, nor on the website of the Special Rapporteur, however, is there a plain language version of the Standard Rules, nor are there practical step by step guides for implementing the Standard Rules and other international standards for persons with intellectual disabilities. The UN disabilities website does include practitioner manuals setting forth practical suggestions on how to apply international norms and standards, although they primarily focus on persons with physical disabilities.

The Special Rapporteur has collected information on the adoption of the Standard Rules by States. He conducted a Global Survey on Government Action on Disability Policy, compiling information on the activities of 126 States in the area of disability legislation and policy.[6] The survey was designed in part to determine the extent to which the Standard Rules had been incorporated into state laws and practice. The survey found that 80% of those countries responding had taken some steps to disseminate the Standard Rules, including translation of the rules into the local vernacular, translation of the rules into an easy to read format, development of educational materials, television and radio programs, and support to research projects and NGOs focused on the rights of persons with disabilities. A series of follow-up reports by the Special Rapporteur continues to monitor state developments in this area. Those reports are made available on the UN's website, providing a useful source of information concerning state adoption of the Standard Rules and a good starting place for finding model programs and policies. In addition, the Special Rapporteur has provided over US $500,000 to fund capacity building projects related to the Standard Rules.[7]

The exchange of information among experts and advocates on persons with disabilities generally has continued since the 1995 Yale Conference.[8] Cooperation and information flow among disability rights organizations was evident in the 1990s. As one commentator observed, the increased cooperation among national disability rights organizations resulted in the passage of disability rights legislation in more than twenty countries during the 1990s.[9] China joined with a number of international NGOs to organize the first World NGO Summit on Disability, which took place from 10–12 March 2000, in Beijing. In addition to sharing positive and negative developments and strategies of NGOs throughout the world, the Summit adopted a declaration on the rights of persons with disabilities with the hope that it would be used as a model for a contemporary UN General Assembly declaration and eventual convention.[10] It is unclear how much of this activity on disabilities in general incorporates the concerns of persons with intellectual disabilities and their advocates. One concern voiced at the Yale Conference was that the primary focus of most international activity is on persons with physical disabilities, with little attention paid to persons with intellectual disabilities. The hope is not that less attention will be paid to persons with physical disabilities (for there is still much work to be done on that score) but that a more comprehensive and holistic approach will be adopted that will focus on all persons with disabilities, including persons with intellectual disabilities.

Since the Yale Conference, and mirroring a development in all areas of human endeavor, the number of websites devoted to persons with intellectual disabilities has increased significantly. As is true with all areas, the quality of these sources of information and their reliability vary. While the UN sites provide links to other useful sites, including those of the major non-governmental organizations working in the area, there is still no one place where a comprehensive and critical overview of 'best practices' and other model developments can be found. Finally, Internet accessibility initiatives have developed with the aim of increasing access of persons with disabilities to the wealth of information provided on the Internet.[11]

III. MONITORING

The recommendations with respect to monitoring fall into two broad categories: (1) monitoring the implementation of international norms, such as the Standard Rules and (2) monitoring violations of the rights of persons with intellectual disabilities. The recommendations are:

1. The United Nations should establish a monitoring mechanism to assess compliance with the Standard Rules.

2. Issues relating to the rights of persons with intellectual disabilities should be included in the US Department of State's annual human rights country reports.

3. Major international human rights organizations and United Nations human rights bodies should expand their focus to include the rights and protection of persons with intellectual disabilities.

As discussed above, the UN's Special Rapporteur on Disability monitors adoption and implementation of the Standard Rules through a series of surveys, conferences, and other related activities. While there is certainly more that could be done in the way of monitoring, the office of the Special Rapporteur provides a mechanism through which monitoring and development of the Standard Rules can take place.

The major thrust of these monitoring recommendations is the 'mainstreaming' of the rights and protection of persons with intellectual disabilities into major human rights advocacy and protection organizations. The sentiment behind the recommendations is that the concerns related to persons with intellectual disabilities be viewed not as a medical or social issue but as a human rights issue. While there have been some positive advancements in this area since the 1995 conference, there is still a reluctance on the part of the major governmental and non-governmental human rights organizations to incorporate the concerns of persons with intellectual disabilities into their mandate.

With respect to the specific recommendation regarding the US Department of State's annual human rights country reports, disability is addressed in the general section of those reports dealing with discrimination.[12] In particular, the reports focus on discrimination in the areas of employment, education, and the provision of other state services, as well as positive developments with respect to programs and policies addressing the rights of persons with intellectual disabilities. The 2000 report on India, for example, summarizes recent programs to integrate persons with intellectual disabilities into their families and communities. The quality of information provided for each country varies and is dependent on the ability of State Department officials in-country to gather and assess relevant information. Some country reports include specific information with respect to persons with intellectual disabilities while others include little if any mention.[13]

The major international human rights NGOs have not made much progress in incorporating the rights of persons with intellectual disabilities into their activities. Incorporation that has occurred tends to focus on a few narrow areas of concern, most notably capital punishment, rather than a systematic focus on the rights and protection of persons with intellectual disabilities.[14] Specialized organizations have led the way by using a human rights paradigm to evaluate the treatment of persons with disabilities. Disability Awareness in Action, for example, has created a human rights database noting the violations of fundamental human rights suffered by persons with disabilities around the world.[15] Mental Disability Rights International ('MDRI') uses international human rights standards to evaluate on a country-by-country basis the protection and promotion of the rights of persons with disabilities.[16] MDRI has used those reports to raise the awareness of the rights of persons with disabilities among various international and regional human rights bodies. These specialized organizations provide a model for the more comprehensive human rights NGOs to incorporate the rights of persons with disabilities, including intellectual disabilities, into their work.

The UN has been somewhat better than the human rights NGO community in incorporating the rights of persons with intellectual disabilities, and more generally of persons with disabilities, within a human rights paradigm. While the Special Rapporteur on Disabilities was created under the auspices of the Commission of Social Development and not the Human Rights Commission, that office has been working to increase the incorporation of disability concerns into the mandate of the major UN human rights organizations. Beginning in 2001, for example, the Special Rapporteur began to work with the UN High Commissioner for Human

Rights to strengthen the attention and protection provided to persons with disabilities by the major UN human rights bodies.[17] The Special Rapporteur's term expires in 2002, however, leaving open the question of whether such efforts will continue or not.

The human rights treaty-based bodies of the UN, as well as the regional human rights systems, have begun to incorporate the protection of persons with intellectual disabilities, and of persons with disabilities generally, into their analysis of human rights violations. One year before the Yale Conference, the Committee on Economic, Social, and Cultural Rights issued a general comment that directly addressed the rights of persons with disabilities.[18] A few statements have been issued subsequently with respect to the rights of persons with disabilities, but they have all been at the level of general resolutions or comments. For example, in 1999, the committee on the rights of women that monitors compliance with CEDAW adopted a general comment that included a reference to the rights of persons with disabilities.[19]

Ironically, while the women's rights mechanisms of the UN have begun the process of incorporating issues relating to persons with disabilities into their work, the more general UN human rights bodies are still working to incorporate women's rights into their activities. Thus, the Human Rights Commission recently requested that all thematic mechanisms incorporate gender concerns into their work; a similar request could be made with respect to persons with intellectual disabilities. The Human Rights Committee—the body that monitors compliance with the International Covenant on Civil and Political Rights ('ICCPR')—adopted a general comment examining all of the rights in the ICCPR from the perspective of gender discrimination; the various human rights bodies could issue a similar general comment with respect to the rights of persons with intellectual disabilities. Such a comment would not only enhance the protection of persons with intellectual disabilities provided by the major human rights treaties, but also provide a model of interpretation with respect to general rights that could be applied by governments and NGOs in advocating for the rights of persons with intellectual disabilities.[20]

One might hope that as the more general human rights bodies systematically incorporate the rights of women into their work they will take advantage of the recent progress made by the official UN women's rights groups to incorporate the rights of persons with disabilities. Along these lines, the General Assembly requested in 1999 that the Secretary General include in his assessment of major UN conferences and summits their contribution to the rights of persons with disabilities.[21] While the focus of the UN on these issues across its major conferences and summits is a welcome development, a recent report on the result of such attention by the Secretary General is that few if any of the major UN conferences and summits place much attention at all on the rights of persons with disabilities.[22]

In addition to developments in the United Nations human rights system, the years since the 1995 conference have also seen some small positive developments in the regional human rights systems. In 1999, the Inter-American Commission on Human Rights issued an important opinion concerning the rights of persons with mental illness in detention.[23] More importantly, in that case the Inter-American Commission used a UN Declaration on the protection of persons with mental illness as a guide to its own interpretation of the American Convention on Human Rights. As of this writing I am unaware of any similar ruling by a regional or international human rights body concerning the use of the 1993 Standard Rules as a guide to interpretation of a general human rights treaty.[24] While the European Court of Human Rights has addressed the rights of persons with intellectual disabilities, the cases have generally involved situations where the disability of the person is not central to the overall claim and resolution of the case.[25]

Andrew Byrnes observed a little more than a year ago that '[o]verall, there has been little sustained examination of the extent to which the conceptual framework and practices of the human rights system are premised on ableist models or fail to address issues of concern to persons with different forms of disabilities'.[26] This is certainly true for the major international human rights organizations and is only slightly less true with respect to the United Nations and the major regional human rights regimes.

IV. ADVOCACY

The conference made recommendations on increasing the development and support of advocacy organizations focused on the rights and protections of persons with intellectual disabilities. Those recommendations are:

1. The UN and international NGOs should support the development of locally based advocacy organizations, particularly consumer controlled advocacy organizations, and organizations that involve family members of persons with intellectual disabilities.

2. The UN, governments, and NGOs should foster leadership and public discourse on the rights of persons with intellectual disabilities.

As noted above, the activity of the major international human rights organizations in the field of disabilities in general is limited. There are, however, a growing number of specialized NGOs that have been working to support the development of locally based advocacy organizations. MDRI, for example, has joined with a number of other organizations to create the America's Group for the Rights of People with Mental Disabilities, a forum for advocates on behalf of persons with intellectual disabilities to come together and share successful strategies and experiences.[27]

Also, as noted above, the United Nations, through its Special Rapporteur on Disabilities, has supported capacity-building projects with respect to implementation of the Standard Rules. The amount of such support has been relatively modest, and there is no indication that such programs have actively sought to foster leadership and political advocacy among persons with intellectual disabilities or their family members or representatives.

Support for fostering leadership and advocacy skills can be found in some regional organizations. For example, the Economic and Social Commission for Western Asia organizes training workshops to promote the empowerment and self-reliance of persons with disabilities.[28]

As laudable as these efforts are, there is still a large gap between the ideal of developing locally based advocacy organizations, and incorporating within those organizations family members and consumers of relevant programs.

V. STANDARD-SETTING: CREATE A BINDING TREATY ON THE RIGHTS OF PERSONS WITH INTELLECTUAL DISABILITIES

As noted above with respect to the implementation of the Standard Rules, there have been few authoritative pronouncements on the rights of persons with intellectual disabilities since the 1970s. Adopting the strategy of advocates for the rights of women and the rights of children, advocates for persons with intellectual disabilities and disability in general have been working towards increasing such authoritative statements, with the ultimate goal of creating a binding treaty on the rights of persons with intellectual disabilities or a treaty on the rights of persons with disabilities generally with specific provisions related to the rights of persons with intellectual disabilities. Efforts to create such a treaty have so far failed, although there is now a regional human rights treaty that focuses specifically on the rights of persons with disabilities.

None of the major human rights documents that make up the International Bill of Rights specifically mention disability as a category that gives rise to international protection against discrimination. It was only in the 1970s that the UN General Assembly declared that the prohibition against discrimination based on 'other status' found in the International Bill of Rights included disability.[29] And it is only in the last two decades that the rights of persons with disabilities have been taken up officially by the human rights division of the United Nations.[30]

The UN attempted to create a Convention on the Elimination of All Forms of Discrimination against Disabled Persons in 1987, but that effort failed to garner majority support within the General Assembly.[31]

The first international treaty on the rights of persons with disabilities was adopted in 1999 by the Inter-American human rights system.[32] While it does not recognize individual rights, it does explicitly prohibit discrimination based on disability.

Efforts to draft an international treaty continue. The declaration adopted at the first world NGO summit on disability in Beijing in 2000 urges both governmental and non-governmental entities to support the drafting of an international convention on the rights of persons with disabilities.[33] In December 2001, a resolution in support of an international convention passed through the General Assembly with the government of Mexico being the major proponent.[34]

VI. INCORPORATION INTO INTERNATIONAL DEVELOPMENT PROGRAMS AND OTHER PLANNING PROCESSES

Recommendations were made with respect to incorporating the rights and concerns of persons with intellectual disabilities in a broad range of international development programs. As with the recommendations made with respect to the major UN and NGO human rights organizations, these recommendations also arise from the sentiment that rights of persons with intellectual disabilities should be 'mainstreamed'. Those recommendations are:

1. International development assistance should be inclusive to make sure that people with intellectual disabilities can take advantage of them.

2. Democratization programs should focus on persons with intellectual disabilities by fostering relevant civil society programs and including the views of persons with intellectual disabilities, their family members, and their advocates.

3. The development of new laws and standards should be inclusive, incorporating persons with intellectual disabilities and their advocates, and people from all over the world.

These recommendations re-emphasize what is already stated in the UN's Standard Rules. The Standard Rules set forth international standards for a national planning process that must take place in every State to ensure full realization of human rights. Under the Standard Rules, such planning processes must actively involve people with intellectual disabilities and their advocates. The training activities, seminars, practitioner guides, and other outreach activities undertaken by the UN and its Special Rapporteur provide an opportunity to encourage and monitor the success in achieving these goals.

Outside of the UN, the World Bank and some of the regional intergovernmental development banks have begun to assess the extent to which they effectively address the rights and needs of persons with disabilities. To date, these efforts have primarily involved conferences to identify and publicize the issue as well as some technical assistance guidelines that direct responsible individuals to identify disability issues in crafting development aid strategies.[35] The World Bank, for example, has established a website to emphasize the need to mainstream the concerns of persons with disabilities into the bank's programs.[36] That website lists World Bank funded programs that include persons with disabilities.

As with the case of encouraging local advocacy programs, there is still a large gap between the ideals articulated at the Yale Conference and the incorporation of the needs of persons with disabilities into the major international development programs. Most importantly, there are still far fewer efforts to incorporate persons with disabilities into the development design process in order to make sure that those programs that do move forward are accessible to those with disabilities.

VII. CONCLUSION

The recommendations for the United Nations and international NGOs build upon developments that began before the 1995 Yale Conference. While some progress has been made in each of the areas for improvement identified by the conference participants, particularly by the UN, there is still much work to be done. The UN and some international NGOs have created useful websites collecting information on the use of the Standard Rules and 'best practices'. However, the 'mainstreaming' of the rights of persons with intellectual disabilities has been minimal. Although the major international human rights organizations have begun to focus on the rights of persons with intellectual disabilities, such focus has not been comprehensive or systematic. Efforts to create binding agreements at the international level to protect the rights of persons with intellectual disabilities have made some recent progress with the endorsement of the treaty idea by the General Assembly in December 2001. Finally, although the concerns of persons with intellectual disabilities have begun to permeate the major international development organizations, such developments have been quite rare. We still have a long way to go before persons with intellectual disabilities are viewed on a par with other individuals as the subjects and objects of the international human rights regime and movement.

NOTES

1. Declaration on the Rights of Mentally Retarded Persons, GA Res 26/2856 (XXVI) of 20 December 1971.
2. Declaration on the Rights of Disabled Persons, GA Res 30/3447 (XXX) of 9 December 1975; the World Programme of Action concerning Disabled Persons, GA Res 37/52 of 3 December 1982; Tallinn Guidelines for Action on Human Resources Development in the Field of Disability, GA Res 44/70 of 15 March 1990; Principles for the Protection of Persons with Mental Illness, GA Res 46/119 of 17 December 1991.
3. T Degener, 'Report: International Disability Law—A New Legal Subject on the Rise: The Interregional Experts' Meeting in Hong Kong, December 13–17, 1999' (2000) 18 *Berkeley J Intl L* 180, 187–188.
4. The Special Rapporteur's website, available at http://www.disability-rapporteur.org (last viewed 2 March 2002).
5. The main page for the UN materials is available at http://www.un.org/esa/socdev/enable (last viewed 2 March 2002).
6. B Lindqvist, *Government Action on Disability Policy, A Global Survey* (1997), available at http://www.disability-rapporteur.org/surveys.htm (last viewed 2 March 2002).
7. *Note of the Director General: Monitoring the Implementation of the Standard Rules on the Equalization of Opportunities for Persons with Disabilities* E/CN.5/2000/3, available at http://www.un.org/esa/socdev/enable/disecn003e0.htm (last viewed 2 March 2002).
8. For example, a major international conference on international standards and disability rights was held in Hong Kong in 1999, following a similar, although smaller, meeting in Berkeley, California, the previous year. Degener (n 3 above) 184–187.
9. ibid 184.
10. L Wong-Hernandez, 'Towards the Development of a Convention on the Rights of Disabled Persons' (Fall 2000) *Disability International*, available at http://www.dpa.org.sg/DPA/publication/dpipub/fall2000/p5.htm (last viewed 2 March 2002).
11. Worldenable, available at http://www.worldenable.net (last viewed 2 March 2002).
12. This is s 5 of the individual country reports, which concerns the status of discrimination based on race, sex, religion, disability, language, or social status.
13. Compare, eg, the 2000 reports on India and Armenia.
14. Human Rights Watch, 'Beyond Reason: The Death Penalty and Offenders with Intellectual Disabilities' (March 2001); J Welsh, 'Intellectual Disabilities and the Death Penalty' (July 2001) *Amnesty International*, AI Index ACT 75/002/2001; cf Amnesty International, 'Bulgaria: Disabled Women Condemned to "Slow Death"' (October 2001) AI-index, EUR 15/002/2001; American Association for the Advancement of Science and Physicians for Human Rights, 'Human Rights and Health: The Legacy of Apartheid' (1998), available at http://shr.aaas.org/loa/index.htm (last viewed 2 March 2002)

(discussing the rights of persons with intellectual disabilities in the context of a human rights paradigm).

15. Disability Awareness in Action website, available at http://www.daa.org.uk (last viewed 2 March 2002).
16. MDRI website, available at http://www.mdri.org (last viewed 2 March 2002).
17. This is pursuant to Economic and Social Council Resolution 2000/268 (28 July 2001).
18. Committee on Economic, Social, and Cultural Rights, General Comment No 5, UN Doc HRI/GEN/1/Rev.4.
19. General Recommendation No 24, Report of the Committee on the Elimination of Discrimination Against Women, UN GAOR, 54th Sess, Supp No 38, at 6, para 25, UN Doc A/54/38/Rev.1 (1999); Commission on Human Rights, 'Human Rights of Persons with Disabilities' (25 April 2000) 2000/51. In addition to these general treatments, the UN has looked at the rights of persons with intellectual disabilities in the context of more specialized concerns, such as capital punishment. UN Commission on Human Rights, 'Question of the Death Penalty' E/CN.4/RES/1999/61, adopted 28 April 1999, and E/CN.4/RES/2000/65, adopted 27 April 2000.
20. The recommendations with respect to incorporating the strategies used by the women's rights movement are taken in part from A Byrnes, 'Disability Rights and Human Rights: Plunging into the "Mainstream"' a pre-paper for 'Let the World Know' Seminar on Human Rights and Disability (Stockholm, 5–9 November 2000), available at http://www.un.org/esa/socdev/enable/stockholmnov2000n.htm (last viewed 2 March 2002).
21. GA Res 54/121 of 17 December 1999.
22. Report of the Secretary-General, 'Implementation of the World Programme of Action Concerning Disabled Persons' (2001) UN Doc A/56/169 and corr 1, s II, C.
23. *Rosario Congo v Ecuador*, Inter-American Commission on Human Rights, Case 11.427, Report 63/99, 13 April 1999.
24. While not directly associated with a human rights treaty, the UN's Human Rights Commission adopted a resolution recognizing the appropriateness of using the Standard Rules as a tool to evaluate compliance with human rights standards concerning persons with disabilities. Res 1998/31.
25. *X and Y v Netherlands*, European Court of Human Rights, Judgment of 26 March 1985, Ser A No 91 (establishing obligation of State to allow criminal prosecution of a person who assaulted a person who was mentally disabled). The European Court of Human Rights has also opined on the rights of persons with mental *illness*, which could be used by analogy to suggest additional protections and rights for individuals with intellectual disabilities. *Johnson v United Kingdom*, European Court of Human Rights, Judgment of 24 October 1997. See LO Gostin, 'Human Rights of Persons with Mental Disabilities: The European Convention of Human Rights' (2000) 23 *Intl J Law & Psychiatry* 23, 125.
26. Byrnes (n 20 above).
27. Americas Group for the Rights of People with Mental Disabilities, available at http://www.wcl.american.edu/pub/humright/disabil/agen.htm (last viewed 2 March 2002).

28. Report of the Secretary-General, 'Implementation of the World Programme of Action Concerning Disabled Persons' UN Doc A/56/169 and corr 1, para 30.
29. Degener (n 3 above) 188.
30. ibid note 33 (citing to Principles, Guidelines and Guarantees for the Protection of Persons Detained on Grounds of Mental Ill-Health or Suffering from Mental Disorder: Report of the Special Rapporteur, Mrs. Erica-Irene Daes, UN Sub-Commission on Prevention of Discrimination and Protection of Minorities, UN Doc E/CN.4/Sub.2/1983/17; and Human Rights and Disabled Persons, UN Centre for Human Rights, UN Sales No E.92.XIV.4 (1993)).
31. CD Siegal, 'Fifty Years of Disability Law: The Relevance of the Universal Declaration' (1999) 5 *ILSA J Intl & Comparative L* 267, 273; Degener (n 3 above) 188–189.
32. Inter-American Convention on the Elimination of All Forms of Discrimination Against Persons with Disabilities, AG Res 1608, 29th Sess, OEA Doc OEA/ Ser. P/AG/doc.3826/99 (1999), available at http://www.cidh.oas.org/ B%C3% A1sicos/disability.htm (last viewed 2 March 2002).
33. Beijing Declaration on the Rights of People with Disabilities in a New Century, available at http://www.dpa.org.sg/DPA/publication/dpipub/fall2000/ p6.htm (last viewed 2 March 2002).
34. 'Disability Buzz' (September–October 2001) 10 *Disability World*, available at http://www.disabilityworld.org/11-12_01/buzz.shtml (last viewed 2 March 2002).
35. Thus the Asian Development Bank and the Inter-American Development Bank have begun to address the relationship between disability and development. Report of the Secretary-General, 'Implementation of the World Programme of Action Concerning Disabled Persons' UN Doc A/56/169 and corr 1.
36. The World Bank Group, 'Including Persons with Disabilities', available at http://wbln0018.worldbank.org/HDNet/HDDocs.nsf/2d5135ecbf351de685 2566a90069b8b6/066274da1ba9e8da852567e0005215e6?OpenDocument (last viewed 2 March 2002).

Appendix
Yale Declaration

This declaration is the result of three sets of recommendations made by the following conference working groups: Recommendations for Developed Countries; Recommendations for Developing Countries; and Recommendations for the United Nations and International Non-Governmental Organizations.

Preamble & General Principles

We affirm the universality of human rights and call on all states to bring about the full enforcement of the rights of people with mental retardation without delay. People with mental retardation have too long been left out of the mainstream human rights agenda of states and non-governmental advocacy organizations.

We affirm the principles of self-determination and autonomy for persons with mental retardation.

Taking into account the social, cultural, and economic differences among peoples and nations, we recognize that we all may gain by working together to share experiences, expertise, and differing perspectives to promote international human rights enforcement.

Mutual respect and recognition of diversity form the basis of international cooperation necessary to promote the rights of people with mental retardation. Regardless of abilities and disabilities, level of achievement, or country of origin, we can and must learn from each other's experiences.

We urge people everywhere to share experiences, expertise, resources, and influence to promote the rights and dignity of people with mental retardation.

We set forth a strategy for effective action to fulfill our common goal of promoting the full realization and enforcement of the rights of people with mental retardation everywhere.

I. International Standards, Domestic Legislation, and Reform

All states must immediately begin a process of reforming their laws and public policies to achieve or exceed international standards and begin an inclusive planning process to bring about full enforcement of human rights for people with mental retardation in their own country. The United Nations Standard Rules on the Equalization of Opportunities for Persons with Disabilities should be used as a guide to this process and as a benchmark to judge its results.

A. Recognition of rights

1. In 1975, the United Nations recognized in the Declaration of the Rights of Disabled Persons that all people with disabilities are entitled to the full protection of international human rights law. The declaration drew upon, and refined concepts of human rights introduced in, the 1971 U.N. Declaration on the Rights of Mentally Retarded Persons.

2. At the World Conference on Human Rights in 1993, the United Nations adopted the Declaration of Vienna, which strengthened the recognition of the rights of people with mental retardation by reaffirming that 'all human rights and fundamental freedoms are universal and thus unreservedly include persons with disabilities.' Section II(B)(6)(63). The Vienna Declaration permits no exceptions to the full enforcement of the rights of people with mental retardation on the basis of the availability of economic or technical resources, and 'calls on Governments, where necessary, to adopt or adjust legislation to assure access to these and other rights for disabled persons.'

3. In response to the Vienna Declaration, the United Nations General Assembly adopted the Standard Rules on the Equalization of Opportunities for Persons with Disabilities ('Standard Rules on Equalization') in 1994, which set forth international standards for the rights of persons with disabilities, including persons with mental retardation.

B. Immediate, Inclusive Planning Process

The Standard Rules on Equalization set forth international standards for a national planning process that must take place in every state to ensure full realization of human rights. Such a planning process must actively involve people with mental retardation, and their advocates and organizations.

C. Information Dissemination

The Standard Rules on Equalization and successful national legislation and practice should be widely disseminated by the United Nations and international NGOs. To this end, the following specific steps should be taken:

1. The Standard Rules on Equalization and examples of successful legislation and practice—such as the Americans with Disabilities Act—should be placed on-line in a way that is accessible to the most number of people around the world.

2. A 'plain English' version of the Standard Rules on Equalization should be drafted and distributed.

3. A 'step-by-step' document on the Standard Rules on Equalization should be drafted and distributed.

4. The Standard Rules on Equalization should be endorsed formally by professional and human rights organizations.

D. The Standard Rules on Equalization

The Standard Rules on Equalization should be used as a benchmark to measure progress in the achievement of the rights of persons with mental retardation. The following specific steps should be taken:

1. An international agency should be established by the United Nations to monitor and report on the compliance of each state with the provisions of the Standard Rules on Equalization.

2. Each nation should designate or establish its own agency to monitor and report domestic compliance with the Standard Rules on Equalization.

II. Increase and Prioritize Resources

States should maximize the use of current resources devoted to persons with mental retardation by emphasizing autonomy, family care and support, and localized services. States should increase resources devoted to persons with mental retardation so as to be in compliance with the Standard Rules on Equalization.

A. Use of Current Resources to Enforce Human Rights

Although resources are limited in many countries, the resources currently available must be used to support services that maximize the realization and enforcement of the rights of people with mental retardation. Funds currently used to support custodial institutions, for example, should be shifted to support the creation of community-based service and support systems designed to maximize individual potential and personal autonomy.

B. Domestic Legislation Should Emphasize Autonomy

Nations should encourage persons with mental retardation to live in the least restrictive environment available. The following specific steps should be taken:

1. The use of institutions should be decreased both for humane and economic reasons.

2. The use of in-home personal assistants and other forms of community-living arrangements should be expanded. Aid and reimbursement

should be provided to family members caring for persons with mental retardation in recognition of their economic sacrifices and the cost-effectiveness of home care.

3. Government funding of assistive technology should be increased to allow persons with mental retardation greater choices of living arrangements as a way of reducing the high cost of institutionalization.

4. Nations should explore alternatives to the use of guardianships, such as mentors and citizen advocates.

5. The legal principle of substitute decision making should be replaced, whenever possible, by supported decision making.

6. Persons with mental retardation and persons living in institutions should enjoy the right to vote.

C. *Increase U.N. Staff and Resources*

The United Nations should increase its staff and resources working on issues affecting persons with mental retardation. There are currently only 28 people throughout the entire U.N. system working on issues of specific concern to persons with disabilities. All U.N. staff that have responsibilities in areas affecting persons with mental retardation should receive training in current standards and techniques for enhancing and enforcing the rights of persons with mental retardation, such as values clarification, person-centered planning, and general systems approaches to providing services and support.

III. Support for Effective National and International Programs

Supporting the development of effective locally based advocacy should be a primary goal of international cooperation among states and international organizations. Collaboration to support advocacy in other states will build on accumulated experiences and expertise while respecting differing interests and perspectives.

A. *Consumers*

Support for consumer-controlled advocacy organizations and consumer involvement in all advocacy efforts should be at the core of international efforts to promote the rights of persons with mental retardation.

B. *Families and Other Allies*

The broadest possible coalitions should be established to promote the rights of people with mental retardation. Families of people with mental retardation should be recognized and empowered to take part in the reform process.

C. Exchange

Consumers and advocates around the world can learn from one another and support each other's efforts by receiving visitors, exchanging information, and building mutually respectful relations. Exchange must be in both directions—people from countries at any level of economic and social development can learn from others' experiences. The United Nations and international NGOs should encourage and facilitate such Exchanges.

D. Fostering National and International Leadership

International NGOs and advocacy organizations should lobby international and national government agencies to increase public awareness of the rights of persons with mental retardation in order to increase leadership in this area. Advocates should increase their use of the media, and should encourage prominent individuals with family members with disabilities and other leaders to speak publicly and frequently on this issue.

IV. Model Programs and Monitoring Progress

Through international cooperation, states and NGOs should support the creation of model service programs that respect the rights of people with mental retardation, maximize the opportunity for individual potential, and enhance individual autonomy. Successes and failures should be noted and monitored by states and international governmental organizations and NGOs.

A. Best Practices

Model programs should support the implementation of the best practices adopted throughout the world. International cooperation can help avoid mistakes made elsewhere, including the support for half-measures or other ineffective measures that do not fully enforce rights or maximize individual potential.

B. Tailoring Strategies to Local Needs

The development and implementation of model programs will allow consumers, advocates, and governments to observe the benefits of innovative, rights-oriented service systems while maintaining local control and learning how such programs can be tailored to local needs.

C. Monitoring and Reporting

International NGOs should supply critical information to the U.S. State Department and the U.S. Congress on violations and protections of the rights of persons with mental retardation throughout the world, so that such violations and protections can be included in the U.S. State

Department's annual human rights country reports. The information compiled should be made available to human rights centers and to individuals throughout the world working on this issue so that it can be used to influence other governments.

V. Development, Democratization, and International Human Rights

The rights of persons with mental retardation and the enjoyment of basic civil and political rights are inextricably linked. Without democracy and responsive government, people with mental retardation cannot seek the full implementation and enforcement of their rights. Without respect for their civil and political rights, people with mental retardation will not be able to take full advantage of democratic governance, and will be less able to make a meaningful contribution to society.

A. Non-Governmental Organization

Non-Governmental Organizations are vital to promoting the rights of people with mental retardation. NGO activity may be severely limited without the full enforcement of civil and political rights and the existence of democratic governments responsive to the concerns of citizens. International cooperation should promote the creation of an independent, non-governmental advocacy sector, in addition to supporting the growth of political freedom and the respect for all civil and political rights.

B. International Development Assistance

All development programs should be inclusive to ensure that people with mental retardation can take full advantage of them. At the same time, international development assistance should especially support the rights of persons with mental retardation through the support of exchanges, model service programs, and advocacy.

C. Support for Democratization

Democratization has come to be respected as one of the pillars of development. All democratization programs must be fully inclusive of people with mental retardation, and special funds should be set aside for the support of advocacy by and for persons with mental retardation.

D. Support for International Human Rights

The number and type of organizations focusing on the rights of persons with mental retardation should be expanded to include:

1. General human rights organizations such as Amnesty International, Human Rights Watch, and the International Committee of the Red Cross.

2. United Nations human rights bodies, such as the Human Rights Committee, the Human Rights Commission, the U.N. High Commissioner for Human Rights, and the U.N. High Commissioner for Refugees.

VI. Improvement of International Law

International cooperation should support the development of international law and standards relating to people with mental retardation.

A. Need for International Convention

People with mental retardation currently lack the protection of a binding, international convention devoted especially to their rights. Treaties have been recently adopted to protect the rights of women, children, and racial minorities, and people with mental retardation and other disabilities deserve no less. In addition to setting forth specific rights and the application of general principles that apply to people with mental retardation, an international convention would assure the existence of an international supervisory mechanism to focus attention on the particular concerns of people with mental retardation.

B. No Limitations on Rights

In the spirit of the Vienna Declaration's recognition of the universality of human rights, and consistent with the requirements of the International Covenant on Civil and Political Rights and the International Covenant on Economic, Social, and Cultural Rights, the rights of people with mental retardation deserve full protection. New international laws should not include limitations on rights characteristic of early U.N. formulations that may be interpreted to permit any nation to postpone action on human rights enforcement. New Laws should set forth rights that are universal, fair, clearly defined, and enforceable.

C. International Laws and Standards

International laws and standards should be set at the highest level for the treatment of people with mental retardation, even if full enforcement is not possible immediately in all countries. Where objective constraints on resources exist, immediate and verifiable efforts to enforce human rights to the maximum of available resources should be required.

D. Inclusive Process for Developing New Laws, Policies, and Standards

The process of developing new laws, policies, and standards should be inclusive, including people with mental retardation and people from all parts of the world. Declarations of locally or regionally based groups, such as the Declaration of Managua, are emblematic of the ideas and initiative for new international standards that have come from developing countries.

E. *Consensus through International Ratification*

International instruments that require ratification within each country are inherently preferable to resolutions of international bodies. The process of ratification allows countries the opportunity to adopt international standards through their own political processes and helps develop world consensus for the recognition and enforcement of the rights of people with mental retardation.

Symposium Participants

Adrienne Asch, *Wellesley College*
Peter Blanck, *University of Iowa Law School*
David Braddock, *University of Illinois at Chicago; Institute on Disability and Human Development*
Robert A. Burt, *Yale Law School*
Donald Cohen, *Yale Child Study Center*
Robert Dinerstein, *American University Law School*
Gunnar Dybwad, *Brandeis University*
James Ellis, *University of New Mexico Law School*
Gary Goldstein, *Kennedy-Krieger Institute, Johns Hopkins University*
Lawrence Gostin, *Georgetown University Law Center*
Stanley S. Herr, *University of Maryland Law School*
Constance F. Kane, *Private Agencies Collaborating Together (PACT), Indonesia*
Harold Hongju Koh, *Schell Center*
Anthony T. Kronman, *Yale Law School*
Mitchell Levitz, *coauthor, Count Us In: Growing Up with Down's Syndrome*
Ruth Luckasson, *University of New Mexico School of Education*
Peter Mittler, *University of Manchester, England*
T. J. Monroe, *President's Committee on Mental Retardation; American Association on Mental Retardation*
John H. Noble, *National Catholic School of Social Science, Catholic University of America*
Roberto Leal Ocampo, *Ambassador, Nicaragua*
Stephen Pincus, *Yale Law School*
Arik Rimmerman, *Bar-Ilan University, Israel*
Marcia Rioux, *Roeher Institute, Canada*
Eric Rosenthal, *Mental Disability Rights International, American University Law School*
Dan Shnit, *Tel Aviv University, Israel*
Timothy P. Shriver, *Special Olympics World Games*

Robert Silverstein, *U.S. Senate Subcommittee on Disability Policy*
Ronald Slye, *Schell Center*
Michael Smull, *University of Maryland Medical School*
Inger Claeson Wastberg, *National Disability Ombudsman, Sweden*
Stephen Wizner, *Yale Law School*

Index

abortion
    feminist theory 329–30
    Inclusion International 43
    mercy-killings 43
    prenatal diagnosis 43, 326
    preventing disability 326, 328–9
    selective 326
Active 27
Additional Protocol to the American
        Convention on Human Rights
        as in the Area of Economics,
        Social and Cultural
        Rights 123
advocacy 138
    self *see* self-advocacy
    UN Declaration on the Rights of
        Disabled Persons (1975) 138
    United Nations, recommendations for
        509–10
advocates
    priorities 3–4
    role 3–4, 139–40
    self *see* self-advocacy
affirmative action
    Austria 164
    Brazil 164
    Canada 164
    drafting human rights instruments 487–8
    Germany 164
    Ghana 164
    Malawi 164
    meaning 164
    South Africa 164
    Switzerland 164
    Uganda 164
African Charter on Human and Peoples'
        Rights 123
African Decade of Disabled Persons 39
America *see* United States
American Association on Mental
        Retardation (AAMR)
    classifications 29–30
    guardianship 447–8
    human rights standards 139
    terminology 29–30, 49
Americans with Disabilities Act 1990
        206–7, 323
    background 206

case law 206–7
core polices
    economic self-sufficiency 278–9
    equal opportunity 268–74 *see also*
        equal opportunity
    full participation through empowering
        274–6
    independent living 277–8
economic self-sufficiency 278–9
equal opportunity 268–74 *see also* equal
        opportunity
full participation through empowering
        274–6
HIV infection 206
implementation 221–2
independent living 277–8
individualization 269
institutional isolation 206
model law 162
purpose 321
reform proposals 221–2
remedies 207
requirements 206
results 203, 206
role 223
service provision 241
template for reform 161–2
Amnesty International 131
amniocentesis 326
'amok' syndrome
    Cambodia 70
    Canada 70
    Filipinos 69–70
anti-discrimination laws
    civil law 167–9
    comparative law 162–75
    constitutional law 164–7
    criminal law 163–4
Arab countries
    cross-cultural perceptions of disability 63
arbitration 217–18
Asch, A 327
Ashoka Foundation 132
Asia
    mental illness 65
Asian Decade of Disabled Persons
        (1993–2002) 39
Association for Retarded Citizens 27

asylums
  see also disability discrimination;
      institutionalization
  architecture 86
  Canada 84–5
  custodial 88–9
  Dix, Dorothea 85
  Europe 84
  historical development 83–4
  management 86
  Mexico City 83
  overcrowding 86–7
  social policy 83–7
  United States 84, 85–6
    custodial asylums 88–9
    intellectual disabilities, first for people
        with 87–8
Australia
  case law 135
  cross-cultural perceptions of disability 63
  disability discrimination 99, 163–4, 167,
      372–3
  education 173
  employment 372–3
  enforcement 173
  intellectual disability 27
  organizations 27
  past disability 171
  reasonable accommodation/adjustment
      172
  sterilization of intellectually disabled
      persons 4–5, 135
Austria
  affirmative actions 164
  disability discrimination 99, 164
  guardianship 445
autonomy
  context of disability, in 154
  drafting human rights instruments 482–3
  exercising 154
  guardianship 429–50
  human rights 154
  independent living movement 154
  meaning 154
  understanding 154
auxiliary aids and services
  equal opportunity 271–2

Barr, MW 89
Beijing Declaration 130
Beijing World Conference on Women
    (1996) 288
biomedical approach 291–2

Birenbaum, A 424
Blacher, J 416, 417, 418, 424
Bolivia
  social welfare law 169
Bosnia-Herzegovina 392
Braddock, D 424
brain fag 65
Brazil
  affirmative action 164
  disability discrimination 99, 164
Bromely, B 416, 417
Bulgaria
  employment 369, 370
  inhuman and degrading treatment 469
Burke, E 140
Burt, R 116

Cambodia
  'amok' syndrome 70
Canada
  affirmative actions 164
  'amok' syndrome 70
  asylums 84–5
  case law 134
  disability discrimination 164, 167–8, 213
  education 134, 173
  employment 364–5
  enforcement 173
  harassment 173
  organizations 27
  past disability 171
  reasonable accommodation/adjustment
      172
Canadian Association for Community
    Living 27
Canadian Association for Mental
    Retardation 27
capital punishment
  mentally retarded persons 3
  United States 140
care and assistance
  Israel 245
  legislation 243–6
  Sweden 246
careers
  self-advocacy 456–8
case law
  Americans with Disabilities Act 1990
      206–7
  Australia 135
  Canada 134
  education 134–5
  Europe 134

European Convention on Human Rights
135–6
international human rights 132–5
involuntary sterilization 135
Ireland 134–5
sterilization of intellectually disabled
persons 4–5, 135
UN Declaration on the Rights of
Mentally Retarded Persons (1971)
132–3
United States 132–4
Universal Declaration of Human Rights
(1948) 135
Wyatt case 132–3
cash assistance
economic self-sufficiency 279
independent living 278
CAT *see* Convention Against Torture and
Other Cruel, Inhuman or Degrading
Treatment or Punishment (CAT)
CAVNET 131
Central and Eastern Europe
inhuman and degrading treatment 469
Challenge 27
challenging behaviour
terminology 27
children
abortion 43
Convention on the Rights of the Child *see*
Convention on the rights of the
Child, UN
discrimination 2
education 43
Education for All (1990) 43–4
having and raising 5
inclusion 33
initiatives 42–4
intellectually disabled persons 6, 415–28
see also out-of-home placement of
children
Jomtien Declaration 43
mercy-killings 43
national plans 43
out-of-home placement *see* out-of-home
placement of children
prenatal diagnosis 43
psychiatric hospitals 43
rehabilitation 33
residential institutions 43
Salamanca Declaration and Framework
for Action (1994) 43–4
United Nations Children's Fund
(UNICEF) 128

World Summit on Children 43
Chile
disability discrimination 167
China
community-based rehabilitation 36
cross-cultural perceptions of disability
63, 64
disability discrimination 371–2
employment 371–2
enforcement 174
preventing disability 334, 336, 337
sex selection 337
social welfare law 169–70
civil disability 302–5
civil rights
disability policy 265
legislation 265
Clapham, A 135
classifications
American Association on Mental
Retardation (AAMR) 29–30
cross-cultural perceptions of disability
60–2
ICIDH 28
ICIDH-2 29
World Health Organization (WHO) 28–9
Cohen, HJ 424
Cole, DA 417
Commission on Human Rights *see* UN
Commission on Human Rights
Committee on Economic, Social and
Cultural Rights
International Covenant on Economic,
Social and Cultural Rights
(ICESCR) 158
Committee on the Elimination of
All Forms of Discrimination 158
Communities Against Violence Network
(CAVNET) 131
community integration
drafting human rights instruments 489–90
community-based rehabilitation
approach 36
China 36
definition 36
examples 36
Ghana 36
Guyana 36
impact 36
inclusion 36–7
India 36
initiatives 36
Laos 36

community-based rehabilitation (*cont*.):
 Philippines 36
 staff training 37
 Vietnam 36
 WHO/ILO/UNESCO joint statement 36
comparative law 161–75
 anti-discrimination laws 162–75
 civil anti-discrimination laws 167–9
 constitutional law 164–7
 education 173
 enforcement 173–4
 equality 171–3
 guardianship 429–50
 harassment 173
 judiciary, role of 161
 legal approaches 163–4
 model law 162
 protected groups 170–1
 reform process 161–75
  ADA, using 161–2
  Standard Rules, using 161–2
  template 161–2
 social welfare law 169–70
 trends 174–6
compensatory privilege 305–7
competence
 cross-cultural perceptions of disability 66
conciliation 217
Consortium on Language, Image and
  Public Education 49
constitutional law
 comparative law 164–7
constructing knowledge 287–317
contracts
 guardians 248
 intellectually disabled persons 247–8
 Israel 247–8
 legal competence to act 254
Convention Against Torture and Other
  Cruel, Inhuman or Degrading
  Treatment or Punishment (CAT) 157
Convention on Elimination of
  Discrimination against Persons with
  Disabilities, proposed UN 130
Convention on the Elimination of All
  Forms of Discrimination Against
  Women (1979) 157
 employment 123, 157
 international human rights 123
Convention on the Rights of the Child, UN
  42–3, 61, 123, 157, 287
 protection of minors with disabilities 123

therapeutic services 123
 treatment right 123
Costa Rica
 disability discrimination 167, 168
 social welfare law 169, 170
criminal responsibility
 intellectually disabled persons 238, 248,
  253
 Israel 238, 248, 253
Crnic, KA 417
cross-cultural perceptions of disability
  59–81
 analysis 62–5
 Arab countries 63
 Australia 63
 changing meanings 60
 China 63, 64
 clashes over treatment of disability
  67–71
 classification 60–2
 clinically specific classifications 65
 club foot case, *Kou Xiong* 67–9
 competence 66
 cultural relativism 59
 culture-bound syndromes 70–1
 definitions 60–2
 Denmark 63
 distortion 65
 DSM-IV 65
 Egypt 64
 epilepsy case, *Lia Lee* 69
 folk texts 64
 Germany 63
 Greece 63
 handicapped 60
 Hawaii 69–70
 Hmong cases 67–9
 importance of cultural information 71
 influence 59–60
 intellectual disability 60–2
 Israel 63
 Italy 63
 Korea 71
 local models 66
 mental illness 60, 65
 mental retardation 60, 65–7
 methodological problems 64
 mind/body dualism 60
 nomenclature 59–62
 policy implications 59
 possession by demons 71
 purpose of analysis 59

religious beliefs 64
research 62–5
'running amok' 69–70
stigmatizing individuals 59
translation, problems of 64
United States 63
cultural groups
    cross-cultural perceptions of disability *see*
        cross-cultural perceptions of
        disability
    naming 50
cultural Other 70

deaf people
    culture 338
    sign language 165–6, 271, 338
Decade of Persons with Disabilities
    (1983–1992), UN 5, 38–9, 156, 287
decision-making
    self-advocacy 458–9
Declaration on the Rights of Disabled
    Persons *see* UN Declaration on the
    Rights of Disabled Persons (1975)
Declaration on the Rights of Mentally
    Retarded Persons *see* UN
    Declaration on the Rights of
    Mentally Retarded Persons (1971)
definitions
    see also terminology
    American Association on Mental
        Retardation (AAMR) 29–30
    cross-cultural perceptions of disability
        60–2
    disability 29
    historical use 61
    importance 26
    intellectual disability 60–2
    international 61
    mental retardation 29–30
    necessary, whether 61–2
Degener, T 467
degrading terminology 27
de-institutionalization
    England 97
    Northern Ireland 97
    Scotland 97
    social policy 94–7
    United Kingdom 97
    United States 94–7
    Wales 97
Denmark
    cross-cultural perceptions of disability 63

Despouy report 128
Diagnostic and Statistical Manual of Mental
    Disorders 65, 293
different but equal principle 3
dignity
    context of disability, in 154
    human rights 154
    Israel 238, 248–9
    legislation taking into account
        intellectual disability 248–9
    meaning 154
disability
    contrasting views 320–3
    diagnosis 289
    meaning 290–6
    perception 289
    preventing *see* preventing disability
    scientific formulations 290–6
        individual pathology 292–4
        intersection with concept of equality
            301–12
        social pathology 294–6
    social construction 321–3
    social formulations 290–6
        individual pathology 292–4
        intersection with concept of equality
            301–12
        social pathology 294–6
    treatment 289
disability discrimination
    Americans with Disabilities Act 1990 *see*
        Americans with Disabilities Act 1990
    Australia 99, 163–4, 167, 372–3
    Austria 99, 164
    Brazil 99, 164
    Canada 164, 167–8, 213
    Chile 167
    China 371–2
    comparative law 213–15
    Costa Rica 167, 168
    employment 172
    enforcement *see* enforcement
    Ethiopia 167
    European Union 99
    Fiji 164
    Finland 99, 163, 164
    France 163
    Gambia 164
    Germany 99, 164, 167, 368–9
    Ghana 164, 167
    Guatemala 167
    Hong Kong 164, 167, 168

disability discrimination (*cont.*):
  Hungary 167
  implementation 205
  India 167, 168, 373
  Ireland 167, 367–8
  Israel 167, 237–8, 241–2, 370
  Japan 372
  Korea 167
  Latin America 370–1
  limitations of law 204–5
  Luxembourg 163
  Madagascar 167
  Malawi 164
  Mauritius 164, 167
  Namibia 167, 171
  New Zealand 164
  Nigeria 167
  Philippines 167, 168
  potential of laws 203–36
  reform proposals 220–3
    Disabilities Rights Commissions 220
    test case strategy 222–3
    White House Office on ADA 221–2
  South Africa 164, 167
  Spain 163, 164, 167, 213
  Sri Lanka 167
  Sweden 167, 214–15
  Switzerland 164
  test case strategy 222–3
  Uganda 164
  United Kingdom 98, 167, 211–13, 238, 369
  United States 61, 97–8, 167
  use of law 204–5
  Zambia 167
  Zimbabwe 167
disability law
  civil rights law 152
  human rights issue, disability as 152–5
  medical model 62, 151–5
  reforms 152
  research 151
  social model 62, 151–5
  social welfare law 152
  United States 152
disability policy 263–84
  appropriation bills 267
  civil rights 265
  core policies 268–79
    economic self-sufficiency 278–9
    equal opportunity 268–74 *see also*
      equal opportunity
    full participation through empowering
      274–6

  independent living 277–8
  discretionary grant-in-aid programs
    265–7
  economic self-sufficiency 278–9
  entitlement programs 265
  equal opportunity 268–74 *see also* equal
    opportunity
  full participation through empowering
    274–6
  independent living 277–8
  laws affecting individuals with
    disabilities 264–8
  loans 267
  prejudice 263
  regulatory statutes 267
  taxation 267, 268
  United States 263–84
Disabled Peoples' International (DPI) 32,
  38
disabled persons
  terminology 27
discrimination
  children 2
  definition 172
  disability *see* disability discrimination
  drafting human rights instruments
    485–91
  ethnic minorities 2
  gay people 2
  HIV/AIDS 2
  intellectually disabled persons 2
  lesbians 2
  mental disability, persons with 2
  refugees 2
  religious minorities 2
  Standard Rules on the Equalization of
    Opportunities for Persons with
    Disabilities 124
  women 2
Dix, Dorothea 85
DPI 32, 38
drafting human rights instruments 467–501
  access to appropriate and professional
    services 481–3
  affirmative action 487–8
  autonomy 482–3
  community integration 489–90
  community-based services 484–5
  discrimination 485–91
  due process 488–9
  growing interest 467
  guardianship 490–1
  healthcare 479–85

highest attainable standard of physical
and mental health 479–85
Human Rights Commission 467
improving use of existing conventions
467–8
independence 483–5
independent organizations 468–9
individualized treatment right 482
inhuman and degrading treatment 468–9
Kosovo 469–70
least restrictive services, right to 484
Mental Disability Rights International
468–70
new convention 468, 491–3
reasonable accommodation/adjustment
487–8
recommendations 467–8
rehabilitation 482–3
right to health 479–85
social integration 483–5
WHO monograph 478–91
Yale Declaration 471, 472–77 *see also* Yale
Declaration
DSM-IV 65
due process
drafting human rights instruments 488–9
liberty restrictions 190–1
proportionality 488–9
unwanted medical procedures 191
Duvdevany, I 419
Dybwad, G 31, 133

Economic and Social Commission for
Western Asia 510
economic self-sufficiency
Americans with Disabilities Act 1990
278–9
cash assistance 279
disability policy 278–9
employment 278–9
goal 278
taxation 279
work incentives 279
economics
equality *see* economics of equality
self-sufficiency *see* economic self-
sufficiency
economics of equality 387–414
data sources 395–401
direct costs 388
findings, research 402–4
discussion of 404–6
indirect costs 388

infanticide 391
Iran 391–2
meaning 388–9
methods of measurement 392–401
data sources 395–401
government stability 394
income 393–4
infant mortality rate 392–3
proxy variables 392–5
religion 393
statistical analyses 401
support services 393
type of government 394
Western medical technology 394–5
neonatal intensive care units 389–91
rejection of Western human rights
standards 391–2
social discrimination 389–92
statistical analyses 401
UN Resolutions 387
United States 387, 389
Edgerton, R 34, 65–6
education
Australia 173
Canada 134, 173
case law 134–5
children 43
comparative law 173
curriculum 33
Education for All (1990) 43–4
effective and meaningful opportunity
272
equal opportunity 270, 272
European Convention on Human Rights
126
Hong Kong 173
inclusion 33
independent living 277
individualization 269
intellectually disabled persons 43
Ireland 4, 134–5
Israel 243–4
Korea 171
most appropriate integrated setting 274
New Zealand 173
Philippines 173
Salamanca Declaration and Framework
for Action (1994) 43–4
United Kingdom 28, 173
United States 2, 5, 173
Education for All (1990) 43–4
Egypt
cross-cultural perceptions of disability 64

employment
  Australia 372–3
  Bulgaria 369, 370
  Canada 364–5
  China 371–2
  comparative analysis 347–85
    Australia 372–3
    bridges from welfare to work 358–62
    Bulgaria 369, 370
    Canada 364–5
    China 371–2
    entrepreneurs with disabilities study
      359–62
    Germany 368–9
    Hungary 369
    implications 356–73
    India 373
    Ireland 367–8
    Israel 370
    Japan 372
    Latin America 370–1
    Manpower study 358–9
    non-union Europe 369–70
    Oklahoma investigation 349–56
    overview 356–8
    private staffing industry 358–9
    role 349–56
    State-sponsored initiatives 359–62
    United Kingdom 369
    United States, implications in 362–4
  Convention on the Elimination of All
    Forms of Discrimination Against
    Women (1979) 123
  disability discrimination 172
  economic self-sufficiency 278–9
  effective and meaningful opportunity
    272
  emerging workforce, studying the 347–85
  entrepreneurs with disabilities study
    359–62
  equal opportunity 269
  European Community 365–7
  Germany 368–9
  Hungary 369
  inclusion 33, 34
  independent living 278
  India 373
  individualization 269
  Ireland 367–8
  Israel 370
  Japan 372
  Latin America 370–1

Malawi 165
Manpower study 358–9
non-union Europe 369–70
Oklahoma investigation 349–56
  ADA implementation 356
  black hole effect 356
  capabilities 353
  core findings 354–6
  economic opportunity 352, 355
  employment integration 352, 354–5
  empowerment factors 354
  inclusion factors 353
  income changes 352
  individual growth 355
  legal factors 354
  overview 351–4
  perception of rights 356
  personal background measures 352
  purpose 350–1
  qualifications 353
open 33
Pathways to Employment scheme 34
quotas 165, 168–9
reasonable accommodation/adjustment
  242–3
rehabilitation 33
research 347–85
self-advocacy 456–8
Standard Rules on the Equalization of
  Opportunities for Persons with
  Disabilities 124
State-sponsored initiatives 359–62
Uganda 165
UN Resolutions 347
United Kingdom 34, 369
United States 34, 362–4
workplace changes 34
Endeavour 27
enforcement 205
  adversarial mechanisms 215–16
  alternative means of dispute resolution
    216–19, 222
  arbitration 217–18
  Australia 173
  Canada 173
  China 174
  comparative law 173–4
  conciliation 217
  England 257
  Ghana 174
  Hungary 174
  impact litigation 216

improving 215–20
India 174
Israel 173, 256–7
mediation 218–19
negotiation 216–17
Nigeria 174
private initiatives 219–20
problem-solving approaches 219–20
quasi-Governmental initiatives 219
United Kingdom 173
United States 257–8
Zambia 174
Zimbabwe 174
England
see also United Kingdom
de-institutionalization 97
Employers' Forum on Disability 222
enforcement of legal rights 257
entitlement programs
close-ended 265
disability policy 265
open-ended 265
United States 265
entrepreneurs with disabilities study 359–62
equal opportunity 298–300
accommodations 271–2
Americans with Disabilities Act 1990
268–74
auxiliary aids and services 271–2
case-by-case analysis 268–71
concept 154
disability policy 268–74
education 270, 272
effective and meaningful opportunity
271–2
employment 269
health care 270, 272
individualization 268–71
interdisciplinary assessments 268–71
Israel 251
legislation 251–2
meaning 153–4
program accessibility 271–2
reasonable accommodation/adjustment
271–2
stereotypes 154
treatment right 272–4
United States 251, 268–74
vocational rehabilitation 270–1
Equal Rights for Persons with Disabilities
Commission 220
equal treatment 296, 297–8

equality 153–4
assumptions 297
changes in understanding 296–301
comparative law 171–3
diversity 171–3
economics 387–414 *see also* economics of
equality
equal opportunity 153–4 *see also* equal
opportunity
equal treatment 296, 297–8
International Covenant on Civil and
Political Rights (ICCPR) 157
intersection with meaning of disability
301–12
juridical 153
Korea 171
liberal theory of equality 296
meaning 297
models 296–301
Namibia 171
opportunity, of *see* equal opportunity
results, of 153
Standard Rules on the Equalization of
Opportunities for Persons with
Disabilities 156
understanding 296–301
well-being, equality of 296, 300–1
Zimbabwe 171
equalization of opportunities
World Programme of Action Concerning
Disabled Persons 156
Ethiopia
disability discrimination 167
ethnic groups
naming 50
ethnic minorities
discrimination 2
eugenics 66, 90–1
preventing disability 334
Europe
case law 134
European Commission on Human Rights
timidity 126
European Community
employment 365–7
HELIOS 365–6
HELIOS II 366
HORIZON 366
TIDE program 367
European Convention on Human Rights
case law 135–6
education 126

European Convention on Human Rights
    (*cont.*):
    fair and public hearing, right to 126
    Human Rights Act 1998 (UK) 135
    international human rights 126–7
    shortcomings 126
    unsound mind, detention of persons
        with 126
European Social Charter 126
    inclusions 127
    revision 127
European Union
    disability discrimination 99
exploitation
    inclusion 34
    intellectually disabled persons 249–50
    vulnerability 249

Fadiman, A 69
families
    access to support services 36
    inclusion 35–6
    Inclusion International 35
    needs 35
    respite care 35
    shared care 35, 36
    short-term care 35
    stereotypes 35
    supporting 35–6, 45
    United States 36
feminist theory
    abortion 329–30
    prenatal testing 329–30
    preventing disability 329–30
    self-determination 329
Fiji
    disability discrimination 164
Finland
    disability discrimination 99, 163, 164
    social welfare law 169
folk texts
    cross-cultural perceptions of disability 64
Food Stamps 278
foreign aid 132
Fourth World Conference on Women,
        Beijing 1995 128
France
    disability discrimination 163
freak shows 89–90
freedom
    legislation taking into account
        intellectual disability 248–9

Friedrich, WN 417
fund-raising 27

Gambia
    disability discrimination 164
gay people
    discrimination 2
genetic testing 327
germ line therapy 43
Germany
    affirmative actions 164
    cross-cultural perceptions of disability 63
    disability discrimination 99, 164, 167,
        368–9
    employment 368–9
    guardianship 441–4
        guiding principles 441–2
        limiting substituted decision maker's
            powers 442–3
        procedural safeguards 442
        protecting zones of autonomy 442–3
        strengthening consumer rights 443–4
    social welfare law 169
Ghana
    affirmative actions 164
    community-based rehabilitation 36
    disability discrimination 164, 167
    enforcement 174
Global Survey on Government Action on
        Disability Policy 505
Goode, B 31
grant programs
    competitive 266–7
    discretionary 265–7
    formula 266
Greece
    cross-cultural perceptions of disability 63
Greenburg, MT 417
Grob, GN 86
guardianship
    alternatives to 429–50
    American Association on Mental
        Retardation 447–8
    Austria 445
    autonomy 429–50
    comparative law 429–50
    criticism of 447
    drafting human rights instruments 490–1
    Germany 441–4
        guiding principles 441–2
        limiting substituted decision maker's
            powers 442–3
        procedural safeguards 442

protecting zones of autonomy 442–3
  strengthening consumer rights 443–4
Inter-American Convention on
    Elimination of Discrimination by
    Reason of Disability 447
Israel 445
minimizing use 430
Netherlands 445–6
New Zealand 446
problems raised by 429–30
self-determination 429–50
Spain 446
Sweden 431–41
  administrator 435–6
  contact person 436
  escort person 438
  evaluation of law 439–41
  forvaltare 435–6
  god man 432, 433–5
  implementation of law 438–9
  kontakt 436
  legal background 432–3
  mentor 433–5
  personal assistant 436–8
  support options 431–41
  trustee 435–6
United States 430, 431
Guatemala
  disability discrimination 167
Guidelines for Action on Resource
    Development in the Field of
    Disability 129
Guidelines for the Establishment and
    Development of National
    Coordinating Committees on
    Disability or Similar Bodies
    (1990) 123
Guyana
  community-based rehabilitation 36

handicapped
  cross-cultural perceptions of disability 60
  United States 60
Handynet 366
Hanneman, R 418
happiness, pursuit of 185–200
  essential lifestyle approach 189–90, 196–7
  liberty restrictions 190–2
  lifestyle preferences 185
  person centered planning 185, 192–6
  service provision 185
harassment
  Canada 173

comparative law 173
Hawaii
  cross-cultural perceptions of disability
    69–70
  'running amok' 69–70
health and safety
  service provision 189
healthcare
  drafting human rights instruments
    479–85
  effective and meaningful opportunity
    272
  equal opportunity 270, 272
  inclusion 33
  independent living 278
  individualization 270
  mentally ill persons 5
  preventing disability 324, 339
  United States 2
Helander, E 36
HELIOS 365–6
HELIOS II 366
Hemp, R 424
Herr, S 471
HIV/AIDS
  Americans with Disabilities Act 1990 206
  discrimination 2
Hmong cases 67–9
Hong Kong
  disability discrimination 164, 167, 168
  education 173
  past disability 171
  reasonable accommodation/adjustment
    172
HORIZON 366
housing
  assistance for independent living 278
  inclusion 33
human dignity *see* dignity
Human Genome Initiative 321, 327, 336–7
human rights
  autonomy 154
  constructing knowledge 287–317
  dignity 154
  drafting instruments *see* drafting human
    rights instruments
  equality 153–4
  meaning 1
  solidarity 154
  universal value, as 1
  values 153–5
Human Rights Commission
  drafting human rights instruments 467

Human Rights Watch 4
Hungary
  disability discrimination 167
  employment 369
  enforcement 174
  inhuman and degrading treatment 469
  reasonable accommodation/adjustment
    172
Huntington, SP 392
hwa-byung 65

ICCPR *see* International Covenant on Civil
    and Political Rights (ICCPR)
ICESCR *see* International Covenant on
    Economic, Social and Cultural
    Rights (ICESCR)
ICIDH 28, 61
ICIDH-2 29
ideology
  mental retardation 55
  naming 50, 51
ILO 127
inclusion
  changes to service provision 33
  children 33
  community living 34–5
  community-based rehabilitation 36–7
  education 33
  employment 33, 34
  environmental changes 33–4
  exploitation 34
  families, supporting 35–6
  future issues 32–7
  health 33
  housing 33
  Italy 44
  Laos 44
  leisure 33
  marginalization 34
  models 33
  moving towards 32–7, 44
  open employment 33
  participation 33
  placement agencies 34
  principle 32–3
  problematic issues 34–5
  public transport 33
  recreation 33
  rehabilitation 33
  Scandinavian countries 44
  self-advocacy 459–61
  Spain 44

  staff training 37
  Uganda 44
  United States 44
  victimization 34
  Vietnam 44
  workplace changes 34
Inclusion International 4, 27, 119
  abortion 43
  collaboration 131
  families 35
  self-advocacy 32
independence
  drafting human rights instruments 483–5
independent living
  Americans with Disabilities Act 1990
    277–8
  autonomy 154
  cash assistance 278
  disability policy 277–8
  education 277
  employment 278
  Food Stamps 278
  full participation and 277
  goal 277
  healthcare 278
  housing assistance 278
  long-term services 278
  meaning 77
  movement 154
  personal assistance services 278
  philosophy 277
  self-advocacy 454
  service provision 277, 278
  skills development 277
  specialized planning 277
  training 277
India
  community-based rehabilitation 36
  disability discrimination 167, 168, 373
  employment 373
  enforcement 174
  mental retardation 66
  preventing disability 337
  sex selection 337
individual pathology 291–4
  biomedical approach 291–2
  functional approach 292–4
individualization
  Americans with Disabilities Act 1990 269
  drafting human rights instruments 482
  employment 269
  equal opportunity 268–71

healthcare 270, 482
infanticide 391
inhuman and degrading treatment
  Bulgaria 469
  Central and Eastern Europe 469
  drafting human rights instruments 468–9
  Hungary 469
  Latin America 469
  Mexico 469
  Russia 468–9
  Uruguay 469
institutionalization
  see also asylums
  conditions 239
intellectual disability
  Australia 27
  contracts 247–8
  cross-cultural perceptions of disability
    60–2
  definitions 60–2
  global trends 25–30
  legislation taking into account 237–61
    access to services, equal 240–3
    assistance and care services 243–6
    care and assistance 243–5
    categorizing legislation 250–1
    civil matters, competence to act in
      253–4
    comparative analysis 237
    contracts 247–8
    criminal responsibility 248, 253
    difference 255–6
    dignity 248–9
    enforcement 256–8
    equal opportunities 251–2
    exploitation, legislation against 249–50
    freedom 248–9
    general versus specific legislation
      250–6
    implementation 256–8
    income maintenance allowance 254–5
    Israel 237–9
    lack of uniformity 239
    legal status with respect to universal
      legislation 246–9
    needed, where 239–50
    protective legislation 252
    specific nature, issues of a 255
    subsistence 243
    UN Declaration 237–50
    universal legislation, legal status
      regarding 246–9

New Zealand 27
organizations 26
partnerships 26
positive themes 26
protective legislation 252
reconceptualization 26
redefinition 26
self-advocacy 26
Singapore 27
social policy on nineteenth and
    twentieth centuries 83–111 *see also*
    social policy
terminology 27–8, 60–2
United Kingdom 28
United Nations 26, 28
intellectually challenged
  terminology 27
intellectually disabled persons
  assertion of rights 2
  children 6
  community, supported living in 26
  contracts 247–8
  criminal responsibility 238, 248
  discrimination 2
  education 43
  exploitation, legislation against 249–50
  future, challenges for 26
  living conditions 3, 4
  meeting needs of 25–45
  mentally ill persons 2–3
  mentally retarded persons 2–3
  needs 25
  needs, meeting 25–45
  positive themes 26
  rape 4, 134
  reasonable accommodation/adjustment
    243
  refugees 6
  self-protection 3
  subsistence 243
  vulnerability 2
intelligence testing
  bias 66
  cultural differences 66
  mental retardation 30, 66
  terminology 28
Inter-American Convention on Elimination
    of Discrimination by Reason of
    Disability 130–1, 447, 474–7
interdisciplinary team 185, 186–90
International Association for the Scientific
    Study of Intellectual Disability 28

International Association for the Scientific Study of Mental Deficiency 28
International Bill of Human Rights 155, 510
International Classification of Disease 293
International Classification of Impairments, Disabilities and Handicaps (ICIDH) 28–9, 61, 293
International Covenant on Civil and Political Rights (ICCPR) 1, 122–3, 157, 158
  adoption 122
  disabilities, persons with 157–8
  equality 157
  monitoring 508
  protections 122
International Covenant on Economic, Social and Cultural Rights (ICESCR) 1, 37, 121–3, 155, 157
  adoption 122
  Comment 5 122
  Committee on Economic, Social and Cultural Rights 158
  omission 122–3
  progressive realization 480, 481
  protections 122
  right to health 479–85
international human rights 1, 115–50
  see also United Nations
  case law 132–5
  Convention on the Elimination of All Forms of Discrimination Against Women (1979) 123
  Convention on the Rights of the Child 123
  disability as subject of law 151–84
  drafting human rights instruments *see* drafting human rights instruments
  emergence of movement 117–18
  European Convention on Human Rights 126–7
  foreign aid 132
  ILSMH Declaration on the General and Special Rights of Mentally Retarded Persons 120
  implementation
    human rights standards 130–1
    intellectual disabilities, implementation of standards relating to 131–7
  International Covenant on Civil and Political Rights (ICCPR) 122–3
  International Covenant on Economic, Social and Cultural Rights (ICESCR) 121–3

legal protection 115–50
national disability plans and recommendations 136–7
national legislation 135–6
nongovernmental organizations 131–2
paradigm shifts
  reports and resolutions 128–30
  world conferences 128
Standard Rules on the Equalization of Opportunities for Persons with Disabilities *see* Standard Rules on the Equalization of Opportunities for Persons with Disabilities
standards 118–21
  construction 287–317
  generally 118–19
  ILSMH Declaration on the General and Special Rights of Mentally Retarded Persons 120
  UN Declaration on the Rights of Mentally Retarded Persons (1971) 120
  Universal Declaration on Human Rights 119
treaties 121–3
  construction 287–317
  Convention on the Elimination of All Forms of Discrimination Against Women (1979) 123
  Convention on the Rights of the Child 123
  International Covenant on Civil and Political Rights 122–3
  International Covenant on Economic, Social and Cultural Rights (ICESCR) 121–3
trends in law 160–1
UN Commission on Human Rights *see* UN Commission of Human Rights
UN Declaration on the Rights of Mentally Retarded Persons (1971) 120
UN human rights statements 124–5
Universal Declaration on Human Rights 119
Vienna Declaration of the World Conference on Human Rights 125
world conferences, paradigm shift in 128
wrongs to be righted by 116–18
International Labor Organization (ILO) 127
International League of Societies for Persons with Mental Handicap (ILSMH) 27, 119

Declaration on the General and Special
    Rights of Mentally Retarded Persons
    120
international standards for rights of the
        mentally disabled
    access to tools for individual agency 5
    core elements 5–6
    inclusion 5
    participation 5
    UN 5
International Year of Disabled Persons
    (1981), UN 5, 38, 287
International Year of the Family 35
involuntary sterilization
    case law 135
Iran
    economics of equality 391–2
    Islamic law 392
Ireland
    case law 134–5
    disability discrimination 167, 367–8
    education 4, 134–5
    employment 367–8
    reasonable accommodation/adjustment
        172
Islamic law 392
Israel
    care and assistance 245
    contracts 247–8
    criminal responsibility 238, 248, 253
    cross-cultural perceptions of disability 63
    dignity 238, 248–9
    disability discrimination 167, 237–8,
        241–2, 370
    education 243–4
    enforcement 173
    enforcement of legal rights 256–7
    equal opportunity 251
    Equal Rights for Persons with Disabilities
        Law of 1998 203, 207–11
    freedom 248–9
    guardianship 445
    income maintenance 238
    out-of-home placement of children 418–22
    reasonable accommodation/adjustment
        172
    service provision 241–2
    subsistence 243
    treatment right 238
    UN Declaration on the Rights of
        Mentally Retarded Persons (1971)
        237, 238

welfare authorities 237–8
Italy
    cross-cultural perceptions of disability 63
    inclusion 44

Japan 125–6
    disability discrimination 372
    employment 372
Jenkins, R 66
Jomtien Declaration 43

Korea
    cross-cultural perceptions of disability 71
    disability discrimination 167
    education 171
    equality 171
    mental illness 65
    possession by demons 71
    social welfare law 169
Kosovo 4
    drafting human rights instruments
        469–70
    UN guidelines 471

Lane 64
language
    see also definitions; terminology
    negative connotations 321–2
    people first language 26–7
    Standard Rules on the Equalization of
        Opportunities for Persons with
        Disabilities 124
Laos
    community-based rehabilitation 36
    inclusion 44
Latin America 4
    disability discrimination 370–1
    employment 370–1
    inhuman and degrading treatment 469
    Partnership Project 370–1
learning difficulties
    study of 25
learning disabilities
    terminology 28
legal competence to act
    civil matters 253–4
    contracts 254
    marriage 254
    revocation 254
Legge, V 62
leisure
    inclusion 33

lesbians
  discrimination 2
liberal theory of equality 296
liberty
  due process 190–1
  restricting 190–2
life, right to
  ethics 390–1
  germ line therapy 43
  mercy-killings 43
  prenatal diagnosis 43
lifestyle preferences
  happiness, pursuit of 185
  service provision 185–200
Lindqvist, B 33, 44, 125, 128
living conditions
  intellectually disabled persons 3, 4
loans 267
Luckasson, R 49, 52
Luxembourg
  disability discrimination 163

Madagascar
  disability discrimination 167
Mahbubani, K 392
Malawi 99
  affirmative actions 164
  disability discrimination 164
  employment 165
marginalization
  inclusion 34
marriage
  legal competence to act 254
Mauritius
  disability discrimination 164, 167
medical model 62, 151–5
'mental'
  terminology 28
mental deficiency
  terminology 28
mental disability, persons with
  discrimination 2
Mental Disability Rights International 4,
      119, 132, 468–70, 507
mental handicap
  terminology 28
mental illness
  see also mentally ill persons
  Asia 65
  cross-cultural perceptions of disability
      60, 65
  India 65

Korea 65
Nigeria 65
South Asia 65
stigma 65
terminology 60
mental retardation
  benign approach 66
  cross-cultural perceptions of disability
      60, 65–7
  definitions 29–30
  evaluation 66
  generalizations 65
  India 66
  intelligence testing 30, 66
  mild 65
  naming 52
    complexities 52–6
    ideology 55
    intended meaning 53–4
    ownership 55
    personal context 53
    power 56
    received meaning 54
    scientific aspects 52
    social context 52–3
  power 4–50
  severe 66
  special religious powers 66
  terminology 28, 29–30, 60
  World Health Organization (WHO) 28
mental subnormality
  terminology 28
mentally ill persons
  see also mental illness
  characteristics 3
  healthcare 5
  institutionalization 5
  intellectually disabled persons 2–3
  meaning 3
  mentally retarded persons distinguished
      2–3
  treatment right 5
mentally retarded persons
  capital punishment 3
  characteristics 2
  intellectually disabled persons 2
  meaning 2–3
  mentally ill persons distinguished 2–3
Merck Manual 65
mercy killings
  children 43
  life, right to 43

Mexico
  inhuman and degrading treatment 469
Mexico City
  asylums 83
Meyer, CE 415, 417
mind/body dualism 60
minorities
  invisible and underprotected 2
  traditional and visible 2
minors *see* children
monitoring
  International Covenant on Civil and
    Political Rights (ICCPR) 508
  nongovernmental organizations (NGOs)
    506–9
  Standard Rules on the Equalization of
    Opportunities for Persons with
    Disabilities 124, 139

NAMI 94
Namibia
  disability discrimination 167, 171
  equality 171
naming
  changing given name 51
  complexities 50–2
  cultural groups 50
  culture 50
  ethnic groups 50
  ideology 50, 51
    mental retardation 55
  importance 50
  intended meaning 50, 51
    mental retardation 53–4
  interim measures 56
  mental retardation
    complexities 52–6
    ideology 55
    intended meaning 53–4
    ownership 55
    personal context 53
    power 56
    received meaning 54
    scientific aspects 52
    social context 52–3
  ownership 50, 51–2
    mental retardation 55
  personal context 50, 51
    mental retardation 53
  power 50, 51
    mental retardation 56
  problems 56

  received meaning 50, 51
    mental retardation 54
  renaming 51–2
  scientific aspects 52
  sensitivity 56
  social context 50
    mental retardation 52–3
  terminology 49–50
National Alliance for the Mentally Ill
    (NAMI) 94
National Association for Retarded Children
    94
national legislation
  international human rights 135–6
  Norway 136
  United Kingdom 135
  United States 136
Nazi Germany 117–18
negotiation 216–17
neonatal intensive care units
  economics of equality 389–91
Nerney, T 430
Netherlands
  guardianship 445–6
New Zealand
  disability discrimination 164
  education 173
  guardianship 446
  intellectual disability 27
  past disability 171
  reasonable accommodation/adjustment
    172
Nicaragua
  social welfare law 169
Nigeria
  disability discrimination 167
  enforcement 174
  mental illness 65
non-governmental organizations (NGOs) 4
  see also individual organizations e.g.
    Inclusion International
  advocacy, recommendations for 509–10
  international human rights 131–2
  international projects 131–2
  mainstream human rights groups 131–2
  monitoring 506–9
  recommendations for
    collection and dissemination of
      information 503–6
    monitoring 506–9
    standard-setting 510–11
  Standard Rules, use of 503–4

Northern Ireland
  de-institutionalization 97
Norway
  national legislation 136
  Ombudsman scheme 136

open employment
  inclusion 33
opportunity, equal *see* equal opportunity
organizations
  Australia 27
  Canada 27
  fund-raising 27
  intellectual disability 26
  terminology for 27
    intellectual disability 27
  United States 27
out-of-home placement of children 415–28
  age of child 418
  human rights implications 425
  intention and decision about 417–25
    age of child 418
    human rights implications 425
    Israel 418–22
    social policy 422–3
    United States 423–5
  Israel 418–22
  motives 415
  parental application for 415–16
  planned placement 415
  policy 415
  research review 416–17
  social policy 422–3
  societal values, shifting 415
  types of placement 415
  United States 423–5
  unplanned placement 415
overcrowding
  asylums 86–7
  social policy 86–7

Panama
  social welfare law 16
Parens, E 327
Parish, S 424
participation
  inclusion 33
Partnership Project 370–1
past disability
  Australia 171
  Canada 171

Hong Kong 171
  New Zealand 171
  Philippines 171
  Sweden 171
  United Kingdom 171
  United States 171
Pathways to Employment scheme 34
Pennay, M 63
People First 97
people first language 26–7
person centered planning 185, 192–6
personal assistance services
  independent living 278
persons/people with disabilities
  terminology 27
pharmaceutical companies
  preventing disability 331
Philippines 99
  community-based rehabilitation 36
  disability discrimination 167, 168
  education 173
  past disability 171
  reasonable accommodation/adjustment
    172
  social welfare law 170
physical disability, persons with,
    discrimination 2
placement agencies
  inclusion 34
policy *see* disability policy
power
  mental retardation 4–50
  naming 50, 51
    mental retardation 56
  terminology 49–57
prenatal diagnosis 43, 326–7, 328, 331
  feminist theory 329–30
preventing disability 319–46
  abortion 326, 328–9
  amniocentesis 326
  China 334, 336, 337
  contrasting views of disability 320–3
  costs considerations 338–40
  deafness 338
  dilemma 320
  disability rights movement 327–8
  diversity, human 328
  economic and commercial influences
    330–2
  eugenics 334
  feminist theory 329–30
  genetic testing 327

genetics 325
governmental influences 332–4
health promotion 325–6
healthcare system 324, 339
India 337
negative perception of disability 324
pharmaceutical companies 331
physician, role of 331–2
prenatal diagnosis 326–7, 328, 331
primary prevention 324–5
  cost implications 339–40
  questioning forms of 326–30
professional influences 332–4
public health 325, 327
reproductive counselling 333
reproductive freedom 333–4
respecting persons with disabilities and 319–46
screening 324–5
secondary prevention 325
  cost implications 339
selective abortion 326
social expectations of perfect child 328
societal influences 332–4
strategies 324
welfare benefits 333
Principles for the Protection of Persons with Mental Illness and for the Improvement of Mental Healthcare (1991) 123
  adoption 129–30
psychiatric hospitals
  children 43
psychiatric primitivism 70
public health
  preventing disability 325, 327
public transport
  inclusion 33
pursuit of happiness *see* happiness, pursuit of

Quinn, G 467

rape
  intellectually disabled persons 4, 134
  mentally ill women, of 4
reasonable accommodation/adjustment
  Australia 172
  Canada 172
  drafting human rights instruments 487–8
  employment 242–3
  equal opportunity 271–2

Hong Kong 172
Hungary 172
  intellectually disabled persons 243
Ireland 172
Israel 172
meaning 172
New Zealand 172
obstacles 242
Philippines 172
Sweden 172
United Kingdom 172
United States 172, 242
Zimbabwe 172
recreation
  inclusion 33
Reeve, A 52, 57
refugees
  discrimination 2
  intellectually disabled persons 6
Rehabilitation 4
rehabilitation
  children 33
  community-based *see* community-based rehabilitation
  drafting human rights instruments 482–3
  employment 33
  inclusion 33
  models 33
Rehabilitation International 32, 119
religious minorities
  discrimination 2
reproductive counselling 333
residential institutions
  children 43
respite care 35
retardate 27
Rimmerman, A 417, 419, 421
Rizzolo, MC 424
Rosemary F. Dybwad International Fellowship 132
Rosenthal, E 471
Rothman, DJ 84, 86
'running amok' 69–70
Russia 4
  inhuman and degrading treatment 468–9

SABE 97
Salamanca Declaration and Framework for Action (1994) 43–4
Scandinavian countries
  inclusion 44
Schwartz, D 34

Scotland
  de-institutionalization 97
Scull, A 86
segregation
  social policy 91–3
Self Advocates Becoming Empowered
  (SABE) 97
self-advocacy 26, 453–65
  advocacy and 463–4
  careers 456–8
  decision-making 458–9
  employment 456–8
  future issues 31–2
  growth 31, 44
  impact 31
  inclusion 459–61
  Inclusion International 32
  independence 453–5
  independent living 454
  meaning 31
  money, making 456–8
  participation 461–3
  social policy 97
self-determination
  guardianship 429–50
  meaning 429
service provision
  Americans with Disabilities Act 1990 241
  equal access 240–3
  essential lifestyle approach 189–90, 196–7
  happiness, pursuit of 185
  health and safety 189
  independent living 277, 278
  interdisciplinary team 185, 186–90
  Israel 241–2
  lifestyle preferences 185–200
  listening skills 188, 189
  most appropriate integrated setting 274
  person centred planning 185, 192–6
  program services 186–7
  reasonable accommodation requirements
    242–3
  severe or profound disabilities, persons
    with 188–9
  support services 186, 189, 190
  United Kingdom 241
sex selection 337
sexuality
  Standard Rules on the Equalization of
    Opportunities for Persons with
    Disabilities 124
shared care
  families 35, 36

short-term care 35
sign language 165–6, 271, 338
Singapore
  intellectual disability 27
Sister Witness International 4
Social Development Accord (1995) 288
social justice 289
social model 62, 151–5
social pathology 294–6
  environmental approach 294–5
  rights outcome approach 295–6
social policy
  asylum model 83–5
  asylums 83–7
  community models 94
  consumer models 94
  de-institutionalization 94–7
  eugenics 90–1
  family models 94
  freak shows 89–90
  institutional model 91–3
  international initiatives 97–9
  national organizations 97
  nineteenth century 83–91
    eugenics 90–1
    freak shows 89–90
    intellectual disabilities, first US
      institution for 87–8
    overcrowding 86–7
  out-of-home placement of children 422–3
  overcrowding 85–7
  political activism 99
  segregation 91–3
  self-advocacy 97
  treatment right 94–7
  twentieth century 91–9
    community models 94
    consumer models 94
    de-institutionalization 94–7
    family models 94
    institutional model 91–3
    international initiatives 97–9
    segregation 91–3
    self-advocacy 97
    treatment right 94–7
  United States
    asylums 84, 85–6
    custodial asylums 88–9
    intellectual disabilities, first US
      institution for 87–8
social welfare law
  Bolivia 169
  China 169–70

comparative law 169–70
Costa Rica 169, 170
disability law 152
Finland 169
Germany 169
Korea 169
Nicaragua 169
Panama 16
Philippines 170
Spain 169, 170
United States 170
socio-political model 62
solidarity
human rights 154–5
meaning 154–5
South Africa 99
affirmative actions 164
disability discrimination 164, 167
South Asia
mental illness 65
Spain
disability discrimination 163, 164, 167,
213
guardianship 446
inclusion 44
social welfare law 169, 170
Special Rapporteur on Disability 5
Sri Lanka
disability discrimination 167
staff training
community-based rehabilitation 37
inclusion 37
Standard Rules on the Equalization of
Opportunities for Persons with
Disabilities 5, 39–41, 43, 98, 99, 122,
123, 223, 287
adoption 156, 505
development 124
discrimination 124
employment 124
equality 156
implementation 124, 128, 510
importance 124, 160
language 124
monitoring 124, 139
national planning 16
non-binding nature 156
philosophy 124
planning processes 511–2
purpose 124
recommendations for use 503–4
rights implementation 124
setting standards 511–2

sexuality 124
shortcomings 124
Special Rapporteur 157
support for 125
template for reform 161–2
stereotypes
barbaric 70
equal opportunity 154
families 35
terminology 26
sterilization of intellectually disabled
persons
Australia 4–5, 135
subsistence
Israel 243
Sundram, C 472
Sweden
care and assistance 246
disability discrimination 167, 214–15
Disability Ombudsman 203, 214–15
guardianship 431–41
administrator 435–6
contact person 436
escort person 438
evaluation of law 439–41
forvaltare 435–6
implementation of law 438–9
kontakt 436
legal background 432–3
mentor 433–5
personal assistant 436–8
support options 431–44
trustee 435–6
past disability 171
reasonable accommodation/adjustment
172
Switzerland
affirmative actions 164
disability discrimination 164

Tallinn Guidelines for Action on Resource
Development in the Field of
Disability 129
Tanno, DV 50
taxation
disability policy 267, 268
economic self-sufficiency 279
terminology
American Association on Mental
Retardation (AAMR) 29–30, 49
aspects 49

terminology (*cont.*):
  challenging behaviour 27
  confusion 26
  Consortium on Language, Image and
    Public Education 49
  conventions 60
  degrading 27
  disabled persons 27
  importance 26, 49
  intellectual disability 27–8, 60–2
  intellectually challenged 27
  intelligence testing 28
  International Classification of
    Impairments, Disabilities and
    Handicaps (ICIDH) 28–9
  international dialogue 27
  issues 26
  learning disabilities 28
  'mental' 28
  mental deficiency 28
  mental handicap 28
  mental illness 60
  mental retardation 28, 29–30, 60
  mental subnormality 28
  naming *see* naming
  organizations, for 27
  people first language 26–7
  people, for 27–8
  persons/people with disabilities 27
  power and 49–57
  retardate 27
  scientific journals 28
  stereotypes 26
  'the' 27
  United States 60
  World Health Organization (WHO) 28
test cases
  strategy 222–3
The Arc 27, 94
therapeutic services
  Convention on the Rights of the Child,
    UN 123
Thomson 90
TIDE program 367
training
  independent living 277
transnational human rights network 4
treatment right
  Convention on the Rights of the Child,
    UN 123
  equal opportunity 272–4
  Israel 238

mentally ill persons 5
modification of policies and procedures
  272–3
most appropriate integrated setting
  273–4
social policy 94–7
Treaty of Amsterdam 126, 127
Trent, JW 90

Uganda 99
  affirmative actions 164
  disability discrimination 164
  employment 165
  inclusion 44
UN *see* United Nations
UN Commission on Human Rights
  enforcement 125
  shortcomings 125
  Standard Rules and 125
  successes 125–6
  working groups 125
UN Declaration on the Rights of Disabled
  Persons (1975) 5, 37, 98, 121, 155, 287
  advocacy 138
  disabled person, definition of 121
  rights 121
UN Declaration on the Rights of Mentally
  Retarded Persons (1971) 5, 37, 98,
  120, 155
  adoption 120
  case law 132–3
  caveats 120
  ideology 239
  ILSMH text 120
  implementation of rights 237
  Israel 237, 238
  legislation, topics for 239–50
  limitations 120
  loopholes 120
  rights 120
UNESCO *see* United Nations Educational,
  Scientific and Cultural Organization
  (UNESCO)
UNICEF 128
United Kingdom
  de-institutionalization 97
  disability discrimination 98, 167, 211–13,
    238, 369
  Disability Discrimination Act 211–13
  Disability Rights Commission 203, 212–13
  education 28, 173
  employment 34, 369

enforcement 173
intellectual disability 28
national legislation 135
past disability 171
Pathways to Employment scheme 34
reasonable accommodation/adjustment 172
service provision 241
United Nations
  advocacy 509–10
  African Decade of Disabled Persons 39
  Asian Decade of Disabled Persons (1993–2002) 39
  Children's Fund (UNICEF) 128
  Commission for Social Development 157
  Commission on Human Rights *see* UN Commission on Human Rights
  Committee on the Rights of the Child 43
  Convention on Elimination of Discrimination against Persons with Disabilities, proposed UN 130
  Convention on the Rights of the Child *see* Convention on the Rights of the Child, UN
  Decade of Persons with Disabilities (1983–1992) 5, 38–9, 156, 287
  Declaration on the Rights of Disabled Persons (1975) 5, 37, 98
  Declaration on the Rights of Mentally Retarded Persons (1971) 37, 98
  disability as human rights issue within 155–61
    evaluation of current use of instruments 159–60
    hard law developments 157–9
    soft law developments 155–7
    trends 160–1
  Disabled Persons Unit 39
  employment resolutions 347
  global recognition of human rights 5
  human rights statements 124–5
  initiatives 37–42
  intellectual disability 26, 28
  International Covenant on Economic, Social and Cultural Rights 1, 37
  International Year of Disabled Persons (1981) 5, 38, 287
  International Year of the Family 35
  internationally agreed standards 39
  language of declarations 37
  paradigm shift in reports and resolutions 128–30
  programmes 5
  recommendations for
    advocacy 509–10
    collection and dissemination of information 503–6
    monitoring 506–9
    Standard Rules, use of 503–4
    standard-setting 510–11
  resolutions 347, 387, 467
  role 37
  Special Rapporteur on Disability 5
  specialized agencies 127–8
  Standard Rules on the Equalization of Opportunities for Persons with Disabilities *see* Standard Rules on the Equalization of Opportunities for Persons with Disabilities
United Nations Educational, Scientific and Cultural Organization (UNESCO) 29
  Universal Declaration of Human Rights *see* Universal Declaration of Human Rights (1948), UN
  websites 504–5
  women's rights 508
  World Programme of Action Concerning Disabled Persons 5, 38–9, 98, 99, 122, 128, 156
  World Summit on Social Development, Copenhagen 1995 5, 41–2
United Nations Children's Fund (UNICEF) 128
United Nations Educational, Scientific and Cultural Organization (UNESCO)
  disability, definition of 29
  special education, promotion of 127–8
United States
  Agency for Foreign Development (USAID) 132
  Americans with Disabilities Act 1990 *see* Americans with Disabilities Act 1990
  asylums 84, 85–6
  capital punishment 140
  case law 132–4
  Consortium on Language, Image and Public Education 49
  cross-cultural perceptions of disability 63
  de-institutionalization 94–7
  disability discrimination 61, 97–8, 167
  disability law 152
  disability policy 263–84

United States (*cont.*):
  discretionary grant-in-aid programs
      265–7
  economics of equality 387, 389
  education 2, 5, 173
  employment 34, 362–4
  enforcement 257–8
  entitlement programs 265
  equal opportunity 251
  eugenics 90–1
  families 36
  freak shows 89–90
  guardianship 430, 431
  handicapped 60
  healthcare, right to 2
  inclusion 44
  national disability plans and
      recommendations 136
  organizations 27
  out-of-home placement of children 423–5
  past disability 171
  reasonable accommodation/adjustment
      172, 242
  redistribution of social welfare rights 1–2
  social policy
      asylums 84, 85–6
      custodial asylums 88–9
      intellectual disabilities, first US
          institution for 87–8
  social welfare law 170
  terminology 60
Universal Declaration of Human Rights
      (1948), UN 1, 37, 138, 155, 287
  adoption 119
  Article 1 3
  case law 135
  deficiencies 119
  disability 119
  intellectually disabled persons, use with
      119
  international human rights standard 119
  negative rights 119
  rights 119
  status 119
Uruguay
  inhuman and degrading treatment 469
US *see* United States
USAID 132

van Maastrict, S 66–7
victimization
  inclusion 34

Vienna Declaration of the World
      Conference on Human Rights (1993)
      3, 125, 128
Vietnam
  community-based rehabilitation 36
  inclusion 44

Wales
  de-institutionalization 97
well-being, equality of 296, 300–1, 307–12
Westbrook, MT 63
WHO *see* World Health Organization
      (WHO)
women
  Convention on the Elimination of All
      Forms of Discrimination Against
      Women (1979) *see* Convention on the
      Elimination of All Forms of
      Discrimination Against Women
      (1979)
  discrimination 2
  rights 508
work incentives
  economic self-sufficiency 279
World Bank 512
World Blind Union 32
World Conference on Special Needs
      Education 128
World Federation of the Deaf 32
World Health Organization (WHO)
  human rights recommendations on
      disability 127
  ICIDH 28
  ICIDH-2 29
  International Classification of
      Impairments, Disabilities and
      Handicaps (ICIDH) 28–9
  mental retardation 28
  monograph, *The Role of International
      Human Rights in Domestic Mental
      Health Legislation* 478–91
  terminology 28
World Programme of Action Concerning
      Disabled Persons (1983), UN 5, 38–9,
      98, 99, 122, 123, 128, 287
  equalization of opportunities 156
  goals 156
World Summit on Children 43
World Summit on Social Development,
      Copenhagen 1995 5, 41–2, 128
wrongful life, damages for 390
Wyatt case 132–3

Yale Declaration 137, 471, 472–7, 517–25
  challenges facing participants 472–3
  drafting human rights instruments
      472–7
  guiding principles 474
  purpose 6
  strategy 473
young persons
  see also children
  initiatives 42–4

Zambia
  disability discrimination 167
  enforcement 174
Zimbabwe
  disability discrimination 167
  enforcement 174
  equality 171
  reasonable accommodation/adjustment
      172
Zola, EK 323